To Run With Horses will touch you in the most personal of ways and reveal how God's presence and love can be seen and known by all of us, even in the darkest of times. This is extraordinary."

> Melvin G Spiese
> Major General, USMC (Retired)

Intelligent. Timely. Moving. Enduring. Manna's *To Run With Horses* has great substance with far-reaching impact. You cannot read this book and not want to be a better person afterwards.

> Dylan Ratigan
> *New York Times* Best-Selling Author,
> Filmmaker, Former MSNBC Host

There are few books that you know from the very beginning are going to change your life. *This* is one of those books. Manna has the ability to write with such clarity and such tenderness concerning those topics that society wishes to hide. It's not easy to share one's pain, and to take off the masks, and yet do it so well that I felt like I was having a conversation with my best friend. Women need to know that they are not alone, and that they will overcome. *To Run With Horses* is the God-given message of hope that resonates through each page. Manna's story is one of challenges, perseverance, faith, and God's enduring love. It is definitely a "must read."

> Alisa DiLorenzo
> Educator, Co-Founder
> ONE Extraordinary Marriage

How do you describe a force of nature like Manna? Seldom does heaven pack so much into one person. From the moment I first met her, Manna stood out and we became fast friends. Quick to pick things up, effervescent in conversation and always looking for ways to build into the future, Manna will take you deeper and further than anyone else in the same space, whether measured by time or book pages. She is extraordinarily gifted and driven by a passion born of the knowledge that she is designed to *run with horses*—an appropriate title for her riveting book. In every way, Manna is exceptional. *To Run With Horses* combines the reflective depth of her Asian roots with the buoyant optimism of an American overcomer and success story. To read this book is to meet the woman. Read it and meet your new friend, Manna Ko.

>Dr. Lance Wallnau
>Author, Speaker, Educator, Entrepreneur

"Mark Twain once said, 'The two most important days in your life are the day you are born and the day you find out why.' In courageously sharing her story, Manna has fulfilled the second most important day of her life–to be a powerful voice for the voiceless and to boldly inspire others to live their destiny."

>Francis Lee
>Chairman of the Board, Synaptics, Inc.

I first met Manna Ko at a leadership conference, and immediately recognized her insight and skill as a business strategist and leadership expert. What I *didn't* know was a remarkable past that's so brilliantly told in her book. *To Run With Horses* is the perfect title because it's a question she's asked all of her life—and most likely, you've asked it, too— *Do I have what it takes to overcome? Do I have what it takes to run with horses?* Now you have an answer. For everyone who's ever dreamed that there was more out there, or believed in yourself when no one else would, this book may just change everything.

>Phil Cooke
>Media and Branding Expert Filmmaker,
>Author of *One Big Thing: Discovering What You Were Born to Do*

I know of very few people that carry and give away more compassion than Manna. Whether advising someone through a marketplace dilemma, standing with someone through a life crisis, or simply "speaking the truth in love," no one is more capable than Manna. So, it is no surprise she, at long last, chooses to tell her own story—and in the most creative of ways. Digging deep and exposing her own pain, she offers hope and healing to others who follow where she came from and endeavor to go where she is now. She risked in love to help others get free, and courageously lets us into her life to tell a story that will capture every reader...and we all win.

> Gary Goodell
> Author, Pastor Third Day Churches

What makes this book so compelling is not just that it's wonderfully written and the story is courageously told, but that the intrinsic virtues of love, hope and honor are so evident from beginning to end. The messages you learn throughout the book will change your life. If you ever wondered if you were ever meant for more, read this book, and wonder *no* more.

> Tommy Barnett
> Founder of *The Dream Center*
> Pastor, Author, Chancellor of
> Southeastern University

As close friends for forty-five years, Manna has always been kind, humble, generous, loyal and true. There is no one more pure, selfless, and inspiring as Manna Ko. You will be riveted by her exquisitely written story, moved by her courage and goodness, and empowered by hope. This book is going to impact the lives of countless people. Good does triumph over evil."

> Brucyne Sud
> Toronto, Ontario, Canada

TO RUN WITH HORSES

From a Stolen Childhood to a Life of Joy -
The Untold Story of Courage, Hope, and Triumph

An Autobiographical Novel

by

MANNA KO

© 2023 Manna Ko

A substantial portion of this material was originally published by Covenant & Gate © 2014-2023 under the title Made for More, now out of print.

All rights reserved. No part of this publication may be reproduced, distributed, or transmitted in any form or by any means, including photocopying, recording, or other electronic or mechanical methods, without the prior written permission of the publisher, except in the case of brief quotations embodied in critical reviews and certain other noncommercial uses permitted by copyright law. For permission requests, write to Covenant & Gate, 2683 Via De La Valle, Suite G523, Del Mar, California, USA. 92014 Email: weloveyou@humannatea.com

I have tried to recreate events, locales, and conversations from my memories of them. To maintain their anonymity, in as many instances as possible, I have changed the names of individuals and places. I also have changed some identifying characteristics and details such as physical properties, occupations, and places of residence.

All scripture quotations, unless otherwise indicated, are taken from the Holy Bible, New International Version®, NIV®. Copyright ©1973, 1978, 1984, 2011 by Biblica, Inc.™ Used by permission of Zondervan. All rights reserved worldwide. www.zondervan.com. The "NIV" and "New International Version" are trademarks registered in the United States Patent and Trademark Office by Biblica, Inc.™ NKJV Scripture taken from the New King James Version®. Copyright © 1982 by Thomas Nelson. Used by permission. All rights reserved. Scripture quotations marked (NLT) are taken from the Holy Bible, New Living Translation, copyright ©1996, 2004, 2007, 2013 by Tyndale House Foundation. Used by permission of Tyndale House Publishers, Inc., Carol Stream, Illinois 60188. All rights reserved. Scripture quotations from THE MESSAGE. Copyright © by Eugene H. Peterson 1993, 1994, 1995, 1996, 2000, 2001, 2002. Used by permission of Tyndale House Publishers, Inc.

All quotations are used with permission, fall under fair use guidelines, or are in the public domain.

University of British Columbia Archives, Jemison photo [UBC 44.1/595-1]
University of British Columbia Archives, photo [UBC 41.1/1592-1]

Composition/Song Title: Beautiful
Writer Credits: Barry Graul, Bart Millard, Brown Bannister, Dan Muckala, Jim Bryson, Mike Scheuchzer, Nathan Cochran, Robby Shaffer
Copyright: © 2010 Simpleville Music/Wet As A Fish Music (admin. by Simpleville Publishing, LLC.)/Wintergone Music/Banistuci Music (Admin. by The Loving Company) All Rights Reserved. Used By Permission.

Cover Design by: Aesthetica Society
Front and Back Cover photo: Jesslan Lee Photography
Editors: Shannon Saia (2015), Tiffany Vakilian (2020), Allison Amerding (2022)

Published by Covenant and Gate, 2683 Via De La Valle, Suite G523, Del Mar, California, USA. 92014. weloveyou@humannatea.com

Library of Congress Control Number: 2023900513
ISBN 978-1-943060-32-0 Paperback

ALSO BY MANNA KO

I Am Born To Run: The Journal
Your Gifts Will Find You™ — Your Journey to Purpose
Know Your Race. Own Your Race. Live Your Race™
Know Your Race. Own Your Race. Live Your Race™: The Journal
My Spiritual First Aid Kit (for Women)
My Spiritual First Aid Kit (for Men)
The Hero In You — 120+ Power Tips for Writers

Children's Books

Sophie and Solo's Fun Adventures™: Yes Yes Sam
Sophie and Solo's Fun Adventures™: Angry McJack
Sophie and Solo's Fun Adventures™: Me-Me Marie
Sophie and Solo's Fun Adventures™: Here and There Claire
Sophie and Solo's Fun Adventures™: It's Okay To Pray

Cookbooks

Chopsticks and Chocolate Chips
Feeding Families and Friends
Feeding Our 4-Legged Families and Friends

Courses

More Than Words
The Hero In You
Your True Identity

For all the little children who understand life
more than grown-ups do,

And for all the grown-ups who wish they were
more like little children.

ACKNOWLEDGMENTS

To PoPo and GongGong who loved me as their own. Were it not for you, I shudder to think what might have become of me. I miss you more than I can describe.

To MahMah. Your life of tenacity and grace is a generational gift and a blessing to our family.

To my visionary father, whose courage, love, and constancy have been my rock of Gibraltar. Your belief in me lifted me higher than the highest of mountains, from where I finally caught a glimpse of what life was meant to be. I would be nowhere without you.

To my brother, "Supersan!" Your kindness, goodness, and selflessness humble me. If I could be half as good as you, then I would have accomplished much in this life.

To my "Mighty Man of Valor," my husband. Thank you for insisting that I write this book instead of a ghostwriter. This book would never have happened as quickly as it did were it not for your unwavering support and devotion to me. I love life more than ever because of you.

To my son, my beloved son…you are my life. I never knew the meaning of joy and purpose until I had you. You are the "bestest" ever and you are my reason for living. 1439 forever!

To my Nava. You are a treasure. Thank you for making God your first love, for making my Tinkie, your second, and for giving me two of the most precious gifts of my life.

To my Justice Prophet and my Joshua Scribe. You are my every thought of every day. I never thought it was possible to love anyone as much as I love you both!

To my Dog Whisperer, Horse Whisperer, and my little ones—I'm so very proud of you all and love you more than words can say.

To Goomah and Goozheng. Thank you for loving me and believing in me. God's love is revealed to us through your lives.

To my extended Ko family and Ko friends, especially my Kai Yeh and Kai Mah and family, I thank you with all my heart for your faithful and loving kindness.

To Pastor Gary Goodell and Georgette O'Brien. I love and thank you with all my heart. It all started to make sense when I met you.

To Amy. You are my true friend, sister, and my MBA. God has blessed me with His best in you.

To Lauren. Thank you for being a consistent champion of my life, and for bringing me such laughter. I'm so grateful for you.

To Denise. Thank you for being a source of strength and inspiration, and for sharing your parents with me. I love you more than I can say.

To Jim. Thank you for your steadfast friendship and faithful prayers. I can't wait for our crew's reunion.

To Cynthia. You are a true gift. Thank you for being my devoted friend. I cherish you.

To my P.I.T. Crew. I have no idea how I could have survived without you all these years. Your loving kindness, tireless intercession, steadfast prayers, and loyal friendship have blessed me beyond measure. I am eternally grateful for you.

To all my friends who lived through so much of life with me. While there are many stories about what I had to overcome in this book, I hope to one day chronicle the great stories we shared. That will be a #1 Bestseller without a doubt!

To Larry Laveman. Thank you for standing by me as I walked through some of the darkest times of my adult life. I will be forever grateful for your wisdom, kindness, and generosity.

To Lo. Thank you, forever! Words escape me when I think upon you and all you have walked me through. "Jet fuel" has a new meaning, and because of you, my shoulders are stronger for others.

To my Volunteer Beta Readers. Thank you for your belief in me, your valuable time, and your constant encouragement.

To my first edition editors, Shannon Saia and Tiffany Vakilian. Thank you for sharing the mastery of your craft with me. I am so very grateful. To my second edition editor, Allison Armerding, you have so aptly and brilliantly helped me to refine this book. Thank you all for believing in me, and for seeing the treasures in this book above and beyond traditional approaches.

Most of all, I thank God, His Son, my Best Friend, Jesus Christ, and my Comforter, Holy Spirit. My heart grows ten times larger with every thought of You, and my knees buckle when I think upon Your majesty and Your great love for me—for all of us. Thank You for loving me so much that You would come after me, fight for me, and die for me. Thank You for exchanging Your life for mine. Thank You for never leaving me and thank You for keeping all Your promises. Thank You for reminding me *we've already won*, and that because of You, victory is a lifestyle. I love you with everything I am.

May this book bring You all the glory.

TO RUN WITH HORSES

TABLE OF CONTENTS

A Message From The Author ... i
Foreword ... viii
Preface ... xii

BOOK I: BRAVE HEART

1	**Touched By An Angel**	1
	Room 316	1
	In the Beginning	4
	My Brother's Keeper	7
	PoPo and GongGong	9
	MahMah and YehYeh	18
	Something is Rotten in the State of Denmark	20
	Not Your Typical Day in the Park	23
	More Than Meets the Eye	26
2	**A Stranger in a Strange Land**	29
	We're Not in Kansas Anymore	29
	Hold the Onions	32
	Social Butterfly	38
	Man's Best Friend	42
	A Day at the Beach	45
	New Kid at School	47
	Fight Club	

Hell's Kitchen	51
Wherever You Go, I Will Go	54
Lunch is Served	58

3 Les Misérables — 63

Making Friends	63
Answer the Phone!	71
Stupid Is As Stupid Does	72
The Thief in the Night	75
Hide and Seek…and Hide	80
The Sound of Music	84
Kramer vs. Kramer	89
So Close and Yet So Far	94
Stupid Face	96
I'm Outta Here	98
Heaven Sent	109

4 The Valley of the Shadow of Death — 113

Room 316	113
Looking a Gift Horse in the Mouth	115
Shamed and Shorn	118
Out of Mind, *Then* Out of Sight	120
Highway to Hell	121
Sticks and Stones	127
I Will Never Leave You	129
Be Strong and Very Courageous	131
No Room At The Inn	133

	It's Easy To Be Weak	133
5	**Deliver Us From Evil**	**137**
	Room 316	137
	True Lies	139
	Kitchen Conversations	141
	Bus Stop	145
	Lost In Translation	147
	Always Dying but Never Able to Die	150
	A Worse Place than Hell	153
	Pistachio Nuts and Wine Gums	157
	The King and I	159
	Pondering Death	162
	The Birds and the Bees	163
	Mommy Dearest	167
	Wash the Dishes, Cinderella	170
	The Emperor's New Clothes	173
	The Coat of Many Colors	175
	A House Divided	177
	Pulled from the Edge of a Slippery Slope	180
	Run for Your Life	181

BOOK II: AGAINST ALL ODDS

6	**Son of a Gun**	**193**
	Room 316	193
	Being a Good Example	197
	Progress Not Perfection	199
	The Devil in Your Ear	201

	Clueless	203
	Edward Scissorhands' Uncle	206
	Bad Company	209
	Your Day Will Come	213
	The Real McCoy	218
	Dirty Rotten Scoundrel	219
	Impartation	221
7	**Dying to Live**	**223**
	Room 316	223
	Boys are Weird	224
	It's a Miracle	228
	An Angel Unaware	230
	With Friends Like That…	235
	One Less Bell to Answer	239
8	**Twilight Zone**	**243**
	Room 316	243
	Mr. Wrong	244
	Weasel Skin Place	250
	It's a Nice Day for a White Wedding	252
	Mother Knows Best	259
	Too Close for Comfort	262
	Someone to Live For	267
	My Superpower	270
	Help Me Help You!	273
	Thanksgiving Gift	275
	The Last Straw	283

9	A Pond of Smelly Frogs	287
	Room 316	287
	Becoming and Overcoming	292
	I Will Arise	295
	Silence Isn't Always Golden	302
	Casanova	308
	Truer than True	312

BOOK III: I HAVE A DREAM

10	No Guts, No Glory	327
	Room 316	327
	Another One Bites the Dust	330
	Ground Hog Day	332
	Negotiating With Heaven	336
	Take the Money and Run	340
	Stealing from a Baby	343
	Humble Pie	345
	True Colors – The Green Old Nanny	347
	Not All That Glitters Is Gold	350
	Signed, Sealed, and Delivered	353
	An Encounter With Heaven	359
	Two's Company, Three's a Crowd	362
	Face to Face with Your Enemy	365
11	Married! Buried!	369
	The Check's In the Mail	369
	Love At First Sight	370
	The Proposal	373

Red Flags	378
50 Shades of "Cray"	384
Time to Say Goodbye	388
"It's *My Precious!*"	400
The Cost of Doing Business	403
The End of an Era	404
When Hell Freezes Over	405
Sleeping with the Enemy	408
I Quit!	411
Wicked	415
Back to School	417
Deliverance	417
Go Ahead. Make My Day!	420

12 Recalled to Life — 427

Talkin' Bout a Revolution	427
Money! Money! Money!	429
Free at Last	432
Wolves in Sheep's Clothing	435
Kangaroo Court	438
The Mass Exodus	443
A Hypocrite or Not a Hypocrite… That is the Question.	444
Alien	450
Ain't No Mountain High Enough	455

13 Everything That Can Be Shaken Will Be Shaken — 465

Room 316	465
The Red String of Fate	466
Famous Last Words	477
My Best Friend	482
Building Windmills	483
Honor's Reward	484
Remove the Hedge	486

	Dancing in the Rain	487
	My Prodigal	489
	Empty Nesters with a Growing Family	491
	Is This Really Happening?!	493
	Et Tu, Brutus?	494
	Jezebel	494
	Servant In Training	501
	The Gift of Enemies	503
	We're Going to Need a Bigger Boat	504
	Needless Casualties of War	509
	A Place of Your Own	513
	The Big Event	514
	Rock of Ages	516
	It's All Yours	518
14	**Happily Ever After**	**521**
	Peaceful Easy Feeling	521
	Dedicated	522
	Mom! I'm Home!	524
	Oh, Happy Day!	524
	The Best Time of My Life	526
	Room 316	528
15	**The Race Set Before Us**	**539**
	The Last Eight Years	540
	It Chose Me	541
	Mended with Gold	542
	My Scars Are My Authority	544
	Our Great Race to Run	546
	A Final Charge	547

Resources   552

Sources   554

What lies behind you, and what lies in front of you, pales in comparison to what lies inside of you.
— Attributed to Ralph Waldo Emerson

BEAUTIFUL

by MercyMe

Days will come when you don't have the strength
When all you hear is you're not worth anything
Wondering if you ever could be loved
And if they truly saw your heart, they'd see too much

You're beautiful, you're beautiful
You are made for so much more than all of this
You're beautiful, you're beautiful
You are treasured, you are sacred, you are His

You're beautiful

And praying that you have the heart to fight
'Cause you are more than what is hurting you tonight
For all the lies you've held inside so long
They are nothing in the shadow of the cross

You're beautiful, you're beautiful
You are made for so much more than all of this
You're beautiful, you're beautiful
You are treasured, you are sacred, you are His

You're beautiful

Before you ever took a breath, long before the world began
Of all the wonders He possessed, there was one more precious
Of all the earth and skies above, you're the one He madly loves
Enough to die

You're beautiful, you're beautiful
In His eyes

You're beautiful
You were meant for so much more than all of this
You're beautiful
You are treasured, you are sacred, you are His…

A MESSAGE FROM THE AUTHOR

Dear Friend,

It's been eight years since the release of my autobiographical novel, and I am deeply touched by all the messages from readers around the world sharing the profound effects my life message has had on them. I'm moved by each exquisite account and am both humbled and honored to have contributed—even in the smallest of ways—to so many beautiful lives.

The last chapter of that book was titled, "Happily Ever After," but as we all know, adventures continue to unfold. One such adventure included going back to graduate school—something I could never have foreseen nor pondered doing again! Yet, in a series of divine appointments, I did exactly that and in the fall of 2022, I completed my Doctorate in Education in Leadership for Change.

Studying to be a "Leader for Change" was a humbling endeavor. Ron Heifetz (a great pioneer in leadership) says, "Leadership is not just a role or a position, but an action." I wholeheartedly agree. Being an impactful change agent is not simply a title, but a way of being. Specifically, leaders must be worthy of the trust of those we lead. That doesn't mean leaders will always get things right, or that they are perfect. Everyone makes mistakes. It's just that good, effective, positive, and sustainable leaders (among other necessary virtues) are also humble and courageous enough to know how to take responsibility for those mistakes, be accountable, make things right, get back up, learn, grow, and use the discomfort of those events to be an even better leader. This is one of the important ways trust is built.

"Change" by definition is not static; it is a journey. And research shows that good leaders are also positive change agents. They know how to conceive, believe, and achieve through their journeys of change, regardless of how long, arduous, or lonely those seasons of change are. The objective is not to simply muddle through issues until we get to the other side, but to use change as a tool—a catapult—for transformation. Said another way, a successful leader does not simply *manage* change—a successful leader *innovates* through it. Instead of being *managers*, we become *innovators*. To innovate through change, however, is not always simple or easy, yet to live a life of meaning, purpose, and depth, this is the adventure we're invited to pursue.

C.S. Lewis once compared life to an egg: "It may be hard for an egg to turn into a bird. It would a jolly sight harder for it to learn to fly while remaining an egg. We are like eggs at present, and we cannot go on indefinitely being just an ordinary, decent egg. We must be hatched or go bad."[1]

---
[1] C.S. Lewis, *Mere Christianity*, (New York: Harper Collins, 2001), 198.

We have to engage with life, which often means engaging with "change." We can't simply hide inside our shells forever, denying a whole world that awaits us. The shell serves a purpose for a time, but after that, it can no longer hold (or hide) what we carry. We have to break out of that shell and hatch. In fact, we're *designed* to break through and break forth because that's part of our great destiny. Or we go bad, and this fleeting vapor called "life," is gone.

However, "hatching" isn't a one-time event. There are many hatching moments as humans because we are always having new dreams and being called to new territories! So, we have many opportunities to break through and break forth from one lesson, one cycle, and one season to the next.

One of my many hatching moments happened recently in a "Mount-Moriah-esque" moment, when I gave back to God something He first gave to me—my made for more message. Very long, amazing, and miraculous story short, I realized that my made for more message was *never* meant to be the final message, the destination point. It was always only meant to be *a launching point*. And as meaningful as my made for more message was to dignify our souls, honor our spirits, and to empower us to live magnanimously (regardless of how we are treated), there is still *more*.

So, last year, I began creating the second edition of my autobiography, and just as the Lord gave me the title for the original book, He gave me this new title as well. God told me to name the second edition, *To Run With Horses*, based on Jeremiah 12:5, which says,

> *"If racing against mere men makes you tired, how will you race against horses?*
> *If you stumble and fall on open ground, what will you do in the thickets near the Jordan?"*
>
> Jeremiah12:5 NLT

The lesson here is essentially saying, *if you're tired when things are easy, how will you make it when things are tough? And even if there have been trials, regardless of how difficult, painful, or even horrifying they have been, those hardships have actually been the most impeccable training ground for your greatest race yet to come. So, pick yourself up, dust yourself off, do what you need to do to get yourself together, and then get back in the race. I'm with you. Now, it's time to stop running with mere men…it's now time to run with horses!*

Made for more was important because it was all about showing others their identity. But now that you know what you're made *of*, you need to know what you're made *for*. And *To Run With Horses* is all about that.

Made for more was about *your identity*. *To Run With Horses* is about *your destiny*.

Friends, in this very important hour of human history, it's time for you *To Run With Horses*. Everything you have seen, heard, and lived through has been preparation for something more brilliant and breathtaking yet to come. You are designed for great and mighty exploits, and you've been allowed to be tested because God trusts you with the pain. He trusts your heart, your character, your will, and your beautiful spirit to be purified, refined, and renewed in the fire, on the anvil, in the dirt, and in the deep waters.

You were designed to be an answer to today's questions. You are disrupters of the mundane, decoders of secrets, and revealers of hidden treasures. You are the light in the darkness, the spark that ignites flames of creativity and ingenuity, pursuers of the forgotten, and the voice for the voiceless. This is your destiny, for "it is the glory of the Lord to conceal a matter and it's the glory of kings to search it out" (Proverbs 25:2). And the role of a king or leader is to search for innovative ways to steward, care, protect, nourish, nurture, provide, and empower those in his care. It's time we shift from might and power to destiny and impact; from selfish gain to collective care; from indifference and offense to love and forgiveness. It is time to stop building our own empires to build God's kingdom, which guarantees life, peace, joy, and love for all.

You may not feel like a king or a queen right now. But isn't this exactly what the enemy wants you to believe? Isn't this how he gets us to abdicate our power, authority, and influence? Isn't this how he gets us to not only deny our destiny, but to also curse it? Friend, just because you don't believe or feel like you're a king or queen, doesn't mean it's not true. History is replete with stories of anointed babies and children (i.e., Moses, King David, Queen Esther) whose destiny was royalty, but they didn't understand its significance until the appointed time. In the meantime, they were in training and being prepared to take their rightful position.

And so it is with you.

But alas, training and preparation are not for the faint of heart. They are for the courageous heart, a mighty heart, a great heart...a champion's heart. Unfortunately, our hearts and our culture has been betrayed by a lie—a lie that defines a "successful life" as good things coming easily, where comfort is the goal and convenience is the way. That we are entitled to get what we want, when we want it, how we want it, and with whom we want it, especially if we "hustle" for it. But a life of ease, comfort, and convenience, despite our own efforts, striving, or insistence, doesn't exist. We don't always get what we want, when we want, how we want, and with whom we want. This is not the heart of a champion. This is the heart of self-absorption, even narcissism. In fact, when I look back at my life, I'm so thankful that what I wanted never came to pass. That would have been a curse, not a blessing!

I recently turned sixty years old, and with much of my life behind me, I can attest that life is not as some advertisements and marketing gurus insist we believe. However, while life is not easy, it is undoubtedly, a great adventure—even a heroic one! As I write this note to you, I'm looking at a wooden carving on my desk that says: "Forget the glass slippers, this princess wears boots!" That's because we can't scale our mountains or run our races in high heels, much less glass slippers! We need something sturdy to support us on long, and even treacherous, terrains.

In 2011, I read a stunning account of the horse Secretariat, the 1973 Triple Crown winner and perhaps the greatest horse in known history. I was undone reading about his epic story, undefeatable passion, and the grandness of his heart. While his victories at the Kentucky Derby and Preakness Stakes were record-breaking, it was his performance at the Belmont Stakes—later dubbed "the greatest race in history"—that left everyone awestruck:

> On the morning of the Belmont Stakes, Secretariat awoke with a seemingly mystical determination. His trainers later told reporters that he was "rearing and bucking, flaring his nostrils and rolling his eyes." He was somehow filled with anticipation for the race. Reportedly "he burst from the barn like a studhorse going to the breeding shed and walked around the outdoor ring on his hind legs, pawing at the sky in a magical, unforgettable instant, now frozen in time."
>
> Secretariat totally intimidated his competition approaching the starting gate; a supernatural atmosphere appeared to surround him. He did not merely walk to the gate—he romped to his position.
>
> The Belmont was the longest of the three races. After the starter's gun had sounded, initially a horse named Sham gave Secretariat a formidable challenge. The first six furlongs were run in a staggering seventy seconds, with Sham incredibly keeping abreast of Secretariat. However, the pace proved more than Sham could sustain, and the challenger injured himself in the last race he would ever run.
>
> Meanwhile, Secretariat continued to command the lead during the second half of the race. As one commentator put it, "It was as though he were running on the wind."
>
> …Setting pace; ***he did not merely want to win—he intended to run the greatest race ever.***
>
> Certain no horse could maintain this pace for so long, many

observers and journalists felt jockey Ron Turcotte was foolish to continue to push Secretariat at this tempo and risk collapse and the loss of the Triple Crown victory. But the jockey had little to do with it: Secretariat was running at his own pleasure. This was a day of destiny. Turcotte later commented that Secretariat had a mind of his own for this race, and he (Turcotte) simply held on and enjoyed the ride.

As the last quarter of the race lay before Secretariat, every fan, journalist, and observer grew mesmerized by the fortitude and sheer talent of this amazing horse, whose victory turned out to be one of the greatest events in sports history. His Triple Crown performance is unmatched in U.S. horse-racing history. It was the greatest single performance he had ever witnessed in a sporting event, recalls legendary golf champion Jack Nicklaus. When this mythic race was over, Secretariat had defeated his closest competition by thirty-one lengths and set an all-time record of 2:24, a feat previously considered impossible.[2]

The author of this piece went on to note, "Secretariat had a secret, which was only discovered at his death. During an autopsy, medical examiners found that Secretariat not only had a perfectly healthy heart but that it was also almost two-and-a-half times larger than an average horse's heart! Secretariat's heart weighed a staggering twenty-two pounds, whereas an average horse's heart weighs about eight-and-a-half pounds."[3]

While every racehorse has a hunger and drive to compete and win, it is said that Secretariat rose far above the rest because of his love to run—and because of the greatness of his heart. God had formed this magnificent creature with a unique gift, and Secretariat used it to its uttermost with every fiber of his being. From the moment I read his story, Secretariat became one of my favorite examples of passion, tenacity, and excellence.

God has also called you and I to have the heart of a champion, and when we look back at our lives, we can see that the many long seasons of hardship were, in fact, training seasons to prepare us for our *Belmont*. We will not fail by adversity. We will be forged by it. For me, I know that a life of comfort and ease would have only lulled me into a path of least resistance, into entropy. I would never have been provoked to fight for my soul or the life of great promise and hope that God had always planned for me. My hardships were truly the training ground that prepared and transformed me to run the race set before me, just as they are for you.

---

[2] Paul Keith Davis, *Books of Destiny: Secrets of God Revealed* (North Sutton, NH: Streams Publishing House, 2004), printed as an excerpt titled "Enlarge Our Hearts" on ElijahList.com, https://www.elijahlist.com/words/display_word/9081, accessed December 13, 2022.

[3] Davis, *Books of Destiny*, https://www.elijahlist.com/words/display_word/9081.

My hope is that by reading about my journey, you too will gain fresh perspective on your story and understand what God has been after all along in your life—to form the greatness of heart in you. You were meant to have the heart of a champion and you are meant *to run with horses*.

The timing and significance of the hour in which we are all living in history cannot be underestimated. In these times of change, God has been preparing an entire company of champions, like you, to run their great race, maybe even the greatest race of life! Your life is a testimony. You have been called, trained, and put in position "for such a time as this." So, take heart, take courage, and take *action*. God is calling you and me to be change-agents for goodness' sake.

Yes, there is a cost to being a good leader—and even more to being a *great* leader. But if we give it all we've got, we cannot lose. And if we give others all we've got, we all win. No matter what people say about you, your dreams, or the mission you feel called to fulfill, you must give it your all. We don't know whom we could bless by stepping into all that we're designed to be, and we don't know how much our courage could actually inspire and empower others. Just remember, as we step out, God will meet us with His favor to run. He is *for* us. No one can be against us, and even if they try, they are already defeated.

So dear friends, I write this note to encourage you, to embolden you, and to challenge you to read this second edition of my story with the deep knowing that your identity is glorious, and you are *already* made for more. I hope you will enjoy reading this new edition with the eyes of a champion and the perspective of destiny awaiting you. This edition has been refined with that in mind, and also includes a few new sections to reflect the ultimate message of knowing your destiny.

You are more than your trials, circumstances, and pain. And while those experiences cannot be changed, or even forgotten, instead of them being used as labels of limitation or chains of constraints to your true identity, let them be badges of honor that signify your position and rank as a mighty woman and man of valor.

You are also more than your past successes for they are only a small sampling of the best that is yet to come. Let your past be great teachers, coaches, and even theologians that direct you to a deeper faith. Let your past be the training ground and the preparation you need for your new assignments in this most important time of history. Let your past build your strength, courage, perseverance, character, and hope. Because dear friends, the best is yet to come.

It's time to choose.

Weights or wings?

Trod by foot, or run with horses?

I hope you choose to release the weights and to run with horses.

Unapologetically for the children™,

Manna Ko

FOREWORD

> The whole course of human history may depend on a change of heart
> in one solitary and even humble individual...
> For it is in the solitary mind and soul of the individual that the battle between
> good and evil is waged, and ultimately won or lost.
> —M. Scott Peck

In the movie, *The Terminator*, Sarah Connor, a moped-riding waitress, lives a mundane life hoping to one day find her "true love." Until then, she serves coffee and pie by day, and waits for her Prince Charming by night.

This predictable pattern is radically interrupted when a robotic assassin from her future shows up. Our hero, Sarah, learns she is at risk when a number of women who share her first and last name turn up dead.

The Terminator has time-traveled from the future to her present time, and anyone bearing the name Sarah Connor is his target. The cyborg assassin doesn't seem like he can fail. He possesses the strength and processing capabilities of a robot, and is armed with the latest in automatic weapons. It isn't long until the Terminator is on Sarah's trail, and there is chaos and bloodshed all around her.

Suddenly, her protector from the future makes his presence known: "Come with me if you want to live."

With no other choice, Sarah jumps in a car with a total stranger, and as bullets fly and cars crash, her protector begins to tell her who she is. He explains that in the future she is a legend and that an entire army wages war, equipped with the foresight and strategies she recorded and passed on to her son. In the future she is part of a heroic fight against the enemy of all humanity.

Sarah, however, just can't believe this absurd story and is certain there has been a case of mistaken identity. There is no way she can be a threat! She isn't a hero...she is just a waitress! She doesn't even have a boyfriend, so certainly there's no son! This nightmare is all a grave mistake!

But her guardian insists that she is, in fact, "Sarah Connor the hero," and his mission is to equip and protect her.

Overwhelmed, Sarah yells out, "I didn't do anything!"

To which her guardian counters, *"No, but you will!"*

You see, just like Sarah, we too have an enemy who knows who we are before we discover who we are. And because he is afraid of you, he has made it his aim to distract you from who you really are and what the purpose of your life truly is. It is his focused objective to undermine your future by luring you off the path of strength, life, and authority, and onto a course of intentional destruction.

The attacks on your life have much more to do with who you might be in the future than who you have been in the past. After all, no one launches a large-scale, systematic assault against something that's not considered a threat.

You are a beloved, royal child of the Most High God, but unless you know this, you cannot exercise your authority and summon all the powers and the companies of soldiers and angels around you to fight and win these battles. Unless you know that you cannot lose (because with God, you have the majority), you will feel alone, helpless and hopeless.

The enemy's approach will look different with each of us, but his goal is the same—he will do all that is within his power to hinder your growth, distract you from your heavenly destiny, and take away your dreams, your calling, your hopes, and even your life.

Manna's breathtaking story is the living proof of this. And as the wiles of the enemy are revealed from day one, the unmistakable and undeniable love and protection of God is there too, also from day one, and onward—through each trial, each affliction, and yes, even through each tragedy.

To Run With Horses is rich, tangible, and palpable. Every part of this book is teeming with substance and grace, even when it is raw and the most real. But that is life. That is honesty. That is humanity.

Manna's boldness in exposing the good, the bad, and the ugly is a sacrifice of love for each one of us. She lays it all down—every icon, every beauty mark, every safety net—so that every reader might be able to stand on her shoulders and grasp a vision of more! With Manna's encouragement, we are able to see further, side-step sinkholes, and bypass yet another unnecessary wilderness trek around the desert.

When I held the proof copy of this book in my hands, and as I touched it and beheld it, I knew…God's fingerprints are all over this. His anointing on this book is unquestionable.

I thank God Manna never gave up. I thank God she pressed in through the darkest and ugliest of times, and I thank God she believed in God's promises over her life more than in the lies of the enemy.

And I pray that through Manna's life, you, too, will discover who you are.

As you read the stories in this book, you will find yourself in similar circumstances—the names and the faces may be different, but that common thread of what we each face as women, and as sisters, will stand before you. The weight of your moment in history is here, in these pages, and you will have the opportunity to make choices that will bring life to your dreams and empower your calling—to be a hero for yourself.

Our circumstances and our culture cannot be trusted to give us the right words to form our prayers. Our prayers must be structured by the Creator of heaven and earth, Himself—the One who is the Architect and the Author of our lives.

It is time for the daughters of this twenty-first century to echo heaven's words.

Remember, the attacks on your life have much more to do with your future than with who you have been in your past. The enemy is afraid of you. That is why he seeks to oppress you. So chase after the enemy! Do not draw back! You are an extraordinary, virtuous, brilliant, and heroic daughter of the Most High God who lives to enhance the lives of others!

You, and everything about you, matters to God. He has a great and magnificent plan for your life.

Now is the time when we must rise up and flourish in love, and in boldness.

Now is the time to awaken the spiritual seed God planted inside you.

Now is the time to remember—you were made *To Run With Horses*.

Lisa Bevere
Pastor, Author, International Speaker
Texas, January 2023

PREFACE

Security is mostly a superstition. It does not exist in nature, nor do the children of men as a whole experience it. Avoiding danger is no safer in the long run than outright exposure. Life is either a daring adventure, or nothing.

—Helen Keller

Benjamin Gilchrist was an accomplished business strategist and former television producer who had been introduced to me by a mutual colleague. After several telephone conversations together, he had agreed to a meeting, and today was the day of our appointment.

This wasn't the first time I had pitched a TV show, nor was it the first time I was asked and/or cast to be on one. I knew what I was doing, and I knew my concepts for *two shows* would be a hit. Yes, many people believe their TV show idea is going to be "the one," but at the risk of sounding over-confident, I was not one of them. Everything I had created was researched, planned out, new, and fresh, *and* its success was also projected by several other sophisticated strategists. The timing of my proposal was ideal for a hungry market.

My meeting with Benjamin went very well and lasted longer than either of us anticipated. The more we talked, the more intrigued he was about my background and my life. He knew a bit of my history from our previous conversations and, of course, he had also done his own research on me. However, he hadn't understood the significance of the *why* behind my passion until now.

After I finished my presentation and answered all his questions, he leaned back in his chair, put his hands together in front of his chest, and silently nodded as his eyes scanned all the papers I had given him. He was in deep thought, and I dared not speak.

Finally, after what seemed like a very long time, he sat back up, neatly assembled all the papers together and tucked them back into the folder. "Manna. You did a remarkable job. Not only is there a market for this, but both could also be homerun hits," he said without reservation. "But I have a question for you."

"Okay. Ask away."

"We have enough content here. Plus, you're intelligent, you've got experience in the industry, and you'll be great in front of the camera. I'm not worried about any of that." He leaned forward and looked at me squarely. "So here's my question: Do you want to have a show for a decade or so and touch a few million people, or do you want to leave a legacy and touch the world?"

I was startled, but immediately responded, "That's a no-brainer! Of course, I want the latter!"

"Then, as fantastic as these ideas are, put them away, and write your autobiography. The enemy of *great* is *good*. Don't spend another minute on this and work on something *great! Write your story.*"

And that, dear reader, is how this all started.

I knew that what Benjamin had just said was true. In fact, I had known it for decades, but I had been hesitant—no, downright resistant—to tell my story.

This was not the first time I had been asked to write my autobiography. People have asked me to document my life experiences in a book for decades. CEOs and business owners in three different countries even offered to help me fund the endeavor.

However, each time I was asked to share my story, two emotions arrested me, one more than the other—fear and, ironically, gratitude.

Fear because so much ugliness had surrounded my life, and it was frightening to consider disclosing both the secrets that I hid to protect others, and those I hid to protect myself. But while fear had me restrained for a time, the second emotion eventually grew stronger and fueled my courage to overcome the first.

Gratitude.

I was grateful, because each time someone asked me to write my story, it affirmed that there was something good and useful about me that could be of help to someone else. While I had spent most of my life trying to survive, this recurring attention to my life encouraged me to persevere beyond mere survival.

Maybe one day my life could be a bridge to help hungry hearts cross to the other side where hope, purpose, joy, and love await…

That thought bolstered me, but I had to wait for the right time. Even the best of ideas is a bad idea if the timing isn't right. "Everything is beautiful in its own time" (Ecclesiastes 3:11 NIV).

When I turned fifty years old, something deep and undeniable stirred inside of me, and I knew. The time had finally come.

It was time to tell my story.

Still, I was not exactly rejoicing over this "opportunity." The thought of diving back into my past and reliving so much pain after I had finally come to such a sweet place of peace in my life was distressing. Where would I even begin? How was I going to tell about such painful things coherently, and dare I say, even elegantly? And how could I bring a reader into (and out of) the depths of it all, responsibly? Did I even have the skillset to do such a thing? I had done a lot of writing in my life, but I had not done any creative writing since grade eleven in Mrs. O'Brien's creative writing class (now over thirty-six years ago).

But more than all of this, did I have the courage to do it…and to finish it?

I thought of hiring a ghostwriter, but those closest to me kept telling me that I had to be the one to do this. So, while it was the last thing I wanted to do, in August of 2013, I surrendered to the inevitable. I cocooned myself and began writing. I prayed for wisdom and insight and asked God to tell me what to write—and He did, one line at a time.

There are a few more things I want to say before you begin.

First, this is an honest book. What I mean by that is that I pull no punches. I've tastefully reworked and softened certain stories, but I did not want to minimize the severity, truth, and weightiness of specific topics. I believe society has whitewashed Truth, and over time we have adopted a backward approach to many life issues. In the desire to maintain our comfort zones, as we seek to live an unbothered life, we have unwittingly agreed to be "tolerant" and "accepting" of things that are intolerable and unacceptable. "Evil" becomes "good" (tolerable and acceptable), and "good" (speaking up, taking a stand, being a voice that speaks Truth) seems "evil" because we're disrupting the status quo, which threatens our addiction to comfort.

But the only way we can make a positive difference and effectively remedy difficult and even offensive issues is by speaking them plainly—with love, patience, self-control, and wisdom, of course, but speaking them nevertheless.

Plus, we are living in an age and amongst a generation of truth seekers who will not settle for anything less than what's "real." Unless we are bold enough to be "real," the innocent and the vulnerable will continue to be unseen, unheard, and unloved, or worse—marginalized, abused, and used. They will continue to feel shame upon themselves and their families if they speak up. This does nothing to further their healing, and even less to propel them to the fullness of their calling and the manifestation of their dreams. And when one dream dies, all of humanity suffers. Think about all the unrealized books, inventions, scientific discoveries, cures, music, technology, art, and so on that could have been a blessing to the world, but are lost—along with the souls who never believed in themselves enough to bring them to life.

As I write this, the media is paying a great deal of attention to domestic violence, bullying, the sex trade, and the effects of pornography. But these issues have been going on for a very long time. We've simply dismissed them, or "tolerated" them for a long list of rationalized reasons (excuses).

Abuse in all its forms is not an issue to be hidden behind closed doors. Today, many organizations can provide the support and advocacy you (or someone you know) may need. A small list of resources is provided for your review at the end of the book.

No, this isn't a new message.

I'm just a new messenger.

So, in this book, I speak honestly, respectfully, and lovingly. I won't patronize you and hide behind flowery words. Yes, there will be some challenging stories, and reading them may cause some uneasiness, but as you continue reading, I believe you will find comfort, relief, and hopefully even answers for some of the adversities that you (or a loved one) may have also endured.

Secondly, I did not write this book for some strange kind of egocentric self-promotion, nor did I write this book in retaliation to anyone, or to vilify anyone. I am simply telling my story as I lived it, and I am telling it because I believe that my story will help others. For a variety of reasons, almost everyone's names, professions, locations, and in some cases, even their gender has been changed or purposely omitted. My life isn't about these people per se or their names. They were simply fellow travelers of life who joined me in a great adventure. And while I wish I never had to experience some of the things I did, each situation taught me powerful lessons that were vital to my growth. I would never be who I am today, were it not for every soul who played their part in my life.

And for that, I am thankful.

Lastly, I want you to know there is a happy ending. ☺

That said, I want to add that our goal ought not to be a "happy ending," but a happy *life* as we're living it. In the midst of our storms, we have to keep remembering, "This too shall pass." Storms don't last forever. Winter turns to spring. Night turns to day, and every morning we can start again. Indeed, in every moment we can make a choice to begin anew. If I can do it, you can too.

As my sweet friend, Filomena, said to me, "Manna, when you win, the world wins."

And so it is with you.

When you win, the whole world will win. So don't give up. There is always hope. You weren't created to settle for a mundane or tragic story. You were made to run with the horses and to win the race set before you. You may not believe it because of what you've lived through, but make no mistake, you have a divine purpose in life. God never sets you up for failure, only for greatness—and in between, there is the preparation. All these trials were to strengthen, prepare, equip, and transform you to step into the bigness of that calling—not just for yourself, but for others.

Whenever you or I choose to persevere through trials, to pursue our calling, and to walk in the truth of who we divinely are, we show others what is possible for them. We show them that they don't have to settle, and that they don't have to be destroyed by the difficulties or traumas that have blighted their lives. They can overcome by choosing to heal, grow, learn, forgive, love, and return good for evil. They can rise above even the worst mistakes, disappointments, and setbacks and fulfill their amazing purpose.

So please don't compare yourself with anyone else. It doesn't matter if you work at Walmart or work on Wall Street. God has uniquely placed you where you will receive the training and preparation you need to excel, fulfill your purpose, and make a difference in the lives of everyone who knows you. Sociologists report that even the most solitary people can influence up to ten thousand people in their lifetime. Somewhere, right now, you are making a big difference to some very special individuals who have been watching you and learning from you. Because of *you*, they could be the next winner of the Nobel Peace Prize, the next president of the United States of America, or the parent of the next Mother Teresa. Or they could be courageously learning to respond to trials with joy and faith, to love their spouse and family better, to serve their community, to develop and share their gifts, and to be fully alive and free!

Robert F. Kennedy once said, "Few will have the greatness to bend history itself, but each of us can work to change a small portion of events, and in the total of all those acts will be written the history of this generation." We can all contribute one small act of faith and one act of kindness at a time for a greater good.

You make a difference, my friend. Don't be discouraged, don't settle, and don't diminish yourself.

Hear the voice of the One who made you calling you to go higher, further, and deeper than you've been before.

In joyful, loving service,

Manna Ko

January 2023
San Diego, California

BOOK I
BRAVE HEART

"If ever there is a tomorrow when we're not together… there is something you must always remember. You are braver than you believe, stronger than you seem and smarter than you think. But the most important thing is, even if we're apart…

I'll always be with you."

— Pooh's Grand Adventure: The Search for Christopher Robin

1 TOUCHED BY AN ANGEL

There is no panic in Heaven! God has no problems, only plans.
—Corrie Ten Boom

Room 316

My shift with Noble Hospice Care started at 4:00 p.m., and it was now 4:30 p.m. I hurried across the parking lot and into the lobby of the hospital, pushed the button on the elevator for the third floor, and took a few deep breaths, centering myself for the next few hours ahead. Three stories up, Mrs. Leah St. John, who once dreaded my arrival (as she had plainly verbalized to me and anyone else within earshot), was most likely now wondering why I was late, and counting the minutes on the wall clock. Her confrontational style was not what I had expected when we first met, but her quick wit and fiery spirit both challenged and inspired me, and I had grown to like her very much.

Volunteering for hospice was something I loved to do. There are a few places where I know all my gifts, capacities, education, training, and spirit shine in their fullest—and sharing with people in the final period of their lives is one of them. People always tell me they feel safe with me, and because they feel safe, they make the most of our time together by being vulnerable, authentic, and real. During these sacred times, some of the deepest, most heartfelt, and transparent conversations can be had. Many people do their "soul's work" here and they are able to experience healing, forgiveness, love, freedom, and restoration all converging in a beautiful crescendo. As a hospice worker, it's been an honor to witness miracle after miracle as people engage in some of the greatest work of their lives.

This was my hope for Mrs. St. John, also.

The elevator dinged and the metallic doors slid open to reveal the nurse's station in the hospice ward. Chatting amongst themselves, the nurses didn't notice me as I stepped out of the elevator. I smiled and was about to greet them when I heard one of the nurses snort, "Ugh, if she calls me in one more time, I'm going to scream!"

"She's ridiculous!" a second nurse snapped. "I can't believe she actually thinks it matters whether or not she has half-and-half or Coffeemate in her tea at this point! I have a thousand other more important things to do than look for creamer!"

In shock, I realized they were talking about Mrs. St. John. One by one, the others added their cruel and exaggerated comments, and after each turn, they roared with bitter laughter.

By this time, I had walked past the small knot of women, but suddenly I stopped as anger swelled in me. *Perhaps they're just tired,* I reasoned, *or overworked.* But try as I might, no excuse could justify their acerbic remarks. *Should I say something? Or should I keep walking and pretend I didn't hear them?*

I thought of Mrs. St. John, lying alone in her bed, and with sudden resolve, I squared my shoulders, spun around on my heel, and approached the nurses' station. The woman who had started the onslaught turned to look at me with lazy disinterest.

I set my purse and bag down. "I can't believe the heartless things you just said—that you would degrade your patient with such a careless, flippant attitude. Mrs. St. John is a human being—a person with a heart, feelings, and *ears.* She's only a few feet away from you! Is this how nursing school taught you to serve a sick woman in her last months, or even days? Either you've forgotten why you're here to begin with or you're in the wrong job altogether!" I waved my hand to include all of the nurses, who now stood staring at me, stunned and speechless.

I looked directly at the woman who had complained about creamers. Her nametag read "Melody." She merely stared at me blankly. I took a deep breath and then looked one by one into the eyes of the other nurses, challenging them to reply. Each one immediately looked away and began pretending to look at charts and place papers in filing cabinets. None spoke. I scooped up my things and walked away, turning my focus to the patient waiting in room 316.

The door to the room was open. After a gentle knock, I walked in, not knowing if Mrs. St. John was awake. The lights were off, but the late afternoon sun filtered through the partially blinds. Except for the slow, rhythmic hum of one of the machines attached to the woman in the bed, it was quiet.

Mrs. St. John was awake and smiling at me as I walked in. "You're not quite as wholesome and uninteresting as I thought you were," she observed wryly. "I heard you giving those women a piece of your mind."

"I couldn't let them say those things about you," I said, still a bit aggravated at what the nurses had said (and also embarrassed that, despite the provocation, I had been so abrasive with them).

She waved away my comments with a frail hand. "I'm used to hearing such things. I've never been anybody's favorite. Besides, I prefer talk like that over people walking on eggshells around me just because I'm dying."

I pulled up my chair and positioned it beside her where I could hold her hand if a moment allowed. Some patients liked this and felt more secure when they could hold hands. Although I wasn't sure about Mrs. St. John, I was close by if she wanted my touch. I poured a cup of water from a pitcher and placed it next to the medication and the nurse's call button on the little table beside her bed.

"You came in here the first time, so prim and perfect, spreading your good deeds like fairy dust," she chided. "Do you know how many people tell me they understand how hard it is? But they don't! How could they? Their words just make me angry. It all seems to come from pity or feigned compassion because it's what they're *supposed* to say. It's their job—and a job they obviously don't much care for, I might add." Mrs. St. John's eyes rolled toward the door and out toward the nurses' station. "And for that matter, I don't know why *you* keep coming back here either. It's not like you have to. Aren't you a highfalutin' big wig out there?" She waved her thin hand in the air again.

I raised my eyebrows in surprise.

"Nothing passes me, young lady," she continued, narrowing her eyes at me. "I asked my husband, Thomas, to do some checking on you. He told me about all your accomplishments and all your big-shot clients. Well, let me tell you something. Just because I'm in here doesn't mean I'm to be pitied. I don't need pity. Never have. Never will." She exhaled, looked out the window to collect herself, and then returned her gaze to me. "Now, though, I see that you're made of stronger stuff than I thought. You have gumption. You seem to be legitimate. I'm glad to see it, and glad to see you're not perfect."

"Perfect?" I said with surprise. "Oh, no. I'm far from that."

"You're in good company then."

She tried to shift in the bed but winced and surrendered to her previous position.

"How are you feeling today?" I asked, reaching for her wrist to check her vitals.

She turned her head away. "No, no. None of that! I'm beyond the point of thinking that it matters how I feel from one moment to the next. And don't you placate me—just when I'm beginning to have hope for you. If we both have to be here, we might as well *keep it real,* as they say." She gave me the same wry smile again. "Let's make it interesting while we're at it. Tell me about *you*. I want to know why you're not so perfect."

"My stories aren't interesting, Mrs. St. John, and I hardly think they would entertain you. I'd rather hear about your life. Please tell me about you," I encouraged, hoping to change the subject.

"I've lived my whole life with myself. Now it's the only thing I have to mull over in all these lonely, quiet hours. At worst, I'm horrified, and at best, I'm bored. Distract me. Don't let me die with my last thoughts being about how I wish I had lived my life differently."

As a very private person, especially in a public and/or professional setting, I seldom shared my personal life, much less with someone I barely knew. I tried to change the subject again, but she met my every objection with a determined stare. When I knew I wasn't going to win, I conceded.

"Fine," I said reluctantly, "but there are so many stories that show I'm not perfect..."

"Really?"

"Yes, unfortunately. If we're going to be *real*, as you suggest, the truth is, I have always felt out of place and different. So, I just assumed there was something wrong with me."

"Interesting." Mrs. St John narrowed her eyes again. "Even as a child?"

"Yes."

"Were you an *unusual child*?"

I chuckled. "Well, I guess that's one way of looking at it."

Mrs. St. John raised one eyebrow and gave me an "all-knowing" look. She settled into her pillow, closed her eyes, and without missing a beat, said, "Just the way I like a good story to start. I'm intrigued already. Start from the very beginning. Begin whenever you're ready."

There was no escape. I took a deep breath, gulped down some water, leaned back into my seat, and began.

"The place is Hong Kong. And the date is October 1962..."

In The Beginning...

I lived with my maternal grandparents in Hong Kong, China. I never knew why they reared me from infancy while my brother, Luke, born only fourteen months after me, lived nearby with my mother, Emily, and my father, David. Many, many decades later, my mother's brother, Uncle Oliver told me no one was ever able to understand why either. He assumed that my mother simply didn't "bond" with me. When I pressed him to explain what that might mean, he hesitatingly confessed that he feared she "just didn't like me." As painful as that explanation was to hear as an adult, it was if nothing else, at long last, "the final answer."

Was I planned? If not, was that bad? Was she disappointed I wasn't a boy? Was I born at a difficult time in my parent's marriage? Was her dislike for me a result of a postpartum reaction? Was she too immature to understand the significance of having a baby? Was I a difficult baby?

What was it?

Many times throughout my life, I sought reasons that would explain my mother's dismissive and often antagonistic attitude toward me. Her obvious detachment was uncomfortable for my family, and since addressing shameful issues went against the unspoken law of our Asian culture, whenever I brought up this topic it was swept under the proverbial carpet with little opportunity for discussion. The few rare times I was able to approach the subject, I was met with vague and obscure comments, which quickly segued into other topics. Whether they were trying to protect me or couldn't understand it for themselves, I do not know. What I did know was the unmistakable sorrow and confusion in their eyes whenever the subject came up, confirming for me that my unanswered questions were, in fact, valid.

Since questions like these (and others) never got answered, I simply learned to live with the doubts and the fears associated with being unloved, unwanted, and disliked. The mystery of those unanswered questions followed me like a cloud I could see everywhere but could never grasp.

"Adult" Manna finally learned to move on by dismissing rejection with bravado and focusing on proving her worth with accomplishments, but "little" Manna was confused, apprehensive, and fragile. Accepting rejection at this vulnerable stage would have meant unspeakable despair, so to find hope to survive, I found other ways to reconcile the abandonment. I reasoned that perhaps the rejection was a function of something that I had unknowingly done. In this way, there was still an opening to restore the relationship.

I didn't realize that this one seemingly innocent thought would end up becoming a life-defining statement for me. I felt like I had to apologize for my existence altogether—for being an inconvenience, for being a burden, for being alive—and simultaneously to somehow find ways to satisfactorily prove my value to those I cared about, specifically my mother.

But as I discovered, no matter how much I apologized, my mother simply did not like me. So, I tried other methods. Instead of apologizing, I did my best to make up for things. I reasoned I must have taken something away from her, so to make things right I needed to redeem whatever she had lost. Moreover, I believed that I must now give her over and above whatever was missing, so she would then see I was not a curse on her life.

Maybe if I was good enough, if I tried harder, worked longer, or if I were smarter, prettier, and achieved more, then she would change her mind and like me.

But nothing changed.

In fact, things only grew worse with every passing day and year—as did the self-defeating beliefs, which began to define my thinking and my life.

I tried everything. I hunted, dug, and frontiered territories I wish I had never explored, all in the quest to find value and significance through my mother's love and acceptance, which never came. Consequently, I spent much of my life in seemingly endless struggles that almost killed me.

My maternal grandfather, "GongGong," was a highly respected medical doctor with an active practice, and was the head of the tuberculosis department at a famous local hospital. My grandmother, "PoPo" (pronounced "paw-paw"), was also educated in the medical field but had stayed home to raise her family.

I was very happy and felt safe with my grandparents. PoPo and I were extremely close, sharing something deeper than a typical family connection. I knew what she was going to say and what she needed, and she knew everything about me, too, as if she had the script of my life. She knew my vulnerabilities, my weaknesses, my strengths, and she also knew my gifts. She knew what to teach, share, permit, and nurture. And she knew how to discipline me, train me, and reach me like no one else could. Countless were the times when I would sense her presence and turn to see her in the room smiling at me.

Yes, PoPo was "love" to me, and all this began as soon as I was given to her. GongGong and I were also very close, but not like I was with my PoPo.

The three of us lived in a flat on the Kowloon side of Hong Kong. One entire wall of the living room was a large picture window with only a short lower wall at the bottom. On either side were floor-to-ceiling curtains. Through the window was a pristine and uninterrupted view of Lion Rock Mountain, so named because the peak itself resembled a lion in repose. I had only just begun to walk, and I found the majesty of that view irresistible. I remember going to that window as often as I could, holding onto the lower window frame to steady myself. I would simply stand there, captivated by the face of the lion. I loved looking at that lion, and though I do not know how I knew this, I knew that the lion had something to do with God Himself.

No one had ever told me about God, but somehow, I knew the Lion and God were one and the same. He was the ruler of all—majestic, noble, dignified, sovereign, and powerful. Yet I also knew that the Lion was loving, merciful, wise, faithful, and true. Something about the face of the Lion commanded respect and even honor, and something told my spirit that He had been in full and victorious reign throughout the ages. The Lion was all-seeing and all-knowing and I so very much longed to go to that mountain, where I believed God lived. I wanted to be there, close to Him.

"Well, you know, Manna," Mrs. St. John interjected, "the Bible calls Jesus 'the Lion of the Tribe of Judah.' He is also called 'the King of kings and the Lord of lords.'"

"Why Mrs. St. John, I didn't realize you knew the Bible so well!"

"And you thought you knew so much about me," she teased. "There was a time when I believed and even memorized the Scriptures—but that was a long, long time ago."

"Oh, you were hiding God's words in your heart, and—"

"Not for long!" she interjected. "I saw the hypocrisy of the nuns who forced me to memorize those verses, and I decided a long time ago that I could figure out life by myself. But enough about me! I want to hear more about your Popo and you."

I hesitated a moment, but then continued.

One night I was up much later than a little girl my age should have been. The house was dark, and I crossed the living room, moving toward the window to see my beloved Lion. However, that night I was greeted by a different sight. The mountain was black and cold. My good daytime Lion had been replaced by a nighttime lion whose face was callous and whose eyes were cold and evil. He was very different from the Lion I knew during the light of day, and it frightened me.

Whimpering, I ducked beneath the main window and crawled along the wall at the base to get away to the other side of the room. I did not like this lion one bit and didn't want him to see me—ever. This became my nighttime routine—crawling along the floor in this part of my grandparents' home to get from one room to another—even when the drapes were pulled closed.

This was when I learned that darkness has a presence, and it was the first time I knew fear.

On weekends, when my father wasn't working long shifts, I would go to stay with my parents, instead of being with PoPo and GongGong. That's when I would see my brother, Luke, and my father's parents, who also lived with them.

I had trouble sleeping without my Popo by my side, so my father would drive me in his car until I finally dozed off. However, he soon discovered that driving alone wasn't enough. I would only *stay asleep* if I could hear music by The Beatles. So in addition to his driving me around until the wee hours of the night, he had to also find a radio station that played their songs until I could fall asleep and stay asleep. I don't know what it was, but something about The Beatles' music comforted me.

My father was wonderful and patient with me, and was the only other haven of love and acceptance I felt other than the arms of my PoPo and GongGong.

My Brother's Keeper

By the time I was three years old, I was fiercely protective of my little brother, Luke. I don't know where this love and sense of guardianship for my brother came from, nor did I know what it meant to be a big sister. All I knew was how I felt, and as far as I was concerned Luke was "mine," and I had been entrusted with him. Yes, it's a strange statement, especially for a three-year-old, but my feeling for Luke was unmistakable. I *loved* my brother with all my heart, and were it not for our age difference, I would have sworn we were twins, I felt that connected to him.

One afternoon while staying with my parents, I sensed a new tension in the air. My mother and father were in the living room, their voices anxious as they spoke to each other. My mother was holding Luke and he was crying.

"We have to get him to a hospital," my father said.

"What's wrong with Luke?" I asked.

"It's okay," my father replied, patting my head with an absentminded gentleness.

My mother was looking for a phone number and trying to calm Luke at the same time. I knew something was wrong. My paternal grandparents were standing nearby, looking worried. My father walked away, busy and distracted.

"What's wrong, Mommy?" I asked.

"Not *now*, Manna!" she said.

Unsure what to do, I went to stand behind a living room chair where I could observe and try to understand what was happening without upsetting anyone.

The adults continued to speak in their cryptic language, and all I could understand was that Luke had to go to the hospital and perhaps have surgery. *What was wrong with my little brother?*

A sense of helplessness started to rise in me. I timidly approached my paternal grandmother, my "MahMah," hoping to find some answers from her. She, too, was a highly revered medical doctor - the first female gynecologist in China. During WWII, she became an emergency and trauma physician, who turned her own home into a hospital after the Japanese bombed the hospital where she worked.

"MahMah," I softly whispered, "Is Luke okay?"

"Yes. Now go and play with your toys while we sort things out."

I didn't believe her, and watching the commotion going on around me, I became more scared and more worried about Luke. I couldn't contain myself and had to ask again. This time I was sent into a room and told to stay there until they came to get me.

Before I knew it, my parents were out the door with Luke, and I was taken back to PoPo and GongGong's home. For the rest of the evening, I tried to play with my toys, but the anxiety in the pit of my stomach lay heavy and untended.

I learned much later that Luke had been rushed to the hospital with a hernia and had undergone surgery to repair the problem. I was finally taken to the hospital to visit him the following day. Once we were in the hospital parking lot, I remember climbing out of the car, and as I stood waiting for the adults to close the car door, I wondered if the doctors and nurses were doing a good enough job taking care of my little brother. I also remember asking God if my little baby brother was going to be okay or if was he going to go to heaven. The thought made me sad, and I didn't know what to expect when I walked into the hospital.

Thankfully, when we walked into the room, Luke was lying in the hospital bed, happy and smiling. My heart filled with gratitude when I saw his face. My parents inspected the stitches and nodded with approval. I surmised that all was well and Luke would not be going to heaven; rather, he would be coming back home where I was sure I could do a better job of taking care of him.

When Luke did come home from the hospital, he seemed even sweeter and more loveable to me. I was very relieved to know he was safe, and my fears about losing him were finally put to rest. But, having Luke back home only begged the question once again of why we didn't live together as a family. *Why could I only see him when I was taken to him? Why was it so normal to everyone that Luke and I should be apart from one another?*

I also wondered why I could only sleep when I had my arms and legs tightly wrapped around my PoPo, and why I could not sleep when I was with my father, even though I also loved him so very much. I wondered why The Beatles' music made me so happy. I wondered why I would see things and have dreams or visions that would tell of the future, but no one else did. I wondered why I was called foolish when I told people what I saw.

And I wondered why there was such a difference between the Lion in the morning and the lion at night.

"Oh, Manna, those are questions too great for a little child to find answers for," Mrs. St. John interrupted. "Such uncertainty …you had such fear at a young age."

"Yes, but my fears didn't come from these unanswered questions. They came from other things…"

"Your mother." Mrs. St. John said instinctively.

PoPo and GongGong

Both PoPo and GongGong always made time for me, and over the course of my childhood, they taught me new things daily and shared life lessons with me through stories of their past. They had been through *two* World Wars, the Great Depression, revolutions, and other radical, life-changing events. Of the many stories they shared with me, what moved me most were the experiences they endured during WWII.

Of course, at four years old, I did not understand fully what war was or how its effects forever change the lives of those it touches. Listening to PoPo and GongGong—seeing them cry as they recounted some of the events that happened to them during those times—was the beginning of that education.

"During the war," GongGong explained, "Your PoPo and I had to escape from the Japanese soldiers very quickly. Thankfully, we were given advance warning about a special recruitment of soldiers coming only for those of the royal court—which included us. We didn't have time to plan an escape or to prepare for a long journey, much less pack all the necessities, or our precious valuables and heirlooms. But we did the best we could as we left our home and everyone we loved behind. We were able to hide a few things, but the Japanese took most of it and claimed it as their own."

GongGong took a deep breath and looked away as the memories became real again. A dignified man, my grandfather stood just over six feet. He was very handsome, with high cheekbones, gentle yet deep eyes, and a smile that would endear anyone to him. He was also a brilliant man and an avid learner, with the ability to understand concepts few others could. In his mid-eighties, GongGong would attend the same university I did, taking classes in astronomy, advanced biology, and chemistry, and computer science. Yes, GongGong was very special indeed. He dedicated his life to medicine and to humanity, ensuring his patients were always treated honorably, whether they were coming in for a simple vaccine or were taking their last breaths. So, to see him sad and tearful as he recounted stories about the inhumanity he experienced during WWII was a sight I will never forget.

"Our family had to separate. My parents and siblings, and PoPo's parents and siblings, all fled in different directions. Our only real plan was to somehow get to Hong Kong.

"It was a frightening time, and there was no way to get messages to loved ones safely and quickly. Communication systems then were very different from what is available today, plus it was wartime. Accurate and trusted information, though critical, was scarce and unpredictable. There was no time to second-guess a decision. Like an animal being hunted, you simply had to trust your instincts for survival. Sometimes, the news that found its way into villages or temporary campsites caught us so off guard we couldn't breathe after hearing it. The information was often so devastating that we didn't have time to feel or to indulge in emotion. There was only enough time to respond and then move quickly. We learned to sleep with one eye open—if we slept at all—and to live with very little.

"Food was a luxury, and water was just as precious. We thanked the heavens for rain and used large leaves to capture as much as we could when the rains did come. We also tried to store as much water as possible in the containers we had, but soon realized the weight of full containers burdened us too much and we could not travel well with them. Who would have thought that the essentials we needed to keep us alive were an encumbrance we could not afford? Many times, we had to sacrifice that treasured elixir so that we could be limber and move quickly in a variety of unknown and potentially dangerous settings.

"Thankfully, we were always provided for. Somehow, some way, we always got water when we needed it, and food for nourishment when we didn't have the energy to go on. I confess, I didn't know much about God at that time and wondered if there was a God at all because of what we witnessed and what we were living through. But my doubts were always replaced with certainty after seeing one miracle after another. In time, I started to just say prayers of thanks, and that gratitude became a salve that soothed my aching body and overworked mind.

"Quiet time was also a rarity in those days, and something I also learned to cherish. We were shaken to the core daily by the sounds of piercing air sirens warning anyone within earshot that an airstrike was imminent. Soon, the rumble of war-planes could be heard overhead, and the booms and deafening explosions of bombs followed, throwing us off our feet. The inconsolable cries of adults, little children, and animals—wounded or traumatized—were almost too much to bear.

"Sometimes there would be no airstrike. Instead, the words spoken by a courier imparting the latest news of the Japanese assault and the territory they were seizing were just as deafening. When there were times of silence, we embraced them."

It was especially moving to hear GongGong speak of PoPo with such admiration in these desperate circumstances.

"Your PoPo was very brave, Manna. I was so proud of her and how she handled everything. One would expect someone of her lineage, surrounded by servants attending to her every need, and cocooned from the roughness of life outside of the court, to be demanding, offended, or entitled. But she was the exact opposite. She was a true lady—an angel. She served others, helping anyone who came by the temporary campsites for rest. She cooked for them, taught them skills for survival, tended to the children and the elderly, and nursed the wounded.

"You see, Manna, although such evil surrounded us, we were still able to share love with one another. That love was in the simple kindnesses—repositioning a blanket over someone to protect her neck and back from the weather, carrying an extra bag for someone who was tired, and sharing what little food we had with one another. Time and time again, love triumphed over evil whenever we took the time to give, and we were always blessed a thousand times more for it later, in ways we didn't expect. Sharing food especially was a sacrifice of love because it was all we had, and we didn't know if we were going to get anymore. That's why PoPo always tries to cook for you now and makes you eat everything on your plate," GongGong said with a smile, touching my face.

"Small groups would gather together and share dumplings, rice, and soups in remote and temporary campsites en route to Hong Kong. Soups were especially popular. A few pieces of meat and bones, some vegetables, a bit of rice, and *a lot* of water could make a very filling and relatively nutritious meal for a large number of people. Sometimes the water quality wasn't good, but because it was boiled, it was no longer toxic. We learned to be thankful for the small blessings.

"Because food was often a rationed commodity and such a treasure to have, PoPo used to say she wasn't hungry and was just satisfied with the watered-down soup. She would say she loved to chew on the bones, so the family could have the meat and the other goodies. This is the beautiful heart of your PoPo, Manna. Even now, as I tell you this story, I marvel at her. She was only in her early twenties when the war broke out. We had been married just a few years, and she was a mother to two very young children—your Uncle Oliver and your mother.

"Yes, your PoPo was amazingly courageous. To stop her mind from being overtaken with fear, she would hum songs, especially in new campsites where we didn't know anyone. Every now and then, when she had a few minutes alone, she would find a quiet place and sit on a rock. She would take a small tattered envelope out of a hidden pocket, and carefully unfold that envelope to reveal one of her most precious possessions—a few photos of her parents and siblings, whom she dearly loved and missed. Never giving in to self-pity, as soon as tears would flow, she would gather herself again, wrap the photos back in the enclosure and return it to its safe home in her clothing."

"Did PoPo pray too?" I asked. I was very curious about my grandparents' experiences with God and hoped they would help explain my experiences of Him.

"Yes, Manna. She did. But you should know it wasn't normal to do that then. China was a Buddhist country, and we were never taught about God's love for us, much less talk *about Him*—except maybe for the occasional missionaries we encountered here and there. But your PoPo came to know God. And yes, she did pray.

"In fact, even though the concept of *God* may not have been the way of life for most Chinese people, during the war, I saw many people cry out to God and believe in Him—especially after seeing and receiving so many miracles. These incidents may seem small by today's standards, but a small act of kindness, a little generosity, and a little compassion now and then were life-savers to us, literally. Yes, they were miracles to us.

"We had heard on the radio that the whole world was at war because a country called Germany had a leader and followers with hearts like the Japanese leader and his followers. They were persecuting Jewish people in unspeakable ways. The news was horrible…" My grandfather stopped in mid-sentence as he remembered those times. After a few moments, he continued.

"We prayed for the Jewish people too. We knew that we had brothers and sisters in humanity suffering around the world…it was a very dark time for all of us. As much as I would like to forget these times, it's also important to remember them. Maybe that's why we're talking about this now. Perhaps it's heaven's way… creating an opportunity to share these memories so that generations after me never forget. We must always remember these atrocities—not to torture ourselves with the memories or to blame people over and over again for the past. We must learn from the past and to never, ever, ever allow ourselves to repeat it. We ensure this never happens again by being kind, forgiving, generous, and thoughtful. And while we must never forget the bad things, we must also remember the good things.

"Remember the stories I'm telling you of people extending love to one another. Overcome evil with love, Manna. Start with small situations as you learn this life principle. Maybe someone at school hurt your feelings. Let it go. There will be times to speak up, but when you do so, speak with kindness. The more you let go, and the more often you speak with kindness, the more you share the spirit of peace. In time, the other children will learn to do the same. And one day, you will not only affect the school, but you'll also change the city—who knows, maybe even the nations!" GongGong beamed at me with an assuring smile.

"Just remember, whenever you are kind and offer a simple act of thoughtfulness to someone, it could be a miracle for them. Always remember this, okay?" He placed his hand on my forehead as if to anoint me with this declaration. "Promise your GongGong you will do your best to be thoughtful and kind. And always remember to show love to others."

Sitting beside him, I no longer felt like he was just telling me a story. It felt more like a dedication, a sacred commemoration. GongGong was passing something on to me—the older, wiser king to the younger, still green princess. My spirit was awakened by his words, just as Graham Greene once penned: "There is always one moment in childhood when the door opens and lets the future in."

"I promise, GongGong. I promise to be thoughtful and kind and to show love to others," I said with confidence. "Maybe one day I will be able to do something to help others, too! Maybe it will even be a miracle for them, just like you and PoPo did!"

"Yes, Manna. I believe you will indeed, and miracles will abound." He smiled.

"Tell me more, GongGong! Tell me more!" I pleaded.

"Well, okay, just a little bit more. Then we will get ready for dinner, and after that, prepare for bed, okay?" he negotiated.

"Okay, GongGong," I agreed reluctantly. "But will you tell more stories about your life tomorrow?"

"Yes." He smiled.

"Promise me, GongGong?" I asked as I looked intently into his eyes as he had done to me earlier.

"I promise," he said, laughing as he swept the hair away from my eyes.

Sure enough, the next day GongGong went on to finish the story of how he and PoPo survived the war. "When the news reports were too frightening, PoPo would pray out loud, no matter who was around to hear it! It was the only thing that kept her from fainting or giving in to the fear that pervaded the atmosphere. When the tears would flow, she prayed through each salty drop. Through seemingly endless days of foot travel and the haunting possibility that we may never complete our journey from Beijing to Hong Kong, she would pray.

"The war was intensifying. Reports of massacres by enemy soldiers were spreading like wildfire. We were told of their cold-hearted accuracy as they dealt death to every Chinese person they saw—even babies, children, the lame, and the elderly.

"We also heard horror stories of concentration camps where the most evil of tortures were inflicted upon the innocent who were captured. Anyone who was caught helping the Chinese, from the missionaries to our allies, were also tortured, dying lonely, painful deaths.

"With these kinds of reports increasing, panic escalated. Any pathways to safety were bombarded. People became crazy—doing horrible things to one another to secure their own safety. Friends betrayed friends, and even family members betrayed one another, sometimes for only a few pieces of silver.

"This was one of the saddest events we had to witness," GongGong sighed, shaking his head. "There is a saying, 'Desperate people do desperate things,' and I can tell you this aphorism is true. The true character of any man is known in and defined by the harshest of circumstances.

"Confucius once said, 'The superior man is aware of righteousness. The inferior man is aware of advantage. The virtuous man is driven by responsibility. The non-virtuous man is driven by profit.' Manna, my hope is that through our painful experiences, we can show you and the family that our character must always stand on a firm foundation of righteousness and virtue. We are to be purposefully living the call on our lives in responsible, loving service to others. Our character and virtue must never be purchasable by vanity, advantage over others, or driven by profit. Wisdom will show you where to stand. Execute your decisions on that scale in life."

"Yes, GongGong." I nodded.

"Good girl. I'm so proud of you. Manna, you are a very special little girl, not like the others. I see your spirit in your eyes. Listen well, heed well, be mindful in all you do, and be self-disciplined—first in your thoughts, which will dictate your deeds."

"Yes, GongGong. I will."

GongGong chuckled so that his head tilted back and forth—a momentary smile to lighten the heaviness of the memories he was narrating.

"What did you and PoPo do next, GongGong?"

GongGong sighed deeply, his smile fading. "I remember watching your PoPo out of the corner of my eye, standing motionless in silent heartbreak as she watched people tear each other apart, trampling over each other—even with vehicles. People even left loved ones behind trying to get through barricades that led to a bus, truck, or train promising to deliver them to Hong Kong. Some of those passengers did make it, but many did not. Patrolling enemy soldiers intercepted their journey. Trucks exploded after hitting hidden mines. Trains rushed off unknown cliffs because the tracks had been destroyed with successive bombs. I think this was when your PoPo came to terms with the reality that her former life as she knew it—her family, her home, her friends, her dream of being a painter, everything—was over. Nothing was ever going to be the same again.

"With no trusted routes to take, we needed to make another difficult decision. We had to part ways with the few servants who had insisted on coming with us. They were more like family than hired help, but even though we were already a relatively small group of about seven, we were still too large in number to maneuver through such dangerous territories. We gave them some of our precious belongings in the hopes that they would be useful on their journey—to barter for food, water, shelter, medical attention, and yes, even bribes whenever necessary.

"Now all that remained was the four of us, PoPo, Uncle Oliver, your mother, and me. Chaos was everywhere, and every place we were told was a safe house was no longer safe. We didn't know who to trust, and each situation was a perilous one. To avoid the growing number of patrolling enemy soldiers, our long days of walking turned into long days of hiking in outlying areas. The cities were just not safe anymore. They were mostly occupied by enemy troops or completely overtaken with active battles. The smaller villages were questionable, as spies and traitors abounded, scavenging for information on the latest escape routes into Hong Kong in exchange for a reward.

"So, we headed to the forest, staying along the river's edge whenever we could. Although it wasn't easy hiking with two small children while carrying our few belongings on our backs, we found the strength to do it because we were together. We never imagined we would be separated from each other, but one day, we were forced to part ways.

"A river ran through the part of the terrain where we were traveling. Since I came from a long line of agriculturalists and was familiar with the region, I knew this river was deep in all but one spot. I also knew the enemy would not consider that river a viable escape route and therefore would not patrol it. While it was not as deep or treacherous as the rest of the river where the force of the rushing rapids prevented any passage, that shallow stretch was by no means easy to cross. It was slick and muddy, and water snakes lived in the mire there.

"I didn't tell your PoPo about the water snakes, though. If I had, she would not have crossed that river. She hated snakes and used to wince and shudder at even the mention of them.

"Our plan was for your PoPo to cross the river with your mother, and me with Uncle Oliver. Once we crossed the river, PoPo and your mother would stay low among the shrubs along the river's edge where they might more easily hide. There, their steps could not be easily tracked.

"I would take the higher path closer to the mountain ridge with Uncle Oliver so that I could watch for the enemy and make sure that PoPo and your mother were safe below us. If I saw anything suspicious or threatening, I had devised a way to alert PoPo with a special sound made from the branches of a certain tree that was indigenous to this region. When blown through a cavity or struck together, this wood made a very different sound than any other of the typical sounds of the forest. If PoPo heard this sound, she would know danger was nearby and she must act swiftly to hide. The enemy though, would not know the difference between this sound and the other sounds natural to that forest habitat.

"But first, we had to cross the river.

"We set out. With your Uncle Oliver on my shoulders, I stepped into the water first. With uncompromising focus, I trusted my feet to find sure footing between the unseen and slippery rocks, testing each step gingerly before firmly planting myself. I had to avoid the areas where the soft mud could cause us to sink too deep, while simultaneously dodging the long strands of floating vegetation, which would wrap around our legs and ankles. Thankfully, we never became tangled in these menacing weeds. If that had happened, we could have fallen and been carried helplessly down to the rapids or dragged beneath by the even stronger undercurrents.

"Meanwhile, PoPo courageously followed with your mother tightly wrapped in a cloth sling on her back. Even though they were behind me, I talked to them the entire time, advising PoPo of what to expect with each step and encouraging her as she made the hazardous crossing. I couldn't afford to take my eyes away from what was ahead of me, so Popo had to speak to me constantly, repeating back my instructions methodically. That way I could know she was all right and still behind me. Because rivers can be noisy, I couldn't rely on my hearing alone. I needed to hear her words to assure me. Ironically, I was thankful for that noisy river, as it prevented our enemy from hearing our communications.

"Suddenly, I heard unusual and louder-than-normal splashes. I immediately held my breath because I was afraid PoPo had fallen. I braced myself, planted my feet as solidly as I could and slowly turned around to see Popo pointing in horror. Several water snakes were swimming past her, raising their shiny, slimy, ugly heads as they did so. Some snakes even slowed to stare at her with their cold and calculating eyes—almost as if they were assessing her. She held her breath and tried to beat them away with some of the loose branches flowing down the river. Then she looked up at me and told me that even more snakes were slithering against the skin of her legs. I knew she wanted to scream, but she could not. She only whimpered and bit her lips.

"Then with total resolve, she began repeating, 'Dear God, help me…help me!' as she determined to get to where I was. I steadied myself again and waited for her midstream, coaching her the best I could, encouraging her to focus on me alone and not to look at the snakes. When she finally reached me, all she could do was cry as she hung on to my shirt, burying her face in my chest. She had come face to face with her greatest childhood fear. I didn't speak. I only held her.

"Somehow, we would make it, together.

"We stood without moving for what seemed like hours—even though I know it must have only been seconds. We didn't have the luxury of time, so with mixed emotions, I slowly let go of her, turned around, found my footing and continued. After all, being stuck in the middle of a river was not a good place to be. Not only were we vulnerable to the elements, we were obvious to the enemy. PoPo braced herself and was ready to continue also. The possibility of more snakes surrounding her was great but being caught by enemy soldiers was even more frightening.

"When we reached the other bank, we collapsed on the hillside. I do not believe either one of us realized we had been holding our breaths. In between our exhaustion and the exhilaration of overcoming such a daring challenge, we laughed and cried uncontrollably.

"After we had rested a while and eaten a few pieces of dried fruit, we continued our trek and braced ourselves to face something much more terrifying than that dreadful river crossing, for this was where we had to separate. It was too risky to travel together. By separating, at least we could delay the soldiers in their search if one of us got caught, thereby buying time for the other one to travel further and hopefully get away. This choice increased the chances that at least one of us, and one of the children, could make it.

"PoPo, with your mother still wrapped tightly on her back, said goodbye to Uncle Oliver and me, trying to give us good advice between her sobs and tears. She kissed your Uncle Oliver all over his face many times and held him tightly against her. I had to look away, pretending to look for a walking stick or some provisions so she wouldn't see the tears running down my own face. I gathered myself and put on a brave front as I said goodbye to my bride and to my little daughter. I had no choice but to believe that I would see them again, but deep down in my stomach, I didn't know. As I thoughts about PoPo taking care of your mother and herself for several days alone, the angst inside my heart and soul was beyond anything I had ever experienced.

"Not wanting to risk losing more time, as there was a substantial distance to travel before the sun started its descent down the other side of the mountain, I pulled myself together and ushered us along our separate ways. PoPo knew what she had to do and I had to trust that she was going to be all right. She would find her way to the village where we agreed to meet."

GongGong paused again, wiping tears from his eyes with a soft white handkerchief he pulled out of his pocket. "As I was saying…I too had to stay focused on the immediate tasks at hand: take care of Uncle Oliver, travel safely through the mountain range, and reunite with my family on the other side.

"Thankfully, the nights were quiet, the days were uneventful, and the enemy did not approach. When I finally arrived at the small village, I did not see PoPo and your mother at first. I had to search for them among the many different groups gathered in various locations. Finally, I saw them huddled together, sleeping near a small campfire. I did not realize until that moment how overwhelming love and gratitude could be. I paused for a moment, watching them sleep with the moonlight above, and thanked God for our safety. Uncle Oliver pulled at my trousers and asked me what I was looking at. When he realized it was PoPo and your mother, he ran to them, calling their names with joy. We cried and held each other for a very long time.

"There were many more nights similar to that one, but I have come to realize that it is only because of those sad and heart-wrenching times that we learned the true weight and power of our love for each other. Yes, we were back together again."

"Oh, GongGong! That's such a beautiful story! And now, I'm with you too! I'm very sad you had to go through the war. War is horrible! How can people be so mean to one another? It is hard to understand."

I jumped onto his lap and wrapped my arms around him. My beloved

GongGong held me tightly, and I held on too, just as tightly, never wanting to ever be separated from him or my PoPo.

"GongGong, we're never going to be separated, are we?" I asked. "I have to be with you and PoPo forever! I couldn't bear it if we were ever separated."

MahMah and YehYeh

At my parent's house, my anxieties and fears were not dealt with so delicately.

In the Chinese language, there was a way to acknowledge and distinguish the maternal grandparents from the paternal ones. PoPo and GongGong were my maternal grandmother and grandfather respectively. MahMah and YehYeh were my paternal grandmother and grandfather respectively. MahMah and YehYeh lived with my father, mother, and Luke.

I've shared a little about my MahMah already. She, too, was a true heroine, helping hundreds of orphans escape to Hong Kong during the war. She personally delivered them (at great risk to her own life) to their distant family members. She then made the perilous journey *back into China* where she continued to heal the wounded in her makeshift hospital at home. MahMah made these trips regularly, and articles were even written about her heroic acts of love.

YehYeh served as a radio engineer with the British Royal Navy in Hong Kong. He was a rough man and dealt with issues and people in the same fashion—abruptly. He traveled often, and when he was home, everything seemed to be an imposition to him, including Luke and myself.

One night, when I was four and Luke was only two and a half, YehYeh had just returned from one of his trips. He overheard me asking my father for a small light to be turned on in the living room so the house wasn't so dark. Before my father could answer me, YehYeh interrupted.

"Manna!" he shouted. "Don't tell me you still can't sleep like normal people! You've been doing this too long. You're spoiled and causing too much trouble!" He turned and directed his attention to MahMah. "Don't give her a light!" he commanded. "She can learn to fall asleep like the rest of us. And don't give her any dinner either! Let her cry all night if she has to. That will teach her!"

My father bristled at YehYeh's interference, but out of respect for his mother, and to a more limited degree, his father, he said nothing. He and his father seldom got along, and they often perceived each other's comments to be personal affronts. It wasn't until decades later that I would learn YehYeh had abused my father, and their relationship had never been healed or restored.

The silence was deafening after YehYeh's warning. He was almost taunting my father, as if trying to lure him into some kind of argument. However, my father bit his tongue, and said nothing. Instead, he took my hand and led me to the kitchen, where we ate a small meal together. Afterward, he took me back to the bedroom, where he sat and talked with me until I fell asleep.

The next day, just before dinnertime, YehYeh called me to his bedroom because he wanted to show me something.

Thinking he wanted to show me something interesting, I wanted to share the opportunity with my brother. "Can I bring Luke?" I called out innocently.

After a moment's hesitation, he replied, "If you want to."

I was quite surprised that YehYeh would want to spend some time with me, especially after yesterday's scolding. *Maybe MahMah talked some sense into him, and he's trying to make things up to me,* I thought to myself. *Maybe he wants to show me a game, or maybe we will read together like PoPo and GongGong do with me.*

Needless to say, I was excited to find out what wonderful surprise YehYeh had in store for us, so I hurried to find Luke, and asked him to come with me. Luke took my hand and followed me down the hallway that led to the bedrooms. The hallway was long and unlit. It was getting dark now, but the door to YehYeh's bedroom stood ajar, letting a narrow stream of light out into the shadowy hallway.

Suddenly, I was no longer so excited to see YehYeh's surprise, and felt suspicious of what lay ahead. That suspicion turned into anxiety—even Luke's hand began to squeeze mine. We moved forward ever so slowly, trying to be obedient. Halfway down the hall we looked nervously at each other, and then forced ourselves to continue, believing that something good and benevolent was waiting for us from YehYeh, though we were growing more afraid with each step.

"YehYeh?" I called out apprehensively.

There was no answer.

I called again and still there was no answer.

We reached the door and I stopped. Luke stood behind me. I began to push the door open, timidly calling out for YehYeh. Just then, I noticed a slight movement behind the door.

I froze.

"YehYeh?"

Silence.

I slowly pushed the door open a little bit more, and as I did so, someone resembling YehYeh leaped out at us, roaring at the top of his voice. His mouth had become a gaping hole, and in his hand, he somehow held his teeth! He shook his dentures at us, manipulating them as if they were chomping away and about to devour us. The man lunging after us seemed deformed. His face was distorted, even twisted with cruel and taunting eyes. We had never seen anyone without teeth before, so we were sure he was a ghost or something demonic!

I shrieked at the top of my lungs and we both turned and ran away, screaming. YehYeh charged after us, holding his misplaced teeth in his hands like a ventriloquist would with his dummy and yelling at the top of his lungs "I'm going to *catch you and eat you up for dinner*! *Arrrgggh!*" His gnawing teeth seemed to move on their own at the end of his outstretched arms.

Up to that point in my young life, we had no idea that YehYeh's teeth were not his own. We didn't know anything about the existence of dentures. All we knew was that a part of his body was no longer where it belonged, and he was threatening to eat us with his teeth! My heart felt ready to burst from the horror.

MahMah was in the kitchen, but upon hearing our screams she came running toward the bedroom, just in time for Luke to jump into her arms. She scooped him up and tried to comfort him as he caught his breath in between sobs. I ran to clutch her legs, but instead of calming me like she did for Luke, she pushed me away, swatting me on the tender part of my head.

I was dumbfounded. *Why did she hit me? What did I do wrong?*

"Stop screaming!" she admonished me. "You're upsetting your brother!"

YehYeh came up behind us, laughing so hard he had to hold onto the wall to remain upright. He continued to rattle his teeth at me, but I wouldn't look at him. I scrambled to hide behind my MahMah's legs, even though I knew this would anger her again.

"That'll teach you not to be so weak," he chuckled.

MahMah rebuked YehYeh, but he dismissed her with a wave of his free hand and went back to his room, laughing and snickering all the way down the hall. MahMah took Luke into the kitchen and sat him down in a kitchen chair where she told him she would protect him and keep him safe. She handed him a treat and something cold to drink.

I was left behind—as if I wasn't even there. MahMah did not come back into the living room where I sat alone, trying to recover from the grim vision of YehYeh's face.

Once again, I was haunted by questions. *Why was I smacked on the top of my head? Why did I not receive any comfort? What did I do wrong? Was I not important too? Was I not a part of this family?*

Something is Rotten in the State of Denmark

A strange feeling that had once come only now and then started to become more frequent, and with each passing day, I grew more afraid of being without my PoPo and GongGong. It wasn't the war stories GongGong told me. The fear didn't come from an external source. It was something internal. Somehow, I *knew* something bad was going to happen, even though nothing on the outside appeared to be different, and life seemed quite "normal."

I was enrolled at a young age in a private school where I began learning to write the complex and elaborate characters of my native language, Cantonese. I was also learning Mandarin at home with my grandparents, which is a dialect as different as if it was another language altogether.

Many days when PoPo would take me to school, an absolute terror would rip through me. I could not breathe knowing I was going to be separated from her. I screamed and cried and clung to her as if my life depended on it. She was everything to me, and I was panic-stricken to be away from her.

In those moments, my grandmother did not know what to do, because I refused to release my grip, wailing even louder if anyone attempted to pry me away from her. Finally, after trying every conceivable method of forcing me from her with no success, the school allowed her to sit outside the classroom door while I attended class. The teacher left the door open so I could see my PoPo anytime I looked over, which I did whenever I began to feel anxious. When I saw her, she would smile and wave to me. Only then was I able to breathe normally again and to return to my studies.

This went on for weeks. Then one morning, just as class was about to start, PoPo fixed the collar of my uniform and said, "Manna, I'm here, so don't worry. Just pay attention to your studies. But you must know that if I sit too long, my back sometimes hurts. If that happens, I will just go for a little walk down the hallway. Or I may need to visit the restroom, so don't worry if you don't see me, okay? I will be back."

She loved me enough to take the time to explain things to me so I didn't feel abandoned. Eventually, I was able to manage without seeing PoPo at the door during class, believing she was just down the hallway. And when I did see her after school, I would run to her and hug her with all my might. We would then walk home and share our day's happenings with each other.

My PoPo was amazing. Even now, as I recount this memory, her love for me still takes my breath away. Unfortunately, there were still times when, seemingly for no good reason, I would be devastated with panic at the thought of being without her. Little did I know that was something I would soon be forced to bear.

It seemed that with every passing day my doubts, fears, distrust in those around me, and need to fend for myself grew. Even at GongGong and PoPo's, where I found love, security, and comfort, my fears were magnified in the dark. I could not sleep without my grandmother in my bed. So she would lie with me each night while I wrapped my arms and legs around her—my way of ensuring that she could not leave without my knowing.

Some nights I woke up to find that she had somehow disengaged herself from my sleepy limbs and was no longer beside me. I would call for her and she would always come into the room, whispering in her soothing voice, "I'm here. Sleep now." She would smooth down my hair and rub my back until I slept again. Although this routine went on for years, my grandmother's patience, love, and compassion never waned.

One summer night when I was five and a half years old, I woke, and the dark seemed deeper than usual. Moonlight filtered through the window and slanted across the bed, making the corners of the room seem endlessly black. PoPo was not beside me. I called for her as I usually did, but her soft voice did not answer. She did not come. A deep fear edged its way through my body, and my stomach knotted as I crept out of bed and opened the door.

Something was wrong. I could feel it. I crawled on the floor underneath the picture window, past the looming night lion, more afraid than ever before that he would see me. I shuddered, and my skin prickled. When I reached the other side of the window, proud that I had accomplished this task more quickly than ever before, I heard voices.

I don't know what made me pause instead of calling out with relief, but I did pause, and I could tell from the muffled tone of the voices that something was indeed very wrong. PoPo's voice was choked with tears, and GongGong was soothing her, although I could hear the distress in his voice too. Suddenly unable to stand it, I burst into the kitchen and said, "What's wrong? What's going on?"

My grandparents were surprised to see me and looked at each other in silence. I could see by their faces that I was right—something was terribly wrong. Their words tried to convince me otherwise, but their eyes betrayed their sadness.

"Oh, Manna, it's nothing you need to worry about," GongGong said. He was stirring his tea on the countertop, but he stooped to bend down to meet me eye to eye. "It's just grownup conversation. Let's get you back to bed."

I turned to my grandmother. "PoPo, what's wrong? Something is wrong. Please tell me," I asked beseechingly.

She looked at GongGong with pleading eyes as if to ask, "What do I do?" She summoned her courage and said, "Come on, darling. It's so late, and you have school in the morning. You need your sleep. I'll come back with you." She held my hand and walked me back to the bedroom. PoPo smiled sympathetically when I pulled away from her and dropped to the floor to crawl past the picture window once more.

When I stood up again, she said, "Manna, I closed the sheers *and* the drapes. No one, including the night lion, can see you through them. You don't need to be scared."

"PoPo, that night lion can see through sheers *and* curtains. I can feel his eyes. He's not kind, and he's not good. He's a bad lion—a very bad lion. I just know it."

We continued to the bedroom, and I held onto PoPo more tightly than ever before. It took me longer than usual that night to get back to sleep because I knew there was more to their conversation and masked looks than they had revealed to me.

"PoPo?" I whispered as I started to drift toward sleep, "I'm never letting you go. And you won't ever let me go, right? I never want to be without you. Never."

"Shhhh," she whispered, smoothing her hand over my hair. "Shhhh."

It was not until much later that I realized she had never answered my question.

Not Your Typical Day In The Park

One Saturday, not long afterwards, my PoPo woke me early and dressed me in my best clothes. The feeling that something was wrong had never left me, but now it was palpable. I noticed that PoPo kept her eyes averted, even though she tended to me as carefully as ever. She told me I would be spending the day with my family because it was Saturday.

"But I want to stay with you today, PoPo," I begged. "I can go with them tomorrow."

"If you go with them today, maybe you will get to go to the park," she answered.

"Why do I have to get dressed up to go to the park?"

"No more questions," she said and kissed my forehead. "They'll be here soon and you'll be on your best behavior, right?"

"Yes, PoPo."

That was the end of the discussion. I wanted to say more. I wanted to tell her I knew more than I said, understood more than what was spoken, and noticed more than anyone realized. But she was too busy attending to things, so I didn't have that opportunity.

I hovered near PoPo all morning, trying to discern the message behind the ominous feeling that would not leave me. I didn't want to be away from her and had to have her not only within my vision, but within my grasp.

Suddenly, I heard the doorbell ring, and PoPo nervously went to answer the door. I heard the usual greeting, but nothing was usual about this greeting—or this day.

Everything felt like it was moving in slow motion. I started to retreat backward in the room, clung to a dining room chair to steady myself, and stared at my parents and Luke as they entered the room as if they were strangers. My eyes were sharp and alert, too afraid to even blink.

My father came to me and kissed me, but my mother directed all her attention to her mother. She did not acknowledge my presence until it was time to go. I looked to my father, trying to smile, but I knew something was very different about this whole visit. He coaxed me to hold his hand as he gently pried my fingers from the chair, but I quickly switched hands, using my other hand to hold on to the chair. He chuckled and remarked on the speed with which I moved. He then took both of my hands and held me in his arms as he walked with me to the door.

I didn't want to show him disrespect, so I only tried to escape a few times, and when he wouldn't release me, I knew better than to fight any harder. I reasoned that I could trust my father, so I stayed in his arms. However, my eyes were still alert as I watched the expressions of everyone else in the room. There were feigned smiles from my grandparents, and their words were few.

My grandparents never walked us to the elevator when my parents came to take me for an outing or to the park, but that day they did. They each hugged me tightly and kissed me many times before guiding me into the elevator behind my parents.

PoPo's voice was shaking and trembling, and she had tears in her eyes. GongGong didn't say much and was desperately trying to smile.

In those days, elevators often had two doors. One was a floor-to-ceiling accordion-like gate, and the other door was glass. Once inside the elevator, the glass door would typically close first, and then the gate would close afterward. The gated door was the one closest to the passengers inside the elevator.

When we were in the elevator, my mother stood in the far-left corner, holding Luke in her arms. My father stood in front of her and was about to push the button directing the elevator to lower us to the lobby. I was standing at the front right side of the elevator.

My father never shut the glass doors, but only closed the gate tightly, so I could see my grandparents through the open slats. PoPo was wiping the tears that now flowed freely down her face and repeated, "Goodbye, goodbye, goodbye…I love you! I love you…" GongGong was waving and smiling, but unable to speak.

I still didn't understand what was going on, or why they were sad and crying. I only knew that the same ominous heavy feeling was now very intense, and I could barely breathe. Whatever was happening was much worse than I could imagine.

As the elevator began to descend, PoPo bent down to catch the last glimpse of me as they continued to call out, "Goodbye, goodbye, goodbye…" As the narrow space between us finally closed, the realization hit me like a lightning bolt. I knew this parting was not simply for a "day in the park."

"No! PoPo! PoPo!" I screamed and screamed with all my might, reaching up for PoPo as she disappeared from my view.

I grabbed the gate and shook it, trying to open the latch, but my father stopped me, blocking the handle with his strong arms. We were falling quickly, and the darkness between the floors was all I could see now. Floor after floor slid quickly upward as the elevator descended.

I flung myself on my father, sobbing. "I want my PoPo! Please, please, I beg you! Bring me back to her! Please!" I clung to him, pawing at him, my body wracked with misery. My mother told me to be quiet, and my father tried to calm me with reassuring words as he juggled a few bags on his shoulders that I had not noticed before. I continued to sob and beg my father to return me to PoPo and GongGong, but it was as if he could not hear me or see me.

And then, suddenly, time stood still.

No one in the elevator moved…it was as if they were captured in a photograph. I believe even the elevator stopped—or at least, it seemed to have stopped. There was no movement and no sound at all—not from my family, not the thumping of the elevator as we passed floors, and not even the hum of the fluorescent lights. Only stillness.

I had thought we were alone—just the four of us—but as I turned, I saw another person. His presence was tangible. Though unexpected, I somehow "remembered" that I was *expecting* him.

His was a vague form—standing but floating at the same time. He was dressed, but he did not wear clothes as we would describe them. He was just slightly taller than me, which I knew was so I would not be afraid.

And he was luminous.

The glow emanating from him produced such brightness it was as if a massive spotlight had been turned on us. If he had been any more radiant, I would have needed to close my eyes.

His presence did not frighten me, nor did it intimidate me. I was simply in awe of him. Though I had never seen him before, I *knew* I had known him for a very long time. He was comforting yet commanding. He was tender, yet powerful. He was kind and sensitive, yet also impartial. He was unmistakably there, as I could easily *see* him, but his facial features were indistinct. When he spoke, his authority was undeniable.

"We begin now."

Although I still felt like my heart had been ripped from me, I also felt a sense of calm at the same time—a peace that surpassed my reasoning.

I spoke to the angel (or so I believed it was) with respect, but I, too, was clear about the message *I wanted* to convey: "No," I said firmly. "I want to go back."

"It is time," he repeated.

"No, I want my PoPo and GongGong!" I said resolutely.

"It is time."

"I'm not ready!" I argued.

"It is time," he said again. "It will be hard, but you must be strong. I will be with you. I will never leave you."

"No!" I objected again. "It's too hard. It's too much!"

"Yes. There will be much to overcome. It will be over forty years of hardship, but the training is essential. Your preparation cannot be minimized, nor can it be compromised. You were made for such a time as this." He spoke precisely and decisively.

"No! I'm not ready…please…I'm not ready…it's too much," I pleaded again, though somehow knowing that nothing I said would change anything about what was to come.

Silence reigned.

We kept each other's gaze for what seemed like an eternity, but I know it was less than a blink of an eye. Finally, he slowly and intentionally repeated the following words one last time: "It is time. Be strong. I will never leave you."

As quickly as his presence had filled the elevator, he disappeared, and his light faded away.

I had no rebuttal.

Just then, the elevator bounced as we descended past another floor. The light resumed its dull, fluorescent cast, and my family returned to their conversation—completely oblivious to what had just occurred.

Surrendering, knowing anything I said or did would be absolutely futile, I took a deep breath, and through the tears still running down my face, I inched backward toward the corner behind me. I clung with both hands to the brass railings that were eye level with me. My knees gave way, and I slowly sank down to the floor, still holding on to the railings.

I whispered under my breath, "Oh boy…here we go…"

More Than Meets The Eye

"My goodness, Manna. You are not what I expected at all!" Mrs. St. John said slowly, zeroing in on my eyes. "Who would have thought hospice would send me someone touched by an angel?"

I smiled and looked down at my hands, not sure if she was mocking me, or trying to be kind.

"So, you *knew* this angel?" she asked curiously.

"I don't know how to describe it. It's not like he had a gender per se, but yes, somehow, I knew who he was and that everything he told me was true. I knew "it was time" as soon as he appeared and when he spoke those words, I was reassured that my life was not a mistake, and that I would be used for the benefit of others—though *how*, I could not imagine.

"Regrettably, I would forget this powerful invocation when I needed to remember it most—during the darkest times of my life. And when I did remember, I worried that because I had made so many mistakes in my life, my opportunities had been lost forever. Instead of being called, I feared I had been cursed. Thank God, He never gave up on me. Long story short, it took a while, but I finally got on the right path."

Mrs. St. John thought a moment, never once taking her sleuth-like eyes off me. "So, you're one of *those*, are you?"

"What do you mean?"

"You're one of those who sees and knows things that everyone else is oblivious to. And your memory…it's photographic! You remember such detail—and you were so young!"

"I don't know how I am able to remember such things, Mrs. St. John," I reflected. "I have always been this way—my memory…it's inescapable. Some may wish for this, but there are also many things I wish to forget."

"How did you know about God so young? You were barely walking!"

"I don't know. All I can say is that I've never *not* known God's presence, and I can't imagine life without Him. Maybe all children are able to *sense* notions of heaven, angels, and God because they haven't been that indoctrinated yet by the world. They just don't know how to express it."

Mrs. St. John paused. "Maybe God only shows up for certain people—like you. I don't know if God shows up for people the likes of me."

"Oh, but He does, Mrs. St. John! God's love is for *all of us*! His love is bigger than our failures and His grace is greater than our self-condemnation. Not believing we deserve such extravagant love, we desensitize ourselves to 'love' altogether, and we make choices for ourselves based on our self-esteem, instead of our true worth. I know I have."

Mrs. St. John's face softened, and she let out a deep breath.

"I have no doubt you saw an angel that day, and I have a feeling there's a lot more to you, Missy!" She smiled but continued staring at me as if to catch something with her eyes. "Or, should I say, Dr. Ko? Remember, I did my research on you! I wanted to know who I was going to be stuck within my last days on this planet. I'm fascinated, and you've got my attention."

Even though her words were strong, I saw the sadness—and the fear—in her eyes. She was searching to find a reason to fight the disease in her body.

"I'm tired," she muttered.

"You should sleep. I'm sorry for rambling on so long." I said as I got up from my chair. "I'll get my things so you can rest."

"If it was only that easy," she muttered. "The medication makes me restless when it should sedate me. I want to move, but I can't, and sleep won't come to me either—kind of like you when you were a little one."

She smiled, and after fighting her bravado, asked, "Do you have to go? I don't really want to be alone right now, plus…your presence calms me. Maybe you have some of your PoPo's essence about you. I hate to admit it, but I feel a little more peaceful when you're around. Maybe you can tell me another story about your childhood?" She wriggled in her bed to get comfortable. "Please, won't you stay and tell me another story?"

I hesitated, but when she reached out to hold my hand, she won me over.

"Okay, Mrs. St. John…I'll stay."

I put my things back down and settled into my chair. "The place is Vancouver, British Columbia, Canada. And it is now the summer of 1968."

2 A STRANGER IN A STRANGE LAND

I am only one, but still I am one. I cannot do everything, but still I can do something; and because I cannot do everything, I will not refuse to do something that I can do.

— Edward Everett Hale

We're Not in Kansas Anymore

When we arrived in Vancouver, we stayed with Uncle Oliver and his family. Their home was in a sweet neighborhood, just outside of Vancouver proper, and we lived there until my parents found a place of their own. Uncle Oliver was married to Auntie Pam, and they had two sons, Adam and Brent. Adam was older than me by a few years, and Brent by only a few months. It was difficult for my cousins to communicate with us at first because they had grown up speaking English and only knew a few random words of Cantonese. We however, only spoke Cantonese, but found a way to communicate through our own version of sign language and our parents' translations.

Uncle Oliver's home had a small brook that ran through their backyard. I remember sitting at the edge of the brook as often as I could and feeling the cool water run through my fingers. I was captivated by how the rippling water danced over the pebbles and stones, sloshing down its path. The lusciousness in the flora and fauna took my breath away.

And the trees!

The trees, oh the trees…they were majestic, noble, and beautiful! It was the first time I remember noticing "nature" and how stunning it all was—and it was the perfect distraction to keep me from thinking too much about my PoPo and GongGong.

Brent taught me how to pick huckleberries from the bushes that framed his backyard, and we spent hours exploring local creeks and trails, pretending we were pioneers. Adam and I, however, were not as close. He used to snarl at me as he walked by, as if to warn me to not get too close. And when we found ourselves in the hallway (going in opposite directions), he would stare at the wall as he walked by—anything to keep from looking at me. Despite this, he seemed to find Luke acceptable. Much later in life, we started to talk and share more together, but in those early days, it wasn't this way.

I can recall the few times the four of us did all play together. There was a berm on one side of their front yard. We would each take turns jumping off it, seeing how high we could jump and how far away we could land on the grass below. One day, as we were playing and laughing together in the front yard, a neighbor walked by and started yelling at us. He cursed and called us some horrible names. I didn't understand the words he said, but I didn't need to know the language to see how offended he was.

Luke and I stopped, our hearts already racing from playing and now racing even more in fear. We turned and hurried back through the front door as quickly as we could, running to Auntie Pam and holding onto her legs. Adam, still outside, didn't seem surprised by his neighbor's outburst, so he just walked down the street to visit another friend.

Brent wasn't perturbed either and continued to jump over the berm a few more times before coming back into the house. When Auntie Pam questioned Brent about the incident, he reported that the man was angry because we were Chinese and had warned us to go back to China because no one wanted us here.

That's when I learned that we were different.

We were "Chinese."

More questions came: *Is being Chinese bad? If so, why is being Chinese bad? What is the difference between being Chinese and what other people are?*

I hadn't noticed our "differences" before, nor did I know the terms "Caucasian" or "white." I just knew that being Chinese was a problem for this person—and, as I was to find out, for others as well.

Within a few months, my parents found us a home of our own, but it was in a different area of the city, and we needed to cross several bridges to get there. I was happy we were finally going to have our own place but was sad to leave Uncle Oliver's. I enjoyed playing with Brent, who always made me laugh. And I had grown very fond of my Auntie Pam, who always made time for me. She taught me how to boil eggs, and she introduced me to the art of eating pistachio nuts (her favorite treat), which I tried to like. They didn't have the same effect on me as they did for her. I liked chocolate much better!

Spending time with Uncle Oliver was also nice. He looked like GongGong and being close to him comforted me. Somehow through him, I felt the nearness of my beloved grandfather, whom I missed more than I could say. Many times, I would just sit by their living room fireplace, pretending I was playing, but I was really staring at Uncle Oliver, thinking I could catch a glance of my GongGong.

As for Adam, well, he never did grow to like me while we were there. Even so, I was sad to leave him because I had hoped that in time we could be friends too, just like Brent and I were.

It seemed like years had passed since we left Hong Kong, though it had only been a few months. My world had radically changed. I was now six years old, and my family and I lived in a neighborhood called Kitsilano, on the west side of Vancouver.

My father wanted to buy a home on the west side because it was close to the University of British Columbia (UBC). He was already planning (and saving) for us to enroll there after high school. The house they chose was a mere nine hundred square feet on the top floor, with an unfinished basement that was dark, cobwebby, and eerie to me. The outside of the bungalow was finished with mauve-colored stucco embedded with thousands of tiny, pressed-in pieces of colored glass—green, brown, red, and gold. I used to pull out the pieces of glass, pretend they were jewels, and glue them onto paper to make bracelets, necklaces, or crowns to wear.

Although these magical jewels on the house reflected the sunlight during the day (which made it pretty, in a bizarre kind of way), the sharp pieces protruding out of the stucco were dangerous. I was scratched many times when I slipped on the wet grass along the side of the house and fell against the stucco.

Finding myself in yet another new place, without my grandparents, and without Brent as my playmate, the feelings of loneliness and emptiness returned. Most nights, I cried myself to sleep.

Luke befriended a sweet little boy named Ronny who lived across the street, and he played there with him almost every day after school (and most weekends as well). Ronny's family was very kind and included Luke in their family gatherings and even evening meals without any hesitation at all. Luke would come home after playing with Ronny totally spent, so he had no problem falling asleep.

I, on the other hand, did not have that pleasant diversion and spent most of my time either staring out the window of my bedroom or sitting at the top of the front stairs by myself, wondering what I was doing there.

One evening before bed, when I felt more lonely than usual, I went to my father and asked, "Daddy, do you remember the song I really liked that always helped me fall asleep?"

"I do, but I haven't heard that song play on the radio for a long time now. And you haven't heard it since we were in Hong Kong. How do you remember that?"

"I don't know. I remember a lot of things…" I drifted, thinking about PoPo and GongGong, but I dared not say too much. I didn't want to come across unappreciative of *the new life I'd been given*. "I remember that song because it made me feel happy," I explained.

"You don't feel happy?" he asked.

I looked down and shook my head, fighting back the rising well of tears.

"Well, I think I can help."

My father went and put a record on the record player. Soon, the sweet strains of my favorite Beatles song, "Michelle," wrapped themselves around me, and I felt my whole body relax.

"Do you think you can sleep now?" he asked when he returned to my bedside.
"I'll try."
"I love you, Manna."
"I love you too, Daddy."

My father turned off the lights and lingered with me a while longer, but just as I started to fall asleep, I heard him step into the hallway. I tried to sing the song again, but I didn't really know the words. I just hummed the melody. I did eventually fall asleep—not to the song, but to the sight of the half-moon outside my window—wondering if PoPo and GongGong saw the same moon, and wondering if I'd ever see them again.

Hold the Onions

When we were still living in Hong Kong, my father had often been promoted, rising quickly to an elite position with the Royal Hong Kong Police force. I remember him coming home one day and telling me that he had been promoted to the Criminal Investigation Department. This division specialized in organized crime and the Bomb Investigation Squad. I didn't know what to say at first, and when I asked him if he was sure that being in the Bomb Squad was a promotion, he laughed.

Soon afterward, he began helping a close colleague in charge of the Dog Squad. *Now, that was a promotion to me!* My father brought home many dogs during that time: pointers, Dobermans, labs, foxhounds, and all kinds of shepherds. The bigger the dog, *and the more dogs*, the better, as far as I was concerned.

My love for dogs started as I watched my father and his colleague work with these beautiful animals. Their loyalty, devotion to service, commitment to protecting at all costs, and unending faithfulness moved me deeply. They asked for nothing in return for their duty and would follow us blindly anywhere because they trusted us. When the dogs weren't working, they were by the side of their handlers, just wanting to be close, eagerly waiting to please them with obedience.

I remember a time when my father introduced me to over nine police dogs in training. It was on these occasions I yearned to stay the night at my parents' home. His favorite police dog was a pointer named "Major," who always stood with distinction beside him. Major was extremely intelligent and obedient, fulfilling commands given merely with the nod of my father's head or a movement of his finger. Even though the dogs were powerful and strong, they were ever so gentle, patient, and tolerant of us kids. The unconditional love given by these animals proved real and true time and time again. My love for dogs has only deepened with age.

Just prior to our moving to Canada, my father was promoted once again, this time to the rank of Detective Inspector for his expertise in solving cases that had been mysteries for years.

Unfortunately, all of his achievements, skills, and abilities didn't translate as they should have in Canada. He was promised a position with the Vancouver Police Department upon our arrival, but for some reason, that opening was no longer available. Consequently, as soon as we settled into our new home, my father spent all his days job hunting. He came home tired and discouraged after long days of looking for work. No one wanted to hire him.

One day, my father told us that he found a job at a building supply store, but at the end of my father's first day shift, the supervisor yelled out "Ko! You're fired! This is your first and last day—no need to come back tomorrow!" My father was not only shocked by this announcement, but also very embarrassed, as the supervisor had yelled this in front of everyone there.

As the employees walked out the exit gate together laughing at him, my father walked toward the supervisor, humiliated.

"Sir, if I may ask, could you please educate me on why you have made this decision so that I may improve my skills and become a better employee next time?" my father asked sincerely.

"You didn't do anything wrong, Ko. It's 'cause you're *Chinese!*" he shouted while handing him the check for the day's pay.

Although this job didn't work out, we were very excited about his next opportunity because he was highly recommended by a mutual friend for the position of warehouse manager. My father went to the interview at the appointed time, professionally dressed and hopeful. However, as soon as he walked in, the supervisor exclaimed in shock, "*Oh!* Our friend just said your name was David. I didn't know you were *Chinese!*"

"Yes, sir. I am Chinese," my father responded politely.

"Well, then I *can't* hire you!" he said as if this should be obvious to my father.

"May I ask why my being Chinese would not qualify me for this position, since I am fully qualified for everything else based on my experience and training?"

"Are you stupid? Look outside! They're all white! How the hell can I ask them to work under you—a colored man? *A chink*? A colored man can't be their boss!" he declared.

In the Chinese culture, giving "face" to someone is a huge matter. In fact, it's one of the most important virtues of our culture—to give respect, honor, and dignity to one another. But in this situation, no such respect was given.

My father took a deep breath, and as he stood before this unenlightened man, he realized there was no point in arguing. The reality was that the supervisor had every right to choose whom he wanted (and whom he did not want) to work with him. And since there were no laws against discrimination then, my father thanked the supervisor for his time and exited the premises.

As he walked out of the office, my father assessed his options. He had saved six months' pay from his work in Hong Kong. He could return, and the police force would be only too glad to take him back as a Detective Inspector. However, unbeknownst to us at the time, our move away from Hong Kong had been my father's desperate attempt to remove my mother from influences that were destroying their marriage. If he went back, he would lose his wife to her unsavory friends, and the marriage would most certainly be over. If he stayed, he could fight for his family. He could give us a new life in a new country with hope for a better future.

Yes. He would try again the next day.

No matter what my talented father did, the only work he could find was as an unskilled kitchen laborer earning a dollar an hour in one of the massive dining halls of a local university.

The kitchen at that time was located in the basement of a large building with no windows. Frank, the chef, tasked my father with preparing not just a few, but *thousands* of potatoes. The potatoes came in hundred-pound bags, which were stacked all the way to the ceiling. To retrieve them, my father (a small-framed man) had to climb a ladder, break open the bag, separate the potatoes into two smaller bags, and bring them down one at a time. He also had to work twice as fast to make up for any lost time collecting the potatoes in this way.

There was a machine that would help with preparing the potatoes, but Frank only showed my father how to put the potatoes into the machine barrels. Beyond that, he taught him nothing. Whatever the machine could not do, my father had to do by hand. After cutting and preparing the potatoes, he placed them in trays and refrigerated them.

Frank hadn't bothered to tell my father that after preparing the potatoes and prior to refrigerating them, they had to be covered with water. This may seem obvious to anyone familiar with cooking potatoes, but since this was all new for my father, this step wasn't an obvious one for him. Remember, this was the 1960s, and at that time it was not common, especially in the Asian culture, for a man to be in the kitchen (unless he was specifically trained to be in the food industry). Moreover, potatoes were primarily a food item used in Western cuisine, so my father had no experience peeling them or preparing them for cooking.

When Frank came in the next day and saw that the potatoes had turned brown, he was so enraged he grabbed my father by the front of his uniform, shook him, and threw him against the wall. Frank called him every horrible racial slur possible. In the hopes of rallying the others in his mockery, he turned to the workers and called out, "Look what this stupid *chink* has done!"

My father managed to appease him by offering to work an extra shift without pay to compensate for the misunderstanding, but that did not satisfy Frank. He had other forms of restitution in mind. Ruled by his hatred of my father's "yellow skin," he was determined to make my father suffer. Somehow, Frank found out about my father's professional background and felt it was his duty to reduce and shame my beloved father into his "rightful place as an unwanted, useless peasant."

From that day forward, my father no longer had to peel potatoes. Instead,

Frank made my father a busboy, picking up all the dishes from every table in the dining hall and washing them—all day long. Because my father had worked in the basement the whole time, he had no idea of the size of the dining hall. Two sets of swinging doors connected the kitchen to the dining hall, one set for entering the kitchen, the other for exiting. Windows on the top of the swinging doors enabled one to see through and avoid possible collisions. As my father looked through those windows, he didn't know what surprised him more—seeing over a thousand people eating in the enormous dining hall, or that there were Chinese students there eating.

A chilling realization came upon him. The Asian community was very small at that time and "our people" knew everything about each other. Any new Asian faces only brought about more gossip. My father thought to himself, *People know I was promised a position with the Vancouver Police. What would they say if they saw I was a lowly busboy instead? They would laugh at me. They would call me a failure!*

He battled in his mind what to do. If he went out with his stainless-steel cart to gather the dishes from everyone, someone might recognize him. They could write home to tell their families that Mr. Ko had not achieved anything but was a failure. It was the worse kind of insult, next to being called "stupid." The shame and humiliation (losing "face" amongst his peers and community) would be overwhelming.

But then, my father talked to himself. *If you haven't the guts to walk through these doors right now, you might as well go home and take the title of "failure"!*

This was a life-defining moment for him. More important than his ego was his love for us. He understood that even though he was a busboy at this time, he was still providing for his family, and there was nothing shameful in that. No matter what others may have said, he was doing the more honorable thing. Though he could not control the actions of others, he chose not to be lowered or defined by them. So, he bolstered himself, pushed open the door with his cart, and went from table to table picking up the dishes he would later wash.

When Frank saw that his plan to humiliate my father failed, he devised another one. Instead of peeling potatoes or bussing tables, my father would peel onions.

Once again, my father was relegated to a task without instructions or tools. Like the bags of potatoes, he had to handle hundred-pound bags of onions. He moved them in the same way, still twice as quickly to make up for lost time, and then peel them—one at a time. The smell and acidity of the onions in the small room of a basement food processing center were almost unbearable, but my father endured.

Imagine. Hundreds of onions that needed to be peeled, daily! As the university's centralized food processing center, this cafeteria prepared a minimum of thirty thousand meals per day. Onions and potatoes were the main ingredients in most dishes for Western cooking. Some days, he was barely able to open his eyes after work and could only stumble onto the bus home like a blind man. After a few weeks, even his hands started to peel. It got so bad that the skin came off in entire casings.

One day, about a month into his onion assignment, the chief nutritionist came in to conduct a health inspection in the kitchen. As soon as she opened the doors to the room where my father labored without complaint, she was so shocked by the offensive smell, she had to step out of it.

When she could bring herself to reenter the room, she bellowed, "Mr. Ko! What are you doing? How can you suffer like this?" She could not help but be moved by his red swollen eyes, now the size of golf balls, and the tears streaming down his face from the noxious smell of the onions.

"Why are you peeling onions like this?" she asked in exasperation.

"I don't know any other way of peeling onions, madam. I have never prepared them before," my father explained.

"Do you mean the chef never taught you how to use the machines?"

"No, madam."

"And where are your gloves?" she demanded when she noticed my father's hands, completely raw and white from the acid.

"No one told me about gloves. Where are the gloves?" he asked.

With utter shock, yet filled with compassion, the chief nutritionist showed my father how to use the machine to peel onions and potatoes the proper way—a way that did not harm him.

"I didn't want to cause any problems," my father told her, humbly. "I'm just very thankful for my job."

"Did no one come to help you? Did no one show you how this is done?" she asked indignantly.

My father shook his head. "Please don't be angry with them. They're all very busy with their own jobs." He defended his fellow workers, even as he thought about how they mocked and laughed at him during each shift.

That was how it was for my father when we arrived in Canada. He did not complain; he simply thanked God for this opportunity to begin again. He was grateful to have a job, no matter how menial, lowly, or reviled the task, no matter how hateful the words said to him, and no matter what vengeance was imputed to him because of his race. My father took it all because he saw our faces ahead of any of these offenses. He knew starting over was going to be demanding, but the ferocity of finding a job in an environment so interwoven with racism was something he could not have predicted.

However, the most brutal of attitudes did not come from supervisors, the chef, or other coworkers…they came from my mother.

With each passing day, my mother's disdain for my father grew. Perhaps she did not like having to adjust to a new city and a new country. Or perhaps she was angry with him for taking her away from her friend Joan, and a social life she seemed to treasure. Maybe it was a combination of these and other things. Regardless of what she was thinking, her attitude toward my father was plain.

Even when my father came home after peeling vats of onions with swollen eyes and raw fingers, she still did not display much compassion. She had started to work again as a nurse (a profession known for its high standard of care and compassion), so her dismissal of him only hurt my father more.

"Emily," he pleaded. "Please tell me how to reduce the swelling in my eyes and recommend some ointment for my fingers."

She only scoffed, "You asked for this!" and walked away, slamming the bedroom door behind her.

One evening, I noticed my father blankly staring out of the window, so I went and sat beside him. "Daddy, you look sad. What's wrong?" I asked.

"Nothing, dear. I'm just feeling a little tired, that's all."

I knew better. "I think there's something more. Tell me, Daddy. Is it because people at work are mean to you because we're Chinese?" I looked down, feeling the shame of this also, and quietly asked the next question, "Why do people hate us so much because we're Chinese?"

"I think people act in mean ways when there is change around them. They feel scared. It's easier to push people away than to take the time to learn about them." He smiled and patted me on the head. "I don't want you to ever be like that though, okay?"

"Okay, Daddy."

My father looked away again. Though he was sitting beside me, he was thousands of miles away, lost in his thoughts.

Then, shaking himself out of his reflections, he said reassuringly, "God will show us a way. He is going to use all these things together for good. We just need to keep believing."

I searched my imagination to find something to console my father. After a moment, I jumped up. I had the answer. "Daddy! I have a great idea!" I proclaimed, "Let's find a job that allows you to work with dogs again—just like you did in Hong Kong! Dogs have always been nice and kind to us, even though we're Chinese!"

My father smiled, scooped me up and gave me a big hug. He told me he loved me so much and as long as I loved him too, then he was always a rich man.

A miracle happened for us the very next day. Our prayers were answered. The Vancouver Police Department finally called my father for the detective position, the very job for which he had applied when we first arrived.

No more onions!

My father was the first Asian man to be hired by the Vancouver police force. In fact, the hiring was such a controversial topic that he was interviewed by the local news and radio stations. The heading: "The Vancouver Police Force Hires First Asian Man."

Social Butterfly

As my parents' marriage continued to disintegrate in front of my eyes, I spent most of my time trying to be the best big sister I could be to Luke. I believed God had brought him into my life as a gift and being with him brought me comfort.

While I had a great relationship with Luke and my father, my relationship with my mother was distant and cold. Despite my efforts to please her, it had become obvious that she loved Luke far more and had unending patience and affection for him.

Interestingly, I was never jealous about Luke receiving her love. My heart was so knitted together with him that I was thankful he was so loved. As long as he was happy, then I was happy. Some siblings end up competing against one another for favor from their parents, but Luke and I never did. He loved and cared for me, and I did the same for him—both with the truest and purest of hearts.

Now that I'm in my fifties, even though he is my younger brother, the roles have reversed over the years. He has become my "big" brother—always looking out for me and doing everything he can to help me through so many of my life's unexpected trials. He is a wonderful man, humble and kind, and his integrity is unshakable. I have witnessed him endure great adversities, but not once did he complain, take the victim's role, or fall into self-pity. He rose to each occasion like a noble warrior. Hence, he has always been like a superhero to me and my nickname for him is "Superman." I'm serious! Whenever I think of Luke, I think of Maya Angelou's quote about her own brother, "I think I have had so much blessing—I've had my brother, who was brilliant. I think my family came closest to making a genius when they made my brother."

Although I had no jealousy for Luke, I did have many unanswered questions about my mother's unmistakable favor toward him. *Was it because he was a boy? Was he born at a better time in her life? Why did he stay with my parents when he was born, but I didn't? Maybe she loves him more because she had more time with him from birth?*

One day, after a particularly difficult event, I tried to rationalize that my mother's indifference wasn't so much to me in particular as it was to motherhood. Being a mother required her to be committed to a marriage and to a family. Maybe she was frustrated that she was no longer free to do what she wanted. After all, she was young, beautiful, intelligent, and (as others suggested) probably spoiled a bit too much by her parents after the war.

My father's issues with her stemmed, for the most part, from her determination to continue to engage in a fully active social life when she had two children at home. She saw him as controlling and demanding, which only propelled her further away from him.

One example of this was on a weekend back in Hong Kong when I stayed with my parents. My father was working a night shift. Soon after he left, my mother got dressed to go out for the evening. MahMah always babysat for Luke anyway, so having me there that weekend wasn't any extra trouble for her.

My mother left without much acknowledgment, just saying she would be back later. I remember the echo of the door slamming closed behind her. By the way Luke reacted—he went screaming after her—I knew that she had been going out a lot and was leaving him behind, again. Worried that Luke's fingers would be caught in the door, I lunged after him, but he fought me off and threw himself at the door. When he realized that, for all the pounding he did, she would not come back, he raced to the balcony where we had a plain view of the front door of the building. As soon as he saw her walk out into the parking area, he started screaming for her. My mother did not look back. He continued yelling for her, begging her not to leave, but she just kept walking until she turned the corner and was no longer in sight.

I stood with my hands resting on Luke's heaving shoulders, trying to console him as he sobbed. I pried my tearful little brother's fingers off the balcony railings, took his hand, and led him back into the living room. He tried to catch his breath through the hiccups he had developed from crying so hard, as he sat listlessly with me on the living room sofa, holding my hand. I wiped his tears with tissues and did my best to distract him—playing games and little tunes on the piano while singing to him.

Playing on the piano and making up songs, pretending they were as good as "Michelle" by The Beatles, became one of my favorite activities—second only to playing with my father's police dogs, of course. My father had traded our old piano and bought me a beautiful, hand-carved, high upright grand made of mahogany. The wood grain was delicate, and the keys felt like budding tulips under my fingers. The design of this piano matched its craftsmanship and when I struck a note and let it ring out, my spirit stood at attention.

My father said that my fingers looked like they were made to play the piano—long and slender, yet strong. I felt special when he said that.

Maybe there is something special about me!

Whenever I played on this piano, I felt like a beautiful princess. And whenever my father was home, I would play and sing for him, even though the songs weren't more than random keys struck together by clumsy little hands. After each song concluded, my father would rise and give me a roaring standing ovation. It made me happy being able to bring him such joy.

I also tried to use whatever gift of music I may have had to entertain Luke and help him feel better when he was down. Eventually, I would succeed in coaching him to join me, as I did again this particular evening. He climbed onto the piano bench and began tinkering on the piano keys, singing made-up songs with me. Together, we entered another reality—one that resonated with music, joy, and togetherness.

In the background, MahMah went into the kitchen to prepare dinner. YehYeh kept to himself, confined to his spooky lair, which we never went back to again after the terrorizing incident with his dentures.

I don't know if Luke ever fully trusted our mother after this. Yes, he loved her and still wanted to be close to her, but something in him shifted that evening, and I was saddened that my beloved brother had to experience his first taste of disappointment from someone he loved.

I did not realize that my mother went out as much as she did until decades later. I was told my mother would often come home in the wee hours of the morning back then. And there were times she didn't come home at all. When my father questioned her, she told him she had spent the night with her parents (GongGong and PoPo) and me. I *never* remembered her staying with us—ever— and I definitely would have remembered it if she had.

This clash of dueling intentions continued to grow until it exploded into one of the biggest fights my parents had had up to that point. It was the fight that ultimately caused us to leave Hong Kong.

My mother decided to go to Japan on a whirlwind weekend with her friend, Joan. If there hadn't already been history of my mother leaving her family, this might not have been such a significant issue. But, there was *so much* painful history, and the unseemly circumstances surrounding her trip were unbecoming of her (especially in the 1960s), which brought great embarrassment to the family.

Personally, I could not understand why my mother and Joan were friends. Joan was not very nice (to anyone), not very smart, and certainly not very poised. She also had a very large face that was scarred from bad acne and her blemish-ridden facial expressions made her frightening to look at. Or maybe it was her thick-set build, which made her a formidable ten-pin bowling partner since she could throw the ball with great power and force down the lane. Ten-pin bowling and Mahjong, or "MJ" (a game similar to but more complicated than gin rummy, played with thumb-size tiles), were my mother's favorite things to do. It was not her other interests, hobbies, or friends that upset my father, however—it was her exaggerated preference for them over her family that caused his concern.

Joan and my mother were always deep in secret conversations, whispering between themselves and then glancing around to see who could hear them. One time, my mother and Joan took us out for lunch at a restaurant in a busy part of Hong Kong. We had to walk a bit of distance to get there, through neighborhoods with large, steep hills. The two of them walked ahead of Luke and me, their heads bent down, speaking quietly to one another as if their crouching backs would shield the conversation from our little ears. I held Luke's hand as we walked behind them, but Joan and my mother were so engrossed in their conversation that they crossed a very busy intersection without us. They did not look back, not once, until I called out for her. Even after they stopped, they were still engrossed in their secret conversation, unconcerned that I had to cross a very busy intersection with Luke alone.

It was terrifying, but Luke and I made our way across the street. When we reached my mother and Joan, my mother snapped at me, "You're so slow and clumsy! Stay closer to us next time!"

"Yes, Mommy. I'm sorry."

Luke and I looked down, ashamed. I made sure we stayed as close as we could to them for the rest of the journey. But we were little, and they were adults, so their strides were much longer than ours. We had to hurry, sometimes almost running to keep up. In an attempt to stay close, I accidently stepped on my mother's heel. She turned around and slapped the side of my head, yelling, "You're so annoying! Good for nothing!"

"Sorry, Mommy. I was trying to stay close, but you slowed down...and well... it was an accident. Don't be mad...I'm sorry!"

Joan snarled at me also, then whipped her head away in disgust, exhaling a loud, "Hmmph!" as she did so. They both turned around, resuming their swift walk and classified conversation. This time, I tried with all my might not only to follow their footsteps closely, but to also look past their feet to see what might be ahead in case anything should cause them to slow down again.

It was a crazy obstacle course, crossing in and out of swarming crowds, street vendors and their crates of goods, and the chaos of free-for-all cars and trucks on the industrious streets of Hong Kong. I managed to stay just close enough—but not too close—stopping early enough to not step on mother's heels when she did stop, all while holding Luke's hand and making sure he was in step until we reached the restaurant. Though exhausted from the ordeal, I was proud that I had followed orders well and avoided another scolding for somehow failing my mother.

However, in staying so focused and so close to my mother, I heard what she and Joan were discussing. My mother was speaking very poorly of my father and talking about making plans without him. In retrospect, this conversation must have been about their infamous trip to Japan.

My heart sank when I heard my mother talk about my father in such a disparaging way. I wanted to throw up. When we were finally seated at the restaurant, I was unable to speak or eat. I just watched the two women talk as if we weren't there.

Many more red flags flew in the days that followed, but instead of fighting her, my father tried to woo her back into the marriage by joining her at ten-pin bowling, and he even played MJ with her. With the additional attention he paid to her, they were able to get somewhat reconnected, and life on the home front seemed to calm down for a little while.

Then my mother discovered she was pregnant again. My father was happy and believed another baby was a blessing that would solidify the family unit. My mother, on the other hand, did not see this pregnancy as a blessing and wanted to terminate it. My father refused to entertain the idea and implored her not to think of such a thing. But my mother and Joan devised a plan, and shortly thereafter, against my father's wishes, my mother had an abortion.

Exasperated, my father could no longer tolerate any more destruction of his family. He wanted my mother to rely on *him*—her husband and her partner in life—not the whims of a selfish, lonely woman who was obviously determined to destroy their marriage. He needed a plan of his own. He could not fight the evil influence of a bad friend in the same way he had before. In an effort to save their marriage and to have some semblance of a normal family, he prepared for our move to Vancouver, Canada. My father worked harder and longer hours, scrimping and saving everything he could from his paychecks. With some additional financial support from both sets of parents, he found a way to make a new life in another country, far away.

I didn't knew why we left Hong Kong or why I was taken away from my GongGong and PoPo, or that my mother had had an abortion, until many decades later. It provided some of the missing pieces to help me understand our move, but it was agonizing to learn Luke and I could have had another little brother or sister. The awareness that another brother or sister's life was just "terminated" was like experiencing a death for me. I cannot explain it, but when I found out, I grieved for this lost sibling that I had never known.

Man's Best Friend

As you can tell, my relationship with my father was glaringly different than my relationship with my mother. While my father was not perfect, he was constant and generous with his love for us. Yes, we've had our misunderstandings, but we overcame them with love, and, like Luke, my father is a hero to me. He taught us powerful lessons about life, provided for us, and inspired us to think creatively—to think "big."

And, of course, he introduced me to some of my best friends in life—dogs.

One afternoon on his day off, my father noticed I did not come straight home from school and went out searching for me, worried something had happened. When he reached the end of the block, he turned and saw me coming from a completely different direction than where the elementary school was located. Surrounding me were six dogs of all different sizes, shapes, and breeds.

He stood on the sidewalk with his hands on his hips, unable to speak at the sight. He did not want to say anything for fear it would frighten me or the dogs, which might cause them to react aggressively. Since he did not know the dogs (how they were raised and trained, if they had been abused, or to whom they belonged, etc.), he proceeded with caution.

A part of him was worried I had taken them from other people's yards and, if caught, would be accused of stealing their dogs—not a good thing for a police officer's daughter. Another part of him simply wondered, *How in the world did my six-year-old daughter manage to collect half a dozen dogs from the neighborhood and coax them to follow her home after school—without leashes?*

As soon as I saw my father, I began running towards him. So did all the dogs. I was excited to have him meet my new friends, whom I had already named and planned on keeping.

When I reached him, he hugged me, and commanded the dogs to all sit and stay, which they did.

"Manna, where did you get these dogs?" he demanded. He was about to scold me, then caught himself. "I mean…where did all these dogs come from, honey?" He directed his attention to a larger dog with short hair—one that I had somehow managed to dress in my coat. My father saw that his two front legs were in the arms of my coat, and the buttons were neatly fastened under his belly.

"Oh, Daddy! I found them!" I declared with great excitement. "They were lost and walking alone without anyone to take care of them! At first, I only saw one, and when I called to him he came running to me. Then I realized there must be others just like him around, so I walked around the block to see if I could find more lost and lonely doggies. I guess I must have walked around a lot of blocks! Look at all the doggies who are lost and scared, Daddy! Just *look* at them! They need us, Daddy!"

"Yes, dear, I see them." He looked at my new friends, who were still obediently sitting, looking at us with tilted heads and big eyes. "How did you manage to have them follow you, Manna?"

"Daddy, you know this better than anyone! All I did was hug them and talk to them. I asked if they wanted to come home with me, and look! Here they *all* are! They just followed me and now they will have a home with us and they won't be alone anymore!" I looked up at my father, who didn't seem as excited as I was.

Realizing I hadn't come straight home from school, I apologized. "I'm sorry I didn't come straight home, Daddy, but now you understand why. Let's go and make sure they have a snack and some water, okay?" I grabbed my father by the hand to lead him back home.

"Not so fast. I have one more question," he said slowly.

"Yes, Daddy. What is it?"

"Well, ummm…why is this larger dog wearing your coat?"

"Oh, Daddy! He was cold! The other dogs have thicker hair, but you see, this one—" I pointed to the short-haired dog—"doesn't have much hair, so it was only fair to share my coat with him. He doesn't have as much covering as the others!" I reasoned. "Can we all go home now?"

"Manna, darling. These doggies already have a home. See these tags on their collars? These are nametags. I know you didn't know that, so it's okay. Daddy's not mad. If we bring the doggies home with us, their owners will be very sad because they will never see their doggies again. We must take them back to their owners, okay?" he explained.

I looked down at the ground and then at the faces of my new friends, who returned my look with sweet, friendly eyes. I was heartbroken that I couldn't keep them. As quickly as I had found new friends, I had lost them.

Seeing my sadness, my father bent down so we were at eye level. He gave me a big hug, then patted each one of the dogs and reached for the individual tags. He acknowledged each dog by name, smiled at me, and then took my hand. One by one, we took each of the dogs back to their owners, explaining that we thought they were lost, but then saw their tags and were now bringing them back.

"Well, that was one way of getting to know the neighbors!" chimed in Mrs. St. John.

"Yes. Can you imagine?" I agreed. "What a sight that must have been in the 1960s, seeing a little Chinese girl and her father come up to your door to return your dog, while behind them sat a pack of other dogs sitting at the bottom of their front doorsteps!"

We chuckled.

"You are too much, Manna. What happened next?" Mrs. St. John asked after taking a sip of water.

My father, knowing I was feeling misplaced and lonely, brought home a beautiful collie show dog for Luke and me not long afterwards. He was sure this dog was a sign of good fortune for us and named him Lucky.

Lucky and I became attached from the moment he came to our house, and he became *my dog*. I hated the idea of his being outside in the backyard, even though it was fenced, and he had a doghouse. I worried about him all the time, and on our first day of rain after getting him, I ran outside with my red raincoat and dressed him like I had with my "lost dog" friend. I knew *I* could come inside and dry off, but Lucky had so much hair he wouldn't be able to dry off so easily. Plus, I was worried he would be cold.

When my father heard the commotion, he called me back inside, but I wouldn't leave until I had Lucky dressed sufficiently in my red raincoat. Lucky just stared at me, licking my face as I maneuvered his front legs into the arms of my coat.

My father helped dry me off and shared comforting words that Lucky would be just fine, that he was bred to be outdoors, and that his fur would keep him warm.

My mother, on the other hand, just walked away and uttered something about my being annoying and useless, again.

A Day At the Beach

Every day, my father pled with my mother to spend more time with us, not only for the basic necessities of rearing a small family in a new country (and a totally new culture), but to also help us in our transition to school in a foreign language.

"The children need you, Emily. They are so young and can barely speak English. They need your help taking them to school and eventually with their homework. They need to be introduced to the teachers and they need to learn the new culture," he begged. "At the very least, spend some time with them. Take them to the park or to the beach before school starts."

But my mother didn't like his pleas. She didn't seem to like anything about him, and they fought often—very often.

One day, shortly before the school year started, my mother conceded and took us to one of the local beaches while my father was at work. Having arrived recently from Hong Kong, these beaches were very different than the ones we were familiar with. They were long and clean, had magnificent, expansive views of the ocean, and weren't filled with massive throngs of people. Only a few logs lay in strategic areas. They sat purposefully, inviting the rare weekday passersby to sit and relax.

My mother walked ahead and looked for a place for us to lay down our blankets, far away from the water's edge. When we found a spot, she settled into a Harlequin romance novel and told us to go and play.

Luke and I had fun creating different structures in the sand and wandering up and down the beach, discovering the world of seaweed and the intricacies of barnacles and mussels that had made their homes in a community of rocks nearby.

My eyes caught sight of a heavy-set European lady wearing a kerchief around her head as she roamed the beach by herself. She held a small pocketknife in her right hand as she walked very slowly, studying the sand and the rocks around her with each step. I noticed that she bent down every now and then and did something with her knife before standing up again. I determined to get closer to find out the purpose of her intriguing routine and was soon standing beside her when she honed in on a cluster of mussels. She bent down and ripped them off the rocks, quickly forcing the shells open with her knife's blade. After slurping up the contents of each shell with large gulps, she haphazardly threw away what was left of each mollusk.

I screamed with horror. I had never seen anything like this and ran away from her as fast as I could. *That was gross! Was there something living inside that shell? Did she just kill it and suck up its guts?*

As I returned to Luke and my mother, I noticed my four-year-old brother had started to venture into the water. He was knee deep by the time I arrived. Wobbling and fascinated by the feel of the sand rushing between his toes, he started to go out further. I told him to stop, but he didn't listen.

A large speed boat rocketed by, and its wake rushed to the shore. The suction of the tide under Luke's little feet caught him off guard, and he fell. Just then, another wave came, covering him, and as it receded, it pulled him further out into the ocean.

"Help me! Manna, help me!" Luke screamed in between gurgles of salt water.

I screamed for my mother to help, but she didn't turn around. I screamed louder, but I had no time to see if she had heard me.

Neither Luke nor I knew how to swim, but as terrified as I was, I had no choice but to jump in and try to save my little brother. GongGong once shared an old Chinese proverb with me: "Being loved deeply by someone gives you strength but loving someone deeply gives you courage." I did not quite understand the meaning of that saying until that moment at the edge of the ocean.

I ran in after Luke, but another large wave hit us, and we were overcome by its strength. Now both of us were being tossed in the current and pulled away from the shore. In between gulps of water, and barely able to see with salty, sandy water in my eyes, I grabbed Luke and shoved him by his pants as hard as I could toward the beach again.

Thankfully, the tide was with us, and he was able to get his footing and run to my mother. I, on the other hand, was not so lucky. Another wave had caught me, and before I went under again, I saw my sweet little brother waddling up the beach toward my mother, laughing with excitement, ready to share his little adventure.

What about me? I thought before the gurgling in my ears, the frigidity of the water, and my inability to find the ocean floor reclaimed all my attention. Somehow, I came up for a moment of air and saw that I wasn't too far from dry sand.

If I can catch the next wave, I might be able to save myself.

With that thought, another wave came and with its momentum, I dug my hands and feet into the seabed with every ounce of strength I had left. The sand was still washing out toward the ocean beneath my feet, but I held on. I closed my eyes and held my breath.

After a few moments, the roar of the ocean in my ears disappeared, as did the water around my feet. The wave retreated into the ocean without me. I was safe.

Sand covered me as I struggled to get up, coughing and spitting out saltwater. I labored towards my mother in heavy wet clothes, pulling loose threads of seaweed off my face and arms. "Mommy! Mommy! You'll never guess what happened! The waves came and dragged Luke and me out to sea! It was so scary, Mommy!"

"Oh, Manna! You're getting me all wet! Stand over there!" she shouted, pointing to where she wanted me to go. "Don't make up stories. It's not good to lie. Now go away and let me read."

I was soaking wet, covered with sand and seaweed. Clearly, I was not making up what had happened. Unable to find words, even if I had been permitted to speak, I stood before the woman I knew to be my birth mother…but I was beginning to wonder *who she was.*

New Kid At School

That September, with little preparation for school or any explanations regarding expectations, I found myself sitting in a classroom where everyone spoke English. I had only started learning the English alphabet in Hong Kong, and my knowledge of the English language consisted of a few basic words, none of which were even recognizable in the setting where I now found myself. In addition, nobody looked like me or dressed like me, and I had no notion of what to say or do. When papers were passed back, I took one and passed it on only because that's what I saw the other kids do.

Lunchtime was also difficult to navigate. My lunch not only looked different than my classmates' lunches, it smelled different. They often huffed and snorted their noses at me, and many sneered even more as soon as I looked at them. They made no effort to talk to me or ask me to play. I would only catch their overt glances and shy away at their laughter.

There were only three Asian students in the entire school—Luke, myself, and one other girl named Jean, who was Japanese. Jean was in another homeroom class, but we were in the same grade. Unlike me, Jean was born and reared in Canada, and she spoke fluent English.

Throughout my four years at this elementary school, Jean and I never got along. One would think there would be some kind of affinity between the two of us. We were both "Asian" and girls of the same age. I thought there would be some kind of rapport since we were so clearly different from the others, but there wasn't. In my last year there, she blurted out, "I hate you 'cause you're a *chink*! I'm Japanese and smarter than you or any other *chink*! My dad says our country took over your stupid country!"

I was shocked by her hateful comments. We were so young, and the very idea that these words came out of a little girl was appalling. I remembered the war stories my GongGong and other survivors of war had shared. These stories were used to teach me lessons on being a better human being—to be compassionate to others and take a stand for humanity. But here was this girl who was also told war stories, only she was shaped by a very different message.

I had never known the difference between races until I experienced how offensive I was to others because of my skin color. Jean, on the other hand, was taught to hate my race, and therefore, me. Even if racism wasn't taught to her directly, it seemed as if it was not opposed or reproved. She still learned it. And that's not right.

But I digress.

Back to when I first started school after arriving from Hong Kong. As I mentioned, Luke had quickly become friends with our neighbor, Ronny, and they were able to overcome the initial language barrier with toys, noise, and boyish antics. I had no such friend, so for the most part, I was on my own.

It was painful being an outsider, so I pretended I didn't need anyone, anything, or any help. But deep down, I *did* need a friend. I *did* need help. I was just too afraid to ask for it. I was afraid of my new city, my new home, the new people, and everything to do with school. Oh, how I longed to see my PoPo outside the classroom door…but no such comfort was there.

Though I was slowly learning English, I was too frightened to fumble through it to ask questions. Mocked by vicious people throughout the day, every day, for being Chinese was already bad enough. To speak and demonstrate my poor English would have been emotional suicide. So I kept to myself and never asked for help, ashamed to show my lack of understanding, but still learning whatever I could the best that I could.

This system worked in some ways, but once, because I didn't speak up when I really needed help, I suffered one of the most embarrassing situations of my childhood. I made a point of using the restroom each morning before school and trained myself to only use the restroom during recess and lunch time. I did not know how to ask to use the school facilities, plus interrupting the teacher to ask for a bathroom break in my broken English would have been humiliating. On this one afternoon, for some reason, I needed to use the restroom more frequently. I sat in my seat, watching the seconds tick by on the clock over the blackboard. I could barely sit still as tears stung the corners of my eyes. I crossed and uncrossed my legs. Finally, it was too much, and my small body gave in to nature.

The boy sitting beside me squealed, "There's water leaking!"

From somewhere else, I heard the words boom in my ear, "It's only under *her* seat!"

All fingers in the classroom pointed to me, and I felt a part of my soul leave my body. The rest of me cowered in my seat, imprisoned by the inability to explain myself and the shame that kept me glued to the seat.

I began to hate my life.

Fight Club

Each day I dreaded going to school, and each night I lay awake listening to The Beatles singing and try to decipher their words. When my father was home, I spent as much time with him as possible. He was kind and patient, always telling us how much he loved us. Sometimes he said this so often I wondered if he was trying to solidify this thought in our minds in an attempt to prepare us for something.

My mother noticed how different my relationship was with my father than with her, and she seemed annoyed by it. She continued to go out, leaving Luke and me alone, and it wasn't too long before I recognized that my mother tried to be away from her children as much as she tried to be away from her husband. I don't know if she was at work, or out with new friends. All I knew is that we didn't see her much.

With my father at work, my mother gone, and Luke playing with Ronny, I was often alone with Lucky and my Barbie dolls. A dog's love and loyalty may seem like such an elemental thing, but Lucky's devotion was everything to me. I was not very old when I learned that love can be conditional among human beings, but with dogs, that is never the case.

In British Columbia, elementary school went from grade one to grade seven in those days. Some of the seventh-grade boys were particularly brutal in their racial taunts against me. One particular week, they jeered and sneered like they always did, but something was different about how they were behaving toward me. I saw, for the first time, the depths of pure hatred for me in their eyes. Contempt for me consumed them, and they were determined, indeed obsessed, with hurting me. Every day, someone from their gang found his way out of his own classroom early and waited outside my classroom to curse me as soon as my teacher dismissed us. On recess and lunch breaks, they followed me around, throwing rocks (and anything else they could find) at me, and warning me that when I least expected it, they were going to beat me up and "leave me for dead."

I didn't know what to do, so I tried to stay with groups of people throughout the day. When school ended, I would leave out of different doors so they wouldn't know how to find me.

One afternoon, I stayed a few minutes late to help my teacher clean up. I liked the way Mrs. MacLean smiled, acknowledging my efforts. She encouraged me to use my new English skills in a kind way. I felt safe and accepted. When I finished helping her, I said goodbye and looked out the classroom door. The hallway was empty. I did not see any of those mean seventh-graders, and with a sigh of relief, I proceeded out the door and walked outside. I crossed the blacktop on the other side of the school because I was sure this would provide me safety.

Suddenly, three seventh-grade boys came running toward me. They had been hiding, waiting for me to leave the security of Mrs. MacLean's classroom, and had followed me.

"Hey, *chink*," one of them called.

I ignored them and kept walking.

"Hey, slant eyes! I'm talking to you!"

The boys lunged at me. One jumped in front of me, blocking my path, while the other two came at me from each side. When I started to back up, they took menacing, confident strides forward and hurled more hateful words at me. "Oh, that's right—you don't understand English! Go home to China, *chink*!"

I tried not to look at them. Instead, I watched the ground and searched for any available opening between them to get away. They continued yelling hateful phrases at me. No matter where I turned, the other two boys intercepted me. They were taller than me and able to move with more freedom, as they didn't have their knapsacks with them.

I looked around the schoolyard, but no one else was nearby. I looked back at the door I had exited from. *If I could get close enough to the door, I can run back inside and ask Mrs. MacLean for help.*

"Where's your rickshaw, chopstick?" one of them mocked.

"You live in a dry-cleaning shop, *chink*?" another one goaded, as he shoved me.

Confused, I shook my head, hoping my answer would appease them.

"No, they probably have a grocery store," one of the other boys fired, and the three of them laughed.

"*Answer me!*" the first boy yelled.

I tried to say, "No, my grandparents have a hospital," but it came out wrong, making them laugh even harder.

"Why don't you run away to your hospital, *chink*? 'Cause if you don't in the next second, after I finish beating you up, you'll really need the hospital! They won't even recognize you by the time we're done with you!"

He swung his arms, so I flinched and backed away. Taking his lead, the other boys let their fists fly at me. What happened next was a blur. One of the punches landed at the same time I was backing up. I tripped over a rise on the blacktop and fell backwards.

Over the ringing in my ears, I heard a shout. The boys stopped mid-swing and turned, surprised—and then fearful. I followed the direction of their gaze and could hardly believe my eyes.

My *mother* was striding toward us over the playground, indignant and ready to defend *me*.

"You stop that, right now!" she shouted.

The boys took off running.

Within moments, we were alone. I did not know what I was in more shock over—the fact that those boys were going to beat me to the point of non-recognition, or that my mother was standing in front of me. It was extremely unusual for her to be home during the day. That, in and of itself, was astonishing. But even more startling was that she defended me! She seemed to care enough to look for me after school, which she had never done before—and never did again after this incident.

Questions flooded my mind. *What had occurred for her to be home? How was it she had stopped whatever she was doing, gotten into the car, and known exactly where to go at the exact to stop a horrible beating?*

It was a miracle!

I got up with clumsy limbs, still shaken by what had just happened. My mother called out a few threats to the mean seventh graders, then turned and just stared at me. I didn't know what to do. I wanted to run to her and hold her, but something told me not to. I held back my tears of fear, shock, and gratitude and mustered enough courage to say, "Thank you, Mommy."

She didn't respond.

I was afraid, so I looked down to the ground.

"Get in the car," she said as she turned and walked towards our vehicle.

I kept up with her quick footsteps, and when we got to the car, I climbed into the front seat. I held onto my Barbie lunch box and homework bag as tightly as I could, trying desperately not to let her see me trembling.

We rode home in silence.

I sensed I was even more of an inconvenience than she thought, so I said nothing. Maybe she did feel compassion for me. I don't know. If she did, she never expressed it in a clear manner.

"Manna, I am so glad I did not know your mother! I would have given her a beating myself for the way she treated you!" Mrs. St. John interjected. Her tone was hot as fire, and I marveled at her strength through her paper-thin skin.

"Oh, Mrs. St. John, I don't mean to upset you. I'll stop."

"No! Don't stop! It's all so fascinating." She let out a deep breath. "I can't begin to imagine what your mother was thinking, and honestly, I'm sad for her. She missed a great life with a beautiful daughter like you."

I smiled. "That's nice of you to say."

She waved this away with a flick of her wrist. "Not tryin' to be nice, dear. It's just the truth. I call it as I see it," she said, shaking her head. "Did things get better between you two?"

"No. Unfortunately."

"Okay then. Fluff my pillows and get me some tea. I have a feeling your story is going to pick up, and I don't want to miss a thing!"

Hell's Kitchen

As great as it was to be with my father all the time, it was still very confusing being without my grandparents. I still felt lonely and sad inside. The only constants in my life were my father, Luke, and Lucky, but it still felt unnatural. Ironic, I know.

In many ways, I felt like a stranger among my own family. In order to fit in, I quickly learned not to ask questions. Rather, I was to adjust to the way things were done in this household—including accepting my mother's careless cooking style.

It wasn't difficult to notice how extremely different her cooking was from PoPo's. Luke gobbled up his food, but I did not like the taste and suffered with it. If I refused to eat the food, I risked making my mother irate, inviting another spanking or smack to my head. Whereas PoPo had allowed me to watch her cook, explaining what she was doing with great patience, my mother would not.

I had enjoyed engaging in conversations with PoPo as she told me stories, taught me lessons about life, or shared plans for our outings together while she cooked. My mother saw my wish for these kinds of conversations as bothersome and annoying. If I even tried to sit by her or talk to her, she would yell, "Be quiet!" or "You're annoying me!" or "Get out and leave me alone!"

I had wanted to believe her bad moods reflected her frustrations about not being out with friends, but it was becoming more and more evident that her anger seemed centered around me. I appeared to be the source of her bitterness. So, in an effort to make her happy (and to not solicit any further acrimony), I did as she asked.

I stayed away from her.

One winter night when it was very cold outside, my mother made soup for us. My father was working a night shift, so it was only the three of us. My mother came into the kitchen where I was coloring and took out a package of ground beef that had been in the refrigerator. I watched her put it into a pot of water with some diced onions and a few shakes of salt and pepper. The ground beef had somewhat of a sour smell to it, but I thought better of asking about it. After the water had boiled and she saw the meat was cooked, she served the "soup" to us in bowls.

We never sat at the kitchen table, but always carried our food into the living room and sat around the coffee table where she enjoyed watching television. My brother and I sat on the floor so our legs could fit under the coffee table.

When we started to eat, I burned my tongue and choked on the grease floating on top of the soup.

Immediately, my mother hit me on the side of my head and said, "Stop making that ugly face! You are so disrespectful to me! This is good food, and you had better eat it! Don't you know there are homeless, starving children in Africa who would love to have this food and your life of luxury?! Don't be so ungrateful again—*d'ya hear me?*"

I apologized and tried to explain that I had burned my tongue.

"Shut up! I don't want to hear another word from you!" she yelled, glaring at me and then said under her breath, "Stupid girl…"

Without releasing me from her hateful glare, she quickly flung her hand at me again. I ducked, and when she saw that I had avoided her strike, she gestured for me to start eating again. I looked at the bowl of "soup" and asked if I could wait until it cooled. She reluctantly agreed. Luke had mixed some rice and soya sauce with his soup, cooling it down, and was able to eat it that way. But with my mother's eyes on me, I dared not move or ask for anything for fear of further angering her.

She ordered me to eat the soup again, and I tried. It had cooled enough that when I took a mouthful, I could feel the texture of the grease on my tongue as well as the "animal" taste of the plain (and sour smelling) ground beef. I gagged, but no matter how I tried to hide the heaving motions from my mother, my body would not stop. Through my watering eyes, I could see my mother becoming more enraged with me. I eventually threw up onto my napkin.

My mother got up, yanked me from under the table by my left arm, dragged me to my room and tossed me across my bed. She left the room in a huff, then returned with the fetid bowl of soup, and with another hit to the side of my head, demanded that I finish my meal in my room.

"I can't stand the sight of you!" she roared, "You stay here until you finish the soup! I don't care how long it takes! *D'ya hear me?*"

"Yes, Mommy," I answered with my head down.

My mother slammed the door behind her.

I sat on my bed and crossed my legs, relieved to be, at the very least, out of her turbulent presence. I stared at the bowl of thickening grease, watching it congeal on top of the strange-colored ground beef called "soup." I wasn't trying to be unkind or disrespectful. The soup simply tasted horrible! And the texture of the fat, together with my burned tongue, was almost too much to endure!

What am I to do? I can't leave the room to flush this down the toilet, and I know I will only throw up again if I try to eat it! How can I get rid of this?

I raised the bowl to my lips to give it one more try, but once the smell reached my nose, I began to heave again.

My bedroom was small, and I shared it with Luke. His single bed was on one side of the room by a wall, and my bed was on the other side of the bed by the window facing our street. I often stared out of that window, dreaming of my grandparents and a life other than my own.

Suddenly, I realized, *I have a window*!

I had a way to escape the torture of eating this "soup"!

However, I dared not simply dump the entire contents out the window. *What if Mother checked on me?* I evaluated the situation. Since she "couldn't stand the sight of me," it would be unlikely that she would want to see me again any time soon. But if she did come back and saw that I had finished the soup too quickly, she would be suspicious. Naturally, she would check outside the window, and if she saw the soup there, my life would be over. I could hear her: "Not only did you totally disrespect me, but you also threw away perfectly good food children in Africa would have been grateful to have!"

This called for careful strategy.

I tiptoed to the bedroom door, so as not to cause any creaking on the wooden floors beneath my feet. I placed my ear to the door to see if I could hear her coming. She was laughing at a television show, so I knew she was still in the living room. I went back to my bed and opened the latch to my window, terrified of the possibility of making too much noise. Careful not to pour too much, I emptied a little of the soup onto the bushes below, ensuring my aim was precise. The deposit had to be made in between the branches so there would be no evidence of the "soup" or the ground beef on any of the leaves. Then I pulled the bowl back inside and quickly closed and latched the window again, just in case. My heart was racing, and my breathing was fast and hard. But the first round of my "disposal mission" had been successful.

I repeated this procedure with small deposits almost a dozen more times, taking well over forty minutes before I was done. I reasoned that this would be the most credible of scenarios in case she checked in on me at any point. Serendipitously, my mother left me alone while she watched one of her favorite TV shows, *Hawaii Five-0*. She would be in a much better mood after she saw Detective Steve McGarrett and his sidekick, Danno, capture the bad guy. At that time, it would be safe for me to leave my room.

As sure as I was of my plan, fear gripped me. I double and triple-checked both the window and the crime scene below before I went back to the door with my empty bowl. I grasped the doorknob, ready to open the door, but felt frozen where I was. Then I realized I had to go out before the program ended or else she would have too much time to focus on me. So, I held my breath, turned the doorknob, and walked out.

Just as the commercial ended and McGarrett was back on the screen, I said, "Thank you, Mommy. I finished my dinner. I'll wash the dishes so you can finish your show." She gave me a quick glare and turned back to the television set.

After showing her my empty bowl, I gathered the other dishes from the coffee table and hurried to wash them in the kitchen sink. When the kitchen was tidied up, I rushed to the bathroom, got ready for bed, and scooted back to my room. I hid under the covers, pretending I was asleep in the dark. The entire experience was exhausting, and my heart raced at the crushing thought that the soup's disposal would be discovered. With the muffled sounds of the television set just outside my bedroom door, my mind drifted to all my trials and misfortunes.

And then, I remembered the encounter with my angel in the elevator.

"God, I told You, I didn't want to do this! I told You this was too hard." Tears flowed, and I whispered, "If I can't be with PoPo and GongGong, can I please come home now?"

Wherever You Go, I Will Go

In time I realized just how difficult it must have been for my father to move to a new country, leaving family, friends, and his growing career in Hong Kong. He sacrificed all his dreams in the hopes of building a new future where his family would have a chance to stay together.

"Daddy," I asked him one night, "Why are some of the words in my favorite song different than the others?" I sang him a verse from "Michelle."

"Those words are different because they're not in English. They're in French."

"It's very beautiful. I would like to speak French."

"I believe you could. You are learning English quickly. Did you know there are places here in Canada where everyone speaks French?"

"Really? I want to go there," I said. "Would you take me?"

"Maybe I could. I'm thinking about applying for some job openings in Montreal where they speak French. You could learn French there. Would you like that?"

"Oh, Daddy! I would like it so very much!"

That night, I felt a little bit of joy in my heart and thanked God for that. Until that moment, I didn't have much to look forward to. Yes, I had Lucky, but I was still quite lonely. Now, there was a glimmer of a chance we could really start fresh with a new job for my father, a new language, and no more mean boys.

I fell asleep asking God to let me speak a different language—a special and beautiful language.

It was the spring of 1969, less than one year after our arrival in Vancouver. My father did end up applying for jobs in Montreal, and on a sunny spring day, he received word from the Royal Canadian Mounted Police (RCMP) that the position he had applied for was his, if he chose to accept it. It was the first time that he had received an offer without all the controversial comments about his being Chinese, and since coming to Canada, it was the first time that he felt truly wanted. Not only that, the salary was better, and the position was perfect for my father.

The only thing was, the job offer was across the country on the east coast in Montreal, Quebec.

He discussed the offer and all the different pros and cons with my mother, and they decided my father would accept the position. My mother suggested that he move there first, get organized, learn his duties, and then find a home and a suitable school for us. Since we were in the middle of school already, my mother said she didn't want to transition us until the school year was over. My father agreed, although he was hesitant to leave us. However, his excitement about the possibilities this new position offered, and the chance to really build a new life for the family, overrode his reluctance.

I heard the excitement in his voice when he talked about this new job, and I shared that excitement, thrilled at the idea of being able to really learn French (and not just the language I thought I had made up). I also looked forward to getting away from "Japanese Jean," the bullies, and the others at a school where I felt totally ill-fitted.

There was much talk going back and forth on the phone and in the house amongst the adults about the move to Montreal. I was not included in these conversations; I only heard muffled voices behind closed doors and cryptic one-sided phone conversations from the heavy black phone bolted to the wall in the kitchen.

Language fascinated me. My parents spoke in Cantonese, the main language spoken in Hong Kong. They also spoke Mandarin, now the national language of China, and, of course, English. In fact, everyone in my family spoke several languages, especially my father, who was able to speak many languages and numerous other dialects.

Maybe my own gift for languages was something I inherited from my family. But I also think my passion for languages grew out of my frustration with how poorly people communicated with one another. I grew up wanting to learn how to connect with others through intentional, respectful, and effective communication. And so, like my father, my love for languages also grew.

"How many languages do you speak then?" interrupted Mrs. St. John.

"Well, until recently I was comfortable with conversations in five different languages. I'm a bit rusty now…"

"Oh, my!" said, Mrs. St. John. "You speak all those languages, *in addition* to being able to communicate with angels!" she exclaimed.

"Oh, Mrs. St. John, like I said, I'm out of practice now, and other than you, I haven't spoken to any angels lately!" I said, smiling.

She blushed, her pale cheeks turning cherry. "Never mind the flattery, dear. And as for being rusty, I have no doubt that once you're back in those surroundings, you'll pick it all back up again, just like that!" she said with a snap of her fingers.

Then she leaned forward and looked at me very closely.

"Ummm…is everything okay?" I asked awkwardly. "Do I have something in my teeth?"

"Hmmm." She hummed softly. "You were right," was all she said as she leaned back into her pillow.

"About what?"

"You *are* unusual."

I smiled and shook my head at her comment.

"Well, now I'm totally intrigued. Keep going, dear! I'm not goin' anywhere, and I've got all the time in the world. Or at least…" Mrs. St. John stopped as she suddenly dropped back into the reality of her situation. "Go on! Don't let our visit end with me sinking into my own world again," she commanded with a wave of her hand.

I took a deep breath, not knowing if I should address her last comment, but the look in her eyes told me she wanted the distraction, and so I continued.

My father was leaving for Montreal, and although he told me he was coming back for us, something simply didn't feel right about his goodbye. For the second time in my life, I felt I was being torn away from something irretrievable.

It was late in the evening, and the four of us had gone to drop my father off at the train station. He invited us to see the passenger car of the train he was going to ride in. My mother agreed, but was agitated. She huffed and went onto the train first, followed by Luke. I walked in next, followed by my father. We walked up and down the passenger car and saw where my father was going to stay on his journey across the country.

That sick, empty feeling I felt in Hong Kong at my grandparents' home happened again, and I felt dizzy from the unspoken tension and anxiety. The air was heavy and haunting. Something definitely wasn't right, again.

My mother hastily walked up and down the aisle of the passenger car and directed Luke to follow her. When she got to the exit door, she picked him up and headed to the parking lot. I continued to follow my father, who was walking in a slow, measured step, assessing his surroundings. We were the only ones in the train car, and in the silence of the evening, I gathered as much courage as I could and asked, "Daddy, can I please come with you?"

My father spun around and looked at me. "What did you say, Manna?" he asked in disbelief.

"Daddy, I want to come with you. Can I please come with you? Wherever you go, I want to go."

He paused and bent down to look me in the eyes. "Manna, you have school… Plus, what would Mommy say?"

"Mommy would be happy I wasn't around," I explained. "And I can continue school in Montreal. It won't be the first time I had to learn how to make it in school in a new language."

"What about Luke?" he asked. "You never want to be without him."

"Luke can come too! But if Mommy says no, Lucky and I can help you get things sorted out first. Once everything is organized, we'll send for Luke…and Mommy."

I had it all figured out.

My father hesitated again, not knowing what to say. He was fighting back the tears, as was I. I didn't want him to leave. Neither of us spoke for a little while. Finally, my father said, "Manna, you don't have your clothes packed."

I looked up from staring at the ground and managed to mumble, "I don't need anything, Daddy—just you."

My father gave me a big hug. I held back the tears with all my might, but soon I found myself sobbing on his shoulders, begging him to take me with him. Even after the moment had passed and we both found our composure, I hung onto him and wouldn't let go. My father did his best to make light of the situation and assured me that our separation was only for a short time. Once the school year was finished, he would send for us.

"We will all be together again. It won't be long, Manna. Only a few months. I promise. Be strong for Daddy, okay?"

I nodded, with flowing tears that wouldn't stop. My father did his best to be convincing, but I didn't believe him. He wiped my tears with his handkerchief and then told me to blow my nose into it. This scenario was all too familiar. Losing another loved one was unbearable, but I did my best to be strong like my father asked.

He stood up again, took my hand, and we walked out of the train together. As we started toward the car, my mother called out, "What took you so long?"

My father didn't answer.

"And what is she crying about?" my mother demanded. She was curt, embittered, and resentful of my close relationship with my father.

"Oh, Emily, calm down. Manna was just being sweet and asked if she could come with me. That's all," my father explained.

"Hmmph," she snorted, and as she whirled her head away from us, she muttered under her breath, "Stupid girl."

My father and I looked at each other. I dared not say it out loud for fear I would get into more trouble, but with my eyes, I communicated with my father, "*See, I told you it would be easier for her without me. Please let me come with you!*"

He patted me on the head, smiled, and whispered so as not to further arouse my mother's ire, "It'll be okay. We'll be together soon."

The parting between my parents seemed cold and impersonal. Their impatience with each other had been increasing, and they continued to argue about the same issues. I didn't expect there to be any changes in our family, other than my father's reconnaissance move to Montreal for us. My father saw this job offer as a way to start completely fresh once again with the family. After all, he was *wanted* at this new job! It had better pay, better benefits, and he believed this move would be less stressful because we had already adapted to the Western culture. He had an identity and a role he could understand and fulfill, and now he had hope.

My mother, however, saw his new job as her opportunity to divorce my father.

Lunch Is Served

With my father now in Montreal, my mother began absenting herself from the house even more often. She said she was working, but she never came home when she said she would. At first, I worried. But when she was gone more and more regularly, I figured it was just something grownups did.

In her absence, I began making lunches for Luke and myself, but found my options were quite limited. I had a choice between stuffing leftover meats between two slices of bread or facing the smelly lunchmeat my mother bought on sale at our local market. I also faced the added horror of unwrapping these concoctions in front of my classmates at lunchtime. My stomach churned at the very thought.

I was also tasked with pouring milk into a thermos for each of us, and when I had spilled a little, she called me stupid and smacked me on top of the head. The times when she was really angry, she would dig her knuckles into the top of my tender head. Apparently, this was a "typical" form of discipline, but to me it was worse than the belt (another "typical" form of discipline). Sometimes I would have to lie down because the headaches resulting from her punishment were so painful.

I dared not tell her that by lunchtime the milk was warm and beginning to curdle around the edges. Each day at lunch, I would take my thermos and find Luke to get his and take them both to the drinking fountain to dump their contents down the drain. We would then get water from the fountain to satisfy our thirst.

Two of the most popular girls in school were Diane and Diana. Both were pristinely dressed, had impressively coiffed blonde hair and lived only a few houses away from each other. They rebuffed any efforts I made at building a friendship, but I soon recognized that no one would ever be deemed worthy enough to enter their elite, two-person clique—especially a new immigrant like me. So, I turned my attention elsewhere. A few of the other girls seemed more accepting of me, and some were quite nice to me.

In time, I befriended two girls, one named Arlene and another named Carol. Both were always kind and sympathetic towards me and my Asian differences. I have often wondered about these two friends over the years and wished I could tell them how much I appreciated their benevolence toward me during a time in my life that was otherwise filled with loneliness and sadness.

They got a kick out of being with me because I was always asking silly questions—silly because of my broken English, and silly because the answers that seemed so obvious to them were not for me. For instance, one time I asked them to explain why a piece of celery filled with peanut butter and sprinkled with a few raisins was called "ants on a log."

Oh, they would giggle and laugh at my ignorance.

At lunchtime, Arlene and Carol not only sat beside me, but also shared their lunches with me. While they eagerly dove into their lunchboxes to see all their goodies inside, I always dreaded opening my lunchbox to find the curdling milk and the ridiculous "sandwiches."

In between breaks in conversation, I remember thinking how much their mommies must have loved them. They took the time to cut the sandwiches, not just into halves but quarters, and then wrap them ever so carefully in wax paper! This may not seem like much to the average person, but to me it indicated a mother who took two more extra steps of love she didn't have to take. They also got juice or Kool Aid, Wagon Wheels, Ding Dongs, and other treats; even their apples were cut into pieces! And they got "ants on a log!"

Do they have any idea of how much love that is?

Every morning, their mommies took the care, time, and thoughtfulness to do something different and special than the day before. Watching my friends open their lunchboxes was like watching them open Christmas presents every day.

There were no treats in my lunchbox. Nothing was cut up. And there were no surprises—only spoiled milk and smelly sandwiches made either from leftovers or expired sandwich meats on sale. I dared not tell them it was I who made these sandwiches, because at least it looked like I had a mommy who took the time to make a lunch. I tried to make the sandwiches look nice, but we never had the fresh fillings to do so. Neither did I tell them that we didn't really have food in the house. Sometimes I could only make us butter and sugar sandwiches as a last resort.

I have to say, though, one day I discovered chocolate candy as filler for my sandwiches! When I brought those sandwiches to school, that's when my friends eagerly traded their sandwiches for mine! My self-sufficiency was rewarded in this way, but deep in my heart, I simply longed to be just like everyone else.

One weekend afternoon, Luke asked Mother for a different kind of lunch meat, and to my great surprise, she took us grocery shopping on Broadway, a very busy street. Since the store was only six blocks from our house, we walked. On our way home, my mother held Luke's hand and carried a small shopping bag in the other. The streets were crowded, and somehow, I got separated from them. As I waited for the crowd around me to clear, I saw that my mother had not only crossed a second major intersection without me, she was already halfway down the next block. The familiar cloak of sadness fell over me once again.

Does she not care about me at all?

Hoping against hope that I was wrong, I called out to her to see if I could catch her attention. "Mommy! I'm okay. I'll be right there!"

She never turned to look. She just kept walking with Luke, engaged in conversation with him.

When the light changed, I hurriedly crossed the last busy street and ran to catch up with them. The noise of the cars rushing by faded. Puffing from the run and anxiousness, I called out once more, "I'm coming, Mommy! Don't worry!"

Luke turned then and saw me. He tugged on my mother's hand to get her attention. After she took a few more steps, she turned to see me running toward her. At that moment, I tripped over a tree trunk that had broken through the sidewalk and fell sprawling in a patch of grass next to the sidewalk. As I went to push myself up, I saw that my hand just missed a pile of dog feces in the grass.

"Oh!" I said, jumping up, "Mommy, I almost fell on a bathroom!"

With a huff and a disgusted look, she rebuked me. "Manna, you're so stupid. That's *not* a bathroom! Get up and keep walking! Stop embarrassing me!" Turning around, she said under her breath, "Good for nothing!"

I followed behind her, humiliated, and not at all sure why I could do nothing right in her sight. Tears pooled in my eyes and eventually spilled over to run down my cheeks.

I walked a few steps behind my mother and brother in silence.

Why does my mother always say I'm stupid? I am not stupid!

In Chinese culture, labeling someone "stupid" was the epitome of disrespect and disdain toward a person. To accuse someone of being stupid was basically branding someone a *loser for life*—someone who would never amount to anything, someone to be pitied and avoided. There were few things more insulting than this.

This incident left me quite wounded and added to my growing list of questions.

What is so wrong with me that I deserve such obvious contempt? What did I do that makes her believe I'm stupid and useless to her? If there are deficiencies on my part, what are they? Why doesn't she explain them to me so I can have a chance to learn, grow, and improve myself?

I didn't realize that I had been looking down as I shared this memory. Without being aware of it, my posture had begun to mirror my heart—sunken and downcast. I pulled myself together, sat up straighter, and noticed Mrs. St. John was wiping away tears from her eyes.

"Oh, no…I'm sorry, Mrs. St. John. I didn't mean to make you sad! See, I shouldn't tell you about my life!"

After a few moments, she said softly, her voice slightly quivering, "Manna…if you were my little girl, I would have gotten groceries another time. I would have held your hand and taken you for walks just to be with you. I would have always crossed the street with you. I would have walked with you to and from school, and I would have learned to sing your favorite song in French with you."

3 LES MISÉRABLES

The most authentic thing about us is our capacity to create, to overcome, to endure, to transform, to love, and to be greater than our suffering.

—Ben Okri

Making Friends

The next day, I chose to come in a little earlier than my scheduled shift. Although Mrs. St. John had been assigned to me for hospice care, she was rapidly becoming more and more special to me. I enjoyed her wit and forthrightness, but the tenderness hidden in her heart was starting to shine through, and that was more compelling to me than anything else I'd already learned about her. She had a beautiful spirit, and I looked forward to seeing more of it each time we met.

When the elevators opened to the third floor, the same assembly of nurses was at the nurse's station. I smiled at them and, unlike the day before, each one returned a genuine smile.

Hearing voices coming from room 316, I tentatively peered in so as not to interrupt a private conversation, but quickly realized the dialogue came from the television set. Mrs. St. John was sitting up, alert and ready to be entertained.

When she saw me enter, she picked up the remote and switched off the television. There was a small basket of coffee creamers on the table next to her bed. She saw me looking at them and smiled. "Thomas, my husband, brought them for me. You just missed him."

"I'm sorry I haven't been able to meet him yet," I told her, sitting down in my usual chair.

"He doesn't like to leave me, but knowing you're here makes him feel better. He worries I lie here alone counting the clock till I leave the planet. I don't tell him I want him out of my way so I can listen to your story!" Leah snickered.

The curtains were pulled wide, revealing another beautiful spring day in San Diego. Looking between me and the scenery outside her window, she said, "Must have been an easy drive in today—you're so early. Everyone must already be out with their families, weather's so nice." Then catching herself from being too sentimental, she added, "Or did a client cancel so you thought you'd come earlier and get this over with?"

"No, Mrs. St. John, no one cancelled. I wanted to come earlier and spend more time with you. Here, I brought you something," I said, handing her the small bag of goodies from a local organic market.

"Gifts? Hmmm, am I declining faster than you thought, and you're bringing me alms now?"

Shaking my head, I chuckled. "You're so silly. One day, you're going to let that great big heart of yours open wide instead of—"

"My mouth?" she interrupted.

"Well, that's not what I was going to say, but if the shoe fits..." We both laughed.

"Why are you bringing me gifts? I don't want you to start getting mushy and all lovey-dovey on me now. I have Thomas for that. Next thing I know, you'll be telling me you're coming because you really like me instead of my being a part of your *shift*," she quipped.

"Well, I've got good news and bad news about that."

Mrs. St. John narrowed her eyes at me, raising one eyebrow.

"The good news is that I already like you."

"I already don't like where this is going..." she teased. "So, what's the bad news?"

"The bad news is that you like me too!" I giggled.

She gave me a playful scowl and turned away to look in the bag. "Let's see what you have here."

Just then, nurse Melody came by on her rounds. I smiled and asked her if she could help me transfer Mrs. St. John into a wheelchair so we could go outside. There was a charming courtyard near the first-floor elevators, and I wanted her to enjoy some sunshine for a while. "You can say it's for medicinal purposes... Vitamin D doses!" I nodded.

"Well, she's on an IV drip...Ah, what the heck! Let's do it!" she agreed.

Mrs. St. John was silenced by my request and Melody's acquiescence. She gave the slightest nod to Melody, like a queen giving approval to a commoner's act of service.

When Mrs. St. John was comfortably transferred into her wheelchair with a blanket about her and the IV drip attached, she looked at me and said, "Well, whatcha waiting for? All this was your idea. Let's get going, shall we?"

"Yes, ma'am," I replied.

Melody smiled and escorted us out to the courtyard.

Mrs. St. John sat under the warm, filtered sunlight of a young lemon eucalyptus tree. I took my place beside her on a sweet little wooden bench that appeared to be hand-carved. A gentle breeze blew her hair away from her face.

She is absolutely beautiful... I thought.

Posture perfect, I could instantly envision her as a young woman—svelte and petite, but hardly frail. I'm certain she used to command any room with her presence, especially with her eyes, which were sharp, alert, and able to discern any signs of manipulation within miles.

Her skin, though slightly slack around the jawline and creased with a few laugh lines around the eyes, was silky and otherwise flawless. Mrs. St. John lacked the typical age spots of a woman in her late seventies and her cheekbones were distinguished, but not prominent enough to take over the symmetry and balance of her other facial features. Her hair, mostly white and kept at ear-length, was soft with loose curls at the ends.

In short, Mrs. St. John was stunning.

With closed eyes, she took long, intentional deep breaths, smelling the lavish bouquet of fragrances from the roses, eucalyptus trees, and gardenia and jasmine shrubs. Her hands lay on her lap, and every now and then she tilted her head as if to focus on the sounds nearby.

I, too, took this time to enjoy the beauty of the day and closed my eyes, meditating along with my companion. When she was satisfied with what she had taken in, she spoke with her eyes still closed, "Did you know that the sun has a smell? As does rain and snow?"

I smiled.

She opened her eyes and looked up at the sky and the wispy clouds above. "Thank you, Manna. It feels good to spend some time out here. It's easier to feel alive when you're a part of the living."

An idea popped into my mind then, and I made a mental note to bring something special for her next time—a reminder of the beauty and the joy of life—my dogs.

Suddenly, Leah snapped out of her meditation and melancholy.

"So, this mother of yours…"

"Oh, Mrs. St. John, I'm sorry about all that. I got carried away yesterday. I lamented too much last evening. It's a difficult subject."

"A difficult *woman* more than a difficult *subject*, I'd say." She reached out and held my hand with both of hers. "And you must stop calling me Mrs. St. John. From now on, I want you to call me Leah. You make me feel old with that 'Mrs. St. John' talk. Old and distant. And besides, 'Mrs. St. John' was my mother-in-law's name!"

She then launched into a wry anecdote about her mother-in-law that had us both laughing. Then her face turned reflective once more. "I don't have the faith in people that you have, Manna. I've seen too much ugliness come from people—people I trusted and loved. And to be quite honest, I'm not sure I have half the faith in God as you do, either."

"Well, I don't know if I have faith in people either, Leah. That's why I put *all* my faith in God instead. I may not have understood what was happening many times in my life, but God always proved Himself to me. While He may not have been responsible for the pain I suffered at the hands of people with free will, He used those struggles for something good. Yes, people are flawed and weak—myself included—but thankfully, God is not us. He is *God*—and bigger than all of our problems, bigger than the people around us, and He has a bigger purpose for us than we can see."

"Come on, Manna. It's not that easy. You can't just say you have faith in God and that will make everything *okay* with what people do to you!" she challenged.

"No, it's not easy. I never said it was easy. In fact, it's often the farthest thing from that. I too, must keep reminding myself to be open to the things I *cannot see*. There's always a bigger picture, a larger story going on behind the scenes that hasn't been revealed yet. Plus, our eyes can play tricks on us. Perception isn't always reality."

"I still don't know if I buy it." She shook her head.

"I get it. Life—and God—are hard to understand. But if God were small enough for us to understand, then He wouldn't be big enough to handle our problems. And I highly doubt the Creator of the universe and all the matter contained within it couldn't handle us and our little problems."

Leah struggled. "So, what do you do when people hurt you, betray you, lie to you, lie *about you*—and then *leave you?*" she demanded, as if seeking answers for herself.

"First of all, before I do anything, I pray. I pray against any offense or a critical spirit, and I ask for clarity, discernment, wisdom, and the courage to then apply what God shows me. I didn't always respond this way, but I've learned this is a much healthier and more productive way of living."

"But what if you are justifiably offended?" Leah demanded.

"The easiest way to be offended is to consistently make everything about you," I replied.

"Ouch!" Leah reacted.

I smiled and lovingly squeezed her hand. "Often, we overreact, or have 'heat' on something because we're looking at a situation with a filter of 'What about me?' But when we care more about being free than being a victim, then we'll see our situations objectively. Sometimes the greatest obstacle to freedom comes not from others, but from ourselves. Our mind is a relentless, uncensored chatterbox if we don't take every thought captive. Seriously! Without that mental cultivation, we remain under siege, bombarded with neurotic monologues based on outdated thinking that has no value for us—and keeps us enslaved prisoners of our own making."

Leah sighed, conceding slightly. "Go on."

"Our paradigms are usually built from 'small thinking,' literally. Our initial assumptions and rules about life were founded when we were *little*, young, immature, uneducated, untaught, etc. Unfortunately, these early thoughts are rarely corrected, revised, updated, or deleted as we grow up. Even though things change, and new people come into our lives, we seldom update those simple mindsets. Instead, we hang onto those rules as if our current survival (and our future) depends on them. And in doing so, we become too entrenched to think about new or different possibilities. We blame others too quickly, become too pessimistic to hope, are dismissive of our dreams, and become entrenched in self-entitlement, living lives of bitterness and mediocrity.

"But when we stop being know-it-alls and are teachable, the impossible becomes possible. Otherwise, instead of living a hero's journey, we'll choose the lesser, and live the way of a coward, afraid to do anything.

"Adversities prepare ordinary people for extraordinary lives. Unfortunately, many give up just short of the finish line, not seeing that victory is just around the corner. If we can simply stop making judgments so soon and keep turning the page, we can see that our lives can be a beautiful story."

"Argh! That's so much work!" Leah protested.

"Yes, it is, but better to suffer the anguish of discipline than to suffer the anguish of regret."

Leah raised an eyebrow. "I want to believe you, *Socrates*, but I don't know." Her voice drifted. "You seem so sure."

"I am sure because I've lived what I'm sharing with you. Treasures are hidden in darkness and God taught me how to mine for those gems there. When I was at my weakest, He was the strongest. And now I know I can completely trust my unknowing world to an all-knowing God."

"How? How did you do that?"

"I stopped getting in the way, and I stopped fighting Him. When I did, every circumstance that was meant for my harm, God used for my benefit, and blessed me even more for believing Him."

Leah squeezed my hand and closed her eyes before nodding for me to continue.

"God doesn't want any of us to be under the blight of darkness, but we live in an imperfect world, filled with almost eight billion people, each with their own free will and their own personal agendas. Unhappiness, trials, adversity, and pain are inevitable. It's not God's fault when we choose to do evil with our free will. And when we are targets of ill-intentioned people, God doesn't leave us alone. He goes through it with us—if we allow Him to. And He will help us find a way through it all too, not just as victimized survivors, but as victorious overcomers. He will bless us when we endure and stay steady on our path, not haphazardly seeking restitution, retaliation, or vengeance, but seeking Him—seeking Love instead. We overcome evil by doing good[1], and He will show us how, every step of the way. In my darkest times, I know God protected me from even worse fates."

I stopped for a few moments as memories flashed before my eyes.

"There are many mysteries our simple minds can't begin to comprehend. And when the queries come and the answers don't, that's when I have to believe *more* in the God who created the universe, who flung the stars into existence with His fingertips, than in the simple thoughts and ruminations of my little mind."

"That's pretty gutsy of you to say—considering what you've told me so far!" she challenged.

"There are seasons in life when we do endure pain, but I've grown wiser, stronger, and kinder from them. I also know that joy is always on the other side. When I go through seasons of difficulty now, I press on. Don't get me wrong—I do ask for God to deliver me from a lot of situations I'd rather not have to go through."

"And does He?"

"Sometimes He does. Sometimes He doesn't. If He doesn't, there's a greater purpose for the trial than my selfish desire for comfort and convenience. Instead of demanding God to rescue me from the problems, I do my best to be teachable—to allow God to use each circumstance as a tool to sandpaper the things in me that are rough and prickly to others. In return, He teaches me how to be strong, courageous, and creative. He builds my patience and my character, and He gives me a new way of thinking—almost like I have a new mind.

"I guess what I'm trying to say is that regardless of the circumstance, God's provision is always there for us. He doesn't let the trials bury us. He uses them to plant us."

"But if you keep asking to learn, you're gonna keep getting crazy people in your life to practice on!" She argued. "I don't know about that! Maybe it's easier to just stay dumb and bitter, like me."

"Oh Leah! You're not dumb and bitter. And you don't protect your heart by pretending you don't have one."

Leah's eyes opened wide. "Touché!"

"Stay soft, Leah. Don't let the world and foolish people make you hard. Don't give in to hate. Don't let bitterness steal your sweetness. It's not worth it…and they're not worth it."

She nodded. "But there are such hateful people around!"

"Yes, what they do can be very hateful. And yes, problematic people and all their silly problems will find us, just as we will find them. There's no way around it. But mighty warriors come from mighty battles, and in time, the little hiccups that once devastated us will be like nothing. We won't be distracted or taken off course by the little things. We'll fulfill greater purposes than we dare to imagine and achieve our own unique and grand destinies. God will use our deepest pain as the launching pad to our greatest calling."

"Bigger fish to fry." Leah said slowly.

"Yes! Exactly. Plus, were it not for those *interesting* people and their equally interesting situations, how else could we effectively offer compassion, love, courage, and encouragement to others, unless we first lived through them and learned from them? As I see it, we should thank them for making us strong! C.H. Spurgeon once said, 'I have learned to kiss the wave that drives me against the rock of ages.'"

Leah hesitated, "Hmm…I'll have to think more about all of this." She paused, leaned forward and raised her eyebrow again. "Until then, I will say you're right about one thing, though."

"What's that, Leah?"

"You are an unusual one." She smiled.

"Leah, you've already said that."

"Well, then I'll say it again!"

"And for the record, I said I was an unusual *child*. I didn't say *I am* unusual!" I bantered, laughing along with her.

"Whatever." She leaned back into her chair. "It's semantics. Unusual child. Unusual person. Same, same." She winked. "But yes, you do intrigue me…I haven't quite figured you out yet. Maybe after you tell me more about your life, I'll have a diagnosis for you." She smiled.

After another moment of reflection, she said, "I have a feeling we haven't even scratched the proverbial surface. Am I right?"

I returned her gaze.

"Then, you must continue," she determined, taking my silence for admission.

"No, Leah." I said firmly. "Really, I've said enough. Besides, there are *so many* other things we could be talking about."

"Please…" She stopped suddenly and then added, "I am only going to say this once and I will never repeat it again. If you tell anyone about this conversation, I will deny it until my last breath—which may be sooner than we all think. Furthermore, I shall never speak to you again because I could not bear you breaking the trust I am going to ask of you."

I remained silent, waiting for her to reveal what this weighty request might be.

"Manna, I awoke this morning with a strange sense that for the first time in my life, I can have peace. I've had a heavy heart and a burdened soul. Sometimes the bitterness oozes out of me, in spite of all my efforts to control my emotions and the thoughts racing through my head. There's an old saying, 'Your tongue is having a fight with your teeth,' and I feel like a perpetual battle is happening in my mouth—my teeth constantly fight to withhold what my tongue labors to express. Sometimes the teeth win. Sometimes the tongue does. There are also times when I couldn't care less about what is going on, and I don't want to waste another drop of energy trying to educate someone. You know, 'Don't throw pearls before swine,' and all that. After all, what's a pig going to do with pearls?" She raised her hands in the air. "I know a lot of people like this, and you've got to admit, you do too, right?"

"Well, I wouldn't quite put it that way," I agreed. "But yes, I know people who refuse to seek wise counsel. And sadly, even after they do, they continue to choose selfishly wreaking havoc and drama in the wake of their poor choices, not only for themselves, but for all those around them."

"See! You know exactly what I mean. Then I bet they come expecting you to fix all their problems!" Leah added.

I nodded. "In Chinese, two sayings come to mind describing exactly what we're talking about. One is, *'S-eye hay.'* Its implication is quite interesting: It's as if to say, 'It's a total waste of *not only* my breath to continue educating the person before me, but it's also a total waste of the *air and oxygen in the atmosphere* altogether to spend one more second or another ounce of energy to illuminate the obviously dull mind standing in front of me!'"

Leah smiled with appreciation and nodded approvingly at my description. "I like that. What's the second saying?"

"You'll like this one even better. *'Sai how suy.'* This means that it's not only a total and complete waste of your saliva to keep speaking, it is a total and complete waste of energy for your body to create the fluid in order to illuminate the dull and thick mind before you."

We laughed out loud together.

"Ah yes…we are simpatico." She smiled and nodded. "So, Manna, no offense, but let's not waste any more oxygen in the atmosphere or saliva in my mouth. Let me say this in all seriousness. I am not sure how to put this, but I realized this morning that there is something about you that will truly help me. After you left yesterday, it took me a long time to fall asleep—not because I was disturbed or burdened by what you shared, but because I was arrested by the unshakable reality that somehow, hearing your life story will be the beautiful pearls *I need* to hear."

Leah leaned towards me again and softly added, "So please, Manna, I know it will not be easy for you to share some things, but if you will take this great burden on, I believe you will carry me to the mountaintop of my life and allow me to see more than I had ever hoped to see."

Leah stopped and exhaled. I could tell that being so transparent was uncomfortable for her. Yet she continued, "I have been imprisoned for too long, and for the first time, I know the keys to my self-imposed prison door are in reach. *I feel it.* Something you say will give me the peace I have been seeking—peace from the torment that has haunted me most of my life."

I swallowed awkwardly, not knowing how to respond to this unexpected and simultaneous confession, declaration, and plea.

She was right.

The burden was great, not only because it was extremely uncomfortable to share my private life with someone I didn't really know (even though I had begun to enjoy our new friendship), but more importantly, I wasn't sure my story was special enough to accomplish such a monumental feat, much less be worthy to warrant being a dying woman's last request.

We maintained each other's gaze for a few more moments. Then, Leah purposefully turned away and straightened both her blanket and her posture. She was sitting at attention again, and with her hands firmly placed on the armrests of the wheelchair, I began.

"My English was improving, and I was getting very good at understanding what was being said, and what was not said…"

Answer the Phone!

I was seven years old now.

In our culture, showing any form of disrespect for our elders (or those in positions of authority) by questioning their choices or actions was an unthinkable act of dishonor. Plus, I never knew what horrors would befall Luke and me next if I spoke up, so I learned to be quiet. Knowing better than to ask my mother questions about her plans, I tried to follow the routines and waited for someone to tell me when we would get to go live with my father and begin our new life.

But things were getting stranger at home, and there were many secret conversations on the phone. Sometimes when the phone rang, my mother ordered us not to answer it.

"What if it's Daddy calling from Montreal or PoPo calling from Hong Kong?" I asked.

"Shut up!" My mother rebuffed. "I told you not to answer the phone! Go outside right now—*d'ya hear me?*"

Frightened and frustrated, I didn't stay inside much. It was almost unbearable to not pick up the phone when it could have been my father or my grandparents calling. I would rather not even hear the phone ring so I wouldn't be tortured by wondering whether or not they were on the other end of the line. I simply couldn't understand why I wasn't allowed to talk to them, nor did I understand why *she* didn't want to talk to them either.

Later, I found out that many times it was indeed my father calling, and she was ignoring his calls. Long distance phone calls were very expensive then, so he could only afford to call when he got his paycheck, and they required specific protocols and the help of an operator to make the proper connections. It was no easy process, so when the calls came in, I knew my father or grandparents had to do a lot to make that happen. Plus, with the three-hour time difference, and my father working many different shifts in his new job, while trying to prepare for our arrival, it was difficult to reach us when we'd be at home and not at school.

When my father was able to finally connect and asked why my mother wasn't answering his calls, she told him that she was either working or taking us on outings, which, of course, was rarely true.

During one of those calls, my father told her he had found a wonderful two-bedroom apartment in a beautiful neighborhood, with a very good, small and friendly school able to take us for the upcoming school year. My mother said she would start planning but never got back to him and kept delaying the process.

My father sensed something was wrong, so he called his aunt, (who had also recently immigrated to Vancouver) and asked her to contact my mother. My mother was shocked when my aunt first called and soon avoided her calls also.

My father then asked my great aunt to check in on us because he had heard (through our small Chinese community) that we were often left alone all day and even all night long. She agreed and came by the house a few times and confirmed what my father had heard.

"David! I'm so sorry," she reported, "the stories are true. I'm so sorry. It's not supposed to be this way! My goodness…Manna and Luke are so young and are almost always at home alone! They told me they were forbidden to answer the phone anymore. And I can't get ahold of Emily either—she's never around."

"Auntie, I don't know what to do. I'm so far away. They were supposed to move here months ago—as soon as the children finished school. The summer is almost over, and if Emily won't answer the phone, how do I get ahold of her? The few times I did reach her, we argued, and then she hung up on me," my father said, feeling powerless. "The job is good here, and I can now make a good living for the family. Do I give this up and come back?"

"No. I will hire you a nanny to help out for now. I know of one not too far away. She is also Chinese, and helped another family I know. She would be glad for the work," my great-aunt offered.

"Thank you so much, Auntie. I am indebted and will pay you back as soon as I am able," my father said gratefully.

"No. This is family. There is none of that. Just take care of yourself and keep working hard. You don't want to lose that job. I will call you when I get things sorted out," Auntie reassured him.

True to her word, we did get a nanny, an older Chinese lady who looked like the stereotypical maids you saw in a Chinese movie. Her salt-and-pepper hair was very short, sharply cut, and held back behind her ears with a large bobby pin on each side. She wore a white or grey shirt with three-quarter length sleeves and trousers that looked as if they had shrunk in the laundry, and she walked with her feet pointing outward in her plastic flip-flops. She wore no makeup, spoke with a bit of a lisp, and when she smiled, her lips revealed a gold upper eyetooth.

She was hired to take care of us, to keep the house tidy, help with the yard, make us lunches, and to cook for us. This seemed to work out well for a while, but something happened which permanently altered the dynamics of our household and eventually drove the nanny away.

Stupid Is As Stupid Does

My mother enjoyed working now more than ever because she liked this new man who also worked there. He was an orderly, a hospital attendant with no medical duties per se, but who performed unskilled jobs—assisting in the cleanup of patients and their beds when they soiled them, helping with cleaning work, and that sort of labor. In those days, this was not a revered position. It was given to those without education who could do menial work.

My mother was not only gone during work hours, she was now gone most of her evenings and weekends too. I would overhear her talking about a man named Scham and soon she spoke more of him than of my father. Her interest in him took precedence over her dislike of me, so for a short time, her indiscriminate rebukes were curtailed.

One evening, my mother started getting ready to go on another date with Scham. I had already prepared dinner for Luke and myself, and while we were watching television before bedtime, I struggled to say something to her. I was afraid to awaken her temper, but I didn't want her to go out again. Within moments, I found myself leaving the living room and walking across the hall to the bathroom. With all the courage I could muster, I cautiously asked, "Are you going out with Scham again?"

She didn't answer, so I pressed on. "Why do you go out with him so much? Is he a friend of Daddy's? Is he helping us move to Montreal?"

Without hesitation, filter, or sensitivity, my mother turned to me and flatly stated, "Stop talking about your father! And stop talking about Montreal! We're never moving there! I never meant to move there, and the sooner your father and I are divorced the better! And you better not ask stupid questions like that when I bring Scham here. *D'ya hear me?*"

Shocked at what I had just heard, I didn't know what to say or how to respond. I didn't even understand what divorce was. All I knew was that we were not moving to Montreal, and it didn't look like I was going to see my father again. I was devastated.

The next day, I somberly asked Arlene at school, "What does it mean when your parents get a divorce?"

"It's when they decide they don't love each other anymore and your father moves away," she said, much too easily. "You'll still get to see him regularly—but not at the same time as you see your mom, and *definitely* not on the same holidays. Don't worry. You get used to it. It's okay."

Unfortunately, what was true for her was not true for me.

It was not okay. None of it was okay.

I was very confused and didn't know how to get answers. With looming threats shrouding us in fear if we ever spoke with our father or PoPo or GongGong, I was left alone with my own thoughts and questions once again.

"Oh, my word!" Leah exclaimed. "Don't tell me your mother left your father for a janitor! If she was going to wreck her marriage and destroy her family, she should have at least chosen a doctor there, for goodness' sakes!"

I smiled at her spiritedness. "I think, in her mind, as a single Asian woman in 1960s Canada—and worse yet, a soon-to-be-divorcée—she felt most people would deem her lucky to get the attention of any man."

"So she settled? She settled for a janitor?"

I exhaled, without knowing how to reply, and continued.

Then the day came when my mother brought Scham to the house. He was introduced to us as "Uncle Scham" because, in our Chinese culture, it was only polite to call close family friends "uncle" or "auntie" as a way of honoring their friendship. Addressing them as "Mr." or "Mrs." would signify that their relationship was distant or that they were strangers. And it was absolutely unthinkable to call them by their first names!

So, here we were with "Uncle Scham"—a "close friend" about whom my brother and I knew nothing. He was about fifteen years younger than my mother, had a heavy Eastern European accent, and light-brown hair. I found out later that he was reared in Germany.

When my brother and I were first introduced to him, he did not say much. He simply sat in our living room and kept his eyes on our mother, forcing the obligatory intermittent smile at us. He was also seldom without a beer in his hand. Luke and I sat mute, watching him while my mother shamelessly beamed at him.

After that first visit, Scham became something of a regular fixture in our lives. He stayed overnight often, and my mother did not care that she wantonly permitted a strange man to stay at our home—even in front of my great-aunt, who would still come by now and then to check on us. Moreover, Scham and my mother would be locked behind closed doors in the bedroom for hours during the day and night, completely oblivious to our whereabouts or our needs.

This behavior (*especially* in those days) was unthinkable—a dignified and self-respecting woman doesn't just have her new dates casually stay the night at her home *with her young children there!* Even by today's more tolerant social conventions, her flagrant disregard for decorum and care befitting of a mother were inappropriate and unseemly.

During one of my great-aunt's short visits (while mother was away), she told us why our nanny had left. I had thought it was because we were misbehaving, but that was not the case. The nanny hated Scham's arrogance and how importunate and boorish he was to her—as if our nanny had been hired to be *his servant*. She hated him for treating us so poorly, and she hated my mother for allowing it.

Scham ate all of the food in the house and left nothing for us. Plus, he would use all the grocery money to buy the kinds of foods *he liked* from his homeland, including gallons of buttermilk he would drink straight out of the glass milk container, leaving a disgustingly smelly thick coat around his mouth; three different kinds of cheeses (that smelled up the whole kitchen) from which he would rip off bites with his mouth; rye bread and beer, as well as a few other expensive items. When the nanny asked my mother for money to get groceries, my mother accused her of stealing the money. The nanny tried to use this opportunity to talk to my mother about this (and other concerns), but the nanny was harshly reprimanded and ordered never to speak about these matters again. When she saw that my mother showed no remorse or intention to change, she could not hold her anger back any longer.

"Scham eats six to eight eggs every morning for breakfast, as well as all the other meats! In fact, he eats *all* of the food, leaving nothing for the children! He also takes all of the other household money and pockets it for himself daily, leaving nothing behind so I am unable get anything for *your children*! What kind of woman are you to tolerate this stranger who is nothing but a selfish opportunist? *He's using you!* Furthermore, haven't you seen how cruel he is to the children? He frightens them with his behavior and short temper, and he yells at them and hits them for no reason! How can you let such a vile person treat your children like this, much less live here?" With a loud breath, she cried out her last denouncement. "On top of it all, you're acting like a tramp! Where is your decency? Your self-respect? You should be ashamed of yourself! Thank goodness your parents aren't here to see this!"

My mother was stunned. She glared at the nanny, but the pride and rebellion in her heart refused to let the truth of these words reach her. Instead, she screamed, "*You're fired*!"

"She shot the messenger!" Leah called out. "And defended that trash, that ill-bred oaf, instead of you kids!"

"Yes," I said slowly. "And without any accountability at home…the unimaginable began."

The Thief in the Night

Out of necessity, I learned to cook by myself on a gas stove. Other than butter and sugar sandwiches (or chocolate chip sandwiches), a baked eggs dish that PoPo once taught me to cook is what I would make if I could get to the eggs before Scham did. I would whip the eggs with some water and a little sugar, bake them, and then serve them to Luke and myself with some leftover rice. If there was a little soya sauce to add, the dish was a gourmet treat for us. Before the nanny left, she taught me how to fry some ground beef with onions and soya sauce and put that over rice too. All in all, not bad for a seven-year-old at a gas stove, and though it wasn't the best of meals, often, these were the only hot meals we had.

Since Scham only had a tiny, rented room on a bad side of town, he spent much of his time at our house, coming and going as he pleased, eating whatever he wanted, and enjoying the luxury of our simple home as if it were his own.

Later on, whenever the question arose from other adults as to how he met my mother, he would brag with his thick accent, "Emily had many hundred-dollar bills in her *vaullet*, and I would *zink* to myself, *mein Gott, zis voman* must be *rich!*" Every time he told the story, he placed great emphasis on the word "rich."

Hearing him speak made my stomach turn. My mother, on the other hand, would smile, as if she was proud that she had had hundred-dollar bills in her wallet (given to her by her parents and my father), but totally oblivious to the fact that this man was using her as his means to enjoy *"ze goot life"* in Canada!

As Scham ingratiated himself into our family more and more, my mother began leaving him to babysit for us when she had to work night shifts.

On one such night, Scham promised we could all watch television if we got ready for bed quickly. He asked us to go take a bath, and we did so immediately. When we were finished, we sat on the floor by the couch and watched TV with him.

Surprisingly, we were having a pleasant time, as Luke and I tried to be nice to him. Deep down, however, we were feeling very awkward, but we didn't want to be disrespectful, so we stayed on our best behavior.

As the evening progressed, we felt a little less guarded in his presence, and during a commercial break, he asked us to sit beside him. Luke climbed on the couch to sit beside him on one side, and I climbed to sit beside him on the other. When the television show ended at 8:00 p.m., Scham announced, "Bedtime!"

Luke and I started to get up to go to bed when suddenly Scham appeared to change his mind. "Manna, help me get Luke ready for bed *unt zen* you can stay up for *vonne* more show because you are older *unt* because you helped me clean *ze* kitchen." I didn't think what he suggested was strange because I had heard similar things from friends who were also allowed to stay up later because they were older and did extra chores.

It wasn't that I wanted to stay up to watch another show or to be with Scham. I was afraid if I didn't do as he asked, especially when it appeared he was rewarding me, that he would report me to my mother as being disobedient or unappreciative. So, I did as I was told and said goodnight to Luke as he got settled for bed.

Scham met me at our bedroom door, and made sure he closed it tight, while explaining himself: "I don't *vant ze* TV to keep up Luke." He then took my hand and walked me back to the living room. He took a blanket and covered me as I sat on the sofa. I thought he was being thoughtful and had no idea he had ulterior motives.

After he had chosen a TV show, he told me he was cold and asked if I would share the blanket with him. Innocently, I said, "Oh, I'm sorry! I didn't mean to take it all for myself."

He then pulled the blanket and loosely threw it over both of our laps. I was sitting to the left of him. When Scham saw that I was excited to see The Beatles come on stage as guests on the popular Ed Sullivan Show, he suddenly put both of his hands under the blanket and began fidgeting with something, but I didn't know what it was.

My hands were outside the blanket, and then, without a word, he reached for my right hand and pulled it under the blanket.

My heart thudded.

I knew something was very wrong as he put more pressure on my hand and forced me to rub my hand around a hairy lump of what felt like skin. I felt the lump of skin get bigger and sweaty. I was afraid, and my seven-year-old brain knew something very bad was happening.

I gulped and could barely swallow. "Ummm...err...what are you doing?" I finally asked, full of fear and apprehension.

"*Nossingk*," he declared under his breath while looking at me with a glaze in his eyes. Somehow, I knew his look was not one a grown man should have for a girl my age.

"What is that under the blanket?" I asked, trying to hide my terror.

"It's *nossink*—just my *zumb*. You're just holding my hands *unt* playing *vis* my *zumb*. Don't be a bad girl now. Be a *gut* girl, *unt* just hold my hand, or I'll tell your *mater zat* you didn't behave."

He held his hands over mine and continued to move it up and down.

Horrified but trapped, I could focus on nothing but his jerking motions and muffled grunts. After what felt like an eternity, suddenly something happened. He groaned out loud, and then released my hand from his strong grip and opened his eyes.

I wanted to scream, but I had no voice. I wanted to run away, but my body was frozen. I stared at Scham in shock, and while I had no idea of what he had finished doing, I knew that something horrible had just happened.

I felt darkness fall over my body, cloaking my entire body and soul with filth and dirt.

Since I had helped change diapers with different family friends' babies, and since I had cared for my little brother, I knew that a girl's anatomy was different than a boy's.

But I did not know much more other than euphemisms, "These are your *private parts*, and it is never right to show them to others or to touch them in front of people." I did not know what masturbation was, and I did not know what molestation or sexual abuse was. Still, I knew Scham had forced me to do something disgusting, and the fact that I had been forced to touch his "private parts" traumatized me.

Scham had tricked me and violated me. Instantly, it felt as though something special had been stolen from me, even though I could not describe what that "something" was. All I knew was that I felt different, and I would never be the same again.

As soon as he released his grip on me, I pulled away my hand. It wasn't until then that I realized he had been holding me down so hard that my right arm was sore from his physical constraint.

"I want to go to bed now," I said, terrified and trembling.

"Fine. Go!" he commanded, maneuvering awkwardly under the blanket. As I left, I turned to look back and saw him look under the blanket and then use it to wipe himself. He caught me looking at him, and waved me away, warning, "You better not tell your *mater* what happened, or I'll tell her you *ver* a bad girl who caused me a lot of trouble...*unt* you know how angry she *vill* be *viz* you for *zat*!"

Without waiting another moment, I darted down the dark hall to the bathroom, whimpering and wanting to scream. I desperately tried to wash and scrub the violation off my hand, which I now felt had contaminated my entire being.

As I cried in the bathroom, the image of the night lion flashed before me. Its darkness made me shudder. How I felt about that lion was how I felt about Scham now.

I looked up in the mirror and had a terrifying realization—there were horrors in this world far worse than I might have imagined, and they weren't on distant mountains.

They were right here at home.

I lay awake that night, wondering what I might do to make sure I never had to be in Scham's presence again.

At the very least, I made plans for how to avoid being alone with him so I would never be forced to do that awful thing again. I imagined telling my mother, but everything inside me knew she would not believe me.

I saw how she looked at him.

Even if she didn't think much of him, she thought even less of me. I also knew how extremely easy it was for her to dismiss me and blame me for any mishaps, and there was no doubt that she would accuse me of lying and causing trouble. And if for some inconceivable reason, she did believe me and decided never to see Scham again, she would blame me for the incident and hate me forever—maybe even send me away.

If she sent me away, where would I go? With no way to find my father or my grandparents, what would happen to me? Worse, what would happen to Luke?

Then the most frightening of thoughts occurred to me. *What if Scham did this to Luke?*

Oh, my God! I could never let that happen!

And so, there was my answer. I would stay, and I would tell no one.

The next morning, I awoke and remembered what Scham had done to me the night before. I staggered around trying to get Luke and myself ready for school. *Did that really happen? Was that a bad dream? A nightmare?* A sickening feeling welled up in my stomach. A retching nausea overcame me, and as I ran to the bathroom to throw up, I knew last night's betrayal and abuse was not imagined. It was real.

I made myself to go to school and, on our short walk there, I continued trying to make sense of what had happened, rationalizing as much as my seven-year-old little girl's mind could comprehend. *Maybe I misunderstood the whole scenario. Maybe this was normal behavior in families. Maybe people did this all the time, but I just didn't know about it. Maybe I am, as my mother said, stupid, and this is only additional proof of my stupidity…*

But no matter what I tried to come up with as a reason, nothing could change the fact that I felt contaminated. This sense of defilement reached the depths of my core.

No, I concluded. No one should feel this way. This was not normal behavior at all.

I already felt misplaced without my grandparents and my father. I felt different for being Chinese and unable to learn English fast enough. I was lonely without friends and felt unwanted and unloved by my mother. But with this new situation forced upon me, I started to believe there was nothing good about me at all.

Though I prayed my mother would never ask Scham to babysit us anymore, unfortunately, he did babysit for us—many more times. And while I tried to avoid him, he continued to threaten me.

"I *vill* tell your *mater* you *ver* being a bad girl if you do not sit *vis* me *unt* hold my *zumb*," he would say.

Just when I didn't think it could get any worse, his brazenness reached even darker depths. Before long, he began touching me all over with his other hand. When I protested or tried to fight him off, he further accused me of being not just a "bad girl," but a *"very bad girl."* He threatened often to tell my "*mater*" if I didn't do as he asked.

"If you don't listen to me, *zen* it *vill* be your fault I tell your *mater*, and it *vill* be your fault for hurting her and causing her more pain during *zis* time of her divorce from your *fater*. You don't want to hurt your *mater* even more, do you?" he hissed.

I did not know hatred until then.

I wanted to speak up, but there was no one to tell, and the ugly blanket of filth and shame grew heavier and heavier.

"Dear heavens!" Leah broke in, "Someone should have used a skinning knife on that filthy animal!"

I chuckled inwardly at her solution.

"Didn't your mother see through that disgusting beast?" she shouted.

"Well, yes and no. While things did not always go well between them, she always took him back. When they had fights, she would scream at him on the phone and then hang up on him. And whenever those fights occurred, she would once again tell us not to answer the phone, just like she did with my father."

Hide and Seek…and Hide

On one bitter occasion, we were given another one of my mother's very distinct orders: "If Uncle Scham ever comes by the house, you are NOT to let him in. No matter what he says to you, *do not open the door to him—d'ya hear me?*"

By now, we knew the tone and inflection of her "catchphrase" by heart. We mouthed under our breath her usual, *"D'ya hear me?"* after every sentence in unison with her, and we did so this time as well.

That weekend, in the afternoon, Luke and I were playing hide-and-go-seek in the front yard. I ran to the end of the block to hide behind a bush, but when I turned around to go to the bush, I saw Scham walking up the street. He didn't have a car, so he always took the bus. He must have just gotten off at the bus stop. He was a couple of short blocks away, but there was no mistaking that it was him. I pretended I didn't see him and ran back to the house as fast as I could, grabbing Luke and whatever toys we had in the front yard, and we both ran inside.

"Scham's coming! Grab the toys! We have to get inside right away!" I yelled. "Hurry!"

As I was locking the front door, I called out to Luke, "Go to the back door and make sure the screen door and the back door are locked. Leave Lucky outside so he thinks we're out at our friend's."

Luke stared at me with terror in his eyes.

"Don't be scared. Just do as I say," I said as calmly as I could.

Luke scurried to the back door and followed my orders. I closed all the windows, shut the blinds, and dead-bolted the front door, as quick as my little legs could rush me around. When Luke ran back to me, I ushered him into our bedroom. We didn't have time to close our bedroom door before I heard Scham walking up the front steps. We pulled our blankets up towards our mouths and I gestured to Luke to breathe into the blanket and not to say a word.

Scham rattled and shook the front door. When he was unable to open it, he went to the back door and shook that.

Both of our hearts had been racing from playing a lively game just moments before, but now they were racing in sheer terror.

The small window built into the front door allowed anyone inside to see who was outside the door, but it also allowed anyone on the outside to see in. Directly underneath this small window was a narrow mail slot, and when Scham didn't see anyone through the window, he tilted the mail slot open and spoke. His voice echoed in the hallway and made it sound like he was already inside. We were absolutely terrified.

"I know you're in *zer*, Manna. Open *ze* door," Scham hollered. "Be a *gut* girl *unt* listen to Uncle Scham. You don't *vant* to make your *mater* angry, do you? She knows I'm coming, *unt* if you don't open *ze* door, she *vill* be *very, very* angry *vit* you!"

My heart had pounded so hard from all that had already occurred, but upon hearing his words, I felt as though my heart actually stopped. *What do I do?* I thought. *Did mother really talk to Scham and tell him to come by? I didn't get her call—the secret code. She would call and let the phone ring twice, hang up and call again. We were outside playing…did I miss her call? If I don't let him in and they did talk, I'll be in so much trouble because she likes him so much. Oh, my…dear God—what do I do? What do I do?*

Luke was frozen in place, curled up against the corner of the wall on his bed. He trembled and seemed to be barely breathing. Only his big eyes peered out of his blanket. I could hear and feel my heart pounding in my chest, and I was afraid Scham could hear it too. I prayed for God to silence my heart so Scham would not hear us, or better, for him to just go away.

Just then, he shook the door again violently. "Manna! *Open* ze *door now!*" he screamed.

I let out the tiniest sigh of relief, knowing then I had been right not to open the door to speak to him. I looked at Luke, shaking my head as if to say, "Don't say anything!"

We were both frozen in place and panic-stricken—not only at the situation itself, but at the very idea that we were being disrespectful, an offense for which we would be in grave trouble. We were fraught with fear. Strange, I know, but that is how it was then.

"I can hear you in *zer!*" he growled. His voice reverberated through the mail slot so loudly it sounded as if he was right in front of our faces.

I looked at Luke and shook my head again, instructing him with my gestures not to say anything.

"I saw you on *ze* street playing! I know you're in here. Open *ze* door *rrrrright* now!" he commanded, aggressively shaking the door again.

We answered with complete silence.

For over fifteen minutes, Scham stayed at the door, ordering us to open it for him. "I'm not leaving till you open *ze* door!" he threatened. "Manna! Open *zis* door now or else you're going to make me *very* angry! *Bof* your *mater unt* I *vill* give you *ze* biggest beating of your life!"

I thought I was going to faint.

I looked at Luke again, his with eyes wide as saucers. I maintained my stand and gestured for him to be silent and not to move.

Silence reigned for a moment.

Scham had stopped his yelling, but I could still hear his heavy breathing through the mail slot.

After a few more moments, we thought we heard footsteps going down the front stairs. I still communicated to Luke with my eyes not to move. I sensed he was trying to trick us. So, we continued to sit in silence for another five or ten minutes.

Those moments felt like an eternity.

But, I had assessed the situation correctly. Scham yelled into the quiet, cursing us with words I had never heard before. Finally, his screams exploded through the mail slot, "Manna! Open ze damn door RRRRRRIGHT NOW! *Got* damn it! OPEN *ZE* DAMN DOOR, YOU *STUPIT* PUNK!"

I don't know how we found the courage to stay still, breathing only under our blankets to muffle any sounds, but we did.

After a while, I heard his footsteps again, but this time the footsteps actually disappeared into the distance. He was really leaving this time.

I waited for another five minutes or so to make sure we were truly safe. When I didn't hear anything, I carefully lifted one of the slats of the old, one-inch vinyl venetian blinds by my window (which had a clear side view of the front door) to see if he was really gone.

He was. The entire ordeal almost took the life force out of Luke and me. We were winded, exhausted, and trembling. It took us a long time to breathe normally again, and we didn't leave our position until the day started to give in to the night.

"What the hell kind of mother would make her children endure such torture? How could she put you two through such horrific ordeals?" Leah jumped in. "It's despicable!"

"I don't know what my mother was thinking. In fact, no one really did—ever. As for Luke, he wasn't the same carefree little boy anymore. Although I hated Scham for what he did to me, I hated him more for stealing my little brother's innocence after that terror-filled afternoon.

"As my hatred grew, so did my anger and my unwillingness to be the 'nice little girl' anymore. With no one to talk to and no one to trust (since both child abuse and sexual abuse were never talked about), I was left alone with what I thought was an isolated curse upon my life that everyone else somehow escaped (or blessedly protected from). Plus, since I had started to feel so defiled and dirty, I didn't think I could be 'worthy' of being 'good' and 'pure' again. So, I succumbed to my lesser thoughts about myself. I became mean, talking back to my teachers (and any other kid that tried to bully me again), and I got into fights. Yes, lots of fights. I figured that if no one else was going to help me, then I had to help myself in the only ways I knew how.

"Unfortunately, this only segregated me even more. Other kids became afraid of me, and instead of making friends, I made walls—big, tall walls."

"I'm sorry...so very sorry," Leah offered.

"Me too. But since I could not leave my situation, I could only do my best to cope, managing with less than adequate skills, knowledge, and guidance."

Leah looked at me, and then looked out the window, far away in thought.

After a moment she said, "I understand."

"I'm sorry, Leah. You see, these stories aren't good. They bring up sadness for you," I apologized.

"No. The poison needs to come out." She looked back at me. "Remember what I shared with you…now, tell me how you got the poison out of your blood. How are you so 'together', so 'with it'?"

"Oh Leah, for a very long time I didn't know what to do, and I was far from having my life 'together' or feeling 'with it.' I was more like the proverbial 'dead man walking' for much of my life. I may have been 'liberated' from my mother and Scham as an adult, but I was still a prisoner of my fears, false beliefs, anger, and memories."

"But you had to have done something to overcome it all. What was it?"

"I did only what I knew to do—I called on my 'Lion.' I called on God. I asked Him to help me. I didn't always remember to call on Him, but when I did, God began healing me of the venom that had infiltrated my heart. Little by little, I became freer and freer."

"How?" Leah persisted.

"God showed me that it was no longer my mother or Scham, but my bitterness and my unforgiveness that kept me captive."

"How can you say that?" Leah shouted angrily. "You had every right to be bitter! Forgiveness is out of the question! Ridiculous! How the hell do you forgive your mother and Scham? Look what you had to go through in one year alone! And you were only seven years old! My goodness, where was *your* God? Where was *my God?* I too have had great sufferings that I cannot forget, and *I will not forgive those who have hurt me!*"

She had begun shaking in her rage, so I placed my hand on her shoulder, trying to comfort her. We both took a moment to gather ourselves.

"I'm sorry, dear." Leah composed herself. "Your story reminds me of… well, *me* in many ways."

I handed her a little water to drink. She took a few big gulps and continued, "You and I were little girls…I cannot wrap my mind around this," she said, as she folded her arms across her chest.

"Yes, I understand how confusing this may seem, and why you or anyone else would ask, *Where was God? Why does He allow such things to happen?*" I gently took her hand and continued. "I shared some of my thoughts about that earlier, but you will only *truly* understand this if you are willing to hear the answer."

Leah took a brief moment to gather herself, and then said, "What do you mean? I asked the question, didn't I?"

"There is a difference between asking to learn, and asking to condemn, with no intention of learning."

Leah let out a heavy sigh.

I continued, "There's also a difference between doubt and disbelief. Doubt is a matter of the mind. It's okay to doubt. We're all learning, and it takes time to understand. Doubt is a natural part of the process. But disbelief—disbelief is a matter of the heart. If your heart is hardened and unwilling, then nothing I say will make a difference. Nothing will be satisfactory, and nothing will move the boulders blocking your path to the freedom you say you want."

Leah looked away, arms still crossed, still laboring with her conflicting thoughts.

After a few moments, I said, "I don't want to cause you pain, but if I stop now, I can't fully answer your questions, or help you fulfill your last wish. If you genuinely seek to be free, then we must do what is uncomfortable. We have to walk that road less traveled and face the things we do not want to acknowledge, much less re-live. So, if your sense of freedom is indeed tied to the sharing of my life, then we will need to go on. But if it's too much, then I will stop."

She narrowed her eyes, breathing hard.

I said nothing as I slowly released her hand and sat back in my seat, waiting for her instructions.

After a few moments, she said begrudgingly, "Checkmate. Now what?"

I smiled. "William Congreve once said, 'Music hath charms to sooth a savage breast, to soften rocks, or bend a knotted oak…'"

The Sound Of Music

My father always wanted us to have the ability to play a musical instrument, not only to soothe and lift our own spirits, but to offer this gift to others as well. Prior to his leaving for Montreal, he enrolled me in The Royal Conservatory of Music—one of the most respected musical institutions in the world. My mother didn't care one way or the other.

I began taking piano lessons at the home of Mrs. Reed, a stout middle-aged woman who seldom smiled and always spoke as if she was enunciating every consonant in every word. My lessons were held two days a week, and on those days, I walked straight to her home after school.

Scattered throughout her living room and dining room were six upright oak pianos—and oak rulers to match each one. She would rap on the side of the piano arm with that ruler as if she was the metronome. If any student misplayed a note, she would violently whack that ruler right where your fingers had been (or were about to land), causing your heart to beat as loudly as her ruler.

She taught several students at a time, conducting overlapping lessons on occasion. Each new piece of music she chose was meant to challenge her students, just as a good teacher should do. But she expected us to play a new piece as well as she had demonstrated it, and I was never able to do that. Frustrated, she yelled as she counted each beat, shouting as she called out each direction, "*Forte! Forte! Staccato! Staccato! I said staccato, not legato!*"

Although she did this with all her students, the others seemed to adjust fairly well to her militant teaching style, or at least they didn't yelp or scream from her (or her ruler's) outbursts like I did. Sometimes, she even threatened to use that ruler on our heads! Needless to say, I was a nervous wreck with her, and the terror of being yelled at, or the prospect of losing my fingers, distracted me from focusing on (or enjoying) the music.

As I progressed and the music became more complicated, it became increasingly difficult to master the piece *and* to keep one eye on the ruler at the same time. If I failed as a natural musician, I knew I didn't fail to exasperate Mrs. Reed.

One day as I was about to play my piece, she handed me two tennis balls. "Open your hands," she instructed in her brusque, no-nonsense voice.

Timid, and uncertain as to what she meant for me to do (and with my eyes peeled for the looming ruler), I slowly opened my small hands.

She smacked the balls into the palms of my hands and said, "Now squeeze."

I quickly did as she had commanded.

"Now, turn your hands over and do not let go of the balls," she ordered. "This is how you are to hold your hands from now on when you play. You are talented, and you can play, but your hands…they need more force! So, I'm going to teach you how to have your entire hand over the keys and dominate the piano!" she explained.

"Okay…I will try," I said timidly.

"You will *not try! You will do!*" she yelled.

I stared at this commanding figure now exposing her ruler once again. "Yes, Mrs. Reed," I conceded.

Needless to say, this new challenge only exaggerated the seeming wretchedness of my piano playing. At home, I tried to practice the piano as much as I could, keeping my hands upright and my fingers in perfect position so as to "dominate the piano." I desperately wanted to pass Mrs. Reed's muster. However, my practice at home had its own challenges. Whenever I practiced when my mother (who also played the piano) was home, she would yell at me from wherever she was in the house, "That sounds ghastly! Play properly! It's torture listening to you!"

I tried to explain that I now had to train myself to play in a completely different way and my fingers were not used to this position, so I was making more errors than normal. But there was no point. She just cut me off and accused me of being lazy, making up excuses, or lying.

So, both at home and at Mrs. Reed's, I endured the wrath of my instructors. By now, Mrs. Reed had made a multitude of new "ruler notches" on her piano arm over each wayward note I coaxed from the keys and over each break in form from my confused and nervous hands.

At home, to avoid any more condemnation, I reverted back to my former "imperfect" hand position. Any progress I had made with Mrs. Reed was now diminished at home. But at least my fingers were able to fly up and down the keyboard (or so it felt), and bearing the weekly reproofs from Mrs. Reed, no matter how frightening, was better than the ongoing persecution from my mother. I chose the devil I knew best and appeased the latter for my own sanity.

As if this was not enough to intimidate me forever when it came to musical pursuits, the time for my first piano recital arrived. Anxieties that had plagued me since early childhood now resurfaced in full force. Performing with my questionable skills (at least in the eyes of my mother) in front of an audience was not my idea of enjoyment. Furthermore, this first recital was not just a *simple recital*. What Mrs. Reed had planned was a full-on evening performance at the relatively new Centennial Theatre in North Vancouver with a seating capacity of almost seven hundred people! I was completely astonished that my mother even allowed me to enter this recital because that would mean she would have to drive me there—over 45 minutes away—*and be there, and be with me*, instead of going out on her own. That awareness, in and of itself, was enough to send panic into my heart, because I knew that I ran the risk of disappointing *both* her and Mrs. Reed—again.

When the evening arrived and I saw the theater and the hundreds of people sitting in the audience, it took everything I had inside of myself not to faint. I began trembling with nervousness, breathing quickly. A lady in charge of organizing the evening gathered all the performers backstage, and we were eventually delivered to the wings where we waited until it was our turn to perform. The performers alternated as they entered the stage—one coming from stage left, and the other from stage right. All of the other children seemed to know what to do. For most of them, this recital was not their first, but for a few others, like me, it was.

Even then, everyone seemed to have had a briefing on exactly what to do and what to expect. I don't remember my mother explaining anything to me, and unlike the other children, I know for certain she did not hold me, kiss me, or encourage me.

The voices of the audience rose as the auditorium filled, and I realized that this event was really happening! I waited; stage left. As my turn came closer and closer, all I could see was a beautiful shiny black concert grand piano in the center of the stage with a spotlight on it. The lights glared off its varnish, and it was simply stunning—and terrifying. I could barely breathe.

One by one those waiting to perform moved closer to the stage as each recital piece was completed with a curtsy or bow and an exit. I was number three in line…then number two.

Suddenly, the girl before me went up to play. She entered stage right, opposite of me. We were around the same age, and she was Asian!

She was beautiful. Ribbons and barrettes adorned her hair, and it was obvious she was wearing a brand-new dress for this special occasion, with nude pantyhose!

Her mother even bought her real hosiery!

When her name was announced and she walked on stage, her parents—and the entire group with them—cheered loudly and gave her a round of feverish applause.

Wow! She must be very loved. Look at how much attention she got from her family and look at how pretty she looks with her new dress. Her mother must love her a lot to do her hair and take the time to dress her so nicely.

I couldn't help but wonder, *Why isn't my family normal like this girl's family? And for that matter, why don't we have dinners at home? Why don't we have normal lunches? Why do we eat weird food and those "soups"? And why does my mother have an even weirder boyfriend who does sickening things to me?*

I used to think it was because we were Asian that we were so different than all of my Caucasian friends. But there, right before my eyes, another Chinese girl my age was obviously deeply loved and cherished, and she seemed *normal*, just like all the Caucasian kids I knew.

I bet she has birthday parties. I bet she has good lunches. I bet no one touches her in bad ways or makes her touch them in bad places…and I bet she's never *called "stupid," "ugly," or "good-for-nothing"…*

As I thought about this girl, my heart stopped racing, and sank instead. I looked down at my old dress and my old dirty white leggings. It was impossible not to notice the tiny, sweater-like balls on the leggings, and that the material around my knees was thinning.

My hair was not styled, or brushed nicely, and it lacked the trimmings of ribbons or barrettes. No personal attention had been given to me prior to my arrival, and I never received any encouragement to play the piano—let alone anyone championing me prior to this evening's performance. My life wasn't at all like the life this other Chinese girl obviously enjoyed.

I was so sad.

Suddenly, I heard clapping, enthusiastic clapping at that. My mind snapped back to the reality of where I was. To my horror, I realized this girl had finished her piece, and I was up next!

The lady helping to organize the event pushed me along with her hand, and instead of going to the center of the stage, curtseying first and then going to the piano, I *ran* from the wings to the piano. There was nothing formal, proper, or graceful about my entrance. I heard sweet laughter from the audience, and a few people who said "awwwww" as if they could tell I was nervous and shy.

My shoes echoed on the wooden stage, and I hurried to sit down at the piano bench. As I sat, the bench screeched against the floor planks, and I was embarrassed to have made such a noise. It felt as though all eyes were on me—judging me for my clumsiness before my performance had even begun.

The overhead lights were much brighter and warmer than they had appeared from backstage. Without raising my eyes to the audience or pausing to gather my focus, I rushed into the piece, playing as quickly as I could. All I wanted was to finish and flee from that stage. By the grace of God, I completed the recital without error, but the selections must have sounded hurried and therefore, careless. When I finished, I rose from the bench, dipped a quick curtsey—never raising my head or smiling at the audience—and rushed into the darkness that waited in the wings, unconscious of anything but the thunderous sound of my pounding heart.

After a little while, relieved that my near-death experience on stage was over, my heart resumed its normal rhythm. I was able to enjoy watching the rest of the performances and I rallied myself to try harder with Mrs. Reed at my next lesson.

My enjoyment was short-lived, however.

When the recital was over, I waited, and waited, and waited backstage, but my mother never came to find me. Finally, after all the parents had come backstage, greeted their beloved performers with flowers or hugs, taken photographs, and left, only two people remained in the back area—a slow-moving janitor sweeping the floor, and me.

I nervously walked out by myself to try and find my mother and Luke. When I found her, she was staring out the glass lobby doors. I ran to her and Luke. I was so excited when I saw them, "Oh, Mommy! Here you are! I was waiting backstage with the others. I'm sorry if I made you wait."

When my mother turned to look at me, her face was set with anger. I expected a smile or a little sympathy for how difficult a challenge I had to overcome, not to mention the complexity of the piece I played without much time for practice. But I received the exact opposite. I shouldn't have been surprised. She glared at me, took me roughly by the arm, and pulled me to a corner at the side of the lobby. When we were out of the earshot of the last few families leaving, she let go of me and bent down so that her face was directly in front of mine. Her face was pinched as she seethed, "I have *never* been so embarrassed in my life."

Her rage seemed to make it impossible for her to even speak, so she did not elaborate on what exactly I had done to cause her such embarrassment. It didn't matter, though. I knew I had somehow failed her, again. She huffed, and spun away from me, grabbing Luke by the hand. She threw open the lobby doors, and stormed outside.

I was left standing alone in the corner. Countless thoughts surged through my mind. *Had she just left me in the Centennial Theatre—not caring if I was going to join what was left of my family? I bet the girl who played before me didn't have a family who acted like this. I bet she was loved, and I bet they all went to have some kind of celebration together afterward.*

I had to quickly decide what I was supposed to do. *Do I follow her? It's obvious she doesn't want me, but would she really just leave me here? How do I leave the safety of this building and try to find her in a parking lot late at night? What if I get lost? What if she's already left? How do I get a hold of my father? How do I get a hold of my grandparents? What do I do?*

I couldn't stay in the building, so, with no other viable option, I slowly proceeded toward the door. The entire theater was empty now, except for the same lone custodian, now emptying the trash in the foyer. When I opened the door, a rush of cold winter wind blew in and took my breath away. It was very dark outside, and it had been raining. The Centennial Theatre was on Lonsdale Street, a very busy main street, and our car was parked across that street in a parking lot. I stopped, looking up and down the street, but I did not see my mother or Luke anywhere.

Did she really just leave me?

A bus pulled away from its stop just then, and as it passed, I saw that my mother had indeed already crossed the street. She was holding Luke in her arms and heading towards the car. I would have to cross Lonsdale Street all by myself if I was not to be left behind.

Cars were zooming by, splashing freezing, dirty water onto the sidewalk as they went. I was soon drenched, and since there was no crosswalk there, I took a deep breath and ran across the street in between cars. When I reached the other side of the street, I called out, "Mommy! Mommy! Please, wait for me! Please, don't leave me!"

She didn't turn around; she just kept walking.

I ran as fast as I could.

The last time she had walked away from me like this, I had been forced to cross West Tenth Avenue and West Broadway by myself. I knew where I was going there; it was our neighborhood. But this time I had no idea where I was and did not know how to get home.

What could I possibly have done to make my mother hate me so much?

My questions from that night were never answered. But I knew I would never put myself in a vulnerable position to be judged and hurt like that again. Even though I continued to play the piano for my own pleasure throughout my life, I decided then and there that I would never perform for anyone on the piano again.

Kramer vs. Kramer

By now, my mother was consumed with the divorce proceedings. My parents' relationship was like a sharp razor—cutting and drawing blood. My mother complained that my father was controlling, and my father complained that my mother was irresponsible. Both were unwilling to concede. And since my father was now living across the country, and Scham had embedded himself into my mother's life, there was no hope of reconciliation.

My mother no longer tried to hide anything from us; consequently, I was present for many of the discussions she had in person or on the phone. I wanted Luke and me to live with my father, so I listened intently to these conversations, following her accounts for clues as to whether my hope might become a possibility. I tried hard to find reasons to stay with my mother, but sorrowfully, I could not make up even one.

When people saw me with my mother, they made the polite remarks adults often make about children. "Oh! You're getting so tall!" Or, "Oh! What a good little girl you are!" Those common expressions were all nice enough, but the one comment I heard more often than any other—the one comment that struck terror in my heart and caused me to step back in fear was: *"Oh Manna! You are the spitting image of your mother!"*

I knew they meant my facial features resembled hers, but to me, those words were like the kiss of death. She was the last person I wanted to resemble. I felt love for her, and tried my best to please her, but I did not *like* her. Worse, in spite of everyone's comments about my mother's "striking beauty," in time, she only grew uglier and uglier to me.

In the winter of 1969, my father was still a relatively new recruit in Montreal, learning yet another language, French—another complication in addition to all the requirements expected of him in his new position in an unfamiliar city. With no family or friends, and with everything else that comes from moving across the country to a completely different culture (again), it was a very difficult time for him. On top of the troubles with his marriage, he was constrained by strict schedules, seniority policies, financial limitations, and distance—he was three thousand miles away and separated by three time zones.

Having believed everything was "fine" before he left for Montreal, my father had left all the contents in the safety deposit box in my mother's care. He also left all the funds in the bank account for my mother's use, and the house and every other investment, though in both their names, were in my mother's care. Online banking did not exist back then.

Since he had every intention of providing for the family, he had used his new salary for his expenses and paid for the necessary preparations for our arrival, including the lease of a two-bedroom apartment to which he was now bound, even though we never came.

On the afternoon of Christmas Eve, my father was at the office Christmas party with over a hundred of his colleagues and supervisors, doing his best to keep his personal sadness from everyone, when a man dressed in the full court uniform walked into the middle of the party and asked for my father. Startled and confused, my father stepped forward and approached the man. Following the exact protocol demanded of his position, the man identified himself as a court bailiff and asked my father to produce his identification. When the bailiff was satisfied, he served my father with a notice of divorce.

The room had gone silent as everyone watched this scenario unfold like some part of a tragic theatrical play.

The court bailiff was noticeably sad himself and even stepped outside of his procedural duties to say to my father, "Mr. Ko. You have no idea how sorry I am to have to do this to you. If there was any other way to avoid this, I would have.

However, there were specific instructions that I *must* deliver this notice of divorce to you on *this day and at this time* during your Christmas party. I'm so sorry." The court bailiff then shook my father's hand, awkwardly wished him a Merry Christmas, and left the room.

Only then did my father remember he had mentioned to my mother (in a recent phone call) that he was going to be at his office Christmas party at that time and location.

My father received "extended compassionate leave" from his supervisors in order to return to Vancouver for the divorce. He arrived before the appointed court date and once again tried to reconcile with my mother, but she was determined to divorce him. With no other option, my father gave up his hope for the marriage and for his family to be reunited.

By this time, my PoPo had arrived in Vancouver and I was beside myself with elation to see her. My mother had asked her to come so she could help watch us during this time of upheaval. My GongGong didn't come that particular time because he couldn't get that much time away from his TB hospital. He did come on subsequent visits.

Strangely, as much as I loved seeing my beloved PoPo, a part of me had already been so broken I did not know how to allow myself to love her in the same way I once had. I do not know if I was subconsciously afraid of getting attached to her—only for her to be ripped away from me again—or if I had lost my ability to love deeply altogether.

My father had arranged to meet my mother, together with PoPo as a witness. He wanted to present my mother with an offer so the trial proceedings could go smoothly and quickly. He proposed that he would take custody of my brother and me so she could have more time to herself. My mother agreed, but she also wanted everything else—all the cash, the house, the rosewood furniture, the piano, and the investments, including the diamonds. She even wanted the gold ingots my father had bought each year on our birthdays as an investment for our future. (Before we had left Hong Kong, my father had been advised to invest in excellent grade diamonds and gold to hedge against currency fluctuations and as an investment for Luke's and my future—our formal education, business, and a home.)

My father agreed to her demands, and they peacefully drafted an agreement between themselves at the dinette table with all three parties signing the document.

With the new agreement in place and with my PoPo as the witness, my father felt confident that they had come to a very generous agreement for my mother. Knowing he now had to be financially responsible for two children, he made some heavy decisions. He decided to utilize the funds he had set aside for his attorney fees for greater purposes—getting us to Montreal, ready for school, and other necessities. His attorney did not think this decision was a good idea, but my father believed my mother would uphold their agreement and terminated the attorney's representation. After all, she was getting everything she wanted, and she would no longer have to deal with what she *did not* want: us. My mother seemed happy and relieved by the agreement and gave no indication that she would challenge or betray it. My father believed that her lightheartedness was due to the fact that she could now be the single woman she had always wanted to be, one with tremendous financial security who would now be able to do whatever she wanted with her life, and her boyfriend.

As for him, the three of us would build a new life—even if we had to start with nothing. It appeared to be a win/win for both of them.

The trial came on a cold and rainy winter's day in Vancouver. I was in the backseat of the car with Luke, since we were expecting to be with my father once it was over. Uncle Alistair and Auntie Christine (my beloved godparents), drove us all there, and we parked in front of the courthouse. Kai Yeh (the Chinese name for godfather) went in with my father to show him emotional and moral support. Kai Mah (the Chinese name for godmother), Luke, and I waited in the car.

I stared at those front doors for hours, and each time they opened, I lunged towards the car window to see if it was my father and Kai Yeh. Luke and I tried to entertain each other with drawings and games, but I could not focus on anything else but what I imagined was going on in that courtroom.

It seemed as though I had only looked down for a few minutes to play with Luke, when suddenly, Kai Yeh opened the driver's side door and climbed in with a rush.

Kai Yeh said to Kai Mah, "It doesn't look good. She got everything *and* the children!"

I was in shock! I couldn't believe my ears. *What is this? But my mother agreed! She said she only wanted the money, the house, the jewelry—she got all that! She doesn't want us! Why do we have to stay with her?*

I was overcome with horror at his words. Grabbing the front seat, I pulled myself towards Kai Yeh and asked boldly, "What did you say, Kai Yeh?"

"Oh Manna…" he said with a nervous tenderness, "Don't worry. It will be okay. Let's just wait till your father comes out."

I wasn't satisfied and wanted to be close to my father right away. I clambered back across the seat to where Luke was sitting and started to open the door. I wanted to get out and find my father, but the door was locked.

Kai Yeh pulled me back. "Manna, dear, you can't leave the car. Your father will be right out. Please, be a good girl and wait patiently for him, okay?"

Not wanting to be disrespectful, and because I loved Kai Yeh very much, I let go of the door handle. Instead, I rolled down the window and leaned out, searching for my father.

Inside the car, Kai Yeh continued his conversation with Kai Mah. "The court said that when the children turn fourteen years of age, they can choose who they want to live with," he paused. "But that is a long time from now. This is a very sad day. David lost everything today."

Later on, I discovered what had happened. In court, my father was left empty-handed. He had relied on my mother's honest testimony and the witnessed agreement she had signed. But without the services of an attorney or any other prior preparation, my father had no additional defense to offer against further court action.

Despite their agreement, my mother had kept her attorney, who was in favor of my parents' agreement and of the arrangements they had made. But in court, at the last minute, he added that since my father was currently living in Montreal, my mother should be reconsidered as the main custodial parent and guardian. The attorney asked that she also receive child support from my father, and that she be made the sole beneficiary of the monthly governmental family allowance fund. His argument was that she would be a single parent, and therefore needed that subsidy (even though she was working full-time).

My father was in shock.

He did his best to argue his case, but he hadn't prepared the proper evidence to prove my mother's neglect and abusive parenting. Because he trusted my mother to keep her word, he did not secure any declarations from the nanny, his aunt, or even from neighbors. No one acknowledged that Luke and I were always home alone. And without an attorney or knowledge of family law, he had no chance.

The judge had explained that it was customary for the mother to receive custody anyway, but he would grant my father "reasonable access." The judge was moved by my father's love and his willingness to concede everything for us, so he granted him visitation every weekend instead of every other weekend.

Unfortunately, with my father living in Montreal, how could he see us every weekend or even every other weekend?

The judge also awarded half the home back to him, but he now would incur half of the expenses also. That decree would not have been so painful to endure except for the fact that Scham was living there for free, eating all of the food my father tried to provide for Luke and me.

If I had known, I would have thrown myself in front of the judge and told them the truth about everything that happened in our house of horrors. But I did not know, and it was all over now.

The judge thought he was being fair in his adjudication. Little did he know he had just sentenced Luke and me to another seven years of hell.

Outside, we waited in the rain, which had partially turned to hail, and came in as a sudden torrent from the sky. The day was dark and gloomy, and the heaviness in the air was unmistakable. It was as if God put my heart on display in the sky.

Finally, from a distance, I saw my father leave the courthouse, his shoulders slumped. He labored to run to the car, fighting his emotions and trying to maintain his strength for us, but as he came closer, I could see that his countenance was one of complete dejection. Even before he got into the car, I knew that what Kai Yeh had said about the proceedings and rulings of the judge was true.

Everything else about the remainder of the day was a blur—except for a few words that still rang in my ear: The court said, "when the children turn fourteen years of age, they can choose who they want to live with."

"When the children turn fourteen…they can choose."

Those words became my lifeline for the next seven years. I carried them like a talisman—a symbol of hope and freedom against the evil that pervaded my life.

So Close and Yet So Far

From that day on, my father's visits were very few. We didn't see him every weekend or even every other weekend. We saw him once every three to six months that first year or so after the divorce.

Day-to-day home life with Scham and my mother was a nightmare. When my father finally could afford to fly back to see us, Scham would cause such a horrible scene that life was almost unbearable. The swearing, the pettiness, the bitter and venomous attacks against my father (and against us) were incessant.

We were already living in terror, in an environment filled with random, unexpected rages and blistering verbal assaults. Not only that, Scham's tirades were often followed by physical demonstrations of hate—assigning Luke and I excessive chores, not allowing us to eat, and actual physical abuse. And whenever my mother was working (or when Luke was away playing across the street), Scham continued to hunt me down and force himself on me. This was our everyday fare of terror.

When it was time for my father's visits, things were even worse at home. On those days, Scham would meet him at the front sidewalk of our house and threaten him, loudly. He caused such a scene that neighbors could hear him and watch the "show" through their living room windows.

He would spit on my father and punch my father in the face and in the stomach. He even threatened to kill my father on many occasions before coming back inside and saying, "You *stupit* kids, did you see how I kicked your *fater's* a—? How great is your *fater* now? Huh? Tell me, you *stupit* kids of his? Tell me! Do you see him out *zer* holding his stomach? He didn't even fight back, he's such a *vimp unt* a loser!"

Scham knew we had been watching the whole thing through the old venetian blinds covering the window. He had not needed to come inside and boast about his *conquest* of my father, but he couldn't resist haranguing us with additional expletives that I dare not repeat.

Even as we witnessed these acts of cruelty against our father, I thought to myself, *Scham is even more of an idiot than we even originally thought*. He knew my father had held high positions with the Royal Hong Kong Police force, the Vancouver Police Department and now as a detective with the RCMP. He also knew my father was trained in martial arts and could incapacitate him with one quick move of his arm!

Scham was delusional, thinking he had any ability whatsoever to make our father appear weak to us.

Luke and I knew better. During these times, our father only grew in stature in our hearts and minds. Our respect for our father multiplied a hundred-thousand-fold as we watched him hold back his retaliation. He knew that if he replied to Scham's rebuffs, while it would be satisfying for him, Scham's humiliation would be heaped on us in full measure once he left. So, my father restrained himself and never once fought back.

My father told me later, "Is it a stronger and bigger man who fights? Or is it a stronger and bigger man to suffer for the sake of another? I knew you were watching us, and I also knew that although I may have won the fight, you were the ones who would have lost. Scham would have been relentless against you afterwards. I could not let that happen."

In those instances, once Scham saw that my father refused to leave without us, he would send me out to get the child support check. Only when I had returned with it, and only after his inspection of it, were Luke and I allowed to leave the house to be with our father, if we were lucky.

Scham knew my father had to save every penny to fly from Montreal to see us for his weekend. Often, after he finished assaulting my father, and after getting the child support check, he would disallow the visit altogether, just so he could inflict more pain on the three of us.

However, as sick and demented as Scham was, I didn't know what was worse, Scham's actions…or my mother's *inaction*. Not once, *not once*, did my mother ever say a word in the midst of any of this, whether the abuses were directed at my father, or at us.

Ever.

The times when my father was denied visits with us, he had no option but to simply turn back. As he walked back to the car he had borrowed for our visit, he would take one last look at us through the window. Those brief moments of eye contact, though comforting, were the most excruciating of all.

He was so close…and yet so far away.

Refusing to give up on seeing us, though, together with his friend and fellow RCMP colleague, Uncle Francis, they came up with another plan. Even though our weekend together was lost, on the following weekday, they would drive to our school and watch us during recess and lunch time.

My father would never come out of the car for fear of us being caught talking to him and then suffering the rages afterwards. So, Uncle Francis would walk out and hand us fresh lunches and relay messages from my father to us.

Looking at each other across the parking lot was all we could sometimes do.

Stupid Face

Following my parents' divorce, Scham had officially moved in and was now with us all the time. He had my mother buy the food he liked, and we would have to eat whatever it was he wanted on any given day. We often had steaks with an inch of fat on the sides of them, and on one particular occasion, when I tasted the fat, I began to gag. Both the texture and animal taste of the meat were so offensive to me that I couldn't help but choke on the food. My mother glared at me as if threatening to give me another beating, but Scham interrupted.

"You're so *stupit*! You don't like *ze* best part of *ze* meat—*ze* fat? Give it to *me*!" He laughed out loud as if he had just won the lottery, then took all of the fat and a hefty chunk of the steak with it. I didn't dare look up, in case I caught my mother's eyes. I just kept looking down at my plate, eating slowly, turning every now and then to see the television show that was on, trying to distract myself from the nightmare in which I was living.

One night, we all went to dinner at an inexpensive Chinese restaurant nearby. It was one of those restaurants that kept the lights so low that patrons couldn't see how dirty the carpet was. This restaurant specialized in an all-you-can-eat buffet, which Scham loved because he could eat as much as he wanted and proclaimed it was "a steal." Luke and I were also instructed to get more of the food items he liked so he could take it from our plates once we were seated. That way, he didn't look like he was going up for *fourths!*

We were seated in a small booth. The table was set with tacky paper placemats decorated with Chinese horoscopes, and dusty imitation flowers in a cloudy vase sat as the centerpiece. When we came back to the table with our plates, Luke was told to sit beside Scham, and I was to sit beside my mother. Luke and I looked at each other, naturally bowing our heads and folding our hands to say the prayer of thanks we had learned from our father.

"*Dear God, thank You for the world so sweet. Thank You for the food we eat. Thank You for the birds that sing. Thank You, God for everythi—*"

I never finished the prayer because Scham had suddenly lunged across the table and hit me across the head. Then he grabbed my ear, squeezed it and pulled on it—hard—many times. I had my eyes closed in prayer, so I didn't see his assault coming. I just felt the pain across my head and the terrible burning sensation on my ear.

I yelped in pain, and my eyes flew open to see his grimacing face. I tried to twist out of his grip and succeeded in freeing my ear, but he reached for my long hair instead and caught a chunk of it, twisting it quickly around his hand to hold me there. I whimpered, and he whipped his other hand across the other side of my head. "Shut up, you *stupit punk*! Who *ze* hell do you *zink* you are—a nun?" he scoffed, laughing out loud. "Did you suddenly become a nun, you *punk*?"

Tears welled up in my eyes, and my scalp, cheek, and ears were burning. I stared right back at him. I didn't care about the "respect" issue anymore, and at that moment, I felt only felt hatred for him. He then released me as quickly as he had grabbed me, and I dropped back into my chair with silent tears streaming down my cheeks. I looked at my mother for help, but she kept her eyes averted.

She said nothing, and did nothing.

When Luke saw Scham attack me, he cried out, "No, no, no!" I nudged him under the table and shook my head, indicating to him to be quiet and not to do anything to further enrage Scham.

Scham yelled at my mother, "What *ze* hell is wrong *vit* your kids?"

My mother looked down, silent.

I glared at my mother. *Mommy, say something! This is about God! If you can't stand up for us, at least you must speak up for God!*

Still, she did nothing.

Scham then turned to Luke and out of pure evil, pulled on his ears. Luke's eyes filled with tears from the pain. Once again, I was in shock, my mind frantically searching to comprehend this madness. *Why did he feel the need to do that to Luke? He had already made his point with me!*

I looked again at my mother. I understood why she did not defend me. But this was *Luke*! Her favorite! Her silence gave no protection to her favorite child, and Luke suffered the needless pain with no defense, and for no reason.

Pure, fiery hatred now burned inside me toward this man. I started to lunge forward to protest his treatment of my little brother, but my mother put her left hand on my right leg and held me down. Scham was on a roll and threatened both Luke and me. "If you ever, ever, *ever* say prayers again, I *vill* beat you so hard, you *von't* need to say prayers! You'll already be dead and standing in front of your *Got*!" He started laughing out loud as if that was the cleverest statement he had ever made.

Luke and I ate in silence, looking down at our plate most of the time. Occasionally, we snuck a few glances at each other, trying to console one another, watching in shock as Scham and my mother engage in carefree conversations between themselves as if we weren't there, and as if nothing had happened.

Later that night, in the room we shared, Luke and I whispered about how much we despised Scham. We took turns making fun of him, and we laughed out loud without any guilt that we were being "disrespectful." In retrospect, we simply had to talk about all the mistreatments. Our sanity depended on being able to vent. Our humanity and our little souls needed to find a way to cope, so we might survive another terrifying day with him.

Soon, Luke and I realized, we hated him so much that we couldn't even speak his name! Giving him a name meant he was a real person in our lives. Worse, we had to address him as "Uncle Scham," using a term demanding endearment and respect. So we created several alternate names we thought would be more suitable to the filthy barbarian who had so disrupted our lives.

First, we tried to find an appropriate name by doing a play on his first name, but none of our ideas were bad enough to describe him. Then we played with his surname, but again, even the vilest of creatures weren't nearly bad enough to describe him.

At last, amidst fits of giddy nerves and anxious giggling, we thought of something perfect. We bestowed upon Scham the nickname we felt was most befitting a blockhead as reprehensible as he: *Stupid Face*.

It wasn't just that Scham himself was deserving of this ultimate of insults. It was even more perfect due to his *expressions*, which often included a bewildered ignorance. His visage clearly demonstrated he had a "stupid face" (not to mention that his face was gruesome to us because of his horrible manners and lack of hygiene).

Yes. Luke and I were in agreement. "Stupid Face" was the perfect name for this monster and what we would call him from now on. And as soon as this was decided, a sudden calm fell over us. We now had an understanding that answered the madness, a way of managing our disgust of Scham.

After all, how could we expect anything good coming from a "Stupid Face"?

We would continue to call him this throughout our lives. Our cousins, Adam and Brent (who also intensely disliked him), also addressed him as "Stupid Face" in our conversations, as did other family members and friends.

Yes, all were in secret agreement that Scham was not worthy of being called by a proper name. Throughout everything that followed, our name for him always gave us some consolation. When we looked at him, we knew we had the power to reduce his counterfeit authority over us to what and who he truly was—a Stupid Face.

I'm Outta Here

Leah shook her head sadly, "And whosoever shall scandalize one of these little ones that believe in me; it were better for him that a millstone were hanged around his neck, and he were cast into the sea."[2]

I looked at her with disbelief as she quoted a Bible verse so fitting for the way I felt at that moment.

"Don't give me that look! Remember, I was raised by nuns. Plus, I told you I was *doubtful*, I didn't say I was stupid!" Leah smiled, and then took my hand. "I know it isn't easy to remember these things. Are you okay to keep going?"

I took a deep breath and nodded.

"Well, as you can see, things were not going well at the Ko family household. I was greatly disappointed by my mother's selfishness, and over time I became more and more openly aggravated at her unwillingness to do what was right as a mother, so I devised a plan to run away from home."

"I hope you made it," Leah said under her breath.

After the episode in the restaurant, my mother was shorter and more dismissive of me than ever. She started calling me names outright. At least before, her name-calling was spoken under her breath or as controlled cuts spurred on by things that irritated her. But one Saturday morning, after hatefully calling me "stupid, ugly, and good-for-nothing" again, I retaliated, unable to control myself any longer.

"*Stop calling me that*! I'm *not* stupid! I'm not ugly, and if I'm not good for anything, then I'll leave!"

I thought my threat would alarm her and bring her to her senses, but I was wrong.

"You're leaving? Perfect! It gets you outta my hair! When are you going? The sooner, the better!"

Despite the small sense of relief I felt from standing up for myself, her words were like a kick to my stomach. I reeled inside in complete shock at what she had said. The bomb that just blew up in my heart was barely containable.

"Monday morning!" I retorted. "And I'm never coming back!"

"That's great for me, but we'll see how long you last out there!" she snorted. She turned her back and walked away from me.

I was *furious*!

But I also felt a sharp pang in my heart, something I didn't want to feel and something I didn't want to admit I was feeling. The hatred that was so familiar for Scham was now starting to grow for my mother. I wanted to love her, I desperately did, but I could find nothing about her to love. I didn't expect much from Stupid Face, but from *my own mother*? Stupid Face I could excuse because he was, well, *Stupid Face*, but my own mother, the one who had carried Luke, and me in her body? Excuse her? Never.

"Luke," I whispered at night, "We have to run away from here."

"What? We can't leave! Mommy will be *sooooooooo* mad."

"She's always mad. Don't worry, I'll take care of you. I'm going to get a job!"

"I'm scared. We better stay here."

"Luke, we can't stay here. I don't think I can take another day of this." I left the unspoken dangling in the air.

Neither Luke, nor my mother, nor anyone else knew the dark ugly secret I was hiding from them—the hideousness of what Scham did to me. Worse, with the progression of time, he was becoming more barefacedly impudent with me—even in the presence of others in a nearby room. As soon as he would start to look at me in his strange, trance-like way, I would leave the room or run outside. But he would always catch me and say out loud so everyone could hear, "Come here, Manna. Be a *gut* girl and listen to Uncle Scham. Come sit on my lap and tell me about your day," he would hiss.

I would do my best to pry myself away, but he would just say, "You're being a bad girl again, Manna! Don't you *vant* to sit *vis* Uncle Scham *unt* talk to me? Do you *vant me* to tell your *mater* in *ze* other room you're being bad?"

When I tried to wrestle my way out of his clutches, he only forced me down harder. Then I would yell, "You're hurting me!"

Most times, he would come out of his "trance" and realize how violent he was being with me and finally let go. But as always, with his unexpected release, many times I would fall forward and collapse on the floor, at which point he would sneer, "You *stupit punk!*"

If I was to run away, Luke had to come with me. I didn't trust Scham around my beloved little brother. I did my best to rouse Luke into excitement about our new adventure together, arguing that no matter what we had to face, anything was better than living with Stupid Face and our mother.

"Come on, Luke!" I'd cheer. "We'll be okay. I promise. I know exactly where I'm going to get a job, and from now on, we'll have great lunches at school!"

"Manna, please don't do this. I'm too scared…I'm just too scared. I can't go!" he whimpered under his breath.

Realizing I had put him in the position of having to choose between my mother and me, I said, "It's okay. Don't worry. You don't have to go."

"I'm scared," he whispered.

Not wanting him to be upset, I jumped up and grabbed both his hands. Looking at him I said, "It's okay, I understand. Don't be scared! I'll still get to see you at school, right? It will almost be like we're together, okay? And I will bring you good food to eat because I'll have a job!" I said optimistically.

Silence. He didn't buy my sales pitch.

Finally, I said somberly, "Luke, you understand that I have to go, right?"

He nodded and looked down at the floor.

"Plus, with me gone, you probably won't ever get in trouble. Mommy doesn't ever get mad at you. Things will be better for you. You just have to help me take care of Lucky for now."

"I don't want you to go," he said tearfully.

"I don't want to leave you either," I said, fighting back my own tears. Then with all the strength I had inside me, I promised, "I won't be gone long. When I get a job, I'll come for you and Lucky, okay?"

He nodded.

We looked at each other for a long time, and then I said, "C'mon, let's go to sleep. Don't worry. Everything's gonna be okay."

I tucked his blankets around him and then went to my bed, staring out the window at nothingness. Luke fell asleep, but I lay awake most of the night, planning. In fact, all weekend long I planned how to make my escape. I went through my closet and sorted out which clothes and shoes I would take, and I walked up and down the blocks of our neighborhood, scouting for a garden shed, an unused shack, an empty garage—anything that looked big enough and dry enough for me sleep at nights. I was suddenly relieved that Luke wasn't going to come with me yet because I didn't know if I could bear him living like I was prepared to do. At least for now, he would have a bed, and there would be some peace around the house without me.

The next day, I walked across busy Tenth Avenue by myself. I traveled and up and down an even busier Broadway Street to see what stores or restaurants I might apply to for a job. I had my eyes on several locations I thought would be perfect, and with some excitement in my step, I went back to our house of horrors, comforted in knowing that it would be my last night sleeping there.

All weekend, my mother mocked me about running away from home, cackling to herself after each criticism. I said nothing back. Her comments only fortified my decision to leave.

On Sunday night, I put my two best Sunday dresses, my dress shoes, a few school clothes, underwear, socks, and one pair of regular shoes into a SuperValue (our local grocery store) bag. I needed more, but it was all I could carry. The Sunday dresses would be good for church and respectable for work as well, and I had enough school clothes to make it through the week. I would be careful not to play too roughly so I didn't dirty the clothes I had. Plus, I reasoned, I would make enough money soon enough to buy the rest of what I needed.

I was eight years old.

Luke followed me everywhere on our "last night" together and watched me pack everything nicely and neatly into the two paper grocery bags. I made five sandwiches for Luke so that he would have enough lunches to see him through the week. I also showed him how to pour milk into his thermos, just in case our mother still thought we drank the curdled milk.

I packed my own meal bag—only two butter and sugar sandwiches—one sandwich for lunch and one sandwich for dinner, because I was certain I was going to get a job. After checking my list and being satisfied I had everything ready, I, too, went to sleep.

On Monday morning, I woke with uneasiness but also a sense of resolve. I collected my lunch and put it in my school bag, and I gathered my SuperValue bags. When it was time to leave for school, Luke and I walked out of the house together. He said goodbye to my mother, and she returned his affection.

She said nothing to me, and I said nothing to her.

Just as I was about to close the front door, she sneered loudly enough for me to hear, "Good riddance!"

I closed the door and pretended I didn't hear her. But I did. And so did Luke, who just looked at me sadly. His big brown eyes told me he had many questions—and much anxiety. I knew he wanted to protect me and do more for me, but he was only six years old and there was nothing he could do. He didn't want me to leave, but he also knew it was very painful for me to stay.

I smiled at him, and we headed off for school. Filled with determination, I believed I would never look back on this day, and I would never have to see my mother again—except for the day I returned for Luke and Lucky.

Ours was an awkward three-block journey. The paper grocery bags had no handles on them, so I had to hold them both in my arms, along with my school bag. They were cumbersome, so I had to stop and put them down several times, gather my strength and courage, and make the trek to school.

Luke kept his pace slow and steady, walking right beside me all the way to school. When I put down the bags to rest, he just stared at me with his great big eyes as if to say, "Are you really going to do this?" while simultaneously pleading, "Please don't do this!"

As we approached the school, Luke saw his friends playing on the blacktop, and I told him to go with them. I assured him I was okay, but he didn't leave me. He walked with me steadily to my homeroom and into the cloakroom.

Each student had a small section in the cloakroom that was maybe twelve inches wide. It was just enough space to hang our coats on the hook attached to the wall, a small place for our boots (if it had been raining, we would have to leave our boots in the cloakroom and change into runners before entering the classroom), and above the hook for our coats was a small shelf.

I carefully stacked my two grocery bags on top of one another, leaning them up against the wall. When I was satisfied, they wouldn't topple over, we just stood there, looking back and forth at the bags and at each other.

Luke didn't move. I know he was afraid to say goodbye to me. I had been his only constant and even though he loved our mother, the two of us shared a bond of trust and safety that he didn't have with her.

"Are you sure?" he asked again.

"Yes, I have to now. You heard Mommy. I *have* to leave now. She said it herself. She's never wanted me, and now I can't come back."

The silence between us was filled with hopes dashed to pieces.

"But don't worry, this won't take long. I know exactly where I'm going to go after school to get a job. And soon, I'll have enough money to come get you and Lucky. It'll be a few days, max! Just don't talk back, stay in your room, and if Stupid Face comes around, tell him you're sick with a cold, have diarrhea, or you've been throwing up. He'll stay away from you."

He nodded.

We gave each other a hug, and right at that moment the alarm sounded for school to begin. He looked at me one more time and ran out of my homeroom toward his classroom.

I took a deep breath. Though excited about a new life away from my mother and Stupid Face, I was sad about leaving Luke and Lucky. I was also anxious from the looming awareness that I might not be able to get a job, and I didn't know where I was going to sleep that night.

I tried to make the best of my day. At the Monday morning assembly, I sang "God Save the Queen" and "The Lord's Prayer." I did my schoolwork, played four square on the blacktop at recess, and traded lunches with my friends. But that deep, sinking feeling never left me. Each time I came in and out of the cloakroom, I apprehensively glanced over at my two bags. I even laughed and passed notes during class, but deep down inside, I was so afraid.

With every movement of the second hand on the clock on the wall above my teacher's desk, I knew the 3:00 p.m. bell that would dismiss us for the day was getting closer and closer.

Brrrinnnggg!

The 3:00 p.m. bell finally sounded.

Pencils, papers, and erasers were all hurriedly shoved into their cases as all the other kids rushed out of their seats. They bounded into the cloakroom, whisked their coats off the hangers, grabbed whatever else they had stored there, and ran out the door. They went outside to eager parents waiting to pick them up, hear about their day, help with homework, and have a warm family meal together—a scenario I had never once known with my mother.

I didn't get up quite as quickly as the others did. Instead, I stayed in my seat, studying the excitement on each of their faces as they raced out to see their loving parents.

I wish I had a family I was happy to go home to.

Not wanting to make a scene and not wanting everyone think I was even weirder than they already thought I was, I took my time packing up my things and made sure I was the last student in the cloakroom. I managed to gather all my things and juggle the two bags in my arms as I walked out of the school.

I walked to a nearby grassy area and sat under a tree to do my homework. Then I gathered up all of my belongings again and prepared myself for the journey toward Broadway Street, an eight-block trek.

But I had to walk past my own street first.

I looked left toward my house and didn't see Luke in the front yard, so I knew he was with Ronny and kept walking. When I approached Tenth Avenue, it was much busier than I had seen it before. That's when I learned about "rush hour." I blundered my way across the busy intersection and proceeded to Broadway.

My sights were on the local paint store.

It never occurred to me that what I was doing was unreasonable. In my mind, it was absolutely possible to get a job, and I knew I would be a very capable and hard-working employee. I would also be loyal, and a very dedicated worker. Plus, I could speak two languages (and even a special one that I prayed for God to give me) and was certain I would be useful and *good for something*!

Just before I approached the front door, I put down my bags, straightened my hair, straightened my dress, and took a quick breath. I reached for the shiny brass doorknob and opened the door. A little bell over the door jingled. I picked up my bags and walked in clumsily. I looked around for an adult to talk to, but no one was around—not behind the aisles of paints, not near the supply sections, nor near the tool sections. After scanning the entire store, I finally noticed the main counter tucked away behind a short shelving unit to my left. Assuming the cash register would be located there, I headed toward that counter as gracefully as I could with my "luggage."

A man walked out from a back room and came down one of the aisles looking curiously at me. He looked around as if he expected a parent to be by my side, but when he saw that I was alone, he walked behind the counter and leaned down to speak to me.

"Good afternoon, young lady," he greeted warmly.

I'm in luck! He's nice and he called me a "young lady!" He didn't call me "chink," "ugly," "stupid," "good for nothing," or "punk!"

"Good afternoon, sir!" I returned his greeting with excitement.

"Are you here by yourself, young lady?"

"Yes, sir. I am. I would like to apply for a job with your wonderful store!" I said confidently.

His eyes seemed to pop out of their sockets. He took a few moments to gather himself before speaking. "Why are you looking for a job? Shouldn't you be in school? You're too young to be looking for a job."

"Sir, I'm looking for a job because I have run away from home. I have everything I need with me, including two nice dresses which I think would be very suitable for work." I pointed to the two crumpled paper grocery bags by my feet. "I plan on going to school during the days, and I will come right after that to work for you, sir. But if you need me all day, I'd be happy not to go to school anymore and work for you all day!" I offered.

Silence, then, "Hmmm…and why do you think you would be a good worker in my paint store?" he asked both in amusement and curiosity.

"Sir, my grandmother is a wonderful artist. She paints all the time and gave me my first paint-by-number-set last Christmas. I stayed within the lines and am very good at that. I am also very good with colors and am able to name every color and mix and match them so they make other pretty colors too," I declared boldly.

I had practiced my speech a dozen times all weekend long, and all my answers seemed very logical to me.

Yet they were met with silence.

The paint store owner leaned further over the counter and stared at me (and my bags) for a long while. I shifted on my feet and tried to meet his gaze as directly as I could. But a part of me suddenly wondered if the kind of look this man was giving me was the same kind of look Stupid Face gave me before he made me do horrible things and I looked away. However, when I looked at him carefully again, I knew this man was not evil. He was actually thinking about what I had said.

"Well now," he said finally, clearing his throat. "I'm very sorry to say this, but I don't have any positions open at the moment."

My smile faded. I tried not to show my disappointment. *What do I do now?*

"Little girl, right next door to me is a toy store. They may have an opening for you," he suggested.

I lit up again. "*Oh, thank you*, sir! Thank you! I will go there right away. Thank you very much, sir!"

I smiled and awkwardly grabbed my two grocery bags of clothes. As I approached the door, I had to put down the bags again and then open the door to let myself out.

He started to move away from the counter as if to help me, but I said, "That's okay, sir. I will manage. Thank you again so much!" I closed the door behind me and stood outside for a moment to catch my breath, and to fight back the disappointment and tears that were not too far away.

I gave myself a pep talk and told myself the toy store would be much more suitable for me, then picked up the two bags and headed next door.

The lady in the toy store wasn't nearly so nice. She laughed a little and said, "Nice try. Why don't you just go home? It's getting dark, and it's almost dinner time. Your mom will be worried." With that, I was summarily dismissed.

If she only knew…

Downcast, I picked up my two grocery bags and left the store. After standing outside the door for a little while, I remembered the Five and Dime store across the street.

Yes! This is even more perfect than the toy store, I reassured myself. *I can totally work there and be really good at selling knickknacks to my friends!*

The only thing was that I had to cross Broadway by myself, with my "luggage" in tow. But I managed to get to the crosswalk and shuffle across the street and into the Five and Dime store.

It was a little dark inside, but I finally saw the owner sitting on a stool in the corner behind the counter, reading a magazine.

"Hello, ma'am. I'm running away from home, and I am looking for a job. I'm very good with fives *and* dimes—and money of all kinds really. I know about Canadian money and Hong Kong money, and when my grandparents come to visit, they always give me some of their spare coins. I know how to count it all," I said anxiously, running all my thoughts together. "Plus, my grandfather has taught me the times table really well, and I have them all memorized! I can really be a good worker for you in your five and dime store!"

"Oh, dear," the woman said, smiling perplexedly. "I'm afraid we haven't any openings at this time. Why don't you go home? It's getting dark, and I'm sure your mom is worried about you."

Again. If she only knew…

I was beginning to worry. This wasn't going at all as I had planned. Feeling dejected, but too afraid to give up and "go home," I headed to the candy store down the street—*Plan D*. I delivered my rehearsed speech, and the lady behind the counter gave me the same answer I had gotten at each of the other shops.

I turned away from the counter, my spirit heavy.

"Wait a second," the lady said suddenly, "I can't give you a job, but you *are* in a candy store…what would you like?"

I had visited the candy shop often with my grandparents, and my favorite treat was the necklaces made of hard candy. I immediately pointed one out, and the girl handed it to me.

"I have a nickel and can pay for this," I offered.

"No, dear, this is my treat. Why don't you sit outside on the bench and enjoy your candy? Then you'd better head back home."

"Thank you very much." I said with a forced smile.

I didn't want to say it was impossible for me to ever go back. I had sworn I would prove my mother wrong. So, I sat outside and chewed on the rings of the necklace, careful not to eat too many. I had to ration this since I hadn't been able to get the job I was certain would come so easily.

With all the courage and hope in my heart I could mobilize, I decided to try getting a job at Peter's Ice Cream, my last hope. If this one fell through, I would be out of options. The only other stores in town were a hardware store, an automotive shop, some clothing stores, and family-operated restaurants that wouldn't want a little Chinese girl working for them.

I bumbled back across Broadway, but despite how good my speech was, I was soon turned away from the ice cream shop as well. The man behind the counter thanked me for my "application" and, like the candy store owner, gave me a small scoop of ice cream and told me to go home.

I found a nearby bench and slowly ate my ice cream cone. *This will be my dinner, and I will save my sandwich for the next day.*

I feverishly thought about every possible option available to my simple mind and looked up and down the street again to see if there were other stores where I might apply, but there were none.

But how can I go home? How can I give my mother the satisfaction of being right, and then be forced to endure another denunciation? How?

It was beginning to get very dark now. The streetlights were lit, the stores were closing, and I had to make a decision. I picked up my "luggage" and started to walk around, looking for an open garage or a shed I could sleep in, but there were none. With nowhere else to go and no other options to turn to, I began my long, solemn walk toward home.

By the time I reached the back lane to my house, night had completely fallen. With no streetlights in the lane, it was difficult to see ahead of me, so I walked even more slowly. Each step brought me closer to the house of horrors. I could not believe that all my plans had fallen through, and I was now walking back towards hell on earth. So, I stopped.

Be strong...I will never leave you.

I exhaled loudly, restrained my tears, and after giving myself another *long* pep talk, I found the courage to continue. When I neared our neighbor's house, I slowly tiptoed to the corner of the fence between our two houses and crouched down. If my mother was in the kitchen, she would be able to see me, so I stayed down low.

But when I peered through the slats of the fence, I saw that the light was on in the living room, which filtered through the kitchen, but other than that, there was no activity there. I took a few deep breaths and then gingerly opened the back gate, pulled my two grocery bags of clothes and my school bag with me as I entered our backyard, and quietly closed the gate door behind me.

Hearing the sound of the gate click, Lucky came running to see me, wagging his tail in excitement. I hugged my best friend hard as he licked my face and threw his two front paws over my shoulders. I couldn't help but notice the stark difference between the love and affection bestowed by my dog and that *not* bestowed by my own mother.

Worried that any commotion may have caused my mother to look out at the backyard, I hurried up the path and hid just by the back stairs—out of view from the kitchen window.

It must have been around 7:00 p.m. Suddenly, I could hear my mother and Luke talking inside and the sounds of clinking of dishes. They must have finished dinner. Just as fast as the noises erupted, they stopped. I kept still, barely breathing. Lucky, who was sitting beside me, poised and attentive, didn't move either. He simply stared up at me, wondering what I was doing. Gradually, the noises inside began again, and I heard the sound of running water as my mother turned on the sink.

With the noise as my buffer, I crept through the unkempt grass to the makeshift shed under the back porch landing. I slowly opened the door so Lucky and I could creep inside. Lucky seemed reluctant to enter that shadowy, cobwebby place—mostly out of confusion, but giving in to his love for me, he came in with me at last. Together, we crouched there amongst the rusty push-mower, shaggy brooms, and discarded tools—items that weren't used much now with my father gone. I sobbed into Lucky's fur, and he sat patiently with me until I was empty of tears.

All of a sudden, the back door opened!

Startled by this, I let out a pent-up breath from crying so hard. Worried my mother had heard me, I froze and listened, but she did not come out. Then I heard her speaking to Luke, but loudly enough to ensure I could hear her also.

"Your sister is so stupid! Did she really think she could run away? She's so ungrateful! There are starving people in Africa who would die to have the life she has! Hmmph! Well, there's no dinner for her! After all, she's supposed to be gone, right? Why would I have food for someone who's not supposed to be here? Hmmph!"

Then she changed her tone, speaking lovingly to Luke, "It's bedtime, darling. Give me a kiss goodnight. I'm going to watch a little more TV."

In another moment, the back door closed. She had only opened it so that I might hear her better. A fresh wave of tears overcame me, and I was determined not to go back inside—no matter what. I couldn't. I just couldn't give her that satisfaction! More tears flowed as I lamented my life.

It was getting very cold now and I was starting to shiver. Lucky leaned into me, trying to comfort me and keep me warm, but even so, it was not enough to keep the damp cold winter night of the Pacific Northwest away. I hadn't packed a coat because I was certain I was going to get a job and a place to stay. But as I sat there in the dank shed, dejected, lonely, and jobless, having just been heartlessly ridiculed by my mother (again), my defeat felt even more punishing.

When I couldn't take the chill any longer, I crept out from underneath the porch. It was fully dark outside now, and the moon was shining brightly over me. I brushed the cobwebs and dirt from my clothes and hugged Lucky. Together, we quietly made our way to the small porch at the top of the stairs, where Lucky stayed most of the time.

In complete humiliation, I slowly opened the door.

I left my two grocery bags with Lucky, knowing I could get them in the morning. I dared not try to maneuver them with me tonight as I crept back into the house. As I tiptoed through the kitchen, I saw my mother watching television. I could not bear to face her. I carefully opened Luke's and my little bedroom door. Luke sat up in his bed, and I put my finger to my mouth indicating for him not to speak, and then turned to ever so gently close the door behind me. I smiled and went to sit on his bed.

"I didn't get the job," I explained in defeat, with my head hung down low. I was so sad that I had disappointed him, that I had been unable to get us both out of this horrendous life.

"That's okay. Did Mommy see you?"

I shook my head.

"Do you want me to sneak you some food? I can pretend it's for me."

"No, it's okay…thank you. I'm not hungry. Let's go to bed. Tomorrow is a new day."

He nodded and lay back down. I pulled the sheets around him, changed into my pajamas, and slunk to bed.

I felt like such a failure.

"Why in the world didn't those shopkeepers do something?" Leah asked in exasperation. "Surely they must have realized an eight-year-old girl wouldn't be looking for a job because everything was hunky-dory at home!"

"Maybe they were in shock seeing a little Chinese girl asking for a job. It was in the late sixties after all. In retrospect, it was probably a blessing that our little 'house of horrors' was kept a secret. If people had learned of our plight, my mother and Scham would have gone through the roof. As it was, we were already stretched beyond description."

Leah let out a long sigh. "I wonder how many other situations like yours were hiding behind closed doors. I think you survived such horrors because you didn't know you had options. Society may not have known what to do to help children like you and Luke back then, but they do now."

"Maybe that's another reason why I'm telling my story now…it's time to set the captives free."

Heaven Sent

It was an unusually warm and sunny afternoon. One would think that on a beautiful sunlit weekend day that our street would be filled with activity. Perhaps children playing in the front yards or riding bikes up and down the street, maybe parents working in the garden, or families out for a midday stroll with their dogs—something.

But this Saturday afternoon our neighborhood was like a ghost town. Not a soul could be seen anywhere for blocks to the left or right of our home. Mother and Scham were also gone, and while that was a relief, everything else felt a little odd.

Luke was with Ronny again, and ordinarily, I would hear them playing in his backyard. Today, however, I heard nothing.

Unlike Ronny's kindness towards Luke, the girls on my street were not very nice to me, so I didn't have friends to play with. Heather, a girl who lived in a home to the left of me, threatened that she would "kill" me if I even walked on the sidewalk in front of her house because I was Chinese. The few friends I did have were from my homeroom class, but they lived many, many blocks away, so it wasn't easy to just go over there to play.

I had already played with Lucky all morning, but ironically, it was in his sweet friendship that the absence of any other kind of affection or love was illuminated. Still trying to pull myself out of the heaviness of my sorrow, I took out my favorite toys—my Barbie dolls that PoPo gave to me. I played with them quietly, indulging all my fantasies about what it would be like to live a privileged life—even just a *different life*. Anything but my own life.

To have loving parents and friends.

To not be Chinese.

I invented imaginary conversations with parents who loved me, who made me lunches, included me in their days, and had Sunday night family dinners with pot roast and potatoes. I imagined growing up and being Barbie. My world through her was amazing. I had friends who liked me and wanted to be with me. I was very successful, had my own big home, lots of dogs, and enjoyed fantastic clothes (something else I didn't have much of)!

The only thing I noticed was that Barbie never laughed…which was okay, because neither did I.

Eventually, my godparents gave me a Barbie camper and Skipper as a playmate, and these two additions felt like a day of liberation. The RV camper was a metaphor for my freedom! I could physically see and touch "a place of my own"! I could be self-sufficient, I didn't need to rely on anyone, and if I didn't like the people around me, I could shut the door and leave.

But as much as I loved my utopian fantasy life, the richness and color of those imaginings made my real life that much starker, colder, and emptier. Suddenly, loneliness overwhelmed me again. Not even my beloved Lucky, my dolls, or my reverie could make me feel better. I put them aside and went to the front door of my house.

I sat down on the top front step of our tiny wartime bungalow and dropped my chin on top of my hands, staring out at the empty street. Instead of being a light-hearted eight-year-old little girl, I felt old, filthy, ugly, and worn.

On that day, the weight of my crazy world suppressed my every breath, and I was totally overcome with despair.

"God! I'm *sooooooo mad at You!*" I yelled through clenched teeth. "You said You would *never leave me*! And now I'm here all alone! I'm hated by every stranger for something I cannot ever change! *And* I'm even hated by my own family! And why, why, why, why, *why did you allow Stupid Face to come into our lives?*

"Wasn't it enough that You took PoPo and GongGong away from me? Wasn't it enough that You took Daddy away from me? I have no friends, I have no family, and You constantly let me suffer! I suffer with Mrs. Reed. I suffer with humiliating lunches at school! I suffer with horrible food at home—if there is ever any food at all after Stupid Face devours everything! He beats us, calls us horrible names, laughs at us when we try to pray to You, and he makes me do disgusting things to him! It's so gross, God!

"Why can't you stop this? Why can't you make Stupid Face pay and suffer for his attacks on us? Why do you let my mother get away with everything? I'm lonely, and Lucky can't talk, so I never can have conversations with him. And You're *never here! Where are You? You promised You would never leave me, but You did!*"

I dropped my face into my folded arms, which were resting on my knees, and wept uncontrollably. When I caught my breath, I whimpered, "Everyone's gone. PoPo, GongGong, Daddy, even Luke has friends. I have no one, not even *You…*"

I hugged my knees and hid my eyes completely.

Then, something very subtle shifted and I felt like I was in a dream. My peripheral vision had gained a white halo around it. Thinking this was the result of my tears, I wiped my eyes and blinked several times to make sure I was focusing correctly. I looked down the street again. It still looked the same—empty. Everything felt very much like the sensation I had in the elevator in Hong Kong, long, long ago.

All of a sudden, a breeze came forward and brushed past me, through me. It felt like feathers caressing my cheeks and eyelids, like thousands of gentle fingers lifting and separating the strands of my hair.

God... is that You?

Without a moment of doubt, I knew that God had come to comfort me. You see, the breeze came only to me. Only my hair moved. Nothing else around me moved—not the little leaves on the bushes beside me, and not the wispy leaves on the trees in front of me. After a few moments, the gentle breeze encircling me intertwined with what seemed like other streams of breezes, and I was enveloped by a breath from heaven—warm, tender, ever so gentle, and soothing to my spirit.

I looked around my body to see if I could notice anything else and saw my t-shirt starting to flutter. I looked up, and the breeze now directed itself to the leaves in the row of chestnut trees that lined our street. Before my very eyes, the leaves of each chestnut tree began to dance in unison. They swayed like elegant skirts rippling in the breeze, first left, then right, in perfect synchronicity. Then little chestnuts began to drop, and when they bounced, they did so with the rhythm of the rustling leaves above.

God was playing a song and singing to me!

A bright light flashed on the lawn and captured my attention. It was the most breathtaking masterpiece I had ever seen. The Master was painting with His own hands, from only one color—green—the most stunning piece of art. With only *one* color, I saw the entire rainbow come to life on the canvas of our lawn.

Then, to my amazement, the grass *also* began to dance for me! It waltzed to the flickers of sunlight that were shining through the leaves of the chestnut trees as they swayed, and the sight made me giggle. Yes, God was with me, and He was showing me how He was in control of everything; the sun, the wind, the temperature, the leaves, the nuts that fell, the grass—*and* the lives and activities of hundreds of people on a very busy "typical Saturday afternoon." He had cleared the streets just so He could summon nature to perform for an audience of one.

Me.

I don't know how to describe this except to say that the breeze that stirred around me now moved *within* me, warming my heart and easing the pain in my soul. Joy rose inside of me, and I saw color in everything—more vividly than I ever had before. The grass was dappled in a multitude of colors, and the sky was a complex and swirling mix of blues and purples. The tiny bits of glass embedded in our stucco house caught the sun's rays and reflected a brilliant prism of color. And the little bracelet I'd made out of these bits of glass and tape now stood ablaze on my slim wrist, and I laughed as I moved my arm, watching the lights dance over my skin.

God had given me these gifts. He gave me a symphony, a ballet, and a masterpiece. I was, for that brief moment, residing in a kingdom different than my current reality. But more importantly, God had shown me He was with me. While I did not understand why such things were happening in my life, I knew He was in control.

Everything was going to work out, somehow.

I was not alone.

He was with me.

Leah tried to hide her tears, wiping them from her eyes as if she was brushing her hair off of her face. And I slowly began to step back from that Heaven-filled afternoon and into my afternoon with Leah.

"It's such a hard life you had," Leah finally said, her voice raspy, "I wish I had the same faith as you."

I squeezed her hand. "We all have faith in something, Leah. For me, my faith is in *Someone*. If we do not lose heart, we will see many miracles in our lives. We will see that God is real and He will fulfill His promises to us. Some people give up too soon—just short of their prayers coming true. They miss their miracles because they shut their hearts off to possibilities, forsaking their reward, just moments before their breakthrough. For others, their faith is in themselves and their own abilities, or worse, their faith is in fear. They believe they will lose anyway, that life is filled with nothing but pain, so they give up before even beginning.

"Sometimes, we create conclusions when we haven't seen the whole picture. It's like reading a few chapters of a book and saying we know how the story is going to end. It's impossible. We need to keep turning the pages. The same is true in life. Just because we don't understand what is happening in one chapter, doesn't mean we won't understand the whole picture if we keep turning the pages. Our pain may not make sense in the early chapters of our lives, but it will have its perfect purpose. It can all be for our good in the end…if we just keep believing."

Leah sat in silence as she considered my words.

Then, as if on cue, a warm breeze swept between us, and she said, "Turn the page my dear, and tell me what is in the next chapter."

4 THE VALLEY OF THE SHADOW OF DEATH

The LORD is my shepherd, I shall not want. He makes me to lie down in green pastures; He leads me beside the still waters. He restores my soul; He leads me in the paths of righteousness for His Name's sake. Yea, though I walk through the valley of the shadow of death, I will fear no evil; for You are with me. Your rod and Your staff, they comfort me. You prepare a table before me in the presence of my enemies; You anoint my head with oil; My cup runs over. Surely goodness and mercy shall follow me all the days of my life; and I will dwell in the house of the LORD forever.

—Psalm 23 (NKJV)

Room 316

The next time I saw Leah, she was in more pain than usual, and when I arrived, Melody was already there with an additional dose of pain medication.

"I told you. I don't want that poison!" Leah objected.

"Well, it's either this or morphine, per the doctor's orders. Choose your poison," Melody said with authority.

Leah turned her head in rebellion and closed her eyes. I moved closer to her and squeezed her hand. She slowly opened her eyes and took a deep breath. "Fine," she scoffed. "Give me the damn pills."

With that, she reluctantly swallowed the pills with a few big gulps of water. "If I didn't know better, I'd say you were trying to kill me with those things!"

Melody smiled and rubbed Leah's shoulder gently. Leah pulled away with a huff. Melody rolled her eyes and left the room.

"She cares about you and worries you're in pain," I offered.

"Whatever," she said dismissively.

I continued holding her hand in silence.

When she was ready, she shared her thoughts about our last conversation, as well as a few stories of her own about her childhood. Some were heartwarming, and some were very sad.

She wanted to keep talking, but the pills soon took effect. No matter how hard she tried to fight it, she became more and more drowsy.

Not wanting to leave on a melancholy note, I promised Leah that next time I would bring her something to cheer her up. I gave her a kiss on the forehead, pulled the blankets up and across her chest, and left her to rest.

Before I arrived at the hospital the following week, I stopped at my favorite florist and bought a large bouquet of sunflowers. When Leah saw them, a smile as bright as the flowers bloomed on her face.

"I wanted to bring you a little bit of summer," I explained.

"Oh! And *who is this*?" she exclaimed, looking at my companion.

"This is Harley," I said, adjusting the leash so she could better see my Bernese Mountain Dog. "I've told you about my dogs—Sadie, Dakota, Noah, Duke and Harley. I only have two left now—Harley and Noah—but I wanted to bring Harley today because he is such a character, just like you!"

"Really! Now that's some kind of dog!" Leah acknowledged.

"Yes. He is. Harley is Duke's brother, but I lost Dukie three years ago. It still pains me to think about it…I've never had a dog like him."

"I'm sorry, Manna. I know how much you love your dogs. Why was Dukie so special?"

"All my dogs love me, but Dukie was *devoted* to me. Plus…"

"What? Plus, *what?*"

I hesitated another half a moment. "Duke saw angels."

"Of course he did." she laughed.

I didn't budge.

"You're serious, aren't you?" she asked, checked by my silence. "Well, I know better than to doubt you. I guess it doesn't surprise me that an owner who has encounters with angels would have a dog who could too," she said, smiling. "Now, tell me about his little brother, Harley."

"Harley is a wonderful dog too. And he has a personality that constantly keeps my family and friends laughing."

"Oh, my. He is special, isn't he? I can tell by his eyes!" she said, surprising even herself. "Other people bring therapy dogs in, but I like yours best so far! He must be a great companion."

"Yes, he is. All of my dogs are that way for me. They bring me comfort and so much joy," I said, looking down at Harley, who thumped his tail appreciatively. When I looked back up, I saw a wistful look in Leah's eyes.

"Tell me, Leah, when do I have the pleasure of meeting your family?"

"Soon, I hope," her voice small. "I'm not ready to leave them…"

"We never are. But this may just be a temporary separation."

"What do you mean?"

"Well, if you believe in God, then you believe in Heaven. And one day, we will all be reunited again."

Leah closed her eyes, and I could see that she was struggling to catch her breath. I had to remind myself that even though her spirit was strong, her body was failing. More medication had been added to her regimen, and the clanging of medical equipment and instruments from the hallway reminded me of the inevitable.

"I've thought about God a lot lately," she said after a moment. "When I first came here, even before you began coming to see me, it was like I suddenly *remembered* God. Thomas, did too. He said he's been having talks with 'the Big Guy' ever since we got the news about how far the cancer had spread…" Her voice trailed off and we sat quietly for a moment.

Suddenly, she pulled herself out of her funk and spoke decisively. "No more about this miserable business of dying. There's just one thing I need to know!"

"What's that, Leah?"

"That low-down, good-for-nothing, oxter! That Stupid Face!"

"Wait. What's an oxter?" I asked laughing.

"It's an armpit," Leah explained. "That's exactly what he was, a stinkin' armpit! A deviant! Tell me your mother kicked him to the curb!"

I laughed some more.

"I wish I could, Leah. I really wish I could…"

Looking a Gift Horse in the Mouth

My relationship with my mother only grew more negligible as the days passed into weeks and months. Nevertheless, she was still my mother. Despite her haranguing and callousness, something in my heart continued to cry out for her love and approval. Even though it didn't make any sense, I refused to give up hope. I tried to please her in everything I did in the hopes of getting any kind of affection in return, such as it was.

One day I picked her the prettiest flowers I could find outside, a bouquet of wild daisies and dandelions, and I brought them to her. I held them with outstretched arms and joy in my heart that I was able to give her a present, but she looked down at them, pushed my hand away, saying, "Get those dirty things away from me!"

On another occasion—Mother's Day—I made her a knitting box out of cardboard. Knowing how she liked to knit, I thought she might enjoy having a box in which to store all of her knitting supplies, instead of the plastic bag she used. I colored the outside of the box with flowers and glued little bits of colored tissue paper, pipe cleaners, and ribbons to it—just as I'd been taught to do in school. I spent hours and hours in my room, trying to get the design just right. When I was finished, I slipped into the kitchen, secreting away a pair of chopsticks and a small ball of string into my pocket and hurried back to my room. I put those items into the box to represent the knitting needles and yarn, knowing she would be upset if I took the real things without permission.

When the day came, I took the box out from my closet and felt a little quiver of excitement. *She will be so happy she has a knitting box, and a very pretty one at that, if I do say so myself!* I had worked on this project for a long time and planned the surprise for her with pure delight. That afternoon, when she didn't seem too busy, I offered the box to her with pride.

"Mommy! I have a surprise for you!" I said with my shoulders back, my head held high, and a big smile. "Happy Mother's Day!" I exclaimed, as I whipped the knitting box out from behind my back.

She looked at the gift with irritation. I had interrupted her while she was watching television and eating a snack. "Oh…that's nice," she said, laying it on the coffee table.

"Mommy, please look at it! You see, I put all the flowers on it myself, and I decorated it with leaves! And see, here—" I said, pointing to another area of the knitting box, "Right here is where the sun shines and smiles on the grass and the flowers! Oh! And look inside! Do you see where the knitting needles go? I used a pair of chopsticks as pretend needles! Isn't that a good idea, Mommy?"

"Mm-hmm," she answered, after tolerating my explanation. "Just leave it here. I'm busy. Go outside and play," she said, dismissively.

Well…that wasn't quite what I expected.

Still, I was very happy I had created such a wonderful gift and I went outside like a "good little girl" not wanting to disturb her any longer. I walked away, filled with the warm glow that can only come from serving someone and giving a meaningful gift that required great thought and even sacrifice.

But as I left her and walked out the front door, an unsettling feeling started to permeate my joy. There was a growing sense that in spite of all my efforts, no gift, no amount of time, nothing was going to please her. I fought off those feelings and continued hoping for the best.

I went outside to play hopscotch by myself and then played in the backyard with Lucky. When I came back inside, I wanted to see if she had at least looked at the knitting box. I would know because it would no longer be in the exact same position on the coffee table. Racing inside from the back door, I ran through the kitchen straight to the living room.

Wow! I thought to myself. *The knitting box is no longer on the coffee table! My goodness! She actually took it! She is using it!*

I was elated, and skipped around the house, believing I had conquered her rejection and defeated the unloving spirit between us. I started to plan how I could show her my love in other ways. *Maybe she will see that I am not "stupid" or "good-for-nothing," but that I am, in fact, "good for something"! Maybe she will treat me like a daughter—like all the other moms I know!*

I ran to my room, grabbed a notebook, and started to think of all the things my mother liked. I wrote down all the different ideas I could think of for special gifts I could make for her. When I was finished and feeling very satisfied with my list, I closed my notebook and put it away. Skipping out of my room, I went to look for my mother.

I went from room to room but couldn't find her. *Did she leave again without telling us? Maybe I didn't see her leave because I was in the backyard with Lucky, or maybe I was too consumed with writing my list of presents to make for her.*

I went about the house one more time. I went down the hallway, through both the living room and dining room (which only housed the piano where I practiced holding my hands like I was holding tennis balls), and scanned the kitchen before going back down the hallway. As I raced down the hallway, my eyes scanned her room, in which the drapes were drawn. Though the room was dark inside, out of the corner of my eye, I saw my knitting box haphazardly thrown into the wastepaper basket beside her dresser.

Not only that, she had thrown other rubbish—used tissues, scrap pieces of paper and the food wrappings from her snack—on top of it.

I came to a dead stop and stared incredulously at the sight. Slowly, I walked to the trashcan, peeled away the trash that covered my gift and dusted off the food crumbs that had fallen from the food wrapper.

Couldn't she have pretended to like it? Even for a little while?
Couldn't she have pretended that she liked me?

I took my gift back to my room. My head was no longer held high, my shoulders were not pushed back, and my heart had sunk into the depths of my nauseated tummy.

My mother didn't come home until after we were asleep that night. I saw her the next morning and decided to "test" her. But first, I went by her room to see if anything had changed in the trashcan. Nothing had been disturbed; it was as I had left it, which meant that she didn't notice that my gift had been taken out.

"Mommy, did you like the knitting box I made you?" I asked warily.

"Yes," she said coldly, without turning to face me.

"Are you going to use it?" I asked.

"Ummm…yes. I used it last night," she lied without missing a beat and with her back still toward me.

"Oh, okay," I said.

She finally turned around and looked at me. I stood there with my eyes welling with tears. She quickly glanced at the wastebasket and saw that my knitting box was no longer there. In an instant, she knew I had found it in the garbage and had removed it. She had been caught lying to me, and there was no way out.

"Go on! Get out! I have to get ready!" she demanded.

She didn't say she was sorry. She didn't try to explain her actions. She didn't even take the time to make up another lie to rationalize why my gift was in the garbage can. She just dismissed me, like she always did. She didn't care about the knitting box I had made for her, or the love I had for her in the making of my gift.

At that moment, I understood that the knitting box was *me*—something that had been created with love but was neither valued nor deemed useful, and which was easily discarded into the trash along with the other items that no longer had use.

Shamed and Shorn

This unforgettable incident only added to the growing distance between my mother and me, and I simply learned to hide. I wished I was invisible or could disappear like Endora or Samantha Stevens on the television show *Bewitched*.

We had a small black-and-white television that received only a few stations with "bunny-ear" antennas on top of the set. Still, I enjoyed watching the few afternoon shows that we did get—*Looney Tunes* with Bugs Bunny and his friends, and *Bewitched*. I loved watching Bugs Bunny, because the cartoon character's antics would make me giggle and laugh—something I didn't do much. I loved watching *Bewitched* because I could fantasize about having magical powers to fly, to be invisible, to help people, and to make bad things right.

Oh, how I used to dream about having superpowers to do good, just like Samantha Stevens. She never used them for selfish, stupid, or illogical reasons—something I detested because I saw these characteristics in Stupid Face all the time. Everything he said (and did) was always selfish, pointless, and unintelligent. Even as children, we were embarrassed by him and worried about what he would say or do in public. What our mother was doing with him, we never knew.

One afternoon only my mother and I were home alone. I was in the living room watching one of my favorite television programs when she called my name from the bathroom where I thought she was getting ready to go out, again.

"Manna? Come here..." She sounded *almost* kind.

This is very unusual. She never calls me without an angry tone.

Nonetheless, I jumped up from the floor, surprised that she had called for me at all, and went to her. "Yes, Mommy?"

When I reached the bathroom, she was sitting on the closed lid of the toilet. It was clear that she'd been crying.

"Mommy, what's wrong?" I stopped at the door. I wanted to race to her, to comfort her, but knowing how she felt about me, I thought better of it, and stayed frozen at the door.

"Come here, Manna," was all she said.

Something wasn't right. I was frightened, but the thought of disobeying her terrified me even more, so I went to her and stood before her. When she looked at me, I noticed a glazed look in her eyes. I leaned forward to try and hug her and was surprised that she received my hug and even lifted her hands up to stroke my hair. I had long hair that flowed down my back at that time, and I liked it very much. It made me feel beautiful—like a princess.

Suddenly, my mother stiffened and pushed me back a little.

"You didn't brush your hair again."

"What? Uhh…yes, I did, Mommy," I stammered, as she pushed me away from what I thought was a loving embrace.

"Don't lie to me, *d'ya hear me?*" She was now screaming.

What just happened?

I saw the anger return again to my mother's eyes.

"I *said*, don't lie to me!" she thundered. "You refuse to brush your hair because you're lazy and good-for-nothing! You expect me to do everything for you! Well, I'm tired of it! *D'ya hear me?* I'm tired of always having to take care of you!"

I stared at her in complete shock, traumatized by the sudden emotional turnaround. She pushed me aside, reaching into the medicine cabinet above the sink. She fumbled for something, and in another moment, I saw she had a large pair of scissors in her hand.

"No!" I cried, "What are you doing?"

"Be quiet and turn around."

"No, Mommy!" I cried, but she whirled me around and in seconds, she was roughly hacking away chunks of my hair. I was too shocked to feel any emotion. All I could do was watch her in the spotted, shabby mirror as I saw section after section of my beautiful long locks fall away from my head.

With every slash of the scissors, she yelled at me, "You better learn to be responsible for yourself—*d'ya hear me?* You can't rely on anyone—especially a man!" she bellowed, "*Never* trust a man—*ever*! Never let a man control you, or your money! All they want is your money! *D'ya hear me? Do you understand me?*" she screamed into my ears.

I wanted to answer, *I'm eight years old, you mean, bad witch! And no, I do not understand! I do not understand any of this! I don't understand your craziness! I don't understand Stupid Face! I don't understand why you let him hurt us! I don't understand why you leave us all the time! I don't understand why you took me away from PoPo and GongGong when you didn't want me anyway! I don't know why you didn't let us go to live with Daddy! And I don't understand why you hate me so much! So, no, you evil witch! I DO NOT UNDERSTAND!*

But I said nothing.

I was trembling and shaking uncontrollably, too afraid to speak. Even breathing seemed dangerous as I stared into the mirrored reflection of her frenzied eyes while she wielded her sharp scissors.

"Stand still! *D'ya hear me?*" she screamed again.

I tried my best to stop trembling, but I could not.

She said nothing else as she brutally finished slicing off the remainder of my hair. She didn't need to say anything else.

She had already said—and now done—*enough*.

The same was now true for me. I would do no more for this woman, and there was nothing else for me to say to her either. So I said nothing, giving in to the shock of what was happening before my very eyes.

In the reflection of the tarnished mirror of the medicine cabinet, I helplessly watched the last bit of my hair fall away. Now, not only was I *Chinese*, not only was I constantly being called "stupid" and "good-for-nothing," but with my hair shorn, I looked like a boy.

My inner feelings of ugliness were now reflected in my outer appearance.

When she was finished, she stared at me through the mirror, but said nothing. She was breathing hard, and her nostrils flared with each inhale.

With resolve, I held her gaze.

"Get out of here!" she suddenly yelled.

I did not move. Instead, I narrowed my eyes and continued staring at her through the mirror. She could use her power over me and try to make me ugly on the outside, but nothing, nothing, *nothing* was as ugly as she was on the inside.

"Go!" she screamed again, as she raised her arm with the scissors still clenched tightly in her hand.

I fled to the safety of loneliness in my little room, and when I caught my breath, I broke down sobbing uncontrollably.

Out of Mind, *Then* Out of Sight

Late one afternoon, my mother was unusually lively, going back and forth between her room and the bathroom, getting ready to meet Scham. It was almost dinnertime, so I went to Ronny's house to check on Luke, but he told me he was going to stay there for their family dinner, so I headed back home.

This was just another evening that went by without a dinner being made, so I went to the local store down the street and used some of the change from the piggy bank PoPo and GongGong had given me to purchase a candy bar to make my "chocolate sandwich."

I took my time walking home from the store, kicking at the scattered lumps of fallen leaves from the chestnut trees above. As I approached the front doorsteps, I heard some faint shuffles from inside, and then the clicking of high heels on the hardwood floor. *She must be ready to leave.*

Hoping against hope that she might still prove me wrong one day about her, I devised another plan to test her, to see if she really cared about us. *Would she call for us and give us last minute instructions before she left? Would she tell us that dinner was made? Would she tell us to only watch television until 8:00 p.m. and then go to bed? Would she leave an emergency number? Would she let us know when she'd be back? Would she give us a kiss on the forehead, tell us she loved us, to not worry, and that she'd be back soon?*

I ran toward a neighbor's house, a few doors to the right. Large bushes framed their front porch, and I hid there, peeking through the branches as I waited for my mother to leave. I wanted to see if she would stop to look for us, call for us, or go back inside to check to see if we were there—anything.

Just then, I heard the clicking of her high heels as she walked down the steps. She went down the path to her brand-new Buick that my grandparents had gotten for her. They paid "$4,000 cash," I had heard her proudly announce to Stupid Face, who had now claimed the car was his, too.

Without missing a beat, she opened the car door, got in, turned on the engine and then drove away. When she reached the end of the block, she signaled to turn right, barely stopping at the end of the street, and completed her turn without hesitation. Within moments, she was gone.

She had driven straight past my hiding spot, never bothering to look around once to call for either Luke or me. I had even jumped out from behind the bushes just before she turned, hoping that she would see me and perhaps come to her senses and realize that she had just abandoned her children without care or protection yet again.

What if we were kidnapped, or a robber came?

But not one of those "normal," logical, or reasonable parental instincts occurred to her. Or if they did, she didn't care. She simply drove away, eyes on the road ahead, leaving me with nothing but a cool chill working its way up my spine.

Most people know the saying, "out of sight, out of mind"—when you don't see someone or something often, it becomes less important to you and you end up forgetting about it. In our case, we were already *not* a thought in her mind, so being out of sight came only too naturally.

I wanted to scream…*No! I do not understand!*

Highway to Hell

Scham's presence in our house became a constant heavy cloud of darkness. His perversion continued as before, and as much as I tried to predict his actions and read his moods so that I might avert his advances, I could not figure out a rhyme or reason as to his sickness.

When he wasn't secretly forcing me to act out his depravity, he would torment Luke and me. He would assign random and preposterous duties for us to perform, and when we didn't do *exactly* what he wanted, he would grab our ears, pull them with great force and twist them until the intense burning sensation brought us to tears. Though he would beat us in other areas of our bodies, he often targeted the ears because he knew it would not cause a bruise or a mark, leaving no physical evidence of his abuse.

When my mother was home, their bedroom door would be locked for hours (even during the day) while we were left to care for ourselves. Luke might not have understood what those closed doors meant, but that brutal man had forced me into an understanding of its implications. What went on behind those doors was lurid and terrible. I hated them both for flagrantly participating in it—and for subjecting me to it.

In an effort to get away from the madness, I continued to play with my Barbie dolls and my Barbie camper, transposing all of my childish dreams—dreams of being older, free, independent, successful, wealthy, and with many friends—onto that imaginary girl. I wanted nothing more than to be that girl.

The time came when even my RV camper reverie took on a negative connotation—once again, thanks to Stupid Face.

My grandparents had come to visit again one summer. I was overjoyed to see them, grateful for the safety their presence provided. While they were visiting, GongGong taught me more fun ways to learn math, how to count using the abacus. He also took me for long walks around the block. PoPo would cook her wonderful meals, and when we sat together, she caught me up on the lives of our relatives in Hong Kong. We enjoyed our sweet time together.

One day my mother announced that we were all going camping. *How bizarre! Why would my mother want to take her parents camping when they just arrived here from Hong Kong?* They had no experience of camping, nor had they ever considered the idea of camping! This entire situation seemed very out of place. Later that day, we discovered it was Scham's idea because he wanted to go and my mother wanted to please him. Thank goodness she had enough sense not to put my grandparents in a tent (which Scham had originally wanted to do). So, my mother rented a small Class C camper, which had the additional sleeping quarters above the driver's compartment, and as we learned on the trip, paid for everything else as well.

The day came, and we all headed out. As you might expect, it was a very difficult trip. Scham had to have everything catered to him—where we went, what we ate, when we ate—and worse, he had no qualms about forcing those choices on my grandparents. He was not only disrespectful and unkind to them, he was also shamelessly rude. Luke and I often found our mouths agape as we witnessed both his debased behaviors and our mother's silence.

If that wasn't bad enough, we had to endure his piffling gibberish and tiresome rants. Still, true to my grandparents' gracious nature, they tolerated his selfishness, his lamentable ignorance, and his dull, ill-witted humor.

At night, PoPo and GongGong slept in a bed converted from the kitchenette. Luke slept in a sleeping bag where a small chair turned into a single bed, and I slept in the bed above the driver's seat with my mother and Scham. My place was against the wall, my mother was beside me, and Scham beside her, at the edge of the bed.

Each night he would pull shut the privacy curtain at the edge of that bed, and then masturbate under the blankets until he finished—even with me right there beside my mother. I pretended to fall asleep quickly each night, holding the pillow over my ears while I fought back shock and nausea. Even at this, my mother said nothing about his reprehensible behavior.

Frankly, I didn't know what was more deplorable—Scham doing what he did while we were all only a few feet away, or the fact that my mother neither said nor did anything about his debauchery, or about how he treated her parents.

Finally, after a long and taxing week, the time came for us to head home. We were battle-weary and scarred from yet another horrifying time with Stupid Face. But just when we thought Scham couldn't be any more despicable, the unthinkable happened.

Stupid Face was driving, and my mother was sitting beside him in the passenger seat. Luke and I were sitting with my grandparents at the kitchenette. After playing and talking for a while, GongGong whispered something to PoPo, and PoPo went to the front of the camper and whispered something to my mother.

My mother said, "Okay," and then said something to Scham.

When PoPo returned to the table, I asked her if everything was okay. She replied, "Yes, we just need to stop for GongGong to use the restroom." He was uncomfortable using the one provided in the camper because the small compartment made him dizzy, plus he wanted more privacy. Not to mention that in those days, the rental campers were not made with today's modern conveniences or luxuries.

It was not an unreasonable request, especially since it was from my mother's father, and it was totally understandable that we stop. Plus, we needed to fill up with gas.

I assumed we would be stopping shortly, but no. Scham kept driving…and driving…

And driving.

I even found the courage to ask to go to the bathroom myself, so GongGong didn't have to bear the brunt of such embarrassing attention. Again, in those days, discretion and privacy for such matters were of the utmost importance, and for Scham to be so spiteful and cruel as to spotlight my grandfather's natural request was humiliating for my GongGong.

I hoped my request would jolt my mother to her senses so that she would finally say something, but almost an hour had passed, and GongGong was now pacing up and down the camper, using his arms to steady himself as Scham abruptly swerved around corners, hoping to cause GongGong to fall.

I could stand it no longer and ran to the front again. "Mommy, please! I really need to go! Why can't we stop?" I asked angrily, knowing I was going to suffer for this later.

My mother again asked Scham to stop, but he refused. She waited a few more moments and asked yet again, but again Scham refused. He insisted we keep driving. We passed by dozens of rest stops, restaurants, and gas stations, but Scham was maliciously making my grandfather suffer. I could even see him smirking in the rearview mirror.

I wanted to scream!

Finally, my grandfather, who was now enraged, walked up to Scham and demanded that he stop immediately!

"We're making good time—settle down old man!" he mocked, laughing at what he believed was another one of his brilliant, witty remarks.

Did I hear him right? Did this uneducated, ignorant, deficient, imbecile just call my grandfather—a medical doctor with his own TB hospital; a noble and dignified man who survived two World Wars, the Great Depression, and many revolutions; a man who rebuilt his and his family's life countless times—an "old man" who needs to "settle down"? Does he not know that it is this "old man" who is financially supporting my mother, who is in turn supporting him?

GongGong gathered himself, but he could no longer tolerate any more of Scham's malevolence. With absolute resoluteness in his voice, GongGong clearly and unmistakably demanded one last time that he stop at the next location.

My mother glared at Scham and *finally* said, "Just stop, Scham!"

Just so he could have the last say, he drove a few more miles, and when he finally did stop, he did so with great petulance. As he turned off the engine, he assailed us with a flurry of filthy curse words that now only seemed befitting for such a foul reprobate.

But no matter how much Scham tried to shame my grandfather, he could never steal his dignity. When we arrived, GongGong, with all the self-control he could summon, exited the camper without a word, and walked to the restroom inside a restaurant beside a gas station.

"How dare that ignorant, ill-bred, idiotic, onion-eyed, uneducated lout janitor dare to be so arrogant and cruel?!" Leah yelled out. "Please, tell me some rogue biker at that gas station kicked his backside back to the fiery pit from whence he came!"

I chuckled at her Elizabethan insult and replied, "Well, no. That never happened."

Leah smirked, "Too bad! I would have kicked his lily-livered, sorry-excuse-for-a-human-backside all the way to Timbuktu if I was there!"

Scham, totally oblivious to the effects of his appalling behavior, stood by the side of the gas station and stretched. He supposed himself to be an athlete in his homeland, and moronically bragged often about his abilities. When he saw a small patch of grass nearby, he attempted to show off a few gymnastic moves, all the while looking to see who might be watching him, as if to impress others nearby.

I was astonished that he did not know how ridiculous he was.

Unable to look upon this detestable Stupid Face any longer, I turned and saw my PoPo standing alone. She was looking around helplessly, not knowing what she should do. *What will she say to GongGong once he exits the restroom? What should she say to her daughter? What could be said? What does anyone say to something like this?*

The distress in PoPo's entire being was more than I could bear. I ran to her and hugged her tightly. She held me tightly back and said under her breath, "Oh, Manna…is it like this all the time?"

Too afraid to put them in the middle, all I could do was cry in her arms. If she only knew.

If she only knew.

Then Scham commanded us to go into the restaurant. "Driving all day makes an athlete *hun-gry*!" he announced. He laughed out loud again as if he had just said the most amusing thing ever. "Emily, get your family and meet me inside. I'm starving!"

PoPo, Luke, and I just stared at my mother in disappointment. She refused to look at us, said nothing, and followed him.

We, however, did not follow immediately. I released my hold of PoPo and took Luke's hand. He had been silent, looking down at the ground while biting his nails. The three of us stood in silence as we waited for GongGong, still jarred by the incident—indeed by the entire trip—and fraught with seemingly endless questions.

Did this kind of idiocy really exist? Or was this some kind of a sick joke? Was this cretin really in our lives? Why was my mother permitting—no, condoning—such abuse, not only to her children, but now to her parents? Why was my mother so weak and so easily corruptible? When would she see the truth and get rid of this beast who was terrorizing our lives?!

Though we had many more questions and thoughts, the one awareness that stood out the most was one I never verbalized. In the midst of my utter disappointment in this woman known as my mother, I realized I had finally completely lost respect for her.

GongGong was wise to have taken his time to gather himself, and when he came back to us, he looked at PoPo slowly, shook his head, and said, "Don't say anything. Let it go."

Nothing could have been said anyway to shift such a loathsome person. He wasn't worth the oxygen or the saliva, so my GongGong chose to save his energy for something more valuable instead; he chose to focus on us.

PoPo took a deep breath and did as he instructed. She gathered us in her arms like a mother hen with her chicks, and together with GongGong, we walked apprehensively towards the restaurant, bracing ourselves for whatever might come next. While I understood GongGong's request, I was at the boiling point of my own tolerance level. I did not know if I had the strength to stay silent and "let it go."

My mother was already inside and knew not to approach her father. She knew he was angry, and justifiably so. But what was not justifiable was *her own* behavior, and she knew that, too. Still, she did not apologize. And the more she said nothing, the more Scham believed he had free rein to do whatever he wanted.

The four of us filed into the restaurant in complete silence and were met with the sound of Stupid Face's harsh voice. "It's about damn time! What the hell were y'all doin' out there? Still learning to read English? It says 'r-e-s-t-a-u-r-a-n-t' right in front!" After bellowing his ignorance to every person in the restaurant, he guffawed hysterically to himself.

The fool had no idea that my grandfather was a gifted linguist who could speak many languages, while the nitwit before us had barely finished high school, and it was questionable whether or not he could even read.

My grandfather steeled himself, took a deep breath, and sat down, saying nothing. My grandmother was more transparent and glared first at Scham and then at my mother, who averted her eyes to avoid her mother's vehement disapproval.

I pursed my lips tightly because I wanted to scream! *How could my mother let this happen to her beloved parents who had done everything for her? I could tolerate her disdain for me, but I was unable to take her treatment of the two people who had only demonstrated love, sacrifice, and generosity to all of us!*

I dug my fingernails into my hands to prevent myself from losing control.

We were seated at a long booth. Luke, my mother, and Scham sat on one side, with Scham on the outside of the booth. GongGong, PoPo and I sat on the other side, and I sat directly across from Stupid Face. I refused to look at him—partially out of disgust, but mostly because I didn't know if I could contain myself anymore. The pressure of it all was becoming too much to bear, and I was afraid I would explode. Thankfully, no one said anything at the table; everyone avoided one another's eyes. The burden of restraint was heavy and palpable, as was the dark energy around us.

Thankfully, it didn't take long for a bubbly middle-aged waitress to come to our table. It was the perfect distraction at the perfect time.

But when she looked directly at me and said, "Well, hello there, how are you today?" I found my self-control painfully tested.

I looked up at her friendly face and leaned forward while simultaneously moving to the edge of my seat. I quickly glanced at my grandparents to my left, and then across to Luke (sitting diagonally across from me). Then I caught mother's eyes. It was as if she knew I was unable to withstand any more. She too, leaned forward—though only slightly. She might as well have been right in my face as her intention was that strong. She gave me one of her most evil glares yet, as if to say, "*Shut up! D'ya hear me?*"

Then I looked back up at the waitress, who was still looking at me. The moment seemed to stretch into lifetimes. I was indeed on the edge—a razor's edge, wanting desperately to scream out and to tell the waitress, "*No! I am not all right! Nothing is all right!*"

I wanted to grab onto her arm and beg her to help my family—to call the police so I could report this deranged madman who had taken our family captive and was heinously torturing us! I wanted her to call the local Social Services department so we could send my mother to an insane asylum where her mental deficiencies and egregiousness might be healed, or at the very least, where she would be severely medicated!

No, nothing was right at all in our lives. Nothing!

I lived a million years in that one moment, battling dueling intentions. I could scream for justice in an attempt to save my family, or suffer in silence, leaving my mother's and Scham's deceptions and illegitimate authority unchallenged.

My choice hung like a heavy raindrop suspended at the tip of a leaf as my mind raced and assessed every option, and consequence I could conceive. With each moment that passed, so did my hope for help.

PoPo knew I was about to say something and grabbed for my hand under the table as if to intercept my outburst. I looked down at her hand, trembling but firm, and knew in that instant that I could not say a word. I could not take the risk. My mother would have easily dismissed me as "just a spoiled child," and then Luke and my grandparents would have taken the brunt of Scham's wrath.

Slowly, I felt my head drop low in despair. I closed my eyes, feeling yet another part of my soul dying as the sense of loss and hopelessness continued to mount.

Only one thought spared me from giving up altogether. Only one thought buoyed me. *In six years, I will be fourteen years old. Luke and I will be able to choose with whom we want to live.*

In six years, we will be free.

Sticks and Stones

The silence from the restaurant continued until we arrived "home"—to our house of horrors behind closed doors.

For the remainder of their trip, PoPo and GongGong went about their days quietly, withdrawn from my mother and Scham. In fact, no one said much to anyone for the rest of their visit. Every day was eerily uneventful, which only made me dread what catastrophe awaited me next.

My grandparents went out quite a bit during the day when we were at school. I didn't know until later on that they were house hunting. They had purchased several homes in the area as investments and were now landlords of several properties. They had also purchased a home in the same town as Uncle Oliver so they could be close to him and his family as well. What I didn't know till later was that, in light of what they were discovering with Scham and my mother, they knew they had to move to Vancouver, sooner rather than later, in order to take care of us. The rental properties were to be their income since my GongGong would no longer be able to work once they moved here.

One day, our neighbor immediately to the west of us, a very nice widow, had her five-year-old granddaughter over to visit. Being older, I tried to teach her different games and even showed her how to turn a tricycle upside down, take a hose, and let the water run under the fenders while maneuvering the pedals so that it would splash all around us. We were having fun, but then she started demanding more and more.

I consented to all that she requested at first, but after *hours* of this, I grew weary of entertaining her, and refused her bidding. She immediately began crying aloud, and before I knew it, she was in such a fit that she was inconsolable.

Suddenly, I felt all this rage come upon me. The more I heard this little girl screaming, demanding that I amuse her, the angrier and angrier I became. *How spoiled! She has no idea how lucky she is! She has a normal life and normal parents! How dare she be so ungrateful? What a brat!*

In a flash, I screamed at the top of my lungs, "*Stop it!* Just play with the stupid bike! You have *no idea* how lucky you are, so *shut up* and stop being such a baby!" Now *I* was the one shaking and trembling uncontrollably.

The truth was, I was jealous of her. I, too, had been innocent at one time, and I was angry that she didn't know how to appreciate her safety, her freedom, and the love of her parents. I was only eight, but I had lost my trust in adults before I was six years old. While I was fighting for my sanity (and at times, feeling like I was fighting for my life), all this little "brat" could do was to demand that I be her clown. I had lost complete control and screamed at her with years and years of pent-up rage.

My unexpected outburst startled her, and she did stop crying, but evident in her tear-filled eyes was the look of fear. I knew I had hurt her feelings. Until that moment I had only ever been the recipient of hurtful words. Now I was their deliverer. *Name calling does hurt people and sticks and stones do break things inside of us. They break our hearts.*

Memories of people saying, "You're the spitting image of your mother" popped into my mind. Then other memories flooded in. Scham spewing his venom at us and cloaking me with his repulsiveness; my mother's contorted face as she butchered my hair; the back of her head each time she left me; her haunting screams of *"D'ya hear me?!* And then, the images of both of them ferociously and intentionally yelling, "You're nothing but stupid, ugly, and good-for-nothing!"

My tortured past bombarded me.

I froze. My greatest fear was that I had become like them—screaming hateful words at an innocent little girl who had done nothing wrong. I had simply found her irritating because she wasn't doing what I wanted. *Oh no! Have I become my mother? Have I become that ugly? Dear God, forgive me!*

Right there and then, I made a vow: *No matter what it costs me, I will never, ever hurt anyone again.*

At the time, this seemed like a good idea. If nothing else, it gave me some modicum of control over my life. I needed a standard and a strategy by which to navigate a family life that had no standards. Morals, kindness, and general logic were completely absent.

Unfortunately, while this internal vow was meant for good, it did nothing to protect me from *myself*. Over the course of my life, I suffered terribly with this as my rudder. I didn't say no when I should have because I didn't want to "hurt someone." And I didn't say yes when I should have because I didn't want to take something away from someone else.

Without anyone to talk to and without any way to understand what was happening in my life, I began giving up. I argued with my teachers and didn't always do my homework. Not knowing if anything I did would make a difference, I stopped trying to be "good" because frankly, most days, I only felt a gossamer thread of hope that my life could be better.

My ambivalence only fueled my mother's displeasure with me. She constantly compared my grades to Luke's, and since mine were less than remarkable, she felt justified to continue her criticism. No matter what I did or didn't do, nothing seemed to work, and I began to wonder if all the word curses my mother and Scham had said to me were true.

Maybe I was stupid. Maybe I was ugly. Maybe I was good-for-nothing. I didn't know what to think anymore.

With nowhere to run and no one to help me, I even became numb to Scham's abuse. Realizing he would finish sooner if I didn't fight him, I succumbed to his perversion. To survive, my mind took me into other realities—whether real or imagined—any other reality was better than the one to which I was bound.

In the midst of his deviancy, I would think about school, my friends, the next birthday party, my favorite television shows, or about places where I could be free like Barbie in her RV camper and go where his repugnancy and corruption could no longer reach me.

I Will Never Leave You

Our lives revolved around three things: my mother and Scham's unpredictable absences, their explosions when they were home, and their abuses. Neither playing with Lucky nor enjoying my delicious chocolate sandwiches could pull me out of my growing despair. One afternoon, I fell on my bed sobbing as anguish welled up within me. I tried to remember the promise I had been given so long ago and cried out to God.

"God, why are You doing this to me? You said You'd never leave me! Where are You?! It's nice that You painted me a picture in the grass, but I need You here *now*! Do You see what's going on here every day and night of my life? Do You see what is happening here? Of course You do…You're God! Don't You think it's *horrible*? How can You let this happen? How can You say You love me? I don't believe You love me! I don't believe You care!"

I screamed my "prayer" as loudly as I could, hoping that if I bellowed it out loud enough, it would reach Heaven itself, and God would finally hear my cries. But this time, there was no response. No symphony. No ballet. No masterpiece. Nothing.

Shocked at heaven's silence, exasperated, and uncertain what else to do, I gave my final ultimatum to God. "Fine! Be that way then! If You're going to be like this, I'm not talking to You anymore!"

In a huff, and with as loud of a "humph" as I could vocalize, I leaped off my bed and stormed toward the door. I slammed it shut as hard as I could as soon as I stepped into the hallway, thinking that I could close the door on God and separate Him from me. I looked back at the door and snorted another, "humph."

"Take that! I'm leaving You!" I threatened.

But no sooner had I finished my last word, I immediately felt the indisputable, unmistakable, and undeniable presence of God fall on me. I was overcome by the warmth, gentleness, and absoluteness of His love, and my knees went weak.

The weight and warmth of His love came so suddenly that I was taken off guard. I expected to have left God in the room when I shut the door. But here He was, all around me. Startled, amazed, and overjoyed all at once, I wanted to jump up and say, "There You are! I love You! I feel You! Thank You!"

But I was too afraid to believe again. I couldn't bear to lose this feeling another time, so instead of accepting God's love and grace, I rejected it.

"Fine. If You're going to be here, I'm leaving."

I stormed down the hall, but the power and tenderness of His presence followed me there. I went into the living room, and He was there, too! I hurried to the dining room where the piano was, and without question, He was there. I went to the kitchen, my mother's room, the bathroom, the back porch…

God was in each place. He was everywhere, and His presence was tangible. Even now, as I share this story, I can remember that glorious feeling of being so enveloped and covered with His love. God didn't leave me. In fact, He followed me everywhere I went.

Oh, how I wanted to believe!

More than anything, I wanted to believe!

More than anything, I wanted to hope, but I was too afraid to open the door of my heart. So, I spurned God again.

"Fine! You can have the upstairs. I know one place where You will *never go!*" I taunted.

The reality was, *I was* afraid to go to that place by myself and whimpered every time I had to go to the basement to do the laundry.

The stairs leading to the unfinished basement consisted of only slats, and it was unnerving to walk up them because you could see through each step. It was dark, and the air was thick with the smell of mothballs from the unopened crates we'd brought from Hong Kong. The windows were small, high, and caked with dirt and grass cuttings that were never washed off. Spiderwebs and dead, dried-up insects clung absently to the white stringy strands that seemed like they had been there since the beginning of time. I slowly crept down the stairs, one at a time, bleating from my own fear. But I had to know for certain that I could trust God. I had to know that He really did love me and that His promise to me was not only to *not leave me*, but to *always be with me*.

I didn't want a part-time God. I wanted an *always* God.

So, I put Him to the test, but to do so, I had to put myself in the darkest place I knew.

When I got to the bottom of the stairs, I turned right, and there, ahead of me, was the dark back corner of the basement. It had been framed for a bedroom, but now it was only storage space for unopened and forgotten crates. I was so scared I was barely breathing, but I had to complete my task. With trepidation, I slowly walked to that back corner where no one dared to go.

The one small window in this room was as dirty as all the others, but allowed for just enough light so I could see the little chain dangling from the single bare light bulb fixture in the unfinished ceiling. The cobwebby room reeked with a must and the pungent mothballs burned my nostrils. Still, I managed to climb over some trunks and toward the far corner of this frightening room. I tried to pull on the dangling chain to light up the room but could not reach it.

So, I tucked myself into that dingy, smelly corner, knowing God would never go there because it was the ugliest and darkest and most forgotten place ever.

I took a few deep breaths and waited. "You won't come here," I whispered, holding my arms around myself in the sunless corner.

Then, all at once, God filled me again with His warmth *and* His light. Even the black and grey room took on warm, sepia tones. I was so stunned, so overwhelmed, that I dropped my arms.

Yes, God was all around me, and His love was like it had been upstairs—palpable, distinct, and real. And now, instead of fear and anger, I could only feel this supreme sense of peace and comfort.

I love you, and I will never leave you.

It was not outwardly audible, but neither was it internal. God was *just there*, and He was telling me with His presence in that deep and utter darkness that there was no place so far, no loss so great, and no action so desperate as to prevent Him from being with me.

Be Strong and Very Courageous

My father would come as often as he could, and whatever times we did have together, we loved. As soon as we got in the car for our weekend visits, and throughout our entire visit, he would tell us how much he loved us.

"Children, Daddy is working hard to make a way for us to be together. I have a contract with the RCMP for a little while longer. As soon as that's done, I will move back, and we can be together more often. Until then, be patient, okay, little ones?"

We nodded, holding back our tears.

"I know it's not easy, but you must be strong and be very courageous. Don't talk back. Just smile and do whatever they ask."

We nodded again, the tears now running down our faces.

If he only knew what he was asking of me...

On Sunday mornings, total and complete dread would wash over us, because we knew that later that afternoon we would have to return to our house of horrors.

On many occasions, I would have rather died than go back there. Still, I said nothing.

"Why didn't you tell anyone?!" Leah interrupted. "You could have told your father, and he would have taken it to the authorities! Then you could have lived with him for certain, and that beast would have gone to jail for physical and sexual abuse of a minor! God only knows what would have happened to your mother!"

"Leah, there was no way I could tell my father. In the eyes of a little girl, he was my hero. I couldn't bear for him to know how tainted and dirty his little girl had become. But much more importantly, my father was a very high-ranking law enforcement official, and so were his colleagues. He was also a martial arts master. I was worried he would have killed Scham!"

"And you thought that was a bad thing?!" Leah jumped in.

"It wasn't the possibility of Scham's death that concerned me. I was concerned about what would happen if my father took things into his own hands! There was no guarantee that my father would simply go to the authorities. Think about it. What normal man would simply go to the authorities after discovering that for years his ex-wife's boyfriend had been molesting and beating his beloved young daughter and physically abusing his young son, while living in *rent-free* in his home?

"Scham wasn't worth ruining another life over. He had already done such irreparable damage to all of us, and I would *never* have given him the satisfaction of hurting my father any more than he already had."

"Hmmm...yes, I can see that's quite a dilemma, and for such a young little girl. You weren't even ten yet! Well, my dear, you were indeed a brave little one. You not only courageously endured such abuse, you did so without relief to protect those you loved," she acknowledged.

"That's nice of you to say, but I wasn't trying to be brave. I loved my family, and I just did what I thought was right to do."

"Please tell me that somewhere in this sad state of affairs your mother realized Stupid Face was no upgrade! Tell me she found some basic common sense, or at least some human decency, and kicked that dolt, that bugger out onto the curb! You gotta give me that!" she declared.

"Well, unfortunately, I'm afraid she never did…in fact—"

"Nooooooooo!" she said slowly with disbelief, anticipating what I was about to say next. "Don't tell me…"

"Yup, she married him."

No Room At The Inn

"Oh, my dear God in heaven! She married him?" Leah shouted, leaning forward in shock.

"Yes, she did, and they chose their wedding day to be the day after my birthday, so there was no celebration for me. They swept that away—like they did everything else having to do with me—and made their day together the focus for everyone else too. Forever afterward, my birthday was a non-event, a mere hurdle on the path to their anniversary.

"Yet there was a wonderful positive side to their marrying; my grandparents moved to Vancouver, and Luke and I were given to them to care for while my mother and Scham lived their own private lives, separate from us."

"What?" Leah shook her head again. "What do you mean they lived separately from you?"

"My mother and Scham moved into a one-bedroom apartment downtown so they could enjoy a new, active, and exciting urban life of their own, childless. We were not wanted. We were not welcomed. It was made abundantly clear when they got a *one-bedroom* apartment."

"Are you kidding me?" Leah declared, flabbergasted.

"No. That's exactly what happened. Worse, while we were forced to live meagerly, once they were married, they lived a life of luxury. When they took Luke and me to see their apartment one day, it was filled to bursting with high-end items and furnishings. They had brand new art, heavy and expensive wood furniture, a plush sofa, a Lay-z-Boy chair, and the most modern glass dining room table I'd ever seen. Sheepskin rugs covered their plush carpeting, and they had a top-of-the-line color TV with the latest stereo console. The console had two separate lids on top that hinged at the back. One side opened to a turntable, and the other side opened to a radio and cassette player. The front of this massive stereo console was carved, with red velvet covering behind it.

"Little did I know that this piece of furniture would one day be the scene of one of the most dangerous beatings I ever endured from Scham."

It's Easy to be Weak

"Argh! I'm aghast at this mad woman you were forced to call your mother," Leah grumbled, furiously. "What was she thinking?"

"I don't know, and like I said before, no one knows to this day. At best, all I can do is speculate as to her motives. Perhaps she resented me for loving my grandparents and my father so openly. Perhaps she was embarrassed at being a Chinese divorcée with two children. Maybe having a Caucasian man somehow validated her…"

"Bah! That's hogwash!" Leah interjected. "Having a pig as a companion doesn't validate anyone! He was nothing but white trash—a manipulating opportunist living off your mother! That's who he was! A lunkhead, a blight on humanity, period! Don't you defend her like that! Plus, she had no problem going out before, when she was still married to your father!"

"I'm not trying to defend her; I'm just trying to find ways to understand her. I've forgiven her many times over the years…but I confess, it's challenging to recount these details to you without a heavy heart." I looked down and took a deep breath.

Leah pursed her lips in frustration. "I understand the heavy heart, but to forgive either of them? Now who's crazy?" she shot. "They're *unforgivable*!"

"Leah, we've all done things that have hurt others. It's not our job to weigh and measure every circumstance, to categorize them, and then to render judgment according to our perception of justice. That only begets more of the same spirit—hatred. I know I've done some foolish and hurtful things in my life, and if I would like to be forgiven for them, and if I would like to have an opportunity for a new beginning, then I ought to extend that same grace to others, too. I don't have to be a doormat, nor do I have to ever see that person again. I just have to make sure *my heart* is right."

"But, Manna, you're different. You learn from your mistakes. Other people don't. Instead of becoming better people, they dig deeper into their cesspool and continue perpetrating their madness on others!" Leah objected. "Scham's a classic! And I'm sure you can think of many others like that, too! I know I can."

"Yes, but we can still learn from those people. We can learn how *not* to be. Anyone who constantly creates or participates in that kind of energy can't truly be happy, peaceful, or healthy. I never want to be like that."

"Like I said, I'm not worried about you, but people like Scham and your mother are unforgivable!" Leah insisted.

I took a deep breath and continued. "Unforgiveness is like a terrorist. It torments you day and night as if you were a POW. It poisons you with bitterness and hatred, stealing your life away, one thought at a time. The only way to deal with unforgiveness is to destroy it."

"How do you do that?" Leah asked, still defiant.

"With forgiveness." I paused. "By forgiving those who have hurt us, we are delivered from handcuffs that chain us to the past. When we forgive others, we become free to create a more beautiful present, and thereby a greater future.

Otherwise, we'll keep perpetuating the transgressions that postpone the healing and freedom available to us. Instead of leaving the trespass as dead—*a completed action that occurred in the past where it belongs*—we keep it alive, allowing it to haunt us in our present. It continues to rob us of our joy, peace, vitality, and meaning. Eventually, we'll lose our focus, purpose, and opportunity to contribute to the lives of others, and suffer a slow, miserable death in the quicksand of self-pity."

"Sounds good in theory, but your mother and that buffoon? You give them too much credit," Leah doubted.

"Leah, forgiveness isn't valuing someone else over yourself. It's not about condoning ill-willed actions, nor is it about absolving the 'perpetrator.' Forgiveness is actually a gift we give to ourselves. When we forgive, we become untangled from the past and free ourselves from the people involved. It's an act of self-care!" I took another deep breath, forming my thoughts. "I'm not saying it's easy, Leah. Nothing great ever comes easily. Blaming and hating my mother and Scham would have been *easy*, but I wanted my freedom more than I wanted to be 'right.' We'll never become the people we were created to be if we keep blaming others for who we are. The weak blame. The strong forgive."

"So, are you telling me it's okay to let all the crazies waltz back into my life again?" Leah challenged.

"No. 'Forgiveness' is not the same as 'trust.' Just because you forgive someone doesn't mean you welcome him (or them) back into your life with carte blanche access. Trust has to be earned. And each situation is different. We must pray for wisdom. I should also add, forgiveness isn't always a one-time event, either. There were times I had to forgive my mother and Scham repeatedly through the day as different memories bubbled up. But with practice, forgiveness became easier and easier. Now, I can honestly say I'm free and at peace." I paused. "But do you know who the hardest person to forgive really is, Leah?"

She shook her head. "Harder than your mother and Stupid Face?! Who?"

"Ourselves. That's why the practice of forgiveness is so important. Forgiveness is for *everyone*, including *you and me*. To forgive ourselves can be the hardest thing we do. Self-forgiveness is an act of love."

Leah was quiet a long time, and as she looked away, far beyond the window scene outside, I knew she was thinking about the many injustices in her life—those she had received, and those she had given.

After I poured Leah a fresh cup of tea, she directed her attention back to my story. "Okay, my dear. You made some points on that round. I'll noodle this a bit and deliver my verdict later. Until then, let's get back to you." She nodded with intention. "All I can say is, thank God you were able to move back with your grandparents! Your life must have been much better then!"

Content in knowing the seed of freedom—forgiveness—was planted, I obliged and continued with the story.

"Yes, it was *much* better, but only for a short time. The damage to my heart and soul had been done and I was a very troubled young girl. I did not like myself, and most of the time I wanted to be anyone but me. The daily refrain of, "stupid, ugly, and good-for-nothing" had beaten me down. Together with Scham's corruption, the ongoing racial discrimination, my beautiful long hair butchered, and being told I was the spitting image of my mother, I began to *even hate* myself."

"That saddens me." she said tenderly. "How did you overcome this? I'm amazed how nothing about you reveals your horrific childhood!"

I smiled.

Leah knew what I was about to say, and rolling her eyes, she answered for me, "I know, I know, I know…God."

"Yup. I can't take credit for His miracles." My smile grew.

"Well, you must be one of the lucky ones. There isn't a trace of anger, resentment, or bitterness in you. Nothing! I know people who've gone through less than you have, and it's all over their faces. Mine too, I'm afraid," Leah said, looking down and smoothing her blanket. "But you…you only seem to smile—unless I've said something to stir the pot of course!" She winked. "Is 'forgiveness' *really* the answer? What's your secret, Manna…? What's the secret ingredient?"

I shook my head and smiled. "Forgiveness is a huge part of our journey, but there isn't just one single secret ingredient. There are many wonderful keys and tools at our disposal. But, if I did have a few simple words of advice—aside from prayer—I'd say, reserve your final decision until the story is over. Until then, have a thankful heart, keep believing because you don't know the whole story, and just stay the course. Persevere to the very end. Too many people give up and pass final judgment on others, and *themselves,* just before the miracle happens."

"That's it? It's that simple?" Leah challenged.

"Simple, yes. Easy, no. Great accomplishments are rarely easy to achieve. But a grateful heart will achieve more than a shriveled up, dark, hardened heart does. A life of joy can be a simple matter of *choice*—one of our greatest gifts."

"That's your story, and you're stickin' to it, huh?"

"Yup. So, Leah…it's up to you. What will you choose?

5 DELIVER US FROM EVIL

"While we must accept finite disappointment, we must never lose infinite hope."

— Martin Luther King, Jr.

Room 316

Leah St. John had now become more of a friend than a volunteering assignment, and I visited her several times per week instead of only once per week. Our conversations had become deeply meaningful and tender, and while her one-liners were still zingy, she had clearly allowed me into the inner chambers of her heart.

We enjoyed a natural ebb and flow in our talks. As I continued to share, so did she. The many tales of her own childhood made us both laugh and cry. Leah's life story was rich and riveting, and the passion in her spirit endeared her to me.

As I heard Leah speak, I became acutely aware of the compelling story hidden in each of us, embedded in each event, each smile, and each tear. Lessons of wisdom, love, and hope, when told, release into the atmosphere opportunities for healing and for goodness to triumph over evil. Through our testimonies of overcoming, we empower others to "fight the good fight of faith" so that we might leave a powerful living legacy of hope and possibility for those following behind us.

And so, in this spirit, Leah and I continued to share. Our time together had become like long-time friends chatting over tea. Her hospital room had transformed also. It changed from being a sterile place, full of medical equipment and a cot on wheels, to more of a warm and cozy den. With the head nurse's permission, I substituted a few of the non-essential hospital items for more personal ones. I took down the humdrum print on the wall and brought in a painting from my home. The old hospital chair that looked like it came from an office consignment store was replaced by a brightly upholstered wingback chair, also from home. And instead of a drab, tan-colored hospital blanket, a handmade quilt with artful patterns now covered Leah.

From time to time, I brought fresh flowers or different foods from fun local restaurants so Leah could experience a bit more of the world "out there" while she was "in here." I introduced her to the world of vegetarian and raw-food *dining*, which she didn't care for much at first, but grew to enjoy.

"It's bad enough that my taste buds are dying along with the rest of my body! Can't you bring me something with flavor or gusto?" she objected before taking her first few bites.

I laughed, saying, "Just try it! You'll love it—I promise!"

She humored me at first, but it wasn't long before she started asking for more of those dishes. In between healthy mouthfuls, she would declare, "Why in the world didn't anyone introduce me to this before? Land's sake—this is delicious! It's like a party in my mouth!"

One day I even overheard her telling a friend on the phone she was now a vegan and touted the benefits of eating healthy as if she had been living that way for decades.

Ah, yes, Leah St. John made me smile.

With each passing day, not only did I grow to love her more, I also knew I was closer to saying goodbye. The inevitable parting was like that proverbial "elephant in the room." But rather than feeling trapped by the elephant, dreading the moment, we chose to focus on the joy we shared as we learned more about each other and ourselves.

After every story, I wondered which one would be the one that held the infamous "key" she had so prophetically declared would free her. We never again referred to that afternoon visit, but that conversation was always present for me—and knowing Leah, it was present for her as well.

Sharing painful, private, and vulnerable memories *was not* my idea of fun, nor was it my idea of what the job description might be for a hospice volunteer. However, just as she had suspected, the stories were reaching her. With each visit, Leah's eyes sparkled a little bit more than they had the last time I saw her. Her countenance continued to brighten, and her heart both softened and began to grow.

During a quiet moment in between stories and tea, Leah said out of the blue, "I appreciate you, Manna."

I looked up from my purse as my hands searched for my glasses.

"Well, Miss Leah…" I paused. "I appreciate you, too."

She fidgeted with a corner of the quilt laying over her and cleared her throat. "Umm, what I mean by that is, I…ummm…well…I really *appreciate* you," she repeated, now using both hands to slowly flatten and smooth the quilt over her tummy.

I put my purse down, smiled, and paused a moment before softly responding, "I love you too, Leah."

She grabbed my hand and held it tight. We gave each other a warm, knowing smile and with tears pooling in her eyes, she whispered, "I'm going to miss you…"

At my next visit with Leah, she wasted no time in asking to pick up where we had left off the previous day.

"You have to tell me!" she burst out, "What happened next? I haven't stopped thinking about it since you left."

"Of course, Leah. Let me take off my jacket first." I had barely walked into the room and hadn't even said hello. "Are you in a rush to go somewhere?" I asked jokingly.

"Very funny. No, I just don't want to be held in suspense. You've kept me waiting for a day and a half to hear the next part!"

"Hmmm, are you sure, Leah? Are you feeling okay? How have you been sleeping? Is the new medication still making you feel badly?"

She begrudgingly indulged me and answered my questions, but I could see that she was restless. When at last I began the slow return to my story, she lay back into her pillow, and neatly tucked the quilt around her. Her expression softened, and the corners of her mouth turned up in a smile.

True Lies

It was now the early 1970s, and Luke and I were living with PoPo and GongGong, not too far from Uncle Oliver's home. I was a "tweener"—older than a "kid" but not yet a teenager.

My mother and Scham had been living their own private, independent lives for some time, and we only saw them occasionally. Since they were now married, they felt justified in demanding their privacy and insisted on having time alone to build *their* life together.

"The kids only get in the way. We deserve this time alone." I overheard her say to my grandparents.

There's a saying in reference to garage sales: "One man's trash is another man's treasure." To my mother and Scham, we were like the unwanted items at a garage sale—dispensable and unworthy to join in the new life they had planned for themselves. We had no emotional value to them, except for the money they could get for us. Thankfully, PoPo and GongGong saw us as treasures and were only too happy to take us in.

My father never knew that we didn't live with them, as my mother and Scham contrived elaborate schemes to hide this fact from him. On my father's weekends, they would either transport us to Uncle Oliver's home or to some other inconvenient and arbitrary public location that my father had to find in order to pick us up.

The few times we did see my mother and Scham, it was for dinner, but the visits were short. Be assured, for Luke and me, this short visit was not a bad thing. We were happy *not* to see Scham often (or for very long), especially during mealtimes when we had to watch him eat. However, not seeing our mother regularly, when we were so young and living in the same city, only accentuated the bizarreness of our "family." They lived less than twenty-five minutes away! Worse, when we did see her, she was never alone. Scham was always with her, and she soon became more like a distant relative than a mother.

We tried to be close to her, demonstrating affection by holding her hands or talking about school, but we did not receive the same efforts in return—at least I didn't. Our conversations were artificial, strained, and unnatural. It only seems reasonable that they would have let us live with our father since they didn't want us anyway, but they wanted the child support money and the government checks to subsidize their lifestyle, so their fraudulent pretense continued.

So, my father was deceived, and my grandparents were held hostage. PoPo and GongGong did not approve of my mother's actions, but no amount of reason could rein in her selfishness. She and Scham were determined to do what they wanted to do. And they did.

Again, this is why my grandparents moved to Canada—to step in with the hope of protecting us. They wanted to give us some sort of normalcy in our daily lives and a chance at some kind of a future. Their sacrifice was great. GongGong retired early, leaving a thriving medical practice. They also sold their investment properties in China (not to mention most of their belongings), and left behind other family, longtime friends, and their comfortable way of life to start over in a new country. They did all this, just so they could take care of their daughter's unwanted children.

After having suffered the ugliness of Scham's arrogance, the consequences of selfishness, and the cruelty of self-indulgence, I made my second vow. I would never cause other people around me to suffer the consequences of my actions, nor would I ever again allow myself to be in the wake of someone else's arrogance, greed, or selfishness.

Like my first vow, as gallant and noble as it sounded, it could never be fully satisfied. In the end, I was (once again) the one who ended up suffering the most. I have since learned this lesson—but not until I had endured much harm, loss, pain, and near defeat.

And though both of my vows taught me self-discipline, compassion, and tolerance, they were short-sighted.

I did not have the experience or wisdom to consider self-care, boundaries, and just plain personal preferences. I had not yet learned the difference between having the gift of mercy and bearing a false burden until late into my forties. So, when I thought I was being kind and compassionate, I was unknowingly taking on hardships and trials that were never mine to bear to begin with.

In addition to the vows that I made, I also developed a keen sensitivity to traits like selfishness, irresponsibility, and stupidity in those around me. By "stupidity" I mean the idiotic absurdity and ignorance demonstrated as a result of arrogance and hubris, not capacity.

I could distinctly see all these qualities in both Scham and my mother, and as I grew older, these detestable traits were kindling to my fury when I saw them, especially when innocent people were victimized.

"Ahh, your Achilles heel!" Leah surmised.

"Yes, I confess I become *activated* when I see these traits in people, especially the stupidity trait arising from someone's arrogance and hubris. That one can send me to the moon fairly quickly."

"Oh, Manna! You can say it!"

Perplexed, I responded, "Say what, Leah?"

"It pisses the hell outta you! You're not just politely *activated*! If I were you, I'd be damn pissed off at anyone behaving even remotely like Stupid Face and that woman who birthed you!"

"Oh, Leah…"

"Well, I'm just calling a spade a spade! Now, *you call a spade a spade!*"

I thought a moment. "Okay. You're right. I do get really pissed off when I see people acting maliciously selfish. When they won't take responsibility or be accountable for their actions, blaming others for everything instead. You are right, I do get really angry." I pounded the edge of the bed with my fist. "Saying and doing stupid things because they're so damn arrogant on top of it all—yes, it sends me into the stratosphere!" I roared.

"Now, that's my girl!" she said.

We both laughed out loud and took a respite from the heaviness of the topic. Then Leah gingerly said, "But seriously, you must have been happy to be back with your grandparents though."

"Yes, I was thrilled to live with my grandparents again. And in the safety of their love and care, I was able to experience life without anxiety or fear for a while."

Kitchen Conversations

Although we had to move to another area of town, I was grateful for the chance to have a new start with a new home, new friends, a new school and real love to bolster our hearts.

And, I could now speak English extremely well, even though I was still the target of much racism. I was about to start a new school knowing no one, but I was not nearly as lonely as I was before. I was free from the daily fatuity of life with my mother and Scham, and for that, I was extremely grateful. Many times, I would lie on my bed and soak in my good fortune. and thank God for this respite. Yes, I was safe again.

Instead of falling asleep broken, and with tears, I fell asleep hopeful, and with a smile.

For a while, life moved more gently, and I spent a lot of time thinking about, and talking to, God. This may sound a little nutty, but I assure you these were some of the most "real" and treasured experiences of my youth. I learned a lot more about life during those precious times of communing with "Papa" (my term for God), and I started to learn about the process of "training for the soul"—how we are equipped and purified through trials and fire for a great calling.

I used to think that the reason Scham was still in our lives was because I had failed God somehow, that I had missed the mark so badly that Scham was some sort of punishment for my misbehaviors. But in truth, I was not being punished. I was, in fact, being strengthened through all those difficulties, so that these painful times could one day be used to help others.

Lucky was given away when we moved, and I was heartbroken.

Being with my grandparents comforted me, but my heart ached for Lucky. I missed my best friend terribly but was happy knowing he was with a family who loved him even more than I did. PoPo knew how much having a pet would mean to me, but she was concerned about her ability to properly care for a dog. So, one day, she surprised me with a beautiful white cat as a friendly companion. She also let me have a few gerbils and helped me make a cage for them. They couldn't replace Lucky, but little by little, I began to let him go in my heart.

In time, I made a few friends at school, and one of them, a kind girl named Kathy, took me in. She was a volunteer with the SPCA in our neighborhood and introduced me to the organization. She knew I loved dogs (and animals in general), and she made me a member of her club. I was overjoyed and felt like I was a part of something meaningful at long last. She would also frequently invite me to her home after school, where we would do our homework together and find ways to save abused or unwanted cats and dogs. Her compassion for the unwanted and abused may have been how she found me and why she took me in. Like a stray, she helped me get back on my feet.

I felt safe and accepted with Kathy. She didn't judge me or make fun of me for being Chinese, or for living with my grandparents. In her eyes, I was normal. She didn't see my race first, what I looked like, or judge me for my family dynamics—and even if she did, those differences were not a barrier to friendship. I was just a girl like her, and she liked me for who I was.

Amazing!

On Saturdays, she took me to a place called Mosquito Creek. Prepared with our tomato and mayonnaise sandwiches, we hiked up and down the creek, imagining we were pioneers looking for a new land. Though we were pretending to brave new territories, it was not a silly game to me. For me, deep in my heart, I was intentionally taking a step toward my future, believing that one day I would permanently get away from my mother and Scham and my memories of life with them. With each step, I determined that I would find "new land" and be free—and not just temporarily like we were with PoPo and GongGong.

Yes, I loved my grandparents and savored each day with them, but I always knew my mother and Scham were in the background, and in our lives. Still, I made the most of my dreamlife while enjoying the comfort of a loving, daily routine with my grandparents. Waking up to them and coming home to them every day after school allowed me to breathe. For the first time since I left Hong Kong, I looked forward to coming "home."

One of the many ways PoPo demonstrated her love for us was through her cooking. An old Chinese saying fitted her perfectly in this respect: "You can taste the love that's in the food."

PoPo made me aware that before cooking any meal, it was only natural to start thinking about the people who would be sharing that meal— who they are, what they like, and what specialties can be prepared to make them happy. She spent hours grocery shopping, looking for the perfect carrot, turnip, or piece of fish.

With this mindset toward food, even grocery shopping became a beautiful ceremony of love. Before you knew it, you were reminiscing about the fun times you had together, contemplating the beauty of their smiles, the light in their eyes, and how much you loved them. Because of PoPo's influence, I too, like a sweet prayer of love, meditate upon my family and friends whenever I prepare meals for them.

We lived on a street with a bus route that would take me directly to school. Every school morning after fixing breakfast, preparing lunches, and seeing us out the door, PoPo went to her bedroom window and waited there until she could see me on the bus when it went by. She also patiently and faithfully waited at her window every afternoon on my way home, scanning each window of the bus to see where I was sitting. Every time she saw me, she lovingly waved and blew me kisses. I blew kisses and waved back, even though other kids smirked at me for doing so.

The love she gave meant everything to me, and no amount of mocking could have stopped our daily rituals.

Every day after school, our routine of love and food continued. As soon as I ran through the front door, I would smell the aroma of some wonderful treat she prepared and had waiting at the table. As I ate my scrumptious snack, she would sit across from me, keeping me company, always prepared to give me "seconds." She asked me about my day and what I had learned. Then she would share her day with me, keeping me current on the happenings of her favorite television programs.

In our kitchen conversations, she taught me her special techniques to make certain dishes. It was impossible *not* to notice the time and care she took in preparing meals for me. But no matter how tedious or laborious the steps were, she always did them lovingly and *joyfully*. Little did I know, I was being let into the generational secrets of our family's recipes. The immensity of her love and generosity of her magnificent heart created precious memories for me that would last a lifetime. PoPo taught me enriching and unforgettable life lessons—the greatest one of all is that *love can be shared all the time, in small and great ways, in everything you do.*

One dish in particular that my GongGong loved was comprised mainly of bean sprouts or "mung beans," as they are typically called in North America. If you know something about mung beans, you know that each sprout has a darker brown root ending, as well as a kind of detachable casing or membrane on the head of the bean. PoPo would first thoroughly wash a very large bag of mung beans. After carefully patting them dry with a towel, she would pinch the root ends off each and every sprout. PoPo then removed any loose casings from the head of the bean—one at a time. Sometimes this process alone would take an hour to do, and it was just enough for one meal. Her fingers looked like prunes by the time each individual sprout had received her attention.

Initially, I thought she went through this elaborate process because the roots or the casings were dirty, but when I shared my theory with her, she simply explained she did this because GongGong liked it better this way. Her work had nothing to do with cleanliness or taste; it had everything to do with her desire to please her husband.

"That was it? Simply because your grandpa liked it this way?" interrupted Leah. "That's some grandmother of yours! Knowing more about your grandparents makes it even more confusing how your mother turned out so, so…odd!" she added.

"Yes, my PoPo was amazing. She went through such tedium, simply because someone she loved enjoyed a dish prepared that particular way."

"Wow. I was never that nice to my husband!" Leah snorted as she laughed out loud.

Although I was tremendously grateful to be living with my grandparents, I was no longer a baby or a toddler, I was a young girl approaching puberty.

I was already so unlike every other typical kid at school and living with my grandparents made the very fact that I was peculiar even more undeniable. I was Chinese, I wasn't wanted, and I didn't belong. I had been told I was "stupid, ugly and good-for-nothing" for most of my life, and together with all the physical, mental, and sexual abuse, I felt worthless.

I did my best to fit in while trying to silence the voices of frustration and darkness in my soul, but nothing worked. Unable to contain the dissonance any longer, I began to despise anything that represented my family. I did not want to be Chinese any more than I wanted to be Manna. My behavior began to reflect this deep dissatisfaction with myself, which turned into self-loathing. I only wanted to die—and prayed many times for death to come upon me.

Meanwhile, my mother and Scham travelled across the globe, spent money wildly, and lived in the lap of luxury. They also traded in the car my grandparents bought my mother and purchased a brand-new car— a white, two-door Buick Century with a red interior. White and red was always my mother's favorite combination, but Scham again acted as if this was his car, bragging as if it was a Rolls Royce! I could barely stomach his talking about it. Plus, they were also secretly buying a brand-new house for themselves, and a speed boat, which I found out about later.

When they purchased a two-hundred-dollar white Persian cat (worth thousands of dollars today) from an elite breeder, that's when I lost my composure.

Not only were they flaunting their extravagance, my mother now flagrantly demonstrated more love for her purebred cat than for her own children—or her parents. Luke and I received no new clothes for our growing bodies, and only a few items for school. We were simply unwanted belongings in a storage container called "'grandparents' house," and my grandparents were their inexpensive nannies.

I silently calculated all of this inequity and confronted PoPo one day.

"Does my mother give you any money at all to help support us?"

"Manna, you shouldn't ask such things."

"I want to know!" I demanded. I wanted to be respectful out of love for PoPo, but not as much as I wanted to get to the bottom of this ignominy. "She spends money on herself and Scham all the time and makes you take care of us! I want to know if she at least pays you for the expenses of keeping a home, food, school supplies, and what few clothes we have. Does she give you even a little of the child support money from Daddy or the government checks?"

"It's disrespectful to ask about such things, Manna," she chided gently. "GongGong and I are happy to rear you and your brother. Yes, she does give me some…but…well, that's the end of it."

But it wasn't the end of it for me, and I told her so—in my intolerant, pre-adolescent voice—and stormed off to my room.

Bus Stop

"Scham was no longer an orderly at the hospital—"

"You mean a *janitor*," Leah said, interrupting. "Come on Manna, tell it like it is. A spade is a spade, remember?" Leah interrupted.

I smiled and continued. "He was now a bus driver, and he loved his new job."

"Of course he would! He wasn't cleaning bedpans like mine anymore!" she joked.

We both chuckled.

"He used to say, 'Everyone I know *vanted zis* job, *unt* I'm *ze von zat got it!*

Now *zer* all jealous of me! I get paid overtime *unt* get benefits too! It's a steal!'" I shook my head. "He was truly embarrassing."

To my dismay, Scham sometimes drove the afternoon bus route I had to take home to PoPo's. On one particular day, PoPo gave me permission to bring a friend home, and I chose a girl who was also a bit of a misfit to play with me. She was taller than most of us, had straight red hair that was bluntly cut at ear level, freckles, and unusually large lips. She had also reached puberty early and was the constant target of the other students' ridicule.

As luck would have it, Scham was driving the bus that same day, and as soon as he saw my friend, his eyes lit up because he saw her shapeliness. His expression was so vulgar that I literally felt nauseous right there and then. I immediately knew I would never take this bus again. If she came back to PoPo's house with me, we would walk, even though it was many, many miles away, or wait another half hour for the next bus to come. I couldn't bear the thought of Scham looking at her in that vile way.

My fears were confirmed when he continued to ask about her each time I saw each him on our rare visits with my mother. This went on for months until I finally told him her family moved to another city. I don't know if that sweet girl did move to another city, but I do remember the boys had been nothing less than abominable to her, and their malice had forced her to leave the school altogether.

That was the first time I saw someone besides me being bullied. When the bullying had happened to me, I thought it was "normal" because I was Chinese, I was a girl, I brought horrible lunches, and had a weird family. But when my friend became the target of bullying, I was stunned, and I was afraid. She wasn't Chinese; she was white! She should have been accepted and included as one of their own, but she had been tormented simply because she looked different.

It was at this time that I made my third vow—I would always help the helpless. This promise seemed to fit well with the other two—that I would never intentionally hurt someone, and that I would never cause other people around me to suffer the consequences of my actions.

Again, although I meant well, I had no idea the depths or the cost of what I was pledging. Not only did I suffer greatly for making these vows, I often stepped into situations that weren't mine to step into—intercepting valuable opportunities for others to learn through their situations simply because I was uncomfortable with seeing them in pain. Worse, I had also unknowingly stepped into the role of playing God, deciding (based on my limited knowledge, ability, perception, and maturity) what was "right" and what was "wrong."

"Oh, Manna, you suffered so much. Yet you still tried to help others..." Leah paused before finishing her thought. "Knowing you now, I have no choice but to admit, God must be real. He *must be.* There is no way you could have come out of this and be so 'good' without Him on your side!"

"Yes, God is real, and though He never wanted for me—or any of us, to suffer such pain, He will give us the courage and the strength to get through it when we call on Him."

"The depth of your faith is difficult to comprehend. It's gentle, yet powerful at the same time. Your courage is evident, though, as is your strength." Leah looked at me with her all-knowing look and then reluctantly admitted, "I know I fuss and protest, but I admit, I can see how God was in your life—it *had to be Him.* I'm starting to believe you."

"Really?"

"Yes, and I'm starting to *feel* a little different too…." Leah touched her chest with her frail hands and closed her eyes for a moment. "Maybe I can grab a hold of this faith like you have…and, maybe, just maybe," Leah now clasped her hands together, almost in a prayer, "God will grab a hold of me like He has you."

"He already has, Leah. He's just waiting for you to hold Him back."

With her eyes still closed, she smiled and rested her hands back on her lap, contemplating the possibility of what I had just said. After a few quiet moments, she opened her eyes again, and with the familiar wave of her hand, ordered me to continue with my story.

Lost In Translation

One of the things I had come to love about Canada was the snow.

I marveled at its existence. Every snowflake that fell was like a kiss from heaven. And when it snowed, it felt as though the world was quiet and still from chaos. Since my grandparents' home was located at the bottom of Grouse Mountain, a favorite local skiing draw, we enjoyed an abundance of snow. I would find myself lost in reverie as I stared at tree branches dressed with white dollops of snow and glistening against the streetlights. Snow was magical for me, and anytime I could see it or play in it I was happy.

One day in class, the teacher announced a new program had just launched at our school called "Outdoor School in the City," and it included a week of ski lessons on Grouse Mountain. All we needed were signed permission slips from our parents.

I was overjoyed. *At last,* I thought to myself, *here's a way I can learn what my friends already know and be a part of their weekend activities! Maybe now I have a chance of fitting in, a way to belong! Plus, it's part of a course curriculum! How perfect!*

That afternoon, I was barely through the front door before I was already asking PoPo if I could attend this course. With my coat still on and my school bag over my shoulders, I followed her to the kitchen. As she prepared my snacks,

I explained the program and all its benefits, and begging for her to sign the permission slip.

"Please, please, *pleeeeeez*, PoPo! Please sign this!" I pleaded.

"Let me get my glasses, dear. Just wait a moment. Take off your coat and eat your snacks."

She read everything and said, "Well, it seems okay to me, but you don't have ski clothes or equipment."

"I don't need it. See? Read this part right here…" I reached across the table and pointed to the paragraph that said the supplies would be provided for a small fee of ten dollars. The remainder was covered by the school.

"Well, it does look wonderful, but I can't be the one to decide this. It has to be your mother."

"What!" I retracted with shock. "What does she have to do with this? She's not a part of our lives, and she doesn't care anyway! We hardly see her, and isn't she in Hawaii again? Please, Grandma! Please, sign it!" I implored.

"Manna, I love you," she said with a smile as she helped me with my school bag and coat. "I know your mother hasn't been…" her voice drifted.

"See! Even you can't pretend she cares! Plus, even if she says yes, it will be too late by the time they get back! I have to give them my permission slip by next week!"

"Sweetheart, as much as I would love to do this for you, I cannot. We must ask your mother for permission. As a matter of fact, they got back last night. So, you will have your answer before the deadline. If she says yes, then either she will sign the permission slip or I will."

With that, she looked at her watch and said, "I can see you're anxious, so let me page her and I'll see what I can do." With that, she got up from the table and called my mother's pager. My mother told her she would come by the following day since she had something for PoPo anyway.

Surprised that she would come by so soon, I spent that evening and all of the following day thinking of things she would say to keep me from going. If it was the ten dollars, I already had it from babysitting money I made. I pulled whatever I had out of my piggy bank and put it into an envelope. I had sweaters, double pairs of socks, a scarf, and gloves already set aside. Not knowing anything about the sport, I could only guess at what I needed as I prepared for her visit.

I was already home from school and helping PoPo prepare dinner when she came in the door and I heard, "Hello…Ma, Pa, it's me, Emily!"

PoPo looked at me consolingly, knowing I was scared to see my mother. She patted me on the head and then turned and called out, "We're in the kitchen!"

After some basic courtesies, I offered my mother some tea. She sat down at the dining room table and talked to PoPo while I nervously busied myself in the kitchen. Part of me wanted to stay away from my mother at all costs, but there was a part of me that still wanted to hug her, hold her, and wrap my arms around her. I hadn't seen her for so long, and she was, after all, my mother. But no sooner had that thought popped up than memories of the past came flooding in, and the decision was easy—stay away from her.

They were talking for a long time, and I was running out of things to clean up. Suddenly, mother called out, "Manna! Come here!" Her voice was deliberate and her tone without feeling.

"Yes, Mommy?" I said, slowly coming out of the kitchen.

"Well, I looked this over, and the answer is no. You cannot go on this ski course," she stated coldly and matter-of-factly.

PoPo and I looked at each other. She was saddened and looked at me tenderly. I knew then that the reason their conversation had taken so long was because she was trying to convince my mother to say yes.

"But why can't I go? The entire class is going!" I exclaimed.

"I said no, and that's the end of it!"

"Is it the money? I have the money from babysitting!"

She stared at me in silence.

"Is it the clothes other than the ski wear they said they'd provide? Don't worry, Mommy. I have that all sorted out. I have it all set aside, plus Kathy said she would lend me whatever I needed!"

Silence.

"It's not a good idea," she said without looking at me. "It's not like you're going to pursue this after the week is over anyway. Forget it!"

"But why?" I persisted.

Silence.

"Mommy, why? I will be the *only* kid in the class who's not going! What will I do in the classroom all by myself when everyone else is gone? Please, Mommy, let me go! I won't ask for anything again. Please, Mommy, please!"

Finally, out of exasperation with my attempts to persuade her, she yelled angrily, "I said *no*! Stop arguing with me! Plus, you're too clumsy to pick up this sport anyway!"

I took a deep breath and swallowed the pain of her words.

Trying to find a way to rework this situation, I softly replied, "Mommy, I know you care about me and don't want me to be hurt, but there are good instructors there and I'll only be on the bunny hills. Please, let me go. Please!"

Irritated, she yelled, "Don't you understand?"

I shook my head. *No, I didn't understand!*

"Let me translate it for you, then. The way you are now…" she snarled as she pointed her finger up and down my body, "You're not very smart, you're not pretty, and you can't do much of anything. It's already going to be hard for you to get married because no one will want you. If you go skiing and break your neck, then I'll be stuck with you *for-ev-er!*"

I stopped breathing. My arms went numb. My feet went numb. Everything around me suddenly became muffled. Even the television a few feet behind my mother seemed muted. Although I was still standing, I felt as if every part of my body had been torn apart, shredded into countless pieces.

My mother, who had been staring pointedly at me as she divulged her true feelings about me, now averted her eyes. I, however, did not release my gaze from her.

Well, that's it then. It's all finally out in the open, I thought to myself.

Only the steel-cold, dark reality lay naked before us all. My mother had finally revealed how she really felt about me. The passing seconds felt like an eternity as the weight of her revelation settled around the dining room. When I was able to move, I simply turned around and went to my room.

My mother stayed a while talking to PoPo, but even when she left, she did not say goodbye. She simply went down the stairs and out the door.

I did not mention the ski trip again, nor did I go. That week, I sat in silence in my classroom doing special work assignments, and when school was over I walked the few miles home, despite the weather. I didn't want to risk seeing Scham on the bus route home. Plus, I didn't mind the cold, the stinging rain, or the snow. At least the inclement weather provoked the numbness and deadened the pain in my heart.

Always Dying but Never Able to Die

This last incident was painful for my grandparents too.

They were in the role of being parents, but their hands were tied. Whenever they wanted to encourage different activities or minister to our growing needs, their authority could not exceed our mother's. As a result, they too were in limbo. PoPo and GongGong didn't know how to handle the different activities we wanted to do, or how to help us with them. They did their best to manage soon-to-be-teenagers in a culture and a generation so different than their own. Furthermore, they had to manage us while learning how to live in a new city in a new country amidst their own life changes as they entered their sunset years.

Yet, despite all these challenges, they were amazing and loved us through every milestone with nothing but joy in their hearts.

The day came when I found out my mother had bought a brand-new, three-bedroom house only fifteen minutes away from my grandparents' home and had been living there with Scham for some time. They also had their two cars, their boat, and their treasured Persian cat. They also purchased another pet, a beautiful purebred German shepherd. Scham named him "Otto" because he, too, was German.

I was *furious*.

Everyone tried to justify their one-bedroom apartment and unencumbered lifestyle after their marriage. But buying that three-bedroom house with a large front (and back) yard, fifteen minutes away, with their same lackadaisical parental involvement was just *wicked* and impossible to explain or excuse.

"Were those two ever evaluated for psychological illness?" Leah asked with all sincerity.

I chuckled at the unexpected question. "No, Leah. But I'm sure that would have made for some very interesting conversation."

"Conversation? Yes, I'm sure there are a lot of interesting conversations in a nuthouse. Or jail, where they belong!"

Outwardly, I smiled at her peppery remark, but inside, I felt that same familiar pang of sadness as I relived the memory.

"I mean, the gall…" Leah added, "How in the world did you turn out so nice and normal?"

"If it weren't for my grandparents and my father, I don't know. As I shared before, it wasn't that Luke and I desperately wanted to be with my mother and Scham. We didn't. We dreaded being with them. But their flagrant rejection and unconscionable neglect of us, *while expecting us (and everyone around them) to be okay with it all* is what angered us so.

Worse, I hated how they put my grandparents into such a difficult situation of having to rear us. But frankly, what I detested the absolute most was their feigned care for us when we were in public. Their counterfeit smiles and saccharine pleasantries only repulsed me.

"We were eventually introduced to their new home, but they only permitted us to see them occasionally, at first, which we didn't mind at all. For overnight stays, I always tried to keep busy and out of Scham's sight, fearful of what might await me if I was alone with him.

"However, when my mother was working, being alone with Scham was unavoidable. At first, I thought he might leave me alone now that he had my mother to himself, but at night when Luke was asleep or outside playing with Otto, Scham would push me down onto the bed that he shared with my mother and carry out his turpitude. Time away from him did not curb his degeneration. I will not share all the heinous things that were done, but what I will say is this: many times, I actually vomited after he was finished."

As I got older, I got taller. Scham could no longer throw me around with one arm—he had to use his whole body to hurl me across a room or to fling me into a wall.

On one occasion, Scham threw me into that heavy wooden stereo console I mentioned earlier. When I fell against it, my spine landed squarely on the corner of that heavy piece of oak furniture. I fell onto the fireplace beside it and started shaking. As I lay there, convulsing, the thought came that maybe the blow had injured my spine, and I could be seriously hurt. After the shaking finally stopped, I tried to get up, but I could not move. My immediate thought was, *he paralyzed me!* He screamed at me to get up, but I could not move. My eyes stared straight ahead, my hands and wrist twisted, my body like a lifeless ragdoll.

He walked up to me, still swearing, and demanding that I get up, but when he saw my eyes, he knew something was wrong. His eyes betrayed his own fear when he thought I couldn't move. But even then, he didn't help me. He just hurried to his room and closed the door, cursing and swearing at me the whole time.

I was too shocked to cry, afraid I could be paralyzed. I dared not to even take deep breaths in case I might jar something else in my spine. I gathered my wits about me, and with shallow breaths I prayed: *Dear God, I need You. I can't move. Please, help me. Help me get up…please…*

I don't know how long I lay there, but gradually, the feeling came back to my body. I carefully managed to get up and found my way back to my room, falling a few more times before I reached the door. I spent the rest of the night alone. My hips and lower back were very sore and bruised for days, but I was grateful that God had answered my prayers, and I was able to walk again.

That night when my mother got home from work, through the thin walls between their bedroom and mine, I heard him telling her how much he hated me. Though she didn't add to his accusations, she hummed in agreement. And not once did she ever defend me.

As I lay in the dark, it was impossible not to notice how both Scham's rages and my mother's scorn increased and intensified.

I was afraid for my life.

Though I was thankful I could walk (this time), I had no guarantee that the next strike would be so favorable for me.

"Dear God, I can't take any more. You've seen it all. I know You said You had a plan for me, but I cannot do this. I'm sorry to let You down, but I told You a long time ago, this was going to be too hard for me. Every day, I die a little, but I never die. It's a slow torturous life. Just please take me now and let me come Home! Please, watch over Luke. I know they don't hate him and he will be fine. Please, let me come Home…"

While I did not have another unexplained symphony or hide-and-seek moment with God that night, I did start to feel His unmistakable presence in my room again, cocooning me in a warm and secure embrace, separated and hidden from the rest of the house.

I knew then God was not going to answer that prayer. I wasn't going anywhere. I had to be brave and keep finding ways to survive another day. But this awareness did not stop my pleading to die and to go back to heaven. Soon, these words became my daily prayer:

"Please take ten years off my life and give it to PoPo. Take another ten years off my life and give it to GongGong. And then take another ten years off my life and give it to Luke. Do this until we all even out, and we can all come Home to You together. Amen."

A Worse Place Than Hell

Scham no longer censored himself. He was open about his malevolent feelings toward us and made it plain that we were unwanted, even during our brief visits. In his own words, we were "sickening to him," especially me. And my mother's silent indifference gave him unrestricted license to openly do whatever he wanted. Scham's abuse was now expected; we just never knew in what form it would come.

Luke and I had different reactions to these traumatic events. He was restrained, quiet, and kept everything inside. He took the curses and the physical and emotional abuse silently. I only saw him cry in private. By this time, he was caught between being a boy and a man. But he did not know how to be a man yet and did not have the authority to defend, protect, or take control of the situation—even though I know he desperately wanted to do so. But Luke is also very kind and has such a tender heart. Retaliation was not in his nature, and out of respect for our mother, he maintained his self-control, saying nothing to her. He simply tolerated the daily afflictions in all of their forms. Feeling enraged, but powerless to do anything effective or sustainable, he directed his anger inward, developing horrible acne that covered his handsome face throughout his youth.

I, on the other hand, was not as valiant as Luke. I did not keep silent. I *could not* keep silent. I *had* to fight back. Even though Scham could seriously hurt me again, my contempt for him increased so much that it often overshadowed my fear of him and fueled my tenacity to fight back. My mother may have been spineless, but I was not.

Since I had lost all regard for them many years ago, and with nothing to redeem either my trust or my respect for them, there was nothing to still my tongue. As soon as Scham began his rampage, rage would course through my veins, and any equanimity or composure I might have had vanished. I would either openly, or under my breath, question the legitimacy of Scham's requests and his self-appointed rule over us. I let it be known that even as a child, I was more aware, more sensible, and more intelligent than he could ever be.

Over time, as if I was an animal ever aware of potential predators, my instincts heightened to the degree that I could even feel the slightest shift in the atmosphere. Survival would only come if I could consistently and accurately predict or detect his shifting moods. I became a great tactician, always armed with options and multiple plans to protect Luke and myself from whatever assault would be launched.

Unfortunately, I was not always successful, and my failure to prevent Scham's assaults only enraged me more. While I found ways to survive Scham's secret corruption, nothing was more painful or more anguishing to me than to see him hurt Luke. My brother was kind, pure, and good, and he suffered great internal conflict between these assaults and his duty to his mother.

I, on the other hand, did not see myself as "good." I was already dirty and covered with shame. Plus, if their accusations that I was "stupid, ugly, and good-for-nothing" were true, then I had nothing to lose. So my verbal challenges to Scham increased in order to shift the attention from Luke. When Scham acted up, I called up the warrior spirit deep inside of me, and I would defiantly stand in front of him every time I could. Fury coursed through my veins and fueled my courage.

Yes, I feared for my life, but if anything happened to me, at least I would have died fighting.

"You were David facing Goliath!" Leah called out. She was frail but her exasperation couldn't be quashed "Where did you find the strength and courage to stand up against this evil beast?"

"I wasn't trying to be strong or courageous. There wasn't time to think. I had to protect Luke. When I sensed Scham was on another warpath, I quickly steered Luke to his room or sent him to do a chore. He thought he was helping me, but in fact, I was clearing him out of harm's way. By the time Luke returned, Scham's frenzy was usually over and I had already been cast away into their unfinished basement, where Otto was chained to an unframed wall. What Scham thought was a punishment was actually a gift. As soon as I got downstairs, I would release Otto from his sentence, and we'd play together."

"I can't believe this was what you had to endure, and these were just *visits* to the mutant, and the 'B' with an 'itch' who is supposed to be your mother!" Leah blurted indignantly. "Thank God you didn't live with them full time! That would have been a sentence to a living hell!"

"Well, we did end up living with them, and yes, it was hell. I continued pleading with God to let me die…but death did not come."

"Oh, my heavens." Leah said, shaking her head.

Before this came to pass, while still on visits, Luke and I always took consolation in knowing we were going to go "home" with our grandparents, but we knew not to ever report the brutalities that occurred. Luke was able to distance and constrain himself, but I was not coping well. There was nowhere to relieve my anger, and no sports or other activities to release my confusion and shock at what happened on our visits.

I was not willing to put my grandparents in the distressing position of having to defend us and confront my mother and Scham. As you now know, our culture did not allow for such discussions and any disclosure of such shameful things would have resulted in the family losing face. PoPo and GongGong had been through enough. They had given up everything for us and I would not taking away what honor and dignity they had left in our family by putting them in the painful position of running interference for us again. They didn't deserve all the extra problems we brought along.

I made every effort not to bring these bad experiences home to them, but hints and shadows inevitably appeared in the form of a bad temper, disrespectful attitude, rebellion, and self-sabotage. Without the tools or the understanding to resolve the conflicting emotions inside me, I was beset with anger, confusion, and sadness, and was prone to sudden, callous outbursts. Eventually, I became unpredictable even to myself. One moment withdrawn, detached, and reclusive, then suddenly electrically charged, emotionally turbulent, defiant, disrespectful, and disruptive. I acted out my emotional dissonance, yelling at and even taunting my beloved grandparents.

After each incident, I was plagued with guilt, remorse, and more shame. I tried to stop myself from behaving like this, but I could not. It felt at times like a spirit of madness was hunting me like the hounds of hell, biting at my heart and soul. If I didn't do something, I was sure I was going to lose my mind. So, unfortunately, while PoPo and GongGong were the only people with whom my soul knew I was safe, they were also the ones towards whom I knew that it was safe to direct my pain, rebellion, and anguish. They were also the least deserving of it.

I hated my life. I hated myself.

Something had to change. *But what?* All I knew was that I loved my grandparents more than I loved myself, and the only way they could be peaceful and free to have a happy normal life as retired citizens was for me to leave.

But how?

Somehow, I had to create so much disorder that I *had to* leave so they could have peace. And so, that is what I did. It wasn't long before PoPo and GongGong had a long discussion with my mother about my behavior and *her* responsibility to rear her own children. After living with my grandparents for almost three years, we were to move back in with my mother and Scham.

On the appointed morning, my mother and Scham came over and told us that they *had* to take us back. Every word they spoke disclosed their secret hopes of being free of us indefinitely. PoPo and GongGong had been expected to raise us until we were eighteen years of age (with only periodic visits with them), but I had foiled their plans.

As the sun shone through the clouds and filtered through my grandparents' living room window, Scham's ugliness was spotlighted once again. His face was disfigured, his lips exaggerated, and spit flew out of his mouth with every curse he leveled at me like bullets aimed at my heart. As I panned the room with my eyes, I saw that my grandparents' eyes and head were lowered, staring sadly at the floor. My mother shook her head, looking at me as if I was the greatest disappointment of her life, and Luke stared out the window, restraining himself from uttering the words he felt, only wishing he could be impertinent enough to speak.

Finally, Stupid Face fired, "Even your *grandparents* don't want you! Now *veer stuck viz* you two!"

PoPo looked up in anger. That was not the truth, and she wanted to speak up against him, but trying to explain anything to this lunatic was pointless. Worse, it would have only inflamed the already dismal straits we were in. I looked at PoPo and quickly shook my head, gesturing her not to worry and not to say anything. I was okay.

PoPo sighed with resignation and sank back helplessly in her seat as with my mother once again silently condoned the insanity. GongGong paced back and forth. Everyone knew Scham had no regard for decency, but it was Scham's unbridled aggressiveness that concerned my GongGong. Too old and frail to contend with Scham, he, too, held his tongue. This was no time for me to fight Scham either. So, with my heart both sunken and broken, I settled into my own pit of defeat. My head lowered also and I took the strikes of another wave of vicious obscenities and ruthless, cutting remarks.

"Be strong and very courageous," I heard in my heart. And with that, I closed my eyes, dug my fingernails into the palm of my hands and waited for the blows to pass.

My grandparents were not to blame. I know that if they had known the truth about everything that was going on, they would have done things differently. But since they didn't know *everything*, they did the best they could. And as I said before, my father did not know we were living with my grandparents at all and had no idea the extent of the horrors we faced daily. He was taken in by a huge ruse that my mother and Scham had contrived, and Luke and I were caught in the middle of the lies, trying to protect him and our grandparents from any more harm and shame. In those days, we didn't know about Social Services, and frankly, even if we had, I don't know if they would have known what to do with us.

When the day came to move, we did so somberly and mechanically. Not much was said. My grandparents were sad and Luke and I climbed into the car. With one look back, I was satisfied to know they were now going to have a more peaceful life.

Only be strong and very courageous…

Luke and I sat in the backseat of the car quietly as Scham leveled another senseless rant. I squeezed Luke's hand, trying to impart some silent encouragement to him. As I stared through the window to the dark rainy day outside, I asked God to forgive me for failing Him so badly, and for failing Luke as well. I couldn't allow PoPo and GongGong to be the brunt of my frustrations anymore. If I had to explode, I would do so to my perpetrators, face to face. This was not my grandparents' mess to clean up. But as strong as I tried to be, I was still shaking on the inside.

How am I going to make it this time? And now, I had brought Luke back into hell full-time with me…

Yes, I hated myself, and I hated my life.

If there was a worse place than hell, we were in it. I wished for my death regularly, but no matter how hard I prayed, death would not come.

With no other option than to live in torture, I prayed that God would help us get through the next few years. I would be fourteen years old by then, and with Luke only fourteen months behind me, I believed we would be able to make the move to my father's house together, and that our sentence to hell would be over. We would be set free.

Pistachio Nuts and Wine Gums

During this same time, my Auntie Pam had been diagnosed with cancer and taken to the hospital. I didn't know anything about cancer except that it was not good. Saddened to hear that she was not feeling well, I asked what hospital she was staying in so that I could go and visit her.

I didn't want to go see her without bringing something, so after school, I took two buses to a local market and used whatever I had earned from babysitting to buy her favorite snacks, pistachio nuts and wine gums. Then I took another three buses back to the local hospital to see her. She was so surprised to see me that first afternoon when I walked into the hospital room. The joy on her face made the entire afternoon adventure worthwhile.

I can still see her delight in my mind's eye, even now.

Although Scham didn't allow us to see much of Uncle Oliver or Auntie Pam, I always remembered them for their kindness and affection when we first came to Vancouver.

At the hospital, Auntie Pam and I would talk, but I was so shy and withdrawn, it must have been quite an effort for her to make conversation. I wanted to share some of the things going on in my world, but I also wanted to hear about how she was doing. Maybe she would tell me stories about her childhood, like PoPo and GongGong did, and I really wanted to know how she met Uncle Oliver.

Auntie Pam did, ask on a few occasions, how things were at home. She must have realized all was not well, but I dared not breathe a word of it. Plus, I wanted her only to think about good things, so she could get better and come back home. We eventually made a pact with each other. She would get better and go home soon, and I would visit her once a week at the hospital until she did. She liked that agreement.

One day, I happened to mention that I would be home late because I was planning to go see Auntie Pam again, but my mother said curtly, "You can't go. She isn't feeling well and doesn't want to be bothered." I was immediately worried because Auntie Pam and I had made a pact—she simply had to get better! I asked my mother again, but she turned and shouted, "I told you, *no! D'ya hear me?*"

In my mind, I thought I would just go the following week anyway, but that never happened. A few days later, we got a call from my mother at the hospital saying that Auntie Pam had passed away, and Uncle Oliver, Adam, and Brent were on their way over.

I was in shock.

I never got to say goodbye!

I felt empty inside. When Luke and I heard their cars in the driveway, we raced downstairs to open the door. Uncle Oliver looked bewildered and grey with grief, his head sunk low, and his shoulders hunched over. He did his best to acknowledge us, but he barely spoke. Adam and Brent were right behind him, and they tried to smile and say hi, but they were also too stunned to speak. My mother came in last and took everyone to the living room. After I took their coats and hung them in the closet, I made some tea. When I came in with refreshments, I saw her give Scham a warning look to prevent him from saying anything foolish. Adam and Brent were standing in front of their father, staring at him, wondering what they should do. Uncle Oliver tried to comfort his sons, but his anguish ran too deep, and every time he spoke, he would bury his head in his hands.

The weight of grief was heavy in the room and my heart ached for them. Not knowing how to ease the pain, but knowing Adam and Brent were about to reach their threshold, I asked if they wanted to come into my room to play. Relieved at having the option, they quickly responded, "Sure!"

Luke led the way, and Adam, Brent, and I hurriedly followed.

We found a deck of cards and began to play Crazy Eights, Go Fish, Slapjack, and Spoons. Soon, we were laughing and enjoying each other's company, even if it was for a few fleeting moments. It was one of the sweetest times we shared together, being available to them during such a time of loss. Adam was even nice to me, offering advice and tips on how to play the games better.

But underlying our chuckling and our laughter was the inescapable reason why we were together to begin with. I didn't know how to make things better, but at least, this was a little reprieve from the stark-cold reality awaiting them outside of my bedroom door.

Suddenly, in the midst of our animated game playing, my mother burst through my door, slamming it against the wall, and vehemently yelled at us, "How *dare* you laugh and play! Your mother just died! You should be sad and sorry! Get out here right now and go sit in the living room!"

"My God, Manna! How horrible for your cousins!" Leah said in shock.

"Yes. My mother had no idea what she had done—again. Adam got up and walked out feeling shamed and defeated, with his head down, even more distraught than when he had first arrived. Brent followed, and I was right behind him, holding onto his shoulders. Luke cleaned up the cards, put them away and came out to join us. We all sat, catatonically, staring at the carpet in the living room, not saying a word."

"Oh, yes, I can totally see how that helped everyone!" Leah quipped sarcastically.

"I know…but there was nothing else we could do. Those were mother's orders. The world felt different without Auntie Pam, and this may sound strange, but as I looked out the window, it felt like even the trees drooped in mourning."

The King and I

My father had completed his contract with the RCMP, and when he was offered a position back in Vancouver, he jumped at the opportunity to be back here with us. He knew we were suffering with Mother and Scham, but he didn't know how much.

Until this position came up, none of his other relocation applications had been accepted. He sought the advice of an attorney, showed him evidence proving my mother and Scham were denying his rights to see us, and shared his suspicions that we were not only neglected, but emotionally abused. But again, the courts generally favored the mother back then, and abuse was not discussed. Nonetheless, my father's attorney was eager to help and believed the judge would at least rule in favor for regular visitation rights.

Having more time with my father would mean less time with my mother and Scham, which would mean less exposure to their "parenting styles." But the attorney did warn my father that things would be difficult. It would be unlikely the judge would grant custody to him since he had only recently arrived back in Vancouver and did not yet have a proven steady income with this new position. In addition, he was a single male parent without family support. His parents had only recently moved to Vancouver, did not drive, did not know the language, and were not as close to us. And lastly, we would have to relocate and start in another school district all over again. The lawyer told him the judge would likely see all these circumstances as too much of a "disturbance" for us.

If they only knew.

While my mother did not want us, she and Scham *did* want all the child support and government supplement checks. It would be very likely she would maintain custody since she could prove she had a steady job, proven income, an established home and family support (PoPo and GongGong), and we were already set in a daily routine with school and friends. Long story short, my father was in for a long and drawn-out battle. Though he was prepared for the fight, he knew Luke and I would be the ones to suffer greatly for it throughout the process. So, after weighing out all the consequences, he decided to leave things as they were and do the best he could with us during the regular visitations.

When we were allowed to be with my father, one of my favorite things to do was to go to church with him. The first time he took us, I instantly felt better. Something was different in this building, different from any other building I'd ever been in. In this building, I felt safe. I felt peace. I felt hope. And I felt strong.

When I was little, I had thought God lived on the mountain, and the only way to be with Him was to scale that mountain. Otherwise, why would He only visit me so infrequently? Now, I felt Him in this building! *I must be getting closer! And we won't be so far away from each other anymore!*

My father's new church was located in Chinatown, where his friends and distant relatives went. I felt like I was part of a family here, and not an outcast like I felt everywhere else. It felt safe to sing, to create, to think, and to play. I found myself naturally mumbling my own special language when I prayed, and I even had the chance to speak Cantonese again without feeling ashamed about it.

The congregation was comprised of both Chinese and Caucasian members, and I saw kindness, cohesiveness, generosity, and goodness demonstrated in everything they did.

At first, because we didn't see my father very often, we didn't always go to Sunday school, which was held downstairs in a big room. Luke and I stayed upstairs with my father and listened in "big church." The sermons were good, but because of the mixed congregation, our two wonderful and kind ministers ended up speaking during the same service. Sometimes Reverend Pan spoke, and then Reverend Burnham would translate. Other times, Reverend Burnham spoke and then Reverend Pan would translate.

Although this was meant to make things easier for the congregants, I only became confused. But, none of that mattered. All that mattered was that I felt love in this place.

In time, when our visits with my father were more regular, we were able to attend Sunday school, and we loved it. We couldn't wait to go to church and see our friends and teachers there. I felt seen, loved, and received, just as I was. Their love for me was greater than the fear and the shame I lived with. Being at church with my new "family" was like a soothing balm—a respite from my life in the house of horrors.

I already knew the Lord's Prayer because we sang that every Monday morning when the school gathered for assembly—along with "God Save the Queen" (which I remember to this day). But when I sang the Lord's Prayer at church, it had a different meaning for me. It became very real, and a few times I even cried with emotion. I started to remember what it was like to talk to God the way I used to so long ago, and slowly, a glimmer of new hope for a better life arose in my heart again.

One day, I watched a few kids go to the front of the church and be confirmed. As I watched, my heart raced because I was afraid that I was going to be asked to go up on stage too. The thought of people in a crowd looking at me terrified me. Memories of my piano recital (and the ensuing wrath from my mother) invaded my mind, and I could hear my heart pounding like a deep bass drum in my chest.

"Daddy, I'm scared. Are you going to make me go up there?" I whispered during the service.

"No, honey. I'm not going to force you...but one day you may want to." He smiled.

"No, Daddy, I will never stand up in front of all these people! Never!" I whispered loudly. *I will never stand in front of so many people where they can see all my flaws, failures, and worthlessness!*

My father simply kissed my forehead and returned his focus to the confirmation ceremony. Relieved and free from any fear of being asked to go on stage, I sat back against my wooden pew. As I listened to the ceremony, I realized that confirmation took place when children who were baptized in their infancy now chose to accept Jesus Christ as their Lord and Savior on their own. It was a public declaration of their love and commitment to God, His Son, and the Holy Spirit. I didn't know about Jesus or the Holy Spirit, but something about this beautiful story captivated me, and I knew I had to learn more.

Now my heart raced and pounded again—not because I was afraid of going on stage, but because I knew with everything inside of me God was calling me. I couldn't refuse to answer. I *wanted* to dedicate my life to Him. I wanted to be close to Him like before.

For weeks after that, this thought would enter my mind, and my heart would race and pound again. I knew then that just like the other kids, I, too, wanted to be confirmed. In fact, I *had to be*—there was no other option. I wanted to be close to God more than anything, and suddenly, I no longer cared about my appearances or feared what others might say about me or see in me. My only care was to have my heart in sync with God's and to be close to Him.

When it came time for our next weekend with my father, as soon as I jumped in the car, I blurted out, "Daddy, I want to be confirmed at church tomorrow!"

"What? Umm…where did that come from?" my father asked.

"I haven't stopped thinking about it, and I know, *know*, *KNOW* I must do this. Please, Daddy, *pleeeeease* tell Reverend Pan that I must be confirmed tomorrow at church!" I pleaded.

"I don't know if they're doing a confirmation service, but I will absolutely ask!" He was overjoyed at my announcement.

To this day, I do not know whether or not they were having a scheduled confirmation service, but the next morning at church, I was asked to come to the front and to declare my commitment to God. No amount of anxiety, no amount of fear—however great—could stop me from running up to the front and repeating the words that the ministers asked me to say.

After I had made my declaration and was excused to go back to my seat, an indescribable joy filled me. I felt safe, loved, and, as strange as this may sound, I also felt strong. I knew that I would never be separated from God again—ever. No mountain, no distance or trouble, no hatred or rejection, no hunger or homelessness, no bullies or gossip, no person and not even the worst of conditions could ever again separate me from God. The King of all kings was not only with me, He now lived *in me*. My King was with me forever.

I will never leave you.

Yes, strength filled me and I knew everything was somehow going to be okay. One day, everything would make sense, and one day, God was going to turn use all the bad things together in my life for good.

Pondering Death

Around this same time, PoPo called to let us know that YehYeh had passed away. (He and MahMah had also recently moved to Vancouver and were living with my father.) My father asked for us to be at the memorial service, and for most families, this would be a normal request. For my mother and Scham, however, this was not the case.

Instead, they were outraged at the inconvenience, and true to their nature, indulged in the usual obscenities before finally permitting us to attend the service.

It was an open casket service, and in the sanctuary sat relatives and friends. Only the immediate family sat in a private back room of the funeral hall where we were able to grieve privately.

I could hear the minister through the speakers in the room, and as he spoke of YehYeh, I couldn't help but wonder if I was attending the right funeral service. I did not know the person of whom he was speaking. I wasn't trying to be disrespectful; I honestly had no recollection of ever knowing YehYeh in that way. My mind flashed back to all the memories I had of him in both Hong Kong and Vancouver, and they were almost all unpleasant, even frightening. The only other memory I had of YehYeh was a sad one. He often locked himself in the bathroom for hours and hours, smoking with the door and outside window closed. The house smelled horrible, but what was even more horrible was I knew YehYeh was trying to kill himself. He was trying to smoke and suffocate himself into a heart attack.

I would knock on the door and ask him to come out to play with me (even though I was scared of him), but he would just shoo me away. I promised him I would be a good girl and do what he asked if he would just come out, but he only responded with silence.

I didn't want him to die. I only wanted him to be nice.

When the service was over, we were asked to come out of the private room and be the first to walk down the aisle to pay our last respects.

I didn't know what that meant.

Suddenly, my father stood up, took Luke and me by the hand to escort us out of the room and into the main sanctuary. I was horrified! *I was not going into a room where there was a dead body!* I screamed and pleaded with my father not to take me into the room and literally dug both my feet into the carpet and pulled back with all my might. He had to use both arms to pull on both my arms while another relative pushed me from behind to walk down that aisle. I knew I *had* to show respect for my family, but *there was a dead man in a casket now only ten feet away from me!* Hiding behind my father, I submitted to his request and stumbled forward, but whimpered the whole walk down the aisle, hiding my head in the tails of my father's blazer, refusing to look up.

Finally, when we reached the casket and had walked by it, my father whispered to me that it was okay to look, but he told me that *as we were walking by YehYeh's face*. When I looked up, I expected to have already walked past the casket, but we hadn't yet, and I saw YehYeh lying in his casket, "resting peacefully." Suddenly, when I saw him, I wasn't afraid anymore. I actually took a moment to intentionally look at him and saw that he was no longer the frightening man I remembered. He looked *different*. The man in the casket *resembled* YehYeh, but the YehYeh I had known was no longer there. It was the strangest awareness for me.

Where did he go? I wondered.

I grabbed my father's hand. "Daddy, where did YehYeh go?"

"He's finally at rest now, Manna."

"Yes, I see him resting, but *where did he go?*" I insisted.

My father looked at me quizzically. He was about to reply, but right at that moment, we were summoned into the lobby area. Before I knew it, we were all standing in an aisle, greeting the guests coming out of the service to pay us their respects and offer their condolences.

While everyone was talking, I slowly leaned forward and looked toward the sanctuary to see the casket once more. I was determined to figure out *where YehYeh went*. To my surprise, the casket was already gone! It was no longer at the front of the sanctuary anymore. I stepped out of the receiving line to see if I could find it, but it was gone.

My father called my name, so I stepped back slowly and turned around. Just as I did, I saw the funeral director and his assistant wheel out the casket, and it was now right in front of me. I gasped, watching as they rolled it to the back of the hearse and then pushed it inside. I was no longer terrified but intrigued.

Why did YehYeh look so different? Did everyone look different once they died? Did Auntie Pam look different when she died? Where did people go when they died? Is the body always "dead" unless the spirit is there? If the spirit can leave a body, then when *did the spirit come into* the body? Where *does the spirit come from? And* where *does it go back to?*

So many questions once again.

The Birds and the Bees

I was now in high school and had become good friends with a beautiful, Indo-Canadian girl named Serena. She had long, flowing hair that moved like gorgeous rich velvet, and a smile that always warmed my heart. She also happened to be well-endowed. And while I detested the way the boys gawked at her, she seemed to manage those uncomfortable eyeballs and comments with great grace.

We bonded over the fact that we were both racially "different" and became good friends very quickly. We often walked to the bus stop together after school, and depending on who got out of class earlier, we would meet at one of our lockers.

One day my class was dismissed quite a bit earlier, so I waited for Serena outside of her classroom instead. The bell rang, and after all the other kids raced out, she finally stepped through the door, reading a book.

"Serena!" I had to shout to catch her attention.

As soon as she saw me, she put away the book and came running to greet me with her usual warm smile. We fell right into step beside each other and giggled over some silly things we had done during the day. After a few moments, she suddenly pulled the book up to her face again and started reading.

I looked at the cover of her book and noticed the title—*The Summer of '42*.

"Why are you still reading?" I asked, "You can read later. Let's talk."

"No, no, wait a second. I'm at the best part. I've been dying to finish it all day!"

"What part is it?" I knew nothing about the storyline of the book, and I wanted her to put the silly thing away so we could spend time together. For a moment, she dropped the book and looked at me, her eyes shining.

"It's the part where the boys are at the drugstore buying a rubber!" she whispered loudly, looking around to make sure no one else heard her.

"Oh," I said slowly, uncertainly.

We continued walking in silence as she went back to the book. While she was distracted, her mind filled with scenes from a book, I was confused, and my own mind filled with questions. In fact, I was *very* confused. *Why would buying something rubbery in a drugstore be so interesting? What's the big deal?* I had no idea. I just knew it was strange.

After a few more steps, I realized I must not be aware of something rubbery that could be worthy of such interest.

I hesitantly asked, "Ummm ...Serena...what's a *rubber*?"

She stopped reading and whipped the book down to her side.

"Oh, my gosh, Manna! You don't know what a *rubber* is?!" she asked incredulously.

I shook my head, eyes wide open, and cheeks flushed, embarrassed at my ignorance.

First looking around to make sure no one else could hear her, she then moved closer to me. "It's for having sex, silly!" she whispered loudly in my ear as if her answer should suddenly make everything very clear for me now. But I still had *no idea* what she was talking about.

We continued walking and she continued reading, thinking the matter had been resolved.

We walked along for a few more steps in silence. Still very confused, but not wanting to appear even more unsophisticated than I already was, I assessed the concept of sex and blurted out, "Oh! I see! Then they better get *two* rubbers!" I said as if I had solved a great mystery, emphasizing the word "two."

Serena stopped cold in her tracks again and gave me a bewildered look. "*What* are you talking about? And why *two* rubbers?"

Feeling like I had finally got it and was instantly Serena's teacher, I replied, "Who's the silly one, now? You need two rubbers because you need one for each boob!"

Now it was Serena's turn to look confused. "*What on earth* are you talking about?"

I huffed, "Do I have to explain it again? Like I said, if they're going to have sex, they're going to need one rubber for each boob!"

"Oh, my gosh, Manna! Is that how you think people have sex? Touching your boobs is not having sex!" she exclaimed.

"Yes, it is! That's why the boys are always looking at your boobs! They want to touch them, have sex with you, and if they do, you'll get pregnant! One day, you'll need to make sure you have two rubbers to protect them, too," I declared.

I hated how the boys stared at Serena and was protective of her, and now I understood why Scham was always trying to touch me. At that moment, I was grateful that he only felt me over my clothes and never touched my actual breasts—otherwise, I could have gotten pregnant!

We looked at each other for a long while, and with each passing moment, I slowly began doubting myself. At first, I was worried I had told her something she wasn't ready to hear. But then I could see by the way she was looking at me that there was an error somewhere in my understanding.

As my best friend, it was now her duty to tell me what *I* may not be ready to hear but needed to. She silently and systematically dog-eared the page she had just been reading, carefully closed the book, took her backpack from her shoulders, and placed the book inside it.

I watched quietly, wondering what had just happened. Serena's sole attention was now on me—not the book that she couldn't wait to read only a few moments ago.

I looked at her with big eyes, wondering.

"Manna, weren't you in assembly for the sex ed video last year?"

I searched my memory to recall the course and remembered that our homeroom class was located at the back of the gymnasium where the assembly was held. I didn't see the video because another friend and I were playing thumb war, hangman, and tic-tac-toe. "Aahhh…well…yes, but I might not have paid much attention," I confessed.

By this time, we had arrived at the bus stop, and we both sat down on a small grassy knoll to wait. My sweet, patient friend went on to explain to me the basics of human anatomy and sex. What she didn't know was that she was basically describing to me many of the vile actions into which my stepfather had initiated me.

I was disgusted. Mortified. In shock.

Overwhelmed by this new awareness, I became lightheaded and reclined on the grass. Staring up at the sky and the clouds above me, I wondered, *how did I not know any of this? Why didn't my mother explain any of this to me?*

All I had heard were bits and pieces of chitchat between friends at school and some gossip about other girls letting boys touch their breasts over their sweaters, but *I never knew* how *it all happened! Could my naiveté have been what protected my soul for so long against Scham's evil advances?*

It didn't matter. Nothing seemed to matter as my stomach now coiled into a knot. All illusion was stripped away, and the glaring truth stood before me. "I don't feel so good," I said to Serena.

I threw my hands over my face, trying to hide the tears that slipped from each corner of my eyes and were now running down my cheeks. When the bus came, I took a seat by the window, and Serena sat right beside me to my left on the two-seated bench. I held my arms around my waist and bent over as if I had been kicked in the stomach. I thanked God that Scham was no longer driving this bus route, as I would have surely vomited on him if he was the driver.

Afraid to tell Serena the dark, ugly secrets of my home life, I simply stared out the window, watching the world as we went by. I wished for the reality of any of the people I saw on the streets other than my own. The time came for me to stand up and pull the chord that would notify the bus driver with a "ding" to stop at the next stop.

"Thanks for explaining everything to me, Serena. Please don't tell anyone I didn't know about this before, okay?"

"Of course. It's our secret. See ya tomorrow!" She smiled kindly and innocently, and waved goodbye, oblivious to the sickening feeling in my body—and to what was waiting for me at home.

"Bye! See ya tomorrow…"

I slowly waved goodbye from the sidewalk as the bus pulled away and drove off. Looking down the street that would lead me home, a new fear fell upon me.

My mother never explained anything to me about puberty, boys and girls, dating, love and marriage, or even the basic "birds-and-bees" talk. Nothing. I was completely ignorant of sex—whether it was just an act, or a sacred part of a sweet and intimate experience between a loving husband and wife. I knew nothing about this matter.

All I *did* know was that Scham had been having some version of sex with me since I was six years old.

My nausea increased, and I endured dry heaves all the way back to the house where my horrors continued.

Can I possibly make it to age fourteen…?

Mommy Dearest

As if I didn't have enough to manage already, my body betrayed me, and the unthinkable happened. I felt an unfamiliar pain in my stomach for two days, and on the third day when I went to the bathroom, I saw a dark-brown blotch on my panties.

Oh, dear God. My period! No, please no!

Thanks to Serena (and the exchanges among the girls at school), I now knew what was happening to me and truly felt that a new curse had befallen me. I dared not tell my mother (and definitely not Scham) of this new development. She already saw me as a massive disturbance in her life, and any additional inconvenience would send her through the roof. And I certainly didn't want Scham to know, as I was terrified of what he might do to me next. So I did my best to keep this secret from them both through that spring.

At first, my periods were minimal, and I could get away with toilet paper folded together. Learning about this entire process on my own was quite challenging, but it was too embarrassing to ask too many questions of my friends. I dare not reveal that I didn't have a "normal" mother-daughter relationship like the rest of them. The entire routine and the secrecy of my cycle made me feel even dirtier and more displaced. When I didn't think I could like myself any less, I now had to deal with this awkward feeling brought on by my own body once a month.

One warm Saturday afternoon, we had a rare treat. My mother purchased ice cream from the store, and we all enjoyed a bowl after dinner. I somehow managed to spill a drop on my shirt, and my mother immediately told me to go wash it out. When I stood up to leave the table, she became cold and stiff.

"Get over here, Manna!" she commanded decisively. She grabbed my arm and spun me around. and held me there, silent for a moment.

"Go into my room, *now! D'ya hear me?*"

She was white with anger, her lips pressed together as she chased me into her room. I threw my arms over my head to protect myself from another beating, but that didn't stop her. She slammed the door so hard that it bounced back open, rebounding off the wall.

"There's a small spot on your pants! You leaked! I know you have your period!" she hissed.

My face grew hot. I dare not say anything, and I wasn't even sure I was breathing.

"When were you planning on telling me?!" she demanded.

I was too afraid to speak.

"*Answer me! You stupid, ugly, good-for-nothing punk! An-swer meeeeeeeee!*" she screamed.

The windows had all been opened because of the warmth of the day, but suddenly, the sounds in our neighbors' kitchens stopped as well as the noise of the neighbors' kids playing in the backyard.

Everyone outside was also now privy to my mother's crazed tirade.

"Did you think you could get away with this? What are you wearing?" she yelled, scanning me with her eyes.

"I used toilet paper at first," I said quietly, full of fright, "and then I used some of your pads from your bathroom. I didn't want to bother you."

My answer, apparently, was not sufficient because my mother went berserk. Her face contorted, her eyes delirious, and her voice almost demonic. "*Who do you think you are?* What kind of daughter are you? *Not mine—that's for sure! I never asked for this!* Sooooo, you think you're a *wo-man* now?"

We stood on opposite sides of her bed, and in an instant, she turned around to the dresser behind her. On top of the dresser was an attached mirror, and in it, I could see my reflection. What I saw was a small, frail, and extremely thin little girl who had somehow stepped into puberty. I was tall, but I weighed less than one hundred pounds.

Dear God, why? Why do I have to be here? What is the purpose of all of this? This is too miserable for any human to bear!

I also saw my mother's reflection in that same mirror. She was facing it and slightly bent over, scrounging around for things in the top drawer. Her mouth twisted as she grumbled to herself. Even in the mirror's reflection she appeared deformed. She was like a rabid animal, saliva flying out of her mouth with every curse she spewed. Every ill word she delivered was a part of the growing catalogue of her hateful assessment of me and her idea of who I was in life.

In that moment, I had no idea who she was. *She may have given birth to me, but she was not my "mother."*

She finally pulled the searched-for items out of her drawer and hurled them at me with all her might, aiming at my head. One by one, feminine pads were launched at me, hitting me all over my body. I didn't know what she was throwing at first, so I used my arms to protect my face and head. Her hatred for me was undeniable as she tried to humiliate me in my vulnerability. I was a simple girl, confused, afraid, broken, *and* in the middle of having her period. Instead of compassion, tenderness, or even regret for not being remotely available, my mother's response was to disgrace me when I was most fragile.

After the first dozen different pads were thrown, she cast feminine belts used to attach the pads before putting on your panties. These were smaller packages but heavier, encased in a hard plastic wrap, so when she fired them at me, their corners stung when they struck my face.

Her last physical assault consisted of three of her old, used 1960s bras from Hong Kong that were hard like cardboard. They had rough seams and darts that ran to the center where the nipples would be. The darts were rough to the touch and, because of the construction of the material (as well as their age), they were also wrinkled and hardened. Even in the midst of her bombardment, I couldn't help but hastily examine them with my eyes—out of shock. I couldn't believe how old, worn, and hard they were and that she actually expected me to wear them.

At first I tried to give her the benefit of the doubt, thinking it was out of kindness that she thought to "save" these for me for all these years, but when I looked at her again, I knew that wasn't the case at all. She simply didn't want to spend a penny on me. My mother didn't care about my sense of self-esteem, self-worth, my introduction into womanhood, or the importance of me developing a sense of femininity or beauty.

The ugliness of the bras represented the ugliness of how she saw me. I looked up from the old bras that were now in my hands and then slowly looked around me. The scattered mess was all over her bed and on the floor. Intimate, vulnerable, and sensitive objects representing one of a little girl's most special and precious times of life were now tainted forever with ugliness, madness, rage, cursing, and enmity.

This meaningful time of my life could have been part of a tender moment of love between a mother and her daughter. Instead, she had declared war. I felt her pure hatred for me once more. Regardless of how hard I tried to forget the past, hoping against hope that I was mistaken (or that I had misunderstood some key mystery about her), I was reminded yet again, that I had not been mistaken. I had not misunderstood her at all.

Tears welled, but I somehow found the courage to hold as much back as possible. Through my tear-blurred vision, I slowly bent down, and in my humiliation, picked up all the items she had thrown at me. When I had them all in my arms, my mother, in her finale, bellowed while shaking her arms at me and pointing to the door, "*Get outta here now! I can't stand the sight of you!*"

As I left with my burden, Scham was awaiting me at the door. I felt naked and exposed before him and was more frightened than ever before of what he might do to me now. He had deftly adopted every new weapon he could find, and this opportunity was the icing on the cake for him.

"Look *vat* you've done! Causing trouble again, damn it! Your *mater unt* I don't *vant* you, and even your pathetic grandparents who you *zink* love you so much, hate you! They begged us to take you back! *They hate you*! Too bad *vee* didn't have a choice! *Vee* had to take you—*unt* if it *ver* up to me, you'd be on *ze* streets or *viz* your punk *fater*!" he yelled in his guttural accent.

I didn't look at him. I just kept walking, hugging the wall on my right and wiping the spray of spit that landed on my left cheek from his spewed venom. When I got to my room, I dropped everything to the floor, crawled under the blankets of my bed that butted up against the back corner of the room, and stayed there all night long. I could take anything Scham said about me, but not the things he said about my grandparents. He had intentionally twisted the truth about them and used those lies like another dagger to my heart.

Again, I prayed. *God, I can't take any more. I know You said to be strong, but this is too much! I tried, but they're crazy! Please, take me Home! And, if You won't do that, then take ten years off my life and give them to PoPo. Take another ten years off my life and give them to GongGong, and another ten for Luke. Do this until we all even out, and we can all come Home to You together.*

As I said, this had become my daily prayer, my only wish, and my only hope against of this life of pain. Even though I had some wonderful experiences with God, what was in front of me daily screamed louder and felt more real than what I couldn't see.

God, I need You...fourteen years of age is too far away.

Wash the Dishes, Cinderella

Scham continued causing havoc wherever we went, and even made enemies of our kind, polite neighbors. I asked my mother countless times to stop Scham from screaming obscenities across the street, but she never did anything.

Some of our neighbors had children, and we would play with them, but they were always nervous whenever they saw Scham. We would apologize profusely to them (and to their parents) for his behavior, but they always responded with "Manna, *we're* the ones who are sorry—sorry for *you*! At least we don't have to live with him!"

While I was relieved that other people could see the truth of who Scham was, my heart was still heavy. There was nothing we could do about our reality.

One day after school, I noticed a bunch of lumber stacked in the front yard. *What is he doing now?* I wondered, shaking my head. Scham had enlisted his brother to help him build a six-foot fence around the house, enclosed with a wrought iron gate in the driveway. He said he deserved to have this because we lived on an "estate."

We were not living on an estate, but a humble, simple, barely middle-class neighborhood at the time.

Within a few weekends, the two of them built the biggest and heaviest fence allowed by the city. They painted it a dark ugly brown, showing the entire neighborhood that he was separating himself away from them.

If building such an ugly fence wasn't enough, he also *taught* Otto to chase after people. On Scham's command, Otto would charge the gate and throw his head through the two iron bars, his shoulders pressing against them. The gates would lunge forward from the pressure and there were times when I thought Otto would break right through them. I would run downstairs and pull Otto back, but passersby only screamed obscenities at me, accusing me of having a vicious dog. "We're reporting you to the police!" they threatened.

Scham had succeeded in his plan to alienate everyone we knew.

These same gates that kept the outside "enemies" away did not keep the true enemy away from us. What they did do, though, was alert us to Scham's arrival after the end of his shift. When we heard the squealing of the gates, we knew that the true enemy had returned. This squeal became our one-minute signal to finish anything we were doing and hide in our rooms. Sometimes we could avoid his wrath this way, sometimes not.

As I briefly mentioned before, Scham kept Otto in chains, bound to a vertical two-by-four in our unframed basement (when he wasn't commanded to charge the fence frightening the neighbors). I was given the job of cleaning and feeding him, which I didn't mind, but seeing him chained up like that broke my heart. I went to be with him as often as I could so he could roam freely downstairs with me. In the evenings, after I had done my homework, made dinner, washed the dishes, ironed all the clothes (including up to ten of Scham's uniform shirts), and finished the other chores randomly ordered, I escaped downstairs to be with Otto.

One evening after I had finished all my duties, I went to take care of Otto. I released his leash and let him bound around the basement. He was so happy. I let him chase me, then I'd pretend to chase him. When he barked, even though it was out of joy, I would stop because I was afraid Scham would hear him. He was so happy to get a little positive attention.

We are so similar, I used to think to myself. Otto, like all dogs, was defenseless and vulnerable to what humans did to him. Otto didn't deserve to be chained up down there. He wanted only to please his masters—to love us and be with us. It broke my heart to see this beautiful creature with such meaningful eyes look at me as if to say, "I'm so happy you're here. Please, don't leave me."

I wish I could have told Otto that I never wanted to leave him. I would have loved him to be with me always, but it was not my house, and I lacked control over our time together. Whenever I could, I would sneak downstairs and sit with him in the dark after everyone had gone asleep. It was actually more comforting with him on the cold, unfinished concrete basement floor than it was upstairs with my mother and Scham.

On one particular occasion, I went to feed Otto. When I opened the can of dog food to mix it with his dry food, the lid cut deeply into my thumb. I dropped the can, which clattered to the ground, and saw that my thumb was bleeding profusely. My entire hand was covered with blood, and it started seeping down my wrist and arm. My thumb throbbed with pain, and I could see how deep the cut was. I reached instinctively for a towel on the dryer and wrapped it around my hand. I grew very lightheaded and slumped to the floor.

Otto was right beside me, licking my face and whimpering. I took several deep breaths and slowly started to get up. Otto sat there, beside me, poised to do anything for me. His eyes eagerly waited for instruction. When I kissed him on the top of his head, he wagged his tail and leaned into my leg. I removed the towel, turned on the faucet and held my thumb tightly as the cold water ran over it to clean off the blood.

I did this a very long time and began to worry that I would need stitches because the cut was so deep, and the bleeding was not stopping. I continued to hold my hand under the ice-cold water as I pressed my thumb even harder.

Dear God, please stop the bleeding. If I inconvenience my mother and Scham, they'll be furious! Please, please, stop the bleeding.

I continued holding my thumb and kept praying. Thankfully, the bleeding stopped after a while, but I was too afraid to release the pressure.

Otto never stopped looking at me with concern.

My fear was *not* for my injury, but for the mess I had inadvertently made. I dared not call my mother and Scham as would most certainly beat me for spilling the dog food or for bloodying an old cleaning rag.

I wrapped up my thumb with the corner of the rag as tight as I could, cleaned up the mess, and finished feeding Otto. I hid the evidence of my clumsiness until I could wash the rag with the other laundry the next day.

When I heard the TV turn off, I went upstairs and secretly wrapped my throbbing thumb with many bandages. I ran into my bedroom and closed the door quietly, believing I had escaped their notice and gotten through a day without one of their rages.

Then, just after midnight, without any warning I heard my bedroom door burst open. Before I could gather my wits after being awakened so abruptly, Scham slapped me across the head! I screamed from the shock and the pain of the hit as he continued to yank me off the bed by a handful of my hair.

"Scham! You're hurting me! Let me go!" I screamed.

"You *stupit* punk!" he yelled back.

"What did I do? I haven't done anything!" I yelled back, trying to catch my footing as he continued to pull me down the hallway by my hair.

He threw me into the kitchen and flipped on all the lights. The brightness blinded me. Through squinted eyes, I saw him lunging towards me. Wincing, I threw my arms up to protect my face and head from another onslaught, but instead of hitting me again, he shoved me with all his might against the kitchen sink.

As I stood reeling from the confrontation, he methodically opened up every cabinet and pulled out all of the dishes, cups, saucers, utensils, pots and pans, baking dishes—everything he could find.

"*What are you doing?!*" I demanded, emboldened by my hatred for him.

"Shut up, you punk! *Zis* is *vat* I'm *doingk*!" he yelled as he lunged for me again. This time, he grabbed my hair with such force that he actually pulled out a handful! He didn't expect this himself, and as he looked at his clenched fist, his eyes revealed his shock to be holding a fistful of my hair.

I screamed in pain, immediately reaching for my head where he had pulled out all my hair. All I could feel was an empty patch, and I cried.

He threw the fistful of hair down on the floor, and I watched in total disbelief as this sick man spat on each of the dishes before tossing them, like Frisbees, into the sink, one by one. Just when I thought I'd seen every repugnant thing possible from this subhuman, his expression changed, as if he had had a flash of genius. He unzipped his pants and desecrated the remaining items before tossing them into the sink.

I stood there with my eyes agape, unable to breathe, and unable to comprehend the revolting madness I was witnessing.

"Now clean it *all* up right now, you *stupit* punk!" he roared. "*Unt* you better do a *gut* job or I'll make you do it all over again! *Stupit, gut*-for-*nossingk*, ugly punk!"

Laughing wickedly, he walked away.

We didn't have a dishwasher; I was the dishwasher. So, I put on gloves to protect my bandaged thumb and washed the filth off the dishes with almost the entire bottle of dishwashing soap and the hottest water I could stand to use. And just to be on the safe side, I also cleaned the entire kitchen, doing my best to sanitize the inside and outside of every cupboard, drawer, under the sink and I even mopped the floor. When I finally took time to look up, the sun had begun to creep toward the far horizon.

The Emperor's New Clothes

Although I was getting older, taller, more daring, and less able to contain my anger, I also knew I was still no match for Scham. He was a grown man weighing well over two hundred pounds. Nonetheless, I did fearlessly pit myself against Scham in one way or another many times. One of these occasions happened quite by accident.

It was a *rare* visit from one of my mother's friends and his wife. Luke and I could not believe it. My mother actually invited someone over for dinner—much less allowed someone from the "outside world" to see the deranged household goings-on. The man knew our family as he and my grandfather had worked in the same hospital. He was a successful medical doctor from Hong Kong in town for a short visit, and my mother felt obligated to entertain him, so he and his wife came for dinner. We were permitted to sit in the living room while the adults conversed, enjoying the company.

The gentleman doctor answered my mother's questions about his hospital. He also shared fascinating stories about the miracles he had seen, and the new advances medicine was making. We all listened attentively. He had a gentle manner about him, and his stories about medicine and family friends at the hospital reminded me of GongGong.

Scham was sitting in his chair, legs spread open, arms flared out, with one hand swirling his rum and Coke in one of my mother's crystal cocktail glasses. His entire demeanor was not only tasteless and unrefined, it was entirely disrespectful and, well, *gross*.

Out of the blue, Scham interrupted the doctor—bursting in loudly with his intrusive accent. He leaned forward, his arms resting on his widespread legs. "*Vell*, I *vorked* in a hospital, *unt* I know a lot about medicine, too! I *vas unt* orderly, *unt* I gotta tell ya, *vee ver za* ones who did all *za* hard *vork*. Do you really *zink* you are *ze* only *vonne* who holds *za* lives of people in your hands? You gotta be kidding me!" he mocked, and then forced a fake laugh as if he had caught our family friend off guard. Then, he turned to my mother. "Tell him, Emily! You're *za* nurse! You see it, too! Tell him how it is!" He pointed at my mother, waving his ugly, thick fingers, insisting that she agree with his dismissal of this highly respected physician.

My mother looked like she had seen a ghost but said nothing.

Scham continued, "All right, if you don't say *anysingk*, I *vill*! I'll tell you *vat* it is to have lives in your hands! I drive a bus! Hundreds of people trust me *vis zer* lives, ev-er-y day! Do you see *zees* hands?!" He put his drink on the coffee table and thrust both of his hands in the doctor's face, as if he was holding onto two large cantaloupes.

"Do you see *zees* hands?!" he yelled again. "*Zees* are *ze* hands *zat* hold *ze* lives of hundreds of people—even *zowsands* of people ev-er-y day *ven* I drive *ze* bus! Do *you* save *zowsands* of people ev-er-y day like I do?" he challenged moronically. "I don't *zink* so! Ha!"

As I listened to his absolutely imbecilic diatribe, my eyes grew wider and wider in disbelief. My lower jaw dropped as if it would hit the floor.

Surely this is a joke! Surely Candid Camera has planned this entire scene, and Allen Funt is about to come around the corner at any moment!

I waited for Scham to say, "I'm kidding," but he didn't. He meant every word and believed he was greater in every respect than the medical doctor and hospital director sitting in front of him.

I conspicuously looked around me, but Allen Funt didn't come around the corner, and I saw no cameras filming for a funny television comedy. This whole sad situation was the horrible reality of my miserable life. Sitting before me was my stepfather, who had just redefined imbecility. And when I looked at my mother, I felt nothing but pity and, once again, the deepest disappointment in who she was.

Our visitors were too polished, too polite, and too kind to show their distaste for this pompous, uneducated fool who reeked of rum and pungent cheese. They simply looked at each other, cleared their throats, and segued into a conversation about the weekend weather prediction.

Overcome by the tension in the room, and the ridiculousness of what Scham had said, I burst out laughing—completely unable to control myself. When I realized what I had done, I pretended to cough as if I had choked on something, but I didn't fool anyone. The family friends also chuckled and gave me a knowing smile as I apologized for "choking" and excused myself.

I made my way to my room, where I continued to laugh wildly.

At this point, I did not even care that Scham and my mother heard my muffled laughter through the closed door. Even throughout dinner, I had to catch myself from not smiling too much for fear that I would be sent into another laughing fit.

After our guests left that evening, I got the beating of my life. But no matter what he did to me, they could never take the satisfaction I had (we all had) that night. We saw Scham wearing the Emperor's New Clothes!

The Coat of Many Colors

Speaking of clothes, winter came, and that particular year we received an unusual amount of snowfall. I didn't have many clothes and what I did have was hardly appropriate. At best, I had a lightweight coat suitable only for moderate weather, and a cheap pair of canvas runners. I wore them all year long for footwear, including throughout the intense Canadian winters.

On one of my visits with my father, he took me shopping and bought me a black and red winter coat. It was beautiful, fashionable, and warm. Luke and I had already learned the hard way. The clothes our father bought for us were never to be worn in front of my mother or Scham. We had done so once before, years ago, and we were so punished for it that we never did it again. Though our runners, especially Luke's, had holes the size of golf balls, we never complained or asked for anything new. It wasn't worth the verbal and physical attacks, so we simply learned to live with very little.

When we were with our father though, he bought us clothes, but we always insisted on leaving them behind, wearing them only when we were with him. My beautiful coat, however, was something my father was not content with me leaving behind. He insisted I take it back with me or else he would talk to my mother. Fearing another rampage, I agreed, but I knew I would have to sneak it into the bottom of my bag. When I returned to my mother's, I had to bury it in the very back corner of my closet, under a stack of books and bed sheets.

One day, snow fell all afternoon, all evening, all night, and it was still snowing when I awoke the next morning. The entire neighborhood was white with pillows of fresh snow everywhere—on tree branches, fences, car tops, and roofs. It was so mesmerizingly beautiful that it was hard to peel myself away from the window to get ready for school.

Oh, how I loved it when it snowed. It always gave me a sense of peace and quiet—almost as if it was covering all the darkness in my life, one delicate flake at a time. All sounds—even horrible ones like the screams of my mother and Scham—were captured by the thick, billowy white puffs. The snow seemed to absorb and soften each blow.

On this particular morning, as happy as I was to see the snow, it also caused me great distress. Even though we lived at the foot of a mountain, I didn't have boots and I had no other outer coat to wear but the winter coat my father had purchased for me.

I didn't have a choice. I would have to wear the coat my father had given me.

At least my body would be warm, even if my feet were not protected. I put on two pairs of socks and brought an extra pair with me to change into at school, knowing the ones I was wearing would be wet and cold once I arrived.

My mother was gone for her morning shift, and Scham was still sleeping from his late shift the previous evening. I folded the coat as small as possible, hid it inside my bag, and carried it with my books. I slipped out of the house as quietly as possible through the squealing wrought iron gate. I even walked a completely different route, adding another two blocks to my journey, just in case Scham should decide to look out the window and check on me.

When I was out of sight of the house, I put on the deliciously warm coat and sighed. My stop was not at a major intersection, so there were no benches, let alone a cover. But none of this mattered to me. Though my feet were numb with cold, I had my new coat to keep the rest of me warm, and I thanked my father under my breath.

After school, my anxiety rose. I knew I had to be very strategic in how to bring my coat back home. As soon as I got off the bus, I immediately took off the coat, tucked it once again into my bag, and hurried the rest of the way home. Inside, Scham was watching television, and my mother was not yet home. *Oh, my goodness! Why is he home? Oh no!*

I had forgotten it was his day off!

Anxiety flushed through my entire body, but I gathered myself and slowly crept up the stairs until I reached the safety of my room. Once inside, I took a deep sigh of relief and felt blessed I had (narrowly) escaped Scham's wrath, both in the morning and this afternoon. I hurriedly took out my coat and hung it up in my closet behind a few other items so it could dry. When I calmed down, I left my room and started performing my growing list of chores. When they were all completed, I went back to my room to do my homework.

Not long afterwards, my mother returned from work. My door wasn't fully closed but she passed by my room several times without greeting me. I was used to this behavior, so that was no surprise, but on her third pass down the hall, she suddenly stopped and put her head in the door.

I looked up, nervously, but she was not looking at me.

"Where did you get that?" she demanded, pointing toward my closet.

I had failed to close my closet door completely, and my mother was eying the sleeve of my new coat. I didn't answer. She turned on me angrily.

"I said, where did you get that?" she yelled sharply.

"David gave it to me...." I replied sheepishly, looking down at the floor. (We were forced to call our father by his first name, and forced to call Scham, 'Dad.')

"I don't want that thing in here, *d'ya hear me*? Take it back the next time you see him, or I'll throw it away!" she ordered.

I didn't reply or look up, too afraid to meet her eyes.

"I said, *d'ya hear me*?" She was now screaming, and she took a step toward me.

She raised her right arm as if to hit me. I flinched and instinctively threw my arms up to protect my face and head again. But the blow did not come because she was walking toward the closet to inspect the coat instead.

"It's *wet*! You *wore it*?" she screamed. Now her look was even more furious. She pursed her lips with the familiar twisting of her mouth. "*How dare you*, you… you…stupid punk! How dare you think you can sneak anything from *him* behind my back *in my house?*"

With those scathing words, she smacked me with her right hand across the top of the head and across the face. It happened so quickly, I didn't have a chance to respond. She then held my arms down with her left arm as she ground her knuckles into the top of my head. I tried to pull away, but she just fought me harder, slapping me several more times across my head.

By this time, her screaming had risen to a fevered pitch, and I began to retreat within myself, knowing what was coming. Sure enough, Scham came into my room after hearing the commotion. The verbal onslaught continued, and finally through tears of pain and anguish, I was forced to agree to give back the coat or else Scham was going to "cut it into pieces *unt* give it back to *him* personally" on my next visit.

After the next visit to my father's, I had to prove that I was taking the coat back home with me so he wouldn't be angry with me either. When my brother and I returned, I slipped it back into my bag and hid it between my mattress and the box springs.

All of this turmoil, simply because we lived at the foot of a mountain, and I didn't have a winter coat for the snow.

A House Divided

Winter at last gave way to spring, and only one significant change came to our domestic arrangement. My mother found out that she was pregnant.

My immediate reaction to her announcement was joy. To have a baby in the house meant having another baby brother or baby sister I could care for and love.

Strangely, instead of being happy, Scham's outbursts only increased with the news of "his child" coming into our lives. As close as Luke and I were, with the added intensity and frequency of abuse, the tension grew to such overwhelming proportions that we directed our inconsolable sadness and unbearable emotion onto each other. With nowhere else to vent our despair, we completely lost control and attacked each other.

Our breakdown was horrible. He hit me, and I didn't have the strength that he did to punch back. So I grabbed his face and dug my fingernails into his cheeks as I pushed him away.

My mother finally peeled us apart and sent us to our rooms. Luke was in his room, stoic but tearful, not saying anything, continuing to hold in his feelings of angst. He went to the bathroom, wadded up a handful of toilet paper, and dampened it with cold water to cool his face and wipe the blood that was running down his face from my nail scratches.

I was mortified. *I definitely wanted to die now.* I had hurt my little brother, and it literally felt like a knife piercing my heart. Realizing what resulted from the intense, unrelenting stress of living with my mother and Scham, I fell onto my bed sobbing hysterically, convulsing as if I was having seizure. My body could no longer handle the strain.

After the major convulsions stopped, my body continued to tremble, and my fingers, hands, and feet were clenched and gnarled as if I had had rheumatoid arthritis all my life.

I couldn't catch my breath, and all I wanted to do was to die.

I began my "mantra" and finished with, *God, please, please, please! I* beg You*! Take me Home now! Hurry, God! Hurry, please hurry…*

I was already sick inside with the realization that I had hurt my grandparents, and now I had hurt my little brother. All I wanted to do was to run into Luke's room and apologize. I wanted to tell him how very, very, *very sorry* I was that I had hurt him. But I couldn't move from the bed. I was still shaking and trembling, and my hands and feet were still twisted and numb.

Without any warning, my mother came into my room. As she looked at me, I began to brace myself for another beating, but I had no way to defend myself. My hands were frozen stiff and knotted up, my feet and toes were turned inward, and my toes were all curled up. All I could do was fall backward on my bed and creep my way into the corner on my elbows, begging her in between my sobbing, "Puh… leez… Mah… meee… puh… leez… don't hiiit meeee… any… more… puh…leeez…."

I was now in the corner of the bed, in the corner of my room. I managed to bring my knees toward my chest and tucked my head close, trying to move my arms to protect my head. My mother slowly walked to me. I yelped preemptively as she came closer, knowing I was going to get the beating of my life for fighting her beloved son.

Then, a miracle happened.

She didn't beat me or grind her knuckles into the top of my skull. For the first time I could remember, my mother actually touched me without rage, force, or hatred for my very existence. Maybe because of her nursing training, she feared I was having a seizure. If so, I'd have to be taken to the hospital where I would have to disclose all that had led up to that point. The secrets of our horrific family life would be known, and she and Scham would be "caught." I don't know. Maybe it was compassion— unlikely, but still a wild possibility.

She knelt down, and instead of wrestling my arms down so she could have a better shot at my head, she massaged my fingers instead, trying to straighten them.

When she touched me, it was if all the tears I had stored up all my life came bursting forth. As soon as I realized she wasn't going to hit me or berate me, I cried even harder and sobbed even more forcefully. I could barely catch my breath, hiccupping and gasping for air as I wailed aloud with all my might.

How could I tell this *woman* before me, my own birth mother, that for her to touch me with a little kindness was all I had ever wanted?

Though the weight and the stress of our lives had clearly become intolerable, the next day, thankfully, though a little awkwardly at first, Luke and I fell into step again and I felt even closer to him. We even hoped that, with the birth of our new sibling, we'd have another ally against my mother and Scham. We imagined this new child would be "one of us," but this was not to be so.

When I was visiting with PoPo and GongGong one afternoon, and I told her of my hopes, her words prepared me for another reality.

"God forbid!" she said with alarm.

I was caught off guard by her reaction. "Why shouldn't I want a little sister?"

PoPo looked at me sadly and gently put her hand up to my cheek. "Don't you see? If your mother has a daughter with that man, you'll be lost all together, Manna. Your mother already ignores you. If she has another daughter, you will be forgotten forever. You must ask for a baby brother."

"But if I get a baby brother, wouldn't Mommy forget Luke? I don't want that. It's better if she forgets me," I offered.

"No, Manna," she sighed, and thought carefully about how she was going to say the next sentence. "Sweetheart, your mother loves Luke, and she will never forget him."

The silence between us stretched for a long moment.

The thread of truth had announced itself once again. No matter how much I tried to ignore it, overcome it, or excuse it, I was not wanted. My mother did not love me, and never would.

"Okay. I understand," I sighed.

When my mother gave birth to my half-sister, Huxley, my PoPo's prophecy was fulfilled. From the very beginning, Huxley was everything to my mother and Scham. If it was possible, I became even more removed from the "family," although they did find use for me. Now, in addition to being the housekeeper and cook, I was also the nanny to *their* daughter. My mother nursed Huxley a little while, but when Huxley woke in the middle of the night, or anytime I was home, I was the one who took her a bottle and sat with her. I also changed her, bathed her, dressed her, and walked around the house with her when she cried until she fell asleep.

I felt no jealousy or animosity for her. I only felt love for this helpless baby. As I sang to her and rocked her to sleep in my arms, I was thankful. Huxley would never have to endure the same kind of life I'd led because she was their *chosen child*.

One day, I overheard my mother proudly explaining to someone how she came up with Huxley's name. "I named her after my favorite actress because she was beautiful, just like I know *my daughter* will be! And I chose her middle name so her initials will spell 'head.' She'll always be ahead of everyone and at the top of my list! It's perfect!"

There it was, again, in no uncertain terms—Huxley held the head position in my mother's life, and this remains so to this day.

Pulled From the Edge of a Slippery Slope

One would think that with his new baby at home, Scham's deviancy would be somewhat quelled, but that was not so. One afternoon, after I had just bathed Huxley and was attending to her, Scham came into the room, and flipped me over, powerfully. He looked possessed, and even more determined than ever.

I begged him to stop and pleaded with all my might. Finally, I shouted, "Please, Scham! Not in front of *your daughter*! She'll be scarred for life! I beg you, please, don't do this!"

But he did not stop.

I managed to free one of my hands to turn Huxley's head away from us. I covered her exposed ear so that she would not have to be a part of this monstrous act in any way.

When he finished his vile deed, I rocked Huxley to sleep and put her in her crib. I then went to wash up and change into fresh clothes, dry heaving all the way to the bathroom.

Scham went in the backyard and I heard Otto barking, so I knew he was with him. I wanted to be with Otto but was repulsed at the thought of Scham. I went onto the front balcony and sat on a lawn chair and then I cried…and cried…and cried. When I had no more tears left, I looked up and over the balcony railing as an unusual thought came to my mind. As disturbing as it was, I believed it was my only way out. I had just turned thirteen years old, and being fourteen still seemed a lifetime away.

There were too many days like this—days I did not know if I could make it, so I began planning another escape. This time, however, I knew I could be employed somewhere. I was no longer a little child; I was a teenager and could do many more things that a little girl could not—*including being paid for letting men touch me.*

Yes, it's sad, very sad that this thought came to me, but it was also true. I knew how things worked now. If Scham had such an insatiable appetite for sex no matter the cost, then so would other men. I had a plan now, and I was determined that I would let men touch me for a price. I would also touch them—for a price. Because of my many years with Scham, I now knew exactly how the process worked.

I thought to myself, *this must be how it works as an adult. This is what men want.*

This is not what I had expected to do with my life, but as a means of survival, I will need to seriously consider this possibility.

Then a cold, stark awareness came over me. I had never dreamed to become *anything*, much less do anything special! I never dreamed of a real career, of going to university, or even traveling. Those were the luxuries of "normal people." I had only ever wanted to die, and when that didn't happen, I could only think about surviving the next day. Beyond surviving to the age of fourteen, my future was never something I thought about.

I got up from the woven plastic lawn chair and leaned over the railing as I looked around the neighborhood. *Where do I start? Who do I approach? What do I say? Do I say something to a man on the bus? Meet them in their cars? Based on my experience with Scham, the routine won't take long—maybe ten to fifteen minutes, so I could theoretically meet four to six men per hour. Maybe they would become regular clients? I could make sure they paid me ahead of time, and this could easily become a regular income. Now I have a viable way of getting free from my mother and Scham. And now I can really come to get Luke and take him away from all of this faster...*

Frightening, I know.

And as quickly those thoughts came, I also wondered, *how many other girls are out in the world, even in my neighborhood, thinking about doing the same thing? People talk about the "bad girls" at school. What if they are "bad" because they're reacting to what is going on at home?*

What if they are in the same position as me?

Maybe I could find out. We could support one another, talk about our pain and share the sadness. Maybe we could all move out together and share expenses. Maybe I could arrange a schedule and a way to take care of each other while we were doing what we needed to do in order to get away? Hmmm...is this how the "bad girls" on TV got started? Were they abused? Were they running away too?

I didn't know the ramifications of what I was thinking. I didn't know that one desperate thought led to another, and that I was scheming to become a "madam" and operate a brothel. How horrifying! Even as I recount this story, it's frightening to see how close I was to falling down a very dangerous and slippery slope. But that's how desperate—how very desperate—I was.

Thankfully, time went by quickly and I did not run away, nor did I sell sexual favors to men for a price. Instead, God created a way to keep me safe by being away from home in another way.

Run For Your Life

Out of the blue, a string of miracles appeared. First, my mother and Scham were suddenly able to arrange a permanent new work schedule to tag-team the baby's care. My mother worked the early shift and Scham worked night shifts. At long last, Luke and I were free of Scham (except for a few overlapping hours) at least five days of the week.

Next, I was also miraculously permitted to join the track team. I loved running and discovered I could do that well—even in my old worn canvas running shoes. Running was the only way I could feel free. All I needed was a pair of running shoes, and I could just go.

Then, a third miracle happened! My mother also unexpectedly agreed to buy me a pair of running shoes after the PE teacher had mentioned on my report card that I had a talent for running and he wanted me on his track team. All the other kids on the track team wore Adidas, but she bought me the cheaper brand, which cost only a few dollars less than the Adidas. I didn't argue against her spite. I was grateful for a new pair of shoes.

So, with my new runners, I ran.

And I ran, and I ran, and I ran.

I ran in the rain. I ran in the sun. I ran in the snow.

When I ran in the rain, no one could tell tears were running down my face. When I ran in the sun, no one knew the redness of my face was from my frustrations. And when I ran in the snow, no-one could hear my sobbing as each flake and snowbank muffled and silenced each cry.

I learned a powerful life lesson then—in the midst of your pain, you have to keep moving, or you will die.

Unfortunately, when Scham was home on his two days off, it was as if he was trying to make up for lost time with us—especially me. On those two days, he was even more unrestrained and daring. I lived in fear of what he might do to me, especially as my body was changing.

After another unwarranted hurricane over breakfast one day, I knew I could not last much longer in this house. One day I would not be so lucky, and I would either lose my mind from the madness occurring in the house, or I would be raped, paralyzed…or dead. Remembering the words my godfather had spoken in front of the courthouse, I knew the time was coming. I was a few days away from turning fourteen years old, and I could at long last be free of this house of horrors.

I was close, so very close.

That night I went into Luke's room and sat on the floor, leaning up against a wall as he sat on his bed doing homework. I struggled for the right words, but there were none. I had to just say it plainly. "Luke, I have to talk to you about something…"

Luke looked at me quizzically, not sure of what it could be that I would go into his room and interrupt him during his studies.

"Luke, we have to go soon."

"What are you talking about? Go where?"

"It's time. We can move over to Dad's now. Remember, the courts said we could go when we were fourteen!"

Luke took a deep breath, looked down at his book, placed his pencil in the middle of it and closed the book.

"I can't stay here anymore," I went on. "I'm gonna either be insane, paralyzed, or dead. You know what I'm talking about."

He blinked at me in the dim room. I could see his anxiety and tried to rally him.

"Luke, don't be scared! Be happy! We made it! We survived, and now we're old enough to make the choice of whom we want to live with. It's time to go live with Dad."

"But I can't yet," he whispered back, "I'm not old enough."

"No, you can! They're not going to fight over that. I'm old enough, and you are with me. So, we will go together. Daddy will be so happy, and the three of us can finally be together. We'll live a normal life, and we won't have to deal with any of this insanity any longer!"

Luke was silent for a long time. "Will you please just wait a while longer?" he asked. "I don't know what to do."

"I won't make it, Luke…" I said, looking down onto the carpet. I found my courage and continued to reassure my little brother. "Don't be afraid. We will have a totally different life once we're with Dad."

"What about Mom?"

"*What about her? She doesn't care about us!* She just cares about Scham and *their* baby. And you know Scham will never hurt Huxley; she's his own daughter! He'll never beat her like he does us! Plus, he'll be so happy to be finally rid of us and have this house to himself and his *own family*."

"Did you tell Mom?" Luke asked.

"*No way*! And you can't say anything yet until we have it all arranged with the school and Daddy. When I know you're ready, then I'll make the plans," I stated confidently, but my heart was racing in fear.

"Let me think about it. Let's talk tomorrow."

"Uh…Okay…" I reluctantly agreed.

I stayed up late into the night, wagering time against my constant companion—fear. Yes, there was a great risk in leaving. I was afraid that Scham might come unhinged when I told him I wanted to leave and take Luke with me—not because he cared for either one of us, but because this move would prove that they were unbearable, and we had had to leave. And more importantly, they would no longer receive the child support money or the government checks to subsidize their lifestyle.

They would lose their free housekeeper and nanny!

Well, "tomorrow" came and went, and Luke was too frightened to make the decision. Finally, after a few weeks, he told me he could *not* go. He was too afraid of what Scham and my mother would do once we told them. I assured him it would be our last beating if they did, but I also told him they wouldn't because I would tell them I would call the police. There was nothing to lose anymore. We were going to be *free*!

I begged Luke to reconsider. He nodded and walked back into his room.

Days ran into each other again, and weeks turned into months. I approached Luke again, and he told me with absolute certainty that he couldn't go yet, but he would soon. He told me to go first to get established, and he would follow shortly.

"I'm not leaving without you, Luke!" I argued.

"I can't go, but I know you *have* to go. I'll be okay. He doesn't hate me like…" he drifted.

"Like he hates me." I finished Luke sentence.

Then, I have succeeded, I thought to myself silently. *The whole point was to take the focus from Luke, but did I buy enough time for him? If I left first, would that cause Scham to be on his best behavior? He would know Luke and I would talk at school, and the rest of the family would know what was going on.*

I was torn, but the urgency in my spirit only grew. It was time, or else something *irreversibly bad* was going to happen.

But how could I leave Luke? How?

It was excruciating. I couldn't leave him, so I continued to deny my intuition. Then, one day after school, Luke suddenly said to me, "Manna, you have to leave. I feel it now. I can't leave yet, but I will be there soon. I promise. I will be okay. I understand it now. *You have to leave.*"

The truth he spoke that day still jars me. It was only because *he said it* that I agreed to leave without him—a decision that killed me inside.

The next day, I spoke with my school's guidance counselor, who helped me arrange a call to my father that afternoon. My guidance counselor was a very nice man and because he was also Chinese, he extended himself sympathetically to me. I only shared the most surface of things with him, but I know he suspected I was hiding uglier details. Thankfully, he didn't pressure me to reveal more when he realized I was going to be moving in with my father. I will always remember him, and the kindness he extended to me that fateful day.

"Hello?" My father answered the phone.

"Daddy, is it true? Is it really true?" I asked without saying "hello."

"Manna?" he asked, startled. "Is that you? Aren't you at school?"

"Yes. I'm calling from the counselor's office. Please tell me. Is it true? Is it really, really true?"

"What do you mean? Is *what* true, Manna?"

"That the courts said that when we're fourteen, we get to decide who we want to live with."

My father was silent on the other end of the phone at first. "Yes. Why do you ask?"

I told my father that I wanted to come live with him. He couldn't believe his ears and started to cry with joy. With tears running down my own face and my voice shaking and cracking, I told him that I had been patient, just like he had asked me to be, and that I had made it. I had been brave and courageous. I had survived and wanted to come and live with him now. I told him that Luke didn't feel like he could leave yet, no matter how I tried to get him to come with me, but I assured him that Luke would be coming soon. "For now, though, Daddy, it will just be me."

My father kept professing how much he loved us, and together we made plans. He said I could move in as quickly as the following Saturday. When I hung up the phone with him, I felt like a weight had been lifted from my shoulders.

It was really happening.

I had made it to fourteen! Now, I just had to survive a few more days.

This was the first time I felt excitement and joy in...I couldn't remember when. I could hardly wait to talk to Luke, hoping that the conversation would encourage him to come with me. But when I told him, he still would not leave. He wanted to stay to make sure my mother would be okay.

In Luke's room that night, I downplayed my excitement but told him I needed to pack. My hands were shaking with fear. *What if they came into my room in the middle of my packing?*

I couldn't take much with me—only what I could carry easily... in case something happened. And I dare not tell my mother or Scham about my plans until that Saturday morning. I knew they wouldn't say no, and even if they wouldn't drive me, I was going to take the bus to get to my father's.

Either way, I was leaving.

I woke up very early that Saturday morning. I did all the chores and more. I cleaned the entire house so there would be nothing for Luke to have to do in my absence. I even prepared a few meals and had them cooling on the counter by the time Scham woke up.

I didn't want there to be any delays, so I also made breakfast. After cleaning up, I asked if I could talk to them. My mother wasn't interested and went to their room. I gave Luke a nod and signaled him to go to his room. I couldn't wait for my mother, so I began with Scham.

"Ummm...I would like to talk to you about something," I said, my voice and hands trembling, my heart pounding.

He grumbled something and didn't even look up from his newspaper.

I continued, "I think it would be best if I go to live with my father. I've already talked with him, and he said it would be okay."

Now Scham looked up, and with his eyes boring into me, he yelled, "Emily! *Emily!* You had better get out here!"

My mother soon came out of their room and asked what was wrong.

"It's your daughter again, making trouble. You'll *vant* to hear *zis*."

He gestured a hand at me, and I nervously repeated what I had already told Scham. My mother's face went through a range of emotions before she bellowed,

"*What did you say?*"

"I spoke with *my fathe*r"—I was no longer afraid to call him by his title and role in my life—"and asked if I could live with him now that I'm over fourteen years old. I remember the judge said I could choose with whom I wanted to live when I turned fourteen, so it's time I go. It would be better for you since I seem to always be making you so upset. Luke is old enough now, and he won't be any trouble to you—he never has been, so that's good. And Huxley is walking, so it's much easier to take care of her. I've gotten her familiar with the *snuggly* when she's sleepy, and she is easily entertained whenever I do my chores. She'll be fine, too," I explained.

"*What?*" she screamed like a crazy person again. "When are you thinking of leaving?"

Not missing a beat, I answered, "Today—now actually. If you can't take me, I can take the bus."

All hell broke loose.

I stood by the kitchen counter as they launched round after round of horrible curses, but this time nothing they said touched me. I was leaving. I was going to be free of them, forever.

"Good riddance, I say!" Scham interrupted.

"What are you taking?" my mother asked.

"Not much. I don't have much—just the necessities. I will even leave Barbie and my Barbie Camper and all her clothes for Huxley to enjoy one day." I thought I was being kind and thoughtful, leaving my most treasured possession behind, but she didn't respond to my charity.

"Luke!" she screamed, suddenly, turning her head towards his room.

Luke came out and braced himself.

"Do you know about this?" she demanded of him.

"*No!*" I yelled out, interrupting her attention. "He didn't know anything, and he wasn't a part of this. I haven't told him anything. He only knows now because everyone is yelling. Please, don't be mad at him. He didn't do anything! I promise!" I pleaded.

My mother glared at me and then looked at Scham, who had already gotten his coat and keys. "Okay, let's go! I'm ready to be rid of her!"

I stood for a moment, afraid to move because my mother was standing between me and my room. *Was she going to hit me as I went to grab my things?*

"I said, 'Let's go!' If you're so eager to get out of here, *vee vill* take you now. Go! Go get your *zings*!" Scham hollered.

With that, my mother turned and went to her room, and I was spared another beating. I retreated to my room, taking Luke by the arm and guiding him away. He went to his room to get his jacket, and I went into my bedroom to get my small bag and my box of clothes. I had packed what I could in an old Woodwards box (a former local department store). I had packed very little; a few T-shirts, two pairs of trousers, underwear, socks, my runners, and the coat my father had bought me. I left behind everything else, including the old 1960s bras.

Luke came to my room and asked to help me with my things. I gave him the box to carry and as I handed it to him, I gave him clear instructions, "Remember, don't talk back and do your homework in your room. If you have to help with the baby, do it outside in the living room or kitchen. Don't worry, with me gone, they won't bother you. They have to treat you *even better* now to prove that I was the bad one and that living here isn't so bad. It's only a couple of days, and then I'll see you at school on Monday. I'll meet you at your locker and you can tell me how it's going then, okay? And if you change your mind at all this weekend, just call. We'll come and get you!" I said this with every ounce of courage I had inside me, holding back the tears welling in my eyes.

My thoughts raced. *How do I leave Luke behind? Maybe I should stay? No! I can't! Dear God…give me strength.*

It was too late to change things now. Everything was set in motion. There was no turning back. I hugged my brother awkwardly, and then the tears came. Scham was screaming at me to get into the car, so I hurried out the door; I didn't even get to say goodbye to Otto.

A few moments more saw us all sitting in the Buick like a family ready for a pleasant Saturday drive, but that image could not have been further from the truth. Instead, it was hell in its full fury.

For the entire thirty-minute car ride to my father's apartment complex, Scham was completely relentless. Without a moment's rest, from the second we were in the car until we arrived at my father's apartment complex, he battered me with hateful and cruel criticisms.

I tuned him out and looked out the window. I was finally leaving this hell on earth, forever.

It is finished, indeed.

My mother was crying in the front seat but said nothing. I held Luke's hand in the backseat and we wiped away our tears as quietly and as discreetly as possible.

When we arrived, Scham got out of the car and slammed the door. My mother said nothing to me. I looked to my left and whispered to Luke, "No matter what, do not look at me. Okay? *No matter what, do not look back.* You must protect yourself. I will see you on Monday, or sooner. Promise me you won't look back."

He nodded and stared straight ahead, showing me that he understood.

I opened the door and stepped out, saying, "Goodbye, Mommy. Thank you for taking care of me and for everything you did for me."

She just stared ahead and said nothing.

I closed the door, looking back at Luke one more time, and then went to the back of the car.

Scham opened the trunk, pummeling me with his caustic words before spitting at me. He grabbed my two items, and instead of handing them to me, he hurled them down toward the curb and across the sidewalk. "*Zer* you go you *stupit*, ugly *gut*-for-*notingk* punk! *Gut* riddance! I hope I never see you again! *Stupit* punk!"

All my underwear and socks now lay strewn on the curb and in the gutter. My T-shirts and simple clothes flew across the sidewalk and littered the steps up toward the main apartment door. My thin little paper box was destroyed, emptied on the sidewalk.

Scham snarled at me, climbed back into the car without saying anything else, and peeled off, no doubt hoping the gravel and dust would spray into my face.

I stood alone, frozen among my scattered belongings as the car drove off. My eyes were fixed on Luke and the back of his head.

He was a good boy. Never once did he turn his head.

In a few moments, they were gone.

Left: PoPo and GongGong on their wedding day.

Below: Luke and I with PoPo and GongGong at Christmas time.

Above: MahMah at her hospital writing a prescription.

Right: MahMah and YehYeh shortly after they were married.

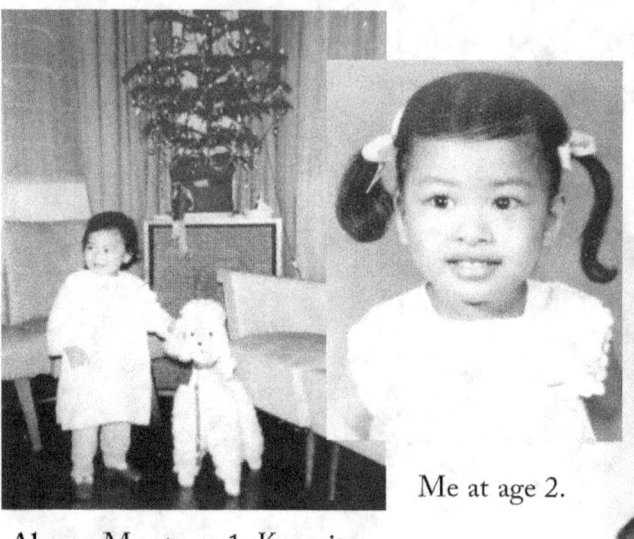

Me at age 2.

Above: Me at age 1. Knowing how much I loved dogs, this toy dog was my Christmas gift from my father.

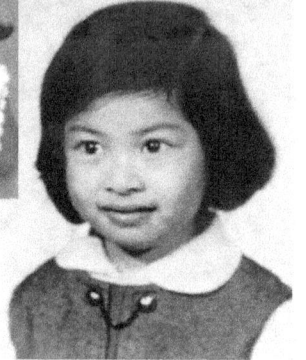

School photo of me at age 3.

Left: My father in his uniform for the Royal Hong Kong Police Force. **Top left:** My father with his police dog, Major. **Above:** My father and Godfather standing in front of our first home in Vancouver.

When together, my brother and I were inseparable.

Luke and I standing in front of our "house of horrors" shortly after my mother cut off all my hair.

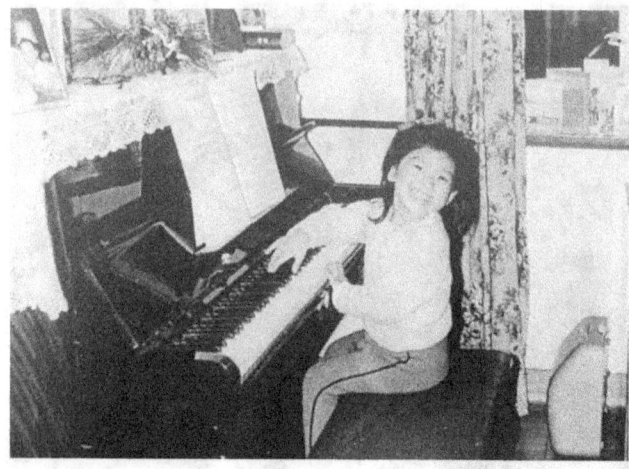

Above: Playing the piano at my father's house. I loved playing for him.

Right: Lucky and me at Spanish Banks beach in Vancouver.

Luke, my father and me on one of our weekends together.

6 SON OF A GUN

He who walks with wise men will be wise, but the companion of fools will suffer harm…

—Proverbs 13:20

Room 316

The day of my next visit with Leah dawned bright and sunny. She was doing remarkably well and had been in good spirits the past few weeks. I expected nothing less when I returned to the hospital, but that wasn't the case.

When Melody saw me walking down the hall toward the familiar door, she stepped out from behind the nurse's station and motioned for me to come with her. She wanted to speak to me away from Leah's door.

"I'm glad you're here. She's been asking for you." Her face showed genuine concern. "It was a rough night," she said. "Hopefully, your visit will help."

I smiled at Melody. "Thank you."

She nodded, and I made my way to Room 316. Entering cautiously, I felt the atmosphere in the room had changed. There was no movement from the bed by the window. I walked quietly to my usual seat and sat down, taking Leah's hand in mine.

I waited until she woke.

"I've been so restless," she said in a garbled voice. "I sleep like a cat now…bits and pieces throughout the day. But it's not so peaceful. The pain wakes me."

"It's normal to have good days and bad days," I said awkwardly, hoping to reassure her.

"Yes, I suppose so. That's life." Leah grimaced as she tried to shift her body in the bed before adding, "and death."

I stroked her hand, saying nothing. After a long pause, Leah spoke again.

"How do you do this? How do you work with dying people when you're young and have so many other 'important' things to do? *Why* do you do this to yourself?"

"Being with you *is* important to me. I don't normally get as attached to patients as I have to you, but still, being with all my patients during this time in their lives is a blessing to me. It doesn't feel like work at all."

"You must have seen lots of people die by now! Doesn't the whole death thing kind of freak you out?" she asked, her eyes bugging out and her hands waving in a mock "scary" gesture. It was only a percentage of her normal energy, but I was glad to see her attempt at levity.

"No, silly goose! Ironically, this can be one of the most precious times in a person's life."

"It's not depressing?"

"No, not at all. It's quite the opposite; I have the rare opportunity to share in the most profound, and often the most real and important conversations people can have. They have no pretenses and no hidden agendas now. Their hearts are open and willing," I replied.

"Hmm…kind of like me, I guess. I told you what I needed because I don't have time to dance around things anymore."

"Leah, I highly doubt you've danced around topics much in your life." I smiled.

She returned the smile and squeezed my hand. It was like shaking hands with a bird. "Well, I guess I did kind of throw you against the wall with my request, didn't I? After all, how could you deny the last wishes of a dying woman?" She smiled again, motioning for her water cup.

"No one has been as determined to hear about my life as you have," I admitted, "and if it were anyone else, I wouldn't have agreed."

We both chuckled and continued talking a little while about other topics. She filled me in on overheard nurses' conversations, the latest recipes from the Food Channel, and other things she found noteworthy.

Finally, she squeezed my hand and said, "So, my dear. The last time we ended, you were thrown to the curb at your father's apartment complex. I'm in awe at the resiliency of your spirit and the kindness of your heart."

"The human spirit is awesome, isn't it? We're *all* braver than we think we are." I reflected. Then, hoping to shift gears, I said, "So, Leah, tell me, are we close to finding those secret keys yet? I'd really like to focus on happier things."

Leah paused. "I know these are not conversations for 'afternoon tea,' or even over a glass—or three—of wine!"

"Or for my hospital visits with my patients!" I added.

"No, they're not…and I want you to know that I am thankful. Thank you for being so open and for giving me hope to sort things out in these last days." Leah smiled feebly and continued. "I'm processing everything you're telling me, trust me. Your stories brought to mind memories about my family, and also about church and Sunday school. I thought about heaven back then, but over time those ideas seemed old and rusty. Honestly, I think I grew skeptical because of…well, people. People are just a pain in the butt! I don't know if I really like 'people.'" Leah shook her head as she spoke. "As a species, we've been given everything, but still we want more—grabbing and stealing from others. We're never content, and in our hunt for more, we trample over others and end up emptier than before!" Leah huffed.

"I agree, being content and thankful is a virtue. That doesn't mean we shouldn't have ambition or aspirations. God put those desires in our hearts, but we need to balance ambition with contentment *and* gratitude. All so we may stay humble and contributory while still experiencing meaning and joy as we fulfill our purpose."

"What do you think *is* our purpose here?" Leah asked.

"Well, we were all created uniquely—each of us is given opportunities to express and to share our extraordinary gifts, talents, and skills with others in service. But I also believe that while we're accomplishing all these great exploits, the underpinning of everything we build is to have a special relationship with God. It's critical to keep that connection real and alive so we don't go looking for our significance in any*thing*—or any*one* else. Otherwise, we'll think our identity lies in those trailing descriptions of ourselves. What we look like or do, how many letters we have after our name, or how much we store up in money, cars, houses, titles, and trophies, which may include people.

"Those things are only substitutes (counterfeits) for 'meaning.' And they're lies about our worth, our true identity. When we understand that our value is based on the fact that God created us to be *like Him*, then our eyes are opened. Everything else is seen for what it is, and not for what we erroneously think it should be. When we get that God loves us all and created each of us for victorious living and for purposeful work, then there won't be any 'one-upmanship.' There won't be any fear that someone else will get more than we do. We'll get that we are all beautifully created with unique gifts and talents, and we can share them in joyful, loving service with each other." I paused before adding, "Yes, the world can be such a different place then."

"You really believe that, don't you?"

"Yes, I do. Because then it'll be possible for us all to *just be nice.*"

"Honey, that's just not going to happen. It's hard enough being nice when things are going our way. How do you expect people to be nice when they feel wronged?" Leah asked.

"As I said, they've forgotten who they are. They're living their lives based on a faulty premise—that they're missing something that is due them. And the underpinning of this premise is yet another misperception. Unfortunately, they assume something is deficient within themselves, requiring them to fight or bully their way into getting what's rightfully theirs.

"What most people don't understand is they're already *more* than enough. If anything, we ought to spend more energy being the best we can be, instead of trying to prove ourselves, pretending, or minimizing someone else so we can feel better. When we can accept and embrace *ourselves*, then we can begin to accept and embrace one another. Why would a girl with brown hair be better than a girl with blonde hair? Why would a CPA be more important than a teacher? We are part of a massive populace that works uniquely as individuals to serve a greater purpose. Why then, should we be fighting, abusing, and killing each other? It's because we don't know who we are, and because of that, we don't fully understand our purpose."

"So, being nice simply means I know who I am," Leah deduced.

"The way I see it, if we could remember our significance and our *true* value, then yes, we would be nice *because* we know who we are. And we would know the value of other people also! If we simply grasp and remember that God created *each one of us*, we would never treat each other in any way other than with kindness and respect. We would each do what we are each supposed to be doing and appreciating others for all that they're being, giving, and sharing also. And when we mess up (which is bound to happen) we can more easily forgive each other, extend grace, and encourage each other to try again!"

"Well, my friend, that's actually quite interesting, even profound!" Leah said with excitement. "I've never had conversations like this before."

"Now, you understand why I love what I do."

"Yes, I do see. I'm also starting to feel that feeling again…"

"What feeling, Leah?"

"You know, that warm cozy feeling that starts in your tummy but is simultaneously all around you like a beautiful down comforter?"

"Oh…*that feeling*!" I smiled.

"I can't tell my kids that, of course. Or Thomas. They'll say my mind is going!" she coughed as she laughed out loud.

I smiled, reaching to check her vitals.

"How long do I have, Doc?" she jested.

I shook my head and smiled back at her. Melody had also stepped in for a few minutes to check on Leah.

Leah turned to me and asked, "Can you make me some of that nice ginger tea, dear?"

"Absolutely. Be right back." I went to the kitchen area where the family and friends of patients could save some of their food during longer visits. There I cut up some ginger and lemon slices and added a little raw honey to hot water. When I returned, Melody had helped Leah sit a bit more forward in her bed. Leah's hands were now folded in front of her, and she was alert, looking like she was ready to take on the world.

"You constantly surprise me, Leah," I said, a bit startled at her sudden change in appearance.

"What? Did you think I was going to die already?! What kind of encouragement is that?" she quipped. She thanked me for the tea, took the cup in both of her hands, and smelled the aroma as if inhaling fine wine. After taking a sip, she sighed loudly. "Now, that's a fine cup of tea!"

"Glad you like it. Did you want to play another game of gin rummy and let me take on the champion? You're up five games to three, I think."

"Well, okay—as long as you continue your story where we left off," she requested. "Now that you've escaped from hell, you must tell me what you did with your freedom!"

"Leah, must we? It's not the most joyful of topics; there are so many other interesting things we can talk about. Plus, I'm concerned the stories may be too upsetting for you," I protested.

"Yes, we must. Don't worry. I'm fine. I was only a little off yesterday…it could have been I was just missing you a little." She winked. "In all seriousness, I'm doing well now that you're here. And besides, if I start to feel a little weak, I have some pink, blue, and green friends here." She tilted her head towards the paper cup of medication on her tray. "I don't keep all those pills around for nothin'!" She winked again. "Now shuffle those cards and start a-talkin' cuz I'm a-listenin'."

"Well, okay. It's a little lighter from here in some ways, but darker in others."

"Everything is. Go on."

Being A Good Example

You'll be happy to know that Luke came to live with us only a few months after the heartbreaking day of our parting. I talked to him regularly at school but didn't want to add more pressure to his already stressful situation by saying too much. He knew I was always there for him, and though we did talk about his moving, I always waited for him to bring up the topic. Luke never said much about his life with our mother and Scham after I left, but it had to be bad enough for him to leave. All I could do was pray that God would move him out quickly—not because he was in danger, but because he simply knew that it was time. God answered our prayers, for we were back together again very quickly.

When he arrived, I ran out to hug him, doing my best not to cry. I also wanted to make sure Scham didn't treat him the same way he treated me once they pulled up. It was such a relief to know he was no longer at risk.

We had no concern for Huxley, though, since she was "their" child and had already been my mother's main focus (and favorite) before we left. Their attention towards her would only grow now that we were out of the picture. Plus, Scham had also forbidden my mother to see us anymore, and not surprisingly, she agreed.

"What? What did you say? Your mother let that daft, dimwitted lunkhead tell her not to see her children, and she *agreed* to it? When is this woman ever going to wake up?" Leah yelled out.

"I don't know, Leah. I don't believe she *wants* to 'wake up.' It's too dangerous for her to wake up. By believing I'm the evil one, the difficult child, the one *deserving* her punishments, then she is free from guilt. If I am to blame, she can tell herself whatever she needs to escape her conscience.

"In Huxley, she had a new beginning, a chance to start over and prove to herself she was a good person—a good mother. She joyfully took Huxley to school, to ballet and piano lessons, and spent every moment with her and doting on her. She even built a pool in their backyard for her.

"My brother and I were soon forgotten.

"Even my grandparents told me that when Huxley saw our photos in their living room, she was told that we were distant cousins of *theirs* (my grandparents), not her siblings. She was reared as an only child and never knew about us until she was a teenager—yet another story I will address later."

Leah, unable to comprehend my mother's behavior, added, "You can never escape your conscience. Didn't your mother realize that? Your conscience will always catch up to you, and if you try to shut it up, it will only scream louder. I don't care what you believe, there is a due accounting for everything in this life—call it consequences, judgment, karma, whatever you want. For all that we have done or didn't do, there's a reckoning! For all that has either caused pain or alleviated it, we reap what we sow! Trust me, I know!" Leah declared, with an emphatic fist slam on the blanket.

"Oh, Leah, my heart isn't out for judgment anymore, although it used to be when I was younger. One thought of retribution trickled into a wish that quickly festered into bitterness. Before I knew it, resentment flowed like a river, meandering through my mind, heart, and soul. It cut into a deep, wide channel that every other thought drained into. It was a lose/lose situation.

"That's when I learned those thoughts only hurt *me!*

"I hated who I was becoming. I hated how I felt. So, I started to 'practice' forgiveness. Eventually, my thoughts about my mother and Scham lessened, and my life's focus no longer hinged on whether they were judged or punished, or not. I was free from them, physically, mentally, emotionally, and spiritually."

"But they got away with so much!" Leah protested.

"Maybe. Maybe not. I don't know the details of their lives, and I don't want to know. I learned what I needed to learn when I was with them, and my journey with them is complete."

"What in the world could you have learned from *them*?"

"For starters, I learned what *not* to be. I also learned who *to be!* I learned what my true weaknesses were (instead of what they had cursed over me). I learned to accept my giftings and not apologize for them, and I learned that I had nothing to prove to anyone.

"Naturally, at times when memories come up, I can (and sometimes still do) get activated. When that happens, I acknowledge the feeling. I take responsibility for it and how it is affecting me at that moment, being thankful that the past is over and has no place in my life now. Then, instead of giving in to a knee-jerk reaction, I forgive them and choose another, more appropriate and life-enriching response. I try to see these memories as 'information,' to be used in service to my growth, healing, refinement of skills, and care for others.

"My life is no longer about my mother or Scham. My life is about how I can be an example of hope, love, faith, courage, and triumph. I want it to be a great example, not a glaring warning."

"That's magnanimous of you, my friend," Leah said soberly. "I wish I had more time to be a great example. Hopefully, the people around me will have amnesia and not remember me as a warning!"

We laughed and finished another round of cards before Leah directed me back to finishing the story about Luke's homecoming.

Progress, Not Perfection

My father was so happy that both his children had returned home to him. After seven years, what had been taken from him was restored. He used to just look at the two of us together as if he could not believe we were really there. But though he was happy, he also realized we were no longer children. Our life together now was different than it would have been had we lived with him when we were younger. By now, Luke and I were both independent and had friends and lives of our own outside of the home.

While we were re-learning our identity, beliefs, roles, new freedom (and of course, learning about our father), he too was learning about us—and learning how to be a full-time father again. He was a single parent working while fitting us into his personal life, which also involved dating. This wasn't a time when being a single father was common, much less a single father with full custody of his two children. We had literally just shown up on his doorstep. The three of us were indeed experiencing a time of great change.

In the meantime, Georgiana and William, my father's older sister and her husband, had just recently moved from Hong Kong to take care of Mah-Mah. They brought their two children, William Jr. and Sarah. We all lived at my father's apartment together at first, but shortly after our arrival, they moved into an apartment two blocks away.

My aunt and uncle, who were very kind and loving (and had the patience of saints), embraced us and loved us as their own. Unfortunately, I was not always so gracious in return. It had nothing to do with them personally, for they were only wonderful. It had everything to do with me.

I was fourteen years old—awkward, hormonal, and had an attitude. Under normal circumstances, this would have been challenging enough for any parent (or guardian) to manage. But I was far from being a "normal" teenager. I was broken, tormented, and wracked with fear. I felt isolated, rejected, and loathed myself. There were no tools to deal with the inner turmoil, and I was still dealing with the painful racism prevalent back then, so that in addition to everything I was already trying to reconcile in my heart and mind, I was even more and more embarrassed by my heritage. With my aunt and uncle's recent immigration to Vancouver, their "Chinese-ness"—and mine—was inescapable.

When I lived with my grandparents, I would sometimes lie and tell people that I was Hawaiian. Thinking back, I can't believe I did that, but that was how desperate I was to be anyone but me. Deep down, I believed that if I could just deny where I came from, then I could deny my mother and all she represented (including Scham), thus giving me a chance to start anew.

Yes, I know this was shallow of me, but that's the way it was. I soon discovered that no matter how I tried to deny it, there was no getting around the fact my family and I were indeed Chinese. MahMah still spoke no English, and whenever we had family excursions, I would ask her not to speak to me in her native tongue. I was oblivious to how that may have hurt my grandmother and my Auntie Georgiana. I saw only the fact that they personified what others hated about me, and rejected our ethnicity because I had learned to hate these same things myself. I could not control anything else in my life, but I thought I could at least minimize the cruel racism that plagued me.

Thankfully, I was eventually healed of this wounded thinking, and now I proudly embrace my heritage.

Shortly after our move, my father had to make another difficult choice. Since all his assets were now in my mother's hands (including his investments to provide for our university education), he decided to move back to Hong Kong to work with his cousin and take an already profitable import/export business to the next level. This way, he could earn more income and provide a better life for us. Neither Luke nor I wanted to leave Vancouver because the city was our home, so it was agreed that Uncle William and Auntie Georgiana would act as our guardians.

As I have already said, my uncle and aunt were two remarkable people. Uncle William drove me long distances and across two bridges every morning, so I could continue going to my former high school and finish the year with my friends (instead of transferring in the middle of the year).

In school, I struggled with chemistry and physics. I had been told I was stupid for so long, I often gave up before trying. Uncle William, an engineer, recognized that I had potential despite my attitude, and tutored me until my grades came up. Soon I was scoring the highest marks of students in my science classes! At last, I understood the concepts that had eluded me before. I began to entertain the idea that maybe I wasn't stupid, ugly, and good-for-nothing after all. And Auntie Georgiana cooked wonderful meals for us and cared for us as if we were her own children.

Our uncle and aunt's new apartment was less than a few minutes walk away, but Luke and I were literally living on our own in my father's apartment. We made our meals, bought our own groceries, and had our own checking account, funded by our father for our necessities. We studied on our own every day, and eventually received scholarships to the local university.

But first, there was high school.

The Devil in Your Ear

I was in the middle of my tenth-grade year when I moved. As I already mentioned, my uncle was kind enough to drive me to school early in the mornings for the rest of the year because we lived so far away. I was now doing well in school, on the track team, and I'd joined the junior cheerleading squad, so my afternoon schedule was very full. There were times I stayed at a friend's house overnight, but I usually took the bus, transferring many times before finally reaching home.

To my surprise, I fell into a happy routine and was enjoying my new life. I had discovered I had a real talent for running the year before, but I didn't know I also had a penchant for dance. My mother had always told me I was very clumsy, so I never thought of trying out for the cheerleading squad until my friend insisted on it. In fact, I loved cheerleading so much I even ended up choreographing several of our dances for half-time shows!

My world had changed so much since leaving my mother and Scham. I was safe, loved, happy, and had friends. I even noticed, although I was Chinese, that the boys liked me.

Yes, for one of the first times in my life, I started to feel I could actually be "normal."

I also got a part-time job at a well-known clothing store that catered to youth and had many locations throughout the city. I started as a salesclerk, earning commission, and did very well, winning many sales awards. In a very short time, I also became responsible for dressing the mannequins throughout the store and in a few of the window displays. Within six months, I moved up the ladder to become head cashier on my shifts at my store. On top of my earnings, my father sent a regular allowance for both of us, so as another "first," I now had nice clothes and extra spending money. I could even afford to take taxis to and from certain school events and parties when it got too late. I was glad to have the cab fare and not burden my uncle with my high school social life travel concerns.

One such occasion was after a football game. As I stood on the field with the rest of my fellow cheerleaders, one of them pulled me aside. "Manna," she said, "You know Richard likes you, don't you? Haven't you seen how he watches you at every practice and even at the games?"

I had seen him, in fact. He often smiled at me while he was on the sidelines, but I dismissed it. Now that I had actually heard the words, a shuddering thrill ran through me. Richard wasn't only tall and on the football team, he was nice, sweet, and handsome.

That night, there was a get-together after the game at one of the cheerleader's houses. Sue and I had become good friends, and she was always so kind to me, inviting me over and including me in her home. It was wonderful to feel a connection like Luke had with Ronny so long ago.

All the girls got ready at Sue's, and I changed into one of my nicest outfits. During the party, Richard came up to me. We talked a little bit, and later he held my hand and kissed me. He was the first boy I ever kissed, and I felt I could have kissed him forever. I had no idea what those feelings were, rushing up and down my spine and in my tummy, or what the tingles were in my hands and feet, but it felt nice. He held me close to him as if he really cared about me and asked me to be his girlfriend. I almost fainted. Sue was smiling from ear to ear, as was another very close friend, Cathy. They were so happy for me because they knew things had not been easy.

After that, Richard and I hung around together at school, and after his own practices he'd come to our cheerleading practices. I was as happy as can be.

Then, things started to change.

Richard had a friend, Bob, who constantly whispered in his ear about how Richard should have nothing to do with me because I was Chinese. One day when I walked by, I distinctly heard Bob say, "Come on, man, why you want to be with a Chink when you can have any other girl at this school?" He made many versions of this statement in his attempt to dissuade Richard from caring about me. It had been some time since I had encountered the intensity of such a racial attack, and I certainly didn't expect to hear it after having recently experienced so many wonderful things in my life. I was taken off guard and felt lost as to what I ought to say or do, or how to defend myself.

Bob stuck to Richard and was constantly beside him, almost as if he had designated himself as Richard's watchdog to protect him from *me*. If I bumped into them coming out of our respective classes, Bob would scowl at me and then lean forward as if to threaten me not to come close to Richard. From then on, if Bob saw me in the hallways, he would urge Richard to turn around, and the two of them would walk in another direction. Within a few days of Bob's constant influence, Richard stopped calling me, stopped talking to me, and even stopped looking at me. He pretended he didn't see me, even during the games.

Our new friendship was over, and my heart dropped in my chest. Just when I began to feel a sense of normalcy, Bob came along and not-so-subtly reminded me that I was inherently different.

All I wanted to do was tell Richard that just being friends was okay. I wanted him to know that there was never any pressure on my part and that I would still like to be friends. But I never had the opportunity to say anything.

A week after our "breakup," I happened to pass Richard in the hall again. He was alone, without Bob beside him to whisper in his ear. We both happened to be in between classes, and the hallway was empty except for us. His eyes met mine, and he looked startled. This time, he couldn't pretend he was on his way somewhere else, and that a random stairway was more convenient for him to take.

This time, he could not pretend he didn't see me. He forced a weak smile and then hurried into the boy's bathroom.

That hallway encounter was the last meeting of our brief friendship. From that point on, I was invisible to him.

"What a weak and ignorant galoot!" Leah exclaimed.

"Yes, it would seem that Bob was," I agreed.

"*No*, I mean Richard! He was a coward!" She huffed.

"I don't disagree," I nodded. "But he taught me a lesson we all need to learn.

"First, we must learn the great power of words, as well as the enormous responsibility we have in friendship. We have the gift (and the weight) of influence in all relationships. Do we exercise this gift wisely so that we are a good influence on those around us? And, just as importantly, who do we *allow to influence us*?

"'Tell me with whom you walk, and I will tell you who you are' is a powerful Spanish proverb that reminds us to use wisdom when spending time with people. We have to watch our relationships, especially with those who are divisive, who create strife, who spread hatred, who gossip, etc. I learned right there and then it wasn't only family from whom I had to segregate myself. I had to really discern *to whom and to what* I would listen with all people and in all situations. Yes, life and death are indeed in the power of the tongue."

"Well, you were better off without him!" Leah stated firmly. "I'm sure all the other boys flocked around you in no time!"

Clueless

Yes, there were other boys, some very nice ones who didn't care whether or not I was Chinese, but I was too shy and afraid to trust that they too might not suddenly have a "change of heart." Perhaps subconsciously, instead of responding to those nice suitors, I liked the boys that I didn't think would ever like me back. It was *safer* that way. After all, if I never had a special friendship, then I would never get hurt.

The older brother of another friend was one of those boys. He and his friends would sit in the stands at the basketball games, and many times I would look up and see him smiling at me. He was just being nice because I was his little sister's friend, but even so, I was beside myself. I didn't know how to handle any kind of positive attention, especially from boys. Plus, he was so handsome, it made me feel even more awkward and ridiculous! So, I simply avoided him, and any other boy.

Football games were large and noisy; the crowd was far away. I had no reservations there, cheering or smiling up into the cumulative anonymity, but basketball games were different. The crowd was too close. I didn't want anyone looking into my eyes because I was afraid they may see that I was really worth nothing after all. I expected anyone who liked me would go the way of Richard, and I feared one day I might wake up and find that this precarious popularity had all been a dream.

The rest of my tenth-grade year seemed to pass in a series of fun and simple parties. I was the girl who didn't smoke or drink, and I was considered a bit of an oddball for having a *huge* crush on Guy LaFleur (of the NHL Montreal Canadiens). These differences, along with all the others, also helped to cast me into the fringes of all my "normal" teenage friends living "normal" teenage lives.

I was tired of feeling ignorant about things everyone else knew. I was tired of feeling like I didn't belong. So, one night after a big football game, I allowed my friend Dave to introduce me to gin and orange juice. Dave was one of the funniest guys in our class. I didn't laugh much, but around Dave, I did. He distracted me from what I believed to be insurmountable inadequacies. When he handed me my drink, I took a sip and was surprised that I couldn't really taste the alcohol. It tasted sweet, like orange juice should, but with a stronger, fresher scent. I convinced myself I wasn't *really* drinking, since it was mostly juice, and accepted two more glasses of the concoction.

Within a very short time, I was very dizzy and could barely keep my eyes open. I was as thin as a toothpick, and the alcohol went straight to my system. Unfortunately, I was barely able to stand, much less walk in my four-inch heels (we had all changed out of our uniforms earlier). Feeling this woozy and out of control frightened me; I knew I needed to get home. Fumbling and stumbling my way into the kitchen, I found the wall-mounted phone by the kitchen desk. No one else around me was in any better shape than I was, so I had to take care of myself. I managed to have enough sense left to look at some of the mail on the phone table to find the address where I was. Then I called a cab to take me home. Thankfully, I made it home without incident that night and managed to crawl into bed to sleep off the alcohol.

Toward the end of the school year, my friend Sue had another party. Her parents owned a sailboat that they docked at the Royal Vancouver Yacht Club. On a recent sailing trip, Sue had met three boys from Vancouver and had exchanged phone numbers with them. We lived in a different area of town than they did, and in those days, traveling outside of your neighborhood wasn't that common. So, it was with great excitement that Sue shared the news that she had invited her new friends to the party, and they were coming!

"Oh, my gosh, Manna! Wait till you meet them!" she said when we were finally face to face. She had asked me to come over much earlier to help her choose something fun to wear for the evening. She already had a pile of clothes on the floor of her huge bedroom, which had once been a rec room. She had many clothes, and I was amazed that her parents loved her so much to buy them for her. Even though I now had a large wardrobe too, I had had to purchase most of it for myself.

"Oh, Manna! The guys are gorgeous and *sooo* nice!" she gushed. "Just wait till you see them!"

I didn't say much. I merely watched Sue change from one outfit to the next as she explained how they had met and how they were coming all the way from Vancouver to North Vancouver (a forty-plus-minute drive) to see her and to meet her friends.

I smiled on the outside, but on the inside, I was starting to have what I now know was a minor panic attack (something never talked about back then, as the concept had just barely been "discovered").

Before I knew it, a dark, sleek Trans Am pulled up to the curb, and three boys got out.

Sue called out to them, "Matthew! Mark! John! Hi!" She grabbed me by the hand to go meet them, but I pulled away and waited in the kitchen, pretending I was having a deep conversation with another girl. I was really hiding. In the distance, I could hear Sue and the boys making small talk before they came into the house.

We were all introduced to one another, and Sue was right. Not only were all three very nice, they were very cute indeed. But when I saw John, my insides turned to mush. Now I wasn't sure if I was having a panic attack or if there was something special about this boy. So many thoughts and emotions surged through me, but I was grateful to at least find my composure enough to smile and say hi.

What in the world am I doing? Stop acting like a goofball and just smile! They live in Vancouver, and you'll never see them again! Just be normal!

In the meantime, Sue was talking up a storm, being the perfect hostess, and making sure everyone was having a great time. She came to find me and threaded her arm through mine, making sure I was also mingling and not hiding in the kitchen.

Throughout the rest of the evening, we talked and shared our plans for the summer. Mark, who was engagingly funny, captivated all of us with his entertaining and mischievous stories. The sweet and endearing Matthew had what I called *smiling* eyes, and you could tell he was very thoughtful and genuinely kind. John was a bit more reserved, which I liked. He didn't say much, but when he did, he was likewise engaging and likable. All the girls seemed to hang on his every word. I found myself watching John more than the others, and each time he caught my gaze, he smiled back. Embarrassed to have been caught looking at him, and worried that I appeared unrefined by doing so, I started to move slowly to the back of the room.

The evening came to an end, and the three Vancouver boys said their goodbyes and drove away. The girls would not stop talking about them for weeks, and our guy friends who were also at the party appeared somewhat miffed that the three Vancouver boys had absorbed all our attention.

However, I simply dismissed the evening. No one could remember what school they attended, and I was certain I would never see them again.

Edward Scissorhands' Uncle

It was now officially summer, and Luke and I went to visit our father in Hong Kong. We had not seen him in a long time, so we were very excited. While we were there, my father noticed that I was extremely shy, insecure, and lacked confidence in most areas. Although I put on a good front initially, whenever too much attention was directed at me or I felt pressed in a situation, I would cave in. He resolved to give me a makeover and enrolled me into a modeling and finishing school there, as well as one in Vancouver upon our return.

Wanting to help me feel more attractive and confident, my father invited me to get my hair done before we were to come home. I had long hair that went almost to my waist and was wavy at the ends. I loved the length of my hair, but I was open to having a bit of a trim and a more *mod* "feathered" look to keep up with the new styles of the mid-1970s, so I agreed.

My father decided to take me to his friend's hair salon. When I expressed my great concern about the place he chose, he assured me that it was the *best* place to go, and they would take *great* care of me.

"He is one of the *best and most sought-after* barbers in Hong Kong!" he told us as we walked into the old shop filled with men in white barber suits cutting other men's hair.

Barbers?

"Dad, I'm really not sure about this. They don't look like they're very up-to-date with hairstyles. I'm nervous."

"Honey, it will be okay," he assured me. "You have a photo of the style you like, right? Just show it to *Grand-Uncle Che*, and he will take care of you. I promise."

I was not comforted with his words of assurance, but before I knew it, both Luke and I were whisked away into two stylist chairs and sitting side by side.

Luke's stylist said he knew immediately what he should do for him and insisted that he have a perm. I watched as his hair was rolled and set in a pungent liquid and lingered as it was eventually dried and styled. Because his hair was so thick, the curls settled into a gentle wave that indeed flattered my brother. We all thought his hair looked great, but he was not so happy about it.

When it was my turn, I told the stylist I wanted my hair to look like the photograph I had brought with me, a brunette version of a Farrah Fawcett hairstyle. Grand-Uncle told me he did a lot of women's hairstyles, and that several of his female clients had also asked for a very similar style, so he knew exactly what to do. I was relieved and relaxed a little bit.

Grand Uncle went through a drawer filled with scissors of all shapes, sizes, and blades, pulled out a "special one, just for me," and started cutting my hair.

Memories of my mother butchering my hair raced through my mind, and I kept telling him not to cut so much, but he said, "Don't worry! I do this every day, and this has been my shop for over thirty-five years! I know exactly what to do. You will love it. Your hair will look just like that photo!"

But I knew something was going very wrong.

He systematically cut over eight inches off my hair; it was now above my shoulders, and he was still cutting. I started to tear up, but I didn't want to disrespect Grand-Uncle or my father, so I dug my fingernails into the palms of my hands so I wouldn't cry. But when I couldn't hold it back anymore, tears started to flow. Worse, my hair was not as thick as Luke's, so when he permed it, it didn't fall into loose, carefree waves. My hair looked like an afro, but even that would have been better than what I had.

My hair was a short, frizzy nightmare!

"Oh, this will loosen in the next few weeks," the stylist explained. "You'll love it!"

I literally wanted to die on the spot! I could barely look at my father, I was so angry with him and his friend whom we had been forced to call "Grand-Uncle." I walked out of the shop with a head of hair that looked like an upside-down pyramid! *Great! Now I look like the Bride of Frankenstein, and I'm starting a new school in a week!*

I didn't want to show my father how upset I was, but I was furious—furious because he would take me to a barber and furious that he didn't listen to me. That night I couldn't eat, and I spent the rest of the night crying in my room. Now instead of feeling somewhat acceptable with my long hair, I was sure that my ugliness on the outside would match the ugliness on the inside, and everyone would see me for who I had always been told I was.

When we returned from Hong Kong, Luke and I were both going to attend a new school. We could no longer ask Uncle William to drive us almost an hour away every morning to school during rush hour. And taking the complicated, two-hour route home by bus, especially with our full after-school programs, had become too much to manage.

The decision was made for us to change schools and start all over. I was sad to leave my friends, no longer run for my track team, or be a part of the cheerleading squad, but my father said we could try for those activities at the new school once we got settled. He tried to reassure me, but he had no idea how much I had come to cherish my newfound identity.

And so, Luke and I began a new school. We were nervous, and even though I felt like I looked like an alien or part of a comedic horror film, we both tried to be brave. We stepped into this new season with hope. Luke was starting grade nine, and I was starting grade eleven.

However, when the day arrived to start our new school, my anxiety surged to new levels. As I looked in the mirror, the reality of my "hairstyle," if I can call it that, glared at me. *How in the world am I supposed to go to school looking like…like… this? I'll be the laughingstock of the entire school!*

I consoled myself with the thought that at least no one there knew me. Today, there is a lot more tolerance and acceptance of different styles and looks, but that wasn't the case back then. Today, wearing a toque (Canadian term for a knitted cap), or a "lid" of any sort would be seen as hip or fashionable, but if I had worn something like that then, I would have been even more of an obvious misfit.

Maybe I can fly under the radar for the first few months, and no one will remember later that I was the girl who looked like the Bride of Frankenstein, I thought to myself as I approached the main entrance.

I walked around, looking for signs and hints of where I was supposed to be going. This new high school was considerably larger than my old school and had many more hallways, levels, and wings coming off each corridor. I had to spend extra time navigating through them, backtracking a few times because I had inadvertently gone the wrong way.

The school buzzer signaled a second time, notifying the students that not only were they supposed to be seated in their rooms already but that the teachers were about to start their homeroom procedures. Yet I was still lost and had not yet found my homeroom.

Finally, I found the right corridor and ran in. I was late. All the other students were sitting in their respective seats and talking among themselves, so when I popped in late, all eyes turned to me.

I could not believe it. It was as if I had actually announced myself when all I wanted to do was to slip unnoticed into the back corner of the classroom. I apologized to the teacher and made my way to an empty seat. After roll call, we were given our schedules and dismissed to our first class. I approached the teacher, apologized again for being late, and explained that I was a new student still trying to find my way around. He was very nice and understanding and gave me some pointers.

The other students were already on their way to their classes, when all of a sudden, I heard, "Hey, Manna!"

I looked up, shocked that anyone knew my name. Part of me wanted to hide because of my "new look," and part of me was curious to see who in the world it could be who knew me.

My throat closed. Standing in front of me was John, one of "the Vancouver boys," beaming a warm smile. I was so shocked I couldn't find the words with which to greet him.

"I almost didn't recognize you. Your hair's different."

"I know…a horrible mishap over the summer," I said, my head bowing down, feeling humiliated.

He didn't pause or slow in his response. "It looks nice. I didn't know you'd be going to school here. Mark and Matthew go here too. I'm sure you'll run into them soon. If you need any help finding your way around, let me know."

"Umm…thank you. That's very nice of you," I stammered.

"Okay—gotta run to algebra. See ya."

"See ya," I said, stunned.

Of the dozens and dozens of schools in Vancouver, how could it be that I would be in the same school, and the same homeroom, as John? And how could it be that I would walk in with my new Bride of Frankenstein haircut? What is happening?

Will the curses never end?

Bad Company

After the first week, I started to feel more comfortable with my new school. I also had a fairly good feel for how the social/cultural life in the eleventh grade worked at this new school. I realized there were several distinct groups, including a large Asian crowd. This was a far cry from my elementary school days when I was one of only three Asians. Now I was in a school where there were Chinese, Japanese, Filipino, Vietnamese, and East Indian students, among others. Diversity was much more prevalent here, and while friendships were made in and outside of one's nationality or culture, there was an unspoken and deeply rooted understanding that one ought to keep with one's "own kind."

I became friends with many different people, including three very special non-Asian girls—Bethanie, Madison, and Christie. They were kind, accepting, inclusive, and just really nice people. We spent a lot of time together and had great fun.

My hair also started to grow out of its horrible "style."

In time, I also met a boy named Byron. He was nice-looking, but it was his apparent shyness that attracted me. I assumed that because he was introverted, he would also be kind, gentle, and safe. We started talking, and before long, we were dating.

Unfortunately, Byron's apparent shyness soon began to morph into passive-aggressiveness. He became more and more controlling and didn't like for me to be with my friends. Not having had a boyfriend before, I wasn't sure if this behavior was representative of how dating should be, so I simply tolerated his behavior and told myself he was this way because he cared about me.

It wasn't long before he wanted our dating to be something "more." He kept trying to be alone with me, wanting to kiss and touch me. I was afraid of his persistence and was wary of sex, very wary of it. It didn't feel like the butterflies-in-the-stomach kind of feeling I had hoped, or even assumed, would happen in a "normal" relationship. When Byron touched me, I had the sense of "this isn't right," but I just assumed this was "me" not being "with it" or savvy to "relationships." I tried to get over it, but it made for awkward moments when we were alone together.

One day after school, he and his friend Doyle came over to my apartment. We hung out for a while, watching television. Suddenly Byron said he wanted to talk to me in private.

"Can we go to your room?" he asked.

Not suspecting anything, I naively agreed and led the way. Once inside, he shut the door. He sat me down on the bed, and he bent over me, kissing me and pushing me backward.

"What did you want to talk about?" I asked, ending the kiss.

"Us. I want to talk about *us!* I love you, Manna, and I want to make love to you. If you love me, you'll want to, too."

A parade of warning signs flashed through my mind. Harsh and repulsive memories of a vulgar man rubbing up on me were followed by those of a young girl dry-heaving next to a tree after she learned what it all meant.

"Oh, I don't think we should. I'm afraid. I could get pregnant."

"You won't get pregnant. I've got a condom. I've done this before. I *really* love you, and *if you love me*, you'll do what I ask."

He leaned over and kissed me then, but when he went too far, I stopped him. "No, I can't."

"Come on. Just try. It will make us closer and more official."

I thought about what he said. Having a boyfriend meant I belonged to someone. I didn't want to be alone. All my life I had done what others wanted to make them happy. I had thought that by pleasing them, I would be liked, and happy too. *Is Byron right? Will we be closer? Will I be happy if I do what he asks?*

How I wished I had had someone with whom to talk. I wished I had parents who were home, so I could have used that as an excuse. I wished I knew how to recognize whether or not someone was telling me the truth.

I wished I had known that I was more valuable than I thought I was.

Since I was a little girl, my trust had been breached, my humanity had been disregarded, and my boundaries had been violated. I didn't know what to think, what to feel, or what to do. I didn't know where to draw the line. No one had ever taught me the sacredness of sexual intimacy.

Then suddenly, something inside me clicked, and I knew none of this was right. It reminded me too much of Scham.

"No, Byron! I can't. I'm too scared…maybe another time. Let me think about it…I'm not ready."

"But if you really love me, this wouldn't be an issue! Come on!" he said, aggravated.

"Now you're scaring me…" I said feebly.

"Scaring you?! I love you! Come on!" Byron was relentless.

He had now forcibly peeled off my pants by holding my hands together and was naked himself from the waist down. He used his elbows and body weight to keep me pinned down, and his knees to force my legs apart. The harder I tried to push him away, the more he forced me down.

I kept trying to get away from his grip, but then...it happened.

My heart sank to even deeper depths of despair and loss. There was nothing loving or gentle or precious or sacred about this first time, and I knew that somehow, I was irreparably changed, used. Forever. I kept trying to force Byron off me, but he continued to do his deed.

I prayed for it to end quickly, and when it did, I lay on the bed, covering myself with my bedspread while Byron dressed and left the room.

I lay there wishing that I might fall asleep and try to erase the past few minutes, but the voices in the front room were distractingly loud. I got up and crept to the bedroom door. When I opened it a crack, all I could hear was Byron bragging to Doyle about how he had just "scored."

I fell against the wall and slid to the floor, wanting to die once more.

The school year finally came to a close, and another summer was before us. I had had a good year scholastically and enjoyed being in classes with some wonderful teachers. Mr. Ramadeen, my geometry teacher, was so kind and patient with me. Miss Marsh, my social studies teacher, encouraged me with her smile and kind words. Miss Glazier, my journalism teacher, was clear, concise, and effective in the way she taught. Miss O'Brien, my creative writing teacher, had the strangest and most comical way of being, and every time I think of her, I cannot help but smile. The antics that went on in that classroom, largely thanks to my mischievous friend Mark, one of "the Vancouver boys," will always be some of the funniest memories I have of high school. And of course, how do I ever thank Mr. Morris, my English literature teacher, enough? I took every class he taught just to be with him, because his genuineness, humor, and belief in me made me feel like I could achieve anything. He was the teacher of all teachers. He not only believed in me, but he also brought out the best in me. Mr. Morris gave me opportunity after opportunity *after opportunity* not only to try, but to excel in every class. Almost four decades later, I still feel indebted to each of these inspirational teachers.

On the personal side, while Byron and I were still together, our relationship was rocky at best. His controlling ways grew, and so did his temper. I only introduced him to my father a few times, but each time Byron was so disrespectful, my father insisted I break up with him. When I did, Byron's fury exploded. He threatened me with a knife, and when I talked him out of using it, he punched a hole in the wall in our living room instead. Not only did he not take responsibility for it, he never even offered to pay for the repair.

I'm ashamed to admit that I didn't have the strength to leave him for good *at first*, and sadly, after every break-up, I ended going back to him because I didn't believe I deserved better. It was a continuation of the life I had known with my mother and Scham—painful and abusive. However, with each of his outbursts, I grew stronger and less attached to him. After what I had to endure to finally be free of Scham, I wasn't going to consciously walk back into a prison again.

Around the time of one of our breakups, I found out that John was interested in me. I was astonished and thrilled at the same time, never believing that such a distant dream could become even a remote possibility. We often talked at school, and sometimes he would take me out in his convertible for lunch or in between classes when we both had a free period.

I thought I was in heaven.

One Friday night, John was on his way to pick me up for a date. Without my knowledge, Byron had been following me and knew that John and I had made plans. To my horror, when John showed up, Byron was also standing there. But that wasn't the worst of it. Byron started to confront John, with escalating rage.

I apologized to John, and not wanting him to be in the middle of something he didn't deserve, we both agreed to postpone our date for another time. I insisted on dealing with Byron on my own.

"Are you going to be okay?" John asked.

"Yes," I said, reassuring him. With reluctance, he agreed to let me sort things out with Byron, hugged me, and said, "Call me later tonight," before he left.

I was so absolutely enraged at Byron for what he had done but was silenced when he threatened me again—only this time he wasn't planning on hurting me, he was planning on hurting himself.

"I will kill myself if you leave me!"

"What did you say?!" I asked in disbelief.

"I already know how I'm going to do it, and then my death will be your fault. It will be on your head!"

I simply didn't know what to do. And then, as if things couldn't get worse, I found out I was pregnant.

There was no one I could tell. I could not heap more shame on myself or my family by telling my father. And I would never tell my mother…or John.

I was alone.

Byron told me to have an abortion, but I had no idea how that would work. I hadn't even adjusted to the whole concept of being pregnant and carrying a baby. After a few weeks, realizing I would be attached to Byron forever, but not having the maturity or the counseling to understand the consequences, I felt I had no other choice, and I agreed.

That horrible, dark day came and went. All I remember was being wheeled into the OR and having a nurse look at me and say, "Oh, dear, you are too young…" I turned my head away and wished to die on the surgery table.

Of course, I'm too young! I'm too young to have seen so much, to have endured so much, to have lost so much! And now to be so naked and dirty, ironically insisting on having something else so precious taken away from me…

When I recovered from the procedure, I tried to buoy myself. I thought of as many other happy things as possible—anything but what had just happened. I convinced myself that I had a chance to begin again, but no matter what distraction I tried to focus on, the grief of what I had done would not leave me.

Time passed, and I tried to go on. John thought I had chosen Byron over him, and while we were still friendly to each other, I was just as sad that I didn't get a chance to know John better. Of course, I was never going to reveal my latest dark secret to him, or to anyone else, so I continued living my days with forced smiles and a heavy heart.

Thankfully, the year was about to end, and I was about to graduate from high school. Another summer was upon us. However, with the trauma of everything that had happened that year, I almost forgot to send in my application to the university. At the last minute, I found the mindfulness to do everything I needed to do, and in the process discovered I had not only been accepted into the University of British Columbia, but I also had qualified for a scholarship.

Byron had never planned on going for higher education and became very bitter that I did. I didn't care. I was determined to better myself, to better my life, and to be rid of Byron and the ugliness of my life represented in him, forever.

Yes, I needed to look to my future. My life was about to begin anew. I was certain of it. I just needed a plan.

Your Day Will Come

It was 1980. There was still the whole summer between me and the beginning of my first year at UBC, where I knew Byron would never go. I had to get away, so I called my father in my misery, and without telling him the details surrounding my despair, he sent me a plane ticket to visit him. I needed to be with a parent, and I needed to get away from my life of madness in Vancouver. On the plane ride over, I was hopeful. Luke decided not to go that summer, so I would be on my own with my father.

I had no idea what was in store for me but was excited because anything was better than what I was living. When I finally arrived at the Hong Kong International Airport, a Chinese man in uniform greeted me with my name on a sign.

"Miss Ko?" he asked with a warm smile.

"Yes?"

"I am your driver, miss. My name is Cheng."

My father has a driver now?

Then I remembered him mentioning something about it because my flight was arriving at a time when he would be in a meeting. I had hardly expected my reception to be so formal. Neither did I expect a personal driver to escort me to a beautiful, new, white luxury car parked just outside the terminal gates. It's common now to have drivers and luxury cars to pick travelers up at the airport, but over thirty-five years ago, this was not so.

I took it in as best I could, touching the fancy upholstery and checking all the buttons lined up on a panel. Each button controlled something—one for the seat movements, one for the windows, several for the music, and even one to control the screen that could separate me from the driver. My heart raced with excitement, and I settled back to enjoy the comfortable ride.

"I'll be taking you to your father's office now," Cheng said.

We drove through the city of Hong Kong, and I marveled at how busy and big it was. I also couldn't help but notice we traveled to a very fashionable side of town and was even more surprised when we stopped there.

"Your building, Miss Ko," Cheng said as he opened my door.

I looked up at the towering, stylish modern building called The Admiralty Center, where my father's office was located, right on the waterfront on the Hong Kong side. Cheng removed my suitcase from the trunk and walked me to the front door, where another man was waiting to take my luggage. This man guided me to my father's office on the twenty-third floor. As we rose on the elevator, I watched the city fall below me.

"Here we are, Miss Ko," the gentleman said, holding the elevator door for me.

I stepped into a beautiful lobby, and to the left was my father's new office with floor-to-ceiling glass doors and windows. It was breathtaking. I suddenly realized what all of this meant. My father had, at long last, achieved what he had been working so hard for. He had "made it."

No more onions for him!

The gentleman helped me with my suitcase and escorted me into my father's private office. To my right was a large conference room, also with walls of floor-to-ceiling glass. Inside I could see my father leading the conversation at the head of the table. Five other men were around him, including two Caucasian men whom I later learned were from the United States.

As I looked out from the door of my father's private office, I noticed the design rooms, showrooms, and another conference room with glass sides, and a large open area filled with a plethora of desks where the employees worked. While I waited, I was introduced to the CFO, who nodded politely and spoke with deference about my father.

The gentleman from the lobby told me my father was expecting me and would be in as soon as he finished his meeting, and then said goodbye. After he left, I couldn't help the tears that came as I walked to the floor-to-ceiling windows and looked out at the magnificent view of the Hong Kong harbor.

My father came in about thirty minutes later to find me sitting in his luxurious leather chair behind his desk. I was caught in my past memories. When I was a little girl alone with my Barbie doll, I had dreamed of being a successful businesswoman in a world like the one my father had created for himself.

I hadn't noticed that my father had come in and was watching me as I pretended to be talking on the phone, negotiating a "big deal," shuffling papers on my large mahogany desk, and writing brilliant notes on an empty notepad with my father's gold Cartier pen—all at the same time.

My eyes suddenly caught a glimpse of him as he stood in the doorway, smiling with amusement. I jumped up and ran to him, hugging him and crying. In a flurry of emotions, I told him how amazed I was at his good fortune and how happy I was to see him again. At last, my father stepped back and said, "I want to show you all of it! We have six weeks before you start university, and we will get to as much as we can before you leave."

I smiled with relief, but it was almost too much to take in.

I was, above all, most delighted to see the joy in my father's eyes as he shared all of this with me for the first time. Later that day, I was taken for afternoon tea, and when we finished, Cheng was summoned again. We were whisked away once more and taken to my father's home—a condo on the tenth floor in the heart of town. I could hardly believe my eyes.

The surprises didn't stop. The next day, my father had to leave for work early. I told him I would be happy to stay at home and entertain myself, but he waved away the suggestion. Instead, he told me I was to go shopping because I needed to prepare for some big events coming up. He gave me instructions to meet a woman named Margaret downstairs within an hour, kissed me on the cheek, and went off to work. In a fit of nervous excitement, I got ready and did as he instructed. When I arrived in the lobby, a lovely, exotic-looking woman was waiting for me. She smiled warmly.

"You must be Manna," she said, reaching for my hand. "My name is Margaret, and your father has asked me to be your personal shopper today."

I laughed out loud.

Here was the dream, and my father was actually living it! The rest of the day flew by in a blur. I was taken from one elite store to another, all of them displaying the very latest designs from top designer labels. I was encouraged to buy anything and everything I wanted. At first, I was reserved and timid, constantly asking Margaret for permission to look at one thing or to approve of another, but she soon helped me to overcome this "obstacle"!

We went to many stores before having a late lunch, and at the end of this adventure, I had at least fifteen different bags full of designer shoes and lovely matching outfits. There were suits, dresses, casual wear, and lovely accessories. Remembering my past—that poor little girl who grew up feeling like an orphan (and dressing like one too)—I felt like now I was on top of the world.

Margaret and I dined at the Furama Hotel (a high-end hotel at the time). Many entertainers and movie stars used to go there, though I didn't know that at the time. A man and two women were sitting in a nearby table, and I noticed them staring at us as soon as we were escorted to our table. All our packages were in the car, so it wasn't as if I was making a scene with all my shopping bags and boxes. I didn't know why they kept looking our way, and shortly after we had ordered our lunch entrée, one of the women at the table came by.

"Excuse me. I hate to interrupt," the woman said. "But I have to ask, are you a model? Or have you done any modeling in the past?"

I shook my head, startled by the question, and managed to say, "Ummm, not for the past year." My father had enrolled me into a year-long modeling and finishing school the previous year, and although I had done some modeling for a few different organizations and events, there were no new events to tell her about. Plus, with all that had happened in the recent past, I didn't want anyone to look at me for fear that they would see my shame.

"We are always looking for fresh faces," she explained, "and a beautiful girl like you could make it quite far in the industry. Let me give you my card. I would love for you to come into the office and audition as the host for an upcoming television show for young adults." (Today, the show would be equivalent to a Nickelodeon channel with programming for teenagers and young adults in their early twenties). "There is a lot of growth and opportunity for you to model, too, since you're so tall. Both avenues could be very exciting for you. I'll personally see to it that everyone knows that beautiful face before long."

For a moment, I was stunned and wondered if she had mistaken me for someone else. I looked at Margaret, who simply stared back at me. She had never been in a position like this before either, and after the lady finished speaking, Margaret asked her a few questions.

"May I ask who you are and what your position is with this company?" she asked, glancing at the card.

The lady explained that she was one of the senior producers of the network she represented and coincidentally happened to be there for an earlier meeting with another talent agent. She said she normally did not approach people. Looking for new talent was outside the normal scope of her work, but as soon as she saw me, she knew that I had "it"—the proverbial "IT"—that would succeed in television, print, or any kind of media. "The point is," she added, "we need to get you in front of the camera and in front of as many people as possible."

We shared a few more pleasantries, but the producer was insistent on setting up a time for me to go to the studio. Margaret studied the card more carefully, and after finally realizing who the lady in front of us was, her eyes popped open, and her eyebrows almost jumped off her face. I understood then that this person must have been a very high-ranking individual indeed.

Not knowing what to tell her, but also not wanting to be rude, I managed to say, "Thank you so much, but I'm only here for the summer before I start university this fall. I will need to show this to my father before we can commit to anything."

"Absolutely. I totally understand, but please do not lose my card. And do call me tomorrow."

The woman thanked us for our time, and I gave her my name and my father's name and contact information. After she left, I didn't know whether to scream for joy or hide under the table.

Did I just have a twenty-minute interaction with a high-ranking influential producer of one of the biggest television networks in Asia? She thought I was beautiful and wanted the world to know it, too! Was I beautiful? Did she not see what others saw in the past? Wasn't I stupid, ugly, and good-for-nothing? Wasn't I the one Bob insisted his friend should not spend a single moment with?

What had happened seemed impossible.

Sitting at the Furama Hotel (known then for its luxury) with my fancy new clothes, being waited on hand and foot, I debated inside. It was hard to believe I was the same girl from Canada.

I looked up from my thoughts at Margaret. Her eyes were riveted on me.

"Do you know what that was?" she whispered animatedly.

I shook my head. She proceeded to explain the intricate details of the entertainment industry in Hong Kong. This was an opportunity of a lifetime—to be "found" in this way. The woman had basically handed me my own television show and built-in modeling career. Margaret flushed with sheer excitement.

I told Margaret that I didn't think I was ready for something like this and had to make sure my father would approve. When we returned to the office, Margaret and I told my father what had happened, and I turned the card over to my father, who tried to hide his concern behind his forced smile.

"What do you think, Daddy?" I asked him.

"I think she is right. You are a beautiful girl, and I believe you have a lot to offer the world. But I also know that industry is a hard one. You are an innocent. You're too green for this, and it's not time yet. Your time will come, but it's not now. If you were to go into that industry now, it would ruin you forever."

He held out his hand for mine and covered mine with his own. I blushed, looking down at the plush carpeting beneath my feet. He could not possibly know how much of myself I had already compromised, or how *ruined* I already felt I was.

Although I didn't mention modeling or television with him again, it seemed that wherever I went that summer (and with each future visit), people always seemed to stop me. They asked if I was someone they had seen on television or in the movies, or if I was a famous singer. One time, when my father was present, a large group of students on their way home from school came rushing up to me. We were in line at the Star Ferry, waiting to buy tickets and cross to the other side. They asked me for my autograph and begged me to sign their notebooks. I told them I wasn't famous, but they refused to believe me. Soon their pleading escalated, and people around us started staring, coming closer. I insisted a few more times that I was not who they thought I was, but the frenzy of their excitement of seeing a "'movie star" took over. I looked at my father, and not knowing what else to do, I submitted to their requests and doodled a fancy signature. For that moment, I was whomever they thought I was, and I had made them happy. They rushed off to catch their ferry, exclaiming joy with each step and comparing autographs with each other.

I was too astonished to move after the crowd dispersed, and I didn't want to take that same ferry ride with them in case they asked me more questions. I saw the joy in their eyes and the smiles on their sweet little faces, and I didn't want to disappoint them.

I'm only me, not someone famous, not someone special, I reminded myself.

My father smiled and said, "Your day is coming. You are still too green, but one day…" He then told me that he had had to tell the producer the same thing and that I needed to simply focus on my formal education for now.

I was disappointed but relieved at the same time. Heaven forbid anyone look too closely at me and learn of my shame.

The Real McCoy

That following weekend was one I shall never forget. I was taken shopping again to find dresses for a few special events—one for the horse races at the Hong Kong Jockey Club, one for a formal dinner at the World Trade Center Club, and a third for a formal high tea party the following day.

Amidst all the information I was learning about my father's new life, came the discovery that we owned a racehorse. Our horse was named The Real McCoy, #4. The Real McCoy was racing that weekend, and we would be sitting in the owner's box to watch him race. Afterwards, we would go down to the paddocks to see him and the jockey and take photographs.

I found the racetrack thrilling to the senses. It had rained the night before, causing the rich scent of damp earth to rise into the stands where we sat. The roar of the cheering crowds and the pounding of the horses' hooves on the track were thunderous. The absolute wonder of watching these powerful, gorgeous animals compete was breathtaking. The Real McCoy was beautiful, and while he was no Secretariat, I couldn't take my eyes off him. Unfortunately, however, he did not win his race, but came in third-to-last. Still, I took many photos of him running his heart out.

After the horses finished their races, we went down to the paddocks to meet the jockey and to be with The Real McCoy. He truly was a majestic horse, and I didn't care what position he placed—to me, he was a winner!

I later surprised my father with a photograph I had taken near the last stretch of the race. After all the other horses had already passed by, a perfect photo op had come for me to take a picture of The Real McCoy to make it look like he was at the head of every other horse—leading by three or more lengths. When he saw it, he laughed out loud.

"Why is this picture so funny, Daddy?" I asked.

"Manna, I know you are only trying to make me feel better, but you can't hide the fact that The Real McCoy almost came in last. Do you see the people in the stands in the back of the photo? Their heads are turned to their right, clearly showing that their focus was on all of the other horses that had already come in ahead of him."

We both chuckled. To this day, it's still one of my favorite photos.

Dirty Rotten Scoundrel

We went home to change and prepare for the big dinner party at the World Trade Center Club. At that time, the members of this very exclusive club were often handpicked. This club, along with the Hong Kong Jockey Club, were considered the most elite of clubs, and we were going to both in one day!

My father, and his older cousin who was his partner, were entertaining Steve, a New York business owner and a long-time client. Steve and his associate had flown in to finalize a contract for one of his biggest orders yet.

For dinner, I selected a pink silk dress from my new wardrobe and took great care in getting ready. When the hour to leave finally arrived, I walked through the lobby of our condominium building on my father's arm, feeling like a princess, and stepped into our chauffeur-driven car. We were driven to the World Trade Center Club and made our way to the reception library where the dinner was to be held. The room was resplendent, and the tables lavishly arrayed.

Slowly, the room began to fill. Everyone mingled and greeted one another. The waiter, who was dressed in formal attire and white gloves, arrived and began taking drink orders. I listened carefully to what everyone else was ordering. Almost all of them were ordering cocktails of some kind. The waiter came to me, and I wavered a moment. I didn't want to embarrass my father with my youth or naivety.

"I'll have a 'Chivas 25 on the rocks, please,'" I said, remembering a TV commercial I'd seen. Everyone always said I carried myself like I was in my mid-twenties, instead of only being seventeen years old, so I thought I would practice and see if it were true. The waiter, gracious and unwavering, took my order, thanked me by title and name, and proceeded to the next guest.

My father turned toward me, his eyes wide, not just because I had ordered an alcoholic drink, but because I had ordered one of the most expensive Chivas Regal scotches available at the time. It was aged over twenty-five years, and a limited release, bottled for our club! The wives whom I had gotten to know smiled at me, and I shrugged my shoulders as I smiled back. I was at least trying to seem like a grownup.

As I saw the server return with our drinks, I tried to lift my head a little higher, and threw my shoulders back a bit more. However, when I brought the crystal glass to my lips, one whiff of the golden liquid told me I'd gotten in over my head. I took a tentative sip and tried not to contort my face as the alcohol burned in my mouth and down my throat. I swirled my glass, playing with the ice in it, hoping it would melt and dilute the powerful concoction, but I only barely managed to take a few small sips during that cocktail hour.

When it was time for dinner, we were formally escorted to a beautiful and elegant private dining room. Five personal attendants waited for the ten of us to enter, including the lead server, who oversaw the entire evening for us.

The dining table itself was adorned with exquisite candelabras, fine crystal glasses, and pure silverware for each place setting. I was seated next to my father's client, Steve, and we made polite conversation.

As my attendant pulled out the chair for me, I studied my table setting, remembering everything I had learned in finishing school. This was the last place I wanted to embarrass my father, especially since I was sitting right beside his client. But I was not concerned. My etiquette was precise not only for the Western culture, but also for the Asian culture. I knew the protocol for both and proceeded with the rest of the evening feeling nervous, but still relatively confident.

Just in case, like I had learned to do so many years ago in elementary school, I watched the others around me and copied what they did. In this way, the dinner passed uneventfully.

The dinner conversation became less ceremonial and monitored as drinks were ordered and re-ordered. I could not, however, take any more of my scotch and just sipped on water.

My father finished telling an amusing story, and just as I was feeling a little more at ease, I noticed some pressure on my right thigh. At first, I thought it was just my being overwhelmed with so many varied sensations, but as I looked down, I saw that Steve had indeed placed his hand on my leg. He had managed to do so under the tablecloth, and with my father seated at the head of the table (and with several people in between), he thought he could get away with this offensive and blatantly disrespectful maneuver. I looked up at him, but he was purposely looking in the direction of his associate sitting next to him. I turned to my father, with whom this man was supposed to be doing a respectable business. I knew he had no idea what was happening.

Inside, my body revolted. I sat as still as I could, not moving a muscle.

I wanted to scream.

Men were the most disgusting, vulgar, and vile creatures to ever walk the earth.

I took the only action I could think of without causing a scene. I excused myself to go to the lady's room and asked one of the wives to come with me. I shared with her what had happened, and when we returned, she walked me to my seat and then simply placed her hand on Steve's shoulder. With only a look, she made it known that nothing else should happen. I also made sure to lean into my seat as close to my other table companion, and as far away from Steve as possible for the rest of the evening.

Finally, the dinner party ended, and everyone said goodnight, but I didn't even look at Steve. I stayed close to my father as we made our way back to the limo.

Impartation

When we were escorted back into our private car, my father leaned forward and gave some directions to Cheng, who took us far away into an unfamiliar part of the city where there were few towers, fewer lights, and certainly no limos.

"What are we doing, Daddy?"

"I want to show you something," was all he replied.

We drove even further still, and at last, my father leaned forward and said, "Slow down, please, Cheng."

The limo slowed. I looked out of the darkened windows and saw that we were on the outskirts of the city. The area surrounding us was rural and very dirty. It was almost midnight. Were it not for the lights of the car, and, ironically, the beauty of the moonlight, it would have been difficult to see much.

My father directed me to push the button to lower the window. I did so, and he said, "Look outside, and tell me what you see."

I looked around. There were no homes or lights.

"I don't really see anything."

"Look closer."

I did. Only then did I see them. "There are big boxes along the roads and into the hillside."

"What kind of boxes?"

"Well, they look like refrigerator boxes; they're big—like for appliances."

"Look closer."

"Oh!" I said, startled when I saw something move. "Oh, my goodness, Daddy. There are people in them!"

As I watched, I saw people moving in and out of the boxes, and I began to understand what I was seeing. "They live in those boxes!"

My father nodded. "There are many reasons why they are living like this. Maybe they were displaced by typhoons, maybe they have had hard luck all their lives, and maybe it was through poor choices. But since we have no way of knowing, we shouldn't judge them. But I also want you to know something else," he said thoughtfully. "You and I are no different than those people living in those boxes. We have had our own rough times. I didn't have a place to live for a while, and I worked four jobs at a time, including peeling potatoes and onions, as you recall. I know things haven't been easy for you either with your mother and her husband, but at least we always had a roof over our heads. By the grace of God, we were given a second chance, a third, a fourth, and so on. By the grace of God, we were given many blessings—unmerited favor and opportunities that we didn't deserve. And now, thankfully, you are about to have the chance to go to university and get an education—something that no one will ever take away from you.

"You can't help the poor if you're one of them. You can't help the weak if you're one of them. You can't help the needy if you're one of them. This applies to all areas of life. God will use everything that happened in our lives for good. We may not understand the purposes of pain and suffering at the time, but in due season, it will all become clearer.

"For now, we are in a season of harvest, and God is blessing us with great favor. But this good fortune is not just for ourselves. That would be in vain. We are given much so that we might give much back. To whom much is given, much is expected. You must steward your gifts and make the most out of them, using them wisely.

"And remember, you must never look down on these people. Rather, you must serve them instead. You too must use your gifts for the sake of humanity. Never squander what you have been given."

I fell back into my comfortable seat with tears flowing down my cheeks, feeling the truth of my father's words in my heart. I also felt ashamed for being so selfish, always thinking about *me* and not about others who suffered in much worse conditions than I ever had.

My father set everything up perfectly with all the shopping, fashionable restaurants, hotels, privileged and elite clubs, and the seemingly unlimited extravagance of it all. It was his intention to crescendo at this beautiful juncture, to see the poor, desperate, widowed, orphaned, needy, and sick.

To see life in such polar opposites impacted me to my core.

I was speechless by the magnitude of this tremendous lesson and unable to say a thing for the rest of the forty-five-minute ride home.

My father knew the power of this moment in my life, and he allowed me to receive this learning in silence.

Unlike other traditional ceremonies or rites of passage, instead of a cotillion, a Sweet Sixteen party, or some other coming-of-age party, I was blessed with the most important event of all—the impartation of my purpose.

As we drove home, I remembered GongGong's words of exhortation to me when I was a little girl, asking me to be kind and to serve others. And now, my father initiated me into that same charge, to use everything I was blessed with in joyful, loving service for others.

In the dark interior of the limousine, I saw then that the pain, fear, and shattered dreams I had were not unique. Though the faces, names, and circumstances may look different in detail, we all share the same collective lessons of life. We all hurt, and we all despair in the loneliness of our private sufferings. But if we rally together, a better and brighter future is possible. We can triumph over adversities together.

7 DYING TO LIVE

We gain strength and courage by each experience in which we look fear in the face…we must do that which we think we cannot.

—Eleanor Roosevelt

Room 316

I never knew what to expect on my visits to Leah. She had surprised me more often than not with her ability to focus, her memory, and even her strength. Today was no different. In spite of her downward spiraling health, when she saw me walk in, she gave me a beatific smile.

"Come and sit beside me," she said. "Tell me how you've been."

"I'm doing great, Leah," I said, trying to match her cheer. "I spoke with my brother Luke today, and told him I was seeing you."

"Oh, I feel like I know him."

"Well, the feeling is mutual, and he sends you his best wishes."

"That's so kind. Tell me how he's doing."

"He's doing wonderfully, thank you."

"He's married, right? And children?"

"Yes, they just celebrated their twenty-fifth wedding anniversary!"

"Really? That's marvelous. Are you close to his wife?"

"Yes. Elizabeth and I are great friends, and she is truly like my sister. I've known her as long as Luke has. They met when they were fourteen years old and were high school sweethearts. They married after Luke got out of graduate school, and have three magnificent children, whom I adore and love as my own. They haven't been without their trials, but Luke and Elizabeth worked through each difficulty together, coming out stronger and closer than they were before."

Leah smiled, "Good for him. He deserves all the happiness in the world."

We heard a knock on the door, and Melody peeked in. Though the door was never closed, she always knocked before entering as a gesture of respect for our deeper conversations.

"I'm sorry to interrupt," she said softly, "I'm just here for the usual routine.

Don't mind me."

Leah was unusually agreeable, complying without her typical grumbling.

"Now, let's get back to you, my dear," she said, returning her attention to me once Melody was done and had left the room. "What happened during the rest of your time in Hong Kong? And tell me that horrible Byron boy was banished forever out of your life!"

"The rest of the trip was wonderful. And when I returned, my former life seemed like a bad dream. I had seen the world outside of what I had been living before, and there would be no returning. It wasn't just the glamour of the dresses and the horseraces and the fancy meals. It was the invitation to a life of excellence, and the suggestion that I actually *belonged* in that life—especially if I followed my father's path of hard work, humility, and generous contribution.

"I think that's why I was so awestruck and enamored watching the Real McCoy run that race," I laughed. "And I suppose it's why we love watching great athletes and artists. There's something about watching someone, or even an animal, who has trained so hard to be the best they can be at their sport or art, or craft perform with all their heart and passion. It shows us what could be possible if we discover what gifts we have been given to offer the world, do the work to develop them, and then use them with all our might, without holding back.

"I knew there was more for me than all I had experienced, more than my circumstances, and more than what I had been told all my life. My eyes were opened on that trip, and once you've opened your eyes, you can never pretend you've never seen before. It was time to put the past and all its negativity behind me, including Byron."

I returned with two big life-changing benchmarks for my new world back at home: one was four suitcases stuffed with an entirely new wardrobe and matching shoes, and the second was a decision I made.

In order to be of most use for the helpless, I would be their defender and advocate. I decided to study law and be a *barrister* (the Canadian term for an attorney).

Of course, as a "fashionista," I knew being an attorney also meant that I *had* to have a three-piece suit, so my father also permitted me to get a *four*-piece, tailor-made, dark grey pinstriped suit before leaving Hong Kong. It was stunning! I loved it, and when I put on that suit, I knew I was truly made to be an attorney.

I was ready to begin my new life.

Boys Are Weird

I started UBC with Madison and Bethanie, two of my three closest girlfriends from high school. Christie chose to attend a university back east, so for the time being, it was just Madison, Bethanie, and I embarking upon our new lives with keen anticipation.

It was the first week of our first year at the university, and the energy was riveting. There were countless first-year students from all over the country (and world) settling into our classes. I will forever carry memories of the long, long walk from "B Lot" to classes carrying over twenty pounds of books and binders. How we kept our bags over our shoulders while trying to maneuver huge golf umbrellas in the rain, sleet, and snow still make me smile—and shake my head.

Yes, I was happy and excited about my future.

Throughout the day, many of the first and second-year students studied at Sedgewick Library. Inside, there were quiet areas to study behind the turnstiles, and "honeycombs" (enclosed circular study cubicles) outside of the turnstiles for group studies. There was also a cafeteria area and many other lounge spaces where students could gather and socialize. My friends and I often met in one of these spots to share our daily adventures and exam stresses.

I was now at my full height of 5'7", weighed 115 pounds, and had a wardrobe of beautiful clothes (which to me represented how far I had come from my days with my mother and Scham). My hair was nicely done in a fashionable style (no one was ever going to butcher my hair again), and I was making friends with new students from all over the world.

Though I had come a long way, my insecurities still rose to the surface when boys started to like me and to show an obvious attraction to me.

I was still obviously Asian, but now at a well-known university where higher thought abounded, and students were from all backgrounds, races, and ethnicities. My being Chinese didn't seem to matter. And while I was relieved by this new reality, I was still uncomfortable with the attention I was getting.

John happened to be going to the same university, and though we had never fully pursued a romantic relationship as seniors, he showed interest again now that we were older and outside of the high school cliques. My girlfriends encouraged me to rekindle my interest in John and welcome his attention.

Under normal circumstances, this wouldn't have been a big deal. But unfortunately, our interest in each other was, in fact, a *very* big deal to a few others. They made it known with unpleasant remarks and underhanded comments that I shouldn't have anything to do with him. I didn't understand all the ins and outs of it at the time, as I was only seventeen. John was maybe eighteen, and we were simply interested in spending time together and dating. Our relationship wasn't about getting married. Apparently, the problem was our different ethnic and cultural backgrounds. While it wasn't an issue for my family or friends, it was definitely an issue for his family and others in his community.

John went against the crowd nonetheless, and we ended up spending a lot of time together. We often studied in the afternoons and evenings and went out on the weekends.

He joined a fraternity, and I, a sorority, of which I eventually became vice-president. There were many events, parties, meetings—and of course, a lot of schoolwork. It was a very busy and effervescent time. My life was so different than what I had known even a year before. I thought I had finally put the past behind me as I looked ahead to my future.

On Halloween, my friends and I attended an enormous party at one of the fraternity houses. We took our time getting ready and goofing around at Madison's home with friends before heading over.

When we arrived the fraternity house, one of the girls who originally disapproved of my relationship with John was outside talking with someone. As soon as she saw me, she grabbed my hand and hurried me into the house, saying, "Manna, where have you been? John has been asking for you for hours! He's inside and asked me to bring you to him if I saw you. Hurry, let's go in."

Did I hear her correctly? John has been asking about me for hours? And wasn't this the same girl who told me I wasn't "allowed" to date him? And now she's leading me up the stairs to see him?

She led the way up the stairs. As soon as she reached the top of the landing, she pulled me around, and I flew in front of her. John came running to me and met me with an authentic warmth I had never experienced from a boy. He wrapped his arms around me and held me tight. "I was so worried about you," he exclaimed. "Where have you been? Never mind, you're here now. C'mon, let's get a drink, and then I want to introduce you to some people," he said after placing a kiss on my forehead.

As we were walking together, John turned to me and said, "You look so amazing, but you have to stay close to me. I don't want anyone else looking at you. You're mine."

I inhaled sharply and tried to control the overwhelming joy that leapt out of me into a simple smile. All of this was more than I could ask for—a new life, a new beginning, and so many new experiences. Life was perfect! I felt that at last I had everything I had ever wanted, including my father's old car to use from time to time (though it often broke down). Now I also had a kind and caring boyfriend and a dream of going to law school. And just when I didn't think I could ask for more, unlikely cohorts were helping to make all my dreams come true. My prince was infinitely charming, and nothing could spoil my elation.

Alas, as is the case with dreams, there comes a time when we awake.

There will always be people who are bitter and spiteful. Because of the darkness in their own hearts, they will do anything to diminish your light and to rob you of your joy. Their goal is to simply make you as miserable as they are.

One rainy morning after my first round of classes, I went to Sedgewick to study for a couple of hours before my afternoon classes. I hadn't noticed the girl leaning against a wall talking to someone, but as soon as she saw me walk down the stairs, she came right to me.

This was a girl from high school (and of the same ethnic background as John), but I never liked her. Behind her saccharine smile was a malevolent heart that wielded a venomous tongue. Now she was slithering her way towards me with her sly smile and wide-open eyes. I knew she had been planning something.

I gave her a polite smile, but immediately looked away and kept walking. She wasn't about to let me go though, and grabbed my arm.

"Oh, don't go! I want to tell you how happy I am for you and John. You two look sooo cuuute together!" Her condescending emphasis on the word cute made it sound as if she was commenting on the cuteness of a camel. "And," she continued, "You complement each other so nicely! He's so blonde, and well, you're so...*not!* And...he's so involved in *our* community! And well, there again...you're *sooo not!*" Then she giggled guilefully and added, before slithering away, "See ya around. Maybe at one of our next community events...or *not!*"

She was known for her seagull approach, "fly-by dumps," and she had masterfully unloaded another deposit.

Sometimes there are snakes in our garden.

John and I were just two kids in our late teens spending time together, but the undercurrent was undeniable, and the cloud of opposition was equally inescapable. Around this same time, several mutual friends confided in me and said, "Even if you were to 'convert,' the fact that you are *obviously* not the same would be too much to overcome."

Those comments took me by surprise since I had not even considered anything more than enjoying the times we were having together. *Why the drama? Why is the fact that we're from different cultural backgrounds such an impasse?*

I kept my spirits up, though. I just kept being me, enjoying my new world at UBC. Unfortunately, what I thought were isolated incidents of pettiness or jealousy, however, had seeded deep roots, and our relationship started to change.

After several months of idyllic dating, John simply stopped calling me. He also stopped returning my calls. When we did unexpectedly meet at school, he was short, cutting, and abrasive. He insinuated that I wasn't smart enough for him and said the pressures he faced at home for being with me were too much. It was for these reasons, it seemed, that he had abruptly and unilaterally ended our relationship.

Are all boys like this? Odd? Strange? Awful?

Byron was abusive and controlling, just like Scham. And both Richard and John just left—no conversation, no discussion.

Boys were *weird*.

For any other girl, this may not have seemed like something herculean to overcome. But for a simple girl like me, who was desperately trying to free herself from her past, to find acceptance and safety in her own skin while trying to make a new life, it was torturous. I could not get past that familiar voice of rejection that told me, "You're not wanted. You're not loved. You don't belong...you'll never belong."

It was all very confusing. Nothing made sense. One minute I was wanted, the next minute I wasn't. One minute I was everything to someone, the next minute, I wasn't.

Was there no one I could trust?

Every time I felt like I had taken a step forward, something bad happened and I fell two steps backwards. In spite of my earnest desire to learn and grow, and in spite of my ardent efforts to overcome each setback, I was always met with the same result—failure. And I didn't know how to climb out of the mire of it all.

The feeling of futility overcame me, and my heart began spiraling down fast.

Maybe I haven't overcome as much as I thought I had.

I didn't know what to do or how to reconcile my "differences" with the world around me. I no longer felt I had the energy or courage to keep looking forward. I tried to figure things out, to look and be a certain way, to be more than enough—only to find there was yet *another thing* I was missing to be accepted. In short, I was tired of trying to be more than what I was, and I was tired of hearing I wasn't enough.

"My poor dear girl," Leah said, "I cannot imagine the heartbreak of belonging and then suddenly not belonging, and then to feel like you had a whole community against you. I was really beginning to like John, and then he breaks my heart too! What a chicken-livered—"

"He was caught, Leah," I interjected. "He was caught between time-honored cultural traditions and the twenty-first century. I respected his beliefs. I just wished he had handled it differently."

"You are always so kind, even when you have been so hurt," Leah rejoined.

"If I am, Leah, it is because that's what I so want out of life—for people to be kind."

It's a Miracle

The winter weather in Vancouver can be very dreary—a lot of rain, fog, heavy overcast skies, blistering winds that blow sideways, and intermittent, unpredictable snowfalls. Whether or not it was an unusually dark winter, I could not tell; all I knew was that it was a very dark time for me.

Though I had the accoutrements and the presentation of someone who had it together, I was far from that. The shell of my life wasn't strong enough to hold up against the battering ram of rejection that struck my heart and mind again. I had a nice wardrobe, a friendly demeanor, academic achievements, popularity, and even the dream of a stellar career as a voice for the voiceless. But it was nothing against the despair I felt.

I had only begun learning about hope and starting to see the possibility of a better life, but my foundation for that was thin, and I was crumbling.

The weight of humiliation was heavy as various people from John's community, one after another, offered ignorant comments of "support":

"I told you so!"

"You'll find someone of *your own kind* one day."

"Maybe if you had blonde hair—but that would be weird, wouldn't it? A blonde Asian..."

"You should move on like John has with his *new* girlfriend."

"Let me introduce you to this guy in my class—he's a geek and kinda weird, but when he finally speaks, he's really nice. And you don't even notice his teeth..."

And so on. Now I can laugh at this, but almost forty years ago, these words were like nails securing my coffin.

One night I was studying late in what was then known as Gage Library (a more "serious" library across the promenade from Sedgewick). Somehow the time had passed so quickly I didn't realize I was there till closing. I had to walk all the way from the library to my car parked in the infamous B Lot miles away. That night was cold and dark and, at 11:00 p.m., not many people were about. I was walking by myself, carrying my large heavy duffle bag of books to an even darker parking lot.

I was scared, but at the same time, I also didn't care what happened to me anymore. It was as if I almost expected bad things to happen to me and was actually surprised when I made it to my car without incident.

As I was driving home, I heard a strange cold whisper in my ear. It told me to end the madness of this empty existence I called a life. While I had often prayed for death to come as a child and teenager, I had never known how to end my life except to plead for God to take me in my sleep. But now I was eighteen years old and knew much more about things. I'm both sad and ashamed to admit that this was the first time I seriously considered taking my own life.

More whispers: *Luke will be fine. He has Elizabeth in his life, plenty of friends, and a wonderful future ahead of him. He is on track now, and his life is going to be great. PoPo and GongGong will be sad, but they still have Luke to love and care for. My father is successful, has a girlfriend, a growing and expansive career, and has a thrilling life of his own in Hong Kong. My friends are fine, and in time they'll forget about the "accident."* Even my mother and Scham's voices somehow joined in...*they'll be relieved I'm gone.*

I heard and rationalized all these thoughts in a matter of moments. As I approached a very large, busy intersection, I noticed the traffic light had turned from yellow to red. To my left, traveling perpendicular to me was a *very large* eighteen-wheeler barreling down the road.

I heard that strange cold voice again say: *Go through the red light. It will be over so fast you won't feel a thing!*

Fear coursed through my veins, and I began sobbing. *My life is such a mess. My heart is broken, and any good that comes my way is instantly snatched away. I can't live like this anymore…*

Instead of slowing down, I moved my right foot from hovering over the brake to press on the gas pedal, gunning the car through the intersection. The red glare of the traffic light fell over the street in front of me.

I was on a perfect path for collision with that eighteen-wheeler.

This is it. Wow! This is how my life is going to end.

I closed my eyes as I raced into the intersection, waiting for the shock of the impact that would be hard and quick.

But there was nothing.

No braking, no screeching of tires, no warning blast of an air horn, no loud noise or sudden, jarring impact.

Nothing.

I opened my eyes, whipping my head to look behind me. All I saw was the eighteen-wheeler's taillights drifting peacefully away down the street I had just rushed through—as though I had never been in the intersection.

I was stunned and quickly pulled over to the curb to try and assess the situation. *What just happened? That eighteen-wheeler must have gone right through me!* My mind raced. *It was as if I was merely a cloud, and that truck simply went through a cloud puff. How in Heaven's name…?*

I sat in the car for a very long time. My reality was stark, and the impact of what I had actually tried to do sent me into shock. I began to shake.

I do not know what happened that night; all I know is that my car should have been rammed on the driver's side by an eighteen-wheeler accelerating through an intersection, and I should not be sitting here to tell you this story.

"Oh, Manna! I know exactly what happened!" Leah sat up as she slapped her hands together. "It was a miracle! A *miracle*! Your angels protected you again! Even an almost blind, dying woman can see that!"

I looked down and smiled. "Yes, Leah. I know this to be true also; there is no other explanation. Obviously, I haven't told many people about this. Plus, I didn't want anyone to 'try this at home!'"

Leah chuckled softly to herself, then smiled and nodded.

"Yes, despite my stupidity and willfulness, God intervened and saved me. He can do anything—defy physics, transport my car faster than the speed of light to safety. And He can give a foolish girl another chance at having an amazing life where He gives her even better dreams to make come true."

An Angel Unaware

Thankfully, the next few days and weeks at school were unremarkable. I quietly reflected on what had happened. But since I didn't have a mentor, counselor, or parents to help me talk out these situations, I felt even more alone with my secret miracle.

I couldn't tell PoPo and GongGong either. My grandparents and I were very close, but they were of a different generation, and I didn't want to worry them about me. I had put them through enough already. So, whenever we were together, I wanted it to be a time of sweetness and to focus on them.

Even though my father's car was a "miracle car" that night at the intersection, it was also very unpredictable (no matter how often we had it repaired). So, I would take a bus like I did in high school, transferring three different times every other weekend to see my PoPo and GongGong.

During those visits, I would clean their house, take them grocery shopping, or drive them to their medical appointments. We would have lunch together, then go home and prepare a nice dinner. In time, I could only go once per month, but we still spoke frequently by phone. They were a source of comfort for me, but I dared not share my fears and worries with them.

Madison and Bethanie also tried to pull me out of my depression with many fun activities, one of which was a tryout for the university's cheerleading squad. I was familiar with that world, and while I was hesitant at first, I finally agreed and gave it a shot. However, when I made the squad, I noticed a very different attitude pervaded the group. Finally, after watching one too many quarrels within the group, we decided to leave the squad.

Shortly afterwards, I began having panic attacks again and decided I would cheer for myself instead of for someone else. I also began focusing totally on my education and pushed through my anxiety-filled days with every ounce of strength I could muster to keep the voices of fear away.

One day in class, I heard a motivational quote about a successful businessman who started to "live his life" as if he was already the person he wanted to be.

I decided to do the same thing. Since I wanted to be an attorney, I began to dress like one and studied at the Law Library. I even went downtown to watch and learn a bit more about the proceedings at the courthouse—all of which helped quell some of my panic attacks, but only temporarily.

Psychology was my major, while English was my other focus. We were trained to study disorders, not have them! The only other time anyone else entertained the idea of having a disorder (or two) was in our Abnormal Psych class, which was hysterical. For the first time, I felt I wasn't alone when students one by one openly confessed they thought they had one or two (or more) DSM IV labels. The fact that they were certain they had a disorder wasn't the interesting part; it was the stories people shared about their inadequacies that were both amusing and comforting to me.

Maybe I'm not so different after all…

I began to hope.

During the spring semester of my first year, I noticed I hadn't really been eating. In fact, my only daily nutrition since New Year's Day had consisted of twenty-plus cups of black coffee per day and one large bran muffin.

I didn't even think about eating.

Maybe it was because I was often by myself, which was very easy to do because then I could just be *me*. I didn't have to perform like a circus animal to gain acceptance (or a few crumbs), and I didn't risk the chance of being hurt again. I learned to enjoy being alone. It was easier, plus in my own world, people were nice.

Nonetheless, I was becoming very thin and not remotely aware that my life was in danger. I weighed one hundred and three pounds and was still losing weight. I didn't mind, because my menstrual cycles became very light and after a while non-existent (which I foolishly thought it was a good thing).

Today, *anorexia nervosa* is an everyday term, but back then, no one spoke of those things, much less suspected I was close to critical condition.

One morning when I was applying my makeup, I noticed that the whites of my eyes were not so white anymore and that I had no pink coloring at all under my eyelids. My hands were very bony as I held the mascara tube in one hand and the mascara brush in the other. I also felt more lightheaded. I blamed that feeling on the smoking habit I had picked up (thinking that's what attorneys did). I quit immediately that day and never smoked again.

The next morning when I looked at my bony hands, I saw tiny veins running up and down my arms through the thin skin of my body and started to think something might be wrong.

I decided to make sure I ate that day, but when I arrived at school, the thought of food made me nauseous. I drank more coffee instead. That evening, Bethanie and I met for our regular mid-week, late-night snack at a local diner after studying at the university. Since I hadn't had my warm bran muffin earlier in the day, I ordered it that night when we were together. The waitress knew us by now and asked, "Your regulars, ladies? Two black coffees, a date square, and a large bran muffin warmed up?"

"Yes, thank you!" we chimed simultaneously. We always used this time to catch up on life, and Bethanie shared the ongoing difficulties she was having with her boyfriend. "I need to get away—a change of scenery," she stated.

"You mean a vacation?" I replied.

"No, I mean a new school," she hesitated. "Manna, I applied to a school in Toronto, and I think I'm going to get in. If I do, I'll be leaving this summer and going to live there."

"*Oh, no!*" My heart sank. "Please! You can't go!" I pleaded.

"I have to, Manna. Our friendship will always be important to me, and I know we'll always be friends—no matter how far we are from one another. But other than you, there's nothing for me here. In Toronto, I'll have more choices…I really need to get away."

There would be no changing her mind. She was leaving.

I drove her home in my father's fickle car and then went home myself. I wondered what life at school would be like without Bethanie next year. I thought about how people come and go in our lives and wondered about friendships—the cost of having them (being heartbroken when they leave) and the cost of not having them (being heartbroken in isolation). I thought about many things, but I didn't think about eating.

The next day at school was like it always was—except for one major difference. My hands trembled when I tried to write. *Odd*, I thought to myself. *Maybe I'm cold?* So, in between classes, I went to The Bus Stop (a quaint diner beside Sedgewick Library at the time) and ordered another black coffee to warm me up. I made it through the day well enough, but I found myself back at The Bus Stop after classes for another coffee before studying.

The waitresses at The Bus Stop were always so wonderful. The ladies there were like mommas to us students, young and old, and I loved going in, sitting on my stool, and talking with them. I particularly enjoyed one named Liz. She had a short, sassy haircut that was wispy and very chic. She stood about 5'4", spoke with a British accent, and had a smile that could melt an entire iceberg.

On this late afternoon, only a few patrons were there. One in particular was a jolly, older-looking man, maybe in his fifties, with a very well-groomed beard. He could have been a grad student or a professor, but it was his warm smile and kind eyes that immediately caught my attention. The counters at the diner were in the shape of a square horseshoe, and the waitresses would walk into the center to serve their patrons on either side. This gentleman sat on the opposite side of the horseshoe from me, and I had a very clear visual of him. When he wasn't smiling and chatting with Liz, he was looking down at his notebook, reading something.

I could not help but watch (and study) this gentleman.

We are always *teaching something*, and there is always a *student* watching. This man was the perfect example of this principle. In the ease of his brief, yet kind, interaction with Liz, he showed me simple kindness could be a possibility in my life also. Yes, I was very much attracted to this man, but not as one might think—I was attracted to the light and joy radiating from him, and, interestingly, I felt *safe* in his presence.

When his order was ready, Liz brought him a juicy beef dip with a full cup of *au jus*, a large basket of French fries, and a side salad with oil and vinegar dressing. When he saw his meal coming, he smiled from ear to ear, and I found myself smiling too. He thanked Liz, shared some small talk...and then, I heard him laugh!

Oh, his laugh! It was unlike any other kind of laugh I had ever heard—ever, or since. It was low and deep. It had cadence and rhythm and richness and joy—oh, the pure joy that came from deep within his soul and resonated all around him with every chuckle and guffaw he bellowed out! It was magnificent!

When I heard him laugh the first time, I almost spat out my coffee and immediately wondered, *Is this for real?*

When he laughed again, I started laughing too. His laugh was contagious! I spun around on my stool to see if anyone else noticed the laughter, but no one else seemed to. So, I pulled out a textbook and began reading until Liz came to take my order.

Suddenly, I heard the gentleman laugh again!

He and Liz were discussing something else now, and they were both laughing together. His distinct and captivating laughter made me laugh out loud *again*. I was so embarrassed, as it was becoming obvious—not only was I staring at him, I was also eavesdropping on their conversation.

I controlled myself as best I could but finally gave in to the moment and put everything down. Since there was no way out of it now, I simply enjoyed this wonderful scene unfolding in front of me. There before me was this wonderful, kind gentleman with a belly laugh that warmed my soul. And there was Liz, a lovely and attentive servant, blessing every patron with warmth and genuineness, greeting her favorite customers with "Hi, Love!" No one had ever called me that before, and I was grateful to hear (and feel) her affection in those words.

I was mesmerized by this man. Watching people eat isn't something I normally do, but on this day, I could not peel my eyes away as he enjoyed his beef dip sandwich with the *au jus* dripping out of the warm, crusty bun. In between each bite, he wiped his lips with his napkin and smiled. When Liz came by, they'd share a quick-witted exchange, and he would laugh his rhythmic belly laugh again. That day, I caught whatever he had—his joy, his laughter, his love for life. All of it was contagious.

Soon, I was feeling lighter-hearted myself, more joyful, and—for the first time in many months—I felt *hungry!*

I called Liz over.

"You ready for your coffee and bran muffin, Love?"

"Actually, Liz," I paused, "May I have whatever that gentleman is having?" I pointed to the fellow with the wonderful laugh.

"He's having a beef dip, Love. You've never ordered anything but coffee and a bran muffin! You must be hungry!" She smiled.

"Liz, I am hungry!" I declared.

"Good girl!" she nodded with approval, "I'll order it right away before you change your mind!" She winked and whisked toward the kitchen.

I continued watching the gentleman eat the rest of his beef dip sandwich, fries, salad, and coffee, and with each mouthful, I grew hungrier and hungrier. And when my meal came, I was able to eat it all!

"I can still picture that man as I share this story with you," I told Leah. "Even after that one-time experience almost forty years ago, I would still be able to point him out if I ever saw a photo of him. That event was pivotal for me.

"Mark Twain once said, 'The human race has one really effective weapon, and that is laughter.' Hearing this man's laughter, experiencing his *joie de vivre*, and seeing the kindness in his eyes while he enjoyed his meal was just what I needed. It was the weapon that broke a spell that had been holding me hostage.

"That was the day I started eating again. Not only was it the first time I had eaten a solid meal in many, many months, it was the first time I had allowed myself to *want* something good for myself. I wanted to laugh. I wanted to eat. I wanted to enjoy life. I wanted to save myself. That man quite literally saved my life."

"You were entertaining an angel unaware!" Leah said excitedly, "Or more accurately, he was entertaining you!"

"Oh, my goodness, Leah! You know that verse?"

"Yes, dear. I know that verse and many others that are slowly coming back to me. Things I learned a very, *very* long time ago, but I wasn't sure if it ever meant anything, until now. Yes, it's starting to come back to me, and the pieces of my life are also starting to make more sense." She paused. "Thank you for taking the time to be with an old, useless woman like me."

"Stop that, Leah. You are not useless. Not one of us is useless. We are all designed for greatness and for accomplishing feats beyond our imagination. Unfortunately, we often settle for much less than we were designed for."

"Well, I thank God for you—and that wonderful man in the diner!" Leah exclaimed and paused before adding, "If nothing else, you are fascinating, my friend. Just when I don't think you can surprise me anymore, another amazing story unfolds. I'm hooked!"

With Friends Like That...

That summer after finals, I went back to Hong Kong to be with my father. We had another wonderful time together, and when I returned to attend my sophomore year at the university, everything was fairly much the way it was before. Life was very busy at school, and Sedgewick Library seemed busier than ever before.

I met another group of students from other areas and became wonderful friends with a girl named Hanna. She was confident and had an inner strength I admired. She had no problem confronting issues, nor did setbacks discourage her from pursuing her dreams because she knew her value. I learned a great deal from her and am thankful for the sweet friendship we shared then and still have now.

Molly was another girl I met that year. She and a few of her friends were taking the same third-year statistics class with me. For some reason, Molly always gave me dirty looks, but even though she rebuffed me, somehow, I knew that one day we would be great friends.

In class, Molly and her friends sat behind me at the lab tables, and I overheard them saying they weren't grasping the concepts. Midterms were coming soon, and by the way they were talking, they weren't going to pass.

So, I "accidentally on purpose" dropped my worksheet in such a way that it floated behind me toward their table.

As I leaned back to pick it up, I said to Molly, "Oops, sorry about that—just have to grab the worksheet." As I picked up my paper, I asked, "Hey, what did you get for number seven?"

"We didn't even understand the question, much less get an answer. What did you get?"

I pretended I wasn't sure if my answer was right, but I explained how I arrived at my answer. They became quite excited and asked me to show them my process. Long story short, Molly's group of friends asked me to study with them so they could at least pass the midterm. I agreed and, just as I had thought, we soon became good friends. We often met in the "honeycombs" to study and in no time, we were laughing together, and on weekends, spending time together.

Yes, indeed, Sedgewick was the place not only to meet old friends but new ones, too. That's exactly where I met my new boyfriend, Landon—a very handsome, tall, dark, and athletic young man in an engineering program. He looked like a model, and I couldn't believe he was attracted to me. Every time he saw me walk through the turnstiles to find a table where I could study, he smiled. Whenever I looked up from my books or went to get a drink of water, he was already looking my way and smiling. I smiled back, feeling shy. Eventually, he came to talk to me more and more each time he saw me. Landon was smart and funny, and it didn't take long for him to win me over.

We had wonderful times together, and I soon met his parents, whom I grew to love dearly. They invited me over for Sunday night dinners and also during the week for family meals in between our studies. They were very gracious toward me, and I will always have a great affection for them and how they opened their hearts and home to me.

There were many times when I should not have accepted their invitation to go over, but I so longed for a family that I didn't know how to say no. When I walked through their front door, it felt like what a home should be—and a home I never had. A mom was home and couldn't wait to see you. The aroma of a home-cooked meal drew you in from the driveway, and the sound of the television coming from the den indicated a dad was there. Landon knew I didn't have anything like this to go home to at my apartment, and because he also knew about my past, he was very kind about including me with his family gatherings.

Things went very well in our relationship, and my life was an endless succession of school classes, study times, dinners, sporting events, get-togethers, and weekend trips away.

Landon also had some very special friends, and I became close to one in particular. Jonathan was extremely kind and thoughtful and is still a dear faithful friend.

Time passed, and as Landon and I started into our fourth year together, our relationship started to fall into a bland routine. One day, as we walked out of the library and headed to our different classes, he kissed me halfheartedly on the cheek and then unkindly remarked, "Your hair isn't like Melanie's…hers is long and flows in the breeze."

Jolted, I didn't know what to do with that comment or the comparison. "And why do you wear mascara? You should be more natural, like Hilary or Terri…"

I wasn't stupid. Our relationship had cooled, and while I knew I had played a part in this happening, I didn't know how to change things.

The time came to think about what we would do after we graduated with our bachelor's degrees. Landon wanted to go to law school also, so we both studied for the LSAT (Law School Admission Test). Landon took the test first, but when the results came back, he learned he had failed the exam. I could see he was wounded, but he said nothing about his true feelings until a week later.

"I can't believe I didn't pass! And you…you! You're only a Psych major! I'm in Engineering! All I can say is you had better think twice about law school, or you'll be like some others we know! They were a cabbage patch group too and only got in because they were graded on a bell curve. Maybe that's how you'll get in, but I doubt you'd be able to handle it once you're in. What a total embarrassment you'd be to your family—especially to your father—if you flunked out. That would be humiliating!"

I felt as if I had been kicked in the stomach. *Oh my goodness…is that true? Will I make it once I'm in law school? What if Landon is right? My father would be so disappointed, and I'd only be proving that my mother and Scham were right. Maybe I shouldn't try…*

I thought about what he said all day and every night for a week, and in the end, I'm sorry to say—so, so very sorry to say—I capitulated and believed Landon more than I believed in my dream. It was better to reject law school than to let law school reject me. So, I withdrew my application. And with that, pulled the plug on my dreams to be an attorney, too.

"Oh, Manna! I cannot believe you listened to that jealous witling!" Leah interrupted. "What a nincompoop! With friends like that, who needs enemies!"

"I know," I said quietly. "It's still something I feel enormous regret over. But I relearned a powerful lesson from that relationship, and that incident.

"Once again, we need to be very careful who we listen to in life. Whether it's the silent voice of the enemy whispering lies about us, our identity, our worth, or our value; or a voice whispering in our ear that it's just "better" to drive in front of an eighteen-wheeler; or the words of a well-intentioned (but ill-informed friend); or the brokenness of someone who professes love to you but is unable to handle his or her own brokenness.

"We need to be much more vigilant about who has our ear."

When it came time for graduation, I eagerly began making plans to celebrate it, but Landon snapped, "Why? You only earned a Psych degree! *That*'s nothing to be proud of! If *I'm* not even going to attend graduation, why should you?"

"But Landon, it's not simply a Psych degree. I earned a Psych and an English degree, and I did well. It was hard…and I had a lot of other things on my mind."

"Really?" he asked, raising an eyebrow, "I wouldn't be so excited to walk and receive a Psych degree that anyone can get. Do whatever you want, but don't expect me to go."

Needless to say, graduation came and went, and I waited with silent and lonely anticipation to receive my degree in the mail.

Even though I had ruled out law school, I wasn't ready to be done with school completely. I applied for the university's Master's program in psychology because it was a safe choice. I *knew* psychology, and no one could tell me I didn't.

I began the program, and Landon went to visit his brother in another city. When he returned from one of his trips, I noticed immediately that he was different. He was even more abrupt and dismissive of me, and I knew instinctively that he had found someone else. When I asked him, he denied it and insisted we enjoy the rest of our weekend plans together before he left again for another trip to see his brother.

One day I realized some of my textbooks and notebooks were still at his house from my last year in undergraduate studies. I needed my materials for a paper I was writing, so I called his mom to try and find them.

She answered, "Yes! I believe I have seen some things. Why don't you come and get it whenever you have time? I'll leave the bag on Landon's bed for you."

We scheduled a time, and when I arrived, the bag was on his bed, just as she said. I found my two textbooks and my binder easily, but I also found some opened letters postmarked from the city he had just visited. When I saw they were from a girl, I couldn't help myself—I read them.

Yes. There it all was. Landon had found someone else indeed.

Even though I had had suspicions, nothing could prepare me for what I read. My heart sank, and I fell into a panic attack immediately. I took some deep breaths, but I was too afraid to let Landon's mother see me that way. I did my best to gather myself, wiped away the tears, explaining them away as allergies. I thanked her, gave her a big hug, and realized I was saying goodbye for the last time.

I called to speak with Landon, but he wasn't available. His brother, who answered the phone, asked me what was wrong. Unable to contain myself any longer, I burst out crying and told him I knew the truth. His brother said nothing— which said everything. I apologized for putting him in the middle, thanked him for the kindness he'd always extended to me, and said goodbye.

Interestingly, through that conversation, I had apparently said goodbye to Landon too since he never called to discuss the situation or to have a conversation about the end of our four-year relationship.

One Less Bell to Answer

After that experience, I felt like I was reeling through space, unattached to anything. I had school, but I grew more and more dissatisfied with it. I sat in class and wondered how I could deceive myself into thinking that anyone would listen to (much less pay to hear) the advice of a twenty-three-year-old girl who was as messed up as I was—even with an M.A. in Psychology. My patients would see through the sham, and worse, *I probably had more problems than they did!*

Through ceaseless thoughts like these, I gradually convinced myself that I had no business trying to be a psychologist, so I dropped out of that program as well.

I had tried so hard to overcome the many disappointments in life, and except for the miracle night when I had defied physics, I thought I was managing well enough. However, with the end of college life, I had become unmoored. Where most people meet change with some foundation of self-identity, confidence, and self-reliance, I had none of that. I was a lifetime behind in that program. My hope had been deferred so many times, I felt lost and hopeless.

By this time, my father had purchased another house on the west side of town, and we moved out of our apartment. This new home became my self-imposed prison, where I stayed safe from the outside world and its people. After dropping out of the master's program, I spun into a cycle of misery and began to unconsciously assume some of the labels I had only read about in psychology books.

I became terrified of stepping out of the house, and I stopped eating again, resigning myself to both anorexia and to the crippling anxiety that had now completely overtaken me. Without any more school bells telling me when and where to be, I realized my life was not governed by anything. I lacked the internal confidence—and the heart—to pick myself up again and forge a better life for myself.

Instead, I lay on the couch curled in a ball under a blanket in our basement rec room all day and night, where my unyielding fears could be distracted by one television show after another. It wasn't long before I knew every morning show, game show, news program, soap opera, talk show, and sitcom by heart.

I had to muster up the courage to even go *upstairs*. It could sometimes take me over an hour to convince myself that it was safe to go into my own kitchen! The fears were like demonic animals biting at me endlessly, tormenting every moment of my life. I was besieged with thoughts of dread, and the only way to drown out those voices was with television.

Thankfully, Luke offered to do all the grocery shopping, so I had no reason to go outside. Each morning though, after falling asleep the night before to the droning of another program, I would awake in a mad panic, trying to catch my breath and seeking some way out of my dark spinning world.

One day I found the courage to write to my father in Hong Kong and to tell him about my life and my fears. Incurring the exorbitant cost of long-distance calls was not an option, so I wrote him a very long letter—over ten pages long, both sides filled. I tried to tell him about these debilitating issues, but he could not grasp the seriousness of it so many miles away. He could not know how my life had crumbled. Instead, he rebuked me, believing me to be ungrateful while he was away working to make a living for us. In despair, and without anyone to help, I almost gave in to the darkness that was consuming me.

I didn't know how serious anorexia was, nor was I aware that I had another illness, agoraphobia, an anxiety disorder sometimes accompanied by panic attacks, in which one perceives certain situations or locations to be extremely uncomfortable or dangerous. My body was very thin and undernourished. My immune system was depleted, and I suffered from one illness after another. When I was too weak to walk, Luke took me to the doctor, who could not believe what he was seeing.

For months and months, I lived in sheer fear and terror. Then one day, I suddenly remembered my life as a little girl and how God was with me in the basement.

I began to pray again.

Little by little, I began to feel the breath of life inside me again, fanning my will to live. I didn't know what the future would hold, but I had enough strength for the next moment, and the next, and the next. I don't even know how to explain it all to you, except to say that it had to have been another divine intervention, for there is no other way I could have come out of that darkness alone.

I was given another miracle.

After succumbing to disabling fear for almost seven months, I finally woke up one day with something stirring in my heart instead of dread and terror. It was hope. Right then and there, I grabbed onto that lifeline, and with every ounce of courage I could muster, I made up my mind to get back into the world of the living. I had been a recluse for so long, I didn't know how to get out of my cave. All I knew was there was a window of opportunity, and it was time.

I approached leaving the house slowly at first. I started with baby steps, literally. I managed to go up the short flight of stairs. It took me thirty minutes with only a few panic attacks, stopping on each step to talk myself out of the anxiety. When I had achieved going up and down the stairs without alarm, I began to approach the back door. In time, I was able to actually open the door to the back porch, take a deep breath, quickly close it, and run back downstairs.

I did this several times a day, every day, until I convinced myself I was safe and could not only open the back door, but step onto the porch itself. Gradually,

I moved farther into the back yard, always leaving the door propped open behind me so I could quickly seek my refuge. Finally, a few months later, I was able to function enough to go to the store a block away. I did what I could; even if it was just a small step, I did it. I kept getting up. And I kept trying, one literal step at a time.

Thankfully, God never left me. When I didn't have the strength, He gave me His. When I thought I was ugly, He told me I was beautiful. When I thought I was good-for-nothing, He told me He had great plans for my future. When I thought I was too broken, He told me I was perfect because He created me. And when I told him I was too dirty to be lovable, He told me I was His treasure, I was sacred, washed clean, redeemed, and I belonged to Him. And when I wanted to die, He gave me His Life.

8 TWILIGHT ZONE

Today, I know that such memories are the keys not to the past, but to the future. I know that the experiences of our lives, when we let God use them, become the mysterious and perfect preparation for the work He will give us to do.

— Corrie Ten Boom

Room 316

It had been two months since I began visiting Leah St. John, and I tried to do something a little different every now and then to make things interesting. I brought both my dogs, Harley and Noah, to visit several times, brought different foods to eat, flowers to brighten her room, books to read, family photo albums to see, and an assortment of dark chocolate to taste—that is, if she was behaving!

Leah St. John found me amusing, and now that I had gotten to know her better, I was more comfortable meeting her tête-à-tête. Plus, the quality of the unexpected kept her alert and on her toes.

This time, however, I came empty-handed. It had been a hectic week with a new client who had hired me to help integrate two corporate cultures after yet another acquisition. I was weary from dealing with a sabotaging executive.

"What? No presents today?" Leah goaded me. "You don't look good—no offense," she said slowly.

"Rough day."

"Are you sure you don't just want to go home and rest?" Leah asked worriedly.

"No. I'm actually happy to be here and to see you. How has your week been going? Have you been behaving?" I asked, smiling.

"The week was the same old thing—a bunch of pills here, a bunch of pills there. An IV change here, an IV change there. Thomas has been in every day. Knowing you are coming in is the only way I can get him to stop worrying. And no, I haven't quite been the angel you want me to be. It's too much fun to keep ringing the bell and seeing who will run in next."

"Oh, Leah, you're a monkey."

"Yes, and darn proud of it! Not ready to just lie here and die! I have to keep fighting—like you. You are a fighter, a survivor, an overcomer!" Leah said, almost shouting.

"Thank you, Leah. I guess I am a bit of a warrior. You and I both have some of that spirited fight in us, don't we?"

"And *that, my dear*, is why I've come to like you so much!" she said with an exaggerated wink and a smile. "I'm bored listening to all the dull stories at the nurse's station and out in the lounge. Hurry and get settled in so you can finish telling me what happened once you put Humpty Dumpty back together again…" She waved her hand again, directing me to resume my story.

Mr. Wrong

Approximately nine months after my victory over depression and agoraphobia, I secured a job working part-time for one of the top ophthalmologists in the country.

I was hired as the receptionist and joined his already large team of other assistants, working the early morning shift, arriving at the office at 6:45 a.m. to prepare for the patients arriving at 7:00 a.m. Not wanting to give in to my fears, I also enrolled in a few courses back at UBC the following session, hoping that if I kept my mind alert and focused on the right things, I would not be as prone to entertaining destructive thoughts.

So, after my shift concluded at 1:00 p.m., I went to UBC for afternoon classes. It was a very hectic schedule, but I was glad for the distraction (and the return of a strict routine). With little time to reflect upon my life, it was easy to pour myself into work and my studies.

Within the first few months of my being hired, several of the other girls started quitting. I picked up the slack, and soon I was doing the work of four employees on my shift alone. I have a gift for organization, so I began creating systems to help manage the doctor's heavy patient load. Mine was a fun job, and I was able to wear a nurse's uniform. It helped me to feel I was doing something important, and I belonged in an environment where I could help others. Soon, the doctor was giving me a raise every other week. I was happy for the income, and the doctor was now saving a great deal of money on salaries.

In time, I also found an apartment and moved out on my own. It was a huge expense to incur, but I was determined to be strong and "grow up."

As luck would have it, Madison also worked in the same area as I did and was actually only two blocks away from me. She was in a committed relationship, and because she was living on cloud nine, she wanted to see me happy, too. That's when I began to hear about one of their sales representatives who worked for a small, local, family-run business.

"Tristan came into the store again today," Madison announced one afternoon.

"He's single, and I think you two would look cute together. Let's go on a double date!"

Madison meant well. She always did, bless her heart. She was always looking out for my best interests and had been my rock for so many years, especially after Bethanie moved. She didn't know how to help me with my brokenness except to look for different ways to get me involved with "life"—in this case, dating.

Every week, she told me more about this Tristan. Everything about her description of him seemed okay until she told me he wore a lot of jewelry. I thought that was odd, and even she agreed that he was a bit flashy. She rationalized that it was part of his flair at work, but I was still uncomfortable with it.

Though I longed for a kind and authentic companionship, I wasn't sure about Tristan. Plus, I was finally starting to feel like I could stand on my own two feet, and I wasn't sure if I could take on someone else's life—especially the life of a man who already seemed a bit…well, odd.

"I know you're not interested, Manna, but would you at least meet him? I told him you didn't want to be in a relationship, but what if the four of us just met for a drink? You'll be with us, so there's no danger or worries. I promise that if you really want to leave, we'll end the evening early."

Her plan sounded reasonable, but I still declined.

Madison continued her coaxing, and finally, a few months later, I agreed to meet for a drink.

"Good, let's get together this Friday right after work! Steven will drive, and you'll come with us," she exclaimed excitedly.

Friday night arrived, and the three of us went downtown to a well-known bar with a nice view of the harbor. On our drive down, Madison told me that Tristan had actually changed his name because he wanted to be more unique and exotic. I shook my head and didn't respond. In fact, I said very little for the rest of the car ride, wondering, *what am I doing?*

As we stepped out of the car, I could only hope for the best and took comfort in knowing if things weren't going well, we could leave, just as Madison had promised.

Tristan arrived within a few minutes of our settling in and sat across from me at the table. He seemed nice enough, but I felt no chemistry. Out of obligation to my friends, I even tried to talk myself into liking him or into at least giving him a chance. However, sitting across from him, his cologne almost pushed me back into my chair. As he drank his cocktail, I couldn't help but notice his manicured and highly-buffed, shiny fingernails. He also wore three chunky gold rings (one inset with several large diamonds), several thick, heavy gold chain bracelets to match his necklaces (note the plural), and the latest Movado watch. He had short, straight, slicked-back hair, and each time he took a sip of his drink, he groomed his thin moustache.

"I'm getting annoyed with him, just listening to your description," Leah quipped.

I smiled broadly. "As the evening progressed, he unbuttoned his shirt another notch to show more of his chest. I almost spat out my drink but explained it away as having simply swallowed wrong."

"You're making this up!" Leah interrupted.

We both laughed. "No, Leah. I'm not. I wish I could say I was, but this is the whole truth, and nothing but the truth."

"Then you clearly hadn't recovered yet from your illness—if you continued to entertain this fellow," Leah goaded me.

"I know. Well, I did tell you that I was only starting to get on my feet again. I didn't say I was *healed!*"

Leah chuckled. "Keep goin', this is gonna be good!"

"Well, like I said, I was still trying to figure things out, and because I still doubted myself, I rationalized that Madison must have seen something I didn't. Otherwise, why would she be so insistent on getting us together? So, again, out of respect to her and Steven, I looked for a reason to at least try. Madison pointed out that at least Tristan was better than the strange men who had been hounding me."

"Wait! You didn't tell me about other guys! Who were these fellows?" Leah exclaimed, sitting up in her bed.

"Well, let's see… there were the two prison inmates who came in as patients for required care when I was working with the ophthalmologist. They both (independently) stalked me after they got out. There was the married car salesman who kept calling me after I bought my first car—a twenty-first birthday gift from my father. There were also fellow grad students who were twenty years my senior who had latched onto me, and a Middle Eastern male student who followed me around in the library. He seemed nice at first, but then he started to leave me bizarre notes in my study cubicle, telling me how good I'd look with a veil and heavy makeup. The worst one of all was the guy who followed me for blocks in his Jaguar, and when he pulled up, pretending to ask for directions, he pointed down, and I saw that he was naked and playing with himself."

"Oh, my soul! What did you do?"

"Well, he tried to grab my arm, but I was faster than he expected, and I ran to the nearest grocery store to hide. He waited outside for me for about ten minutes and finally drove off."

"Did you call the police?"

"I didn't know what to do. I was so scared and just wanted to get away. If he had come into the store, I would have told the owner. I left a few minutes after he drove away, but looking back, I should have called the police. But in those days, these kinds of things weren't common (or if they were, they weren't discussed). As women, we simply weren't trained for situations like that the way we are now."

"What in the world?! How could all these things happen to you, Manna?" Leah declared. "It's like the Twilight Zone!"

"I know! For most of my life, I had wondered why I got transported to a strange land called 'earth' where people were odd and hurtful. Then I thought that maybe there was a curse on me, or I was jinxed. The randomness and the range of bizarre things that have happened in my life have truly been mind-boggling."

"You should write your life story—an autobiography! I'm sure I'm not the first person to say that to you," Leah encouraged me.

I smiled.

Leah gave me a knowing look, "Good! I want a copy—autographed!"

"Absolutely…and I think you'll quite like it," I grinned.

"I already do because it's about you!"

"Well, that's sweet of you to say, but there's going to be a new character involved, and I have a feeling you'll approve."

Leah's eye's opened wide. "Really? Who's that?"

"You, Leah! You'll be in the book!"

Leah beamed with joy. "Well, then, we have lots still do, don't we? Tell me what happened after you saw super stud."

"Well, after that double date night, Madison told me that Tristan had come into the jewelry store many times, asking about me and wanting to see me again. 'He really likes you, Manna!' she insisted. 'You should see him again. He's not everything you're looking for, and he is a bit different, but at least he's not a *real* weirdo.' Translation: *He is weird, but not as weird as the others, and since he's the best you can do, you might as well make it work.*"

"Oh, Manna, *settling* is never an option," Leah shook her head.

"I know that now—many decades later—but at the time, I didn't. I thought I was being 'reasonable,' 'logical,' and even 'appreciative' for what I had! The haunting words spoken over me for so long kept whispering in my ears: 'You're stupid, ugly, and good-for-nothing.' Those curses made me think I shouldn't be so demanding or 'extravagant' with my dreams; rather, I should be thankful for *any possibility* I had—even with Tristan. A battle raged in my mind between what I longed for and what I thought I deserved. I was at a crossroad."

A few more weeks passed, and something was wrong with my car. The warranty had run out, and I wasn't going to go back to the dealership, in case the married salesman tried to ask me out again. Steven told me about someone he had used, so I brought my car there.

I spent the morning in the grimy front office of the repair shop in a remote area of town where two mechanics recommended extensive repairs to my vehicle. As the hours wore on, my repair bill rose. By the time I got my car back, I had begun to suspect they had lied to me. The major issue involved the clutch of the car, which they said they had replaced. Come to find out, they had only adjusted it, but charged me for a brand-new one, along with other supposedly necessary parts, plus labor, of course.

I asked them to go over the itemized repairs they had made, but they abruptly dismissed me. When I insisted on discussing the bill, they became aggressive and pushed me toward the car that was still parked inside their garage. Realizing I was alone in the bay with their escalating tempers, I quickly got into my car. The door had barely closed behind me before I heard them laughing as they walked toward their office door.

Their echoing voices carried to me, "Stupid Chink…and a girl to boot!"

Tears stung at the corners of my eyes. These were supposed to have been "nice guys" and friends of Steven. I felt betrayed, but I was also too afraid to take a stand for myself alone in their garage. We didn't have cell phones those days, and without a secure way to call for help, I buckled. There had already been too much drama in my life, and I didn't want any more of it. So, I drove away—confused, sad, alone, and with seven hundred and fifty dollars less in my bank account.

As upsetting as it was to have been taken advantage of, I was equally shocked at the sudden racial slur that had been thrown at me. I could not seem to shake the unfair ethnic label. On the one hand, men generally found me very attractive, and had gone to extremes in recent years trying to court and date me. On the other hand, there were men who belittled, impugned, and slandered me with malicious, discriminatory daggers. It felt impossible to establish a true sense of value or worth with such inconsistent and polarized mirrors, and I was mystified as to how I might get along in a world that had already prejudged me.

I began to feel the cocoon of anxiety close around me again, but I had rent and utilities to pay, and there were great responsibilities at work and at school. I couldn't afford to give in to the fear that started to swell again inside me, so I steeled myself and fought the battle in my mind once again.

When I told Madison what had happened, she immediately advised me to reconsider Tristan again. "What you need is a good guy, Manna—someone to be with you all of the time. Then you won't be taken advantage of, and you can tell the rest of the world to go to hell! I know Tristan isn't what you were hoping for. He isn't educated, but maybe it's okay to just have a simple guy. Steven says he's been the company salesman for a few years, and he seems to be decent. You really ought to give it another shot."

When Madison finished, an unforgettable sadness loomed over me. *Is this how it is going to be? Am I really going to settle for someone who took more time to get ready, and who wore more jewelry and more cologne than I did? Has it come to this? Has it really come to this?*

With no one else from whom to seek counsel and no one to encourage me with the possibility of a brighter future, I conceded. *Maybe Madison is right… maybe I had better think twice about burning the bridge with Tristan.*

Very long story short, I agreed to see Tristan again, even though my feelings for him did not change. I still thought he was odd, but not so odd that I couldn't talk myself out of being disturbed by his peculiar ways. And he was "decent." He wasn't always trying to force himself on me (which was what most men always seemed to want), and I knew he wouldn't hit me, hurt me, or have an affair.

So, a month or so after our awkward beginning, we were now an official couple. Although our relationship still wasn't what I wanted, and I didn't have all of the feelings a girl should have when dating someone she really likes, I told myself, *Just be thankful for a "decent" guy.*

I also found myself sighing a lot, but I managed to quell my sadness with practical thoughts. I rebuked myself for appearing to be ungrateful and demanded that I be less sensitive. I acquiesced and accepted the thought that love simply wasn't in the cards for me, so I might as well take it on the chin, deal with life like a big girl, and just keep things going—neat, tidy, and feeling nothing.

Within a short time, many friends were getting married, and I numbly watched one friend after another walk down the aisle to their true love. I rejoiced for them as much as my damaged heart could, and as happy as I was for them, I didn't believe that I could be so lucky. To have such a beautiful relationship—one in which you loved someone fully, and even more, that person loved you back, was not for me. I didn't even know if I could imagine it or dream it, much less believe in it.

I also reflected on the marriages of the people around me. The truth was that I didn't know anyone who was truly, truly happy. Yes, there were a few couples: my grandparents, my Uncle William and Auntie Georgiana, and my godparents, but they were of a different generation. Their lives were also culturally different than the life that I was living, and, unfortunately, their example seemed out of reach to me. As for other relationships, while they were far from being horrific, many marriages seemed to be made up of distant and dissatisfied people living together.

Maybe this is the way marriages are, I thought to myself. *Maybe you're not supposed to stay happy—just stay married. Maybe the fire dies, but at least you have someone around to talk to. Maybe my dreams were wrong, and I needed to change my thinking. Maybe this was the way things are done after all.*

After a few months of dating, Tristan casually and unemotionally suggested that we get married, tagging that thought to the end of another sentence. At first, I didn't know if I had heard him right.

Did he just say what I thought he said? Where is the romance? Where is the proposal? Where is the tenderness, the sweetness, the thoughtfulness behind something so special? Where is the excitement, the joy…the love?

"Where was the ring?!" Leah interrupted.

I laughed. "There was no ring at first, and when he did get me one, it was a small dinner ring (not an engagement ring) from a sample line he was selling. His standard joke was, 'I told you I'd surround you with diamonds and gold! I just didn't tell you they wouldn't belong to you!' Then he would laugh out loud, thinking this was really funny. It wasn't."

"Unbelievable," Leah shook her head.

"It wasn't the ring or the size of the stone that mattered to me. It was the size of the heart I was seeking. In time, he did purchase an engagement ring, but it wasn't until much later that I learned it was a very poor-quality zircon that became cloudier and foggier with each passing day."

"That sounds like a bad omen," said Leah.

"Quite," I agreed. "When Tristan gave it to me, I asked him to repeat his proposal, and he did so noncommittally, as if he was asking what I thought about ketchup with my fries. So, I paused and said again, 'If you're asking me to marry you, could you at least say it with some kind of sweetness—maybe even make it more fun or romantic?' He said, 'Why? You get the point.'"

Leah groaned.

"Trying to hold on to my last shred of hope that marriage should be more meaningful, I told him, 'Then the answer is no. I will not marry you. Not like this.' He just smirked at me and said, 'Like what? What do you think this is, Disneyland?' I walked away without responding. But, I'm sorry to say, I didn't walk away *from him*."

Weasel Skin Place

Shortly after that, Tristan was given another territory in another province. He traveled back and forth at first, and then he told me he would have to relocate to one of the cities there—Rutherford, his hometown. He tried to convince me of its merits, but there was nothing in Rutherford that was similar to my life in Vancouver. At that time, the only attractions were oil refineries and an indoor mall. The weather was wretched and unspeakably miserable. The winters were cold, averaging temperatures of -15°C (without the wind-chill factor) and incessant snowfalls which often left up to six inches of solid ice on the roads for most of the winter. The arid climate in the summers on this flat, brown landscape caused nosebleeds and made skin itch so badly that even applying baby oil didn't bring relief.

I wished him luck and thought our relationship was over. But Tristan didn't want our relationship to end, and he called me several times per day while he was away, regardless of the long-distance calling costs. The distance awakened something inside of him, and he began professing his love for me. Ultimately, he said things that assuaged my concerns about him, and long story short, when he came back after one of his long trips away, I rationalized my fears once more, tucked my dreams back into their box, and agreed to marry him.

We set the wedding date to be the same as my PoPo and GongGong's wedding day. I wanted to honor them, but also hoped that by choosing the same day, we would be ensured a long and successful marriage, just like they had had. (They celebrated over sixty-one years of marriage before GongGong passed away.)

TWILIGHT ZONE

Tristan told me that his stint in Rutherford would only be for one year, at the most, and convinced me that my "sentence" there would be minimal. Plus, I could fly home anytime I wanted to see my family. But it was the summer of 1986, and Vancouver was abuzz with Expo '86. The city was alive and vibrant, and I did not want to leave. I had naively thought I would still live in Vancouver after we got married and simply visit him on weekends. I had no intention of actually moving to Rutherford. However, after talking with Tristan one evening, I began feeling guilty. I wasn't trying harder to be "a good wife." So, I finally agreed to go to Rutherford to get to know the area a little bit better before making any final decisions.

As my plane flew over the city preparing to land, I was astonished to see how flat, dry, brown, and barren the landscape really was. The only indication of life I saw was the odd farm silos and smoke streaming from oil refineries. There were also mazes of subdivisions with track-homes that seemed only inches away from one another, sectioned into parcels and closed in by concrete walls.

I felt my anxiety rise as the plane pulled up to the gate.

When Tristan picked me up, I tried to be optimistic and cheerful, thinking that maybe on closer inspection, more places of interest might be revealed. But as we drove, I saw only more brown, dry, and barren land, and more silos and oil derricks. Flat nothingness was all around us.

"Where are the people?" I asked.

"I guess they're either working in the oil fields or at the mall."

Oh boy...

Not long afterwards, we slowed down to turn left at a huge intersection off the main highway and headed toward a massive building with a blue metal roof that sat on that busy corner. It looked like an institution.

"What is this place?" I asked Tristan as we drove toward the building.

"This is where we're living."

You've got to be kidding me...

We exited the highway, and there was nothing else around us in any direction I could see. As we pulled into the driveway, I looked up and saw that the sign above the building read, "Erminskin Place."

"Ummm, Tristan...what does *Erminskin* mean?"

"Well, I'm pretty sure 'ermine' is a weasel, and 'skin' is *skin*, so I guess this is Weasel Skin Place!" he explained, laughing.

Of course, it was.

My future husband lived in a place named after a weasel.

Has it really come to this? I let out a loud sigh.

Tristan took my suitcase out of the trunk, and I followed him somberly to the lobby. His apartment was on the second floor, and after walking down a very long corridor that funneled into two other additional passageways, we finally arrived at B215.

Tristan opened the door of his apartment, and all I saw was dark-brown carpet leading down another long entryway. As I walked in, through the dim light that filtered through the vertical plastic Venetian blinds, I saw that the living room contained only two pieces of furniture—an old rusting woven patio chair and a matching folding lounger with a faded cushion on it. Tristan pointed to it as he explained how he had just brought it in from the balcony. He dusted it off with his hand and motioned for me to sit on it.

Both pieces looked as if they had been outside for a very long time. I went back and forth, staring at the furniture, and then at him. I thought he was kidding at first, but he was serious and assured me it would be quite comfortable. I pretended I didn't hear what he said and quickly looked around the apartment.

That was when he told me it was his parents' apartment, and the reason it lacked furniture was because they had moved it to a suburb of Vancouver, in the home where they now lived. We could bring *my* furniture from Vancouver and make it seem more like home. "But for now, we can use this patio furniture."

I put on another brave front and tried to be nice, but my anxiety began to grow. Again, Tristan asked me to relax in the lounger, so I submitted and sat in it as he requested. As soon as I did, water that had accumulated in the lounger from the rainstorm earlier that week poured out all around me—soaking not only the carpet but also my beautiful outfit.

I started to cry; I couldn't help it. The tears just flowed, and I held my face in my hands for a long time.

I wasn't trying to be a princess. I wasn't trying to be ungrateful or discontented. I just knew with all my heart that I was *not* supposed to be marrying Tristan but only agreed to because I thought I deserved nothing else. I knew that moving to Rutherford was *not* what I was supposed to be doing, and this was *not* the life I was supposed to be living. But I had given up so much of myself that I didn't know how to want (or expect) more. Whatever hope I may have still felt had been snuffed out by the rainwater in the patio cushion, reminding me of my reality.

Under different circumstances, if I had been in love and with the right person, this event would have been cute, sweet, and funny. It could have been a very romantic moment, and I would have jumped up to hold my beloved and kiss him, saying, "This is a great home and a great new start for us! We will build wonderful memories here together!" And the scene would have been something adorable to giggle over as we celebrated many, many, many anniversaries.

But I wasn't in love. And Tristan wasn't my beloved.

It's a Nice Day for a White Wedding

Tristan began changing and seemed lost in his own world. Whatever virtues he had convinced me he had before were no longer visible. So, leaving my home, family, friends, job, school, and our new family dog, at a time when our city was growing and filled with possibility, was almost too much to ask. But it was asked, and I can't believe I'm saying this, but I did leave.

I gave up on wanting more for my life, and with no demands on me now, I reasoned that hiding in Rutherford for a little while would keep me safe. After all, who would threaten me if I had nothing to offer, nothing they'd want to take, and nothing they'd think was valuable? I chose to sacrifice my dreams. I chose to play small, wage little, be unseen, and go unnoticed.

Interestingly, while Tristan and I became distant and lived more like polite roommates, I became very close to Tristan's family. His parents, whom I called Nanny and Pa, were kind people who seemed to love me genuinely and took me in as family.

Tristan was the youngest of four children. Marjorie was the oldest, and she and her family lived in Rutherford. Simone was the second oldest, and she and her family lived in the same Vancouver suburb as Nanny and Pa.

The third child was a baby boy who had died shortly after birth. As one could imagine, that loss was devastating, and Nanny never seemed to recover from it, so when Tristan was born, he became the "golden child," replacing their young baby boy who had died. I suppose Nanny and Pa meant well, but as a consequence of never having dealt with their grief, they raised Tristan with an attitude that he could do no wrong. Tristan was literally (and figuratively), "spoiled"—as in *ruined*.

When a child is reared with no boundaries, no responsibility, no accountability, no rules, no consequences, no vision, and no sense of others, he becomes a monster—as I was about to discover firsthand.

I didn't see this dynamic at first. All I saw were seemingly loving and doting parents who were attentive and always there for their children and grandchildren. They organized evening dinners or weekend gatherings and were ready to help with anything that was needed. Holidays and events were held either at their home or at Simone's since she lived only blocks away from them. When we were in Rutherford, gatherings were held at Marjorie's. No matter where we were, our times together were always fun, warm, and loving. If we weren't playing with the children or watching a few favorite television shows, we played cards. Gin rummy was the game of choice, and we would sit and talk for hours and hours.

Marjorie and Simone were amazing—extremely kind, thoughtful, loving, generous, and very fun! We laughed a lot (and cried a lot) together over the years. In short, I loved being with Tristan's entire family, and at long last, I felt like I belonged somewhere. It no longer mattered to me that Tristan and I weren't the perfect couple. It didn't matter that I wasn't in love with him like I should have been. It was enough that I loved his family, and they loved me. Frankly, the only reason I even followed through with the marriage was to be close to his family. If I was in love with anything, I was in love with the illusion that, if I were married, I'd finally be a part of something special. I could finally be "normal."

With this sense of closeness forcing my anxiety into the corners of my mind, I muddled through the process of planning our wedding. But no matter how hard I tried to escape my true feelings with displacement, distractions, and rationalizations, my unconscious pain and grief revealed itself in my choice of the wedding theme.

My future mother-in-law was mortified when she found out I was having my bridesmaids wear solid black, tailored blazer dresses. I wanted something they could use afterwards, and the dresses were clean, sharp, elegant, and very professional—perfect for working in a law firm (or funeral home), but maybe not so perfect for a wedding.

I tried to explain to her that I was after a sophisticated look, which required equally sophisticated flowers, so I chose four or five white Calla lilies simply wrapped with a white ribbon as the wedding bouquets. To me, they looked best this way—sleek, long, crisp, and also very elegant. Ironically, I had *no idea* what my choices would truly look like until after I saw the wedding photos. The bridesmaids dressed all in black and carrying stark, white lilies looked like a funeral procession as they walked down the aisle!

The morning of the wedding, as the limo brought my bridesmaids and me closer and closer to the church, I started to get lightheaded, unable to catch my breath. I started saying under my breath, "Oh, my God! Oh, my God! Oh, my God..." By the time we had arrived, I was *whimpering* that same phrase out loud—and two octaves higher.

Molly (my friend from UBC) was one of the bridesmaids. She pulled me aside and wisely said, "Manna, you don't have to go through with this. You know that, don't you?" She was very matter-of-fact, and though I recognized the truth in her words, I was unable to speak. The words flowed from Molly so easily. She made it seem so simple, but it was the farthest thing from being simple, or easy. Molly was strong. She knew her worth, and I envied that. I remember thinking, *One day, I will be that strong too.* But at that moment, I was still "me," fighting the duality of what I knew in my heart and what I justified with my mind.

We stared at each other, and then I fumbled, "No, I'm okay...I'm just nervous. That's all."

She didn't buy my explanation, but what else could she do? We were only minutes away from walking down the aisle, and how could she have her typical "to-the-point conversation" with me now? Eventually, she surrendered to the day as well.

As I looked around, everyone was so happy—everyone but me. I was heartbroken. As the bride, I did my best to put on a happy face, but I felt empty inside. I looked at my ring, which was growing cloudier by the day, and thought about the symbolism of it. It was cloudy, murky, and fake, just like our relationship, and now this ceremony. I felt like an imposter. There was no authenticity, purity, or truth about the day (or my heart), and I began to feel even worse about myself.

The organist began playing. All the bridesmaids went ahead of me, and then it was my turn. My father, who had flown in from Hong Kong for this special occasion, stood to my left, ready to walk me down the aisle. He took the first step, but I was frozen in place. He stepped back and looked at me, beaming, encouraging me with his smile. He stopped, took a breath, and tried again, but I was still frozen in place. I couldn't seem to take the first step. The organist replayed the introduction to the procession march yet again, but this time, my father turned and asked me, "Are you sure about this?"

I looked at him with terror in my eyes. I thought about my life and what a mess it was. I turned to look out at the crowd of one hundred and fifty, my family and friends and Tristan's. *How can I disappoint everyone here? They think so much of me. They think I am happy. They think I am together. They want me to be happy. How can I tell them I'm miserable, frightened—terrified? I don't have a clue about what I'm doing.*

The music played once more. I shoved my heart back into its cavern again and thought to myself, *Well, at least there'll be a nice party afterward…*

I nodded to my father, and this time I took the step forward with him. Trembling all the way there, I looked at the faces of my friends to either side of me, and then I saw my grandparents. Both were happily smiling, and all I could see was PoPo's look of pure joy, and I felt her love. All she ever wanted was for me to be happy. Her whole life had been devoted to making sure I was taken care of, and now she believed Tristan was going to take care of me and protect me for the rest of my life. My heart sank as I looked at her, radiant and crying with joy. I knew then that I had to make this marriage work. I didn't want her to worry about me anymore.

When I reached the altar, and it came time to say our vows, I said mine wrong. I couldn't seem to hear what the minister was saying, nor was I able to repeat what he asked me to. Sometimes he sounded like he was speaking in super slow motion; at other times, it sounded like I was listening to him speaking underwater.

I knew the gist of what he was going to say, but I still wasn't able to focus. So, I read his lips, and after a few attempts, I managed to say the vows accurately. I caught Molly's expression, who was looking at me with both love and concern. Again, I wished I was as strong as she was…but I didn't have her strength, I didn't have her confidence, and I didn't have her courage.

I felt like a failure.

The ceremony ended, and the organist played the music again. The next thing I knew, we were ushered back down the aisle to happy family and friends who were excited to share in the celebration of our new life together.

Yes, I will make this marriage work!

Yes, it was a nice day to have a white wedding…even though everyone wore black.

I managed quite well the rest of the afternoon, but when the evening came to an end, and it was time to go back to the hotel room, I was panic-stricken. I had no more people around me to talk to (or introduce to one another), and there was no more food, wine, or music to distract me. There was just Tristan and me.

The stark reality of that fact and the significance of what it *should* have meant was almost overwhelming. For most people, this is one of the sweetest times of the entire day—the wedding night—when the beloveds finally have their alone time together. But we were as far apart as two planets in the solar system—lightyears, even galaxies, away.

That sinking feeling in my stomach returned…you know, the kind of feeling you have when you know you have made the biggest mistake of your life.

Then suddenly, a movie of our relationship flashed before my eyes, but now I saw it all with no filters. The scales were lifted from my eyes, and I could clearly see everything for what it was! I saw again how he acted the night we first met, his excessive attention to self, his insensitivity to the needs of others, his detachment, his irresponsibility, his growing arrogance, and his entitlement. When Tristan didn't get his way, he would sulk, be angry, and stop trying. He wouldn't look for solutions or other options, and he refused to create possibilities or work harder. He simply gave up, demanding that someone else fix things, and until that occurred, he felt entitled to amuse himself in any way that pleased him.

I gasped for air.

I could no longer pretend, ignore, or rationalize his behavior, nor could I justify my reasons for being with him—no matter how nice and wonderful his family was.

Yes, I know, most people would have already come to this conclusion after day one, but people make different decisions when their lives are founded on fear. While their choices may appear foolish or even stupid to others, they're actually doing the most logical thing possible—surviving.

I wouldn't fully understand till much later in life that when you are in survival mode, you do the least possible in order to conserve energy. Your mindset is simply to prolong life so that you can survive another day. Higher-level thinking comes when your body doesn't think it's going to die the next minute. It is only then that you have the time to make other choices. Being in a constant state of fear doesn't allow that kind of thinking to occur. You don't believe you have choices. Of all times, I began understanding these things on my wedding night!

"Oh, Manna. I'm so sorry. That event should have been the happiest day of your life, and you should have been smiling ear to ear with joy, even more than your PoPo!" Leah said sympathetically.

"Yes, but it was my faulty thinking that got me into such a mess. I foolishly believed that *caring* about someone was enough to make a marriage work. It isn't. Marriage is a covenanted relationship—not one to undertake as a plan to escape another reality. And as much as I think Tristan believed he loved me, he, too, was looking at me as an answer to escape his reality. He was running from something, but neither he nor his mother revealed the secret he was running from. I didn't find out what his secret was until twenty-one years later."

So, that night, I was overcome by the glaring reality of my mistake.

Oh, dear God—what have I done? Somehow, I have to fix this and get out!

I could not accept this untrue marriage as my fate, and for the first time in my adult life, I found the courage to ask for more. Instead of running away and hiding, I was going to stand up for myself.

But how? How am I going to fix this? What in the world am I going to say? We just got married in front of a ton of people! PoPo…GongGong…Oh, dear God, please help me!

We walked to our room in silence, both avoiding the awkwardness of the unspoken. Our wedding night was supposed to be filled with romance, but romance takes time, thought, effort, generosity, patience, and a caring heart. Romance is mysterious, playful, and even heroic. Tristan held none of these virtues or ideals.

In a flash, I knew what I would have to do. *The marriage has to be annulled. I will find a way to start over again, somehow.*

We had arrived at the door of our suite at the hotel. Tristan opened the door, and I watched him walk in and disappear around the corner. He didn't open the door for me, nor did he carry me over the threshold. I held the door open with my left hand and took off my shoes with my right hand. I watched him go into the bathroom to get ready for bed. I went straight to the living room of our suite, sat down, and massaged my feet.

When Tristan came out of the bathroom, I thought he would at least come and say goodnight. Instead, he crawled into bed and fell asleep. I stayed in the living room, turned on the television, and watched Johnny Carson reruns, crying myself to sleep on the couch.

I awoke early, and the sun was rising beyond our window. The new light of day made the glaring reality of what I had done even more arresting. The inevitable hung over me ominously, and what I had to do now lay very heavy on my heart, but there was no other option—I had to speak to Tristan about this mistake and somehow rectify the situation. The absoluteness stared at me, and I was petrified as I went into the bedroom and woke him, telling him that I needed to talk to him.

"I'm sorry I fell asleep," he said, still groggy from just waking.

"It's okay. I need to talk to you."

He had no desire to talk. He tried to gather me to him. He thought my resistance was because I was upset he had fallen asleep the night before. I wanted to cry, but I was afraid. I resisted and tried to make him aware that I had something else more important to talk about.

But fear and the old habit of doing what was expected of me kicked in, and we consummated the marriage. I tried to vacate my mind during the process and lay there, waiting for him to finish. I thought that if I did what was expected of me, then he wouldn't be so angry with me when I told him I wanted to annul the marriage. I could appease him by telling him that we were still together, but not married.

I kept looking for the right time to say something, but one moment led to the next, and before I knew it, we had gotten ready for the day, checked out of the hotel, and were headed to his parents' place for dinner that afternoon.

We weren't going on a honeymoon because he had no money, and I had used up my savings for the wedding and items needed at Weasel Skin Place. Not having a honeymoon was totally fine with me, as the thought of being alone with him for a week or two at a romantic getaway was alarming. It was better to tell everyone we were saving up for our future instead.

On our way, I was silent for most of the drive. I stared out the window, wondering how I was going to bring up the topic of annulment, and how I could make this easy and palatable for him. When we passed the halfway point between the hotel and his parent's home, I knew I was running out of time. I couldn't bear going to see his parents without having the conversation first.

We were on West 41st Avenue going westbound, about to stop at a traffic light at Oak Street. To my right was the former bus depot where all the buses that ran the streets of Vancouver parked. Those buses were all bound for somewhere… how I longed to be on one of those buses going "somewhere," for the vehicle I was riding in was going nowhere.

I mustered the courage that I needed to speak, and right then, Tristan turned to me and asked, "What are you thinking about?"

This is my chance! I grabbed it. Unfortunately, I wasn't as eloquent as I had hoped. My words came spilling out of me in awkward, redundant, frantic fits. I took all the blame on myself, accepted responsibility for my choices, and offered to make restoration.

"Oh, Tristan, I'm so sorry. I made a terrible mistake. I'm not ready to be married. I don't have the capacity or the ability to be a wife right now. I can't do this. Can we please simply annul the marriage? I won't leave you. We can still be together, but I need more time…I'm too afraid…I can't be married…I just can't! I'll return all the gifts to everyone and pay everyone back, and even reimburse everyone who traveled to the wedding. I will also take the blame for it all. You can say anything you want—please, let's just annul the marriage…I can't be married…I just can't. I'm so sorry. I know this isn't what you want to hear, but I need to be honest with you. I'm so sorry."

The longer I talked, the angrier Tristan became.

"Stop it!" he finally yelled. He pulled the car over, grabbed my left forearm, and pulled me to him, dragging my body toward him so that my face was only inches from his.

"I know you don't love me, but we're married, and that's the way it's going to stay! You're stuck with me, and I will never let you go! I see the way all the guys look at you, but they can't have you now. You're mine now! You're mine until death! You will not talk to me about this again, do you understand? End of discussion!"

He threw my arm from his grip, and I turned back to the window and hugged the door as close as possible. I thought about opening the door and running away, but where would I go? We were still legally married.

The bus station faded behind us, as did my hope for freedom.

I felt doomed. Tristan had said, "until *death.*"

Mother Knows Best

The delightful relationship I had enjoyed with Nanny also started to change. Even though Tristan and I lived in Rutherford, she became more and more involved with all aspects of his life—especially his work life—much more than I thought was appropriate. She would tell him what to do but express it in a way that didn't seem like she was telling him what to do. Rather, she would cleverly bring up conversations, plant her idea, and then dismiss it, as if it was no big deal, knowing Tristan would take it from there and run with it.

With me, she told me how to cook for Tristan, how to do his laundry, and how to bake his favorite desserts. She would slide in a criticism (or three) in between compliments, and then dismiss her comments altogether as if they meant nothing. "Manna, you're like a chef, taking *all day* in the kitchen to prepare a 'simple' dish! And just look how much *weight* Tristan has gained in such a short time! I would gain weight like that too if I ate your meals every day. I've never had your flair—using butter or wine or having a cupboard full of spices and herbs like you do. My cooking was simple and natural without all those heavy, filling sauces. I'm old, so I cook the old-fashioned, wholesome way so you can taste the food. My style of cooking worked to feed a large family on a budget. But since you don't have a budget, I guess you don't worry about basics like that. Did you ever take home economics?"

"What the hell?" Leah piped in.

"I know. It gets worse, unfortunately. She also spoke with me about money issues."

"Where was Tristan in all of this?" Leah demanded.

"He was there, and he knew exactly what was going on, but said nothing. Over the next year, I told him many times that I thought something wasn't right about his mother and her interference in our lives. Each time he responded coldly, 'You're not used to that because you never had a mother who cared about you. Be thankful that someone cares. Remember how much you loved her before we got married? Stop being overly sensitive!"

Not wanting to be unappreciative of my newfound, loving family, I sucked it in and dismissed her increasingly intense daily comments.

I don't know who fueled whom, but between Tristan and Nanny, work conversations were rampant about what Tristan "deserved" and what he was "owed." At one time, Tristan did well without having to work hard. But the market changed, and sales orders were fewer in size and frequency, which is the reason Tristan had been given this added region to grow.

Nanny, however, viewed this as unfair, and perceived Tristan was "suffering," having to work "so hard." She accused the owners of being unreasonable and unjust. Why she was even involved in his business to begin with is another issue, but the fact that she had Tristan's ear (and he had hers) was the main concern at this point. Eventually, Tristan also believed he "deserved" to have the same commission as he did before, even though he had fewer sales.

Nothing about the situation was very logical.

Tristan's work schedule grew more and more inconsistent, and when he came home, he was filled with frustration, spouting his entitlements loudly as he threw his keys onto the counter. When I tried to discuss things with him, he would reject my ideas. With a wave of the back of his hand and a loud, "pffft!" he would fall onto the sofa to watch TV.

His laziness and illogical thinking were starting to wear on me, and when Nanny saw that I wasn't in total agreement with her son, she directed more unnecessary, spiteful comments at me. It felt as though I was in a strange three-way relationship, but it was *I* who was interfering with *their* marriage.

In the meantime, Marjorie did her best to include me and to make sure I felt welcomed into the family and at home in Rutherford. She also tried to include me with some of her friends in a league sport in which she was very involved.

"Manna, join the club with me, please? It will be so much fun!" Marjorie said, sweetly.

"What kind of club is it?"

"It's a curling club. You'll love it!"

I gasped.

"And you'll get your own matching jacket with the rest of the curlers too!" she said in a sing-song way, trying to incentivize me.

I forced a smile. "Curling? Really?" I barely got my words out. "You really *curl?*"

In Vancouver, I enjoyed an active, athletic life. I played tennis, trained at the gym, ran miles along the beach, and went boating with friends. But curling?

While some may have enjoyed that sport, I found the idea of pushing and sliding stones on ice mortifying. I mean no offense meant to the sport. It's just that the invitation was also unnerving (and depressing) because this club represented the only option for me in Rutherford. Had I been married to someone I loved, were I not so sad about leaving my family behind, and were it not for the peculiar dynamic between Tristan and his mother, I would have seen curling as a fun new adventure. I would have been happy trying something new and different because my attempt would have come from a foundation of love. I was starting a new life with my wonderful husband!

But since none of those things were true for me, this sport only resonated with me as another somber reality of my dismal life.

I loved Marjorie for thinking of me and for her unending efforts to make me feel at home and loved. However, I just couldn't see myself curling. To do so would have meant I had completely relinquished all hope and sentenced myself to this place—and this life—permanently. Temporarily dealing with three-to-six inches of ice on the roads for months and months on end, having to plug in your car at the end of the day so your engine doesn't freeze in the winter, nose bleeds and cracking skin due to the dry climate, or feeling like you've got bugs crawling over your skin in the desert-like summer was more than enough.

So, after thanking her profusely for the offer, I politely declined.

I had convinced myself to live in a world of defeat and failure, but a world of "something more" kept summoning me to remember. I couldn't put my hands on it, see it, or define it, but something always called me back to life. Like a lone thread in a tapestry, I hung on to it, believing that one day the entire picture would be revealed to me.

So, in the spirit of trying to make the best of my new life in Rutherford, I started working for the Elizabeth Arden makeup counter at one of the local malls. In less than three months, I had increased their sales by two-hundred-and-fifty percent and made friends with the other girls working in the same makeup department.

I must admit, while the success was invigorating, I enjoyed being out of the house and away from Tristan.

We had been fighting daily because I was frustrated with his swelling arrogance and his poor work ethic. He refused to build his territory, so his paychecks were not sufficient to make ends meet. When I asked how we would pay his parents next month's rent, that's when I discovered he had never paid them. Tristan used whatever money he made as spending money. I confronted him with this falsehood, and he exploded with anger before leaving the apartment. Moreover, the better I was doing at work, and the more money I was earning, the less he thought he needed to work.

"I'm happy to support us if there is a good reason for it," I told him, "but I will not agree to it if you *choose* to do nothing and *expect* me to support you."

Our quarreling became so bad that I threatened to go back home to Vancouver. When he knew I was serious, he looked for another job, but when the titles he wanted or the pay he expected wasn't forthcoming, he decided to stay where he was and "work harder."

While I did well in my sales position, I knew I could only go so far there. I was also starving for intellectual stimulation and thought about going back to law school at the local university.

In spite of the haunting words Landon had spoken over me years earlier, I was older now and found the courage to begin anew. Instead of starting with a heavy course load, I chose a light curriculum with classes I didn't have the luxury to take before, thereby increasing my grade point average even more for my application to law school.

Since Tristan's income wasn't enough, I had to work increased hours on top of my studies to pay for all expenses. I didn't mind. I was happy because my mind was sparked with learning, and I had more reasons not to be home.

It was exhilarating to be back at a university with people committed to higher-level thinking and who had a vision and purpose for their lives. I became the top student in the class, scoring almost perfect grades on all my exams, and my dreams about becoming an attorney again seemed closer. I just needed to believe in myself and not in the things that were spoken *to* me or *over* me.

Too Close for Comfort

Try as I might to bring in extra income and better myself with school to provide a brighter future for us, things were not getting better with my marriage. Tristan and I had very little in common and even less to talk about. When we did talk, our conversations escalated very quickly and always turned ugly.

During crabbing season, the fishermen never have to cover their buckets filled with crabs. They know they will never lose one because each time one tries to climb out, another pulls it back down. Sadly, I felt this way in my marriage. Whenever I felt like I was finally getting ahead, I was pulled back down into the bucket of hopelessness.

One day, Tristan and I had a huge and horrible fight.

He refused to try harder at work because I was providing most of the income now, and I was furious. Unbeknownst to me, Tristan began receiving monthly support from his parents. However, instead of talking forthrightly to her son, Nanny often called *me* to "discuss" our finances, blaming me for our lack, and the unhappiness Tristan apparently shared with her. She did approve of my desire to go back to law school because then *I* would be able to support her son in the future, "But until then, Manna, how are *you* going to pay the bills and support the family? He's so stressed and under too much pressure from his company. You should ask your father for money."

I was horrified at her solution, and one so casually offered! Long gone were my sweet days of conversation with her. Now, our conversations were to the point and as respectful as I could be, but that too was becoming more and more difficult with each communication.

"Nanny, it's a sales job. He only earns money when he works. And it's not my father's responsibility to support *your son!*"

When I tried to talk to Tristan about his mother again, he accused me of being jealous of her. "You should learn to love me like she does!"

On this particular afternoon, I'd had it with all of Tristan's excuses; I had reached my boiling point. I dared not tell my family how horrendous my situation was, and how ashamed I was of where my life had gone. I had a lazy, spoiled child for a husband and an overbearing mother-in-law. I was stuck in a place I didn't belong away from my family—especially my PoPo and GongGong, who were getting older and needing more help.

All my mistakes came crashing in on me. My life was a mess.

Tristan's vulgar language intensified as well, and on this day, he said horrible things, using my past against me in ways that I will not share. He called me every vicious name he could think of, including my mother's and Scham's mantra.

When I heard this, a switch in me flipped, and I lost it. "Get out right now! And don't come back! I'm leaving on the first flight tomorrow and filing for a divorce!"

Though it may sound tame as I recount this to you, let me assure you, it was the fight of all fights. This was the fight that would end any relationship. Nothing was spared. All weapons were used, and the result was absolute destruction. I was devastated.

He stormed out the door, and I knew he wasn't coming back.

I sat in the silent aftermath and cried. Yes, my life was a complete mess, indeed. Even my enjoyable classes were not enough to stimulate me out of my depressing marriage, and I saw myself as a failure once more. Law school seemed so daunting and so far away again, as did any hope for a brighter and happier future. I was living in an apartment I had futilely tried to make into a home, and everything in it was only a reminder of the mess my life was. *I know I said I would go back home, but how can I face my family and friends? How can I let PoPo and GongGong know what a loser I am?*

Other people would have simply packed their things and booked the next flight out. If that were me today, I would have done that very thing... but I didn't. I still lived without a solid foundation of truth, identity, or self-esteem. While I often succeeded in talking myself into a better state of mind, this fight revealed how unanchored I really was. This tempest threw me off the line, and I was once again on the negative side of the equation.

In the dreary silence, each moment felt like a lifetime. I was confused, terrified about admitting my failures to everyone at home, and dreading the thought of having to face another day of more disappointments. I felt more alone than ever before. The depression I had been trying to stave off for years reemerged with a vengeance.

Just then, I could hear that heavy shadowy voice once again against my ear: *You don't have to feel any more pain. You can be with God. After all, isn't that what you've always wanted?*

I did want it. I did want to go back to heaven. Everything was a mess, and I could not do anything about it.

I just wanted some peace. I just wanted to go "Home."

I cried out to God. *I said I didn't want to do this. I said it was too hard.*

The darkness was palpable, its heaviness increasing and enveloping me. Sobbing my way to the bathroom medicine cabinet, I decided to end the personal hell I was living in. I took out a bottle of Tylenol, poured a glass of water, and gulped handfuls of the pills. Then I lay down on the bed, thinking, *I'll fall asleep and wake up in heaven.* I closed my eyes and apologized to God. *I'm sorry I failed You. I'm sorry I didn't make it. I'm sorry I made so many bad choices. I'm sorry that a few people will be hurt. Please tell them that I'm sorry once I'm gone. It will be better this way. I will be a better guardian angel than a human...*

I cried and cried as I thought, *This is it, I guess... Tristan is gone, and no one will find me till it's too late. He said, "Till death do us part." I guess it is time after all.*

My sadness and remorse for not doing what I had promised God I would do with my life was real. Though I didn't know what that was exactly, it was obvious I had not accomplished it. In the absolute silence of the moment, the darkness came, and my eyes grew very heavy.

I had no idea how much time had passed between that last thought and when I heard a sudden bang. The thunderous sound jarred me out of my slumber. I was barely able to open my eyes, and my mind was very groggy and fuzzy. I thought maybe I was dreaming, or that I was in heaven. But I wasn't dreaming, and I certainly was *not* in heaven.

I had been curled up in a fetal position, and through barely opened eyes, I saw Tristan hovering over me. When he saw the bottle of pills on the nightstand, he grabbed me. With both hands, Tristan shook me violently and called out my name, panic etched into his face.

All the while, I could only wonder why he was there. *Why did he come back? There is no logical reason for him to be here—none! That fight was the fight to end all fights. I kicked him out and told him I was leaving. Why is he here?*

Then I felt something warm inside me, and I knew... God had intercepted this event and made Tristan come back to get me.

"Why are you here?" I slurred.

"I don't know... I can't explain it," he said. "Something stopped me from going further. I literally felt I had no choice but to turn around and come back. It's kinda creepy, actually. All I knew was I had to come back, and now I know why. We've got to get you to the hospital."

The next thing I knew, I was in the car, and after racing over a huge speed bump, I opened my eyes and saw the hospital "EMERGENCY" sign. I was taken inside, and after answering a few questions, I was given something black to drink and handed a bucket.

That's it? No explanations? How odd. I took half a bottle of Tylenol, and they're just giving me something to drink…and what do I do with this bucket?

I was wide awake by now, alarmed at what I had done, and ashamed that everyone around me knew about it.

Suddenly, I became very nauseous, and before I knew it, I was throwing up.

That's what the bucket is for…

It felt like I vomited for hours. Tears ran down my face from all the vomiting. Just when the nausea finally subsided and I had a few minutes to breathe, the queasy feeling returned, and I was vomiting again. I threw up more that day than I thought any one person could be capable of in a lifetime.

The nurses checked on me periodically, but not with kindness or concern. Their hostility was conspicuous. I had just tried to commit suicide with an overdose of pills, and I felt no bedside manner from them at all. They took my vitals when I arrived, gave me more charcoal to drink, and every thirty minutes or so forcefully whipped open the curtains drawn around my gurney, looked at me crossly before leaving again.

I didn't need to be scolded, either verbally or silently, with disapproving expressions. I was doing a great job of berating myself already. What I needed was someone to hold my hand and tell me everything was going to be all right. Tristan stepped out a few times during the whole scenario, and I didn't blame him. When he came back, he sat in a small chair by my bed with nothing to say.

I felt even more humiliated than before I took the pills.

God, I wondered, *Why, why,* why *won't You just let me go?*

"Did you get an answer?" Leah asked.

I paused, trying to decide how to answer this question. "Well, actually, I did."

"You *did?*" Leah sat up a little. "What did you hear?"

I let out a deep breath, leaned forward, and said, "I heard and instantly felt in my spirit the words, '*I sent you for a purpose. My plans will not be thwarted.*'"

Leah raised her eyebrow and tilted her head to me. She waited a moment and then said, "*Thwarted?* That's not a word a girl in her mid-twenties back then would say. Hmmm…interesting."

We both took a deep breath, and after Leah had pondered my response, she continued, "And what do you mean, 'you heard and felt in your spirit'? And how is that different than the other voice that told you the other times to kill yourself?"

"Well, the *dark voice* was always an uneasy one, with no peace or sense of calm. It always wanted me to do something that would harm me, put my life in danger, or demand I overreact with retaliation to defend or vindicate myself. I never felt *good* about anything *that voice* told me. I only ever felt sadness, fear, anxiety, or desperation.

"The *voice of God*, however, always encourages me, shows me strategies for the future, and lifts me up for a purpose bigger than what I'm able to see, or believe, at the time. When I hear from heaven, my spirit feels calm, even if the message is a tough one to receive. I feel a sense of peace in me and around me. It's a knowing that surpasses language and human understanding. When I *hear* from God, there is a quiet strength in my soul…something comes alive and rises from deep inside, and in an instant, I know the truth in the situation—every lie is exposed."

I paused to look at Leah, and when I knew I hadn't lost her, I continued. "And when I say I *hear* God, I don't always hear a tangible voice. Sometimes I *feel* His words, I *feel* His voice. But I *always* 'hear' God when I'm reading the Bible, and whenever I'm *open-heartedly and truly* seeking Him. God reveals Himself to me in breathtaking ways, and I always end up feeling lighter. It's difficult to explain something so wonderful. It is too good for words, too big to contain, too amazing to comprehend with human language. So, for now, Leah, please trust me when I say, when you hear from God, *you will know it*."

Leah kept her gaze on me, eyebrow still raised. I met her watchful eye back, and when she was satisfied with her evaluation, she whispered, "Fascinating." Then, without skipping a beat, she added, "Then what happened?"

I took another deep breath and continued.

When I was stabilized, and there was nothing left to throw up, the on-duty psychiatrist came into the room.

"Are you Manna Ko?"

"Yes."

"Do you know what you did?" he asked phlegmatically.

"Yes," I replied remorsefully.

"Are you going to do it again?"

"No, sir." I shook my head.

"How do I know that you won't?"

"Because I never, ever want to throw up that much again!"

He looked at me over his glasses and nodded. "Sign here," he said, handing me a piece of paper on a clipboard. After I had signed the document, he turned and walked away. There was no, "Good luck," no "Do you need someone to talk to? We have some good therapists we can recommend." Nothing. A couple of questions, a quick look over the rim of his glasses, a "sign here," and *voilà*, I was free to go. Yes, that was the extent of the psychiatric care I received after a serious suicide attempt.

Someone else came shortly afterward, asked me to sign a few more papers, and then released me to go "back home."

Really? Go back there with Tristan? Don't you know that's how I got here to begin with?

As we walked through the emergency room sliding doors in silence, I prayed, *God, please give me hope. Give me something to live for.*

"Oh, Manna…no one would ever suspect you were so broken." Leah shook her head.

"Yes, I'm astonished myself as I relive this with you. I have come a long, long way."

"Yes, thank God! You had another miracle then…but some are not so lucky," she said sadly.

"I know. Now that I know the depths of that dark emptiness, I can boldly tell those who believe they are lost, unforgivable, 'too different,' or hopeless, to never, never, *ever* give up. I would tell them to stop listening to the enemy of their life and to not believe the lies spoken over them (or quietly whispered in their ears). I would tell them to focus on what is true, noble, just, pure, and lovely. I'd say to focus on good reports, on virtuous and praiseworthy things. And I would remind them to keep believing. There are new days, better days, ahead. There is hope. I know. I was there, and if I can do it, they can too. Just please, believe."

Someone to Live For

Tristan and I had been married seven tumultuous months. We had not been intimate one time since the bleak morning after our wedding. We were newlyweds, without any emotional or physical intimacy between us, and in addition to all the other disappointments, I felt doomed to be the sole provider and the head of the household.

Over the Christmas holidays, Tristan suddenly thought he should try harder to make our marriage work—or at least that's what he said one morning. It was the first weekend of the new year, and I woke up earlier than usual that morning. Fresh snow had fallen and covered the ugliness of the hardened ice and dirt on the roads. Since everything was quiet, I went back to sleep a little bit longer. We were babysitting Marjorie's child at noon, so I knew I had plenty of time to get ready.

I had just fallen back asleep when Tristan rolled over without any warning and said, "I think we should try to be more than just roommates."

Still groggy, he rolled on top of me and had his way as I stared at the alarm clock on my bedside table. Strangely, it read 9:38 a.m. *the entire time.* The digits on my clock never once changed. When it was over, I went into the bathroom to shower, hoping to wash off the soil I felt. *Had my life really sunk this low?*

As the hot water washed over me, I sobbed, "God, I can't do this!"

You can. You will.
"Why? Why should I?"
You're pregnant.
I froze and stopped breathing.
"*What?* What did You say? What…did…You…*say?*"
It will be a boy.
I stood motionless and speechless. But something in me knew.
I was pregnant…but how?
My mind raced in a thousand directions with even more questions. *This was impossible! This was the first time we'd been intimate in seven months! How could this be?*
I dried myself off hurriedly, grabbed my robe, ran back into the bedroom, and told Tristan I was pregnant.
"You're crazy," he said, annoyed with my pronouncement. "There's no way you can be pregnant! That was just a few minutes ago! It doesn't happen that fast! Stop talking nonsense!"
"I'm telling you, I'm pregnant! I know I'm pregnant!"
"Fine." He put down the remote to the television and looked at me impatiently. "How do you know you're pregnant?"
I hesitated.
"Well…? Are you going to tell me how you know or not?"
I braced myself. "God told me."
He roared with laughter, shaking his head as if I had lost my mind, and returned to his television show.
I went back to the bathroom and stared into the mirror.
I'm going to be a mom! I'm going to have a baby, a baby boy!
Interestingly, Tristan and I were never intimate again. And for the remainder of our marriage, we lived just as he had described, as roommates. Little did I know, we were meant to come together that one time to fulfill God's purpose—to have Michael. It was just as He had told me, and nothing could thwart it. God also had a plan for my son's life, and I was chosen to be his mother.

"Oh, Manna, I wish your marriage was more of what you had hoped for," Leah said tenderly. "Thankfully, Thomas and I have had a great marriage, and we had fun trying to get pregnant! The alarm clock was the last thing I thought about!"
We both laughed, and Leah urged me to continue.
I exhaled. "It defies human reasoning that I could know I was pregnant or that I was able to feel this microscopic change in my body, but I did. I didn't need a test kit to prove it, nor did I need the doctor to tell me that the 'bunny died' (the euphemism in those days). I *knew* because God told me.

"Ironically, I had purchased a brand-new journal a few weeks earlier, but I didn't know why I had bought it until that moment. It was to be my journal for my baby. In that journal, I began writing to my son, my Michael, telling him how much I loved him and how much I couldn't wait for him to come into my life."

"It's mind-boggling! And why did you know his name would be Michael?" Leah asked shaking her head in awe.

"The name Michael means 'most like God.' 'Michael' was also a powerful archangel, and I knew that this name would befit my son. He would be a great man of God and a great warrior for Him."

"Hmmm….why doesn't it surprise me that someone who talks to angels, had a dog who saw angels, would name their child after the most powerful angel of all!" She chuckled.

When Tristan saw me writing, he asked what I was doing.

"I'm writing a letter to my baby boy," I told him straightforwardly. He raised his eyebrows, rolled his eyes, and walked away, mumbling something about me having "lost it." But I didn't care what he thought. I knew God had once again done what He said He would do—He had given me hope and a reason to live.

God gave me one of the greatest purposes of my life. Not only did He give me the gift of being a mother, but He had also forgiven me for what I had done with this gift before. The God of second chances (and the 1,000+ chances) gave me another chance at happiness and another new beginning.

Peace, joy, and strength filled me from the inside out, and for the first time in my life, I felt special, precious, important, and worthy.

We got ready to go babysit and headed out the door. Traveling to Marjorie's house, I gazed out the window engaged in a hundred different thoughts while Tristan was focused on an accident on the other side of the highway. We had just passed an exit ramp and began our descent down a very large six-lane bridge that also served as an overpass. Suddenly, something told me to turn and look straight ahead. As I did, I saw in the distance that a car ahead of us had spun out of control on black ice. I screamed, "Tristan, slow down!" but he was looking the other way. Even when he turned to look straight ahead, he still didn't react. He was paralyzed with fear. We were about to have a head-on collision traveling at sixty miles an hour—on ice!

"Pump the brakes! Turn into the shoulder!" I screamed.

When he didn't, I reached over, grabbed the wheel, and turned it toward the wide shoulder on my right. At that moment, Tristan awoke from his shock, and finally took his foot off the accelerator and stomped on the brakes, only to lock the brakes and throw the car into a spin.

This time, I thought for sure, *I am going to die.* I simply closed my eyes and waited for the impact.

By the grace of God, our car stopped, and we didn't collide with either the concrete divider or another car. But we weren't out of harm's way yet. We had spun to a stop and were now facing the oncoming traffic. A row of cars was coming towards us now, and though they tried to avoid us, they were sliding directly at us! Some were able to stop, some managed to take another lane, and a few others had lost control but managed to swerve around us. Miraculously, one by one, the cars passed us until we could gather ourselves, restart the car and turn it around to drive in the right direction.

That was too close for comfort! I didn't want to die anymore. I wanted to *live*! I had something to live for. I had *someone* to live for!

The following Monday, I called my doctor and asked to have a pregnancy test. He didn't think I was pregnant and explained that even if I took a pregnancy test, it was too early to have a definitive answer. "Take some antacids and call in a few weeks," he suggested.

Nothing I could say convinced him otherwise, and since there were no over-the-counter tests available in those days, I had no choice but to wait.

The coming weeks were interesting ones as I felt my body change. I became very forgetful and couldn't remember the simplest of things. Even driving became a strange experience. We had a standard, or manual shift, and any other time, I could handle that car with my eyes closed. But now, I couldn't seem to remember what to do. I felt really *dumb*, and it became a challenge for me to focus; the simplest of things seemed to confuse me.

Weeks passed, but the doctor still wouldn't believe me. He insisted it was still too early to know for sure, but he humored me and agreed to the pregnancy test. A few days later, when I returned for the test results, he came into the examination room where I waited and shook his head in disbelief. He announced, "Yes, Manna. You are indeed pregnant."

I walked out of the office beaming and floated to my car.

In the months ahead, in spite of my burgeoning belly and my memory lapses, for the first time in my life, I felt beautiful and invincible, because I was the carrier of a great treasure.

To this day, although I have flown in private planes, resided at elite hotels, been chauffeured in limousines, walked the red carpet adorned with jewels and dressed in expensive gowns, and met princes and dignitaries around the world, I have never felt more special and more beautiful as I did when I was pregnant with my son, Michael.

My Superpower

Tristan and I had never talked about having children, and the news of my pregnancy rocked both of us. He was happy but fearful about this growing responsibility in his life. I was excited about the chance of doing things right and being a great mom—the kind of mother I never had.

Interestingly, one would think since Tristan and I had come together physically, overcome a near-tragic car accident, and now had a new baby on the way, things would be better between us, but they weren't. Our marriage only got worse.

I did my best to encourage him, brainstorming with him and digging up as many good qualities about him as I could grab. Unfortunately, this couldn't sustain us, and Tristan soon gave in to his default, citing a variety of excuses for his failure.

It was exasperating, and I was losing my patience with it all. Plus, with a baby now on the way, I couldn't afford to waste any more time or energy on this dysfunction. Law school was no longer an option, and I was unwilling to tolerate Nanny's daily calls asking me "where the money would come from" to support her son. I was losing respect for both of them and needed to focus on a healthier way of living.

In my heart of hearts, I just wished Tristan could be "normal"—that he could be a man! I wanted him to grow up and stop complaining about what he didn't have and what he thought he was owed. And when things didn't go as hoped, I wanted him to figure it out—not run to his mother! It was unnerving for me to think my life would forever be like this, so I decided to move back to Vancouver and rear Michael there. After all, if I had to do and be responsible for everything anyway, I might as well do it alone. I wasn't thinking about a formal separation, but if we had to separate, I'm sorry to say, I was only too happy to do so. In the meantime, my father, who was still living in Hong Kong at the time, insisted I stay at the family home until we decided what we wanted to do.

Thankfully, the company Tristan was working for opened up another division in Vancouver around this same time, and he was given the opportunity to run it. Within a few months, we were headed back home.

I arrived back in Vancouver overjoyed! Life fell into an easy routine for a while, and I spent a lot of time with my grandparents. Even though I was pregnant, I still helped them with cleaning, laundry, and their weekly shopping—just as I had when I was younger. But it was easier now as they lived very close to where I was renting. My mother had talked them into selling their home to her, so my grandparents found a smaller home on the Vancouver west side.

My mother then tore down my grandparents' older home and built her custom home on that site. Apparently, Scham had made so many enemies with their neighbors, they needed to move and start fresh. My father's heirloom jewelry and diamond investments my mother had promised to hold for us in trust no longer existed, so we all assumed those items had been sold to provide for her lifestyle. That, or were given to Huxley.

I had not seen my mother in years. I had, despite everything, tried many times to connect with her, and both Luke and I gave her Mother's Day, birthday, and Christmas cards through PoPo, but she never took them home with her. I even invited her to my wedding, but she didn't come. Still, with a baby on the way, I hoped for a fresh start and wanted to leave the past behind me.

Though painful memories still popped up now and then, I harbored no bitterness and only wished to share this special time with her, as a mother and daughter should. I wanted to share the birthing process and motherhood with her and had hoped my pregnancy would be a way for us to get to know each other again. Plus, I wanted Michael to have the opportunity of getting to know his grandmother. But it would not be so easy.

In my third month, I suddenly started spotting. I was very scared. My doctor told me I might be miscarrying, but I refused to accept that diagnosis and prayed against it. I wanted this baby more than anything, and I knew I was supposed to have Michael. There was no way I was going to miscarry. I prayed for God to let me keep my baby and laid in bed without moving for hours.

My prayers were answered, and by that evening, I had stopped spotting. After a few tests later that week, it was confirmed that my baby was fine, growing, and healthy.

I continued to spend time with my grandparents every day, and we had great fun together. PoPo made me fantastic and delicious meals and having her nearby when I was feeling so vulnerable, afraid (especially of the delivery process), and alone was like my lifeline.

After eating very little for the first trimester due to horrible morning sickness, I found myself constantly hungry throughout the rest of my pregnancy. I ate everything PoPo made for me and began gaining a lot of weight. I couldn't stop eating! Some days I would eat eight to ten meals per day, especially dinners. And as you know, eating was never really something I enjoyed, so this entire experience was very surprising for me.

My appointments with my doctor always left him shaking his head. He was surprised at both my strength and my weight gain, which was all up front. From behind, people could not tell I was pregnant, but when I turned around, their eyes almost popped out of their sockets. When I sat down, I was *literally* an arm's length from the table, my tummy was that big. In my last trimester, I could no longer see my ankles without twisting my torso into a funny, sideways position.

"Oh, my! How much weight did you gain in total?" Leah asked.

"About seventy pounds!"

"*What*? Did the doctors not worry about you? Not psychologically," she winked, "but health-wise?"

"No. Other than the weight gain, my test results were excellent. And I didn't care about the weight. I was simply relieved to know I was going to have a healthy, full-term baby. I wrote in my journal to Michael regularly, telling him how much I loved him and how much he meant to me. I had not felt a love so strong, so deep, and so powerful—ever. The love that I had as a mother for my baby was, and continues to be, amazing. I would do anything to ensure the best for him in life, and I finally understood what it meant to be a 'momma bear' or a 'momma lioness.'

I was fiercely protective of Michael and would have killed anyone who tried to hurt him, and would not have thought twice about it."

"I've never heard you talk like this," Leah said with eyes wide open. "I see commercials on TV about superhero shows all the time. Sounds like you're one too, only your superpower is being a mom."

I nodded in agreement.

I loved being a mom to Michael from the moment I knew he was created. And throughout my pregnancy, I continued to cherish my quiet times with him. I sang to him so he would know my voice, and I played Mozart and other great classics for him so he would have an appreciation for beautiful music. Sometimes he would even kick when he heard certain familiar pieces.

Around this time, I contemplated the two distinct polar extremes of motherhood I had experienced, neither of which were healthy or what I would call normal. On the one hand, there was my mother. Now that I knew what it was like to be carrying a child, to feel the "butterflies" in my tummy when he got big enough for me to feel him move, to see his hands and feet kick against my tummy, to watch my tummy roll as he moved, to hear his heartbeat and to see his ultrasound photo, I couldn't understand how my mother could not love me. I couldn't understand her distance and her disassociation from me.

And then, there was Nanny, who doted on and catered to every one of Tristan's whims and wishes, well into his thirties. She couldn't see that her pampering was not *love*, but a form of abuse. Instead of rearing her son to be a contributing, responsible, and accountable member of society, her obsession with him ruined him, creating an entitled, demanding, and incapacitated man who thought of no one else but himself; a person who either crumbled with a little pressure, or exploded with vulgarities when he didn't get his way.

Now that I was an adult and no longer voiceless like I was as a child, I was able to choose how I could be the best mother possible to my son. I asked God to give me wisdom, the ability to show compassion when I needed to, and tough skin, resolve, courage, and steadfastness when I needed that even more. I determined to love Michael, but never wound him—either with cruelty or with kindness.

Yes, I would do everything in my power to rear Michael well, and in ways that would honor the calling in his life. I also prayed that Michael would know what that calling was early in life, would rise to it, and honor God back with his life.

I had not yet followed that calling so far in my own life, but I was determined to make sure my mistakes would not be in vain. If nothing else, the lessons of my life would be used to serve Michael.

Help Me Help You!

In the meantime, Tristan worked between two retail stores in prime locations of Vancouver, and sometimes I would go help him in between my own part-time jobs. But my heart always sank when I came into the store. I often saw him dousing glass cleaner over one small display case. He would then polish it with ten sheets of paper towels and repeat this routine with each case.

Not only did the waste of supplies and the inefficiency irritate me, it was the waste of that most precious commodity of all—time! I asked him in fun ways what he did to bring in new business, and he answered, "Nothing." I asked him what he was doing to draw in customers who were walking outside, and he said, "Nothing." I asked him who was in charge of marketing, and he replied, "I dunno…me, I guess." I asked him if he had made any suggestions to management about what he could do to bring in more business, and he said, "Nope." I asked a few more common-sense questions, including, "What are the top three bestsellers? When are the busiest times of the day? When are people most likely to buy—times of day, special occasions, holidays, seasons?" When he didn't know the answers, I immediately gave him about ten different marketing ideas, and drafted them on some copy paper and asked him to present it to his boss.

"Tristan, the owners gave you a great gift—an opportunity to come back to Vancouver and run these two stores. Their overhead must be huge being located where they are. You owe them your loyalty and help in recovering some of their overhead with revenues from sales. It should be easy. They're in prime locations, tourists are everywhere, weekend shoppers are everywhere, and you don't have to travel! This is what you asked for! And they gave it to you on a silver platter!"

"Whatever!"

"Tristan, this shouldn't be taken lightly. Quite frankly, if you're not part of the solution, you're part of the problem, and if their company fails, you will lose your job, too!"

I hated saying these things, and I hated that I was in the position of having to say it. Were it not for our past, I would not have been so direct, but I felt as though Tristan had to be shocked into reality. He had not been able to produce results (again) and was on a razor's edge with the company. Plus, we were about to have a baby! I was worried about our finances and could not bear my father subsidizing our expenses because my husband was too lazy to work.

Naturally, Nanny always came quickly to Tristan's defense, excusing him for not following through because he was too "stressed" with the recent move, his new job, and a baby on the way. "He's under too much pressure," she would say.

No matter how much I helped Tristan, and no matter what I wanted *for him*, unless he was willing to work for it, nothing would change. No amount of great ideas, encouragement, support, excuses, or even confrontations were going to make any difference.

I decided to "stop wasting my saliva."

Thanksgiving Gift

On the first weekend of October that same year, I began to feel deep cramps. I had already been quite uncomfortable the day before, but not as badly. I didn't know what contractions felt like and wasn't sure what to expect. My due date had already gone by, but my doctor just told me to wait.

It had already been very difficult to breathe with the full seventy pounds I had gained, when suddenly I felt the sudden urge to sneeze, and it wasn't one of those little tidy, polite sneezes, either. Normally, this wouldn't have been a big deal, but I was so large that I knew instinctively there was nowhere for the pressure of the sneeze to go. I held my tummy as tightly as I could with one arm as I covered my mouth with my other hand. The sneeze came loud and fast, and with nowhere for the pressure to escape to, I burst a blood vessel in my eye and simultaneously cracked a rib with a loud pop. I felt a sharp stab of pain on the left side and buckled over, catching myself on a piece of furniture.

The pain continued for the rest of the day, but it wasn't from my cracked rib. It was in my lower back, and I could barely move. When the pain was almost unbearable, we decided to go to the hospital. I slowly followed Tristan down the stairs of our apartment building, stopping every few seconds to catch my breath and wince in pain—from the broken rib, the now steady and heavy cramping, and the growing, stabbing feeling in my lower back.

Is this labor? I thought to myself. *Really? This can't be labor! It's too painful! No woman can go through this kind of agony and survive, much less be open to repeating this process again with another child later!*

Every mother with whom I had talked said giving birth "wasn't that bad," and they were fine the next day. Many even wanted to plan another baby soon afterward, but with the excruciating pain I was experiencing, I deduced there must have been something wrong. Or, if this was indeed labor, there was *no way* I could ever have another child and go through this again.

We finally got into the car, but the stabbing sensation in my lower back overtook me. Its intensity and sharpness surpassed any other ache that wracked my body. As we drove, every crack in the asphalt, pothole, or bump we went over en route to Grace Hospital (the newest women's hospital at the time), was like a knife jabbing me in the spine.

When we finally arrived, Tristan went ahead of me to the registration desk. The doctor had pre-registered us some time ago and secured a private room for us. I followed as quickly as I could, knowing the faster I could get into a room, the faster I could receive the infamous "epidural" that would rescue me from the pain.

The woman at the desk greeted me with a half-smile and appeared to be irritated that I had disturbed her evening. She barely looked at me as I spoke to her.

"Miss, my name is Manna Ko, and we called about fifteen minutes ago to let you know we were coming in," I said with clenched jaws, gripping the counter with my hands as another contraction wave went through me.

"I need your insurance card and your driver's license," she said mechanically, typing on the keypad without taking her eyes from the computer screen.

"Here it is. Can you please have them start preparing the room and the epidural while we are checking in? I'm not trying to be difficult, but the pain is like hot, searing knives in my spine, and I would appreciate your help as quickly as possible," I asked as nicely as I could.

Unmoved and ignoring me altogether, she continued, still without looking at me, "Do you have the papers your doctor provided for you?"

"Miss, I'm in extreme pain...and my husband already gave those to you. Could you please have the nurse prepare the epidural?" I persisted.

Suddenly, another contraction gripped me, and I sank down to my knees. When it was over, Tristan grabbed me by the elbow to help me up.

Ignoring the fact that an almost two-hundred-pound pregnant woman now in labor had collapsed in front of her, she said nonchalantly, "I just have a few more questions and some papers for you to sign."

"I'm sorry, but are you always this rude to someone in excruciating pain and about to deliver a baby? My husband can sign the papers! *Please* help me get to a room, and please tell the nurse to give me my epidural right away!" I said sternly.

"I'm sorry, ma'am, but I'll need to get all the proper information first. After I finish inputting everything, we can get you to a room."

She was most certainly *not* sorry, and maybe even enjoyed her power over me a little too much. But when she saw me sink to my knees again, now flushed and sweating from the pain, she relented and finally called for a wheelchair to take me to my room.

In the room, I was hooked up to monitors and left to languish. I was given warm socks and a warm blanket, but I still hadn't received my epidural. After what felt like hours, at long last, I finally received my elixir. The night passed with my feeling only pressure and a slight amount of pain. My labor continued into the next day. When I asked when my doctor would be coming, I was told he had just left on vacation and my baby would be delivered by whichever doctor was on call.

What? He never told me he was going on vacation. There wasn't any conversation regarding another doctor. What do you mean he is on vacation? What do you mean, "whichever doctor is on call"?

Elizabeth, the attending nurse, saw the terror in my eyes and sat down beside me. She explained that she was a midwife and had performed many deliveries. She was also the mother of two children, so she knew what to expect. I looked into her eyes and saw her kindness and compassion. She introduced me to the other nurse in the room and assured me that they would be with me the entire time and I would be fine. She tenderly touched my forehead with one hand and held my hand with her other hand. She smiled and held my gaze, not moving. I took a deep breath and relaxed into her strength.

Throughout the next night, Elizabeth was my touchstone and my anchor. I knew I could get through this labor with her help. Memories of how I had learned about sex and babies came to mind, and I tried to breathe through my anxiety and think of other things. Elizabeth played different types of music for me in the room, and in between checking my vitals and my epidural, measuring my dilation, and other necessary tasks, she sat beside me and engaged me in sweet conversations to take my mind off of the actual delivery process.

Elizabeth left the room now and again, but during one of her examinations, she told me it was almost time to deliver my baby. I was anxious, afraid, and excited all at the same time. Then she told me it was time to take out the epidural so I could prepare to deliver my child (the protocol in those days).

Unfortunately, as soon as the epidural was removed, I felt the full strength of the contractions again. Tristan was in the room and tried to help, but he was the last person I wanted to see. I also knew my mother-in-law was waiting for the call, and I was worried that she would try to take over Michael's life too.

I folded into both the physical and emotional pain.

As my labor progressed, the midwife called for the doctor on call. But in spite of her repeated requests made to the doctor's lounge, he didn't come. Finally, Elizabeth, who was also frustrated, asked the other nurse to page the doctor again. She came back and reported he was "having tea and a scone and would be down afterwards."

I looked at her, bewildered, wondering if I had really heard her correctly. Then, with a smile, she said, "I would love to be the one to help you deliver this baby, but I cannot. Since we are in the hospital, I must wait for the doctor and his orders."

I nodded as I groaned and grunted through another fierce contraction. When that pain subsided, and I was able to catch my breath, I turned to Elizabeth and pleaded with her, "Please, Elizabeth, I can't do this. Please, can I have the epidural again? My back…please? This is going to kill me."

"I can't, honey. The doctor has orders that you have to be off the epidural within the hour of the expected time. If I could, I would give it to you. I'm so sorry. You can do this. I'm here with you."

She held my hand tightly as wave after wave of contractions heightened and intensified. I could barely breathe and sweat profusely from the pain. That was when I was told the fetus wasn't in the proper position. Michael was pressing on my spine, which explained the abnormal level of pain.

Again, I beseeched Elizabeth, "Please, Elizabeth. Make it stop—just for *one minute*. I need to catch my breath. I'm not a wimp, really! This is the worst pain I have ever felt in my life. I just need this to stop for a minute…please. It's too much! Or is something else wrong? Am I dying? If I die, can I please see my son before I do?"

She held my hand with both of hers and looked at me lovingly. "No, Manna, you're not dying. I know this really hurts, but it's not going to be much longer. I can see the baby's head! Keep breathing…"

I groaned as I squeezed the midwife's hand.

"Don't leave me," I whispered. "Please don't leave me…"

"I'm not going anywhere."

"Everybody has before, but Elizabeth, please don't leave me…" I was discombobulated, exhausted from the twenty-five hours or so of labor, and not sure what I was saying to this woman.

"I won't. I won't leave you, dear. I'm here, and we'll get through this together. You're doing great, and it's all going to be okay. You're a beautiful soul, and you're going to be a great mom." As she breathed with me and held me, the rest soon became a blur, and all I can remember is Elizabeth telling me to push.

I did what I thought was pushing, but the pain sometimes had me either trying to lift my pelvis off the table or turning over. Another nurse had to hold me down on the opposite side. They tried to comfort me, encourage me, and help me to be as comfortable as possible, wiping my forehead and face with a cold compress, stroking my arms, and smiling as they directed me to push.

All I could hear was the sweet lilting tones of the nurses' voices. And when the on-call doctor finally came, he treated me as if I was a disturbance to his "teatime."

Everything started happening quickly then. It felt like cotton was in my ears as I heard all the orders being called out. But the pain was so fierce I began to doubt Elizabeth's assurances. "Are you sure the baby's okay? Am I dying?"

Thankfully, nature took over, and the pain dulled as it spread throughout my whole body. At last, I experienced the miraculous release. The doctor disinterestedly went through the motions, and with little to no bedside manner, he took Michael and gave him to the attending staff.

The next sound I heard was a wail, followed by the tardy doctor's voice saying, "It's a boy." The nurses immediately took the baby and performed their post-birth procedure on him. He was cleaned up, wrapped up, and delivered into my arms.

I was still in shock and unsure what to do. Elizabeth inclined my bed slightly so that I was more comfortable seeing and holding my baby. He was so heavy!

"Elizabeth, are all babies this heavy?"

"No, honey, they're not, and I have to congratulate you! You just delivered a ten-pound baby!" she exclaimed.

"What?"

"Yes, my dear. You are very brave and very strong. And at 9:38 a.m. on this special Thanksgiving weekend, you delivered a ten-pound baby boy!" She hugged me, and as she smiled lovingly at me, she wiped my forehead with another damp cloth.

Did she say what I thought she said? Did she say 9:38am? In a flash, I realized Michael was born exactly nine months to the minute of his conception! And it was Thanksgiving (in Canada)! It's God's perfect gift at the perfect time!

I couldn't take my eyes off my baby boy and thanked God for my little Michael. At last, he was finally here.

Then, out of shock, I asked, "Where are his eyelashes?"

Elizabeth giggled and assured me that they were there. Michael had big eyes, and though they were closed at that moment, his beautiful face was perfect and absolutely spectacular. I was in love! Tristan was standing by me now, but all I could do was stare at my baby. Elizabeth asked if I had considered any boy names, and I told her that I had always known I was having a boy and that his name would be Michael.

"That's a nice strong name. Why Michael?"

"Michael means 'most like God.' And that is also the name of the strongest archangel in heaven!"

"That's good. There is incredible power in a name. Do you think he'll be called 'Mike' for short?" Elizabeth asked.

"No, I will do everything I can to make sure that does *not* happen. He is definitely a *Michael*," I stated emphatically. "He will never be abbreviated, pared-down, simplified, or diminished. He is *Michael* in every sense of that name."

"I'm happy you're standing up for that. I did the same thing with my son Daniel. All of his friends wanted to shorten his name to Dan, but like you, I insisted that he be called by his true name." She smiled and looked at Michael and added, "Welcome to the world, Michael. You have a very brave mommy, and she loves you with all her heart. You're going to have a great life, Michael!"

Then, she apologized as she explained that she had to take him away for monitoring and observation. Michael had swallowed meconium and needed to be cared for by the neonatal team for the next twenty-four hours.

That news alarmed me, and I was afraid to let my baby go, but Elizabeth assured me this was a common occurrence, and that Michael would be all right. I watched uneasily as the nurses walked out of the room with my baby bundled in their arms.

I was left alone in the delivery room except for some aides. Then, as if I hadn't been through enough, the indifferent doctor came back into the room. He put me through undeniable torture for the next forty-five minutes for the after-birth process. A large animal veterinarian would have had more bedside manner than this man, and when he was done, he threw off his gloves, not looking me in the eye or addressing me once. Instead, he gave instructions to the nurses and coldly left the room.

Elizabeth came back and gently attended to me. She then said goodbye to me, wished me well, and gave me a hug and kiss on the forehead. A nurse's aide helped me into a wheelchair and pushed me toward the elevator where she would take me to my room.

She wasn't as gentle or as attentive as Elizabeth. I was shoved into the elevator feet first, where I stared at the back wall of the shiny metal box as we ascended to the third floor. *Where was the love? Where was the dignity? I had gone through hell and didn't even get to have my baby with me! Now, I am shoved into an elevator without even the decency to turn me around? Seriously?*

When the doors opened, I was spiraled around and pushed silently down the hall and taken into my private room. Between the bed and the window stood a plastic bassinet for the baby on a stand, but no baby was in it.

Then the nurse spoke, "Okay, get into bed!"

I looked at her like she was crazy. She stared back at me and then conceded to help me rise from the chair and settle into the bed. When she saw I wasn't exaggerating or trying to be difficult, but was actually in serious pain, she excused herself for a moment and asked me to wait until she returned. She came back quickly with a stepstool and a "donut cushion" for me to sit on.

The entire situation was thoroughly embarrassing. As I climbed into bed, the nurse wasted no time showing me the necessary things about the room and a tray that held small baby bottles of sugar water.

"Well, that's it! You're all set!" she said and left before I could respond.

What do you mean, "That's it"? Ummm...no, that's not "it!" What am I supposed to do now? Where is my baby? When will I see him? Is there any pain medication you can give me? And what exactly does, "You're all set" mean? I have no idea what to do or what happens next. So, no, it's not all set! It's not all set at all!

In the silent, empty room, I felt my aloneness again. Tristan had left for work and wasn't going to be back till later. I sat on my bed with the blankets wrapped around me, looked down at my belly, and then out toward my feet. I realized it was the first time in months I had been able to see my ankles! I whipped my right leg out from under the blanket and saw my lean legs and ankles again. Relieved, I breathed a huge sigh of relief. Then I noticed my belly was flat again. I was no longer arm's length away from anything!

Wondering what had become of my stomach but feeling encouraged because my feet were back to normal, I assumed that my stomach would be okay also. Yes, I knew it had been stretched and had borne the brunt of the pregnancy, but since I was always strong and athletic, I felt confident that these nine months wouldn't have destroyed what I had worked so hard to maintain all these years. I peeled back a layer of blankets and lifted the light-blue hospital gown up to peer underneath. Where my "abs" had once been, there was now an unsightly, doughy blob.

Yes, my tummy lay flat, but the skin was no longer taut. I yelped in disbelief at what I saw with my own eyes. I poked and pulled at it, trying to assess the level of damage that had been done. Of course, since no one was there to advise me beforehand—nor afterward—that this was natural and that my body would return to normal, I was frightened and quickly covered the offensive sight.

Tears pricked at the corners of my eyes and slowly ran down my face. With the birth of my baby, it seemed as though my body was worn and deformed. The familiar feelings of ugliness, inadequacy, and unworthiness all crept up on me again. But this time, I felt even uglier. Gaining seventy pounds and then losing it would not leave me unmarred. The only time I had felt beautiful was when I was pregnant with Michael. Now, it was just me again, and I wasn't sure if there was anything beautiful about me. My mother's and Scham's mantras echoed in my ear, and if no one had wanted me before, no one would now. Feeling helpless and hopeless, I broke down in tears.

They gave Michael back to me the next day. The nurse who presented him to me said, "Okay, he's all yours! He's hungry, and that sugar water isn't going to last long. You'd better start feeding him right away!" she commented casually, and then started to leave the room.

What do you mean? How do I feed him? What do you mean?

"Ummm, excuse me, nurse, but I'm not quite sure what you mean by that. I've never done this before, and no one has ever told me about how to feed a baby. Do you mean formula? Do you mean nurse him? If so, how is that done? I'm sorry, can you please explain this all to me?"

She stopped and looked at me, astonished at hearing my confession of ignorance. She came back into the room, lifted Michael out of the bassinette like he was a football, and asked me to partially disrobe. Michael was crying, so in between his screaming and the gruff orders from the nurse, I was very stressed and anxious. She put him to my left breast, and Michael clamped on with a vice grip that made me yelp out loud.

I screamed to the nurse, "Get him off me, please! Please, make him stop! It hurts so much!" She showed me how to make him release and gave me the bottles of sugar water to give to Michael instead. Drinking that fluid calmed him down for a little while, but when he started crying again, I knew I didn't have any choice but to try the nursing again.

Anxiety filled me.

I took a few deep breaths and tried a few times more, but Michael was so strong that I had to peel him away each time. Finally, after the fourth try (and several bottles of sugar water in between), I let him grab hold as I held my breath. My toes were scrunched up in pain, and I learned to brace myself for his feedings from then on.

Thankfully, I was able to produce a good supply of milk for him, and over the next six months, I even expressed milk in between feedings and stored them in the freezer because there was so much of it.

During one of my checkups, a month or so later, one of the nurses examined me and commented on how full and large my breasts had become. *That's a strange comment*, I thought to myself. Then she explained she was very happy to see I was producing a lot of milk, and jokingly said, "Looks like you have enough there to feed a brood of offspring."

"Pardon me?" I asked, confused by her comment comparing me to animals and their offspring.

"Well, so many new mothers can't produce milk…I wonder if you would mind sharing your milk with other babies?"

Am I now a cow?

The way she said it sounded like women would be coming to my home with their newborns, and I would be bringing one baby after the next to my breast. I knew I wasn't savvy with all the new birthing and baby care trends, but I had never heard of strangers nursing other people's babies. Some insight and education about expressing and donating breast milk would have been helpful, but since none was offered, I was left to my own thoughts.

"Well, think about it, and let us know," she offered nonchalantly as she wrote in the chart.

Still stunned at what she had asked of me, I didn't ask her to explain what she meant. And frankly, I didn't want to hear the answer either—just in case it was exactly as I thought. From the horrible on-call doctor in the delivery room onwards, I was feeling more like a farm animal every minute. But the most horrific experience happened just before I was released from the hospital.

After everything I had been through during labor and then post-labor, just when it didn't seem like it could get any worse, something happened that ripped a hole in my heart.

I wanted to have Michael circumcised and understood that it was a routine procedure occurring soon after his birth. Another doctor came in from a well-known OBGYN group in town at the time. After he finished the procedure, he came into my room. Surprised to see anyone, much less a doctor I didn't know, I sat up.

"I'm Dr. M., the doctor who performed the circumcision on your little baby boy."

"Oh, good morning, Doctor. Thank you."

"Do you hear that?" he asked.

"Hear what?"

"The baby crying down the hall."

"I hear a lot of babies crying," I answered him.

He shut the door and walked toward the bed. "I'm talking about the one who's crying the loudest. That's your son," he said, "crying and screaming louder than all of the other babies after you asked for him to be circumcised! I hope you're happy!"

After leveling that condemnation, he simply turned and walked out.

I sat there a moment in stunned silence. I swore that I would love and protect my child, and this abusive and hostile man had told me in no uncertain terms that I had brutalized my own son. I watched him walk away, breathless. And then I screamed. And screamed and screamed until the nurses came running in. I was sobbing and hyperventilating. I couldn't catch my breath to tell them what had happened. Finally, they succeeded in calming me, and I told them what the doctor had said as tears streamed down my face.

"Oh, dear, it's okay," one of the nurses offered, "It all seems worse than it is. The doctor told us that you were suffering from postpartum depression. It's normal to be emotional at this time. Let's just calm down, and we'll bring your son in as soon as we can."

I'd been set up!

The doctor had prepared them for my reaction, knowing what he was going to say and knowing that he was going to accuse me of hurting my child. He obviously didn't believe in circumcision, but to attack me so violently and so coldheartedly was nothing less than sheer evil.

I wanted to take action against him, but I wouldn't have stood a chance as there were no witnesses and no evidence of his having said those comments to me. It was my word against his, and I wouldn't win with the kind of clout he had. He set me up, and he knew it. There was nothing I could do; I was the fragile mother with "postpartum depression."

The Last Straw

"Men!" Leah hmphed. "Those beasts! Cads! I wish you'd had someone wonderful like Thomas in your life. It must have been hard with a baby but tell me you left that oaf of a husband!"

I chuckled. "Yes. We ended up parting ways, but not right away. Tristan continued his pattern of pretending to work but blaming others for the lack of results. His mother continued to meddle and accuse me of not providing well enough for her son."

"You just had a baby!" Leah exclaimed. "And she wanted *you* to provide for *her son?*"

I sighed. "Yes. And it only got worse from there. Let me give you the backstory first."

The real estate market started to boom, and as an investment for my future, my father purchased a sweet little house for Michael and me to have as a nest egg. It was a small wartime bungalow, simple, clean, and had great potential. It needed some light remodeling and touchups, and my father helped with that as well. Nanny and Pa also contributed by cleaning up the house, and paying for an inexpensive kitchen countertop, and a new fridge and stove. Marjorie and Simone also gifted us with a new washer and a dryer as both a housewarming and baby-welcoming gift.

Knowing I was very good with people, my father suggested that I try selling real estate for work, especially in a growing market.

"You could work part-time and choose your own hours while taking care of

Michael," my father said confidently.

So, in between some light remodeling and caring for a brand-new baby, I studied and earned my real estate license. When Michael wasn't quite a year old, I began working part-time as a real estate assistant. Nanny would babysit, as would my father, who had returned from Hong Kong for a while.

My part-time job turned into a full-time job very quickly, but we were still not making enough money. I took on another job as a typist in the evenings for students who needed papers typed from handwritten notes. Computers were not available then, only typewriters, and because I was able to type quickly and accurately (a skill I attributed to my piano-playing abilities), I was able to finish quite a few papers in a relatively short time.

Needless to say, Nanny hovered over Tristan in my absence.

Worse, interest rates were around 14% then and were it not for my father's ongoing help to subsidize our expenses, we would have lost the home and any modicum of dignity I had left. Unfortunately, none of this fazed Tristan. Instead of working or looking for more work, he continued to play golf with his father during the weekdays and watch TV once he got home.

One day, after another heated argument, he angrily yelled, "Fine! Quit your nagging! I'll get my mom to help if you don't want to ask your father again! My mom will gladly help if your father doesn't want to!"

I was mortified. Tristan simply did not "get it." It wasn't about anyone else being responsible for us; it was *his* responsibility!

When I heard Tristan say these outlandish words, I knew the marriage was over. The last domino had fallen, and I saw with devastating clarity that I was married to a man who had no integrity, character, or moral compass. I was done trying to be logical or reasonable, and I was no longer going to invest any more effort into educating him or his mother. All I needed was the right opportunity to discuss our separation. Until then, I would have to tolerate a few more aberrant events.

One day after work, I came home to find Tristan watching TV (again) and Nanny doing *only* Tristan's laundry! I went to the bathroom where the laundry hamper was and noticed, on closer inspection, that she had separated out all my laundry from her son's. I felt violated that she would go through my personal things, and then clearly demonstrate her dysfunction by only doing *his* laundry—a grown man's laundry! And in *my* home! There were *too* many things wrong with this picture to discuss, but you get the point.

Nanny would also ask me about what I was going to cook for dinners or prepare as desserts on the weekend. I thought she was making conversation, so I always answered her openly. Once (months before, when I was still trying to make our marriage work), I told her I was planning on making Tristan a lemon meringue pie because that was his favorite. Wouldn't you know it, that very afternoon she came over with a lemon meringue pie!

This craziness happened regularly.

The last straw, however, was coming home after working a twelve-hour workday to find Tristan lying on the sofa. He had one hand on the channel changer and the other holding a beer. Michael was in his highchair, with food all over his face, and when I went to pick him up, he had a dirty diaper that had seeped through his clothes. It was obvious that he hadn't been attended to for a very long time.

Just then, Nanny called. We didn't have a call display then, so I picked up the phone. "Manna, it's Nanny. I've been thinking," she said in her familiar dry voice, "Since you're only working as an assistant, and your typing job is sporadic, when students aren't writing papers, maybe it would be possible for you to take on another job. Or you could ask your father to give you more money. After all, where do you think money's going to come from? The sky? You have to do something! Your poor husband is just so stressed out right now."

I held my breath. *This wasn't happening…was it? Really?*

Leah interrupted. "Never miss a chance to shut up, as they say! She should have stopped while she was ahead—about the time you two got married! What did you say to her?!"

I told her I had to go and hung up the phone.

The following day, I told my father what had been going on. He wasn't surprised and offered to support me in whatever decision would be best for Michael and me.

The problem was that Tristan had a very explosive temper and one of the foulest mouths I had ever known. I was worried for my safety as well as the safety of our home. I would have to plan things very carefully.

When I thought everything through, I prepared myself to ask him for a separation. I was scared and didn't want to follow in my parents' footsteps of divorce, but there was nothing else I could do.

Sure enough, when I got home after a long day (holding three open houses back-to-back), Tristan was splayed out on the sofa in his usual position watching TV. Michael was once again in the highchair—dirty and unchanged. I took care of Michael and then addressed the issue.

"Tristan, I need to talk to you," I said, bracing myself.

"What do ya want?" he said rudely.

I exhaled and said resolutely, "I want a separation and am asking you to leave now. This should not be a shock for you. We've been fighting since day one. I've done everything under the sun to try and help you, but I can't keep working these crazy hours, having my father and your parents support us financially, and being the blame for everything wrong with you. I will not allow Michael to endure such poor care when I'm at work, and I can't afford to keep you in the same lifestyle as your mother did. You can go back to her and your room there. Please leave quietly now without any disruption. Take what you need for now, and we can arrange for your other things later. Lastly, your temper and your abusiveness frighten me, so I've asked my father to wait for my call. If he doesn't hear from me in thirty minutes, he's been instructed to call the police to come over immediately. I've done everything I can, and now I'm done. There will be no discussion about this matter. I will not change my mind."

Nothing I said surprised Tristan. He was angry, but only because I had finally stood up to him. He rose from the couch and came towards me, swearing viciously and threatening me. I remained calm and reminded him that he had thirty minutes, or the police would be coming to the door.

When Tristan yelled again, Michael clung to me even harder, crying. I asked Tristan to stop his ranting as it was upsetting Michael and told him this only confirmed my decision to separate.

When Tristan finally left, my father came by with a friend who was a locksmith. As a favor to my father, his friend had agreed to change the locks no matter what time of day or night it was.

It is true that out of something horrible, blessings do come. Though the situation had been incomprehensibly difficult with Tristan and his mother, it was exactly what I needed to give me the strength to step out on my own.

Leah took my hand in hers and smiled. "I haven't shared everything about our marriage with you, but I do assure you I did everything in my power to make that marriage work. I loved Tristan's sisters and their families, but I loved Michael (and myself now) more. I wanted more for the both of us, and I was willing to do whatever I needed to provide a healthy and safe home and life for us.

"The divorce was finalized within the year, but not without its battles—especially from Nanny. But at least it was over."

"Good for you!" Leah whooped. She raised her hands with an unexpected burst of vitality and motioned to give me a high five. "That's my girl!"

9 A POND OF SMELLY FROGS

The truth of the matter is that you always know the right thing to do. The hard part is doing it.

—Norman Schwartzkopf

Room 316

On my next visit to see Leah, I was surprised to be greeted in the hallway by the sounds of talking and laughter coming from her room. I stood outside of Room 316, uncertain if I should enter. I glanced over to see if Melody was at the nurses' station, but no one was there. After a few moments of hesitation, I decided to go in and see if Leah would prefer I come back at another time. When I entered the room, five faces turned around to meet me. Behind them, Leah was smiling proudly from her bed.

"You must be Manna," one of the younger women said. "Mom's told us so much about you. I'm Abigail. This is my sister Ruth, and my brother Peter. That's our father, Thomas, and that's Aunt Rachel, Mom's sister."

We shook hands as I was introduced to each family member, and we shared a few warm pleasantries.

"This is the first opportunity for us to be here at the same time, and we were just reminiscing," Abigail explained. "Our mother has greatly enjoyed her visits with you, and we love how you have made everything so comfortable for her." She gestured to the different items I had contributed to the room. She took a deep breath and continued. "We can't tell you how much this means to us. We know you have done well beyond the scope of what hospice does—"

She stopped suddenly, unable to finish her sentence. Her last few words quivered as she held back tears and emotions.

"Now, Abby, don't you start getting all sensitive on me," Leah interjected. "I'm not goin' anywhere yet. With Manna here, I'm too busy to die! She won't stop talking!" She turned to me and winked before continuing, "I'm too busy to go anywhere!"

Thomas was standing beside the bed, holding Leah's hand and gazing down at her. His adoration for her was obvious, as was his sorrow. Leah looked up at him and smiled.

After a few uneasy moments, Aunt Rachel explained she had been sharing a funny memory when I entered. I apologized for interrupting and asked her to continue.

Rachel looked just like Leah in features and stature, but her hair was done in a stylish up-do. She wore mascara, and her nails were painted a brilliant candy-apple red to match her lipstick. It was easy to imagine Rachel and Leah in their younger years with their many suitors coming from near and far trying to court them. They must have been quite a pair together.

Rachel continued her funny story, and when she delivered the punch line, we all erupted with boisterous laughter. Of Leah's three grown children, Abigail seemed the most comfortable in the room. She was gracious, thoughtful of the others, and very attentive to her mother. She was also extremely courteous, offering me her chair while she scurried out, insisting on making me a cup of tea from the family lounge outside of Leah's room. I hesitated, still unsure if I was interrupting the family visit, but Leah insisted I stay and join them. I sat down and glanced over Leah's chart between polite exchanges.

The others hung back and were a bit more reserved. Ruth looked not only like she had been crying but seemed as though she might start again at any moment. When Abigail returned, she saw my gaze upon her sister.

"Manna…may I talk to you outside for a moment?" she asked as she handed me my cup of tea.

"Of course," I said, following her back out the door. I glanced at Leah and jokingly said to her, "Behave!"

Leah rolled her eyes and shooed me out the door with her hand.

Abigail led me to the family lounge, but her easygoing disposition turned to apprehension as soon as we sat down. A few moments later, the rest of the family also emerged, one by one, and joined us. Each face bore the marks of their individual concerns.

"First, let me say how nice it is to meet you. With our hectic schedules, we've been coming at different times of the day, somehow missing you each time, and even missing each other. Peter arrived late last night from out of town, so this is the first time we've seen him, too," Abigail said, smiling at her brother. Sighing, she continued. "Thank you for everything you're doing for our mom. You've made a remarkable difference. We don't know how long it will last, but we're thankful for every moment."

"She seems happy and even nicer!" Ruth added.

"Yeah, you don't feel like your head's about to be lopped off the second you speak," Peter muttered.

Abigail looked at Peter compassionately and then turned back to me to ask, "Do you think this change of heart is real? Or—" She stopped mid-sentence, pursing her lips, and looked away as if to gather herself. Thomas put his hand on his daughter's shoulder, and I glanced up at him. His face was etched with pain.

"Or what, Abigail?" I asked, gently encouraging her.

"Is this what happens when people get really *close* to dying? Do they finally give up fighting and *soften*? Like Ruthie said, are they nicer because they know they're going to die soon?"

"That's not a simple question to answer, but what I can say is, regardless of your mother's physical condition, she is not the same person she was when I first met her. I don't know what she was like before, but I think it's safe to say she was a spitfire."

The children chuckled at my aptly chosen description of their mother.

I turned my attention back to Abigail. "I don't know exactly how close to dying she is. She has good days and bad days, but her vitals seem okay. As you see in your visits, her mind is alert, and she is still aware of all that is going on around her. She surprises me with her strength sometimes." I smiled at the thought of some of our banter.

"Your mother has come face-to-face with her own existence, her mortality, and the purpose of her life—the 'Why am I here?' questions. Is she more than just matter glued together by 'goo' or held in bondage through an encapsulated sac called skin? What was she meant to accomplish? What will happen once she takes her last breath? Where will *she* go? Is there a heaven? Is there a hell? How does she ensure she gets to heaven instead of hell?" I paused and gave an encouraging smile to everyone. "She's an eager student of life right now, and that passion fuels her. She may not be asking these questions point-blank, but she is asking them. Plus, her keen interest in my life history seems to be helping her find some missing pieces to her own life. She wants to find resolution, healing, hope, and even humor in all that she has seen and experienced."

"I have a hard time believing Mom is so open," Peter said skeptically.

"As difficult as it may be to believe, I assure you that your mother is not only open and curious, she is eager to learn. She is also the most vulnerable she has ever been. She's pretty determined to 'get' what she missed before. Somehow your mother knows that forgiveness, peace, and freedom are at her fingertips—all available to her as a last gift."

No one spoke as they contemplated their own personal memories of Leah.

Peter awkwardly broke the silence. "Well, this certainly isn't anything like what I expected when I walked in this morning!" he quipped. "I came to see how Mom was doing with death. Instead, I'm getting an update on how she's doing with *life*!"

Everyone nodded in agreement.

After a collective heavy sigh, Peter continued. "I guess those aren't questions just for Mom. They're for me too—maybe for all of us…" He glanced around at his family. "I want to start living too. I've lost too much time to death—dead jobs, dead relationships, dead dreams…"

I thought it would be best to give the family some private time, so I excused myself and went to retrieve my things. When I returned to the room, Leah's eyes were closed. She was reclined a little lower than when I had first come in, so I thought perhaps she was sleeping. As I reached for my coat, Leah opened her eyes and smiled.

"You've been gone so long…I assume you've solved all the world's problems by now," Leah muttered, not missing a beat.

"No, not yet. We go global next week."

She chuckled. "I like you, Manna Ko."

"I like you too, Leah St. John," I said, smiling.

She breathed in deeply and closed her eyes again. "So, what do you think?"

"About what?"

"About my family! What else?"

I pulled up my familiar chair and sat down beside her.

"I'm happy you finally got to meet them," she continued softly. "How are they doing?"

"They're doing fine, Leah."

"What about Peter?"

"Peter is doing fine, too. He loves you very much."

Her eyes opened. "He's a good boy, Manna. It wasn't easy rearing him on my own. Thomas was stationed away a lot, and we didn't see much of him, but I did the best I could. Peter was always my sweet little 'Petie'—even despite the trouble he'd get into with his impetuousness." She took a breath and closed her eyes again. "Peter was a very special, gifted child. I knew that the moment he was born, but without a lot of resources, I didn't know how to nurture his gifts."

"You did a great job, Leah. He's a good man."

She didn't respond. Instead, she fell into steady, rhythmic breathing. I thought maybe she had fallen asleep when suddenly she spoke again. "How do you know Peter loves me very much?"

"Even though we just met, it's impossible not to notice his love for you. It's in everything about him. It's in his nervous pacing, in how he folds his arms across his chest when he doesn't know what to do or say. But mostly, it's in his eyes… there's no doubt in my mind how much he loves you. Plus, the bond between a mother and a son is inseparable and indivisible."

A tear rolled down her cheek. "That's good."

She gave me her hand and I held it with both of mine. Soon, many tears rolled down her cheeks as she told me story after beautiful story of Peter when he was a little. Each memory she shared summoned another. Before long, the tears were replaced with laughter as Leah excitedly recited many wonderful memories of her family with me. We laughed and cried together as she sang the merits of each of her beloved children. She also divulged antics she and her sister masterminded and professed her ardent love for her husband.

I don't know how much time had passed, but during a particularly long story, Leah began to tire. After a few deep yawns, she fell fast asleep in the middle of one of her tales. The emotions of the day had finally caught up with her.

As I stood to straighten her blankets, Peter came back into the room and gasped at the sight of me covering his mother. When I reassured him that she was only sleeping, he blew a huge sigh of relief. No longer able to maintain his stout bravado, Peter broke down sobbing. He wept on my shoulders and declared his love for his mother. Whatever happened in their history was being washed away with each tear. Even in its imminence, death could not steal the promise of restoration and the gift of new life. Everything was being made new.

After this day of sharing, I felt it was important for me to see Leah even more frequently. Although I saw no obvious physical changes in her condition, my spirit sensed something else, so I arranged my schedule to have more time with her and came the next day.

"How did the rest of your visit go yesterday? How great to have everyone here all at once!" I said as I pulled up my chair.

"Yes, indeed, but way too much crying going on after you left…do you always have that effect on people?"

"Sometimes it's worse. Consider yourself lucky."

She smiled. "Do you know what's strange, Manna?"

"Tell me."

"Life. Life is strange!" she exclaimed. "As wonderful as it was to all be together yesterday, why couldn't we have all come back together sooner? Why now? Why didn't this happen before?"

"Oh, Leah," I sighed, "sometimes it takes a life-changing event to wake us up, so we can see what we've been missing and finally take a stand and claim what was always meant for us. Unfortunately, some people never have this opportunity. But you, Leah, you and your family are a few of the lucky ones. Not everyone embraces this kind of opportunity for rebuilding and healing like you and your family have. It's a new beginning for each one of you!"

"Hmmm…always looking at the bright side of things. And I'll be darned—some of what you're saying is actually starting to make sense to me." She pulled me with her hand, inviting me to come closer. I did so, shuffling my chair beside the bed.

"What would I do without you, Manna?"

"I'm not sure if I'm of any help, Leah. Sometimes I wonder if I've been too much of an imposition. I worry my stories are too much of a burden for you to hear."

"Are you kidding? Hearing about your life makes me feel normal!" She laughed out loud.

"You can't say I didn't warn you," I replied.

Leah chuckled. "Yes, you did, but I didn't believe you. No one would ever guess what you've been through—and I know you've only told me the highlights…I suspect there are more eyebrow-raising stories."

I nodded.

"Manna, though it comes at a great price for you to share your stories with me, by doing so, I win…my family wins. And one day, when you tell your life story publicly, we will *all* win—the world will win! What you think is a mess will be the *message* we need to hear to open our hearts to more…so much more." She leaned forward and gave me another one of her all-knowing looks. "I know because you did that for me."

I took a deep breath and let out a loud sigh. "I'm glad I've been able to help you even a little…though as for 'the world,' I don't know. You're much too kind."

"Hmph! Kindness has nothing to do with it! You'd be selfish if you didn't tell people your story. You'll give them hope, just like you did for me. You'll see…people may have heard a similar message before, but it's time for another *messenger*. And I believe that's *you*." Leah leaned in closer to me and narrowed her eyes again. "You know what I'm saying is true. I can tell in your eyes that you already know this."

I nodded again.

"Good girl. I can die now."

"Oh, stop it! You're not dying yet!"

"Ahh, the operative word is 'yet'! So, let's get going, shall we?"

"Go where?"

"Goodness sakes, do I have to spell everything out for you? Get goin'—finish telling me what happened after you and Tristan got divorced. By my calculations, you left off when you were in your late twenties. No offense, but by looking at you, you're not in your twenties anymore! We have a lot of catching up to do, and I don't have forever, ya know!"

I smiled.

How in the world does she remember everything?

Becoming and Overcoming

I was excited and expectant as I began my journey to unlearn my past and to create a new future. Instead of focusing on what I *didn't want*, I began to focus on what I *did want*, including who I wanted to become. There was still much to overcome, but I was stronger than I had ever been and was determined to pursue my dreams for a great future. My son deserved it, and so did I.

While I was happy to be away from the dysfunction, I wasn't happy about being divorced. I was sad to have had a failed marriage, but I was more concerned about how this would affect Michael and our relationship with Simone, Marjorie, and their children.

Yes, I know I made many decisions out of fear and desperation rather than wisdom and assurance, and I take full responsibility for all that's come of it. I apologized to Tristan and his family, my family, and especially to Michael. And then I did my best to look forward, mitigating the damages and repercussions from all that had occurred.

I also tried my best to keep things amicable with Tristan, so the transition would be as easy as possible for Michael. They had regular visits together, but unfortunately, I soon discovered Tristan wasn't actually spending much time with Michael at all. Tristan took Michael to his parents after picking him up, and that's where he stayed while Tristan went out with his friends—sometimes not even coming home until it was time to return Michael to me. I tried to talk to Tristan about spending more one-on-one time with Michael, but the last thing he wanted to do was to listen to me. In fact, Tristan's bitterness, verbal abuse, and volatility towards me only intensified. Needless to say, I kept our conversations short and succinct, keeping the focus only on the safety and timeliness of Michael's return after their visits.

Frankly, I was very reluctant to let Michael go with Tristan at all, even though they were court-appointed visits. Tristan was my son's father, but he'd begun to frighten me more than ever before, not because of his treatment of me, and not even because of his eventual death threats against me. I *was* frightened because I was witnessing a soul who consistently chose darkness, and the effects of his choices were glaringly evident with each meeting. His entire appearance had changed. First, it was his choice of clothing, wearing black from head to toe, always with a black trench coat. He had lost over fifteen pounds within a month, was sniffling all the time, and he reeked of alcohol and cigarette smoke. His face was gaunt, his skin was sallow and pale, his hands trembled, and he had dark circles around his eyes.

In spite of all the red flags, my attorney said I didn't have enough to justify my attempts to disallow Michael to be with his father. Apparently, my disapproval of Tristan's personality, attitude, and lifestyle choices were not valid legal reasons for the court to stop visitation rights. Unless I had evidence of abuse or of my suspicions that he was using illicit drugs, I had nothing to stand on.

So each time I let Michael go out the door with him, it was with great trepidation and fear, followed by much prayer. I did have some measure of comfort knowing that Michael was with Tristan's parents, who, regardless of their ill feelings for me, were caring toward Michael.

While I was uncertain about Michael's relationship with his birth father, my relationship with Michael continued growing and deepening.

As an infant and later as a toddler, I noticed how very different he was from other children. Seemingly older and wiser than his years, he seldom cried (except when I had to leave him to go to work), and was very attentive and focused, surprising even the doctors with his maturity and learning abilities. He was also inherently loving, thoughtful, and well-behaved. Instead of what one might expect of a typical toddler, Michael rarely complained. He was the first to share, the first to help others, and effortlessly demonstrated a heart of gratitude.

My father eventually retired (the first of many attempts at retirement) shortly after Michael was born. Together with my new stepmother, Shirley, he moved back to Vancouver to be close to the family and his first grandson. I had gotten to know Shirley, who was the Comptroller of my father's company in Hong Kong, when I visited during my summer breaks at UBC. Even though she was much younger than he was, I encouraged their relationship because she seemed to be kind, was diligent at her work, and appeared to genuinely care about my father. After a few years of courtship, they were married the Christmas before my graduation from UBC. Shirley had a daughter from a previous marriage, but her ex-husband had custody of her—a topic we never talked about.

"That's odd, especially in those days," Leah noted. "You know that only too well!"

"Yes, I agree."

"Do you know what else is odd?" Leah added. "Don't you think it's strange that you were once again faced with a situation where a mother did not have her daughter?"

"Yes, I've thought about that too over the years."

"Was it because she was a girl?" Leah asked.

"I don't think so. We never knew why she didn't have custody of her daughter. We only knew never to talk about it. Shirley was a very quiet person, keeping her emotions measured and controlled around us.

"In the beginning, we simply thought she was shy, but after several decades, her emotional distance was undeniable. She no longer worked after she married my father, and as a couple, they participated in different church activities, dinner parties, outings, and even went on many vacations together. I knew she could be sociable and interactive, but I didn't experience that side of her often. Regardless, we were not as close as I had hoped to be."

"Don't worry about that, Manna," Leah offered. "A stepparent needs to integrate many dynamics when *stepping* into a family that isn't their own. Her emotional distance may not have been as much about you as it was her dealing with her own demons."

I nodded in agreement.

In time, through marriage, Shirley became a Canadian citizen, and they both stayed in Vancouver for a while to help me with Michael when I returned to work.

On one such day, while Michael was riding in his car seat at the back of my father's car, my usually talkative son quietly looked out the window, deep in thought.

My father, surprised by Michael's unusual silence, asked, "Michael, darling, what are you thinking about?"

"Da" (Michael's nickname for my father), "I'm thinking about how much I love you." This amazing response came from my two-year-old son.

"Really, Michael?"

"Really, Da. I was thinking about how much I love you and how much I love being with you."

Not known for his silence either, my father was rendered speechless.

I Will Arise

I had been working long, long hours as an assistant to a top producer. Around my one-year mark in that position, a brand-new, more progressive firm had opened, and its presence began to challenge the established goliaths of real estate. I knew it was time for me to leave and fly on my own. Though the move would be risky, I took the chance. Armed with excitement, possibility, and the promise of a new future, I went to speak with my manager to give him my two-week notice.

His typical friendly manner disappeared, revealing another side of him I was not expecting. He spent the next fifteen minutes rifling one attack after another, and in his cool, steely way, not only took credit for all that I had done and achieved but wished for my imminent failure without him.

I shook my head in shock and disappointment at seeing his true nature. Instead of demonstrating leadership I would embrace and under which I would be proud to serve, he demonstrated severity and oppression. My decision to leave had been confirmed.

"Have you finished?" I asked calmly, after enduring his diatribe.

He stared at me with cold eyes and silence.

"Well, I want to thank you for the opportunity to have been a part of this office for the past year, but unlike you, I *do* wish you and everyone here all my best. Now, if you will please excuse me, I must get back to work." I rose slowly and walked out of his office.

For the remaining time I was there, he never once looked at or spoke to me. Still, I worked even more conscientiously than before. In addition to the manuals and processes I had developed, I left copious notes, itemizing step-by-step procedures for my replacement. I documented everything I did and left thank-you notes for my difficult boss and my cold-hearted manager.

They didn't expect any of this. They thought I would do only the minimum since I was leaving, but I intended to leave with excellence, dignity, and grace.

On my last day, nothing was said to me, and no well-wishes were extended. I walked out of the back door unceremoniously as if it was just another day at the office.

When I reached my car, I was thankful that my life was going to be new, exciting, and in my control. And I was thankful for what I had learned to do—and *not to do.*

The next day, I woke with joy and anticipation.

I walked into my new company and was greeted with joy and a warm welcome. The atmosphere was like family, and I took a deep breath of relief. They asked me to choose my desk from whichever ones were still available and then they showed me around. The desk I chose was in the corner of the first floor of a multi-level open office. It also happened to be adjacent to Susan, who was the assistant to one of the founders (and one of the top producers) of the new company.

Susan was a hard worker, loyal, very smart, and kind. She extended her help to me out of courtesy at first, but over time, we became good friends, and she became like an "auntie" to Michael.

I remember my first official day of work there. I came impeccably dressed, brought all of my office supplies and stationery with me, and set up my little corner cubicle neatly.

It took me less than five minutes.

What am I going to do for the next eight hours?

I sat staring at my empty desk, and fear crept in. *What am I doing? I have a two-year-old at home who needs me. I'm a divorcée, alone, and have no steady income. In fact, I'm starting in a whole new business based solely on commission! There is no guaranteed pay or benefits, and I have almost no money to my name. I am afraid of talking to people, and I'm not sure I even like people—they're mean and calculating, and they are only nice until they don't need you anymore. Plus, I'm Chinese! Yes, that's important in a growing Asian market, but for the first time in my life, I'm not Chinese enough! Who would have thought I'd ever say that? I don't fit in with any of the other Chinese top producers in the industry, but I'm Chinese enough that I don't fit with all the Caucasian top agents either! Who will want to work with me? I have no contacts! This is an industry all about "who you know" and how much money they have! Oh, my goodness! What am I doing here?*

The words of my former manager crashed through my mind, but I dug deep and forced myself back to the present.

I looked around me. Only a few people were in the office that day, but they knew what they were doing and were definitely focused on their tasks. Susan was on the phone with her boss, talking about industry-specific legalities about which I knew very little. *How does she know so much? I wish I knew what she knew! I wish I knew what I was doing!*

I took a deep breath and stopped looking around me. I returned my focus to what was in front of me instead, and the only things looking back at me were a heavy beige phone with a row of flashing lights at the bottom (alerting the top producers of the calls that were waiting for them) and two telephone books—the white pages and the yellow pages.

Start dialing, I heard an airy and indistinguishable voice say.

"What?"

Call people listed in the white pages starting with the letter "A" and see if they want to sell or buy a house!

"Are you kidding me? That's ridiculous! I will not invade people's privacy by calling them at home to ask them to sell or buy real estate with me! That's insane! I'll never do it! *Never!*"

Silence.

I felt paralyzed. Here I was, all dressed up, with literally nowhere to go. I fought back the anxiety—and what seemed like dozens of new voices in my head telling me what a mess I was in. Then I heard the most frightening voices of all—the combined voices of my mother and stepfather: *You're stupid, ugly, and good-for-nothing!*

I gasped, and with a resolve that came out of nowhere, I straightened my shoulder, grounded myself in my seat, and opened the telephone book.

I had no script. I had no plan. But with no other option, I braced myself and started dialing.

In those days, many homes had answering machines to record incoming calls. While I was making calls, if an answering machine clicked on, I simply hung up. If there was no answer, that was even better! Either outcome resulted in huge sighs of relief from my little corner cubicle.

As I went down the alphabet, people did start to answer, and somehow, I found the courage to start talking to them. I introduced myself and told them about the new firm. For the most part, people were very nice to me. We enjoyed some pleasant, but brief, conversation, and I ended each call with the simple offer that if they, or anyone about whom they cared, needed any assistance with real estate to please contact me. I jotted down names and other comments to help me remember the people and their individual needs in a separate notepad beside my telephone book.

One day, I realized that my little notepad had grown into a binder filled with labeled and color-coded information—leads and possibilities! Soon, I had made friends with complete strangers who had at one time been only names in a telephone book. Whether it was with their home, a revenue property, or a business, I soon became a trusted advisor for them and their referrals. That binder represented the very humble beginnings of a shy, fearful, and wounded young woman, determined to arise and use her wings.

I did it!

I overcame what seemed like an impossible mountain to climb. Who would have thought that a telephone book was such an immense mountain? But it was for me. Those three inches of paper represented every fear of what I thought awaited me on the other side the telephone line—rejection, mockery, callousness, criticism, chastisement, racism, and every other imaginable derogation. But, as intimidating as this list was, the greatest fear chasing me was a lie I was afraid would be true—that my mother and stepfather were right.

I can't give up. I'm more than what they said, and my value, worth, and goodness isn't based on their inability to see it. Keep fighting. Be strong! I told myself.

In the end, my success wasn't based on how many contacts I had or how much money I made. For me, success was based on my ability to overcome and to know my true identity. And at that moment, success was victory over something as innocuous as a phone book.

It may sound silly now, but doesn't every excuse sound silly once we prevail and get to the other side? Every excuse, every fear, and every lie sound so real, so credible, and so logical at the time we're about to do something extraordinary. Even if what you want to achieve seems small at the time, it's actually extraordinary because it's those little breakthroughs that forge new patterns for us. So, whether it's taking a chance at a once-in-a-lifetime opportunity, signing up for a new class, leaving a bad relationship, asking for forgiveness, or believing you're bigger than a phone book—anything that causes you to step out of an old groove that no longer serves you is something extraordinary.

Every morning and every afternoon, I called people for one hour. The rest of the time I spent either going to all the different "agents opens" (open houses held for realtors to preview/review a current property for sale) that were planned a different day of the week for each regional area of the city, or learning from the office managers at their in-house training get-togethers. I also took every class I could that was offered by our real estate board to learn even more about the industry. As my knowledge and skills improved, so did my confidence.

One of the other office top producers was Jean, who also served as one of the acting managers of the new company I joined. Out of the goodness of her heart, she asked me to co-list a nine-hundred-thousand-dollar new home with her within two weeks of my walking in the door. She basically handed me half of her commission check. In return for this opportunity, all she asked was that I do the open houses and the showings and be responsible for the marketing of the home.

Jean believed in me and saw something she called "greatness." I was humbled beyond words and determined to make her proud, proving that her confidence in me would not be in vain.

In less than six weeks, and in a down market, we were given a miracle—we received an offer. Jean taught me all the details of contract negotiations and how the process worked from beginning to end. I was astonished at her kindness and goodness toward me. Were it not for her taking me under her wing with such unconditional love and generosity of heart, I would have had a much more difficult start.

I have always remembered Jean's sacrifice. Even several decades later, I made a point to find her to thank her again for all that she did for me when I started my career in real estate.

"So, there are good and trustworthy real estate agents out there?" Leah joked.

"Yes, Leah. Jean was not only a good person, and trustworthy in real estate sales, she was a good person and trustworthy in all aspects of life. She is one of those special people who come into your life at the right time and change it for the better—forever."

"I was especially grateful for her help, but now that I had stepped out on my own, the pressure was really on. As an assistant at the other company, I had worked over sixty hours per week. Now, I was working even longer hours, up to ninety hours per week, but at least it was for my family. Working part-time or choosing my own hours was not a possibility. I was a single mom who had to provide for Michael's and my present, as well as for our future."

"How in the world did you work ninety hours per week? That's crazy!" Leah interrupted.

"It was crazy, but the real estate market cycles weren't always predictable, so I had to work when work was there."

With determination, my credibility, experience, negotiating acumen, strength in market knowledge, and, especially my visibility, grew. I share that not out of arrogance, but to simply illuminate how far I had come.

One day, I overheard a conversation in which I was called a "top producer." I remember looking around to see whom they were addressing, and when I realized it was me they were referencing, I didn't know how to embrace the title. Sure, it was a nice recognition of my accomplishments, but to me, the recognition symbolized something greater—that I had overcome my limitations, inadequacies, and fears. I was an overcomer!

Before long, I had an assistant of my own and achieved my Real Estate Broker's license in addition to my sales license.

Time passed. As much as I enjoyed working at this company, I eventually moved to another company that provided more international networking and relationships. It was a great struggle to leave, but it was time to grow and expand again.

I wanted Michael to have options, so I embraced hard work. My past was behind me, and I enjoyed building long-term relationships based on a foundation of trust, integrity, and respect with colleagues, peers, associates, and especially with my clients. My intention wasn't only to be a "promise maker," but also a "promise keeper." I made a point of never stepping out of the door unless I knew I had everything ready to deliver on the promises I was about to make. I wanted to thank and honor my clients for the trust and belief they had in me and excelling at what I did was one of the ways I showed them that. Every little detail was carefully planned, and the next ten steps of every transaction were also carefully prepared. I worked every day, and eighteen-hour-plus days weren't uncommon, hence the ninety-hour work week.

But I loved what I was doing and what I was able to provide for Michael, so time flew. Days flowed into months and months into years. Before I knew it, television, radio, newspaper, and other kinds of media attention were directed at me. I was humbled and honored for the opportunity to represent my industry.

As we all well know, no one ever achieves anything great alone. God always sends a great tribe of people to come alongside us to help us on our path. And when I say "great," I don't just mean in size and number, but "great" as in wonderful and amazing. Sometimes, that tribe is only meant to be with us for a season. Sometimes, it's for a lifetime. Only time will show us how we fit into each other's lives and for how long.

Granted, it's not always easy when our tribes change. We can misinterpret the change as something wrong or bad when often it's simply a matter of growth and a new assignment. But at this special time of my life, I was blessed with an amazing tribe of "earth angels" who stood with me in the fiercest of storms, and for that I will be eternally grateful.

Several such angels were Julie and Jeffrey and their family. They were godsends to me, and their home daycare was the perfect loving, nurturing, and growing place for Michael to thrive before attending school. I honestly don't know what I would have done without them.

Further, almost all my clients were wonderful and accepting of the fact that I was a single mom. They received Michael with love and acceptance when my father or childcare wasn't available. However, in spite of their generosity of heart, there were times when I could not bring him with me. When I was in contract negotiations or presentations, it was then when my tribe came to my rescue. "Auntie Suzie," "Auntie Susan," and eventually, my full-time assistant, Jennifer, Dolores and Jeff, Helen and other dear friends became my earth angels, caring for Michael while I worked. My gratitude to them runs deep, wide, and long.

As my business grew, I had less and less free time. Feeling badly that Michael didn't have a *normal* childhood routine, I would often apologize to him, but all he would say was, "That's okay, Mommy. As long as we're together, I'll go wherever you go."

Such was the heart of my beautiful little boy.

When Michael came with me to my open houses, he would fill his backpack with toys and books for the afternoon. And of course, he always brought his treasured blanket—a quilt that I had made for him when he was a baby. I generally did *six* open houses every Saturday and Sunday for years. The first one was from noon to 2:00 p.m., then 2:15 p.m. to 4:00 p.m. and then from 4:15 p.m. to 6:00 p.m.

This was no easy feat, even though the homes were always selected to be within close proximity to each other. Signage, directional arrows, balloons, and sometimes food all had to be strategically planned out and executed with precision timing. As soon as the initial preparations were done, then Michael would set up at the kitchen table, where he would read or play with his toy dinosaurs.

One time, I had so many groups come through an open house, I was almost unable to serve each one with the care and attention they required. Questions abounded as I juggled each person and moved from room to room. Michael heard me whisper under my breath, "I wish there were two of me to handle all the people today…"

Without missing a beat, Michael went to greet the next couple coming in the door. As I was working with a family in the kitchen, I heard Michael say, "Hi! Welcome to my mommy's open house. This is a five-bedroom home with a three-car garage. It also has…" He continued to repeat almost word for word everything I had been saying. The couple was very delighted and laughed out loud as they listened to my three-year-old "assistant" do his thing!

"My name is Michael, and I'm three years old," I heard Michael reply to one of the couple's questions. "I know this house very well because we've been here lots of times." Then he extended his hand and welcomed them in as he began explaining, "This is the living room with a gas fireplace, and over there is the dining room…"

By now, the family with whom I was working was silent as they stretched their necks to see Michael in action. I had also turned around, and with my mouth agape, excused myself and slowly tiptoed toward the living room. Poking my head around a wall, I saw the couple bent over to listen to Michael explain his purpose as my assistant. "My mommy works every day so that she can take care of me. It's just the two of us, so I come to help her…" He caught his breath, and then as if he had a flash of insight, with a huge smile on his face, he said, "Would you like to buy this house? It's beautiful, and I know you will love living here!"

I gasped.

Oh, my goodness! He just asked for the order!

I rushed out from behind the wall, and Michael excitedly called me over "Mommy! Come meet these nice people! They want to buy this house!"

Smiling, I introduced myself and apologized for my son's boldness, but they were enchanted. With a wink, the wife asked if it would be okay to have Michael show them the rest of the house. They smiled graciously, and Michael took them by the hand and showed them the rest of the house.

I watched speechlessly as my little boy led them to another room. As sweet and adorable as the entire conversation was, my heart was cut with sadness. He was only three years old. *What am I doing bringing my little boy to an open house? Did I have any other options for childcare that I didn't think of? What else can I do as a career that could afford me to take weekends off? He needs to be playing. Is this "play" to him? Or…is this hurting him?*

Countless thoughts somersaulted in my mind.

As Michael's voice drifted down the hallway with this kind couple, I took a deep breath, dug my fingernails into the palms of my hands to distract myself from crying, and thanked God for the greatest blessing and joy of my life—my son, Michael.

Silence Isn't Always Golden

"What a wonderful child!" Leah boomed. "And, I have to ask—did the couple buy the house?"

I smiled. "No, they didn't buy that one, but they became my clients, and I not only represented them in the sale of their existing home, I also represented them in the purchase of another one."

"Who knew that out of the mouths of babes? Well, you deserved every success, Manna." Leah squeezed my hand. "Now, tell me, with so much attention on you, you must have had a boyfriend, or two—or seven!" She winked. "I can't imagine anyone not being smitten by you and wanting to sweep you and your wonderful son off your feet!"

"Oh, Leah, you are too much." I smiled. "In those years, I was mostly focused on my work, and whatever free time I had, I spent with Michael. It wasn't until I was established, many years later, that I was able to take a few days off, and even to have a holiday. And to address your question, yes, there were a few courters, but… well, let's just say things didn't work out."

"Hmmmm…always so diplomatic and kind. Sounds to me like there were lots of smelly frogs all wanting to be kissed, but not a-one of them was a prince at heart!" Leah declared. "Fess up! I smell a pond full of them!"

I chuckled. "Oh, Leah…"

"Hey, I just call it as it is. A spade's a spade, remember? Now, tell me, what of those frogs?"

"Let me first say that I'm very thankful for each friendship I had. They were part of a priceless lesson I desperately needed to learn."

"What's that?"

"To date my value, not my low self-esteem."

"No offense, dear, but isn't this the same lesson you should have learned with Tristan, too?" Leah said as she patted my hand reassuringly.

"Yes, it was. But in many ways, this lesson was too 'advanced' for me back then. I had to first learn to value life. Until I understood that my life was valuable *first*, there was no way I could understand I was deserving of anything else.

"That's powerful," Leah said, nodding her head slowly.

"It took me a long time to realize this and, like I said, in terms of meeting the many so-called 'frogs,' each one was necessary for my healing and my growth."

"So, after sloshing through the smelly pond, did you find your prince?"

I smiled. "Yes. It took a while—a long while—but yes, my prince did come for me."

"Ooooh, very intriguing. Amuse me. Tell me about a couple of them en route to Prince Charming," she exclaimed excitedly as she adjusted herself in her bed.

"Well, first there was Preston, who I originally met in university. He was kind, gentle, and had an air of refinement about him. His temperate and amiable disposition was so different than any man I had known, and I was very attracted to this. We lost touch, but when we finally ran into each other again almost a decade later, I shared this reflection with him in a warm and candid conversation. He was surprised to hear it, and in his endearing way, dismissed my compliment as part of his British upbringing. 'We were always taught to be appropriate and proper—even if we were dying inside,' he said."

"I remember wondering what it would be like to be with someone like that—educated, accomplished, refined, and reared in a good family. I wondered if an unwanted, damaged misfit like me would ever be worthy of someone like that."

"But Manna, how can you say that? You overcame so much and accomplished so much! And, *you are kind, generous, and educated yourself!* Plus, you reared a child on your own! What in the world were you thinking?" Leah interrupted.

"Oh Leah, that's kind of you to say, but back then, even though it wasn't that long ago, the mindsets of people and society were different. I was a divorcee and a single mother of a little boy. In my mind, the negatives screamed louder than the positives. Sure, I had my bachelor's degree, but I had not yet finished grad school, something I thought would validate me somehow. I may have been successful in real estate, but I had been working up to ninety hours per week to earn commissions that weren't paid until months later. I had one of the biggest blessings of my life in being the mother of an amazing little boy, but I had gained seventy pounds during the pregnancy. Thankfully, I had lost the extra weight quickly. But I was left with loose skin around my abdomen, and after nursing Michael I also had very loose and saggy breasts…and, of course, there was the nagging and inescapable reality of being Asian.

"I believed the odds were stacked against me, so I simply banished any further thoughts of Preston, even though my heart secretly hoped for someone like him one day. I wanted someone kind, intelligent, respectful, and accomplished. Why accomplished? Because that symbolized to me someone who persevered and had self-discipline. It exemplified the heart of a man who wanted to succeed in spite of distractions or excuses.

"Preston also represented hope—hope that someone could have the character and qualities I admired. And hope for the possibility that a person like this would love me with my shortcomings and would one day even overlook the loose skin… the loose yellow skin."

"I know I keep saying this, but I can't believe what I'm hearing! Look at you!" Leah said, almost shouting.

"It sounds crazy as I hear it coming out of my own mouth, too, but it's the classic situation of a broken little girl trapped in time, old beliefs, and lies. I was getting stronger day by day, but I was not yet fully healed. No matter what kind of affirmation, confirmation, or validation I received, I couldn't yet *see* it in myself. And frankly, there were times I wasn't even sure *what I looked like.*"

"What do you mean? Look in the mirror, silly girl!" Leah persisted.

"What I meant to say was, though I had many wonderful compliments and noticeable attention, when *I* looked in the mirror, I still saw myself with wounded eyes. As a little girl, I used to cringe when people said I was 'the spitting image of my mother.' Then, as I grew into a teenager, all I saw was a despised 'Chinese girl' looking back at me. Thankfully, over twenty-five years later, I am a completely different person. What didn't belong, I found the courage to face and let go of, so I could discover the true *me* inside. The work isn't done, and like that old saying goes, 'I'm not where I used to be, and I'm not where I want to be yet, but I thank God, He's not finished with me either.'"

I took a deep breath and exhaled loudly. It wasn't easy remembering those agonizing times and who I was then. I was embarrassed to confess out loud my foolish thinking and my weaknesses. Leah looked at me strangely. She had both the eyes of a compassionate friend and the eyes of a perplexed professor. Searching for another way to explain my low self-esteem during those times, I suddenly remembered something I studied in school.

"Leah, are you familiar with Dr. Emoto's fantastic work on water crystals?"

Leah shook her head.

"He was an author and entrepreneur who explored the idea that matter responds to negative and positive thoughts, and/or energy. Using water molecules, he discovered that evil, ugly, selfish, jealous, and toxic thoughts all affected water crystals in very destructive ways. Similarly, thoughts of love, gratitude, generosity, peace, and prayers all affected the crystals in beautifully profound ways, forming the most breathtaking designs and symmetry.

"Since a great majority of our bodies are composed of water, energy, thoughts, words, music, and such all affect us. If a person is cloaked and filled daily with ugliness, negativity, abuse, and violations, then this body becomes as toxic as these feelings. In time, the body only resonates with that frequency of toxicity, as it has become 'familiar' and 'comfortable' with it, eventually dying of disease. It doesn't matter whether we are in an environment of negativity (or if we *are* the negative environment, perpetuating ugliness), the body becomes whatever we think about and are surrounded by. The Bible talks about these matters too, but we don't realize its significance and its impact until we see it manifested in our very lives by the way we think, speak, and act, and by what we endorse, comply with, submit to, and settle for."

"Okay, I get it, but it's still hard to believe someone like you couldn't see the truth about yourself once you started getting ahead. How could you believe you were ugly?" Leah added.

"Leah, like the water crystals, my cells didn't know how to resonate with positive attention. When one is as damaged and as broken as I was, one becomes accustomed to and even comfortable with callousness and loneliness. We get involved in (and stay in) lonely or abusive relationships because we're familiar with those things. Yes, it sounds ridiculous, and it *is* ridiculous to the normal mind, but for people like me back then, mistreatment was *normal*. We shun, avoid, ignore, or don't even see the possibility of something else good in a nice relationship with another person until we get the help we need.

"That said, with the personal development work I was doing, and with my little victories here and there, I suppose I must have had a flicker still alive in my soul when I noticed Preston. But even so, waves of anxiety washed over me when I agreed to our first date."

"A date? Now we're talkin'! That's my girl!" Leah shouted with approval. She coughed a tiny bit, but when I reached for her with concern, she smiled. "Oh no, I'm not missing this! Keep going!"

I was still nervous about going on a date with Preston. My divorce had just been finalized, and I couldn't remember the last time I went on a date. My single life seemed so far away. I tried to tell myself it was just *a friend* reaching out to me, and I should just *calm down!* But my nervousness only increased as the weekend approached. I dressed in my most flattering jeans and chose a bra I trusted to hold everything together.

"You're a nut." Leah joked.

"I'm serious! It may sound funny now, but it wasn't funny at all back then. While I had returned to my pre-pregnancy weight, nothing was in the same place as it had once been. A few months after I stopped nursing Michael, I had to run to the store to get some diapers and a few other groceries. I quickly put on some sweatpants and threw on a T-shirt with a sweatshirt on top. I hurried to dress Michael as well, and off to the store we went. When we returned home, I first unloaded Michael in his car seat and placed him safely inside. I then hurried to retrieve the bags of items I purchased at the store. Only then did I realize that in my rush, I had neglected to put on a bra. As I jogged back toward the house, I noticed a strange feeling on my chest. I had the sensation of my breasts swinging in opposite directions under the baggy sweatshirt I wore.

Ummm…why are my boobs flapping? Not "bouncing"' but flapping! Why is one going to the left and the other to the right? What has happened to me?

Leah was laughing and nodding again. This time, she was nodding with familiarity. Thankfully, there was no cough. "Okay, okay, okay…I know *exactly* what you're talking about! I'm with the program now. Continue."

Preston and I met at a local beach and went for a nice late afternoon walk. He was single, as handsome as ever, and had a successful business of his own. He was genuinely happy to see me and embraced me with a welcoming hug. In the hours that unfolded on that visit, we talked about many things, catching up on what had occurred in our lives since graduation.

Not long after catching me up on what he had been up to, he confessed his affection for me, and said he'd had feelings for me ever since we met in our university days. He explained that he had never approached me because I was with Landon, and when he heard I had gotten married, he had given up hope.

Then, Preston said, "When I found out you were divorced, I felt that providence had stepped in to give us both what we should have had in the first place."

I was dizzy after hearing this. Ten thousand thoughts flew around in my mind, and I remember stopping—unable to move any further when he admitted these feelings to me.

He had liked me? He hid his emotions and his feelings so well! How could I not see any of the signs? There are usually signs! How did I miss this and then marry someone I didn't even love (or like!) because I didn't think anyone else could love me? And there he was, this whole time!

Still being the gentleman, he didn't try to hold my hand or be too bold in any other way. He wanted to honor my "space" and let this revelation sink in.

He continued, "I don't know how you feel about all of this, Manna, or how you even feel about me. I'm sorry to share so much all at once, but I let so much time go by, and I didn't want to lose another chance of being with you again. So, there it is…a decade in a nutshell!" He smiled.

My heart melted, and tears welled in my eyes. As they fell down my cheeks, he brushed them off with the back of his fingers and held me in his arms. I wanted to cry and cry on his shoulders, but I did not. I kept myself together, and when he let go of his embrace, he kissed me on the forehead.

Preston and I dated for several months, and it was intoxicating. At dinner one night, he looked deeply into my eyes and said, "Manna, do you know what your name means? It means a "windfall"! You're an unexpected gift of good fortune from heaven itself! And that's exactly what you are to me."

I almost fainted hearing him speak these words to me.

We spent almost every day together initially, and he professed his love and care for me, and for Michael as well. We introduced each other to our friends and colleagues, went to parties together, attended art events, and went on romantic dinners. We also enjoyed fun outings, and sweet tender times together making dinners at home. I supported his passion for creative arts and his athletic pursuits, and one day, he even surprised me with a romantic weekend getaway at a boutique bed and breakfast retreat on one of the Gulf Islands during one of the weekends Michael was with Tristan.

Often, he would just hold me and whisper, "Thank you, thank you, thank you." These moments were priceless, and for the first time, I felt like I *truly* belonged and that I was safe—safe with Preston, and safe in his arms.

Shortly afterward, Preston started training for a prestigious sporting event hosted by another country. It was then that things started to grow cold between us. At first, it started off as not seeing each other much during the week, keeping in touch with phone calls. But even that stopped, and then weeks, and eventually months went by without our having any contact at all.

"What the hell?" Leah interrupted.

"I know…it was so strange. It was as if I never existed. Not wanting to impose, when a few of my calls weren't returned, I stopped calling too. I kept busy with Michael and my career, which kept growing."

Leah interjected and didn't hold back. "He fell off the face of the earth! He didn't say anything to you when you were in college, and he didn't speak up again now! Face it, he just didn't have the jewels to talk straight with you!" Leah sighed with agitation. "And I was just starting to like him…"

It was a very, very confusing time. I was hurt, and not knowing what to do, I left Preston alone. It's a horrible feeling to be unwanted, and the last thing I wanted to do was appear as though I was trying to force myself into his life.

After four months had gone by without one visit or one call, one day, I'd had it. I called him and asked if we could meet. Interestingly, he wasn't surprised to hear from me and agreed to meet without hesitation. We decided to meet at the same beach where we had started our relationship.

I arrived early that afternoon and sat on a park bench overlooking the beautiful Pacific Ocean. I was the only one there that afternoon, so he was able to find me easily. He sat down beside me and awkwardly said, "Hi."

I was no longer enamored by his handsome looks, his achievements, his talents, or his abilities in any other endeavor, and after some initial niceties, I asked him point-blank what was going on. He said nothing; he only stared at his feet.

Say something! Are you sick? Do you need help? What is going on with you? Are you having an affair? Are you always like this in a relationship? Did I do something to offend you? Say something!

He didn't say a word.

"Preston, talk to me. Please tell me. What have I done? What have I done to warrant such coldness and your silent dismissal?"

He looked ahead at the waves running to the shore. After an uncomfortably long time, he finally said, "I don't know what to say. I don't know, Manna."

That's it? What do you mean you don't know? Of course, you know! Please, talk to me!

After another agonizingly long silence, I found the courage to say what I had to say. "Preston, I love you, and you said you loved me. But it's obvious you no longer feel that way because love doesn't behave like this. I don't know what is happening in your life because you have cut me out of it completely. I am sorry if you are going through something. If I can help, I would love to help. If not, then let me free you of this bizarre arrangement we have fallen into and liberate you from any unspoken ties you have to me. Even though we've only been together a short time, we've known each other for over a decade. I deserve more than this cold silence. I've only been good to you. I did my best to support you in every endeavor you pursued. And if you do not tell me what I have done to cause you to be so repelled by me or our relationship, there is no way I can grow, become better, or apologize."

Preston, who was now looking at me, still said nothing.

With a sigh, I continued, "Preston…I need to be free from this arrangement, too. It's horrible to be discarded like I meant nothing to you. I have feelings, too. If nothing else, please at least give me the dignity of my humanity to just end it. Why would you drag me on, tormenting me for months like this? I expected more—much more from you. You know what I have been through, and to experience such coldness from you is unacceptable. Plus, I have a son who was getting close to you! But you suddenly disappeared from his life also. You told me you never wanted to let me slip through your fingers again—that you believed Providence was moving. You said that's why we had a chance to come back together after all these years. I felt safe with you, and I opened my heart to you…but obviously you've changed your mind." I paused, took a deep breath and finally added. "I deserve better. I really, really do."

"I know you do…I know you do," was all he said.

We sat in silence for a long time, looking out at the ocean. When it was clear that Preston was not going to add any more to the conversation, I turned to him. With sadness, and a heart still full of love, I said softly, "Preston, please don't feel you have to stay and sit with me. I'm fine. Thank you for taking time to meet with me. You can go now if you want."

He looked at me and awkwardly said, "Okay…Ummm, goodbye then." And he got up and left.

Casanova

Time passed, and my career continued to flourish. I served on real estate boards and spoke at numerous events. The media coverage continued to grow as I was nominated for awards, and I even did a little modeling again. Soon, I was able to purchase a home in one of the nicest areas of town, had a new condo at Whistler Mountain, enjoyed membership at an elite private tennis club, and drove a BMW convertible. I even had a personal shopper at a beautiful and elite upscale clothing store.

Michael was doing very well in a French immersion school, was taking piano lessons, playing soccer, and learning tennis. We had a beautiful golden retriever named Sydney, and everything was, at long last, "perfect." I was in my mid-thirties and in my prime. Life was glorious, and I felt like I was finally out of the woods of the craziness in my life.

It was an exhilarating time, and I met lots of new people from all areas of life, including another of those infamous "frogs."

His name was Trevor. He was a simple guy just starting out in his business, but what I enjoyed about him was a sense of playfulness and his penchant for adventure. He enjoyed life and always had something fun he wanted to do. And while this carefree attitude was refreshing in the beginning, it became a challenge for us later on.

Initially, things seemed to go well, but there was always something unsettling about him. I just couldn't put my finger on it. Instead of trusting my spirit, I let things slide and tolerated behaviors I never should have. I reasoned that every relationship had its ups and downs. Unlike Preston, Trevor seemed open to working on them. So, I stayed, and I continued to rationalize the red flags.

Long story short, Trevor meant well, but he was young and struggling. He wanted to be successful too, but couldn't seem to "get traction like me," (he used to say) and was envious of my success. He often accused me of having a charmed life, and attributed my achievements to random luck, not perseverance and hard work. The ongoing recognition I received only fueled his underlying resentment. Instead of encouraging me and being happy for me, he diminished me with cold and calculating remarks, using my insecurities as weapons. He also manipulated situations to keep me in chaos and uncertainty so he could have the upper hand.

"The confusing part was he was very attentive and wanted to spend a lot of time together (which many deduced were due to the benefits of my career and all that it afforded me—and therefore him," I explained to Leah. "In conversations, and eventually in our couple's counseling sessions, he—"

"Couples counseling, really?" Leah interjected.

"Yes," I said slowly with a sigh.

"Keep going, I *gotta* hear this."

"Well, I shared that I was becoming increasingly bothered by Trevor's suggestion that I should bear the brunt of the financial obligations since I was earning more. This reminded me of Tristan, and I was going to have *nothing* to do with that. Adding to the chaos, while he professed his love for me one minute, the next minute, he would be eyeing and flirting with some voluptuous blonde somewhere.

"I'm so sorry, honey," Leah interrupted again. "I hate to say this, but Trevor loved what you represented more than he loved you. I bet he thought he hit the jackpot with you. Figured he'd just walk into a beautiful home, the condo, the private club, and everything else—probably eventually partnering with your business too!"

"Well, yes, that did come up eventually in counseling also. It was difficult to hear such things, but I still tried to make things work. To that end, a dear friend asked me to take a special personal development workshop that he had also taken earlier in the year. He said it wasn't like any of the others, and it had transformed his life. He wanted me to have that same experience. I trusted my friend and signed up right away."

"How was Trevor with Michael? Was he good to him?" Leah asked, shifting gears.

"Trevor was *okay* with Michael. He wasn't *great* with Michael, but he was nice enough—more like a friendly neighbor than a father figure."

"And how did Michael feel about Trevor?"

"Michael was always nice to everyone. So, he was nice to Trevor, also, being obedient and polite, but they weren't super close. Michael needed a *father*, not someone who simply played that position or title when it suited him. Luke and my father did the best they could to mentor Michael, but it wasn't the same as having a great father at home."

"I know this only too well, Manna. Things were also tough at home with Thomas away so often on duty. It's not easy when the family is separated—even when the parental relationship is strong."

"No, it's not."

"Well, you did a great job with Michael—I can tell. You can see it in his eyes in the photos you've shown me."

"I wasn't perfect by any means, but I did my best. I loved Michael more than life itself, and he was going to have the best home life I could give. I was going to be the mother I never had."

"I think a lot of people coming out of abusive homes feel the same way," Leah noted.

"It's not easy to be a parent. It takes a greater force to help us keep it all together." I sighed.

"What you mean to say is it takes God to keep it all together! Seems like anything, everything, is possible with God, if we just ask Him for help and then do what He says," Leah corrected me.

I smiled and raised an eyebrow.

She raised her hand, showing me her palm as if to say, "Don't go any further with that," and then gave me one of her *looks*.

Well, the workshop itself was wonderful. It was an eye-opener indeed, just as my friend had promised. I immediately registered for the second phase of the course, which was an intensive five-day retreat away, and the third phase after that, which was substantially longer and more involved, but it was worth every moment.

I was learning so much.

I was also noticed by several of the lead facilitators who encouraged me to take their advanced leadership courses and train to be a facilitator myself. I was thrilled, because something resonated in my spirit about healing, overcoming, and sharing the wisdom I had learned to help others get free too. Little did I know then, this was the beginning of my training for a part of my career twenty years later. Peggie was one of the lead facilitators and course developers, and she became my wise woman and coach. She was wonderful then and is even more marvelous now as a friend. I will be forever grateful to her for all that she taught me.

In the meantime, Trevor continued flirting with other girls in sly ways. His methods were designed not to be overly offensive to me, but they were unmistakably evident. He excused these encounters as his nature—being "fun and playful" or "bringing joy into people's lives." Interestingly, he never demonstrated this "nature" to men, only women, and single women at that. I realized then that he was acting with other women in the same way he had acted when he first started dating me—playful, coy, and flirtatious.

Trevor was still looking for the person he felt would best decorate his life. Although he told me over and over and over again I "was the best thing to ever happen to him," something inside of him insisted he was missing out on another conquest or on the perfect young girl in his life. Consequently, I was simply a placeholder until he found his perfect beauty.

Trevor began noticing my growing strength, and though he was still not one-hundred-percent committed, he worried he was losing his grip on me. He insisted that we spend more time together, and soon many of his clothes and other belongings found their way into my home.

Nervous and not one hundred percent committed myself, one day, I panicked. *God*, I whispered, with my head in my hands, *please show me what to do in this relationship.*

I had a good cry, and when I gathered myself together again, I went into my home office and focused on something more productive¾ writing my next newsletter for work. When I sat at my desk, I noticed a pile of books in the corner of the room, hidden loosely under a plastic bag.

That's odd, I thought to myself. I prided myself on neatness and organization, and this was out of the ordinary. Not to mention the fact that *every one* of my books were always neatly categorized in my bookcases. *How did I miss putting these books away?*

I went over to the pile of books and began picking them up, one by one. I looked at each cover to see where they would belong in my bookcases but was soon horrified to see the topics of the books. They were books on relationships, but not wholesome academic, wise, or honoring books about improving them. Rather, they were books on manipulation, control, and how to dominate women. These books taught psychological and behavioral techniques on how to use intimacy and sensuality as tools to trap women into physiological attachments.

I scanned through the books. Their contents touted various tricks and tenets of mind control, manipulation, and seduction for men to beguile women. As I reviewed the chapter titles, and a few of the pages within those chapters, a flood of memories bombarded my mind of how Trevor had used these methods and procedures *with me*.

I was sickened.

I trusted him, and had unknowingly fallen for those dirty, fraudulent, and deceptive tricks. Little did I know that our romantic moments had only been a part of the protocol he had mastered. I had been baited, and I had fallen wholeheartedly into a trap that was both beguiling and loathsome.

There could be no more rationalizations, excuses, or justifications. I had to get out of our dysfunctional relationship. Unfortunately, I'm not proud to say this, but as strongly as I knew I had to get out, I was simultaneously petrified to leave.

Truer than True

Around this same time, my health took a sudden change for the worse. I suffered from debilitating migraines, and the incapacitating panic attacks (where I could barely breathe) suddenly returned.

I thought I had escaped this long ago when I couldn't leave the basement of my father's home. Yet, here it was again, but with even more intensity than before. The sense of imminent doom and the darkness that covered me was comfortless, and I felt like I was observing my own death—one frantic gasp at a time. The fear was gripping; it stole any sense of reason or hope I had. The darkness of these episodes was real, and beyond my ability to chronicle.

Desperate for answers, I researched everything I could at the time to discover what was wrong with me. With no Internet in those days, in between an exhaustive workload, I spent hours at the bookstore and in the library. I pursued anything written about the myriad of symptoms I was experiencing. I was driven to learn everything I could about my symptoms and what they all meant.

I discovered that my *condition* was called "codependency." The dictionary describes it as a type of dysfunction where one person supports or enables another person's addiction, poor mental health, immaturity, irresponsibility, or underachievement. Among the core characteristics of codependency, the most common theme is an excessive reliance on other people for approval and identity.

Well, that was me.

And when I couldn't get that approval (which symbolized my worth and value), I would panic. According to the textbooks, the panic attacks were the result of "severe anxiety disorder," and mine were so crippling that at times, I believed only death could bring relief.

I met with a counselor again, but he only wanted to label me and give me behavioral homework tasks to do. I recognized the fact that reactionary behaviors designed to overpower another unpleasant behavior were not the answer, so I found another counselor, and another, and another, but no one could really help me get rid of the root of the problem; they all focused only on what I call distraction techniques.

I found some comfort in meditation techniques associated with philosophical schools of thought and spiritual disciplines. But, in due time, I realized that in many ways, those ideas or principles were even more self-abusive. I was told to override my thoughts, fears, worries, anxieties, pain, and memories with "happy" thoughts. Moreover, several "spiritual masters" told me I was bringing these things onto myself in this current life. That these effects were the due consequences of a previous, poorly lived life. Furthermore, if I were *enlightened* enough to learn these lessons now, then I would not cause my future self any more pain. However, if I didn't become enlightened enough (or made more errors), then I would be forced to come back. I'd have to redo this lesson until I become so evolved I won't have to be burdened by life on this planet at all.

How depressing! Everything—my future, my serenity, my health and well-being, my dreams, my relationships, my career, my soul, and my *eternity*—everything hinged on whether or not I would *get it now*, or it would affect my future, which would then affect my next life, or lifetimes!

I was petrified. Petrified of my current life and petrified of doing anything for fear that I might cause myself more pain in "my next life."

This thinking spiraled me into deeper depths of anxiety and hopelessness. If I aligned myself with this belief as a foundation, then I would neither be smart enough, nor would I learn enough to save myself. I could not be kind enough, nice enough, or compassionate enough. I could not be forgiving enough, work enough, or be generous enough. I could not detach enough or meditate enough, and I could not fast enough or surrender enough. Nothing was *enough*.

That's when I was told I was too *attached* to this thinking, so now I was in danger of not *being* enough.

"Are you making this up, Manna?" Leah asked incredulously.

"I wish I was. It sounds absolutely ludicrous, doesn't it? But as we talked about before, everything is easy to see for what it is long after you've overcome the obstacle. All trials seem like nothing after we've surpassed the testing, and time has washed our memory banks. But I assure you, while it may seem clear now, it was anything but that back then."

I understood and could agree with the principle of self-responsibility and attraction—an "as a man thinketh" kind of attraction. But I could not comprehend or agree with many of the other principles the so-called spiritual masters were trying to teach me, much less worship them or those principles.

So, I went back to what I knew—I went to church.

Unfortunately, in those days, many of the services seemed mechanical. Of course, not every church I visited was like this. Some churches had great pastors who gave very meaningful messages, but I was too confused and afraid to stay. In retrospect, what I was most afraid of was people, not the church or the services.

I wasn't ready to share my heart again, and quite frankly, I didn't know how much I had left to give. I reserved whatever I felt I had left of myself for Michael—and for the strength it took to work with some demanding and difficult people who thought nothing of using me for their selfish gain. The more successful I became, the more people I met every day. I needed the energy to be present, alert, and on my game. No matter what I gave to everyone who came to me, for some, it was never enough. Eventually, I learned how to release those kinds of clients (and friendships)—those *vampires* of time, energy, heart, and hope. And by doing so, I began to reclaim parts of my fragmented heart. But that was still not something I had mastered at the time.

With nowhere else to turn, I remembered I could talk to God from anywhere, just like I used to as a child. I could be with God in my father's sweet little church, and I could be with God at home.

Can it be that easy?

I was torn. My spirit resonated with this thought, but somehow, I knew it wasn't the entire story. *What am I missing? What is wrong with me?*

I was desperately seeking answers and the truth. I was desperately seeking God. I wanted to hear Him again and have the connection I'd had with Him when I was a little girl, but I didn't know how to find Him. I looked to fill my "God void" with other people, other things, and other beliefs, but they were all so limited and elusive. Plus, none of them felt *right*. I didn't care about all the polarizing beliefs, protocols, rituals, and cultures. I didn't care about the how-tos. I simply wanted my God!

I wanted the God of my childhood. I wanted my Best Friend, Who summoned me in the elevator. I needed the One Who came after me in the hallways and in the dank, cold, and smelly basement to show me I wasn't alone. I craved the One Who sang to me through windblown leaves, Who painted me the masterpiece in nature. I wanted my Lion on the Mountain back! *Where was He?*

"Sweet Manna," Leah whispered with compassion, "I wish I could have been there for you. I may not have known what to say or how to guide you, but I would have stayed with you and listened to you until you felt safe."

"Oh, Leah, you're doing that for me now. Even though I go back and forth on *what* to share (and how much of *that* to share), in many ways, you are giving that little girl a voice at long last. And I thank you," I said as my eyes filled with unshed tears.

Leah squeezed my hand.

"Do you want me to stop? Are you tired? Have I worn you out? I'm sorry, maybe I rambled on too long again today..." I was concerned and a little embarrassed that

I may not have been attentive enough to Leah's needs.

"No, not at all! Are you kidding me? Like I said, this is good stuff. You are speaking about much of what I have wondered in the stillness of my own heart on many, many, lonely nights. You are helping me…more than you know. Please tell me more about your spiritual journey," Leah encouraged.

"Well, all right. But first, let me say this—what I'm sharing are simply the experiences of my own life and what was occurring for me during those times. My intention is to humbly give you my testimony of how God has been so very present in my life. Even when I couldn't see Him, hear Him, or feel Him, He was there. *He was there.* It just took me a while to know what was real and what wasn't, what was Truth and what wasn't. I just thank God that He never left my side."

"But Manna, how can you know God was *clearly* there so often, and then doubt it so easily again?"

"That is a great question. I believe it's part of the human condition. How many times do we doubt our abilities to do something we've done repeatedly when we're tested suddenly? It's the same way with faith. Even though God had shown up for me so many times before, when a new challenge came, my heart and faith were tested. *Did I really believe? Did I really trust God?*

"I once heard someone say, 'a faith that cannot be tested is a faith that cannot be trusted.' The walk of faith is mysterious. 'Believing' in the unseen Truth even when the world and your circumstances are shouting another message is strange! But God isn't afraid of our questions or even our challenges. He wants to prove Himself to you, to show you He is there for you, but we must acknowledge His presence and invite Him into our circumstances first. Because I challenged God, He showed up, and with every new encounter with Him, my walk of faith grew stronger."

Leah nodded. "Well, that makes sense—the ebbing and flowing of learning and life."

"I know it can sound a bit of a neurotic, going back and forth with my doubts and my belief that God is *for* me. But frankly, I *was* a bit of a basket case back then. Just bear with me as I explain my experiences from the past. I sometimes have to jump into the present and then back again. Am I too confusing?" I apologized.

"No, not at all. I just want to make sure I'm tracking. Life isn't always black and white." She smiled. "So, is that why you're thankful for such difficulties? Because you grew closer to God?"

"Yes. My relationship grew and deepened with Him through each adversity, and I learned rich lessons in each circumstance. I also learned the difference between the true and living God and what was just a god, a counterfeit."

Leah's eyes opened a little wider. "I want this too. I want to know the truth about God, too."

This time, it was my eyes that opened wide.

"I know, I know," Leah confessed. "You aren't the only person I used to annoy with my protests. I used to have heated debates over religion and spirituality, always accusing people they couldn't handle the truth…but maybe it was me. Maybe *I* was the one who couldn't handle the truth. But I'm ready to hear it now. I *have to* now…"

I paused and thought about how to express my next thoughts. "Even though the overall principles of what the 'spiritual masters' told me didn't make much sense, I recognized a hint of the truth in some of what they did say. So I stayed on this track, hoping *my Lion* was right around the corner. Regrettably, in my zealousness to find the truth for my own healing, I was more vulnerable than I realized. One thing led to another, and before I knew what was happening, I fell deep into bizarre mystical practices that left me even more confused than when I started.

"As I look back, I now know there is a difference between what is *true* and what is *Truth*. Something *true* may be 'accurate' and 'correct,' but it may not be *Truth* because it is not complete—it's not *the whole truth*. It's only a partial aspect of the truth. *Truth* is complete, whole, and total. It is a principle that is inerrant, foundational, and real. It is not only the umbrella that covers everything underneath it, but it is also the bedrock and the underpinning of any precept that follows above it. I believe this is where many people become confused—myself included. We assume that if something is *true*, it is also *Truth*. This isn't the case at all."

"Ahh…" Leah leaned forward in an "aha" moment. "There's the rub."

"Yes. That's where we are so easily deceived. We don't want to admit that we're misinformed. However, not all information is good or useful, and knowledge of *misinformation* only begets more misinformed people."

"I think I get it. If I believe that the world is flat, then everything else will be shaped according to that belief. The original information is wrong, so everything based on that will be wrong too."

"Exactly. And that is what happened to me. I went down one smelly pipe after another, hunting and digging up every school of thought, naively hoping this next practice would help.

"It didn't. Worse, I had unknowingly opened the door to the *occult*, which, by definition, means 'to shut off from view; eclipse; not easily apprehended or understood.' *Merriam Webster Dictionary* includes a myriad of synonyms such as 'belie, blot out, conceal, enshroud, mask, obscure, suppress and veil' to describe this world. Instead of finding illumination, revelation, and truth, I was buried underneath a mountain of lies and sophisticated manipulation.

"Thankfully, my discernment grew. It got to the point that whenever I was in the presence of someone who had or was actively practicing in the occult, I had a physical reaction. It's still true to this day. I can smell it a mile away."

"You make it sound so ominous," Leah said.

"Make no mistake, Leah. The spiritual world is real. It is intense, powerful, and has consequences that would shake anyone to sobriety.

"So, yes, in this world, we will have tribulation, but we needn't fear. God has already overcome the enemy.

And because God is in us, around us, and for us, no one can ever truly be against us. The enemy can try, but no weapon formed against us will prosper, and we will always be victorious because Jesus intercedes for us, and legions of angels encamp around us. Greater is He who is in us than he who is in the world.

"Yes, there will be opposition, but we've already won the war. We fight *from* victory, not for it. God has already provided The Way. We just have to keep our wits about us—take every thought captive, think with a new mind, and trust in Him even when things don't make sense."

Leah thought a moment. "Well, it makes sense—if there's good, then there will be evil. If there's light, there will be darkness…I wish I could see life the way you do."

"The biggest battlefield is in our mind, Leah. I know because I learned the hard way…It seems like we're all prone to this learning style until we realize there is a *better* way. That said, I also believe God allows us to learn through the fire. Otherwise, how do we truly understand and overcome our fears and obstacles? Mighty warriors come from mighty battles, and we can't win a battle unless we're in one. But once we have victory in a certain area, we will also have authority over that area. And with that authority, we can help set other captives free too."

Leah nodded. "You've come a long way, my dear…and by golly, you did learn by fire, didn't you?"

"Yes. I was seeking answers in all the wrong places, with all the wrong people, and in all the wrong ways. Little did I know then that God was all I ever needed."

"Let me ask you another tough question," Leah asked, one eyebrow raised. "How did you know God was the *only* way?"

"I became a sleuth. I learned everything I could about *spirituality*—and the multitude of disciplines, practices, and associations under that label. And I studied the Bible. To me, the contrast between partial truths and *Truth* was undeniable. I could give you example after example, but for now, let me just say that the Bible is both true and Truth. While other schools of thought promised to help me find a little peace, it was nothing more than short-term relief through distraction. Moreover, the issues themselves were never resolved; they were only masked or redressed, almost as if putting a cover on a chair would change the reality of the chair."

"Reminds me of something my ol' Gramps used to say on the farm: 'Don't put lipstick on a pig!'" Leah spoofed. "It's still a flippin' pig no matter what you do!"

I chuckled.

Leah paused and then narrowed her eyes slightly. "I have to ask, Sweetie, are you sure your lack of success in other…modalities…wasn't due to, well, 'operator error'?"

I smiled. "That's a fair question. And the answer is 'no.' In my pursuit to get help and to find peace, I was a fastidious student who learned quickly, and I obediently applied each step given. Sadly, I ended up looking more like a fool and a radical spiritual nut than a healed and whole person."

"It's difficult to imagine all that you've been through." Leah paused and let out a deep breath. "There is no other explanation…"

I tilted my head, not sure what Leah was referring to. "Explanation?"

"You are a walking miracle. God must be *real!*"

Leah looked out the window, and I knew not to interrupt her. She held my hand tightly and then asked, "Tell me, Manna, did any of your honest seeking at least help you with your anxiety, migraines, or panic attacks?"

"No, unfortunately."

"Then how did you get over it? I'm assuming you don't have them anymore."

"I started to link the similarities between the time I was experiencing panic attacks upon my graduation from UBC and what was happening in my mid-thirties. The predominant theme was some kind of illness or any situation where I felt totally out of control. Even the slightest cold would set off an attack because I would be too weak and vulnerable to help myself. In those times, I often felt the most alone."

"A simple cold could cause you a panic attack?" Leah asked. "There must be more to it."

"There is. When I was about eight years old, my mother and Scham took us fishing to a remote lake. It was springtime, and we were surrounded by beautiful trees and fields of wild grass. Within a half-hour of our arrival, my eyes started itching and turned beet red. My nasal passages began clogging, and it was becoming difficult to swallow. I couldn't know it then, but I was either having a severe reaction to the allergens in the air, or I may have been bitten by some insect native to that region.

"Being a nurse, my mother directed me to just lie down and 'rest' in the back seat of the car. She didn't offer any other kind of comfort, antihistamine, or even a tissue. I was simply ordered back to the car while they continued fishing at the edge of the lake. I was told not to cause any more trouble since they had come all that way to go fishing.

"Soon, I was having a difficult time breathing, and it was increasingly harder to swallow. Naturally, not being able to breathe terrified me, causing even more anxiety. I rallied the strength needed to get out of the car, find my mother, and tell her I couldn't breathe.

"With the palm of her hand, she impatiently smacked me on the head. 'I told you not to interrupt us anymore! Scham is going to be really angry if he sees you here again!'

"She threw down the cheap fishing rod we had bought at the Army and Navy surplus store, grabbed my arm, roughly escorted me back to the car and essentially pushed me in the back seat again with one last verbal warning to 'stay there!'"

"Dear God! Couldn't she see your eyes?" You may have been having an anaphylactic reaction!" Leah exclaimed.

"Looking back, I believe I was, but what was I to do? By that point, I could barely open my eyes. With no other choice available, I simply told myself to calm down and breathe as best I could. I lay back down on the seat, and that was the last thing I remembered. When I woke up, we were driving back to town."

"You could have died, Manna!" Leah shouted.

"I know, but once again, you see how another miracle saved my life. You can also see how being vulnerable and weak was not a good place for me. Whether I was a little girl outdoors with severe allergies, or alone in my room with a bad flu, I felt terror in the powerlessness. Whether an illness after graduation from a compromised immune system or a cold when I was the sole provider and a single mom—being sick or feeling vulnerable would send me into a horrific panic attack. Unconsciously, I had surmised that since no adult was going to help or protect me, the only way I could be *safe* was if I protected myself. If I could work, pay the bills, and stay healthy, then Michael and I would be fine.

"A cold or the flu may be unpleasant, or even rough, to the average person, but for me, it had a different meaning; it meant that I would be vulnerable, alone, and a burden—maybe even die. Of course, it took me a while to put all the pieces together, but once I did, the power of the panic attacks and the anxiety over my life started to break. I still get headaches now and then, but that's just an indicator to me that I'm working through some things."

"Okay, now I have to ask another tough question…in order not to be vulnerable, did you become one of those crazy control freaks?" Leah asked, half-seriously and half-jokingly.

"That's a fair question, too. While it was true I needed to have stability because I now had Michael to protect too, I can honestly say yes—and no!" I smiled.

"What's that supposed to mean?"

"I wasn't a control freak with others. By then, I knew full well that people will do whatever they want, whenever they want, and however they want—irrespective of any insight or wisdom you might be able to offer. Few are truly open-hearted enough, humble enough, or willing to heal and grow enough to be teachable. So, I learned not to expect too much out of people. Instead, to maintain peace (or at least what seemed like peace), I became a people-pleaser. *I controlled myself.* I adopted great self-discipline in everything I did and went out of my way to keep peace by ensuring other's needs were met, even before my own. This fit well with the vows I had made as a child, and my little equation seemed to work, for a while. But as you know, this wasn't sustainable or truly empowering."

"So, you lived in your own world, basically," Leah kidded.

"Maybe. I figured if I was nice, then maybe they might be nice back."

"Were you successful?"

"Not always, but it still felt *better* to be nice, if that makes any sense. I feel more peaceful, happier, and lighter when I choose the way of kindness, irrespective of how others choose to behave."

"Are you telling me you don't harbor any bitterness inside of you? Not even a little bit of resentment about the past, or when people are intentionally unkind?"

"Leah, I'm human, and as I shared with you when we first met, *I'm far from perfect!* Of course, there are times when I am triggered, and my 'flesh' wants to cry out at the offense and be critical. But I have to discipline my thoughts, take them captive, and talk myself down. I do my best and wait to respond, biting my tongue. Inevitably, things always work out much better this way; less collateral damage is done, and relationships are not sacrificed but lifted up."

"Is it *that* easy?" Leah asked.

"No, Leah. It's not easy at all."

"Then how do you do it?!"

"By the grace of God." I smiled.

"I knew you were going to say that!"

"It's the truth."

"It's truer than true!" Leah added with a smile, then paused. "This whole idea of an *unseen* God Who works in your life so consistently…well, after spending time with you, I'm starting to believe this is possible. God *had to have been there for you*, even when you didn't *see* Him…there's no other way…no other explanation! It *must have* been Him directing you, protecting you, and teaching you…I can't find the words quite yet, but I think I'm starting to *feel* it—right here!" Leah pointed to her tummy.

"The seat of the soul. That's where He is all the time as a deep part of you, your core."

Leah thought a moment. "So, one more question. If you were so afraid to get hurt or to be out of control, you must have been kinda…boring! Tell me you had some kind of excitement! Did you ever pick up skiing or anything? You lived in such a beautiful city where the beaches and slopes were both less than thirty minutes away? Plus, you had a place at Whistler! I bet it was breathtaking up there. Tell me you weren't boring!"

"Hmm, I don't think I was boring, although others may have thought so! And yes, I did try to ski. It took everything inside of me to even get on those silly skis, but yes, I did learn. I didn't go beyond the green and blue runs, but at least I tried it."

"Good girl!" Leah shouted, releasing my hand to motion for a high five.

"Leah," I paused, "being with you is so easy. Our times together remind me of being with my PoPo or Auntie Georgiana. I love it. But speaking out loud about my failings is not easy. I'm not proud of my past, and I'm ashamed to admit some of the choices I have made. I was a shell of a person, fragile as a raw egg on the edge of a countertop…"

Leah took a deep breath and pushed away the retractable tray by her bed, so we had nothing between us. She slowly reached over with both arms outstretched, and I stood and reached back for her.

Like a mother with her daughter, she held me in her arms for a very long time. At first, my hug back to her was polite and appropriate, but then…I felt she was giving me a *mother's embrace*. I tried to pull back, but she would not release me. She clutched me with all the strength her frail body could muster, and I sank into her warmth and the genuineness of her hold. First, a tear or two escaped from my eyes, and then I wept.

And I wept, and I wept.

Leah continued to hold me, smoothing my hair, caressing my back. She blessed me with a mother's love, and in her frail arms, she took the burden of all those tears upon herself as she whispered, "I love you. You are precious. You are smart. You are beautiful, and you are meant for so much more than all of this…"

Left: Age 13, just before moving in with my father.

Below: Me and my father after my horrific visit to the barber.

Above: Age 17, my father and me.

Right: Me at the World Trade Center with the head chef.

Above: Visiting my father before starting my second year at University.

Right: The Real McCoy.

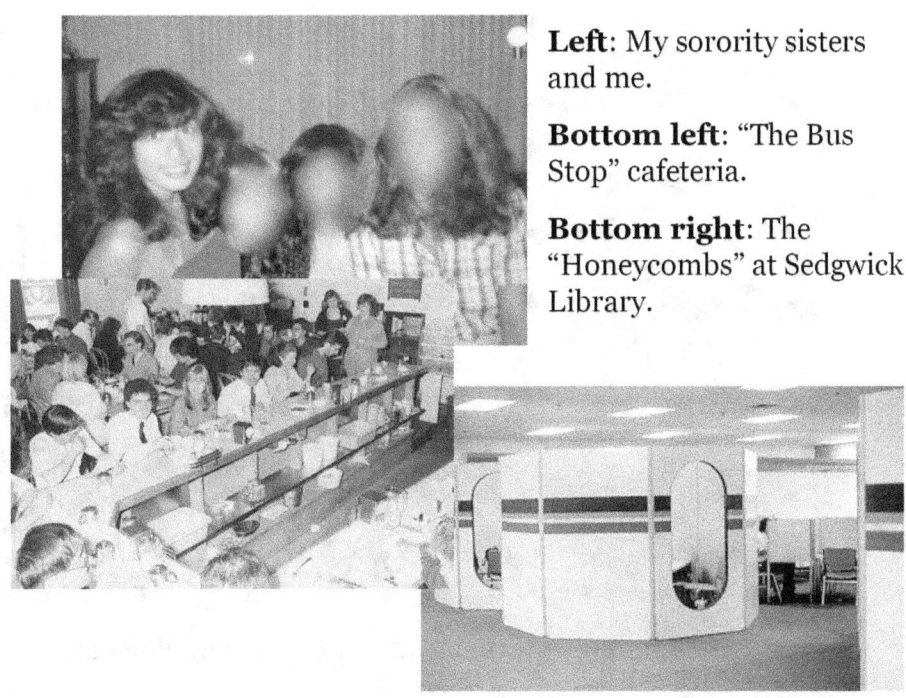

Left: My sorority sisters and me.

Bottom left: "The Bus Stop" cafeteria.

Bottom right: The "Honeycombs" at Sedgwick Library.

Left: My dad and me on my wedding day with Tristan.

Below: My bridesmaids all dressed in black.

Me (8 months pregnant with Michael) with PoPo and GongGong.

Above: My first real estate headshot and one of the newspaper features on me. On the right is my first home co-listed for sale with Jean.

Left: I finally learned to ski in my 30s!

Below: Me and Sydney.

[i] We have an enemy—the devil and his minions—and they hate us with a furor we can't begin to comprehend. Let me explain why. In the beginning, the devil was known as Lucifer, and he was a beautiful and very powerful angel. But when he decided he was equal to God, he was cast out from heaven. He learned he was nothing close to being God, and with his wounded pride, he denounced God and made Him his enemy for all eternity. Lucifer then became Satan, or the devil, (the father of lies, the accuser of the brethren, the adversary, and the antithesis to all that is good) and took one-third of the angels with him. With his company of fallen angels (now 'demons'), Satan's sole purpose now is to destroy, devour, and kill anything God loves—namely us.
[ii] John 16:33 (NIV) "I have told you these things, so that in me you may have peace. In this world you will have trouble. But take heart! I have overcome the world."
[iii] Isaiah 54:17 (NIV) …no weapon forged against you will prevail, and you will refute every tongue that accuses you. This is the heritage of the servants of the Lord, and this is their vindication from me," declares the Lord.
[iv] 1 John 4:4 (NIV) You, dear children, are from God and have overcome them, because the one who is in you is greater than the one who is in the world.

10 NO GUTS, NO GLORY

Do all the good you can, by all the means you can, in all the ways you can, in all the places you can, at all the times you can, to all the people you can, for as long as you can.

—John Wesley

Room 316

The next time I came to visit, I was pleasantly surprised to find Leah waiting for me outside in the courtyard where we had enjoyed many of our other visits. I went to her, gave her a hug, and pulled up one of the patio chairs. She looked like she had been in deep thought and seemed eager to talk to me.

She asked me to sit a little closer to her, so I did as she requested. From underneath her blanket, she pulled out a medium-sized box, wrapped in a beautiful, metallic, silver linen paper with a thick cobalt-blue sash and bow. The presentation took my breath away.

"Leah! How in the world—what is this all about?" I exclaimed with surprise.

"This ol' girl still has a few tricks left in her!" She winked.

I held the box, running my fingers around each detail. The satin sash was three inches wide, and the bow in the center was punctuated with a stunning crystal brooch that looked like a small crown.

"That brooch was given to me by my grandmother," Leah said proudly. "I want you to have it."

I gasped, "No, Leah." Taking a deep breath, I continued, "I'm honored, but I can't take this. It's too much. It should stay in your family—with one of your daughters or granddaughters. Just the thought of you even considering giving this to me means more than I can ever say."

I handed the box back to her respectfully.

"Manna, *I want you to have it,*" Leah said firmly, pushing the box back to me. "This belongs to you."

I didn't understand her comment and looked at her curiously as she continued. "You had cause to doubt your value as a child but doubt no more. You are a beloved treasure. You *are* a gift. I know why you were named 'Manna.' I'm sorry your mother never saw the treasure in you, but that is not a reflection of you—it's a reflection of her."

Speechless and moved by Leah's affection and generosity, I looked down at the gift on my lap.

"Treasures are considered treasures because they are rare, distinctive, and hard to find," she continued. "Only through excessive adversity and even death are the ordinary transformed into the extraordinary. A speck of sand deemed an irritant turns into a luminous pearl. A hairy worm bound to a life of lowliness transforms into a radiant butterfly, perfect in symmetry and design. Only after death and lying in apparent unending darkness until its appointed time is that butterfly able to fly—higher and farther than where it could ever have traveled before. And as you know, diamonds are brilliant only after enduring enormous intensity, pressure, fire, chiseling, and buffing. You get the picture."

I nodded.

"And do you know what else? Do you know what each treasure has in common?"

"Tell me, Leah."

"Humble beginnings. Each treasure was once seen as something annoying, ugly, worthless, and common—as something to discard. Each treasure also has *time* and *timing* in common. *Time* is how long the process of transformation requires. Sometimes we beat ourselves up for not *getting it* sooner, but we only do the best we are capable of at the time. *Timing*, on the other hand, is divine. *'Everything is beautiful in its own time,'* and at that appointed time, the treasure will be made known. Do you know what else? Treasures are always meant to bless others. They don't see themselves as special, nor were they created to serve themselves. They are *created* to bless others." She paused, smiling. "I share this because everything I just described is *you*. You are a treasure to me, Manna. Please, let this little gift be a small symbol of how much you mean to me." Leah wiped her eyes with a tissue and motioned for me to open the gift.

Humbled beyond words, with tears escaping now from my own eyes, I slowly untied the sash and released the beautiful brooch. Leah nodded, smiling with pleasure.

I pinned the brooch to my lapel and delicately continued opening the box. Inside was an exquisitely crafted, gold antique frame housing a finely painted butterfly surrounded by a garden of flowers. My eyes fixed on how the artist managed to so skillfully paint the precision of the shadows, the fine lines of a distant branch, the fading of colors within the throat of a trumpet lily. Each stroke was captivating. It was superb!

"Leah, I honestly don't know what to say. This is one of the most beautiful paintings I've seen in a long, long time—and the frame. It's so delicate and skillfully crafted. Leah, I can't—the painting, the brooch…it's too much…"

"None of that, my dear. This is for you, and I want you to have it as a parting gift from me to you."

"What do you mean 'parting'?" I asked, immediately alarmed.

"Well, let's face it. I've been given a bit of extra time—which I suspect you had something to do with, by the way." She winked. "But we all know why you're here to begin with. And as for how much more time I have left...well, let's just say that while I still have my senses about me, I thought I had better get this done. And just so you know, that's not a painting."

"It's not?" I asked in amazement as I looked back down at the gift. "Is it a photograph?"

"Nope." She shook her head in playfulness.

"I don't understand. If it's not a painting and it's not a photograph, what else could express with meticulous accuracy the breathtaking beauty of such a scene?"

"It's embroidery," she answered slowly.

"*What?* This is embroidery? Impossible!" I grabbed my glasses out of my purse and studied the "painting" again.

Leah chuckled. "Do you like it?" she asked again, playfully.

"Leah! *I love it!* Now I see it! But each thread is almost thinner than the finest silk threads of China!" I exclaimed.

Leah laughed out loud now.

"I'm glad you approve. I made it," she admitted.

Now I was totally in shock. My mouth hung wide open, and I grabbed the frame again to study the artistic magnificence of every stitch. The fact that this was fine needlepoint and not a painting completely took my breath away

"Leah! I had no idea! You see, this is why I didn't want to talk about me all the time! There are so many more wonderful things to learn about you! That's it. From now on, I'm not saying one more thing about me. I have to hear about you!"

Leah giggled some more. "This took me almost a year to do. I have a bigger garden scene at home that took almost three years to finish." She beamed. "Bet you didn't think this ol' gal could do more than bark orders, did you?" She laughed out loud again—proud she had brought me joy. "I'm glad I got to surprise you."

"Yes, you did." I took another deep breath and looked at the framed butterfly again. "You totally did. I'm speechless."

"Abby helped me put this all together. I had to tell her to do the bow a few times until it was just right, but other than that, she did a good job."

"Abigail knew about this?"

"Absolutely! They all do." She stopped and swallowed the sudden swell of emotion. "We love you, Manna..." Leah started to cry.

"Oh, Leah..." I got up from my chair and knelt by her wheelchair. We hugged each other for a long time, weeping with both joy and sadness.

Washington Irving once said, "A mother is the truest friend we have; when

trials, heavy and sudden, fall upon us; when adversity takes the place of prosperity; when friends who rejoice with us in our sunshine, desert us; when trouble thickens around us, still will she cling to us, and endeavor by her kind precepts and counsels to dissipate the clouds of darkness, and cause peace to return to our heart."

My mother wasn't that true friend, but I had the privilege of knowing a few women who were—my PoPo, MahMah, Auntie Georgiana, and my Leah.

Over one of Leah's favorite meals (which I picked up on the way to the hospital on our next visit), she finally obliged me and recounted stories about her childhood. We laughed out loud as she shared silly pranks she pulled on the boys in the neighborhood, her first driving experience, what she thought when she first saw a television show, who her teenage idols were, and how we both loved Audrey Hepburn.

"Now, we've gotten off track a bit," Leah said seriously.

"What do you mean?"

"Well, I still don't know how things ended with Trevor, what happened in Michael's life, how you got to the States, and how you got here—into my life. So we better get back to business. You can't leave me hanging."

"Leah, I thought we'd take a break from all of that and focus more on you. We had so much fun talking about your life just now, and I'd love to learn more about you. Truly."

"Well, if you're bored talking about yourself, then we're all in trouble. I know of no life more interesting than yours. Now since mine is almost over, you'll have to hurry and finish. And…if you're lucky, *then* I'll tell you about my first time getting arrested."

"Arrested? The *first time*? You were arrested more than once?"

She laughed and, ignoring me, adjusted her blankets, pulled up her tray to better reach her glass of water, and like a Cheshire cat, smiled and waved the back of her hand at me, motioning me to continue.

"Oh, Leah!" I said frustratingly. "There's no way to fight you on this, is there?"

"That's the same thing the judge said after I got arrested."

"Argh…Leah! You're simply impossible!"

"That's the second thing the judge said," she winked. "Now, let's get busy, shall we?"

Another One Bites the Dust

My relationship with Trevor continued down its tumultuous path. And as strange as this may sound, I awoke one day feeling something different in the air. I *knew* Trevor had decided to make a commitment to me.

For most women, this would be a good feeling to have. However, it was the last thing I wanted to happen. I knew we weren't right for each other, and while I had been afraid to leave him before, my strength was building, and it would only be a matter of time before the inevitable happened. Ironically, while I was trying to find the courage to leave, Trevor was trying to talk himself into staying. It was not love as much as it was an economic decision.

No sooner than I felt that check in my spirit, Trevor announced he had planned a little weekend trip for us, and I instinctively knew that was when he was going to ask me to marry him. I did everything I could to dissuade him from going through with this trip, but he was insistent and told me everything was already set and paid for.

I was stuck, and since he already paid for the trip, I reluctantly agreed to go.

The day came for our trip, and when we arrived at our destination, that same ominous feeling—that warning sign with which I had become so familiar—came over me again, this time even stronger. Without a doubt in my mind, I knew Trevor planned to propose at dinner that night, so I did everything possible to negate that opportunity. At the restaurant, I talked a mile a minute and engaged a fun couple sitting next to us in conversations throughout the evening. I asked our server a ton of questions about the sights to see and basically extinguished any possibility for romance to occur.

I wasn't trying to be callous or insensitive. In fact, it was because I was sympathetic to Trevor that I behaved in this way. I wanted to spare him the embarrassment of having to go through the whole evening and then the proposal itself, only to have me say *no*—not to mention it would have made the rest of the weekend entirely awkward and maybe even ugly. I was not going to say yes to marriage again unless I was completely in love and knew my future husband felt the same way.

"Good girl," Leah nodded with approval.

When Trevor asked for the check, I knew the moment of opportunity had passed. His countenance confirmed it, and I was finally able to take a breath. I gulped down more wine and let out a discreet sigh of relief. The dinner, as well as the remainder of the weekend, ended with clumsy conversations and superficial niceties. The moment had indeed passed, the question was never asked, and the ring was never presented.

When we returned home, Trevor grew increasingly agitated. Instead of talking about his disappointment over our weekend, he became even more abrasive. Then, one afternoon, he stormed into my office, threw an invoice at me, and said, "That's the cost of the ring. You owe me for this, not to mention half of the trip."

"*What did you say?*"

"You heard me! You owe me!" he said with restrained force.

At that very moment, I knew my angels had indeed been protecting me that weekend. God had given me the insight and the strength to avoid Trevor's design.

In addition to the engagement ring's invoice and the weekend's invoice, he also presented a list of other expenses he thought I owed to him for the past six months as well. I guess that was his way of saying, "It's over; now, let's settle up."

Strange, I thought. *I never itemized all the things I paid for…*

In fact, that kind of thinking never even occurred to me. Surprisingly, he still possessed the ring and had no intention of showing it to me, much less giving to me in return for the payment. I was saddened to see his true character now unveiled, but at the same time, I was relieved and ever so grateful. I didn't need any more evidence. This was exactly what I needed to confirm everything I had felt in my heart—I deserve better.

It was finally over. And no, I never paid him.

Groundhog Day

With my newfound freedom, I was able to start focusing on myself again. With a skip in my step, I decided to "go for it" and fully dive into my life—no longer just living on the periphery of it. Michael and I went up to our place at Whistler often, I created better systems and processes at work (which made me more effective and allowed me to have more personal time), and I spent more time doing fun things with my family.

After some time, an opportunity came for me to go on a little vacation of my own. Other than the trip with Trevor (which was anything but a vacation), this was the first trip I took with the intention of relaxing. It would be a "real" vacation—my first in over twenty years, and I was looking *so* forward to it. But the strangest thing happened just before I left.

I had to go home early one afternoon to review some files I had left in my home office. No sooner had I taken off my shoes and put down my bags, I saw Preston open my front gate and walk up the path to my front door!

I was in shock!

What's he doing at my house? I haven't heard from him in years!

He didn't ring the doorbell, but I heard my mailbox open and close. Immediately after, I heard his footsteps walking back down the path and the sound of the gate closing. I waited a few minutes, then went to see what he had left in the mailbox. A square-shaped envelope was inside, addressed to me. I went back inside and sat down on the sofa in my family room. I took a deep breath, not knowing what to expect, and opened the envelope.

It was a beautiful card and a two-page love letter in which he explained he did love me despite his bad behavior, and always had. He was too frightened to know what to do with those emotions, and instead of sharing them, he ran. He expressed his emptiness at not having me in his life or seeing me at home when he walked in the door at the end of the day, and confessed the emptiness he felt when, having accomplished his semi-pro event abroad, I was not there to celebrate his dream with him. He also confessed he was the only one to blame.

The letter continued. Preston told me how much he appreciated me, apologized for how he had treated Michael and me, and pleaded for another opportunity to rekindle our relationship. He recognized he was undeserving of that chance, but he would give anything to have it. He promised me he would give all of himself to us and assured me he would never take me for granted again. He asked me to take as much time as I needed before responding, as he knew this was a huge request.

"I will wait for you," he declared, *"no matter how long it takes."* Even if I said no, he said he would still wait, and keep asking because he now knew there could be no one else other than *me* in his life.

His letter was one of the most beautiful letters I had ever read. The beauty wasn't simply because it was eloquently written. It was because I knew how difficult it was for him to write it. And he had to have been thinking about this all these years.

After reading both the card and the letter over and over again, I put down everything, fell back against my sofa and groaned out loud. I closed my eyes, and then the tears came.

I did not want to live in the *what-ifs* after reading his letter, but it was impossible to stop my mind from shuffling through the unnecessary pain that happened that sad day at the beach, and since then. Most of all, I couldn't help but wonder what could have been. There was so much joy we could have experienced, so much we could have achieved and built, and so much love that slipped through our fingertips—not once, but twice.

He once said how fun it would be to be a family together, but that never happened. Maybe the time was now. I simply didn't know.

Can I trust him? Can I trust him with Michael? Has he learned to communicate his feelings now? What happened to have transformed him so? Is he really ready for what he says he wants? And am I willing to put my heart—and Michael's—on the line again?

The next few days were strange. While I was secretly overjoyed and cautiously contemplating the possibility of a future with Preston, I was also tethered by concern. After much prayer, I called him. He wasn't home, so I called his office. His wonderful receptionist, Kaya, was still there, and she was very happy to hear from me. We had a sweet time catching up, and she told me Preston was hoping that I'd call. I thanked her for relaying that message and told her I was leaving for vacation the next day and would call when I returned. She was thrilled and was looking forward to seeing me.

My trip away was wonderful. I made new friends, enjoyed the sun and the white beaches, tasted great food, and I laughed. I laughed a lot. For the first time in a long, long time, laughter came back to my life, and gratitude filled my heart.

When I returned home, I took the next week to settle back in with Michael, get in touch with all my clients, and go through all my mail. I opened another envelope from Preston, but this time, it was on his professional stationery. Inside was an invitation to an afternoon reception for the grand opening of his new office in less than one week. I didn't know he had moved his business and thought I would wait to contact him and surprise him at his party instead. It would be the first time we had seen each other in years, and meeting again in a lighthearted environment and in a spirit of celebration seemed like a great idea. Plus, his first letter had said *to take my time, and he would wait for me—no matter how long it took*. That was only a few weeks ago, so I didn't think much more about waiting a few more days.

When that day came, I went home early from work and got ready. His office wasn't far away from my home, and I arrived in no time. I parked and decided to check my makeup and noticed my hands were trembling as I pulled down the visor to look in the mirror. I didn't know why I was checking since I had just freshened up at home only a few minutes before!

Just calm down! I told myself. *This is a wonderful surprise, and the gift you bought for him is perfect! He'll be so happy to see you! Remember what he said in his letter. It couldn't be more ideal! Now, get out of the car and go in!*

I flipped up the visor, exhaled, and opened the door. The sound of music, laughing, and talking filled the air. The excitement was all around me. People were coming and going, and scores of others milled about the entrance.

A few mutual acquaintances came up and said hello, and someone directed me to where Kaya was. As soon as I saw her, my heart smiled. It had been years since I last saw her, but she was as before—wonderful and sweet. As I started to approach her, she noticed me and excused herself from her current conversation. Her eyes opened wide, and she called out my name with excitement. But as quickly as she smiled, she caught herself, and suddenly her disposition changed. She became a little more serious.

I was confused but brushed it off as my misinterpretation of the situation. I should have known better.

We made some small talk and discussed the brand new and high-tech office. Then, Kaya turned her head, nervously looking back towards the long hallway that led to the other offices behind her.

"Preston is in the back somewhere. It will probably be hard to find him with all these people…but we can try," she said, almost as if to discourage me from seeing him.

Something's not right.

Kaya led me through a sea of people, each group moving as if they were waves of bodies going from one location to the next.

And then I saw Preston. His back was toward me, and as always, he was graciously listening to a client relay what seemed an exhaustive story. Kaya took his arm, apologized for interrupting the conversation, and said, "Someone special is here to see you." She rubbed my arm, smiled almost consolingly, and walked away.

That's odd. Really odd.

When Preston turned around, I could not believe how much he had aged.

He looked worn—like one of my older professors at school with bushy eyebrows and deep-set lines in his forehead. I also saw the same conflicting response upon seeing me as Kaya had displayed. He hugged me but was careful not to embrace me long.

What is happening here?

"Umm, Manna, uhhh…it's so great to see you! Thank you for coming," he said courteously as if I was a friend of a friend of a friend whom he had met once but couldn't remember when.

I smiled, too stunned to find the wherewithal to do anything else.

Preston sighed and then put his hand on my left shoulder, "Why don't we step outside; it's so noisy in here."

This isn't good.

He led me out a glass door that opened into a small courtyard.

Like I had done earlier with Kaya, we made some small talk about his new office. When there was nothing else to discuss about that, Preston looked down in the awkward silence.

I decided to get to the point and not waste time. "Preston, thank you for your card and letter. I came back from vacation and saw your invitation to your grand opening. I thought it would be nice to surprise you and for us to see each other after such a long time at this special event commemorating you and all your hard work. Congratulations."

"Umm, thank you…it *is* a wonderful surprise to see you."

I gave him the gift I had bought him for the grand opening. "Oh Manna, you didn't need to do that," he said, flustered. "Thank you so very much—it's just great…really great. You're always so thoughtful. Thank you. Really, thank you."

Silence.

Oh, my goodness. Here we go again.

Not dreaming we would be having a repeat performance of almost five years before, I found myself in shock that I was actually going through this once more. "Okay, Preston. This is silly. I'm going to leave because clearly, you are very uncomfortable with my presence here. This is your special time, and you should be enjoying every moment of it. I don't want you to be anything but happy on this eventful day. I'm sorry I came."

He said nothing.

I reached over to give him a hug, and he awkwardly offered to walk me to the door.

Walk me to the door? Are you flippin' kidding me?

"No, that won't be necessary. I don't know why you said what you said in your letter, or why you invited me to your party, but no matter. There's obviously nothing we have to say to each other anymore. Goodbye, Preston."

And with that goodbye, I turned and reentered the building. Preston did not follow. The cacophony of noise was almost deafening, and like a cat on a hot tin roof, I maneuvered around the masses of people as quickly as I could, desperate to get out of there.

Together with the commotion of all that was going on around me, and the sound of my heart pounding in my ears, I did not hear my name being called. It wasn't until I felt someone pull on my arm that I turned around.

Kaya had both compassion and love in her eyes. She took both of my hands in hers and smiled. I bit my lip and tried to return her smile. I didn't want to speak because I was afraid I would put her in a difficult position. Preston was her boss, mentor, and friend, and her loyalties belonged to him and to him alone. She owed me nothing. I didn't even expect her to say goodbye.

"Manna, it's not you," she said sorrowfully

I exhaled slowly, trying to compose myself while simultaneously fighting the intense impulse to bolt.

"I'm sorry, Kaya," I blurted. "I thought this would be a fun surprise. I don't know what could have changed in a few weeks. I'm sorry to have made you or Preston uncomfortable. It was a mistake for me to have come. Thank you for always being so kind and gracious to me." As I reached over to hug her goodbye, she whispered something that almost made my knees buckle.

"*What? What did you say?*" I asked incredulously, pulling away from the hug.

"Yes, Preston is going to have a baby."

Stunned, speechless, and light-headed, I listened as she told me he had been in an on-again, off-again relationship, but had ended it because he knew she wasn't *the* one. But what he thought would be a simple break up turned out to be much more complicated. She was pregnant and keeping *his* baby. Preston felt he had no other option but to stay with her.

Oh, dear God…

I thanked her for being so kind and for putting herself on the line for me. I said a final goodbye and walked out the door.

Negotiating With Heaven

Shortly after this disappointment, I received a call from my Uncle Oliver. Since I rarely heard from him, I knew it had to be bad news. PoPo had suffered what seemed like a minor heart attack and was in the hospital.

My beloved GongGong had passed away six months earlier due to complications arising from a minor condition. He had taken his last breath (and a part of my heart) on the evening of March 11, 1993.

It was now six months later, and though PoPo was strong and resilient, she was overwhelmed with the loss of GongGong—her husband, best friend, and companion for over sixty-one years of life.

When I received the call, I was six hours away at a business conference. I packed everything in my car as quickly as possible and raced home. Reaching the city's old landmark hospital in record time, I raced through the heavy front doors, and bee-lined directly to "Information," where they directed me to the location of my sweet PoPo.

My heart was in my throat, and though I was alert and present to everything around me, people's voices were muffled and distorted. The world around me could not move quickly enough, and the only thing I knew was, *Get to PoPo!*

Finally, I arrived at the ward where my grandmother was. I saw the ICU sign and the placards that forbade anyone but authorized personnel to enter. I looked through the windows of the two large security doors blocking me from a person who had loved me so wholly and completely since my birth.

I knocked loudly, but no one seemed to be on the other side. I knocked and rattled the doors again, but still, there was no movement from the desk only ten feet away, and no nurses or any other medical staff were in sight. My breath was shallow, and I tried not to panic. I looked behind me and ran down the hall to see if there was someone else nearby who could let me in, but again, no one was there.

I was frantic. I raced back to the forbidding doors, searching for any signs or buttons I could push that would notify people on the other side of the doorway to let me in. Thankfully, I found a small call button almost hidden beside several other signs and pushed it several times. A slow-moving nurse dressed in the typical white dress uniform of the day eventually came to the door. She was shorter than me and had a gentle manner about her. "Please, nurse, I need to see my grandmother. May I please come in? Please?" I said, trying to control myself.

"I'm sorry, but who are you? And what is your grandmother's name?" The nurse replied, friendly but still irritated by my continuous buzzing.

After answering her questions, I continued, "I just found out she was here—I was away for work and raced back to see her. I don't know anything else. Please tell me, is she okay? I need to see her—I need to see PoPo—" I rambled, trembling.

"Oh, I see," she whispered slowly, assessing me. "Unfortunately, visiting hours ended well over an hour ago. Your grandmother is resting now, and we are watching her. I'm sorry. You'll have to come back in the morning."

With those words, she released the door, and it started to close. I instinctively blocked the door with my arm and stuck out my foot as an added restraint against the door.

I looked at her name badge and pleaded, "Nurse O'Brien, please. I mean no harm. I don't know how to explain this, but I need to see my PoPo. She means *everything* to me. I can't bear *not* to be with her. I just lost my grandfather only six months ago. My grandma needs me, and I need her. Please…" I paused. "I beg you. Please let me see her. I promise to be on my best behavior, to be quiet, and only to sit by her side. Please…" I pleaded with tears now streaming down my face.

She stared at me in silence as she breathed through her now flaring nostrils. Hers was the longest stare I had ever known. Perhaps she had compassion for me, perhaps she was afraid of the commotion I might cause, perhaps my angels intervened. Maybe it was a combination of all of those things, but after a few more moments, she finally yielded. "Follow me—but you must be quiet, and you must not get her excited!"

I nodded many times and exhaled deeply.

Following her down an indistinctly lit hallway, I noticed how dim the entire ward was. And except for the rhythmic tones of oxygen machines and intermittent beeps from other medical equipment, it was palpably silent.

We rounded a corner and continued down another hall before stopping at the entrance to my grandmother's room. She turned to me and, now smiling, said, "Remember, do not to make a fuss and do not get her excited! Control yourself!"

"Yes, Nurse O'Brien." I nodded several times. "I will. I will. Thank you so very much. Thank you, thank you..." I bumbled before stepping inside the doorway.

The little light by the night table wooed me in. My grandmother was looking the other way into the far corner of the room as if she was in deep thought. I tried to be quiet, but as soon as she heard me walk in, she turned and smiled.

Unfortunately, I *could not* contain myself, and the thought of doing so didn't even occur to me. Without an ounce of restraint, I bolted toward my sweet grandmother, crying out her name, "PoPo!" I fell onto her tummy, sobbing uncontrollably, and held her in my arms with all my might—doing the exact opposite of everything I had just promised Nurse O'Brien.

In that moment, nothing mattered except that I was with my PoPo. Maybe if I could hold on tight enough, she could never leave me. Death could not have her. She was safe in my determined arms.

I sobbed, blubbering uncontrollably for ten minutes or more. The threatening reality that my beloved PoPo could be taken away from me *forever* was not something I was prepared to accept. It may have been one thing when I was a little girl when I had no say and no power. But as an adult, I was never going to let that happen again. It may be one thing to separate us by oceans and continents when I was little, but I was not going to let anything separate us again. I know this sounds ridiculous, but at that moment, I was ready to challenge life and death itself, and I hung onto my PoPo with all my might! Nothing was going to tear me away from her again.

I grabbed some tissues after composing myself and pulled up a small chair to the left of her. "Please don't leave me, PoPo. I know you're really sad now that GongGong is gone. I know your being here is a result of your sadness, but we can make things better. Please don't leave me," I pleaded. "Please, I can't live without you. Please, PoPo, don't leave me. I will die. I don't know how to live without you!"

I started sobbing again and buried my head in her lap, wrapping my arms around her as tightly as I could.

PoPo didn't reply. She simply looked at me with sorrow in her eyes as she quietly combed my hair with her fingers. I looked up at her, and with a shaking voice and trembling lips I pleaded, "PoPo, you have to promise me. You can't die.

You have to stay. Please, promise me...PoPo, promise me."

She took a few slow, deep breaths, closed her eyes, and sank her head against her pillow. Her countenance was not one of someone in repose, but in serious contemplation. When she opened her eyes, she did not look at me at first. She looked up to the ceiling, and her eyes moved to the left and then to the right. She did this many times, as if in silent discussion with...*Someone*.

This explanation may sound very strange, but at that moment, I knew she was negotiating with God for more time here with me. She wanted to go home to heaven to be with GongGong and to see her parents, her beloved siblings, and dear friends, but her love for me was so strong that she was willing to endure— just for me—more loneliness, disappointments, and sadness in the ensuing years. She knew what was ahead of her, but instead of choosing peace and comfort, she chose to stay with me.

Every moment of her silent negotiations was like a decade to me, but I waited patiently, never once letting go of my hold of her, just like when I was a little girl in Hong Kong.

When the heavenly agreement was finalized, she looked at me, brushed my hair again with her fingertips, and rested her hand on my right shoulder. "Okay, Manna. I will stay."

I cried some more, but this time with relief and gratitude. We started to discuss the possibility of her living with me after she left the hospital, but she was certain neither my uncle nor my mother would approve of it. I could not understand why they would be so disagreeable to this living arrangement, but all she kept saying was, "Don't cause trouble. There's been enough in this family already. Just let it go. I'll be fine."

This conversation was one of many exasperating discussions in the years to follow. I didn't want to disobey PoPo, and I didn't want Uncle Oliver or my mother to be angry with her, thinking she was putting me up to it. But when PoPo was clearly getting too old to live by herself, I did eventually bring it up to my uncle, who quickly dismissed my offer, just as she had predicted he would. No matter what legitimate reason I offered, nothing would change his mind.

Life continued much the same after PoPo's release from the hospital, and I continued to see her a few times per week, cleaning her home, having lunch with her, and/or taking her to her doctor's appointments or to buy groceries. She cooked me more delicious meals, and then we'd enjoy a few of our favorite shows together—*Lawrence Welk*, *Ironside*, and *Murder She Wrote*.

One of PoPo's favorite pastimes was to find good deals, especially when grocery shopping. She would weave from one market to another, concentrating on the ticket prices for each item. Some of her favorite stores were next door to each other, but others were located many blocks away. This wasn't an issue on warm days, but in the cold rainy weather of Vancouver, it wasn't always easy to maintain this routine, carrying heavy bags of groceries into one store after another, only to save a penny or two per pound for yellow onions. Often, we would load the car with what we had and then drive to another location. I would have to find another parking spot in the frenetic streets of Chinatown, fill the meter with coins, and repeat the ritual. We'd go from store to store in the pouring rain, carrying umbrellas, looking for bargains, and accumulating more bags to carry. I didn't know how to tell her we were spending more time and money plugging the meters than what we were saving on the price per pound of vegetables.

One day after shopping (and getting soaking wet when a bus zoomed by and splashed everyone waiting at a crosswalk), I lost my temper. I told PoPo it was foolish to be doing what we were doing. "Next time, we will only go to a few of your favorite stores instead of spending all afternoon looking for a sale here or there and sometimes never finding them."

Her expression sank, and I knew I had hurt her. I felt horrible, and to this day, that memory still haunts me.

Time with our loved ones is so, so precious—and fleeting. Take the time to do the little things with your beloveds. They may be silly to you, but it may be the only source of joy or meaning they have. One day, these little things will be great treasures for you, and you'll only wish you were inconvenienced more before.

What I wouldn't give to have that opportunity again to be with my PoPo, to spend the afternoon with her looking for apples, ginger, bok choy, and the choicest pieces of chicken in the rain...

Take the Money and Run

In the meantime, Tristan's secret life was now a full-blown public mess. He was arrested for grand theft (to support a drug habit and other "businesses"). There were also *people* "looking for him." He was on the run.

Interestingly, even after everything he and I had been through, I was the one he called when he was released on bail. We agreed to meet, and as soon as he saw me, he ran toward me and held me, sobbing. I felt the weight of his remorse as his shoulders heaved while he cried in my arms. He apologized for messing up our marriage and thanked me for always being fair and letting him off the hook so easily.

"Tristan, I didn't want to cause you pain. I simply wanted us to do the right thing and be nice to one another. I'm sorry for my part of what happened, too," I said sadly. "We were both young, foolish, and ill-equipped...but you can begin again. I know there are still things to sort out with the courts, but you can start fresh now."

I asked him to get into the car, and we talked some more. He regretted ever being with his past girlfriend (who introduced him to his abject world) but didn't think he deserved more.

There was that lie again—that we are unworthy and undeserving of more. So, we settle, going down a path of crazy-making and never really know how to get back on the right track. That's why it's so important to know the Truth. The "stairway to heaven" may be a steep climb, but it's better than speeding down the "highway to hell."

For the next month, I helped Tristan the best I could. Though I now know it was very unwise, I secretly met him in dark alleys, gave him a brand-new waterproof sleeping bag, warm clothes, food, and a little cash. We also met at out-of-the-way diners where no one would imagine him to be, and I treated him to warm meals and took time to encourage him, strategize with him, and speak life and hope into him.

At one of those dinners, he told me the courts had been lenient with him. He was required to pay a hefty fine (permissible in installments) but could be a free man if he did community work, along with a few other requirements, since it was his first offense. He told me he wanted to move back to Rutherford once he completed his obligations, which would be soon. He could start over since no one there knew his current situation. He also told me his relationship with his ex-girlfriend was finally over. "I'm never going back to her. I'm ready to start over now."

I sighed with relief. Tristan was still not out of the woods, but this was a step in the right direction. He asked me to pay for his bus ticket when that time came, and after listening to his plans, I agreed.

Months passed, and then one day, I received a call from an unknown number. It was Tristan. He was ready to leave, and as promised, I agreed to meet him at the bus station.

After I purchased the ticket, we sat and talked. Then I handed him an envelope.

"What's this?" Tristan asked, surprised.

"It's a little something so you can pay for some necessities and a small room at a youth hostel for the next month until you get on your feet. I know your friends will help you, too, but I didn't want you to feel abandoned and helpless." I held back my tears as I looked at the devastated life sitting before me.

He opened the envelope and looked back up at me with eyes as big as saucers. "Manna! How much is in here?"

"It's thirty-five hundred dollars in twenties, so it will be easy for you to use as you need it. It's plenty to help you get started, but Tristan, this isn't play money. This is equivalent to seven thousand gross dollars for me. I hate to say it like that, but you need to know the reality of what it means for me to give this to you. You've often accused me of "rollin' in the dough." I want to dispel that myth for you. It's been very difficult for me to make a career in real estate. If you only knew the sacrifices I've had to make, and the cost and toll it takes on me, and on Michael. The money in this envelope is from my savings for Michael's future, for his education and other necessities...but I'm giving this to you because you promised me you have learned from your past, and you really want to start over." I looked down and paused before speaking again. "I believe in you and want more for you than you have settled for. If you are ever tempted to use this money foolishly or to go back to your old ways, then think of it as *Michael's money*. So, again, please, use this wisely."

"Yeah, sure," he said, eyeing the thick stack of cash in his hands. Just then, an announcement came over the loudspeaker for the passengers to board the bus. Tristan jumped up, "Time to go."

But something wasn't right in my spirit. "Not yet." Holding his hands, I forced him to look at me. "I need to know you are really going to take this new beginning seriously."

He stared back at me blankly and said nothing.

"Tristan, you are better than the voices you've been listening to," I continued, hoping to rally his spirit. "Do you remember all the success you had before? Well, you're going to have even greater stories than that in the days ahead. One day, you'll be able to use all these experiences for good. You'll share your victory with others and help them get back on track, too."

Tristan looked at me with empty eyes, wanting to believe.

"You have to be strong. I can't do this for you; no one can. You must finally do this for yourself. Everything that's happened could be part of a divine setup—the perfect plan to free you! You have it in you to triumph over this! *You can do this!*"

He continued to stare at me, his eyes revealing his torn spirit. He nodded, "I have to go. The bus is loading."

"I'm not letting you go until you can look me in the eyes and tell me you aren't going back to the old ways. Promise me."

He exhaled, gave me a hug, and said, "Yes! Yes, I promise."

I felt a battle waging for his liberation. I was willing to stand with him, but would he be willing and able to stand up *for himself?*

The announcement blared over the speaker again.

"I gotta go," he said. "I'll be fine. Now, stop talking so I can get going *to my future!*" he said with a roll of his eyes.

Oh dear...the moment of promise had passed.

My heart sank as his old self returned. I comforted myself with the fact that at least he was leaving town. All I could do was pray. The rest was up to him. It was just a matter of choice.

It always is.

"Call me collect when you arrive, okay?"

He nodded and then waved goodbye.

Stealing from a Baby

Almost two months passed, and I had not heard from Tristan. I began to worry. During the divorce, I'd had no choice but to distance myself from his two sisters and their families. I was saddened to have lost them in the divorce and had often contemplated the irony of it all; it was only because of my love and affection for them that I had even married Tristan!

It had been years since we last spoke, but now I thought about calling Simone and Marjorie to see if they had heard from Tristan. I was apprehensive. Maybe they blamed me for the downward spiral of Tristan's life. I didn't know.

Some more time went by, and I finally found the courage to call Simone to ask about her brother. It was awkward at first, and she told me she hadn't heard anything either, but soon, our conversation flowed more easily as I felt the discomfort of the past start to fall away. Over the following year, we were able to rebuild our friendship, and my nephews started to become a part of my and Michael's life again.

Almost four months had passed since Tristan and I saw each other at the bus station, and I had still not heard from him. So, I decided to call his old cell number one more time, hoping it wouldn't go to voicemail again.

"Hello?"

"Tristan! Is that you?" I almost shouted with relief.

"Yeah—who's this?" he snapped.

"Tristan, it's Manna," I replied hesitatingly.

"What d'ya want?" he retorted with irritation.

"Umm," I stuttered with shock. "I was worried about you and wanted to see if you were okay. I thought you were going to call me when you got to Rutherford."

"Yeah, well, I didn't." He said with hostility. "You're not my keeper! I don't have to check in with you!"

"No, no, you don't." I was taken aback. "I wasn't trying to be your *keeper*. I just wanted to make sure you were okay…where are you?"

"In Vancouver, where else?"

"*What?* I thought you left on the bus!"

"I got off after you left," he blatantly admitted without remorse. "What d'ya want? Your *precious* money back?" he taunted.

"Well, now that I know you didn't use it for its intended purpose, yes. That would be the right thing to do."

Tristan used some vile expletives and then blasted, "It's *my* money now, and I'll do whatever the @#$% I want with it! Are you an *Indian giver* now?"

I was *furious* but composed myself and pulled over in my car.

"None of that language is necessary. Do you remember what I told you about that money? I was saving it for Michael—*our* son! If it's not used to help you with your future, please return it."

I bit my tongue from saying more. I *so* wanted to remind him of the time he had asked Michael to bring him his piggy bank on one of his visits, lying that he was going to open a bank account for him, but had taken the money for his own selfish use instead, but I didn't. I had been generously adding to Michael's piggy bank, so he would be excited to see how much he had already accumulated and be inspired to save more. There were several hundred dollars there, but Tristan had deceived his own son and stolen that money from him.

I also fought back the urge to remind him that he had never paid child support, plus a litany of other offenses. I wanted to *level* him, hoping this would be the ground on which his knees would fall, and he would meet his true self. But I didn't.

He had brought out the worst in me *again*. I was incensed and took a deep breath to calm myself down. I refused to be drawn into his cesspool of hostility or to dignify his baseness.

Suddenly, a verse I had learned as a little girl came to my remembrance, "Be kind and humble. Don't be hateful and insult people just because they are hateful and insult you. Instead, treat everyone with kindness. You are God's chosen ones, and He will bless you."[3]

I took another deep breath. *What if I didn't want to be kind and humble anymore?* A third long breath.

Slowly, I came to realize my job was not to educate Tristan, nor was it my role to save him or free him. It never was. My job was simply to "be nice," to plant the seed and to show him there was another way. It was Tristan's job to do something with those opportunities *for himself*.

I also realized my outrage was not just at what Tristan had done or what he was saying. My aggravation was at the loss of a great opportunity for his freedom. When I understood this, my anger lifted, and what remained was, surprisingly, compassion. Just then, a peace filled me, and it felt as though something powerful had happened in the unseen realm. I was no longer entangled with Tristan. Whatever had connected us before was severed, and I had been released from him forever.

Unfortunately, just because I was at peace didn't mean he was. He began hurling vulgarities again, and his hateful invectives drew me back to our conversation. "Are you listening to me? Huh? Whatcha gonna do about it, b!#^&?"

"Tristan, I told you what I would like," I responded calmly.

"*Ha*! You're more stupid than I thought. And besides, the money's gone. End of conversation!" He hung up the phone.

That was the last time I heard anything about him until his mother called me seven years later.

Humble Pie

At the height of my career, to ensure I stayed humble, a wonderfully humiliating experience brought me back to earth.

There I was in my mid-thirties, and with my "no guts, no glory" attitude. I was literally on top of the world. In addition to my other blessings and successes, I had begun modeling again. I served on real estate board committees and led workshops both nationally and internationally. I was unattached, successful, and "living the dream."

On one unforgettable day, I was downtown at one of the city's more famous business towers and had just finished giving a presentation to a law partner at a prestigious firm. He wanted to sell his large extravagant home located in a coveted neighborhood. After being awarded this multi-million-dollar listing, I was feeling particularly full of myself as I came down the elevator. As the elevator door opened to the grand lobby, I noticed two groups of handsome businessmen in their equally attractive designer suits, holding crocodile skin briefcases, waiting for the elevator. They stepped aside as if the *sea* parted for me while I did my catwalk out of the elevator.

I was dressed to the nines in a designer red dress, adorned with a five-strand pearl necklace and matching earrings, soft hose to match my supple leather shoes, my Louis Vuitton purse slung over my shoulder, and my matching briefcase in the other hand. With each step, my ankle-length Italian handmade coat swung and danced behind me. The glorious three-story lobby boasted floor-to-ceiling windows and betrayed the men's eyes as I saw their reflection watching me *glide* through the lobby. The guards ahead of me were also watching me, as were the attendants at the concierge desk. They were all probably wondering, *Who is that goofball?* But in my grand delusion, I assumed they were admirers.

I felt like a princess at a ball, sauntering down the exquisite lobby, thinking I had a captivated audience of new admirers. However, that feeling did *not* last long.

The valet had seen me approach and brought my car around. Moments after the doorman opened the heavy glass doors for me, I missed a step on the outside entrance steps, and literally did a flying lunge forward, landing on all fours after rolling down three or four more stairs. To say I was horrified was an understatement!

Both of my knees were scraped and bloody, and my expensive silk hose ruined. The palms of my hands were also scraped and bloody, and my ego—yes, that silly thing—was totally crushed!

Immediately, I *knew* this fall was a lesson for me to learn. I got up as gracefully as possible, swooshing my hair back off my face. After I brushed the dirt off my beautiful coat, I turned back and gave a glaring look *at the stairs*—accusing them with my eyes of being ill-functioning while muttering something about how the inept architect had failed *miserably* in designing the entranceway to this formidable building.

Then, out of the corner of my eye, I noticed a few heads from inside the lobby of the building straining to see if I was okay. I dared not turn my head to look. What I saw out of the corner of my eye was enough! Once I got into the car and was a block away from any *witnesses*, I dropped my head on the steering wheel and repented for my arrogance. I think I sat parked in the car for about thirty minutes—unable to move beyond the much-needed, but terribly humbling, encounter.

I can honestly say that even though that incident happened over *two decades ago*, I have never forgotten that scene, nor that lesson. And I have never been full of myself like that again.

"Didn't like the taste of humble pie, did ya?" Leah managed to say in between her laughing fits.

"This is just further confirmation of what I was saying before. Lessons come to teach us how to be kinder and more authentic human beings, and as a verse I memorized says, 'Do not think of yourself more highly than you ought to think, but to think soberly…do not associate with high minded things (self-exaltation), but to associate with the humble. Do not be wise in your own opinion.'"[4]

"And '*Pride goes before destruction, a haughty spirit before a fall,*'" Leah said, pleased with herself. "Get it? Before *a fall? Get it?*"

"Yes, I get it. And yes, I'm fully aware of that verse. Thank you for adding to my pain, Leah."

"I guess God was more interested in your character than your comfort zone, little one!" Leah continued through her chuckling.

"I know. I know…that's why I'm sharing the story. It was 'a necessary evil,' so I didn't go too far down a smelly path of 'I'm all that!' But what I find more interesting than my horrifying trip down the stairs is that even though I had a lifetime of humble beginnings, it only took a few years to get my head so big God had to allow such a powerful lesson to humble me.

"I realized then that Jesus Himself never took credit for anything, never demanded accolades, nor did He demand to be served or to be outfitted like a king, even though He was one! Instead, He walked with everyday people, ate with them, shared with them, and served them. His character never erupted with self-aggrandizement. Rather, He gave deference to His Father, redirecting any attention to God, remaining humble while He did amazing things on this earth. If Jesus did this, then, *how dare I ask, or expect, to be exalted?*

"I knew then that I would always do my best to develop a character of humility—not shame, but a humble and modest heart. More than my fear of being embarrassed, I desired to be more like Jesus that stirred in my soul that day.

"Either I choose to fall on my knees willingly (in prayer and humbleness), or I will be taken down at the knees (as a consequence of being on a man-made pedestal)."

Leah looked down. "I will start on my knees too…and maybe there's still time for me to stand tall…"

We held each other's hand for a moment and noticed she was starting to feel sad. Not wanting to end on that note, I changed the subject. "Well, anyway . . . I have digressed."

"No, it was exactly what I needed to hear," Leah said, still smirking. "You've been true to your words…"

I tilted my head. "What do you mean?"

"You are indeed, *faaarr* from perfect, just like you said at the very beginning," Leah replied.

"Very funny," I smirked.

"I'm sorry…I'm not laughing *at* you, I'm…well, no, *I am* laughing *at* you. I can't lie. But all your stories just make me love you more. You're perfectly imperfect, and that's just perfect!"

I smiled. "Well, I'm glad I amuse you."

"You do, my dear. You do. Now, let's get back to business, shall we? What's up next?"

True Colors—The Green Old Nanny

There are seasons in our lives—and some last longer than others. The harder seasons are always the ones we wished were shorter in length and intensity, and the seasons of ease, we wish could last *forever*.

I'd had a season of levity and success, but that season was not without storms.

Although I was blessed with some great friends who stood alongside me, I was not without my fair share of disappointments and betrayals either. One such friend, whom I shall call Patsy, worked in the same office as I did. We became very good friends, and I loved her playfulness and her sense of humor. She embraced Michael as if he was her nephew, and I as if we were sisters; we were inseparable. We shared everything together—all of our failings, losses, brokenness, family issues, hobbies, the secret hopes for our lives, and our elation when some of our dreams became realities.

We traveled together and spent many weekends at each other's homes, sharing meals, entertaining, and just talking. I helped Patsy through a major health crisis, she shared life secrets (which I have kept to this day), and she empathized with me as I struggled in my relationships and with my fears.

As I have already explained, after the birth of Michael, my body changed dramatically. Today's options were simply not common then, and as time went on, regardless of the reassurances, I became increasingly consumed about what I saw as "deformities."

I was fit and exercised daily. I wore a size two and had a twenty-three-inch waist. By anyone else's standards, I looked great, but to me, my body was warped, and my heart and mind were in daily turmoil. Such were the thoughts of a wounded young woman who didn't know her identity beyond the outward appearances—looks, career success, and material gain.

Our culture has become much more open today about all sorts of private matters, but in those days, personal issues like these were considered very, very intimate, and handled with the utmost sensitivity.

Plastic surgery (also not very common twenty years ago) was an option, albeit an expensive one. I agonized over the idea for over a year, and finally, I booked an appointment with a plastic surgeon to discuss my possibilities. A few weeks later, I had a partial tummy tuck and breast augmentation.

I finally had relief from the emotional torment of my physical body and shared this private victory with a few of my closest friends who knew these steps were taken for my self-esteem, not manipulation. The breast augmentation was not radical, nor did I flaunt myself or dress inappropriately.

The one person whom I thought would be most happy for me was *my friend*, Patsy, so I was surprised when, underneath her feigned smile, I detected hostility. Still, I did not know the depths of her jealousy and bitter resentment until almost a year later at a New Year's Eve party.

The theme was "black and white." The men wore tuxedos, and nearly every woman, including myself, wore a black dress. Unlike some of the revealing "body-con" dresses we see today, the style back then was more modest, yet still beautiful.

That celebratory evening, everyone was having a great time—laughing, enjoying a delicious meal, and drinking multiple rounds of wine. At one point, a kind and jovial gentleman at the table, who was a friend to everyone there, decided to pay a compliment to each of the ladies. As it happened, I was the last to be acknowledged. "And Manna, you look beautiful too—as always," he noted.

No sooner had he concluded his compliment, Patsy, who sat across from me, narrowed her eyes, and yelled out, "She's not that beautiful and perfect! You can have a pair of perky boobs too for $5,000!"

Everyone gasped.

I was mortified!

Elise, another friend with whom I had shared my private victory, was seated beside me. With her mouth agape, she grabbed my arm in shock and stared at Patsy, as did I. No one knew how to respond, but *not* to respond would only serve to embarrass me further, so we all chuckled awkwardly as another guest quickly changed the topic. Elise, being the sweetheart she is, waited for an appropriate amount of time to pass and then excused herself to go to the ladies' room, asking if I would escort her.

I knew she wanted to give me a way of escape, and instead of going to the ladies' room, we went to the lobby where we could talk. Elise was utterly dismayed at the spitefulness of Patsy's remark. It was then that she confided that she knew of Patsy's jealousy of me but had no idea she would be that intentionally cruel.

"Manna! How awful! Even if plastic surgery *is* commonplace today, such ugliness from *a friend* would still be despicable!" Leah interjected, rattled.

I felt too disgraced to stay at the party, but I knew my sudden departure would only solidify her attempt to humiliate me. Thankfully, the music began shortly afterwards, and people were headed to the dance floor. This distraction was perfect, and I discretely retrieved my belongings and left. Elise covered for me, telling everyone my babysitter had called because Michael wasn't feeling well, and I had gone to take him home.

I didn't receive a call from Patsy that night to see if Michael or I were okay (which would have been her normal response). Neither did I receive a call the following day, or the day after that. Since we normally spoke many times throughout the day, her silence was an obvious indication she knew what she had done, and she was unwilling to discuss it with me.

After the fifth day, I called Patsy. She was cold and distant. After some moments of uncomfortable silence, I finally asked about her remark. Instead of apologizing, she unleashed her hitherto hidden anger toward me.

"I'm sick of you getting all the attention everywhere you go! You're successful, and you have a great son. You're nice, you're talented, you speak all these languages, and *you have the world at your fingertips*! Everyone loves you! It's just *not fair*!" she wailed into the phone. "The last time we were together at the park, someone thought I was Michael's grandmother or old nanny! Do you know how that made *me* feel? I'm not *that much* older than you! What the hell? I'm sick of it! *You can't have it all!*"

I was speechless. *Who is this person? Where is the friend whom I have loved, cared for, done so much for, and who has done so much for me?*

All I heard on the other side of the phone was huffing and puffing. I didn't know what to say, but I finally addressed the simplest comment first. "Patsy, I had nothing to do with the woman at the park, and I don't think you look like—"

"Oh, shut up!" she interrupted. "I know you didn't have anything to do with her comment, but she never said anything about you! I'm sick of you always getting the compliments and the attention! What about me? I hate standing beside you, and I hate always feeling old around you! Someone had to let the world know you're not perfect! Someone had to knock you down a few rungs!"

I remained silent for a long time. What could I say to someone clearly in so much pain, who saw me as the source of it—no matter how irrational that was?

"Why didn't you talk to me about these feelings? Why did you want to humiliate me—"

"I didn't plan it, but the opportunity came, and I took it! It was *perfect!*" she said firmly, with joyful emphasis on the word "perfect."

"So, you don't see anything wrong with what you did?"

"Nope."

"Wow…so, you don't feel bad about *any* of it?!"

"You had it coming," she seethed. "Like I said, I'm sick of everyone thinking you're so great!"

"Oh, Manna…" Leah said sorrowfully. "I don't know what to say or how to console you for that kind of attack."

"It was painful, but like Ralph Waldo Emerson says, 'What you do speaks so loudly that no one can hear what you are saying.' What Patsy did spoke more about her heart than what she could ever say about me. Out of the abundance of her heart, she had spoken."

"Well, then, if she had an abundance of anything, she was full of *manure*!" Leah huffed. "In thinking she could minimize you, she reduced herself! Did she ever apologize?"

"No, she never did. In fact, over the following months, she not only demonstrated no remorse—she grew more bitter and hateful towards me. Her husband encouraged her to repair our relationship, but she would only toss her head in indignation whenever she saw me. Needless to say, our friendship ended that fateful night."

"I can't believe her!" Leah exclaimed. "She was green with envy, and it made her sick—sick in the head! I feel sorry for her husband, and anyone else around her! It's best she stayed in your past. There's a reason why she didn't make it to your future. I'm glad she was taken out of your life early!"

"Yes, her true colors were revealed to me early. I guess this is all simply part of life's curriculum."

"And what course would this be called?" Leah asked.

"Well, I'm reminded of a Chinese Proverb, 'Outside noisy, inside empty.'"

"That's good, but I like my European ancestry's saying better, 'Not my circus, not my monkeys!'"

Not All That Glitters Is Gold

The sad lesson from Patsy is this: there are people in your life who will only love you when you're small and seemingly insignificant. They love to see you struggling, suffering towards your goals. They know of your sacrifices and what you've had to overcome, but when your harvest comes, they are furious. They are eaten alive with bitterness, jealousy, and resentment. Why? Because they're unwilling to do the hard work themselves and only continue digging a deeper pit of deception, loathing, and self-pity. It's an abyss that is dark, slimy, and endless. Furthermore, though Patsy and others may have envied the attention I was getting, what they didn't understand was that not all that glitters is gold. Some of the attention I was getting was terrifying.

I had recently moved into a new office, situated in a prestigious area above a well-known shopping mall. Upon entering for work one morning, I found an envelope under the door. The enclosed note was from a "secret admirer" who said he had noticed me in the mall.

I thought nothing more of it, but my intuition told me to file the letter—not throw it away. A week later, I found another envelope under my office door. This one contained the same handwriting and shared the same sentiments as the first note, but this time, the writer was a little bit more elaborate in describing his emotions for me. I was uncomfortable with what he had shared and immediately asked the receptionist and other colleagues if they had seen any strangers near my office. Each person I queried said they had not. I filed that note with the other.

Later that same week came another note, and the next week, still another. The messages became increasingly more graphic, and alarmingly, more violent. I became frightened and called the police. An investigator reviewed all of the notes and basically told me the fellow was a stalker. He advised me on what to be aware of and how to protect myself. Unfortunately, without any witnesses, there was nothing else he or the police could do at the time.

The detective gave me his card and a number to call if this continued, or if I felt I was in a dangerous situation. He assured me he would have a report written and officers would make their presence known around the mall more frequently. But that assurance gave me no comfort as far as what happened *before and after* office hours and during long stints at open houses where I was often alone or with Michael.

The next day, I found another note waiting for me under the door. I was afraid to open it this time and called the investigator right away. After discussing my options, it was finally suggested I get a protection dog. I researched several places specializing in this kind of training and asked my father to come with me. After all, handling dogs had been one of his specialties. We narrowed our search to three facilities and made appointments for them.

The one most memorable was the facility that trained Rottweilers. When we arrived, the trainer asked me to sit on a chair in the reception area while he went to bring the dog he thought would be perfect for me. He left through a Dutch door that led to an outdoor hallway. The top half of the door remained open, but he was careful to ensure the bottom half was tightly closed.

After a few minutes, I heard the sound of footsteps and panting from down that same hallway. I stood up and eagerly ran to the half-opened door. Suddenly, before seeing the trainer or the dog, I saw a huge shadow filling up the entire lower half of the wall directly ahead of me. *Is that the shadow of the dog?*

As the trainer approached, he asked me to step back from the door and to wait for his directions. I did so, but since I loved dogs and had no fear of them, I didn't step back very far. When the trainer opened the lower half of the door, he revealed Saldat, a young Rottweiler weighing over one hundred and fifty pounds with a head the size of a beach ball—literally.

I gulped and slowly stepped backward. The trainer had him on a leash and was in full control of him, but all I could see was the enormity of his head and the massive body attached to it. I gulped again, and slowly—ever so slowly—continued my journey backward until I absentmindedly fell into the same chair in which I had been told to sit earlier.

Saldat came closer and closer to me. I was unable to speak, my eyes fixed on him. Saldat was now toe-to-paw with me, and we were almost eye-to-eye too because of his massive size. Then, without warning, he playfully plopped his head on my lap. With his big brown eyes still looking up at me, he blinked as if to say, "Hi!" I laughed out loud with relief. His lower lids were almost drooping like a Basset hound, and he simply blinked again as if to say, "I love you…are you my new master? Can I come home with you now?"

I fell in love with him instantly and threw my arms around him. He turned his head sideways and received my embrace with many joyful snorts. My father and another longtime trainer who had come in unnoticed were all chuckling too, as they were curious about Saldat's approach. Though they knew he wouldn't harm me, apparently, he had never before behaved this way with anyone else, so they did not know what to expect.

When it was time to go, the trainer tried to pull Saldat away from me, but he tugged against the leash, straining his head toward me, and gave me his paw. He wanted to stay with me, and I wanted him to do just that, too. In fact, I wanted to take him right then and there, but my father insisted we meet with the other facilities and said we would be in touch very shortly.

We met with all the other trainers and their dogs, and though I desperately wanted Saldat as my own, we were afraid I wouldn't be able to control him because of his size. He would love me and protect me for certain, but I did not know if I would have the strength, when needed, to pull him back or restrain him.

In the end, we chose a smaller dog, a female German shepherd, but because of her specialized training, she was being saved for a situation that required her particular skills. However, the trainer agreed to let me have her temporarily with the understanding that, should the situation arise, I would return her. If I still needed a guard dog, they would find me another one.

While it was very embarrassing to walk around with a guard dog, we settled back into our routines after the initial novelty of it wore off. My colleagues and clients were supportive and, if nothing else, this unfortunate situation brought a heightened awareness of safety for all of us in the industry, especially the women.

A few months later, the detective in charge of my case called to inform me the stalker had finally been caught. Apparently, the guard dog presence around me worked, and he had moved on. The detective told me the man was a contractor working in the mall and was caught doing the same thing to another woman working in another office.

Serendipitously, the dog trainer called shortly afterwards to see how I was doing and to tell me they required their guard dog. Since my case had been resolved, I was no longer in need of a protection dog, and I let my new friend go.

This experience reminded me of how wonderful it was to have such a special friend, and I knew it was time to have a dog of my own.

Within a month, a client called me and told me she could no longer keep her dog due to a work transfer to another province. She asked if I knew of anyone who would be willing to take her pet. My eyes lit up at the thought.

Sydney, a beautiful two-year-old golden retriever, was soon a part of our little family.

Signed, Sealed, and Delivered

Although things had settled down, and I was no longer living in fear of being stalked, feelings of sadness still stirred in my heart. I didn't know why, since I seemed to have "the world at my fingertips." I went to see a counselor, and he quickly sensed the deep wounds underneath my armor of strength.

Over the next year, we talked about how I had overcome recent trials, and naturally, we discussed the ordeals of my childhood. We also worked through the disappointments surrounding my marriage, its failure, the madness surrounding the in-laws, the strain and pain of the divorce proceedings, the stress of being a working single mom, and how best to effectively rear Michael. I needed guidance on how to provide him with a consistent and loving home, how to teach and nurture him, and how to best fill the role of a father in his life. We also talked about what it was like for me to build a new business with no guarantee or consistency of income, how to be a good steward of my finances, and the pain of betrayal in relationships.

In one of our sessions, the counselor summarized my life in ten-year increments and showed me how—no matter what was thrown at me, I had overcome each decade with few to no resources.

I hadn't seen my life from that perspective before.

I had only seen my life as an unending list of battles I simply managed. His approach made me curious, and I wanted to learn more. I wanted to understand what skills I had unconsciously used to overcome obstacles, and how to apply those skills (and new ones) to get better and to do better in the future. I wanted to know how to finally put the past behind me.

I may have been victimized, but I was no victim.

He asked me to journal my thoughts. Instead of asking, "Why are these things were happening to me?" I was to ask, "How are we (God and I) going to get through this together? What is God teaching me through this? What is God revealing about me that needs correction and/or healing by going through this? How will I be better once this trial is over? How can I bless others while I'm going through this trial, and afterwards?"

When I finished writing, I put down my pen and exhaled loudly. *No wonder I was getting the wrong answers! I was asking the wrong questions!*

By asking better questions, I had the foundation to finally rebuild my life, not just dress it up. This gave me much needed hope that my life wasn't so messed up that I couldn't start over again. There was hope to live the life I was created for.

The counselor also asked me what I wanted to do to complete this decade's cycle, to put a metaphorical *period* at the end of this phase—something to not only liberate me but also catapult me into the next season of my life.

I contemplated the question, and after sharing a whirlwind of dreams, ideas, and goals with him, I looked up and saw he hadn't been moved by my passionate monologue.

"What's wrong? Does that sound crazy? Too much?" I inquired, worried I had revealed yet another foolish quality about myself.

"No, Manna, not at all," he replied. "That's all great! Knowing you, it's not only achievable, you'll probably accomplish it all by next summer. However, you didn't answer my question."

Perplexed, I recounted our conversation, "But isn't that exactly what you asked? How I want the next decade to be?"

"Not quite. I asked how you would like to *complete this decade*. How would you like to put a period at the end of this decade that will close this chapter of your life, so you can be clean, untangled, and free to start *a new chapter*?" he responded carefully.

I had naturally gravitated toward something fun, or something that would give me a reason to live. It had become a part of my nature to keep looking forward, to find the good in my circumstance. Some have even called me foolish or idealistic. I wasn't always able to find that hope, that silver lining, but I thank God for His divine interventions so that I could try again the next day.

The counselor kept his gaze on me

What is he asking me to do, exactly?

I looked down at my hands, fidgeting.

"Have you ever told your mother what Scham did to you?" he continued. "Have you ever confronted Scham himself?"

I stopped breathing when I heard those questions.

Discuss the perversion of my mother's husband with her? With them? Discuss anything sexual with her—or him? This is the woman who hurled menstrual pads and belts at me while screaming her hatred for me like a lunatic! Talk to Scham about anything, much less his sexual and physical abuse? Does he know what he's asking? Seriously?

After taking some time to control my emotions, I replied, "They would never listen. It would be a complete disaster."

"How do you know this for sure? It's been many years since then," the counselor insisted.

I debated the impossibility of his request for the remainder of our time together (and the majority of the next session), until the counselor finally came to his senses.

He then suggested another way for me to release my emotions; to give "that little girl" a voice after all these years. He asked me to write everything I wanted to say down in a letter, as an exercise to get my past out of my mind and my body and onto paper instead. At the end of the letter, I was to forgive them, and by doing so, he assured me I would be free of them once and for all.

It was not an easy exercise I could just robot through. In fact, it was brutal, and I had to stop many times. I procrastinated and wrestled with the task night and day for weeks. Eventually, the time came when I knew that the pain of remaining the same was greater than the fear of doing something different,[5] so I went back to my computer and began again.

I wrote and wrote and wrote, pouring out my heart, sobbing, and even shouting at my computer as if I were talking to each transgressor individually. I pounded out page after page, addressing each bully, and divulged the shameful secrets from our house of horrors.

Things I had tried to forget came crashing through. All the Technicolor memories assaulted me, one after another after another. I could not type fast enough, and what I could not type, I recorded onto a portable tape recorder for later transcription. I even recorded my sessions with the counselor, so I could later listen to what I had overcome. I allowed the disclosures to remind me of who I truly was, instead of what they had cursed over me.

I was not dirty and used; I was whole and precious. I was not stupid; I was intelligent and a very fast learner. I was not ugly; I was beautiful. It didn't matter if my mother didn't like me, or my hair got butchered. It didn't matter if I didn't have white skin or that my body changed after having a baby. I was *beautiful*. I was not useless or "good-for-nothing." I was created by God, Who has a great plan for me. And in spite of everything I had been through, my life will all be used for good.

After managing my life through denial, decorum, distraction, and displacement, I was able to assess my inadequacies accurately. I started appropriately acknowledging my strengths. I weighed my losses with my gifts in each circumstance, and though it was still painful, I was able to see how the trials had shaped me into a better person. I let myself go to the darkest places of my memory, reached for my lost soul, and brought it back from brokenness into healing.

In that one weekend alone, while Michael spent a few days fishing with my father, I typed over a hundred and fifteen pages. Finally, when I was too fatigued to feel any more anger, I took the necessary pieces from that outpouring and began crafting my letter.

On a new blank page, I began to write again.

It would be another two weeks before I could go back to reading what I had written, and admittedly, it took many more rewrites before I was able to share it with my counselor. My first attempts were not pretty. Rage roared through the first few pages. Bitterness and resentment came next, followed by self-righteousness, judgments, and condemnation. No, it wasn't pretty at all, but I gave myself permission to let the pus out of my heart. This opportunity was for me and for my liberation—not for anyone else. The ability to even contemplate forgiveness and be "obedient" to the process did not (and could not) come until I had acknowledged my pain and released all those other layers first.

I liken this process to a walk through a deserted field full of abandoned (but still active) land mines, which I found myself stepping on. Sometimes, I exploded with rage. Other times, my heart was blown to pieces. Completing this assignment was truly one of the most agonizing journeys I had ever taken. But I'm grateful I did because that was when my healing began. I had to get rid of the poison inside of me before I could do anything else.

The letter my counselor had asked me to write ended up becoming two letters—one to my stepfather and a separate one to my mother. Though exhausting, demanding, and painful, writing those letters proved to be as the counselor had predicted—liberating and empowering. I felt like a huge weight had been lifted off of me, and for the first time since I could remember, my breathing normalized. Before this, the only time I had been able to take deep breaths was when I was running—one of the other reasons why the counselor suspected running was so important to me.

With my new perspective, the counselor asked me once again to consider speaking to my mother and Scham. He suggested I use the letters as a beginning step for that conversation.

I refused at first, but after a few uncanny "coincidences" that confirmed what he was saying, I finally agreed. With the support of my counselor, I refined the letters, doing the best I could to be in as much equanimity about the matter as possible.

The day finally came, and I sent the letters, each one double registered, to their respective places of work. Since Scham had still forbidden us to see my mother, the only way to contact her was through messages given by PoPo, or on her pager. Not wanting to involve PoPo, I paged my mother, explaining that she and Scham would each be receiving a letter from me.

"Oh my! The suspense is unbearable!" Leah sat up. "What happened?!"

"Not what I had hoped, unfortunately. I was so naïve. Just because I was on a journey of healing didn't mean the members of my family were."

On a cold, rainy, windy October afternoon, a call came through on my office line.

"It's me. I got your letter," was all my mother said.

I took a deep breath and braced myself. "Hi, Mom…when did you get it?"

"A few days ago," she answered pointedly.

Hmmm…they must have conferred with each other then…

"How are you, Mom?"

Silence.

I struggled to make some kind of conversation. "I always ask PoPo about you, and she tells me you're really busy with all of Huxley's activities. I'm happy you have the time now to enjoy those things…"

More silence.

I continued, "Ummm…I left messages for you to call me. Since I'm not allowed to see you and I don't hear from you, I didn't know what else to do but write you a letter."

Nothing.

She wasn't going to make this easy, so I dove in. "Mom," I sighed. "The things in our past have been painful and very destructive. I need to move on. And the only way I can see to do that is to talk to you about them. Could we do that?"

Nothing.

"My intention in sending the letter was not to hurt you, but…I needed…" Not able to find the words, I tearfully blurted out, "I love you, Mom, I just want…I just want…*you!* I miss you. I miss having a mom. I needed you when I was little, but I'm no longer little. Can we start fresh now? I would love to have you in our lives—even if it's only every other month for a quick visit. I'll take whatever you can give me. You only live thirty minutes away. It can't be that hard to meet…"

Those were the pleas of the little girl inside of me. *What is so wrong with me that you hate me so much? Tell me so I can apologize and fix it and be better! Don't leave me in torturous place of limbo!*

Still nothing.

Not knowing what to do with the cutting silence, I remained quiet a few more moments myself.

Is she upset? Is she rejecting my offer to start anew? Why isn't she talking? What is she thinking?

Suddenly, there was a check in my spirit, and I knew to gird myself for what was about to come.

"Manna, I want to talk about what you accused Scham of," my mother said callously.

What? What did she just say?

I was dumbfounded.

She never said a word about my heartfelt plea, my profession of love, or my invitation to be a part of our lives. Neither did she try to comfort me in my obvious sadness and genuine desire and need for a mom—*my mom*. At that moment, she had revealed her position, and although I was afraid to speak up to her, I had no other option. This was finally my time to give that little girl inside of me a voice.

"Mom," I said firmly, "I'm not *accusing* Scham of anything. I'm *telling* you what he did. You were there to see how he beat us! Do you really want me to remind you of each incident? And you know in your heart he molested me many times! It's sickening even having to discuss this, much less to have to prove myself to you. I can't believe you're even challenging me on this! Don't you remember how even *you* used to try to hide me in the bathroom when I was little? Why do you think I learned to hide there? It's the only room that has a lock on it!"

I heard her breathing, but she still said nothing.

I continued, "I'm sorry I had to write a letter, but I had no choice. And I'm afraid for Huxley."

"You leave her of this!" she shouted, "She's fine. You don't have any proof!"

Are you kidding me right now? You're defending him?

I bolted out of my chair and stood up resolutely. "I do have proof," I said decisively. "I have diaries, journals, and counselors who will verify everything I've said. Even the counselor at my old high school knows the truth. It's in their records. The only reason I didn't pursue this then was because I was *only trying to protect you!* I have friends who witnessed my bruises, and they were my confidants when I had no one else to turn to." I let out a huge breath and continued. "And while we're at it, do you really think our old nannies, your nursing friends, neighbors, and the rest of the family did not know how abusive Scham was? Every neighbor around us would gladly testify against him. Furthermore, *Mother*, do you *really* think a child could make up all these things? How did I, as a seven-year-old, know about molestation until Scham violated me?"

Neither one of us spoke for a long while.

Why is she taking his side? Why isn't she saying she's sorry for all we've been through? She saw how Scham beat us, how he treated us. I certainly know she remembers how she treated me! This is madness! Lunacy!

Then, of all the atrocious things my mother had ever said or done to me, nothing could have prepared me for her next statement.

"I don't believe you, Manna," she said coldly and determined.

Everything started to go white around my vision, and I felt lightheaded. All I could hear was the pelting of the cold October rain against the windows as her last words repeated themselves in my head like a ghastly echo in a horror movie.... *I don't believe you, Manna.*

Breathe. I had to tell myself. *Breathe.*

Finally, I responded, "Are you calling me a liar?"

No answer.

"Are you saying you would rather believe that lowlife than your own daughter? He's done nothing but bring destruction, division, and suffering to our entire family! And you're choosing to believe *him* over me—your daughter, someone who's done nothing but try to please, help, and even protect you all her life?!"

Silence.

"Mom! Say something!"

Nothing.

My heart was pounding, and I was breathing heavily, but still, not a word came from my mother.

Finally, after a long while, I spoke.

Solemnly, I said, "Your silence is deafening. Your *non*-answer shouts louder than anything you could ever say. It's one thing to be an unwanted child, but to be discarded over and over again in my life is almost unbearable." I exhaled and continued slowly, "I wish I had been adopted. At least then I would only have been given up once. But you have given me away not just once, but *many times, every day* of my life. But today is the last day you will do that. Today, I put a final period on this madness. It's over. I've done everything in my power to try to fix, restore, and heal whatever this unspeakably cruel relationship with you is. I'm done."

Silence.

Despite what I said, I *desperately* wanted to be wrong. Yes, even in spite of everything that had just occurred. Hoping against hope there could be even a nano-sliver of a possibility that my own mother would fight for me, I dared to ask, "Do you have nothing to say, *Mother*?"

Silence.

I exhaled and said, "Well, then, you've said more than enough. I know you have a full and wonderful life with Huxley, and it's almost time to pick up her up from ballet, so I'll let you go."

Silence.

My heart was shredded. Tears steadily flowed now, and I could not see the phone on the desk through them.

Still, no sound came from the other end.

I slowly pulled my hand away from my ear and lowered the receiver to replace it on its cradle. My head followed the receiver, as the little girl inside of me *still* clutched onto the dead hope she would hear her mother call her name.

My hand was now only inches away from the phone base, but my mother did not say a word, and she did not call my name.

I placed the receiver on its cradle.

Click.

The final period.

An Encounter With Heaven

"Leah, are you okay?!" I managed to ask as I reached over to help her adjust her pillows and handed her a glass of water.

"What kind of question is that?! How the hell is anyone supposed to be okay after hearing that?! It's bad enough to hear the story on its own merit, but to know the history! That was a chance of a lifetime for your mother!" Leah was incensed. "Jiminy Crickets and General Jackson!"

"I'm sorry, Leah. I told you these aren't easy stories to hear."

"Dear girl!" Leah exclaimed. "I'm fine! I worry about *you!* How can you tell these stories with such composure?!"

I let out a loud sigh. "It's been a *long* walk of healing, Leah."

Leah took my hand and let out a huge sigh too. "Yes, I'm sure it has. But look at you now…" Leah looked away for a moment and then said, "I wish I had met you many years ago. I would have doted on you the way you deserved and toughened you up a bit more. Through you, I would have learned the things I needed to, too. Then I wouldn't have wasted so much of my life. The nuns at school taught me about God…seems like eons ago now. I once had a relationship with Him the way you do, but I'm afraid it's too late for me," Leah said sadly with resignation.

"Leah, we both have scars that remain, but if God has done such amazing things for me, I know He can do that for you, too! It's never too late to hope, dream, and do something we've always wanted to. It's never too late to begin again, to change our old habits, and to learn from our past. It's never too late to apologize to those we've hurt. It's never too late to forgive those who have hurt us, and it's never too late to know God's love and to welcome Him back into your life."

Leah closed her eyes tightly, holding back the tears.

"I can't believe you're here trying to comfort me when you're the one who's been hurt so badly."

"Leah, this is what life is all about, to recognize how we have been so richly blessed, so we might be a blessing back to others."

Leah opened her eyes, tears falling on each side of her cheeks. "Manna," she said softly, almost childlike. "Will you help me? Will you help me find this peace that you have? I so want that…I want to know this, this 'peace' before…"

"Yes, we can do it right now if you want. How do you feel about saying a little prayer with me?" I asked.

"I would love to."

"Okay, repeat after me…

> Dear God, I am tired and weary. I don't know what else to do or where else to go. It's difficult to trust in things or in people, but I am willing to trust in You. Please forgive me for all my wrongdoings, known and unknown to my conscious mind. I often live by habit and am not always aware of all my mistakes, shortcomings, or weaknesses. Please forgive me for the things I do, which I know are wrong but can't seem to stop myself from

doing. It's been much easier to blame others—and You—so I didn't have to take responsibility for it all. I'm sorry. The results of living this way are painful, and what I've settled for is no longer acceptable. I want to change my ways and am ready to do so with You. I don't know how to do this or what this will look like, but I am willing to try and to learn. I need You, and I believe in You. I declare by faith that you are the one true God. I believe that Jesus is Your Son and my Lord and Savior, and because He exchanged His life for my own, I am now saved, redeemed, and free. I can be with You forever. Please show me how to live a full and meaningful life. Whatever time I have left, I want to make the best of it. Soften my heart so I can be more like You. I dedicate my life to You now. Protect me and guide me. Live in me now and be with me forever. Thank You, God. In Jesus' Name, I pray. Amen."

I looked up and saw a steady flow of tears flowing down Leah's cheeks. I remained silent, letting the beauty and wonder of this precious moment sink in.

Leah started to smile, and with eyes still closed, she tilted her head and leaned her shoulder away from where I was sitting. I continued watching curiously.

What is going on? Is she having a conversation with someone beside her?

Then, as if to answer my questions, she opened her eyes and looked at me with her Cheshire-cat look again. "I bet you're wondering what's going on, huh?" she asked teasingly.

"Yes, kinda!" I responded, eagerly waiting for her to fill me in.

She closed her eyes again. "I promise I'm not making this up, but I'm listening to the most beautiful music in the world! It's like nothing I've heard before, and trust me, Thomas and I have been around the world. No symphony ever sounded like this!"

I smiled and nodded, knowing exactly what she was referring to.

"And…" Leah continued, "I heard a voice say something very curious to me."

I waited in suspense, but I dared not interrupt. She slowly rocked back and forth, side-to-side, moving to the rhythm of the music only she was hearing. Finally, when I couldn't stand it anymore, I asked, "What did the voice say, Leah?"

"I heard a very distinguished gentleman say, 'Welcome to the family! We're having a birthday party for you!'" She opened her eyes and started giggling repeatedly.

"What's so funny?"

"It's not my birthday!"

"Well, maybe it *is*…"

We spent the rest of the day talking about what Leah called her encounter with heaven.

"Now, you're not the only one who was touched by an angel!" she said proudly.

I explained that not everyone *needs* to have this kind of experience after inviting God into their lives. Many people don't *feel* anything different afterward, and that's totally okay. We are all created differently, and we experience things differently.

We talked a lot about "life," and by the end of the visit, we resolved that our simple human minds could not begin to comprehend the weightier matters of it. After all, if remembering where we put our car keys is challenging, how in the world could we dare assume we could understand the mysteries of the universe?

Just then, Melody came in with Leah's dinner. "No more stories," I smiled as I helped adjust her bed for her evening meal. "Time to have a bite and then get some rest. It's been a big day."

Leah gave me a long hug, but before I walked out the door, I turned around and said, "Happy birthday!"

Leah beamed a smile that will warm my heart for the rest of my life.

Two's Company, Three's a Crowd

Our next visit was filled with excitement and animation. Leah looked ten years younger and had a sparkle in her eye I hadn't seen before.

"Oh, my goodness! You look amazing, Leah!" I proclaimed.

"Why are you so surprised? Did I look that bad before?"

"No, of course not, silly goose, but something is very different about you today."

"I had a good sleep," she joked.

"Is that all?"

"I put on some makeup," she added without a moment's hesitation.

I smiled and gave her a big hug.

"Leah, I forgot to ask you last time, but when *is* your birthday on this side of heaven?"

"My birthday isn't for a few months, so don't you go fussin'. I'm too old to force a smile through these bad teeth and pretend to be happy just so everyone else doesn't feel guilty. Plus, I highly doubt I'll still be here…now promise me you won't make a fuss!"

The reality (and pragmatism) of her statement hit me, but I did my best not to show it. "Okay," I said. "But you can't stop me from doing something for you."

"You've done plenty already," she winked. "You have given me more than I could ever imagine, and I'll be forever grateful." She took my hand and squeezed it tightly. "How about we go to the courtyard again? It feels better when I'm outdoors and in nature."

"Let's do it."

We found our usual spot and settled in. Leah shared a few comedic stories of the lady in the room next door, and some ongoing drama at the nurses' station.

"But enough of that, my dear," she said, waving the subject away. "In your last conversation with your mother, you mentioned Huxley. Did you ever see her again?"

"Actually, I did end up seeing her again, but when I did, she was no longer a young child but a young woman in her early twenties. To make a long story short, I felt as though I needed to make up for lost time and offered to take her under my wing. I gave her a position as my assistant, training and teaching her everything I knew about my industry. I imagined that, basically, she would walk into a ready-made business shared with Michael one day. She was only working odd jobs at the time and jumped at the opportunity to work with me. The promise of a successful career was too good to pass up.

I introduced her to every contact I had, took her to the finest restaurants, gave her carte blanche to everything I had on the computer, helped her financially, and blessed her with gifts. It felt like she was my own daughter, especially since she was mine to basically care for the first two years of her life. But I may have been too 'motherly' for her."

"What do you mean?" Leah asked.

"I worried about her because her personality and behaviors were rough and coarse. She had a terrible temper, a sharp tongue, and her skills of manipulation and control were too honed for anyone her age—any of any age."

"Uh-no. The 'spoiled rotten' child!" Leah jumped in.

"My mother and I had still not seen each other or spoken since our call that dreary fall day, but through Huxley, I was told my mother was agreeable to meeting."

"Made sense, since you basically showered 'her daughter' with a great life," Leah retorted.

"Yes, one which she never had to work for or sacrifice for, like I did."

Leah harrumphed.

"My mother bought Huxley an expensive, brand-new condo in an up-and-coming area of the downtown core. And she maxed out credit cards to pay for all the furniture, decorations, and so on to make it perfect—just the way Huxley wanted it. Then, she helped her get a brand-new BMW."

"*What?*" Leah shouted.

"I know. There's more, but, well, you get the picture."

Huxley knew I hadn't seen *her* mother for a very long time, so she took it upon herself to arrange a meeting between the two of us. I wasn't sure it was a good idea, but Huxley assured me it would be fine and that my mother was looking forward to it.

My mother is looking forward to seeing me? *Really?*

Despite having thought I had closed my heart to her after our infamous phone conversation, the "little Manna" inside burst with excitement at the thought. So, after weeks of Huxley insisting on a meeting, I agreed. What I didn't realize was my mother was perfectly content with having just "one" daughter, Huxley. And while she was open to *seeing* me, having *a relationship* with me was something completely different. I was like a third shoe to her—useless. But the day came. I parked the car and waited with Huxley and Michael for my mother to come.

When I finally saw her for the first time after so many years, feelings of love overwhelmed me. I tried to stay calm, reviewing the instant mental slide show of all the different experiences I'd had with her. I was torn between excitement and *extreme* caution.

Then, suddenly, I realized I was looking at *my mother*, and I threw caution to the wind, ran to her, and threw my arms around her. I no longer cared about the past or what had happened. I just wanted to have *my mom*. So, there I stood, sobbing on her shoulders, crying out loud, "Mom, I've missed you so much! Oh, Mom, I love you…I love you…" I blurted in between my sobs.

Huxley was overcome by emotion, too, and had to walk away. Michael, still so young, did not know my history with my mother, but he knew I was sad and clung to my leg, trying to comfort me. Tears also ran down his cheeks out of compassion because he rarely saw me cry.

"What did your mother do? What did she say?" Leah asked excitedly.

"Nothing."

Leah pulled her head and shoulders back in shock. "What? What do you mean, *nothing*?"

"Just that. Nothing."

"Nothing?!" Leah shouted, frustration starting to boil. "You're sobbing on her shoulders—her firstborn that she hasn't seen in what, seven? Eight? Ten years? She didn't say or do anything?"

"No. Not at first."

"Why? Was she sad? Did she even hug you back?" Leah persisted.

"No. Her arms stayed straight by her side."

"*What?*" Leah exclaimed again, flabbergasted. "Well, what *did she say* when she finally spoke?"

"Stop crying."

"That's it?!" Leah shouted. "*That's it?*"

"Yes."

"What did you do?"

"I stopped crying. And I never cried for her again, ever."

Leah simply shook her head in disbelief.

"Then, many months later, I was presented with another test—the ultimate test," I said slowly. "I agreed to go to my mother and Scham's new house for dinner."

"*What…did…you…say?*" Leah gasped, the shock almost making her wheeze. "Yes, dinner with my mother… and Scham."

Face to Face With Your Enemy

y mother and Scham were thankful for all I was doing for Huxley, so they invited Michael and me over for a casual dinner.

All my life, I had tried to create some semblance of a relationship with my mother, but despite my staunchest efforts, nothing availed me to her. And after our last meeting, I had shut my heart off to her for the last time. Yet here was another opportunity to connect with both of them.

Maybe the counselor was right…

Still, I politely declined the offer.

But, once again, Huxley kept insisting I go. Finally, after many months of excuses, I agreed to dinner.

When I rang the doorbell, Huxley opened the door and invited Michael and me in. I brought flowers and a few gifts, entering nervously. My mother greeted me at the top of the stairs, welcomed me to their home and quickly showed me around.

When we got to the kitchen, I came face-to-face with Scham for the first time in two decades. This time, however, I was no longer the little girl he knew. I was a grown woman, standing nearly as tall as he was, and I might add, with many years of martial arts training under my belt.

Of course, I had no intention of fighting him, but now I knew I could defend myself if I had to. I was no longer little and helpless.

It took every bit of strength, every ounce of courage, and a battalion of angels to help me stand face-to-face with my abuser. But interestingly, there was no anger, resentment, bitterness, or any thought of retaliation towards him. None at all. The only emotion I felt was compassion. True compassion. I didn't want to be his friend, but I knew instantly, down to the core, my hard work had paid off. God delivered what He promised—freedom."

It wasn't easy preparing for the visit, nor was it easy at any time during the visit. Every moment was like an exclamation mark, and I remember almost everything. We exchanged some social niceties, and I thanked him for inviting us into his home. He seemed sincerely happy to see us. His accent was still noticeable, but not as heavy as it was before. Scham was no longer the young, strong man of his youth. He suffered spine problems and wore thick glasses.

He asked us to sit down at a small kitchen table. We all cumbersomely maneuvered around it. I was uncomfortable, but talked myself down, trying to enjoy the opportunity of being with "my family," as bizarre as we were. As we all settled into our seats, Huxley went to her room.

I never told her anything about her father, nor did I tell her anything about her mother. To this day, I've never personally shared what her parents were like to Luke and me. Nor does she know what her father did specifically to me. To have burdened her with such issues would have been unfair.

""I can't even *begin* to imagine what it was like for you to see him again," Leah responded in awe. "Why didn't you tell her later? I'm sure you had lots of opportunities to talk."

"Well, our relationship didn't go much further after that."

"Uh oh..." Leah said quietly.

As they spoke, I faded in and out of the conversation, looking around inconspicuously. I wanted to see if I recognized anything from my life with them before. The beautiful upright piano my father had purchased for us as children was gone. In its place was a beautiful new baby grand for Huxley, who had completed the majority of her private tutelage at a renowned music academy. Like my reaction to Scham, I was surprised to discover I felt no animosity or jealousy toward her. She was an innocent coming into this world, and how we were treated wasn't her fault.

When it was time for dinner, my mother asked us to go to the dining room. At that time, Scham made the most amazing statement as he stood on the opposite side of the dining table. *"Vell,* you guys have dinner now. I'll go," he said with a sheepish tone.

All of us stood dumbfounded, not knowing what to say, but I knew deep down why he was so uncomfortable and wanted to leave.

"Why are you going?" I spoke up.

"You guys are family; eat by yourselves. I deserve to eat *outside vis* the dog, *ver* I belong." He said it half-jokingly, but in his heart, he meant exactly what he said.

"No, Scham, don't go. It would mean a lot to me if we could enjoy this time *together*...please," I asked again.

No one had spoken up but me. Scham looked at me but couldn't hold my gaze. Again, jokingly, but with heart-wrenching sincerity, he insisted that he deserved to go outside where "dogs belonged." My heart was so moved by his humility that I reached across from the table and grabbed his hands—the same hands he had used to hit me, throw me across the room, yank out my hair, and molest me—and asked him to stay and enjoy dinner with all of us.

Michael looked up at me with great big eyes and leaned into my legs. Huxley, while not knowing all the details, obviously suspected something, watching to see what her father would do. My mother looked away, silent. Eventually, Scham agreed to stay, and we all sat down for what appeared to be a "normal" dinner.

But it was anything but normal!

It was *amazing,* for I had achieved the impossible. I had met my enemy face to face and felt nothing but compassion and peace. Forgiveness is for the forgiver indeed.

"I'm flabbergasted," Leah finally said after a few minutes of silence. "I never suspected you would have seen him again. And then, to have no feelings of anger or retaliation? That's way over the top!"

"Yes. It was nothing less than a miracle."

"It had to be," Leah grimaced. "Did you see Scham again after that?"

"Yes, several times. In fact, and he even came to my wedding."

"*What?* You're going to give me a heart attack!"

I smiled. "Yes, but I'm getting ahead of myself."

"Well, hurry up then!" Leah said excitedly. "Honestly, nothing surprises me anymore with you! The next thing you'll tell me is that you had dinner with the President or some other world leader!"

"Well, now that you mention it…I didn't, but my father was personally invited by Menachem Begin to have afternoon tea at his private residence in Tel Aviv many years ago."

"Of course, he was!" Leah said as she hit her forehead with her hand, jesting exasperation.

11 MARRIED! BURIED!

Out of suffering have emerged the strongest souls; the most massive characters are seared with scars.

—Kahil Gibran

The Check's in the Mail

"There are so many twists and turns and ups and downs in your life," Leah said, shaking her head. "Unless I knew you, I would have a hard time believing all these things happened to one person."

"I know. It's crazy, isn't it?" I concurred.

"And by the way, it doesn't surprise me that your relationship with Huxley didn't work out; she was raised fully by your mother and Scham! Sounds like she got everything she wanted anyway," Leah concluded. "At least you and Luke had other solid family members, and other than Patsy, I'm sure you had good friends."

"Yes, other than the obvious, my family is great, and yes, I have wonderful friends who were godsends to me back then. Were it not for them, I don't know how I would have made it through those tumultuous times. However, as in all things, to know what is true and pure, whatever we deem 'valuable' needs to be challenged and tried. Whether it's rope, to know its strength to carry weight, gold to know its purity, love to know its commitment, or faith to know it's real, relationships also need to be tested.

"While not every friendship is meant to travel on the same road forever, I believe true friendships can endure trials, different callings, distance, and time apart—and *still* be genuine, caring, and supportive.

"One such example is with a woman I'll call Barbara. We were great friends, and it was with this affection that I agreed to loan her money to buy her own condo. At first, I had only agreed to a small amount, but when it came time to move forward with the contract, she told me she needed five times as much. Hearing the amount actually made me lightheaded. I knew I was not supposed to loan her that amount of money." I paused. "I'm embarrassed to share the next part…"

"No! Don't even tell me…"

"Yes, I did. I didn't have the courage to say no. I foolishly believed I was breaking my agreement to her if I didn't loan her the money. Barbara had her heart set on this condo, and she and her significant other had already started making preparations and telling people about it."

"You're *kidding* me!" Leah moaned. "You believed that crap?"

"Yes, I know how absolutely ridiculous it all sounds. Were the situation to present itself today, we wouldn't be having this conversation. However, as I have said many times, I'm not proud of some of the choices I've made. I'm very embarrassed to show my people-pleasing dysfunction and lack of strength once again. There are only so many times I can reiterate how wounded I was and how little I thought of myself. I was afraid of people and afraid of their rejection. It's easy to be brave from afar; it's much more difficult when the battle is inside your soul. So, yes, I regretfully loaned her the money."

"Oh, Manna," Leah said sadly.

"I know, it wasn't good at first, but it did turn out for good in the end," I assured her.

"What happened?"

"Unfortunately, when it came time to repay her loan, she denied I had loaned her the money."

"*What*?" Leah shouted, sitting up in bed as if she were about to get up, find, and fight Barbara. It was as endearing as it was adorable and comic.

"It wasn't pretty, and attorneys were involved. I'll spare you the ugly details. Suffice it to say she did eventually make payments, but not all of it was paid back. I let it go and didn't push for the remaining balance. I cared more about her than I did about the money.

"Besides, if anyone was to blame in this mess, it was *me*. I could have refused to make the loan, but I didn't. My loss was the cost of that lesson. Learning the principles of self-honor was no one's responsibility but my own. I was thankful to be repaid what I was and thankful I didn't lose more."

Leah thought quietly and then added, "Do you remember what Hamlet said? 'Neither a borrower nor a lender be, for loan oft loses both itself and friend, and borrowing dulls the edge of husbandry. This above all; to thine own self be true, and it must follow as the night the day, thou canst not then be false to any man.'"

After she quoted Hamlet, Leah took my hand, looked into my eyes, and said, "I'm glad you're learning. Always remember, to thine own self be true…you canst be false to *you*!"

Love at First Sight

In the midst of Barbara's buying her condo, she took a computer technology workshop and loved it. She learned so much that she hired the speaker to help her with her business. She implored me to go with her to the next conference, believing it would help me streamline my work, and have more free time for myself. The only negative was that the seminar was being held in Portland, Oregon.

I politely refused because I was so busy and didn't want to take the time away to go to the weekend event. "That's exactly why you need to go," Barbara responded.

For the next two months, she was relentless. When I had no more excuses, I agreed to go with her. I figured I could make it work since I had been asked to speak at another event in the United States and could fly directly there from the conference.

Barbara thought it would be fun to make a road trip out of this event, but as we came into the city, I began to have a sharp stomachache and bent over in pain. The closer we got to the hotel where the conference was held, the worse the pain became. "Barbara—what is going on at this event? Something isn't right," I noted with trepidation as we pulled up to the hotel entrance.

I should have taken note of that inexplicable occurrence, but I had not yet come to understand my giftings and discernment. All I knew was that something was going to happen at that event, and I had a horrible adverse reaction to it.

We pulled up to the lobby, and she turned to me, excited for our trip. "Don't worry!" she smiled confidently. "It's just a seminar, and you don't have to buy any tapes or sign up for anything if you don't want to." With that, she eagerly bolted out the door and opened the trunk of the car to start unloading our suitcases.

We checked into our respective hotel rooms and started to unpack. *Maybe I'll go to the gym and work off some of this anxiety,* I thought to myself.

I walked through the lobby with the headphones to my Walkman on, making my way toward the fitness center. En route, I passed three men seated in the lobby, talking. I didn't yet have the music turned on, and I heard one of the men say, "Oh, my God, *who is that?*" No one else was in the lobby, so I felt flattered to think this comment might have been meant for me. I did not look back but continued on to the gym.

When I returned from working out, the same three men were seated in the same lobby chairs, apparently still discussing business.

"There she is again," I heard. "I have to find out who she is." This time, I noticed who did the talking. The elevator doors opened, and I stepped in. When I turned around to press the button for my floor, my eyes met the eyes of the man who had made these comments about me.

The following morning, I ran late. I was talking to Michael on the phone before he went to school (he was staying with my father while I attended the conference). Barbara had already gone down, and I met her at the entrance. She found us third-row seats, center to the stage, and I watched the room fill to almost five hundred participants.

Eventually, the room quieted, and we were welcomed. A man came onto the stage, made some announcements, and then introduced the speakers. The room burst into applause, some giving a standing ovation. Still unsure what I signed up for, I turned to see several men (including *the man* from the lobby) jogging down the aisle. They hopped onto the stage, greeting the crowd as the sound of clapping faded. When the man from the lobby looked around at the crowd and saw me, he exclaimed, "Oh, my God! It's you," with his mic on.

I was so embarrassed!

"It's you! It's you!" he repeated.

The entire crowd began looking around, first at him, and then at me. Not knowing what else to do, all I could muster was a smile and a nod. I felt Barbara glaring at me and then felt her kick under the table.

"Did you meet Barry out in the lobby earlier?" Barbara whispered through her smile as if she was a ventriloquist. "How does he know you? I know you've never met before!"

Pretending I was taking notes, I jotted an answer on the side of my notebook, like we were in a high school classroom. I explained what had occurred in the lobby. I had no idea who he was and still hadn't been properly introduced to him. I supposed his reaction was because he had recognized me from yesterday.

The rest of the seminar was like something out of a strange storybook. Each speaker gave their presentation, but Barry spent most of his time walking the aisles as he taught. He made a point of getting closer to me, walking back and forth in our row. He went out of his way to work from my notebook, and on breaks, even though he was swarmed with people, his eyes kept darting my way.

"He can't take his eyes off you!" Barbara screeched in a controlled whisper, "I think he's come by our row about five times this morning alone!"

"What do I do?"

"Well, do you like him?"

"I don't know. He seems nice, I guess…but I don't know anything about him. Until you mentioned this seminar, I hadn't even heard of him."

"Well, obviously, he's American…oh, and he is separated with a couple children."

"Separated? Separated and getting divorced? Or separated and working on their marriage?"

"Definitely getting divorced! He told us at our last appointment. He just hasn't made it public yet," she continued. "You should give it a shot! He's smitten by you!"

"But he lives in the States! I don't want to have a long-distance relationship, and there's no way I'm moving!"

"Maybe he'll move to Vancouver!" Barbara suggested.

I gave her an "are you kidding me" look. "Not if he has young kids and established business in the U.S."

When the group was dismissed for lunch, Barry jumped down from the stage before another crowd gathered around him. He leaned over the row of tables and invited us to join him and several other clients for dinner that evening.

At dinner, he ensured that we sat together, and when our meals came, acted as if we had been together for years. He pushed his plate toward mine, and we shared some of each other's entrees.

He had somehow asked Barbara about me earlier on a break, so our conversations went easier than they might have had we started from scratch. We engaged in interesting work conversations, together and as a group, and the evening went by as if we had all been longtime friends.

When dinner was over, Barry asked me to stay behind and talk. I still wasn't sure if I was interested in him, although I was attracted to his message and his desire to help people. We ended up going for a long walk along the hotel's walkway, which paralleled a long river. As we rounded a bend, we both looked up, frozen at the sight of the biggest moon either of us had ever seen. It seemed to sit on top of the river, straddling each side of the bank.

We continued walking on the pebbled path lit by the warm, golden moon and stopped at a wooden bench that seemed to be waiting for us. Barry gave me his suit jacket to keep warm, and we sat and talked for hours. He was very candid about his past and forthcoming with the questions I asked. I was touched by his candor, and his childlike excitement to be with me.

He asked me about my dreams and what I ultimately wanted to do. Then, he asked me to help him—to partner with him in reaching his clients, all eager to learn and wanting to make a difference in the world.

I was both startled by his invitation and humbled by his request, but I didn't think of it as much more than polite flattery.

The Proposal

Barbara was beside herself that Barry and I had connected, and even more excited about the possibility of my having a future with him. Although she was projecting into the future much too quickly, I admit I, too, was curious about the idea. But with so many logistical issues to address, I eventually dismissed our meeting as a fun chance encounter.

Barry, however, saw things differently. His affection for me only grew. When he learned I was leaving early, he asked someone else to finish his portion of the program so he could take me to the airport.

He nervously fidgeted with his umbrella as we rode in the cab on the way to the airport and was very uncomfortable about saying the inevitable goodbye. When we arrived, he insisted on walking me to the gate (TSA still allowed people to do this back then) and stayed with me till until I boarded

When the announcement came for the passengers to begin the boarding process, I stood up. Barry stood up with me and grabbed both my hands.

"Manna, you can't go. I just found you. I need more time. I don't want you to go…you can't go!" he stumbled. "Come speak for me!" he pleaded. "You don't need to go to any other events from now on. Travel with me! I told you, I need your help. You have something everyone needs. Love and compassion ooze out of you! And you've accomplished so much, you can show others how they can endure and succeed, too. Don't go!"

"Barry, you're so silly. I'm only going for a few days. Let's talk after we both get back from our respective trips and get settled," I answered, noticing I was starting to feel an attraction for him. I even began giving myself permission to imagine what sharing a dream of serving others together would look like.

"When will that be?" he asked, then answered, "That's too long!"

We both laughed. I looked at him endearingly as he tried one objection after another. Finally, when I had to go, he gave me a great big hug and whispered in my ear, "I can't let you go..." he paused. "Manna, will you marry me? You are everything, and I mean *everything* I have ever wanted, and...well, you're *'it'!* You are *'the one'!* You are *the only one*, and I don't know how to let you go. Tell me you'll marry me!" With a magnificent smile, he pulled back and waited for my answer.

Is he serious right now? Did he really just ask me to marry him?

He continued, "I know what my request must sound like, but you have to trust me. I've journaled about someone like you! I've dreamt of someone like you, and when I saw you a few days ago, it was like God delivered you right to my front door. I know you have to catch your flight, so just say yes! Say you'll marry me."

"Barry...I...I...I don't know what to say," I stuttered in bewilderment. "We just met! I'm sorry...I can't marry you." I tried to answer delicately. "Can we just date and see how things go?"

He stared at me, his eyes searching for something else that would convince me. He hoped I would say yes, but he knew I had to say no. "I understand, but I'm not letting you go. Call me as soon as you land. And just so you know, you *will* be my wife one day!"

With another hug and a kiss, I walked down the jetway and looked back to wave goodbye before going down the ramp.

This man is serious.

With a "what just happened here" kind of awkwardness, I smiled and waved goodbye to my future husband.

"I know you're telling me the truth. You can't make up stuff like this!" Leah shook her head. "Your life is better than fiction!"

"I know, Leah. I—"

"This is only going to get better. Keep going," she directed.

Things went very well at first, and we saw each other almost every other weekend. I flew to his events and spoke for him, just as he had asked, and he flew to Canada to see me. Michael also joined me on many of those trips because I didn't like leaving him behind. He was thrilled to be a part of everything and even insisted on dressing up in a suit and tie to help Barry and his team.

Barry and I appeared to have similar dreams about making a positive difference in other people's lives, and we spent countless hours planning, sharing, and working towards this dream together.

This is the way it's supposed to be, I thought to myself.

He was quirky, but his eccentricity and childlike excitement whenever we were together endeared him to me. Although he was a bit awkward as a father figure, he seemed sincere in his attempts. I loved him for trying as hard as he did. It wasn't long before I started becoming truly attached to him.

Maybe *this time*, my dream would come true.

On one of our weekends together, we were quietly working, writing out programs, and discussing how they could be used to help his clients. I felt something in my spirit, so I looked up from my notes and worksheets.

At that moment, I saw Barry with different eyes. Instead of seeing him romantically, I was given a vision of his giftings. Sitting in front of me was a brilliant man, writing and scribbling away, taking in all the ideas we had created, structured, and refined together. If anyone could deliver those ideas with impact, it would be Barry. He was a great presenter. He had a real finesse for showmanship and was blessed with a platform of influence that many could only dream of.

He noticed me staring at him and put down his pen. "What? What are you looking at?" He smiled.

"I just really *got* something."

"What is it?"

"Barry, do you know how blessed you are?" I asked, smiling.

"I know. I have you!" he answered quickly.

"No, not because you have me, silly goose. You are blessed because God has given you so many gifts and great favor. Do you know what you have here?" I asked, extending my hands over the table strewn with papers, notebooks, and colored markers.

"I like the sounds of this. Tell me more," Barry said, leaning back in his chair and putting his pen to his mouth.

"Do you realize you have a community of thousands who listen to you and believe in you?"

"Yeah, I know. It's cool, isn't it?" He laughed out loud.

I smiled. "How do you handle it all? It's such an immense responsibility."

He shook his head. "What do you mean?"

"People travel across countries, incurring all the related expenses to pay to learn from you. They trust you and are willing to try anything you tell them."

"Yeah, I know. Like I said, that's cool, right?" Barry replied, still uncertain as to the point I was trying to make.

"It's much, much bigger than that. Barry, do you realize that under the umbrella of doing *business*, you are given the opportunity to bless your clients' lives exponentially? It's not just ideas, plans, and tools that will increase their revenues, you also have a unique platform to show them how to serve, contribute, and give back to their families, clients, peer groups, communities, and cities! It's huge!"

"Hey! That's great! I like that concept. Let's tell the team!" he reached for his phone.

As wonderful as Barry was, he was impulsive and often acted hastily. In the short time we had been dating, I had already seen him latch on to random ideas without much thought, and then run with them like a man with his hair on fire, right into a dead end.

"No, not yet," I said, putting his phone down. "Let this sink in first. This isn't just another *new, better, different,* or *next* marketing or promotional idea. If you truly understand and honor this gift, then your platform will really grow."

Barry jumped into his journal, "I'm writing this all down!"

"Barry, please," I said softly, as I stopped him from writing. "This isn't a technique. Please don't make this a campy talking tool. This is a timely word for *you alone*. If you will honor this gift, be a leader with a servant's heart, steward your finances and resources, and acknowledge the people around you who serve you faithfully, the sky is the limit."

Barry gnawed at his pen and nonchalantly said, "Yeah, I know."

"Did he? Did he *get* it?" Leah asked doubtfully.

"Well, yes and no. *Yes*, because he began researching everything on *stewardship* and *servant leadership*. And *no*, because in an instant—'Bam!'—all the existing curriculum (which took a great deal of time and hard work to develop) was scratched, and every topic for the next few months focused on *stewardship* and the importance of being a *servant leader*."

Sadly, the sweet times we shared together became fewer and fewer as he transitioned me into a "work partner." Where he had once been attentive, thoughtful, and endearing, he became increasingly demanding, unpredictable, and even antagonistic. I finally addressed the painful situations he orchestrated.

"I'm so sorry, Manna," he replied, in his usual, charismatic way. "When we're not together, it drives me crazy, and I can't think right. I worry about someone else stealing your heart away from me, and I can't focus. I need you with me. Will you move to the States? Your impact is already huge; everyone loves you!"

"But my whole life is in Vancouver…I don't know how I can give that up."

"I know it's almost impossible for you to think about, but *please* think about it, seriously. Until then, I will try to be better. I'll even go see someone to help me work through everything." He hesitated and then continued, "I'm dealing with my ex-wife and kids too."

He began recounting many difficult stories about his ex-wife, and, feeling I should be more empathetic, I apologized and rallied myself to be more understanding.

Unfortunately, this behavioral cycle became a common pattern during our two years of dating. Barry would set off a bomb in our relationship, apologize, promise to do his personal work and healing, cry, plead, and make more promises. Then I would feel bad that I wasn't more patient and vow to try harder. In public, he regularly confessed his battle with alcohol, and though he had been sober for a long time, he had not dealt with the behaviors surrounding his addiction.

I desperately sought professional support to help me understand and cope in this relationship, but instead of addressing Barry's unwillingness to be accountable and to seek authentic help, the focus was always on managing his explosions and my need for extra coping skills. This process only made me even more anxious because the onus was on *me* and my coping capacity versus his responsibility and how *we* might create a healthier relationship *together*. So, sadly, instead of making strides in my personal autonomy and healing, I became more entrenched in codependency and fear.

At one point, I actually terminated our relationship. Living in constant fear of the next storm that might be launched at me was no way to live.

Several of Barry's friends called, asking me to give him one more chance because he was totally distraught without me. As hard as they tried, I could not be convinced there was hope for a future together.

A few weeks later, Barry's best friend called. Kent was a kind, brilliant man with a pure heart. He was not only Barry's confidante and mentor, but he was also a consultant and partner in several business ventures. Apparently, Barry's eruptions weren't uncommon to anyone who had been around him. Kent even shared many of his own experiences of Barry with me.

We enjoyed rich conversations, and I had grown to trust Kent. I knew he was able to give me answers, strategies, and hope that counselors could not. He openly admitted Barry's weaknesses, but he also added that our long-distance relationship was causing Barry unprecedented stress because he had never been "in love" before—Barry was ill-equipped to know how to navigate such foreign territory.

Long story short, Kent pleaded a very credible case for his friend and promised to help me keep him accountable. He believed both of us had great promise and together, we could do much to help many. Kent believed it would be a worthy request for me to consider moving to the States. He wanted me to give Barry a chance he deserved to prove himself to Michael and me.

Needless to say, Kent's pleading worked, and after more thought, I was willing to give Barry another chance. Immediately after that, Barry proposed a second time, and before long, I was preparing our move to the U.S.A.

Red Flags

The excitement of the upcoming marriage consumed Barry, and it was the high he needed to distract him from old behaviors. Things were still difficult, but since he openly admitted his weaknesses, sought help, and was accountable to others now, I was hopeful for our relationship.

Please don't misunderstand, I'm not saying I was perfect—as you know, I am far from perfect.

Leah smiled.

However, my deficiencies did not assault or wreak havoc in my spouse's life—or the lives of his children. My failings were obvious: people-pleasing, an inability to say no, and over-compensation to validate my own worth. My identity was not based on my ability to dominate people. My identity was based on proving whether or not I was even worthy of being alive—of taking up *space* on this planet. Domination, superiority, or oppression were the furthest things from my mind because, quite simply, I was too busy settling for crumbs, which, in hindsight, was how I found myself in this relationship.

Unfortunately, since Barry's travel schedule only increased, and since we were not living in the same city and spending our lives together daily, I didn't see the full manifestation of his dysfunction until it was too late. So, in my idealistic naiveté, I resolved to prove my commitment to Barry (and to our future together), and made the massive sacrifice of leaving my whole world as I knew it——my business, my family, my home, my country, and my beloved PoPo—and moving to another country to enter wholeheartedly into his life and his world.

I could not imagine, much less believe if anyone had told me, the enormity of what lay before me, and the destruction I would have to overcome in the coming years. Had I known, I would never have given up everything I had sacrificed to build my promising future, and what would be my last year with PoPo.

Time moved very quickly after I accepted Barry's proposal, and soon I had to sell my business and start the immigration process.

I had positioned Huxley and another dear friend, who had been in the business for a very long time, to take over my business. Unfortunately, my friend was unable to fulfill her agreement due to unforeseen personal matters, and suddenly, Huxley was missing in action.

She had been behaving strangely over the previous few months—not returning calls or even showing up for work. I was still paying her, but she did a minimal amount of work and kept her distance from me and the business. Even though Huxley had agreed to be a bridesmaid at my wedding, she was distant through it all and unavailable in every other way.

I would discover later that she had made copies of all my contacts, processes, and systems. She had also taken several commission checks while I was in the States and did nothing to manage operations as promised. Without resources like the Internet offers now, I was truly dependent on the honesty and integrity of the people to whom I left my business. With my main person unavailable, and Huxley misappropriating funds, I asked another friend to help me.

"Did he?" Leah said.

"Unfortunately, he took the business and never paid one penny for it, either through referral fees or regular installments. Because of my many years of hard work and client relationships, he essentially earned my income on top of his, but he did so without integrity."

"No! He got *your* database and all you put into the lives of those clients!" Leah shouted. "What a scoundrel! How dare he just take your chest of gold!"

I nodded, both aggravated and sad at the memory.

"Don't worry, Manna. That purloiner will get his just desserts. A person can't be given such a gift, and then betray the giver, without getting what he's got coming to him. It's that thing called *karma*. You'll see." Leah patted my hand with hers.

It was so heartwarming how she tried to comfort me as my memories flooded back.

"And if Huxley had anything to do with this, well, it will be double for her. She was 'family,' such as it was. There is a universal scale of balance, and they'll reap what they have sown. You can count on it."

"I don't wish them ill will. I just wish they had honored their agreement and did what they said they would do."

During this time, my life with Barry consumed and exhausted me. Immigration and Naturalization Services (INS) monitored me closely after we petitioned for a green card based on marriage. Unfortunately, many unscrupulous people requested green cards disingenuously, which meant extra procedures had to be followed to ensure Barry and I were legitimate. Until then, Michael and I were given the status of "Legal Alien on Advanced Parole."

The worst part was my restriction to leave the States. I had to wait another six months before INS said I could go home to see my PoPo. In the meantime, Barry seemed truly happy for all of us to be together. He talked about Michael's sweet and wonderful nature to everyone, both on and off stage. In our private family times, he would often say to Michael, 'You're going to be *my* son, and I'm so proud of that. You're the son every father would want, and I'm so thankful *I'm* the one who has that privilege!"

Michael would cry and hug Barry ever so tightly at these words of commitment.

A time of intimacy like this between a new father and a new son in a blended family is sacred, and since Barry spoke so often of his excitement about Michael, I trusted him to honor the innocence and purity of Michael's heart. Barry had two children of his own, and I assumed his fatherly role was guaranteed.

But as quickly as Barry would profess his love to us, he would switch gears. Suddenly, he treated us as if we were strangers—or worse, enemies. Looking back, I see clearly there were red flags—many red flags.

"Now when I meet people in a similar situation, I tell them unequivocally to *stop* and turn around. Pray and ask God for wisdom, strength, and the courage to do the impossible—to leave! HEED THOSE RED FLAGS! *And* one *red flag is all you need!*

"I wish I had possessed the self-confidence and the self-worth to say no and to go back home—even if it meant my tail was tucked behind me. I could have rebuilt and started over. I could have rebuilt. My clients would have welcomed me back, and I would have found a way to recapture what was lost."

I let out a heavy sigh and looked at Leah. Her loving eyes encouraged me to continue.

"As I recount the eight years of my life with Barry, know that I do so with mixed feelings. I feel regret that I did not have the courage or the strength to believe more in myself, or to believe that I deserved better. I feel sadness for believing I deserved pain, abuse, and even terror. Most of all, I feel remorse for having allowed this turmoil to reach Michael's life.

"I'm grateful we have a God Who turns all things out together for good, Who intervened when He did, Who provided for and blessed me in each situation, and Who used each circumstance to teach me the priceless lessons of knowing my true identity, value, and worth.

"Yes, God is good all the time—even in spite of myself."

Because of the INS rules and the time constraints it created for us, Barry and I had to marry first in the States before having a formal ceremony in Vancouver at a future date. We pledged our vows in the mountains, sharing this special occasion only with Michael and a handful of dear friends. Michael, nine years old at the time, served as one of the groomsmen.

Thankfully, the Barry who showed up at our sweet little ceremony was the man with whom I had fallen in love.

Several months later, we prepared for our larger wedding celebration in Vancouver (which even included my mother and Scham as a gesture of my wanting a new beginning with them). Lamentably, Barry's personality started to shift again, and the ugliness of his dark side erupted with a vengeance. After our rehearsal with the pastor the day before the formal ceremony, he launched one of his cruelest attacks on me. We were just blocks away from our hotel, where all our guests were joining us for dinner that evening. I cannot even repeat what he said and did, but his actions so shocked and disgusted me that when the car stopped in the middle of traffic in between lights, I opened the car door and ran.

Racing to my bridal suite, I managed to get to my room without causing too much of a stir. Thank God, Michael was with my father in another car. Barry had another room reserved for the evening, so I knew I wouldn't have to see him right away.

I cried and cried.

When I calmed down, I called my bridesmaids. They were already downstairs preparing for the rehearsal dinner, so it was easy for them to come up to my room. When I told them what had happened, a simultaneous, "*What?*" erupted from them.

After the initial reactionary comments, we all sat together quietly—some on the bed, some on the sofa, some on the floor. The only sounds to be heard were a vacuum cleaner down the hall and our own heavy, intermittent sighs.

Though it was relatively quiet in the room, my mind was barraged with screaming thoughts. I analyzed, and qualified each separate reflection, weighing every choice before me. And when I felt I could speak them aloud, I presented them to my friends.

We discussed the possibilities and viabilities of each choice, but we all knew that unless Barry sought intensive counseling, medication, or even an intervention or in-house program, nothing was going to change. In fact, it would only be worse because I would be in another country without family, friends, a support system, or the familiarity of my own surroundings.

We were also exceedingly aware that the clock was ticking—the rehearsal dinner would start in thirty minutes! Though we discussed the advantages and disadvantages of each choice, the conclusion was ultimately the same: I could not marry Barry.

In spite of everything, I knew I had to call off the wedding. I was not going to have another black wedding day again.

"When are you going to do this?" one of the bridesmaids asked.

"I don't know…"

"It has to be soon. Forty people are downstairs about to have dinner to celebrate you!" said another.

"I know…how do I get myself out of this mess? I thought I was doing the right thing! The way we met, how we had such similar dreams, or so it seemed…" I reflected out loud. "I know there are no perfect people…I was willing to work on all the issues, but this is just too much. He's—"

"Sick!" interrupted another. "Manna, problems occur in every relationship, but I know of no other person so ill, so impaired, and so debilitated in human relationships as Barry! And I've known him longer than you have!" she stated with conviction. Then, she gently took my hand and said, "Manna, yes, you've made a huge difference in his life, but you must ask yourself if you are willing to live a life of abuse! It's killing your soul! I've never seen you so distraught…and what about Michael?"

Her insight was confirmation. The thought that Barry could be damaging to Michael was all I needed for me to make my decision. I know not every man can be a perfect father, and I know that in spite of my love for Michael, I was not the perfect mother. But at least I did my best to be a good parent—one who loved, cherished, and honored the blessing of being a parent, and one who was willing to do whatever was necessary to rear him well and right. If Barry had such defective thinking with no sensors or filters *now*, then it was bound to erupt again. I refused to let Michael be caught in the repercussions.

The decision was made, and I steadied myself for the next steps. "Well, that's it then. The wedding is off, and I will make the calls myself…to everyone…later this evening."

"We'll stay with you, but what about the rehearsal dinner?"

"You guys go down and just keep it light," I responded. "I'm sorry to put you in that position, but I don't want to cause a commotion downstairs. It will be easier when I speak to each person one by one later."

"So, are you not coming down?"

"No. I can't face Barry…or anyone else…not just yet." I struggled with how to diplomatically, yet sensitively, deal with this situation. "Well, maybe I'll come down in a bit…I don't know."

"What do we tell them?"

I struggled with an answer. "Please tell them I'm not feeling well," I suggested.

Just then, Barbara stepped up to me, placed both her hands on my shoulders, and looked at me eye to eye. "Manna…I don't want you to go through another moment of torture with Barry, either. But not going through with this ceremony won't change anything. You're already married, remember?"

Oh my God! She's right!

I felt lightheaded. I backed up and sat on the bed—about to faint. I felt helpless and hopeless and like my life was over.

Apparently, the dinner went by smoothly. Barry entertained everyone, putting on the perfect show. He adroitly handled the fact that his bride-to-be was not in attendance at her own rehearsal dinner. No one was suspicious because he was so happy, going from table to table engaging in flattery and being attentive to my family and friends. The evening went off without a hitch, and my absence was dismissed. It was a simple case of a fragile bride overwhelmed with emotion and nerves. While this statement may have been *accurate*, it was not entirely *true*.

Yes, I had emotions that kept me from coming downstairs, but they were not the emotions of a joyful bride; they were emotions of terror and dread, as if I was going to be buried alive.

I contemplated going downstairs many times. My PoPo, my son, my father and Shirley, and Luke and his family ware all there. Surely, I could tell them!

But then, Barbara's words echoed in my mind: "Manna, you're already married!"

The threatening rules the INS officer had told me also flooded my mind. Removing my petition with INS now would put a long-term mark on my name. They had already taken so long with a simple visa process, I'm sure this would complicate my ability to travel in and out of the States even more. I might even be denied entrance. This situation would affect my ability to accept speaking engagements, and my flexibility in working with the new business ventures I had already begun—another quagmire to contemplate.

I stayed in my room, still dressed in my rehearsal outfit, staring blankly out the window. Tears ran unattended down my cheeks as I assessed my options. No matter which way I turned, I felt trapped. I was snared in a lose-lose situation.

It was dark outside now, and the city lights cast a surreal glow into my room, along with the muffled sounds of the Friday night activities of downtown below, where our hotel was located. Just then, the phone rang. It was Barry calling me from his room. Dinner was over, and everyone had left for the night. I could say nothing. I simply listened as he attempted to explain his earlier reprehensible behavior.

After a long silence, I finally said, "Barry, I can't go on like this."

"Let's go to counseling together," he suggested.

I hesitated. "What will that look like *this time*?"

"We'll see Larry together," he offered. Larry was a very gifted family therapist who had been referred to me by one of Barry's employees immediately after we started dating.

"You've said that before, but you don't consistently go for your individual sessions, or for our couple's sessions. Instead, you schedule golf or some random conference call to avoid seeing him."

"I know…I'm sorry," he admitted. "I thought you were going to leave me anyway, so I didn't bother trying. Then I thought if I pissed you off enough, you'd leave me sooner rather than later."

"What?!" I asked with alarm. "What does that all mean? Are you saying you set me up?!"

"Yeah, I guess I did. Now that I see you really are going to leave me, I'm scared half to death. I spent the night with your family and a lot of time with your grandma. They all love you so much, and the more I spend time with them, the more I'm aware of how amazing and precious you are. I was a fool, and I'm so sorry. Please, can we try again?" He paused before continuing, smoothly, "Please marry me tomorrow, and I will make you the happiest girl in the world. I will prove to you that your sacrifice of leaving your family, especially your grandma, will be worth it. You'll see."

After a long while, I said tearfully, "I want to believe you…but you scare me. The things you say and do are…really cruel! For all that I've been through, I never expected assaults like this from someone who claimed to love me as much as you have. I have left relationships for far fewer offenses. And I will never let you hurt Michael."

"Manna, I am so sorry. I love both you and Michael. He's the best kid, and I would never do anything to harm him. I promise I will treat him the way I wish I were treated as a little boy. You will never have to worry about Michael with me. He'll love being with me, and with my kids, and we'll all make it work as a family together. You'll see!" he promised desperately.

Through tears, he continued, "I love you more than anything and am scared to death to lose you. I know I've hurt you a lot, especially today, and I am very sorry. My past is hard and dark, and I know…I know I have a lot of work to do. I'm the one to blame for everything; I admit it. It's all out on the table. I don't deserve you, but I am willing to do anything I can to keep you."

And so went the conversation for the next few hours—more confessions, more pleading, more tears, and more promises. He said everything I wanted to hear and everything I desperately wanted to believe.

It had never occurred to Barry that we were already married.

But Barbara's eerie words were all I could think of. No matter what Barry said, I knew I had to face the music either way. With his fervent promises and my determination to keep a watchful eye over his interactions with Michael—and since we were already married—I gave in and went ahead with the ceremony.

50 Shades of Cray

The time soon came to move to the United States, and my departure was not without its tears. Leaving my family—especially my PoPo—was like leaving a part of my soul behind. I intended to fly PoPo down to see me (and for myself to return) often. I just had to wait until everything was cleared with INS, so I kept everything else intact (my homes, club memberships, and financial accounts, etc.) as it would have been too difficult to leave any other way.

Michael, on the other hand, was extremely excited and eager to start fresh in the U.S. Tristan was nowhere to be found, and we encountered no obstructions or delays in our INS filings.

When we arrived, Barry told me the area in which he wanted to live. He shared his dream of having a home in one of the most prestigious neighborhoods of an already exclusive zip code. I was astonished at the size of the home he was interested in, and even more, alarmed at the size of the mortgage.

"I don't know if having this much debt is a good idea, honey," I suggested.

"Don't worry. In the U.S., you get to write off a million dollars of your mortgage. I forget, how much is your mortgage in Vancouver?" he asked.

"I don't have one. I paid it off a few years after I bought it. The Whistler property should be paid off soon, too."

"Great! Then you can help me pay for this new house," he said matter-of-factly.

"But I left my business, and I'm not earning an income now. Even if you can write off a million dollars, it's still a two-million-dollar mortgage! How can I help make such a big mortgage payment?"

"I'll put you on the payroll. Now you can finally get paid for all the work you've been doing. I'll get—oops, I mean, *we'll* get—more money out of the company, and you'll help pay the mortgage. Don't worry, I know what I'm doing," Barry assured me.

This conversation marked the beginning of my awareness of how extremely unhealthy Barry's relationship with money was.

While we'd had discussions about money before, they'd been superficial and theoretical. Dating long distance is one thing, but dating long distance between countries is another. Dating long distance between *cultures* is yet another. I'm not referring to a culture of ethnicity or race, but a culture of stewardship, value, and honor.

Let me simply say that Barry *loved* money.

He did not see money as a tool of exchange in the economy of life¾money was his identity, his oxygen, his lifeblood. It was also one of his weapons of choice. When he felt he was on the upswing, he was happy and willing to share, sometimes even lavishly. However, if things weren't going as he liked, he would use money as a weapon, withholding it to manipulate, shame, or demoralize others.

Such was the case on our first anniversary. I had planned a beautiful evening. I had hoped to start with a romantic dinner at a restaurant known for its wonderful food and ambiance in a sweet area of town. From there, I wanted to take a peaceful walk along the water's edge afterwards. But I became concerned when we headed for the car and noticed Barry was bringing his journal with him. I knew immediately our night was not going to be romantic. It was not even going to be good.

You see, Barry also used his journal as a weapon against people.

If he were in one of his paranoid states, he would unashamedly scribble journal entries about you right in front of you, making sure you knew he was recording his interpretations of the interchange. Between paragraphs, he would look up and then write some more, using his arms to hide his words. Barry's journal was his pretend authority figure, his personal judge, to whom he would report your actions.

Don't get me wrong—I believe journaling is a wonderful exercise. I journal also. However, I don't use my journal as a weapon of data made from fatuous, unfounded, derailed thinking. Barry did. He would even wave the book in the air, threatening to "tell on you" as if his transcribed fantasies carried weight.

So, on our first anniversary celebration, Barry brought his imaginary judge to our "romantic" dinner. When I eventually asked why, he told me he wanted to discuss our household budget.

He wasn't earning as much as he had hoped that quarter, and because he had bought the big house *for me*, he thought it would be good to discuss *our* spending.

"But Barry, this is our first anniversary. Can we do that tomorrow, please?"

"No. I want to handle it now and implement everything *by tomorrow*!" he stated emphatically.

Before the meal had been served, he had read me a list of faults he had recorded about me. Each one was titled, dated, and followed by several paragraphs of delusion. I sat quietly, watching his macabre face spew his venom. Page after page after page, Barry revealed what I would call his mental disorder.

But he thought nothing of his desecration and acted as if everything was normal, even wonderful! He was very proud of himself that evening.

I, however, was heartbroken.

Not only did I not eat, I couldn't even lift a utensil.

To make matters more bizarre, Barry never once mentioned the household budget during dinner. Nor did he bring up any great family fiscal plan he had for us. He was simply upset that he didn't bring in as many sales as he had hoped that quarter, and I was the closest target for his frustration.

"He is a sick, *sick* man!" Leah shouted. "He had more than just an alcohol problem! He had a mental problem *and* a money problem, too!"

"Yes, Barry was addicted to money (and other things), and like all addictions, what satisfied you before, is never enough the next time. In Barry's case, steadily increasing sales was not good enough. What I'm describing is not just growth in business; I'm talking about greed, even mania. Money (and its accumulation) was Barry's *god*, and his relationships, no matter how close or respected, were secondary, or last. If he didn't get what he wanted, whoever was in his firing range received the brunt of his fury. Hence, Barry was entangled in many heated disputes (and lawsuits) by loyal and trusting allies who no longer tolerated the broken agreements.

"Everything he did had something to do with how he could control money and people. I've seen him fearfully clutching his jar of loose change as if for dear life, to lavishing five of his consultants with Rolex watches for no reason. But make no mistake, a heavy toll was always exacted from every recipient of his apparent generosity. Every gift would eventually obligate a piece of the recipient's heart and dignity."

"What misery. I'm so sorry," Leah said, shaking her head.

"I did my best at the time with the strength and knowledge I had. But what I couldn't do for myself back then, I do for others now. Whenever I'm asked for advice on relationships, I always tell them to make sure they really *know* who they are dating. You need to know them in their day-to-day life and in their surroundings. You need to know how they are—at home, when they stub their toe, or when they're sick. You want to see how they treat people when they're at a gas station, when they pay for groceries, or when someone sneaks ahead of them in line at a store. You want to see how they are in the humdrum of daily activities, and how they are with their family, friends, coworkers, associates, neighbors, and strangers on the street. Don't date a 'project,' and never marry one!"

Barry spent the first few days after our return to the U.S. with me in *our home*, but even then, most of his time was spent on the computer. When I asked him if there was anything I could help him with, he looked at me irritatingly and quickly shut down his computer. I thought his behavior was odd, but I blamed myself for interrupting "such a gifted man who was called to help so many people," so I learned not to disturb him when he was in his home office.

The next day, he suddenly announced he had to go on a trip and would be gone for five days.

"Oh, I didn't know you were traveling. Is there anything I can do to help you?" I asked.

"No, thanks," he answered, never looking up from his packing.

"When are you leaving?"

"The car's coming to get me now. My flight is in a few hours."

"*Now?* When did you know about this? Why didn't you tell me before?" I was flustered. "Honey, we just got here a few days ago. I was hoping we could spend some time together. You were going to show me where the grocery store and the bank are located. We haven't been out of the house for days, and I don't have a clue where anything is or where to go for supplies. There's hardly anything in the house."

"You were a top realtor in your city, right? You'll figure it out. It's easy," he said sarcastically.

I took a deep breath. "Umm…honey, I don't have a car, and I don't know anything about this area. Couldn't you please take even thirty minutes and just show me around? Can you catch a later flight? Why are you in such a rush? I don't know anyone here and have no idea who to ask to help me."

"Yeah, well…the limo is coming to pick me up. Use my car," he replied, without addressing my other questions.

The doorbell rang just then. It was Barry's driver. He closed his suitcase, threw me his car keys, and handed me a hundred-dollar bill. "Here, this should be enough for a few days. You have your own money too, right?" he coldly added, hurrying to the door.

Strangely enough, in front of the driver, he was completely different. As the driver put his suitcase in the trunk, Barry said the oddest thing to him: "Do you see my wife there? Isn't she gorgeous? I'm a lucky guy! Now let's hurry to the airport, so I can do my work and get back to my hot bride!"

I was absolutely shocked.

I stood at the doorway, unable to speak. *What was* that *all about? Who says things like this?! And did he* really *just hand me a hundred-dollar bill for food and necessities in a new, unfurnished mansion for the next week?*

I closed the door and stood in the foyer for a few moments, wondering if I had imagined what had just taken place. Jarred that Barry would be so heartless—not telling me he was leaving for almost a week, knowing we had literally just moved here, knowing we had no groceries, supplies, or car except his "to borrow," and no idea about the community or even how the system worked differently here than in Canada (to name a few insensitivities)—I went to my office to try and learn some things on my own using the computer.

That's when I remembered having the business card of a wonderful gentleman, Mike, whom I had met at one of the events where I had spoken. He was pure in his intentions and had offered me his assistance if I should ever need it when I moved to the area.

I found his card and gave Mike a call. He was more than happy to help, and he spent the afternoon showing me the nuances of each area, and where to shop for the things I needed. To this day, over two decades later, he and I still remain the best of friends.

Time to Say Goodbye

Unfortunately, with every day, Barry's mercurial behaviors didn't simply increase; they also intensified. His moods arbitrarily swung from elation and euphoria to despair and paranoia, and I had no idea how to prepare for, or how to manage his capriciousness.

Then, as if things weren't bad enough, another series of situations evolved concurrently. I had a strange and frightening sense that my beloved PoPo was not doing well, that she was dying. Unfortunately, I was still dealing with the INS (who, over four years, lost my file three times), and I felt lost in how I could maneuver in such a convoluted system. Getting back home to see both PoPo and MahMah (who was also declining in health) was not going to be easy. I felt helpless.

Michael also started a new school, so I was steeped in learning all the different aspects of an American school system and preparing the necessary documents and procedures for that as well. We were also trying to integrate Barry's two children into our relationship, but when I began to witness Barry's jealousy toward Michael, my anxiety escalated, and I was unwilling to leave Michael unattended.

Still trying to deal with the damages and lost income from my own business, while simultaneously managing all the projects Barry had given me to build his business, my health began to deteriorate. My doctor was seriously concerned about my weakening system. If the cause of my declining blood test results was not found, he would have me hospitalized to try and get me stabilized.

"Manna! It's plain as day! No matter how you slice or dice it, living with Barry was toxic, and it was killing you!" Leah said pointedly.

"Yes, I know that now, but I didn't see it at that time. Back then, I was just trying to preserve my sanity and keep all the different shades of crazy away from Michael and me."

"I'm almost afraid to ask," Leah said slowly, "but what happened with your beloved PoPo? How did you know she was dying?"

"I must warn you, it will sound strange."

"Seriously, Manna?" Leah interrupted sarcastically with one raised eyebrow, "What about your life *hasn't* been strange?"

"You're right." I paused momentarily. "I had a dream..."

"You...had a dream?" Leah repeated with doubtful hesitation.

"Yes. In fact, I had a very vivid dream of my PoPo's passing, but I'll just summarize it for you. In my dream, I checked her in at the hospital. When we were there, she sat facing me, her legs straddling mine as if she was a child. Her head rested on my shoulder as I was speaking with the nurses at the counter. In my dream, I was with her for ten days. Then she would go to heaven."

"That a pretty clear message," Leah said soberly.

"Without an ounce of doubt, God gave me this warning dream months in advance, so I could prepare for what was about to come. I wouldn't have been able to handle the loss otherwise."

I was desperate to be with PoPo, but unless I was given the papers to travel from INS, I could not leave the country. So, I called her daily to check in. I never told her my prophetic dream, but I didn't need to. She knew her time was also coming.

"Darling, I don't have much time. I don't know if I can wait this time. How much longer do you think? When can you come back? I want to see you before I go..." PoPo replied. I could hear the sadness in her voice.

"PoPo, please, try. Please try to stay like you did last time. I will call my immigration attorney again to see if we can do anything else to speed up the process," I continued to plead.

"I don't know...I'll try...please hurry," PoPo said cautiously.

Three months later, I finally received my papers. Within hours of the documents reaching me, I booked my trip home to Vancouver.

"Hurry, Manna. I don't have much time," PoPo urged.

"I'm coming, Grandma. I'll be there on September seventeenth. I just booked the flight," I said as bravely as I could.

Interestingly, my counselor in Vancouver (and his wife, who co-counseled with him) asked Barry and me to spend some time with them at the same time. They invited us to join them for a two-day retreat a few days *before* I was to see my PoPo.

They had been helping us since we first dated, and we had continued our sessions with them by phone after we married (along with our in-person sessions with Larry, our marriage and family therapist in town). But with our escalating issues, they thought it would be best to have some uninterrupted and more focused sessions with us.

Barry refused to go, and he refused to come to Vancouver to support me with my grandmother, so they *strongly* suggested I go alone.

"Excuse me, let me get my head around this. Did you say you had three counselors for your marriage?" Leah asked.

"Actually, we had more than that—five at one time—but at this particular time, yes, we had three therapists working on our case."

"That's a lot of counseling, Manna," Leah sighed, shaking her head. "A *lot* of counseling."

"I know…and that still wasn't enough."

Leah shook her head and motioned for me to go on.

When I was offered the retreat for myself alone, for reasons I could not explain, I knew I had to accept the opportunity to get away. Little did I know that this was going to be part of the miracle about to happen.

During what should have been a wonderful time of our lives as newlyweds, I was discovering that the man with whom I had fallen in love was only a small part of the real man, dominated by his dark consciousness. Despite the confusion, sadness, and fear, I knew I had no other option but to fight for my marriage. It was my second one, and there was no way I would walk away without doing everything in my power to make it work.

All of this is to say I was faced with two urgent situations.

The first was seeing PoPo. In both our spirits, we knew she would be leaving me soon. The second was an unrelenting knowing that I desperately needed those days with my counselors, away from Barry. I needed the time to regroup and regather some strength and resolve. Without this preparation, I would be in no position to handle what would be required of me in the days ahead.

As it turns out, I was right to do so.

It wasn't until later that I understood the full extent of why I *had* to see my counselor before I saw my beloved PoPo. What I had thought would be an intensive retreat to strengthen and bolster me for my precarious situation with Barry turned into a beautiful time of healing to prepare me for my grandmother's passing. The retreat hadn't been planned that way, but in every conversation and exercise, all my focus instinctively turned towards my grandmother.

God orchestrated a beautiful opportunity—a gift of time—to prepare me for what was to follow.

I prepared as best I could for letting go; for separation, death, loss, grief, and faith. When I returned from the retreat, I went immediately to see PoPo, who had moved in with my mother six months earlier. I learned that PoPo was extremely disappointed with my mother and grew sadder by the day, being there.

She told me my mother had "changed." No matter how PoPo had tried to defend her daughter in the past, there was no denying it now. Instead of being thankful, loving, and tenderly caring for PoPo, my mother constantly argued with her. Moreover, my mother and Scham had sold their cars and boat to pay for Huxley's luxuries and had no car to drive PoPo anywhere. They took the bus wherever they needed to go.

I didn't want PoPo to suffer for my mother's choices, so before I moved to the States, I bought my mother a car. That way, she could take care of PoPo with more ease and convenience. But even after being given such a generous gift, my mother only criticized the car. She kept telling me I should return it because it was a burden for her! Day in, day out, mother only continued to grumble. She didn't like the color, the seats, the make, or the model. It didn't fit in her driveway. It disrupted her life. It was an inconvenience to have the "thing" in her driveway. After ten days, I returned the car and took a loss on it. She didn't want my gift, even if it was to help her mother, my PoPo.

In fact, every gift I had given her was passed on to Huxley.

I know it isn't easy being a caretaker, but my mother had spent a lifetime as a professional nurse, as well as a home-care worker. She was trained for this, plus this was her beloved mother. This was the one woman who had taken the brunt of all her mistakes and suffered for all her choices.

Couldn't she have shown some compassion and love for her mother?

When I arrived and rang the doorbell, PoPo rushed out of the house and into my arms. I was so overjoyed to see her that all my troubles were forgotten in her presence. She didn't say goodbye to my mother, who was inside, and my mother never came outside to say hello to me.

PoPo didn't say much at first, so I made lots of conversation to distract her from her unhappiness at home and to keep her spirits up. When she did start talking, it was heart-wrenching. All of PoPo's stories were of how disappointed and sad she was because of how my mother treated her, and how alone she felt. She didn't want to "stay around" anymore; she wanted to "go Home."

"Life is no fun. It's just no fun at all," she said firmly. And then, while still looking out the window, she carefully reached for my hand and squeezed it tightly. "I'm glad I got to see you. There isn't much time left…" she stated calmly, but quietly.

Too afraid to address the truth of her comment, I swallowed hard and offered another option. "PoPo, I know we talked about this before, but Uncle Oliver and mother wouldn't agree then. Now that they have both taken care of you, and it hasn't worked out, would you *please* come live with me? I know it's in the U.S., but I can arrange for great healthcare for you, and we can be together. I know it's a lot to ask, but I think it's time we really consider this option."

"I don't know…" she replied sadly.

"PoPo, I hate to see you so sad. Please come back with me. There's plenty of room for you at my house, and I want you to live with me. There's a beautiful garden, and you can help me with all the roses. Michael misses you too, and we can all be together. Then when you're settled, we'll take a trip to see your brother in New York. You haven't seen him in so long—we can make this all happen quickly, and we'll be together," I continued.

She sighed and said, "We'll see."

We pulled up to the street to her favorite grocery stores and started shopping. Suddenly, I felt a strange emptiness in my tummy. Something was about to happen, but I didn't know what that would be.

I watched my PoPo as we walked up and down aisles, looking for the right crackers and treats to take away the strange taste in her mouth caused by her dentures. We prodded and turned over every apple and other exotic fruit displayed, but nothing seemed to interest her. "That's okay…I don't really need anything now," she said quietly, putting down one of her favorite fruits.

We then went to have a special lunch at one of her favorite restaurants, to enjoy something she hadn't had for a long time. Since my mother had not taken her out, she wasn't able to eat any foods she liked—only what my mother made for Scham.

The still-present emptiness in my stomach was joined now by a painful heaviness.

I watched my beloved PoPo. Age spots landscaped her eyes and cheeks. Her upper eyelids were heavy, limiting some of her vision, and seeing her sorrowful countenance broke my heart. She tried to be cheerful, but her eyes betrayed her true feelings behind the superficial conversation, and the strained smiles.

The server came by and placed our order in front of us. PoPo seemed happy to see one of her favorite dishes delivered to her, but no sooner did the smile come it was replaced with the inescapable awareness of her loneliness and sorrow. We prayed a blessing over our food and continued our attempts at pretending all would be well.

The truth was, my PoPo was tired and weary. She'd had enough.

Five years earlier in the ICU, she had heroically agreed to stay for me until I was strong enough and able to handle life on my own. But now she no longer had the strength—or the heart—to stay.

Just then, PoPo looked up at me, and without saying a word, revealed the deep sadness in her eyes. It was as if she was pleading with me, asking permission to finally let her go. When our eyes met, I knew...

It was time.

But anxiety washed over me. I let out a deep breath, not knowing what would be next. And then, peace covered me and filled me. The fear and grief I was feeling about losing PoPo were replaced by an inexplicable sense of comfort and assurance.

As my most faithful and staunchest ally in life looked back down at her meal, I felt the Holy Spirit tell me to say something from my heart—not to verbalize it, but to think it out loud.

Sweet Grandma...I understand. You can go now. I love you, and don't want you to suffer anymore. I want you to be happy. Thank you for loving me and for staying all this time. I'll be okay.

No sooner had I finished "thinking those words out loud," PoPo lifted her head and looked at me deeply. "Thank you," she said as if she had heard my silent words. She smiled at me, and then she slowly looked down again to finish her meal.

I gasped in horror. *Oh, my God! What have I done? I don't mean it! I take it back! Please, God, I take it back! Don't let her go. Please, she's all I have. She's my lifeline. I don't mean it! Oh, my God! What have I done?*

The moment had passed, and I felt our agreement was sealed. There was no turning back. PoPo never looked at me that way again the rest of the meal. I wanted to talk to her about what had just happened, but I felt restrained. Words were frozen in my throat. Besides, where would I begin? How would I even start? I attempted to start a conversation about this several times, but no words came. There was nothing else to say.

It was time.

Unsure what would happen next, I started to feel anxious again. But then, a wave of that same peace washed over me once more. Each time I became anxious, another covering of peace wrapped around me. This happened over and over again as we headed back to my mother's home.

We drove home with a profound understanding in our spirits, but in my mind, I was not sure I could let my sweet PoPo go yet. My eyes were still swollen and puffy from the previous days' crying and sobbing at what I've come to think of as my "pre-loss grief retreat." PoPo asked me why my eyes were swollen, but I couldn't tell her I had been with my counselors for the past few days sobbing inconsolably. I couldn't explain that I was learning how to deal with her passing. Instead, I told her my allergies were bad, and I had forgotten to take my antihistamines.

Before taking her home, I detoured and went for a long scenic drive and stopped at a park where there was a large waterfall. There, we walked and attempted to talk about our wishes for the upcoming year, even though we knew they weren't going to happen. She had to stop frequently to catch her breath, but she wanted to keep walking. I was concerned for her blood pressure and did not want her to be overly exerted, but she assured me she was fine. On we walked, and her face lit up as we stared out at the rushing water, allowing the mist from below to refresh us. We held hands at first, but she looped her arm through mine. There was so much love and joy in simply being together.

Her eyes looked so far away, and everything about her felt like she was in between worlds. She was torn about leaving me, but she had no desire to stay in suffering any longer.

As we walked back, the dark cloudy day gave way to the unexpected light and warmth of the sun. I remembered having a vision of too much blood rushing to her brain and through her heart. I became worried and suggested we sit down for a brief rest. She agreed, and we found a park bench where we sat. I took some photos of her.

PoPo was starting to feel tired, so we headed home. When I walked her to the front door to say goodbye and confirm our arrangements for the next day, she seemed somewhat disoriented. I was perplexed, but I thought this was due to our emotional day together. Little did I know things were already well in motion.

The next day, I rose early to prepare for another day with my PoPo. It was a beautiful fall morning in Vancouver.

Then the phone rang.

My mother's voice was on the other line. "I found Grandma lying over her bed this morning. The ambulance is on its way."

"*What?* Is she breathing? What happened?" I asked in fear and panic.

"I think she had a stroke. She's awake but not able to talk—the ambulance is here. I'll see you at the hospital."

Dear God…so fast! This is happening so fast! Is this my fault? I said she could go home yesterday, and in less than twenty-four hours…oh, dear God!

The vision I had of the blood rushing to her brain and PoPo's disorientation when I said goodbye flashed in my mind. She must have been having a series of small strokes, even as we were together.

I immediately headed to the hospital by my mother's home, over thirty minutes away. I don't know how this happened, but I arrived at the emergency entrance before the ambulance arrived. As I paced back and forth at the entrance, I found myself uttering nonstop, "Oh, my God! Oh, my God! Oh, my God…"

My thoughts then turned to my beloved grandmother. *Where was the ambulance? Where was my PoPo?*

I kept pacing and muttering, absentmindedly stepping over the entrance mat, causing the automatic doors to make a loud whooshing sound each time.

Suddenly, Luke walked up to me. His calm demeanor and comforting smile gave me some relief, but nothing could take away the impending reality of what I knew was about to occur.

The ambulance finally pulled up, and the attendants took my PoPo inside. She smiled and tried to wave when she saw me. One side of her face was paralyzed, and her smile was disfigured. My heart ached to see my sweet PoPo suffer and be so helpless.

Luke asked if I wanted to go in, but I shook my head. I wasn't able to stop trembling and crying. The last thing I wanted to do was to give my PoPo the burden of worrying about me, so I asked Luke to go in to check in on her without me. I would remain outside until I could find my strength to go in.

Fighting the panic in my heart and the stark reality of what was happening, I watched Luke walk toward her. I told myself to be strong and to go in, too. I eventually did, but I could only follow for a few steps because I could not control my weeping. From where I stood, PoPo's temporary room was in my full view. The curtains weren't drawn, and I was able to watch the doctors and medical attendants move about her. When they left, Luke went up to PoPo, and I watched her face beam with joy as she saw him standing by her side. She smiled as best she could. Even with her lopsided smile, she was adorable and precious, exuding loving kindness.

I gasped for air as I felt my body weaken at the sight.

PoPo tried to hug Luke with both arms, but her right side failed her. She momentarily looked at her right shoulder and arm, and I could tell from her expression she was trying to assess and understand what was happening. Still, her disability didn't stop her from showing her affection. When she saw she could successfully use her left arm, she reached up to touch Luke's face and rubbed his cheeks with her palm. She tried in vain to speak and sighed in surrender, but she still tried to smile.

"Don't strain, Grandma," Luke said softly. "It's okay. I love you too. Just rest, everything is going to be okay. The doctors are taking good care of you. We're all here. Manna is just outside and will be in shortly." He tried to comfort her, as she was obviously troubled. My mother was by the other side of the bed and said very little as she watched the machines monitor PoPo's condition.

The shock of this entire scene unfolding before my eyes was almost too much to take in. Fighting the feeling of everything closing in again, I walked back outside.

Luke noticed me wobbling and came to where I sat on a bench outside of the sliding doors. When I saw him, I jumped up and started crying even harder.

"Luke, this is it…this is it, isn't it?" I asked, gasping for breath through my sobbing and trembling body.

"Yes, Mann (his nickname for me). It's time," he answered as he pulled me close for a comforting hug.

I don't know how long I stood sobbing into his chest. Thousands of memories poured through my mind. The idea of losing this beautiful, dignified, noble woman crushed me. PoPo came through royal descent, had been through two World Wars, the Great Depression, uprisings and revolutions, economic upheavals, monumental changes in the industrial, technological, and economic booms, great personal losses, countless sacrifices, and now, the betrayal of her own body as she tried to move and speak.

Oh, the unanswerable questions of life…

Doubt and disbelief knocked at my heart's door, and I fought the temptation to blame my mother—and even God—for the pain and suffering in PoPo's life. I breathed deeply, trying to center my thoughts.

Then I remembered all I did know about God. I remembered His nature, His goodness, His patience, and His provision. I remembered all the times He had saved my grandparents from worse than what they had suffered, how He had provided for them all their lives. And I thanked Him for giving me them as loving "earth angels" for as long as I had them to watch over, provide for, and fight for Luke and me.

Instead of asking the ugly, base question of "why," as if I was entitled to more, I simply thanked God for all that I did have and all that He had given me. Instead of asking questions that would only foster bitterness and anger, I began to fill with unspeakable gratitude.

My repetitive, *Oh, my God! Oh, my God! Oh, my God…* turned into, *Thank You, God! Thank You, God! Thank You, God!*

As soon as I started to shift my heart to the Truth of all that God had done for us, my heart shifted from victim thinking and self-pity to courage.

I remembered the dream God had given me, well in advance, to prepare me for this time. He had used all those months to strengthen me. He also created a divine appointment in the form of a two-day retreat to equip me for this fateful day. With good counselors supporting me, I had been able to begin my grieving process in advance for what would be the test of my life, no less than forty-eight hours later.

Yes, God knew everything that was happening, and He had provided a way for me to stand in the middle of the storm.

My PoPo was eventually moved into a private room, and the family worked courteously together to quell any distress PoPo may have felt or sensed from us. I walked around the room, assessing it. I planned to stay with PoPo for as long as it took. I had a nanny who had graciously agreed to stay with Michael during this time, so I had the flexibility to stay as long as I was needed. At PoPo's bedside, I positioned a larger chair, which would be my bed in the days to come. Just then, I overheard my mother and Luke in a conversation outside in the hallway.

"Luke," my mother whispered. "You had better watch Manna. She's not going to be able to handle this…"

"Of course, she will. It won't be easy, but she'll be fine. God has been preparing her for this time," Luke replied.

"I don't know," my mother said uncertainly. "PoPo is all she knows… they're so close…maybe too close."

I suspected it may have been one of the first times my mother realized that *her mother* was the only mother I had ever had. Perhaps this was her guilt speaking, revealing her awareness that losing PoPo would not only be like losing a real mother, but my very lifeline.

Hearing my mother speak gave me a sliver of hope. Could she actually be concerned for me? Then I heard her say, "I think she could have a nervous breakdown, and then who can help her? I'm not taking care of her! That's for sure! You'd better watch her!"

There it was again. Her fear of having anything to do with me. Who makes comments like this, much less a mother about her child? Who predicts the worst for their child and then denounces their willingness to stand by them?

Right then, a nurse came in, showing us the different buttons and functions of the monitors. She adjusted PoPo's pillows, inclined the bed, and left the room. I sat on PoPo's bed with her. Unsure how much of her brain had been damaged by the stroke, or if her memory or language function was impaired, I spoke to her in Mandarin—her native tongue. She touched my face with her hand and looked upon me with loving eyes. With her eyes, she told me how much she loved me and was proud of me. She brushed my hair away from my face with her hand and played with my hair like she had when I was a little girl. We looked at each other, and in those powerful moments of silence, she spoke with her touch, her eyes, her heart. PoPo said more through her spirit than any other language could convey.

Then, she leaned forward and grabbed both my hands, squeezing them tightly. Tears flowed from her sad, sunken eyes. Without speaking, she was exhorting me to be strong and courageous. Everything would be okay.

We were together for half an hour—touching and sharing, and when I felt I could manage some words through my own stream of tears, I spoke to her again in Mandarin. She replied with her hands, telling me to stop talking and to surrender to the inevitable.

I could hardly take it in.

Yes, it was time.

Then, all of a sudden, her eyes looked just past me, and she started to track something moving to the left and eventually to the wall behind her. She strained, arching backward, following the movement. She turned back at me and tilted her head toward the same area as if to show me what she was looking at. I prayed for God to open my spiritual eyes even more, to see what PoPo was seeing, but I couldn't. She extended her working arm upward, reaching, reaching, wanting to grab hold of something or *someone.*

The nurse came in to check on her IV, hardheartedly commented that PoPo was hallucinating, then walked away again. Her comment was the farthest thing from the truth. PoPo was lucid and as clear as she had ever been. Just because she couldn't speak didn't mean she was hallucinating! She grunted, in an effort to tell me what she was seeing.

"What do you see, PoPo?" I asked.

She looked at me exasperated, wanting so much to explain what she was seeing. She looked up and reached out again with all her might.

"Do you see GongGong?" I asked, struggling.

She looked back at me, and her eyes told me to try again.

"Do you see an angel?" I asked, guessing.

She looked at me with frustration and reached up again.

"Do you see God?" I asked.

She gave me another look, and reached backwards again, grunting as she strained with all her might to grab onto something. Exhausted, she slumped back down in her bed and closed her eyes. When she looked at me again, her eyes were pleading.

I tried again. "PoPo…are you reaching to take the hand of Jesus?" I said, whispering almost incredulously.

She nodded.

Oh…my…!

In the profundity of that moment, I prayed. I thanked God for His presence and asked Him to take my beloved grandmother, so she would not have to suffer any longer. I didn't want her last moments of consciousness to be in fear, desperation, or anything else that could torment her. I continued praying in silence, holding Grandma's other hand as she repeatedly attempted to reach for the hand of Jesus. PoPo was trying to be lifted out of this body, out of this reality, and into the beauty of heaven. I tried to control myself, but tears flowed down my face as the inevitable became closer and more and more real.

Later that evening, I was told PoPo would be receiving morphine shots through her IV so that she wouldn't be in pain or suffer anymore "hallucinations." I explained that my grandmother was not hallucinating, but no one believed me.

For the next ten days, the morphine did its job, and PoPo slept soundly. Many times, I wasn't sure if she was sleeping, but she was too drugged to fight. Still, I talked to her, reminisced with her and thanked her for every memory and every sweet and wonderful thing she and GongGong had done for me.

Occasionally, I fell into fits of despair and despondency, wailing and groaning when the reality of losing my PoPo forever pierced me. At times, I climbed onto her bed and hugged her. I told her it was my turn to hold her now, telling her she was safe, and she had nothing to be afraid of.

I was beside myself.

The prayers I had prayed as a little girl, asking God to take ten years off my life and to give them to PoPo and GongGong until we evened out and died together had not been answered. They would both be going Home first, without me.

One afternoon, Scham came.

I started to leave so he could have some time alone with PoPo, but he asked me to stay. He tried to comfort me and stuttered in his awkwardness. It took a lot of courage for him to come by himself, knowing I would be there. A lot had happened before this event, not the least of which was how Huxley treated me after everything I had done for her. Scham could have chosen to be cold and angry toward me in defense of his daughter, but he didn't.

He told me he knew there was more to the situation than he had been told; he knew what his daughter was like. He also told me how hard it had been for him to lose his youngest brother to cancer, and he understood my sadness. We talked about his brother, and I shared with him my own happy memories of him. Ours wasn't a long exchange, and afterwards, he left to go home.

As I watched him leave, I couldn't help but notice how different things were now between Scham and me. I thanked God for turning around the most hideous of situations and for having brought healing, forgiveness, closure, and wholeness to me.

Over the next few days, visitors came and showed their kindness toward the family, as did the two counselors who had worked with me mere days before my PoPo's stroke. They were in awe at how God had orchestrated our time together. Because I had that time to prepare, with each passing day, I had the strength to find a little more peace in accepting the inevitable.

On September 29th, PoPo opened her eyes for the first time since the nurses started giving her morphine. My mother, who was in the room, advised me not to be too excited because we were told this could be a reaction to the medication. But as I looked at my grandma's eyes, I saw they were intentionally open, and she was trying to say something to me.

When I told my mother this, she went toward the bed to check PoPo's pulse. She looked down and said slowly, "It's almost time."

What? She's leaving! Oh, no…oh, no…oh, no…

I pulled my chair closer toward the bed and looked right into PoPo's eyes. She had been sleeping on her side, and I was now face to face with her. "I'm right here, PoPo. I'm right here. It's going to be okay. Don't be scared. Everything is going to be okay," I said. My eyes were full of tears, but she was even more beautiful in my sight. She seemed to glisten and glow.

She closed her eyes again. I looked up at my mother to see her turn away, tears in her own eyes.

Oh, my God, this is really happening. Oh, my God…oh, PoPo, sweet and precious PoPo…

PoPo opened her eyes once more, and with determination, she held them open for a few more seconds.

"I love you, PoPo! I love you. Thank you for everything. I love you…I love you…Thank you for everything…Oh, Grandma, I love you…" I cried out, sobbing.

And then, my beloved PoPo slowly closed her eyes for the last time as she took her final breath.

On September 29th, at 2:39 p.m., my PoPo was gone.

PoPo was now freed from her suffering.

After taking some time to gather myself, I stood up from the chair where I had spent the past ten days. The nurses came and checked PoPo's pulse, and after a few moments, nodded to confirm that she had indeed passed. I continued to watch, speechless, as they turned PoPo over, so she was lying on her back. They pulled her sheets neatly up around her chest.

"We'll let you have some time together now. Let us know when you're ready. Take your time," the nurse said.

I walked over to my beloved PoPo, and as I looked upon her, I could barely recognize her. As I reflected on the last few minutes of her life, I was amazed to witness the process of her spirit leaving her body. Little by little, it left. Soon, all that remained was the shell that had housed her soul and spirit for eighty-seven years. I can honestly say that *who* was left behind did not look like my PoPo. I slowly walked around the bed in bewilderment, unable to avert my eyes from what used to be my PoPo.

I now had no tears to cry and no words to say. I was numb from all that had occurred, shocked by the reality that my world was now forever changed. I was emptier because my precious lifeline called PoPo was no longer with me. I staggered at the accuracy of my prophetic dream and how it had unfolded before my very eyes, in awe at how God had provided for me every step of the way.

After kissing PoPo on the forehead one last time, I walked toward the window and stared out into the busy world below. Everything was the same, but nothing was ever going to be the same again.

Without PoPo, what will I do? What will life be like without her? How will I manage? Who will I talk to? All I have known is PoPo…without her, what will keep this side of the family together?

"It's MY PRECIOUS!"

The next two weeks were chaotic at best.

Uncle Oliver allowed me to present the eulogy, which was far from easy. I spoke of PoPo as an amazing human being who had repeatedly sacrificed in her life for the entire family—not just for me alone. I tried to offer comfort by letting loved ones know that PoPo had known her time was near, and she had not only been prepared to go but had been eager to take the hand of God. Lastly, I reminded everyone that more valuable than the cash and the rare curios, artifacts, and paintings she and GongGong had collected was the priceless gift of having had her in our lives. When the memorial was over, I naively thought we could all find a new way of being a family together.

"That doesn't sound good," Leah interjected.

"No, it wasn't good at all. As much as we had experienced together, especially with the passing of PoPo, I thought there would have been a humble resolve to start fresh. I wanted my family to do what it would take to keep the family together. But that was not the case."

I sighed and went on to relate what happened next.

When the time came to go over the will, my mother was furious to discover that I had inherited as much as she and Uncle Oliver. Essentially, my grandparents said I was equal to their daughter and son; that I was like another daughter to them. Although I was distributed a cash amount that was according to my grandparents' wishes, the rest of the estate was not distributed fairly at all—nor as they had wished.

And when it came time to distribute a few special pieces of PoPo's jewelry, only Uncle Oliver, Luke, my mother, and I were there. Everyone else had rejected the opportunity, wanting equivalent cash disbursements instead.

When it came time to choose PoPo's engagement and wedding rings, I asked for them. PoPo had promised them to me because of all the stories we had shared together about their engagement and wedding, and how GongGong had saved every penny to buy the rings for her. Relative to the other pieces, these small stones weren't worth much, and were the least valuable items we had before us.

To me, however, they were priceless because of the memories and the promise they had made to each other.

When I tearfully and humbly explained why I wanted them, my mother interrupted me violently. If Uncle Oliver hadn't been sitting there, she would have lunged to hit me. She yelled at me, delirious, her mouth twisted, looking as if she had lost her mind. "I'm taking it! My mother only had one daughter, and that's me—*not you*!"

"Emily, that's not necessary. Calm down," Uncle Oliver said sternly, and then looked at me. "Manna, the only way to do this is to divide the two rings. Which do you want?" he asked.

"Uncle Oliver, how can I possibly choose? One symbolizes everything GongGong had to do to buy PoPo that ring when he had no money and was trying to go through medical school. The other one symbolizes all they went through together after marriage, and how they provided for us as a family," I protested.

"*I want them!*" my mother screamed again as she lunged for Uncle Oliver's hands.

Uncle Oliver looked disapprovingly at my mother and then turned to me again and said, "Manna, please choose one."

I hesitated and took the one I felt meant the most to my grandparents, the engagement ring, even though it was the least expensive of them. When they had nothing, they gave each other the best they had. The wedding ring was just as important (and had more diamonds), but their engagement ring was their promise to each other when they had nothing else to offer and in spite of all that went against them.

No sooner had I made my choice than my mother grabbed the wedding band out of my uncle's hands and stared at it, looking every bit like Gollum from *The Lord of the Rings* with his "precious."

She continued to hurl vicious comments at me, but I said nothing, steeling myself after each hateful remark. But when she wouldn't relent, unable to withstand anymore, I finally confronted her.

"I have done nothing but be a housemaid and nanny for you and *your precious daughter*, whom I gave the chance of a lifetime to help again as an adult! How dare you speak to me this way after every horrible thing you've done to the family and *me*? You're the one who took all of PoPo's best and finest things and hid them away in your basement. You *stole* everything PoPo wanted for me! I received nothing except the scraps after you and everyone else went through her things! All I ask now is to have a few special pieces that mean nothing to you, but because they mean something to me, you want to rob me of those too! Haven't you appropriated enough? Haven't you stolen enough life out of me, Luke, and our whole family? *Haven't you done enough, period?*" I shouted.

Uncle Oliver held my hand, and with his touch, tried to assure me that he knew more than he let on. But that was not the time to hash out the past. Luke was quiet, torn between what he knew was true, and his obligation to still respect his mother.

Where I found the self-control to disengage from my mother, I do not know. I bit my lip, and as soon as the process of dispersing the last of PoPo's jewelry was completed, Luke and I left the house.

That was October 1998. I had just buried my PoPo, and whatever trace of latent hope I had for my mother also died that day.

It was finally over.

The Cost of Doing Business

Uncle Oliver was in charge of dispersing the remainder of my grandparents' assets and told me he was going to hire Christie's or Sotheby's to appraise them. I asked him to let me know what that final appraisal amount was and, if it were acceptable to him, I would pay the estate for the curios so that PoPo and GongGong's belongings would not be scattered into random homes around the world where no one would know their history or the sacrifices that had been made for each piece. He agreed.

When I was told the amount, it was no small matter. However, I was grateful to have earned and saved enough, and I cashed out over half of my investments to pay the estate. I also had to pay the hefty penalties and taxes for cashing out my investments early, but I was happy to do so to keep my grandparents' belongings in the family. The monies were wired and sent, and the process of organizing the pickup of the artifacts began.

A week later, I received a call from Uncle Oliver. "Manna, we changed our minds," he said frigidly.

"Umm…I'm sorry. I don't understand. Who's 'we,' and what did you change your minds about, Uncle Oliver?" I asked.

"We changed our minds about selling the curios to you."

I was stunned to speechlessness.

"Manna, did you hear me?"

"Yes. I'm trying to understand what you mean," I responded.

"It's simple. We decided that we don't want to sell the curios to you, and we are going to give you your money back."

"Why? Did you get higher offers? Do you want more money? If that's it, let me know. I'll figure it out," I offered.

"No. We just don't think it's a good idea."

"Who's we?" I asked again.

He never answered.

"Uncle Oliver, I cashed out most of my savings and had to pay a lot of penalties and taxes on all of that money, which you have already received. If you want more, then let me see the appraisals, and I can get you more money. I really don't want Grandma and Grandpa's things sold to strangers and distributed all over the world. Please. I will pay the difference," I offered again.

"No. The decision has been made. You'll get your money back."

"But we agreed!" I pleaded.

"The decision has been made. Whatever we can't sell, we'll draw names for afterward," he answered curtly.

"That's it? No discussion? What about what I would like to do? Wouldn't it be best to have these pieces stay in the family?"

"No. The decision is made. There's nothing more to discuss."

"What about all the expenses I had to pay to set up accounts and wire monies to you? What about the taxes and penalties I had to pay? Will I get that back?"

"No."

"*No*? How is that right, Uncle Oliver? We're family! We had an agreement," I asked with tears streaming down my face at the thought that my beloved uncle whom I adored, to whom I had looked up all of my life, whom I thought and believed was my ally and friend, was now like my enemy. He shared no kindness, no empathy, no emotion. My uncle had simply dismissed me. And then, the final cut...

"That's the cost of doing business," he stated heartlessly. "There's no more discussion." And with that, he ended the call.

"*That's the cost of doing business?!*" Leah shouted, leaning forward with shock.

I took a moment to lean her back and get her settled in the bed comfortably. "Yes," I said sadly. "That's exactly what he said before he hung up, and that is something I will never forget. Needless to say, we haven't been in touch since then.

"A few years ago, Luke retrieved the artifacts that were attributed to me per the lottery draw for the things that did not sell. And I was not surprised to see the least valuable, least desired, and the fewest amount of pieces had been distributed to me. Plus, the celadon bowl GongGong had promised to me as he taught me the fine nuances and the mastery of appreciating such artifacts were never given to me as Uncle Oliver had promised."

There was a long silence. I looked up to see Leah looking out the window, wiping tears from her eyes.

"Don't be sad, Leah," I said with concern. "In the end, I had the greater treasure. I had something indescribably rare and beautiful with my grandparents. Something no one can ever take away."

The End of an Era

I began this part of my story by saying the health of both my grandmothers' was declining. Well, within a few months of PoPo's passing, my MahMah also passed away. It was the end of an era.

"*What?!*" Leah gasped.

I had been traveling back and forth for my PoPo's memorial (and all the other matters I shared earlier) and was now making plans again to go back to Vancouver for my MahMah's services. Though we weren't as close, she had softened a great deal over the years, and so had I. Our relationship had grown to be sweet and easy, and her sudden passing sent me reeling, especially on the heels of having just lost PoPo.

Amid such loss, I expected some compassion and tenderness from my husband. But instead, I was met with callousness and cruelty.

"I forbid you to go to the funeral!" he yelled.

"It's my grandmother's funeral! You can't forbid me to go! You should be coming with me! You never came for PoPo's funeral, or to see me at the hospital as she was dying! Have you no heart?"

"What about your work?" he blasted.

"*What did you say?* Didn't I leave shortly after PoPo's memorial and fly straight to your event to deliver a standing ovation talk for you? Didn't I deliver an entire floppy disc of documents for your trainings, so everyone could be on the same page? And didn't I write two newsletters for you while I was in the hospital? *Is this some kind of sick joke?* Both my grandmothers just died within a few months of each other, and you're worried I'm not working hard enough?"

Even with counseling, Barry refused to show kindness or compassion and kept insisting I not go to the funeral.

I went anyway.

When I came back, Barry did not once ask me how I was feeling after the loss of these key people in my life. He *did* ask about my inheritance money, but went right back to his routine of golf and excessive time on the computer.

Michael and I were not even on his radar.

When Hell Freezes Over

Barry's children were young at the time, and I noticed immediately that we had different parenting styles. Living with Barry and seeing him in day-to-day reality was *very* different than dating him long distance. I had made excuses for his way of living in hotel rooms because I told myself he was always busy or focused because of the high demands on him. But now I could see that how he lived at home was not much different. I was neat and organized. He was haphazard and dirty. While this wasn't the end of the world, what was appalling was his lack of personal self-care and the absence of even elementary etiquette.

"How bad could it have been?" Leah teased. "He wasn't instigating belching or farting contests with his children at the dinner table, was he?"

I said nothing, returning her look with a raised eyebrow.

"Oh, my word!" Leah chimed in. "Money doesn't buy class, does it? And don't we all know people who have money, but still act like farm animals? Unless his kids were trained differently by their mother, I'm sure they learned his poor habits, too."

"I don't know how Joyce was with them."

"Was she nice to you?" Leah quizzed.

"I only met her a handful of times, and she was civil. But behind my back, well, that was another matter altogether. The many unkind things she repeatedly said were reported back to me. But I felt compassion for her. From her point of view, I was the *new wife* who had come in to reap the benefits of all she had suffered for. But she had no idea I knew what she had endured, and she had no idea what was going on behind our seemingly *beautiful* marriage.

"Barry and I were still newlyweds, but our marriage was already a hot mess. Still, I could not give up. Not one stone went unturned, and I tolerated more than I can talk about, just to avoid more issues to fight about. Unfortunately, while my determination to contend for the marriage was fierce, Barry's entrenched dysfunction and his unwillingness to overcome them was stronger. He opposed me and everything the counselors suggested."

"I'm so sorry." Leah shook her head. "Did Joyce at least appreciate your care of her children?"

"I don't know if she knew the extent to which I did care for them. Even though the children's visitations were meant to grow their relationship with their father, what I witnessed was anything but that. Because Barry was so lacking in relationship skills, the burden fell on me to constantly navigate a very tenuous connection between them. Sure, they had fun together at first, but within a few hours, bedlam would break out. The children may not remember it now, but it was often hell during their visits, and it never took long before they would ask if they could be taken back home.

"A counselor once remarked that after every visit, I would lose a month of my life because of the energy and heart it took to manage all of their dynamics.

"One time when we were on a trip together, I asked the oldest one, 'Have you and your father always fought like this?' They said, 'Yup! We hate him! He's always *sooo* mean, and I can't believe the things he says to us!'

"Barry was also ruthless with his bizarre standards of perceived *excellence*, and the irony was how little he lived up to those standards for himself. He had a disturbing obsession with body image and would swing from overeating to excessive exercising and fasting protocols. He imposed his rules on his children (and me) as well, and when we didn't meet his standards, he mocked us.

"All I wanted to do was to help Barry rebuild his relationship with his children. I was successful often enough, but just as often, I became the scapegoat and the mutual enemy, so they could find a reason to rally together.

"In the middle of dealing with Barry and his kids, I was also helping Michael adjust to his new change of environment. He had valid feelings about leaving behind our family, his friends, and his soccer league and tennis team. And I was helping him understand the loss of his great-grandmothers at the same time. He was in the midst of starting at a new school, making new friends, learning new material in class (such as American history instead of Canadian history), learning new colloquialisms that helped him to feel like he belonged, and dealing with my traveling for work more frequently than before. Worst of all, he had had to reconcile the ambiguities of Barry's so-called 'love,' and of course, processing our integration as a 'family'—a family Barry promised he would do anything and everything to have and to build.

"Overall, Michael adapted to the new changes very well and had a great time meeting new friends and being a part of a new life here. And though he was disappointed that Barry never followed through with any of his promises to him, we were still very happy together and relieved by Barry's absence.

"In fact, we were *happiest* when Barry was away for work every other week. During those times, we had a joy-filled home life, and I still made fabulous lunches for Michael with a love note for him every day hidden somewhere in his knapsack."

"Sweet little boy. How about Barry's children? How were they to you?" Leah asked.

"They were distant at first but warmed up to us quickly. Their home life was filled with negative reports about me, so it was always a battle to start fresh each time we saw them. It wasn't their fault. They were caught between two worlds."

"You're an angel," Leah said, shaking her head.

"I don't know about that. But I was kind, and I was consistent."

"So, who told you Joyce was talking trash about you?"

"Many people at the office, mutual friends, even the children told me what their mother was saying about me."

"Right from the horse's mouth, so to speak," Leah said, disappointedly.

"Yes, but when the kids reported these comments to me, I just listened. I wanted them to know they were safe, talking to me about anything. My intention was not to put them into a battle between their mother and me. Rather, I turned these comments into opportunities for teaching them character-building lessons they could relate to. Instead of using their mother and me as subject matter, I used current examples with friends or school activities as a focus. We talked about using our words to speak life, hope, and possibility instead of using them to hurt, judge, or condemn, especially since we did not always know the truth of every situation."

"Like I said, you're an angel! I would have given up a long time ago! Nope, not my circus and not my monkeys!" Leah said defiantly. "How did things work out with the kids over time?"

"Michael and I built a good relationship with Barry's kids, and they even insisted I participate in some of their school activities. I did my best to support them, but I also knew when not to overstep so as not to pose a threat to Joyce."

"Dear God, Manna, what a minefield! I hope those kids know how much you did for them," Leah added.

"I doubt they do. When our marriage ended, Barry refused to let me say goodbye to them. I would never have put them in a position to choose sides—they had already done that once. I only wanted to tell them I loved them, that I was sorry I had to go, and if they ever needed anything, they could call me."

"Oh, Manna," Leah stopped, thought for a moment, and then continued, "I hate to say this, but no matter how nasty the stories were about you before, they only got worse after you left. You do know that, don't you?"

"Yes. I know."

"Did Barry ever ask to see Michael?" Leah asked.

"Not at first. Years later, long after our divorce was finalized, he asked to see him once."

"What did you say?"

"*When hell freezes over!*"

Sleeping With the Enemy

My marriage, right from the beginning, was one dysfunctional episode after another. The great changes Barry (and Kent) had assured me of never happened.

Even our first night together as newlyweds in our new home was tragic. Instead of a night of warmth, love, and intimacy, Barry randomly started recounting details of every sexual escapade he had with other women! The topic in and of itself was shocking, especially on our first night together in our marriage bed. I only tolerated his discourse because I was too stunned to speak.

In the battlefield of my mind that night, I tried to find a reason for what was happening. *Maybe he's going to tell me he is remorseful for those flings? Maybe he's going to tell me how he wished he had waited for me instead?*

No. There was nothing logical or sane about this, so I interrupted him. "Barry," I said, trying to muster as much composure as possible, "Where are you going with this? This is our first night together in our home! It's just wrong for you to be talking about this! Can we talk about *us* and how we're going to start a new life together, instead?"

"You interrupted me in the middle of my sharing!" he blasted.

"Are you saying it's *normal* for you to talk about past sexual episodes with strange women on the first night of marriage in a new home with your wife?"

"Yes!" He seethed. "I'm sharing! You're supposed to be my 'safe place!' Now listen or get out!"

I flung the covers off, grabbed my robe, and went outside to sit in the backyard. I was fuming with rage. On what should have been a sweet, intimate, and memorable evening together, he had entirely dishonored me as his wife.

Barry's sexual anomalies continued to reveal themselves. He openly gawked at young girls in my presence, saying I should be like them—my 5'7", 123-pound figure was not up to his standards. My husband was obsessed with bodies—his own and other women's or younger girls'—which led to his other addiction.

Barry's computers kept freezing unexplainably. Time and time again, different technicians worked on both his desktop and laptop. The technician finally told me (after fixing Barry's computer for the umpteenth time) the source of the computer issues. All problems were the result of numerous viruses downloaded from the multiple *porn sites* he had visited. The technician was very embarrassed to have to tell me this. Were it not for the fact that Barry refused to return any of his calls, I may never have learned the reason. But at that point, he felt he had to at least let me know.

It was humiliating to make the discovery in this way, but at least finally I knew why Barry acted so strangely whenever I came into his office while he was "working" on his computer.

The only other story I will tell is the dreadful abuse I took on our first Christmas together as husband and wife.

I wanted to do something special and sweet for him, so on Christmas morning, I got up early to get ready. Barry was curious and seemed excited about the surprise. He promised he wouldn't leave the bed and would wait until I returned. I quickly went into my closet and put on an adorable red Santa bra and panty outfit with a cute matching apron outlined with faux fur, a Santa's hat with a white pompom, and white go-go boots. My heart was racing with anxiety because I hadn't done anything like this before, and knowing how critical he had been of me made me even more nervous. Still, I wanted to try and to bring some life and hope back into my marriage, which was not yet even one year old.

When I was ready, I loaded three large and beautifully wrapped Christmas presents for him in my arms.

"Honey, are you ready?" I asked sing-songily from my closet.

"Yeah, I'm ready," he answered.

I put on Bing Crosby's "White Christmas," and walked in dressed as "Santa," bearing gifts with a childlike heart and a smile to match. I felt very vulnerable in my costume, knowing I was allowing him to assess and critique me, but my desire to surprise and please my husband outweighed my fears.

Barry's eyes opened wide as he twisted his lips. I was expecting him to be happy, but to my utter horror, he berated me with a snarl.

"What the *hell* do you think you're doing? You look absolutely ridiculous!" He coldly laughed out loud. "Who are you trying to be? Take off that stupid costume! Is this what you think is a fun surprise for me on Christmas? What a joke!"

I was paralyzed by his hateful words. My mind raced as I tried to decide what to do. My smile vanished, as did the color from my face. I felt a cold chill of evil cover me, and the alarm in my expression could not be hidden.

I did not want to give him the satisfaction, but I could not hold back the tears that flowed like a running faucet down my cheeks. Unable to comprehend the wickedness of what my *husband* had said, much less find the words to reply, I threw the boxes onto the bed and backed away from him toward the bathroom door. As sick as this sounds, I knew if I turned away from him, he would have another excuse to critique me from behind, and I refused to give him that opportunity.

I tried to find my breath. And when I reached my closet, all I could do was to pace back and forth, trying to comprehend the incomprehensible. I fought the urge to scream, to kick in a wall, to retaliate. Instead, I undressed, threw away my outfit, put on some sweatpants and a sweatshirt, and went to the backyard where I prayed for God to help me.

Barry never came after me, never apologized, and never said anything to me about that incident again. When I addressed this in our couple's counseling, he dismissed it as *my issue* with sex.

When I heard Michael rustling around, I shared Christmas with him alone and then suggested we go to a restaurant for brunch. He asked about Barry, but when I told him he wasn't coming with us, he knew we'd had another fight.

"Why is he always so mean, Mommy?" He looked down and then said slowly, "It must be really bad this time for us to leave on Christmas morning…I'm sorry."

Sad to realize how much Michael had heard and witnessed in spite of all my efforts to protect him, I responded, "I'm the one who's sorry. I wanted more for you…for us." I sighed. "Wounded people sometimes wound others…"

"But you don't hurt people, Mommy, even when they're mean to you! If people know what it's like to be treated mean, shouldn't they be nicer to one another?" Michael asked innocently.

Out of the mouths of babes…

"Yes, Michael. We should be nice…"

But not wanting the heaviness to usurp the reason for the season and on the beauty of this day, I jumped up and said, "Enough about that. Are you hungry?"

"Yes!" Michael replied with a huge smile.

"Me too! Let's go, shall we?" I said as cheerfully as I could.

"What restaurant will be open on Christmas morning?" he asked as we drove away from the house.

"I know of only one—Mendel's," I answered with a smile.

"Why? Why would Mendel's be open on Christmas morning?" he asked curiously.

"Because it's a Jewish restaurant."

We both laughed.

When we arrived at the restaurant, Michael opened his door and exclaimed, "Mommy! Wow! There's a twenty-dollar bill right here!"

I looked around for other cars, thinking we could return the money to the owner. But no other cars were there.

"It's a sign," I said.

"Of what, Mommy?"

"It's confirmation that God knew we'd be here, and it's a sign of provision! Breakfast is paid for!"

We laughed and held hands walking into the restaurant, enjoying our first Christmas in America together.

"Oh, Manna…I don't even know what to say…" Leah paused and then continued, "How does one even try to comfort you after experiencing such…such crudeness?! He's a deviant! And he needs to be locked up before he hurts more people!"

"It's not easy to share these stories, but I believe accounts like these can help others. By making these experiences known, maybe collectively, to a society whose religion is *backwards tolerance*, perhaps we won't tolerate such madness any longer. When we find the courage to tell the truth, we release ourselves and others from distorted projections that may have been hurled onto us.

"Plain and simple, some things are offensive—they're not to be tolerated and not to be endured. If the outcry is great enough, maybe our dampened sensitivities and lax boundaries will be reevaluated. Instead of condoning the deplorable and the disgusting, instead of incorporating perversion in any form into our daily lives—instead of living with feigned compassion and counterfeit forgiveness masked as *acceptance and tolerance*, we need to say, 'No!'"

I Quit!

It was becoming very clear that I had to finally say "No!" too. It was time to leave Barry.

But my final immigration papers were not yet ready. I thought about going home to Vancouver and starting all over again. My clients would come back to me, and even if they didn't, I would begin again. However, without my proper papers, I would still have problems going in and out of the country. Those issues would severely hinder my career opportunities—something I had to carefully think about since I would be on my own financially again, starting from zero.

My immigration attorney was kind, and his assistant, Sherry, who helped me with many of my documents, advised me to try and seek support and counseling. Little did she know we already had a handful of different therapists, including a corporate therapist (or "coach") to help the partners, consultants, and the management team deal with Barry.

Not only that, I had a crew of health practitioners to help me survive the abuse in my marriage. I was under the care of three medical specialists. One was a cardiologist who put me on a heart monitor for six months. He could not understand my irregular heartbeats and sudden escalations in blood pressure. Another was an internal medicine physician. He could not understand why my body was failing and why my comprehensive blood tests were at dangerous levels. And I had an immunologist, to whom I was referred as a last attempt for healing. Perhaps I was allergic to something or had an autoimmune disease that was causing my hair to fall out in such drastic proportions, my scalp was starting to show.

In the middle of one of my exams, my doctor asked me, "Were you in a bad car accident?"

"No, why do you ask?" I asked.

"Because your back is in spasms before my eyes. I only see this kind of injury with people involved in major car accidents!"

I took a deep breath, "No, I wasn't in a bad car accident," I admitted with defeat. "Just a horrible marriage."

All my doctors were concerned and told me to see a counselor. Like Sherry, each was stunned when I told them we already had five of them.

While Barry was excellent at outward appearances, I was not. My failing health could not be hidden. No hairstyle could hide my scalp, no amount of makeup could hide the dark circles under my eyes, and not even the most coveted of designer outfits could hide my ongoing weight loss.

Though our marriage was now showing the *outward* signs of disrepair, I felt I had no choice but to still keep trying. I was constantly lining up more health practitioners, programs, and retreats. I was also going to Al-Anon meetings, and even attending more counseling sessions with Barry. We had brilliant therapists, but neither their skills, techniques, nor well-designed couples' exercises brought unity to our marriage. Each process only revealed the depths of Barry's disorders, and unless he fully committed to doing the work needed, my marriage was hopeless.

Each of our counselors had different thoughts on Barry, but essentially characterized him as a "dry drunk," a narcissist, a pathological liar with bipolar tendencies, and a few other personality irregularities. Our lead counselor even said, "Manna, I'm sorry to say this, but you don't have a marriage. You have an arrangement."

His words revealed the truth of the situation. The therapist was right. We had an arrangement: Barry manifested, and I did damage control. We had an unspoken agreement that I would work harder on his problem than he did. That was not love.

Barry's dysfunctions soon openly spread to our working relationship. He grew increasingly jealous of me, and on several occasions, I found him sneaking into my office to download my work onto floppy discs, claiming the work as his own. While he loved the appreciation I received from his clients, he hated me for the attention he felt I was "stealing" from him. So, he sabotaged me, demeaning me and lying about me in ways that would cause upset and fear in his partners and close associates. He even pitted the employees against me, several of whom I had once considered friends. In spite of the countless hours I had devoted to developing systems, processes, manuals, programs, and so on, he only saw me as his competitor—not his partner, friend, and certainly not his wife.

"There are always yes-men and yes-women who can be bought for a price. It sounds like you met a few of them!" Leah deduced. "Just remember, they didn't sell out on you; they sold out on themselves!"

The final straw came when Barry's impulsivity and lack of self-control reared its ugly head again. He wanted to implement yet another "new concept" without any discussion, planning, or preparation, and immediately started rescheduling his curriculum. Doing this would throw everyone from marketing to shipping into a tailspin, and invalidate his previous trainings. The effects would have been very damaging, and the company could not take another implosion (especially after overcoming a succession of them). So, with nothing to lose, I went to speak to him about the issue.

"Barry, may I come in?" I asked as I knocked on his office door.

"Uh, err, sure!" He clicked off his computer and looked at me. His eyes used to sparkle when they saw me. Now they were just empty eyes.

"Barry, we all know what's on your computer, so don't bother trying to hide it. Unless you're willing to try in our marriage, there's nothing I can do. I refuse to compete with porn sites."

He looked down and hung his shoulders.

I continued. "Somehow, you've made me your enemy and your hated competitor when it was you who asked for my help. Search your heart and ask whether or not I have given you my best with your business, your kids, your associates, your estranged family, and even with your ex-wife."

He looked at me, and to my surprise, he began to soften.

"Ask yourself if I have ever done anything to hurt you or to betray you," I said with tears in my eyes.

Barry looked down.

"Barry, I love you, and I have only wanted the best for you. I don't know how I became public enemy number one."

"I know, I know…you have done everything you could," Barry admitted. "Tell me what to do!" he pleaded.

"Barry, you know what to do. I can't tell you any more than the counselors already have. You just have to choose if our marriage is worth the effort. And if you're asking me about the company, all I can say is this: You have a great business filled with people who love you, believe in you, and want to serve you. You have clients who follow you, listen to you, pay to see you, buy all of your products, and basically do anything you tell them to do. Please, seriously reconsider executing the concept you were just talking about. Your clients are paying for your wisdom. Why would you sabotage them? Why would you create perpetuate more this chaos?" I asked boldly.

After a few moments, he looked up at me and confessed, "When I create chaos, I can control people."

Oh, my…did he just say that?

Barry continued. "People don't seem to stay with me. I had to find a hook! And chaos works! When I throw new things at them all the time, they stay, looking to me for answers. It's perfect! It's—"

"Manipulation!" I interjected. "Barry, I understand innovation, progress, and growth, but none of the past few concepts fall into those categories. Your clients are confused and complaining. They're frustrated and overwhelmed. One day you sell them an 'ultimate' plan and all the goodies to go with it. But then, the next day, you tell them to do something completely different and go in another direction. 'New and different' works in the right context, but you can't build long-term on chaos. Chaos is not a plan! Maybe for war, it is, but it's not for clients who trust you. And now you're seeing the effects of chaotic management—from lower sales to all the attrition. There are clear reasons why they're leaving. We need to take responsibility for that and then course correct."

"But I have to keep everyone on their toes!" he replied as if he didn't hear a single thing I said. "And this new technique I'm using is great!" He began to shout, back in his own world again. "I'll always be number one...I'll always dominate this market!"

"But that's just more manipulation!" I objected. I tried not to join him in volume, but it was becoming difficult. "Mind control, even with the best of intentions and the purest of hearts, is a tremendous responsibility *and burden*; it's not to be taken lightly. And without clean intentions, it's a dangerous weapon that can create much harm. Don't go down that road."

Barry leaned forward over his desk and looked me squarely in the eye and shouted, "This is *my* company! Neither you nor anyone else is going to tell me what to do!"

That's when the topic of two significant business associates who had been in lawsuits with him came up. He admitted he had betrayed them and rationalized that he did so to "get ahead of the game."

Just then, his phone rang, and he shooed me out of his office with a wave of his hand. Shaking my head, I left. Whatever opportunity there may have been for open and genuine discussion was gone.

Barry's conversation became very boisterous and energetic. And, as if I hadn't heard enough, he began discussing *me* and my upcoming role at the next event, despite the opened office door.

"I'll force her to retire...but she's a great trainer, and everyone loves hearing her speak," he said calculatingly. "It won't be easy."

Suddenly he erupted with excitement. "That's a great idea!" he shouted in response to what was said on the other end of the line. "I'll tell her to speak at the end of every event. Yes! That way, everyone can still see her and hear her message. People always sign up after she speaks! Yeah! That's great! She'll be our *closer* from now on!"

My office was next to his, and the foolish man did not know I could hear everything he was planning. Or maybe he did, and he was so far in his hubris that he didn't care.

Did he just say he's going to force me to retire? And, did he just call me a 'closer'?!

He's the one who asked me to help him, to build his business and to work side by side with him! Now he's 'forcing me to retire'?!'

When he finished the call, he bolted into my office—as if genius had struck him again. "I have the answer!" he announced. Then, with no concept of tact or diplomacy, much less sensitivity or tenderness, he continued, "We're not going work together anymore! At first, *we* were afraid of sales and signups falling after you leave, but we've got it figured out! You'll just come in at the end of the events, and do your talk about love, serving others, and the community. *We'll still blow the charts off the signups!*" He laughed, unashamedly. "It's perfect! You're a great closer—one of the best ever! *We all* love the idea! Come on, you have to admit it, this is *brilliant*!"

I stared at him from my desk, leaning back in my chair. "So, Barry, who *all* was on the call with you? Second, when were *we* going to discuss *my retiring*, or rather you forcing me out of a business I helped you grow and of which, by your own admission, I am such an instrumental part? Third, when were *we* going to discuss the new speaking arrangements to which you obligated me, and fourth, when did I become a *'closer'?*"

"Well, you *are* a great closer!" he answered, ignoring all the other questions.

"Am I simply a marketing tool for you too?"

"Don't get hung up on semantics. You drive sales!" he said, bouncing with energy.

"But I share from my heart. I mean all those things I say. It's not a marketing tool for me!" I rebutted.

"That's why you're 'the closer'!" You mean what you say, and your authenticity is felt by everyone in the room! They believe you, that's why they *have* to sign up!" he continued with exhilaration.

"But, Barry, do *you believe* in what I'm saying? Do *you believe* the intention and the purpose of what we are doing is *to love, serve, and build community?*"

"Whatever sells! Stop analyzing everything!" he said, annoyed.

I let out a huge breath, knowing we were on two completely different planets. "So, just to be clear, you only want me to come in at the end of your events, be your 'closer,' and drive sales."

"Finally! Yes! Now you get it!"

I slowly stood up and leaning forward, I said, "Yes. *I do finally get it.* Now, *you* listen to me very carefully. I will *not* be your closer. I will *not* allow you to use me any longer and be a pawn for you to use to manipulate your clients or anyone else! I am *not* retiring. *I quit!*"

Wicked

Around that same time, Joyce's attorney notified us that Joyce was suing us for more alimony and child support.

Under duress from Barry, I had been forced to pay Joyce what she had already been asking for with my own earnings, not to mention paying for all of her random, yet constant, miscellaneous expenses for her children, all of which totaled *well over* five figures monthly. I still have every check stub to prove it. Barry said I was to pay her out of my salary, and he would take care of our expenses.

I'll spare you the countless arguments about this, but long story short, I was enraged that almost every penny I earned went to his ex-wife and his children, and there was next to nothing left for myself or for Michael.

For my own spending money or anything to do with our own household, I was often forced to ask, and sometimes even beg, Barry for every penny, having to give an account for the necessity and the purpose of each item. It was humiliating and insane.

"You're kidding me! *You had to pay his child support and alimony?*" Leah hollered.

"Yes! Like I said, insanity reigned in that house! Trust me, I fought hard against this, but in the end, I had no choice but to comply. I was living with a very unstable person, and his outbursts were almost unbearable as it was. To force this issue when he was already so aberrant, and especially with his love of money, would have been emotional suicide.

"And frankly, there were many times I wanted to give up and literally *die*. My life was such a disaster, and I had grown weary of fighting and pretending and hiding from the outside world the incessant emotional tsunamis that left nothing but destruction in their wake. But the thought of leaving Michael in his care or guardianship frightened me even more, and so I fought to make it, for Michael.

"One of the saving graces was that Barry's travel schedule required him to be away for almost a week, every other week. Our counselors each noted that were it not for this 'gift' of time away from him, my well-being would have been questionable. During this time, we could all do what we needed to do to recover."

"What a wicked, wicked, evil man!" Leah gasped. "How did you manage to get away?"

"Well, unfortunately, it didn't happen immediately. I was torn about what to do. We were in between two worlds. I had just taken Michael out of a very full life in Vancouver. In spite of all that was happening in my marriage, I had managed to establish a relatively 'solid' home environment for him in the U.S. Pulling him away again would have been too much turmoil, and I couldn't do that to him.

"Plus, though Sherry from INS could not understand the delays herself, she assured me my papers would be approved 'any day' and encouraged me to be strong and to be patient. Our conversations always ended with her reminding me of the consequences if I left before my papers were ready. Sherry also continued to refer me to other counselors, and I continued to cry in desperation.

"In the meantime, avoiding him as best as possible was my only option. One lonely afternoon, when I didn't think I had the strength to carry on one more day, I cried out to God again.

"How could I have misunderstood Your message? It was so clear! So real! I know the calling You had for Barry, and for me. But if Barry won't do it, how can I? Barry has stripped me of everything, and I have nothing of my own anymore. If sharing the message of love, hope, and community was not possible with Barry, then how else can I do it? Dear God, please reveal my next steps..."

Back To School

In another divine series of events, I managed to make every application deadline (and be accepted) for the right program at the right school for the following semester. Then, after many years of intense studies in accelerated programs and heavy course loads, I eventually graduated with an M.A., a Ph.D., and several other certifications in the field of health and wellness. I didn't finish all of my schooling until after I left Barry, but at least I was doing something I loved, and I was able to focus on something more uplifting than the dreaded reality of my marriage and my home.

Not only did I find hope again for my life, my coursework was the excuse I needed to further distance myself from Barry. When not involved with Michael's activities, I was in class or practicums or sequestered in my office. There, I could hide in my readings, research, and writing. At school, I rediscovered my passion for learning. I was able to absorb, retain, and recall information well and quickly, achieving near-perfect scores on all my work. I was thrilled to successfully achieve and surpass every benchmark in my curriculum. No, I was *not* "stupid, ugly, and good-for-nothing."

My intention was to one day open a wellness center that would be a resource for women who suffered conditions similar to my own. I wanted to provide a place where people could learn about their role in their own health and well-being and receive fantastic leading-edge care.

"That sounds wonderful," Leah said. "And so like you!"

I smiled.

Thinking about helping others gave me joy, and little by little, I began to remember my gifts and purpose. When I started to understand my own worth, Barry's attempts at making me feel worthless stopped working. Although his escapades were still shocking, in many ways, they became expected and no longer affected me as strongly. My "skin" became tougher, and my heart, which was no longer available to him, was now only reserved for me and for Michael.

Deliverance

Finally, the long-awaited phone call came from my immigration attorney.

The papers were done, my green card was ready, and it was only a matter of filling out some final documents. At long last, my deliverance had come!

What should have been a six-month process (at the time) had been, instead, a four-year sentence in hell. I was a prisoner behind the beautiful doors of Barry's *dream house* in one of the most coveted neighborhoods of the U.S.A.

But now, I was allowed to be free!

Initially, Barry was hesitant to sign the papers. He found every excuse to avoid doing so. I prayed for there to be no more hindrances and for God to pave the way for Barry to sign. When I did, a gentle feeling of peace washed over me, and I knew everything was going to be okay.

My sentence was coming to an end.

The morning came for us to sign the papers, and just as God had assured me, Barry did so without question, rebuttal, or attack. I walked out of the downtown building with such a wave of relief I almost collapsed before reaching one of the outside benches in the front courtyard.

Barry looked at me oddly and wrote another entry in his journal.

Sadly, Barry's escalating negative reports about me were not restricted just to his journal. Conversation after conversation was repeated back to me by well-meaning individuals. Barry accused me of being with him for his money, the green card, and a litany of other indictments. He had always inappropriately revealed his unseemly personal thoughts to anyone who would listen—even publicly—but now, he was blatantly mendacious with his tales about me and our marriage.

It was one thing to be the direct target of Barry's attacks, but now I had to learn how to handle myself in the face of cruel and bald-faced lies told about me publicly by my own husband. Some had ticklish ears and were eager to listen and to spread gossip. Others were innocent and unsuspecting of his bulletin announcements. Either way, I had learned a very difficult lesson: to be free from the need to defend myself or to prove myself right by proving someone else wrong. I had to trust that *who I was* spoke louder than the lies spoken about me.

As we headed home from the lawyer's office, I realized there was truly nothing to hold us together anymore. He had killed every bit of love I had for him, and as this reality hit home, tears pooled in my eyes.

I had loved him deeply, tried so hard, and sacrificed *too* much for him, our marriage, our "family," and the promises of a fantastic future together. I did my best to find some residue of love for him, but there was nothing. If anything was left, it was hidden so deep it felt irretrievable.

"Not my circus! Not my monkeys!" Leah reminded me. "So, did you leave that night?!"

"Ironically, however, I didn't leave right away."

"What?! I would have had moving trucks waiting for me when I got home!"

"Well, we did go straight home, and as you can imagine, the ride was unpleasant. The energy was heavy, and the silence was deafening. But the strangest thing happened as soon as we walked in the door.

Barry stood by the garage door, crying as he stared at me. I turned to look at him, startled by his sudden and baffling display of emotions.

"Barry, what's wrong? What happened?" I asked.

He wouldn't answer. He just stared at me.

"Please, talk to me. Why are you crying?" I asked again.

He hesitated, then walked around me, going into his office. He threw his keys and journal on his desk and stared at the wall. I cautiously followed him—not sure if another lambasting was about to be unleashed at me.

Should I wait? Does he want time by himself? Did I do something I didn't know about again? Is he not feeling well? What should I do?

Finally, my compassion for him overrode my apprehension. I waited by the door, careful not to get too close. I took a few deep breaths to steel myself, and asked again, "Barry...what's wrong?"

He turned around and said, "I have feared for this day." He then plopped down into his desk chair and cried in his hands. When he was able to calm down, he looked up at me, sat back in his chair, and with resignation, he began. "I want to tell you the truth about *everything*."

Oh no...what now...what is he going to say now?

"Please, sit down." He motioned for me to take a seat in a small leather chair in the corner.

"I have dreaded this day," he repeated. "I told you I never thought I deserved you, and I tried to push you away when we were dating. It almost worked, but when it looked like you were really going to leave me, I panicked and begged you to come back. I thought being married would be the answer. I thought if you were here with me, I could control you, and there'd be no way you could leave me." He took a breath and continued. "Every day, I saw your goodness, and in your light, I couldn't help but see my darkness. The more love and generosity you gave, the more I hated you. I could never compete with you, so I had to crush you instead. When you and Michael moved here, I was happy, but I soon realized I had nowhere to hide. You would find me out sooner or later. I couldn't have you be *right* about me, so I had to make you wrong—very wrong." He cried again and continued through his emotions. "But you still kept trying. No matter what I threw at you, you never gave up. So I gave up instead, and I stopped caring about you. When I found myself softening, I talked myself out of it—I told myself not to care. I told myself you were only out for money and the green card. I forced myself to believe you were evil, so when the time came for you to leave, it wouldn't hurt so much." He exhaled deeply and finally said, "Now, you're free. You have your green card, and now you're going to leave me!" he wailed.

Completely dumbfounded, I fell back into my chair.

He planned all this? He intentionally designed ways to try to break Michael and me?! He threw us under the proverbial bus for the past six years? This whole thing has been a setup?!

Barry exhaled and continued, "I destroy everyone around me. I hurt them, and…I should just kill myself like Kent did." He stopped and looked away into the distance with empty eyes.

My mind tried to process what he said. *I've never heard him talk like this before. He's never shown interest or regard for life or death, even after Kent committed suicide. It seemed insignificant to him. He's so impulsive. Unpredictable. Erratic. Unstable. And now he's talking about his own life…would he really take his own life? What should I do?*

Before I knew it, these words came rushing out of my mouth, "Barry, thank you for being honest. If you really love me and are willing to go back to our counselors, maybe we can make this work…"

What did I just say?!

"Really? You'll stay?" Barry whirled around in his chair.

Oh, my God! What did I just do?!

I exhaled, "On one condition. You have to get help. You *have* to commit to *both* individual and couple's counseling once per week. I know that's a lot, but there is *a lot* of work to do. If you really want this marriage to work, then getting help is critical."

Barry jumped out of his chair, raced around his desk to me. He swung me around, repeatedly telling me how much he loved me.

In that moment of ultimate choice, when I believed his life was in danger, I chose to stay in my chains until I knew he was safe. He was either telling me the truth, or The Great Manipulator had just given his best performance yet.

Soon enough, I would either find freedom in the relationship, or I would be free of it.

Go Ahead. Make My Day!

The next two weeks went by relatively uneventfully, but the quiet before the storm was hauntingly eerie.

It was midweek, and I had just come home from a late afternoon class. Michael walked in the front door, somewhat dazed, and clearly upset.

"Michael! What's wrong?" I asked, running to him.

He was trying to hold back tears, but he began crying.

"Honey, tell me what happened," I insisted.

"Barry took me golfing, but then he started calling me names in the cart for no reason. After we teed off, he asked me to get into the cart, so I did. We drove up to my ball. He slowed down and told me to pick it up because we weren't going to hit in the rough. He wanted to place it in the green and use the irons from there."

"Then what happened?"

"Well…when I bent down to pick up the ball, he gunned the cart! I fell out of the cart and hit my head."

"Oh my gosh!" I exclaimed, examining his head for wounds. "Did Barry stop?"

"No. He was so mean! He called me a klutz, and a few other really bad names. Then he called me a 'momma's boy' and told me to go running home to 'Mommy'!"

I was so angry I could have killed Barry for hurting Michael!

"You and me both!" said Leah, waving her fists in the air.

Michael looked out of sorts, so I took him to the emergency room. He may have had a concussion, and I didn't want to risk him not being seen.

When we got back, Barry was home. I waited to see if he would tell me about the incident or ask where we had been and what we had been doing, but he said nothing. After about half an hour, I went to his office.

"We just got back from the hospital," I stated, ready for the confrontation.

He looked at me, irritated that I'd interrupted him. He pushed some keys on his keyboard and then stared at me blankly. I knew what he was doing, but that wasn't as disgusting as how he had abused my little boy. I was furious and closed the office door.

"What did Michael ever do to you? He looked up to you, and you told him to call you 'Dad,' but you're anything but that! You're despicable! Why did you even ask him to go golfing with you? Was that a setup too? You do that so well! Why did you tell him to pick up the ball and then gun the cart?"

"I didn't gun the cart!" he lied.

"If you didn't gun the cart, then why weren't you with him when he came home?! And why do his clothes have so much dirt and grass on them?!" I demanded.

He didn't have anything to say.

"You had to have gunned the cart because of the kinds of stains on his clothes. It took force to do that! That wouldn't have happened if it was *just* an innocent fall or a mistake of your foot! You set him up on purpose! You wanted to hurt him!! You didn't even have the decency to see if he was okay after he fell! Instead, you called him names and mocked him and made him *walk* home! Is that what men of character do? Is that your definition of being a *father*?!" I screamed.

He looked at his desk and then looked up and said, "The course is only a few blocks away. It's not a big deal!"

He completely missed the point, again.

This time, I held nothing back. "You're sick! You're *sick in the head*! You know that right? ! Going after a little boy because you're jealous of him *is sick!* Just because you can't be normal with your own children doesn't mean you have the right to go after *my son*! He could have had a concussion! You never even cared to ask how he was when we got home. Instead, you sit there hiding behind your porn sites, acting so smug as if you've done nothing wrong! You're flippin' *sick!*"

He looked at me with empty, shark-like eyes, "Are you finished?"

I leaned over on his desk and looked at him squarely.

"*Yes! I am finished and done!*" I shouted, livid. "I'm *done* with your illness! I'm done living with a narcissistic pathological liar, abuser, and thief! Yes, *I am finished*!" I left, slamming the door behind me.

I called my counselor and arranged for an appointment. By this point, Michael and both of Barry's kids were in counseling also, but this time I made the appointment for only Michael and me. We discussed the situation, and the counselor was very concerned. He asked to see Barry, but Barry refused.

The counselor insisted on having a session within the coming week to discuss this incident. Otherwise, Child Protective Services would have to be called. After hearing that consequence, Barry agreed.

This was when I learned Barry had never scheduled regular appointments as he had promised. Were he not threatened, he wouldn't have gone on his own. I knew then, there were no more excuses. It was time to leave, and I began to carefully plan our escape.

That weekend, I had a Saturday morning class. Michael was home sick with a cold, which I believed was probably a reaction to the shock and the stress of what Barry had done.

Barry had made plans to be with his children, so I thought Michael would be safe at home without me. Our nanny was off that weekend. I reasoned that, with his own children around, Barry would focus on them, and no harm would come to my son while I was at school. With our impending counseling session to discuss Barry's undeniable abusiveness to Michael, I assumed Barry would be humble and conscientious about his behavior.

In between classes, Beth, a classmate, asked to speak to me outside and said it was important. I was concerned she needed help of some kind, so I naturally agreed to talk to her. She asked me to step outside because she thought it would be best to have the conversation in private.

We found a quiet, out-of-the-way spot. Leaning up against the outside wall, we made some small talk, and then she finally shared why she wanted to talk to me. "Manna, I'm sorry I was so vague about meeting with you. It's not easy for me to say what I have to say, but I need to ask," she shared hesitatingly.

"It's okay, Beth. Ask away," I replied unsuspectingly.

"Manna, we've been in lots of classes together, and I've been watching you. I need to ask you if your husband is abusing you. The signs are everywhere. I know you're trying to be strong and brave, but *we all know*. I volunteered to speak to you on behalf of the others. There's help for women who suffer from domestic violence. There's help for you and your son. You don't have to stay…you don't have to be abused any longer."

Everything started to go white around me.

I had fainted.

I fell to the ground, my papers flying out of my binder and my books strewn around me. Beth tried to help me up, but when I gathered myself, I could not find the strength to do so. Instead, I sat on the pavement, leaned against the side of the building, sobbing. Beth comforted me as best she could.

We discussed the choices before me, and needless to say, we both missed that class and the following one.

To this day, I will always thank her for her boldness and courage to speak to me. I needed to hear the truth, and I needed to deal with the reality of my life. I could not hide it anymore. I could not manage it anymore, and I could not deny it anymore. Her conversation was confirmation.

I was an abused wife.

My health was weak, and I was down to only 115 pounds. I had tried so hard to make it, to fight for my marriage. But other people I barely knew had seen the truth. They recognized the signs I'd been trying to manage and hide. Yes, it was confirmation. I deserved better.

Michael deserved better.

No sooner had we finished speaking than my phone began to vibrate. I looked down and saw it was Michael.

I excused myself and took the call.

"Mom! BA-RRY HIT...HE...HIT ME! HE HIT ME! Michael was screaming hysterically on the other end of the line. He was crying and gasping for breath, and I wasn't sure if I heard him correctly. I tried to tell him to calm down and tell me what had happened. Even then, he could barely get out the words, but eventually he told me the chilling story of what had happened. I girded myself and tried to stay calm to hear and understand everything Michael was saying to me—especially after what had occurred less than an hour before in my conversation with Beth.

Michael told me Barry had picked up his kids and was insisting Michael go to eat with them.

"It's okay, Dad. You guys go ahead. I'm still sick with a cold and am going to stay in bed. I don't want to get anyone else sick either," Michael had explained to Barry.

"*Stop arguing with me*! You're coming with us, and I won't take no for an answer!" Barry had bellowed.

"Dad, please don't yell. Why are you so angry? You're scaring me."

"Don't talk back to me, boy! Or I'll make you pay for your back-talking!"

With that, Michael had locked the door to his room and hid in his bed.

Barry then tried to kick his way into the room, but when the door wouldn't fully open, he charged at it with his shoulders. With the weight of his body and the force behind it, Barry had broken through the door, peeling it away from the doorframe. He then charged at Michael and hit him.

"He hit me—because I d-didn't want to g-go to b-breakfast with him," Michael said, sobbing.

I asked where Barry was, and Michael told me he left after Michael threatened to call the police.

"I'm coming right home. I'll be there in fifteen minutes."

I gathered my strength and rushed home, angrier than I had ever been in my life. I rushed to Michael's bedroom. The door was destroyed, and I found my son sitting on the bed, trying to calm down from what had taken place. I saw a welt on his arm, and his face was flushed.

I, too, was flushed, but red with fury. I prayed for God to control my instinct to attack Barry with everything I had.

It may sound silly, but with my many years of martial arts training, I knew I could really, really hurt Barry. Even though I was small, I was strong, fast, and skilled at my craft. Plus, I had rage. I had the fuel behind me to move a semi with my bare hands. He went after my son...*and now he would have to deal with me.*

Barry was nothing but a bully, a coward. He was a caitiff, with no substance and no backbone or character. He would fold with my first strike...but I was not sure I would stop at the first...or the tenth strike. I had to calm myself down and to think. I had to be wise and not fall into another one of his traps.

I assessed the damage done to Michael and the room. I took photos of the doorframe, the door, the walls, and I took photos of Michael's arm and face. Then I held my son in my arms and told him I was so sorry and promised him Barry would never hurt him again.

I did what I needed to do to prepare legally by taking all the evidence I could, including the photos I mentioned, recordings, and other documentation. I then did my best to mitigate the emotional damages done to a little boy who wanted nothing but to believe in the man who said he was proud and excited to be his *father*.

I had no idea what was going to happen next, but because Barry was now clearly unable to disguise the secret of who he really was—or lie about it, as he had always done so masterfully—I had to be prepared for anything. My mind raced with what to do and how to cautiously proceed. Until I found a new place, Michael would never be left alone with Barry again. My nanny (who hated Barry also and eventually testified for me against him) helped me, as did another consultant who worked with me at home on a few other matters.

Later that afternoon, when Barry came home, I confronted him.

Swear words came out of my mouth that I won't repeat, but they were the release I needed. Otherwise, I was afraid I might have physically attacked him.

All Barry could say to me when I confronted him was, "He talked back to me."

"He talked back to you?! That's it? He *talked back to you?* Even if that was true, was that worthy of breaking down a door, destroying the door frame, denting the wall behind it, and *hitting an innocent child?! ARE YOU FLIPPIN' NUTS?!*" I shouted in a fury.

I remembered he was a pathological liar, and I was not going to let him be unaccountable for his deceit or his madness any longer. He debated with me for fifteen minutes about the events, but I was immovable. I was unwilling to retreat from this fight, and I was unwilling to let him get away with one of the most abominable and detestable actions anyone could do—abuse a child, a child who trusted, loved, and believed in him.

Finally, Barry shouted, "I'm sorry, okay? I'm sorry! Now get off my back!"

"You're sorry? You're not sorry! *You're only sorry you got caught!* You're not remorseful, humbled, or even ashamed of what you have done! You'd still be dumping your crap all over me, Michael, and anyone else you can get your hands on—if you hadn't been caught! But now your game is up! No matter how clever your pathological mind is to fabricate another lie, you can't hide! And you can't shroud yourself under mind-control techniques, semantics, or even report this in your journal to your secret authorities! The truth is the truth!" And then I added, "I will even quote your ex-wife—*one day, the truth about you will be revealed!* And here it is, in your face! *You are a sick man! A sick, sick man!* You need extensive, intensive help in a locked facility! And you better get it soon before you have more blood on your hands!"

"So, are you saying you believe your son over me?" Barry asked in his demented way, completely ignoring the issue at hand again. All he cared about was that he was *right*. He had no virtue, character, or moral compass to address his abuse nor was he willing to be held accountable for it.

"*Are you kidding me? Are you flippin' nuts?* Look upstairs, you fool! Have you seen the bruises on Michael? Have you seen the doorway? The walls? And how do you expect to explain this to the contractor who's got to fix everything? I have photos of everything, and there's *no way you can lie your way out of this one!*"

"Whatever! It's either me or Michael! Choose!" he threatened loudly, totally missing the point again.

Then he rushed up to me and grabbed me. To his surprise, I easily maneuvered out of his grip. He lunged for me again, and adrenaline coursed through me. "Do you want to hit me, too? Try it! Go ahead—*I dare you,*" I taunted. "*Make…My…Day!*"

He flinched, the wretched dastard that he was, and backed away while cursing me. As if there was even a question, he demanded again, "I asked you to choose between Michael and me!"

"*You are totally* insane*! You're even sicker than I thought!* I won't even dignify your lunacy with a response. Tomorrow, I will find an attorney and file for divorce. I can't do a thing about how you torment your own children, but you will never have anything to do with Michael's life again."

I paused, then walked deliberately towards him.

When I was within inches of his face, I delivered my last message to him very, very slowly.

"If you *ever, ever, everrr* touch Michael again, *or even look at him the wrong way,* make no mistake, I *will* kill you with my bare hands!"

12 RECALLED TO LIFE

The most glorious moments in your life are not the so-called days of success, but rather those days when out of dejection and despair you feel rise within you a challenge to life, and the promise of future accomplishments.

—Gustav Flaubert

Talkin' Bout a Revolution

It was the best of times, it was the worst of times, it was the age of wisdom, it was the age of foolishness, it was the epoch of belief, it was the epoch of incredulity, it was the season of Light, it was the season of Darkness, it was the spring of hope, it was the winter of despair, we had everything before us, we had nothing before us, we were all going direct to Heaven, we were all going direct the other way...

I typically started my days at 5:00 a.m., but on this particular morning, I was awakened a little earlier than normal by this passage from Charles Dickens' *A Tale of Two Cities* that kept repeating in my mind—*it was the best of times, it was the worst of times...*

That's strange, I thought. I hadn't really looked at this classic since my undergrad studies. It was still dark at 4:14 a.m., but I felt compelled to get up and read that section of the book again. My room and hallway were aglow with moonlight, and it was easy to walk to my office and to find the book. When I did, I turned on the desk light and sat down in my chair. The page opened immediately to the first section title, "Recalled to Life." Astonished, I let out a deep breath and read the familiar passage.

The message was clear. I was being awakened back to my life.

Before an oak tree can manifest its fullest purpose, it must first start as a seed and be completely broken. Yes, the outside is broken, even crushed, and the insides bleed out. Everything looks like it's falling apart. To someone who doesn't understand life, new beginnings, or breakthrough, this would look like total devastation.

And that was how I had felt about my life until now—broken and devastated.

But this morning, I felt hope, a small but powerful reminder that something great was going to come from all the destruction. Smiling, I looked up toward the ceiling and thanked God for showing me those words and for preparing me for the new season ahead.

Anyone who has lived with and escaped from an abusive relationship or marriage knows I haven't told much. In situations like mine, what I have chosen to share barely scratches the surface of the madness of such a life. Barry exhibited every sign of a classic emotional abuser. He mistreated me and then apologized profusely—feigning false humility and responsibility while professing his undying love for me, telling me he *cherished* me above all things. And promising me the abuse would never happen again.

Wanting to believe him because I loved him and believing there was something *I* could do to make things better was a quagmire. The fact was, no matter how much I wanted to believe Barry, his dysfunction was no longer deniable, excusable, or defensible. His masquerade had unraveled.

Michael and I needed to get out of there.

It may be easy to say, "You should have left earlier," but that, unfortunately, simply isn't true. Not only did Barry control our finances with the intensity and skill of his psychological warfare, he also controlled every moment of my life with chaos. It was not easy to determine what was real and what wasn't. Confusion, disorientation, bewilderment, turmoil, and demoralization were the daily fare. I was in a no-win situation, and I labored over the pros and cons of every reason to stay, and every reason to leave…countless times. Because Barry was so unstable, I never knew what he would do next. All I knew was that whatever he would do would *not* be virtuous, kind, respectful, or honorable.

I expected only the worst because that's all he demonstrated.

His theory of chaos and control dominated our marriage (and professional life), and for the most part, it worked. But now I was finally preparing for a new life, free from that insanity. I just had to be wise in my strategies.

In another malevolent encounter, Barry had kicked me out of the master bedroom and demanded I sleep in the guest bedroom. Trust me, it wasn't that I *wanted* to sleep in the same room, it was how our separation was handled that only confirmed his baseness.

But in spite of everything he had done to me, the one thing Barry will have to atone for more than any other is the way he treated Michael. There is an ominous heaviness to what Barry did, inviting Michael to be his son, and lulling him into trusting and surrendering his heart to him, only to turn around and abuse him. *This violation*, more than any other, will be the one for which he will have to answer to greatly one day.

"Yes, indeed," Leah affirmed. "He will be judged, and he will be found wanting…and his millstone will be just as heavy as Scham's."

A Tale of Two Cities may have been about the rise of the French Revolution, but I was in a revolution of my own. I would be free, but first I had to go through another two years of unnecessarily vicious divorce proceedings. While I was in a season of quiet introspection, healing, and accelerated learning, Barry's hubris and noxious thinking only escalated—and it was all directed at me through the divorce process.

Since Barry had "kicked me out" of the bedroom before our divorce, I assumed I would soon be kicked out of the house next. Unfortunately, nothing reasonably priced was available to rent right away. So, until I found something suitable, we all had to find a way to live together. Thankfully, Barry was away for work a lot, and when he was home, Michael and I spent a lot of time out of the house.

To find peace, I began pursuing God like I never had before. I desperately wanted to understand His will for me, and what the purpose was for what I had gone through with Barry—and in my life in general. No family member, friend, classmate, colleague, counselor, or medical doctor was able to offer me any answers I needed. I had to go beyond "man" to a higher authority.

What had I done wrong? What were my deeper beliefs that got me into these situations? God, please reveal Yourself to me again. Please show me Your plans for me—plans for peace, a wonderful future filled with hope.

Little by little, revelation after revelation, the pieces of the puzzle of my life came together. My faith grew, and though I still wobbled, unsure of my footing, God's love lit my path.

And like it was in *A Tale of Two Cities*, it was springtime for me. My prison doors were opened. At long last, a season of light, the promise of spring, and the accompanying hope came.

Money! Money! Money!

In spite of Barry's charisma and talents, the truth of his character (or lack thereof) was coming out. A wake of enemies trailed behind him, and his reputation for mistreating people didn't lag far behind. But, instead of humbling himself, healing, growing from his mistakes (and making restitution for his actions), he only became more entrenched in his delusions.

If he wasn't possessed by money before, he was now.

I vividly remember him rolling a large, cumbersome container full of loose change down an entire flight of stairs because he didn't want me to have any of that money. He looked like the hunchback of Notre Dame as he snarled with each step, "This is mine! This is *mine!*"

There may have only been several hundred dollars in that container, to which we had *both* contributed over our six years together. I mention this not because I wanted the money, but because I will never forget how disfigured Barry looked as I watched his illness manifest all for a jar of coins and bills. He had sold his dignity for so little.

Without any discussion or notice, he cancelled all my credit cards. He also closed out our joint bank accounts, taking all *our* money and leaving me literally penniless. When I asked him for *my* money back, he ignored me. After a while, I was forced to ask him for some basic support until I could get on my feet and secure a good job. To my request, he replied, "You want to leave me? Then figure it out yourself!"

He was trying to control me again with money, forcing me to stay in the same home with him. But this only intensified my resolve to leave. When I found the right home, my father loaned me money for the first few months' expenses. I began planning my secret escape, but it would be another two weeks before I could move into our new home.

I had to be patient and exercise self-control.

In the meantime, Barry continued instigating attacks, trying to goad me into altercations. He even kicked both my puppies in the stomach, hoping to infuriate me. I did everything I could to control my temper. My only focus was on leaving, and my resolve was like steel.

And, just so you know, I had my puppies checked and they were fine.

A few times, I thought about my mother and wondered if she had ever considered leaving Scham. Regardless of what she may (or may not) have considered, I did what she did *not* do. I was willing to face my greatest fears and address my greatest weaknesses because I loved my son more than anything. My fears, though fierce at times, were not greater than my love to provide for my son and to give him a loving and safe home. No matter what trouble was ahead of me, I would never let Barry hurt Michael again.

Michael and I would soon be free. We would begin again.

I could have called Child Protective Services (CPS), and armed with all the evidence I needed, I could have put Barry away in jail for a long time. I could have destroyed his business and any false reputation he had with any of his clients—and his family and friends. I would have been interviewed by the authorities and maybe even the media. There would have been little to say; the evidence spoke for itself. The inconvenience to me would have been minimal, but the damage to Barry would have destroyed his whole life.

I considered pressing charges, but I did not want to put Michael or Barry's children through the public humiliation, and I wanted to spare his clients from the drama as well. All I wanted was to part ways, to be fair in our financial dealings, and to never have anything to do with him again.

But Barry did not once take a high road. He tested me daily with his rampages, not knowing the grace I continued extending toward him. Many times, I was fingertips away from calling the police or CPS. But I waited, strategizing my escape. When my new place was ready, I planned my move to coincide with a time when Barry was away for one of his trips.

A few friends and befriended moms helped me move. I took only what was mine in the house and left the items we had purchased together. Knowing how Barry was with money, I had no choice but to be firm in what was mine before marriage, since I knew I would receive nothing from him.

The move went smoothly, and I was soon living in a little rental house located in a quiet, gated community where I knew Barry could not easily gain access.

The reality of everything was sinking in, as well as the fact that I had not said goodbye to Barry's children. Not trusting Barry at all to do what was right, I prayed about how to convey my love to his kids in a way that would honor them and not put them in any more turmoil than necessary.

Do I call Joyce?

I paced and paced and paced around the house. She was the last person to whom I wanted to talk. She already had such animosity toward me...why would she want to relay anything heartfelt from me to her children?

Still, I braced myself and dialed her number.

"Hello?" she answered.

I hesitated and then spoke, "Joyce...this is Manna. I'm sorry if I'm interrupting you, but do you have a few minutes?"

"Uh...sure."

At that moment, a thousand thoughts flooded my mind. I wanted to tell her I was sorry for all she had been through. I wanted to let her know I held no ill will against her and that I even understood her bitterness toward me. From her perspective, I was walking into the life she believed she deserved after suffering all those years of abuse from Barry. In her mind, I hadn't paid the price she did. But she did not know the price I did pay—and that Michael paid. She did not have to tell me one thing about what she endured, because I lived it also.

I also wanted to acknowledge her and validate her. Barry had confessed many things he had perpetrated upon her, and no matter how he tried to justify it, my heart cried out for her—woman to woman, sister to sister.

I wanted to share so much with her and to tell her I loved her children. I had done my best under the most brutal of circumstances and had given them everything I could. I wanted to tell her how sad I felt that now I would no longer have time with them. And though I did not expect to be a part of their lives now, I had hoped I could be, one day.

Just as I was leaning toward sharing some of these thoughts, Joyce said curtly, "Well? What is it?"

Immediately, I knew I could not share my heart with her. I exhaled and said, "I'm sorry, but have you talked to Barry lately?"

"No. Not really, just about the kids' schedules."

I took another deep breath. "There's no easy way to say this...I've asked Barry for a divorce. I wanted to tell you this myself because I want you to know I'm sorry that I could no longer stay…I tried. I really, really tried." That was all I could find the strength to say as I held back the tears.

"*What*?" she yelled into the phone loudly.

I understood her shock, and she confirmed it by saying, "I can't believe it! Barry makes it all look so perfect! You guys look like you had a perfect life!"

"It was far from perfect, but I want you to know that with everything I had, I gave it my best."

"Wow…" was all I heard on the other line.

After a few moments, I continued. "Joyce, my concern is for the children. I don't think Barry will arrange a visit, and I don't want to put them under any more strain than this will already be. I will do whatever you think is best for the kids. Just tell me, and I will do it."

She said nothing.

I could not contain myself any longer as the reality of saying goodbye to the children was now undeniable. "Joyce, I'm so sorry. I tried…I really, really tried," I said, eyes filling with tears.

I would not tell her how Barry treated me or how he had treated Michael. Badmouthing Barry was not my intention for the call.

Then an interesting thought popped into my mind—maybe this situation would be the opportunity Joyce and Barry would have to restore *their* friendship. They had been at ferocious odds with one another since day one. For all of her efforts, she was not able to enlighten, educate, or even crack the fortress of Barry's mind. And neither was I. Maybe now, as a unified front with me as their common enemy, they could rally together and find ways to work together for the children.

Finally, Joyce said sarcastically, "Well, I guess you never know what's behind closed doors, do you?"

I did not respond, and there was no point in elaborating. "Joyce, please consider how you would like to handle this with the kids. I'm open to whatever you say. Don't hesitate to call. You have my cell."

"Okay," she said stoically. "Goodbye."

I knew then that she was never going to call me. I hesitated and said, "Goodbye…please tell the kids I love them…and I'll miss them."

I heard the click on the other side of the phone line, and with it, my relationship with Barry's children ended. I never saw them again.

Free At Last

The divorce proceedings took over much of my life since Barry wanted to "make me pay." I was referred to a good mediator, but Barry was unwilling to go that route. The mediator then referred me to a good attorney, but I soon discovered she was the best friend of Barry's attorney. My case was then moved to another attorney known for his no-nonsense attitude, who promised to help me divide our assets fairly and to make Barry accountable. Unfortunately, that attorney suddenly died in the middle of my case, and I was forced to find yet another lawyer and go through all the details of my case again.

Yes, it was the best of times, it was the worst of times.

In terms of my financial requests, I was not asking for anything unreasonable. I still had no access to our bank accounts and was only asking for some immediate support to meet my basic needs. Many advisors had said I asked for too little.

Even one of *Barry's* financial consultants confided that I was asking for too little because Barry had hidden more from me than I ever knew. Though I was thankful for the information, my intention was simply to be free of him, to have returned to me what was mine before our marriage, and to receive what I had contributed during our marriage. I did not want revenge, nor did I want to "take everything from him" (as he had accused me of attempting to do).

As if the divorce wasn't difficult enough, Barry also began stalking me. He parked down the street from where I lived and would "coincidentally" be at a grocery store, Michael's school, pet supply stores, and other locations to harass me.

The judge saw the truth behind *everything*, even in the preliminary filings, and rebuked Barry for his maltreatment of us. He awarded me both steady monthly financial support and the restraining order I had requested.

Strangely enough, none of this curbed Barry, and he found other ways to badger me. Every week he bombarded me with irrational, cretinous allegations, forcing me to incur more attorney fees. Many of these accusations also required my attorney and me to appear in court, either to present a motion for him to stop or to defend myself. Barry was so bitter he wanted to barrage me with all kinds of legal fees. That way, any support monies I had would be spent on defending myself instead of my basic personal use. He intended to slowly bankrupt me. What should have been a clean and easy divorce (less than a ten-year marriage and no children—though he had desperately wanted them, and I *thank God* I had the sense not to) ended up taking over two years and cost me almost half a million dollars.

Unbeknownst to me, he had also bought the allegiance of several people. People I had once counted as good friends and associates now revealed their true characters as they lied in sworn statements. One person blatantly lied on sworn documents and in a deposition but did not expect me to have as much evidence as I did. Because of my preparation, his dishonesty was revealed, and his testimony was rendered useless. Now, I wasn't expecting mutual colleagues or friends to side with me. But what I didn't expect was the number of so-called friends and colleagues who lied and acted spitefully against me.

I learned a great deal during this time—not the least of which was a deeper lesson on the true meaning of friendship. I knew what friendship meant to me, *but what did friendship mean to someone else?* I was awakened out of my own naiveté as I realized the companionship some people offered wasn't always sincere. Like

Barry, I was merely a tool to be used to forward their own goals.

After over two years of this madness, one Wednesday morning, weak and weary from all his attacks, I drove to my favorite location at the beach and prayed like I've never prayed before. I pleaded with God to make Barry stop his attacks, to end the divorce, and for him to *just leave me alone*! I also reminded Him of all the promises He had given to me as well as those He had spoken of in the Bible. I declared them, one by one, out loud and proclaimed them over my life, especially the one where He promised He would never allow more than I could bear. I was at that point now; I could take no more.

And as He had done so many times in my life, I felt God soothing my heart and comforting me with a peace that transcended description and understanding. Then, just like I knew Barry was going to sign the papers for my green card months before, I knew Barry was going to sign divorce papers that day. Nothing had been scheduled or discussed. I just knew…somehow, God was going to answer my prayer.

This was the day I would be free, at last!

Within the hour, I had an unexpected call from my attorney to meet with him, Barry's attorney, and my soon-to-be ex-husband in my attorney's office at 2:00 p.m. And sure enough, everything was negotiated and finalized that very afternoon.

In some people's eyes, I *gave up* over two million dollars and settled for a small fraction of what was fairly due to me, but I did not see things in that way. Even my attorney wanted me to stop the negotiations several times because he said he couldn't let me give up so much. What he and others did not understand was that my soul and my freedom were worth more than money. I knew with all my heart that once I was free, I would be able to earn whatever I needed, and favor and blessings would shower me for my faithfulness and my refusal to be ugly, vengeful, or greedy.

No matter what the sickening experiences of the past eight years were, they were all about to be put behind me.

Yes, Michael and I were free, and we would never have to see him again.

"Praise the Lord! I want to sing Handel's 'Hallelujah Chorus' right now!" Leah shouted with jubilation. "You must have danced all the way home!"

"I wanted to, but I didn't. I kept my composure, and when I got into my car, I phoned my family and a few friends, who were waiting to celebrate with me when I arrived."

"You got your life back!" Leah continued.

"Yes, I did," I agreed. "I established a settled home with constancy, safety, and joy. During the week, Michael and I had a fun routine. We'd go to my health club where he trained with coaches, as he was now on the school's varsity tennis team, and I trained to run marathons. And we had great weekends, too. On Friday nights, Michael would have his friends stay over, and on Saturday nights, he would stay over at another friend's house. Many times, his friends just stayed over again on Saturday. I loved it! I loved having 'life' and laughter back in my home.

"Sometimes I entertained at home, and we had wonderful parties there; other times, we just relaxed. And on Sundays, we went to church, where Michael assisted me when I taught Sunday School.

"I made new friends, ran several marathons, and picked up tennis again (my favorite sport), now that I had joy back in my heart. In time, I purchased a home of my own (in another gated community where I felt safe from Barry) and got another dog. I now had three Golden Retrievers. Yes, all in all, we had a great life.

"Though this was a time of great testing, training, healing, and refining, God kept His promise to not allow more than I could handle and showered His blessings upon me. He restored the brokenness of my heart and taught me the priceless lesson of leaning on Him for my provision and strength. It was a time of hope indeed."

Wolves in Sheep's Clothing

When Michael and I moved to the United States, we began attending a local church where one of the associate pastors helped me greatly. Even though it was a very, very large church, he didn't treat me as a number. He was a kind shepherd with a true pastor's heart. Were it not for him, I don't know how I would have overcome those horrifying years with Barry. Unfortunately, he ended up moving to another state, but I did my best to live what he had taught me to do—to keep my eyes on God alone.

Barry only came to service with me once. He refused to go again because he believed he could do a better job teaching "inspirational messages" than the pastor.

Michael and I continued going to church though, he to the youth group, and I to "big church." But because I had been living the secret life of an abused wife for so long, I had become extremely shy and uncomfortable around people. I kept to myself, hiding amongst the large crowds where it felt safe.

There was so much wisdom in the Bible, and I couldn't learn fast enough. As soon as I had separated from Barry, I signed up for Bible study classes, and eventually served on several volunteering assignments. Over the next two years, I was a Sunday school teacher, a special counselor for The Billy Graham Crusades, the floral designer for the church, and a volunteer both for the prison ministry and for special church events.

I slowly began to come out of my shell, contributing behind the scenes in areas that did not require a lot of personal socializing. As a special counselor, I was only called for more challenging cases. As a floral designer, I designed and created the silk floral arrangements in my garage. I taught Sunday school with Michael as my helper because I loved children and didn't have to be with adults. The prison ministry work was just buying, wrapping, and delivering gifts to the families of the incarcerated. And when I volunteered for special events, since so much needed to be done, there was little to no time for mingling. I was able to perform my tasks faithfully and alone.

It wasn't until I left Barry that I realized how deeply damaged I had become. Little by little, my naturally outgoing personality had been replaced by a shy, confused, and frightened frame of a person. Although I could put on makeup and dress to fit in in the outside world, I felt like my shattered pieces were only glued together—except the glue wasn't set yet.

In short, I was a walking mess.

I had little-to-no confidence, was still underweight, and if a person looked at me the wrong way, I would feel my knees buckle. My pulse would race, and my typically low blood pressure would spike. I thought it was easier to be alone and to find peace in my reclusiveness.

Worries about agoraphobia surfaced again, but I remembered my old pastor's encouragement and focused on God and my future. I forced myself to keep venturing out into the world in some way every day.

In time, a man named Calvin found his way into a friendship with me, and we eventually dated for a very short period. He was tall and dark, and while others thought him handsome, I realized he was anything but that as I got to know him.

Other women seemed to be attracted to his looks, in spite of his odd hairstyle (he sprayed foam-hair on his scalp to hide the growing bald circle on his head), but I was more attracted to how he represented his relationship with God to me. I later learned he had lied about his work, his finances, his business ventures, and his contacts. For all of his feigned self-righteousness, he was as disturbed as Barry. Part of his masquerade was pretending to be humble by volunteering only for cleanup positions—even cleaning the toilets. To me, his pretense was even worse than Barry's, because this man said he was a Christian! It was then that I learned about the men who "pray to prey." He was only the proverbial wolf in sheep's clothing.

"Dear heavens! Foam hair?" Leah exclaimed. "That's just not right! But neither does anything else seem right about him!"

I smiled at Leah and continued.

In a short time, Calvin started talking about marriage and wanted to move forward with a wedding as soon as my divorce was finalized.

Red flag! Pay attention!

He was behaving just like Barry.

One Sunday evening, when I was working on my computer, I noticed an email from Calvin that had been sent earlier that same day from *my computer* when I was teaching Sunday school.

That's strange! How could I send myself an email from home when I was at church?

When I opened the email, I noticed it was actually a forwarded email from another friend from my inbox to Calvin's email that he accidentally sent back to me! I looked at the original email from my friend and didn't see anything dubious or incriminating about it. It was innocuous, with nothing but a link to an inspirational message from one of my favorite authors.

After more digging, I found over a hundred emails in my *sent* folder to Calvin from *my* computer! I was alarmed because I had never sent any of these emails to him. As I further studied the contents of the sent folder, I realized that all the emails Calvin took from my computer (and sent to his own email address) were all from men—relatives, friends, business associates. Worse, *every* email was sent on consecutive Sunday mornings when I was teaching Sunday school!

To make a long story short, Calvin knew where my hidden key was, used it to enter my home without my permission when I was teaching Sunday school, accessed my computer, and forwarded to himself my private information and correspondences from any male who was in my life. What he did was illegal on multiple grounds—breaking and entering, premeditated theft of personal information and intellectual property, stalking, and so on. He was another obsessive control freak.

Needless to say, I was *furious!*

I immediately called and confronted him. He didn't apologize for his actions at all. Instead, he rationalized his behavior by saying he was protecting me from other men who wanted to pursue me. I had no idea what he was talking about, and it was then he told me other men were interested in me. I hadn't been aware of these other intentions, but he didn't believe me.

"So, you broke into my home because you think someone else likes me?" I yelled. "You think you had the right to break into my house, use my computer without my permission, search through my personal emails, and steal information because you think other men are interested in me?!"

"I'm just trying to protect you. And while we're on the subject, I don't want you to drive your convertible as much, either. Drive your SUV," he replied, completely oblivious to the point I was making.

"*What?!* What are you talking about?!"

"Well, I know you like your convertible, but I don't want you driving with the soft top down anymore. The soft top must always be up. Otherwise, too many men will see you, and you will cause them to fall in their flesh!"

"*He should be locked up!*" Leah shouted.

"That's exactly what I said to him, right after I told him I was going to call the police. But first, I called another pastor I trusted, so he could be made aware of this *madman* running around church pretending to be pious, godly, and righteous. I called Pastor Earl, who agreed, and asked me to change the locks on the house.

He also said I should do more research around the house to see if he had taken anything else."

"Calvin wanted to control and isolate you, exactly like Barry did!" Leah deduced. "And he stole information from your computer and ingratiated himself into your life without remorse—exactly like Barry did, too!"

I sighed. "I know. It was alarming!"

Leah reached for my hand and gave it a compassionate squeeze. "So, what did the police say?"

"I never called them."

"What! Why not? He should have been locked up!" Leah shouted again.

"Pastor Earl asked me to forgive him and not to press charges. He promised me he would deal with Calvin."

"What did that mean, 'deal with' him?" Leah asked disapprovingly.

"Pastor Earl said he would ask Calvin to leave the church, but he pleaded with me not to destroy his life. I respectfully disputed with him for over an hour, but in the end, I agreed to extend mercy to Calvin, and to let the church authorities deal with him."

Kangaroo Court

Months went by, and just when I thought life was back to normal, Pastor Earl called, asking me to come to his church office to talk about the flower arrangements theme for the next month. I agreed and went to see him after a business meeting the following afternoon.

When I arrived, the receptionist buzzed Pastor Earl, who came out to greet me. When I entered his office, I noticed his office furniture had been moved. The desk was pushed along one side of the wall, so the other corner of the room could be made larger. The back of a small folding chair was jammed into that corner, facing two larger single chairs placed unusually close to that single chair. I turned around to look at Pastor Earl, and he extended his arm, motioning for me to sit in the single chair.

That's strange, I thought. *Why would he arrange his office like this? Why did he ask me to sit in the chair in the corner? Is he going to sit in the other chair? Who's the other chair for?*

As I sat down, another wonderful youth pastor, Pastor Scott, whom I also loved, came into the office. Neither pastor oversaw my flower design work, however, so I became very suspicious. I had been set up—but for what?

They took the seats facing me, and there were maybe twelve inches between their feet and mine when we sat down; we were uncomfortably close. These two men literally had me cornered in a small room, and I lacked any information about what they were about to say to me.

The hot afternoon sun shone through the Venetian blinds, casting long shadows over their faces. Perspiration beaded on their foreheads as they proceeded to tell me the purpose of the meeting.

"Manna, we just love you, and all you do for the church...you are such a servant. We love your heart and how you faithfully, even sacrificially, give every week and every month. But, ummm...we have to talk to you about a delicate matter."

"Of course. You can talk to me about anything," I responded, innocent of what lay behind their flattery.

"Well, a lot of talk is going on at church about you," one said.

"*Pardon me?*" I asked, baffled by such a statement.

"Well, quite a few men have come to me asking for permission to date you—even though your divorce may not be finalized," Pastor Earl said. "Men appear to be paying close attention to you."

I was stunned by the topic of the conversation. It was not their position to hold this meeting, nor had I given them authority to speak on my behalf to any potential suitors (even *if* I was interested in dating, which I was not).

Further, this didn't seem to be *my* issue, but something that they should be speaking to the "men" about.

However, out of respect, I allowed the conversation to continue. "I'm not sure what you are talking about. The only person I *dated* was Calvin, but as you know, he's a sick man and a criminal. Needless to say, that relationship has ended."

"Well, there's another situation. Duane (a supposed elder at church) reported harsh things about your moving from one man to another."

"What? Not only is that untrue, but...Duane?" *I have only ever been polite and kind to him. Why would he slander me so?* "What is he saying?" I asked with shock.

It was then I learned Duane had whispered his accusations about me to Pastor Earl *while I was getting baptized!* Apparently, Duane was upset with me because I had turned down the affections of one of his friends. Frankly, his friend was very odd, but unlike Calvin, who was able to cloak his deceit, this fellow was outwardly foolhardy and known for his gross exaggerations.

Instead of keeping this to himself, and counseling his friend privately, Duane believed the fabrications of his odd friend and irresponsibly (and inappropriately) made it a public matter.

"Are you saying that I'm here, *cornered* in a room by two men—under false pretenses, I might add—because you chose to listen to a man maliciously gossip about me *during my baptism?*" I asked squarely.

They looked at each other and then looked back at me.

I continued, "Did it occur to you that you could have simply *called* me to talk about these things? And did you correct Duane about *his* behavior?"

They exchanged another brief look.

This kangaroo court continued for the remainder of the afternoon. They further disclosed that, unbeknownst to me, several men were apparently displaying their interest in me to each other and jockeying for position to date me. This growing interest caused the pastors to be concerned, and they assumed it must have been *my fault*—that I must have been "leading them on." In their minds, no other explanation could explain their attraction to me.

Throughout the grueling interrogation, they also questioned how I dressed outside of church (professionally and casually during my off-work hours), including what I wore to exercise at the gym. Shocked that we were even having this conversation, yet again, out of my respect for them, I politely answered each accusation. Before I finished my second sentence, they stopped me and admitted they knew I had always been acceptably dressed and never improper, but they "had to ask, *just in case*."

"Who are the men who have been talking about me? You can't accuse me like this, and ask such insulting questions, which I have openly and forthrightly answered, without giving me something of weight to justify this illegitimate persecution. Please give me the names of these people."

They danced around my request, but I persisted. Eventually, the two pastors gave me the names of the men but followed their disclosure with another flurry of questions. They asked, "How did you meet them? Did you seek them out? What did you have in common with them? What kinds of conversations did you have with them?"

Appalled, I shook my head in disgust, biting my lip so I wouldn't say something I would regret later. I felt frozen with outrage. I staggered at the crudeness of these men whom I had *once* respected and trusted. Worse, they didn't see how shameful and reprehensible their own thinking and actions were.

They waited in silence as I struggled with my self-control. "I don't know any of those people!" I said firmly. "I don't even recognize their names! Yes, I smile and say hello or good morning to *people*. I speak to men and women en route to the sanctuary for service, or as I'm delivering the floral arrangements. But that does not qualify as a 'conversation,' much less the ugly things you're accusing me of."

They looked at each other, perplexed. "Are you sure you don't know these men?"

"I'm sure!" I said sharply. "I don't have a clue who they are!"

They looked at each other again. Then Pastor Earl, the one I knew the most, trusted the most, confided in the most, and the one who had counseled me and helped me the most—hurt me the most. Just when I didn't think this kangaroo court could get any worse, he asked, "What about Sunday school? Do you have extra or inappropriate conversations with the men who pick up their children before or after service?"

What did he just say? What…did…he…just…say?

I fought back the tears. The horror of his question was too much. Trembling, I answered, "I cannot believe this! You, of all people, Pastor Earl…I trusted you. I confided in you, and you know me better than anyone at this church. You were my pastor, and now you are the accuser? I can't believe you could ask me such a perverted question." I grabbed a tissue, and then answered him straightforwardly. "Pastor Earl, other than saying, 'Hello, what is your child's name, and do you have your ticket?' with dozens of other parents either simultaneously dropping off their kids or picking them up, *no, I have not had extra or inappropriate conversations with any fathers!*" I shook my head. "I'm in shock…I can't believe this is happening right now! You have broken my heart—both of you."

"Err…ummm…well, ummm, we just don't understand…ummm, we don't know what to do. There's just been so much attention and talk about you…and, ummm…" They both stumbled.

Then, as if a brilliant insight flashed before Pastor Earl's eyes, he blurted out, "Okay. Why don't we do this—when the parents come to pick up their children, you will only be permitted to speak to the mothers, *but if the fathers come to the door,* then only Michael may speak to the men."

My jaw dropped, and my eyes popped as I battled again to make sense of what I had just heard.

"*What did you just say?* Did I hear you correctly? Are you basically forbidding me to speak to *any man* at church, and are you telling me that my twelve-year-old son is the only one who can speak to the men on my behalf? *Do you hear yourself?*"

Pastor Earl nodded, still unmoved by the atrocity of his words. Pastor Scott, however, could not look at me. Instead, he looked out the window.

What the hell *is going on here? Is this some kind of sick joke?*

Finally, I found the courage to speak up. "Do you do this to every woman who attends this church?"

"No…ummm…we've just had a lot of men…ummm, well, you're getting a lot of attention now that people know you're getting a divorce, and we don't…"

"So, you immediately assumed I was doing something inappropriate to bring all of this attention to myself? I've been a member of this church for years now, and I've done nothing but serve quietly and faithfully. I've been going through a horrendous divorce orchestrated by hell itself, and instead of being kind and compassionate, you're leveling one defiling accusation after another at me. Did it ever occur to you that you chose to listen to juvenile gossip? Did it ever occur to you to keep *the men* in check? Did it ever occur to you, especially since we *had* a good friendship that you could have simply talked to me about this, instead of deceiving me into this *ambush, and bullying me*? Where did you apply God's principles of love and wisdom in any of this?"

"Well, we…errr…it's just that you're in a position of leadership, and you are so well-known here," Pastor Earl said, flustered.

"And what am I known for?" I demanded.

"Well…uhhh…for your joy and faithfulness when you serve…for your time and thoughtfulness in all that you do," he responded.

"So, if I'm known for that, and you've allowed me to be in a place of leadership, doesn't that prove that I'm trustworthy?" I interrupted. "You even did a background check on me! Doesn't my credibility mean anything? Instead of looking at me and winnowing every part of me through whatever bizarre and perverted filters you have, why don't you look at the men and qualify, bridle, and rebuke them?! Monitor *them*! Examine *their* thoughts, their words, and inspect their actions! Did you corner the men under false pretenses and accuse them of things like you are doing to me? Isn't it obvious something is awry here?"

Still trembling, but now with shock and anger, I continued, "By the time my divorce is over, my ex-husband will have tortured my son and me for almost a decade. I came to this church thinking I'd find refuge and shelter here in God's house. Instead, I see the devil and all his minions running rampant! All I wanted to do was to serve my Lord, to bring Him my gifts, and to bless others with them. If I'm guilty of anything, I'm guilty of being naïve—naïve to the wiles of predatory men at church! Just because I smile, am polite, and courteous, doesn't mean I'm flirting, or making a move on a man!"

They said nothing in response.

Leah interrupted. "What a pair those two were! Real men, especially pastors, dignify others, not humiliate them! They were truly the devil's pawns! And furthermore, if men can't keep their weenies in their pants, that's *their* problem! How dare they project that onto you and accuse you of their own twistedness! I hate it when men don't take responsibility for themselves, and only blame women for *their* lack of self-control. Sickening, really…"

I sighed. "It was horrible. I couldn't believe the absurdity of what I was hearing, and worse, that it was coming from the two men whom I trusted most at church."

"Pastor or no pastor—they gossiped and took action based on it like ignorant prepubescent adolescents!" Leah did not hold back. "How did this scam end?"

I slowly recounted the words I said to them—words I will never forget. "I said, 'Pastor Earl, this ruse is over. Whatever you do regarding the men at this church is up to you, but I never want to hear about this again. I have a clear conscience, including how I trusted you in coming to this meeting. In spite of your hurtful interrogation, I have respectfully answered each offensive question. You've said more than enough, and I've heard more than enough. So, if you'll excuse me, this meeting is now over.'

"I stood up, and they did too so they could move out of the way to let me out. They awkwardly thanked me for coming and told me they looked forward to seeing me on Sunday.

"Without responding, I hurried out of that office and out of the building. I took a few long breaths once I got to my car and fumbled to call my longtime friend, Jim, through the tears that were now flowing. Jim was not only a dear friend, but he was also a deacon at the church, and he was outraged when I told him what had happened that afternoon. Jim called the two pastors right away and confronted them. Later, he told me he knew a few of the men the pastors were referring to but never said anything to me because they were simply what he called, 'guy conversations.' He didn't know things had gotten so blown out of proportion, and he was infuriated.

"The next day I came home to a long voicemail from Pastor Scott, who apologized profusely. His voice shook as he told me he was unable to sleep after what had happened and asked me to please forgive him. He asked if I could stop by his office the next time I was at the church, so he could apologize to me in person.

"I cried as I listened to his voicemail, and I was touched by his sincerity and his humble heart. But I heard nothing from Pastor Earl. Ever."

The Mass Exodus

"I know not all churches are this dysfunctional, but with all this nonsense going on, why didn't you leave?" Leah asked.

"Well, I thought about leaving right afterwards, but leaving suddenly while I still had a lot of responsibilities would have brought more attention and gossip. Plus, it wouldn't have been fair to the other volunteers, who didn't know what was going on, to suddenly disappear and leave them with all my work. I decided to stay, taking the high road and working through the conflict. Interestingly, it wasn't long before I noticed many other people had left that church, an event the remnant termed 'the mass exodus.'

"When I came in to exchange the monthly floral decorations (some arrangements were in pots with a thirty-six-inch diameter), my large and elaborate designs were nowhere to be found. After looking all over the premises, I finally found these costly arrangements destroyed. Some had been thrown into the corner of a remote closet, and the rest were left in the dumpster at the back of the building. Horrified, I went to the church office to see if I could get answers from the head pastor (who apparently permitted the trashing of my floral arrangements), or Pastor Earl. But they were either 'out of the office' or 'in a meeting.' I asked them to call me, but no one did."

"Ever?" Leah exclaimed.

"Never," I replied.

Confused and distraught, but not wanting to put the front desk staff in an uncomfortable position, I quietly left the church building.

As I walked back to my car, a kind staff member chased after me in the parking lot. "Manna, I have to talk to you."

I stopped and turned around to see Mary smiling as she caught her breath. "I'm so, so sorry about *everything*. I know it's all been very hard on you, and it breaks my heart to see you treated this way. I want to fill you in, but promise you'll keep what I'm about to say confidential."

I nodded. "Of course, Mary. Thank you. Thank you for doing this…"

She took both my hands and began. "They think the only way to keep you out of the limelight is to take away your ministries, starting with your floral work because your flowers are so beautiful, and everyone always asks who does them. By taking this away from you, they believe you'll get less attention. Kid's church needs help, so they're not going to pull you away from Sunday school. Plus, since Michael is with you, they think it's okay. And the other positions, well, they don't get a lot of focus. I'm so sorry, Manna. It's not right, and it's not you. They're intimidated by you…and be careful of Maude. She pretends to be your friend, but she's jealous of you…and ummm…let's just say, she's not a friend…ugh…I've said enough. I should go. Don't worry, honey. It'll all work out. I'm so sorry…" And with that, she gave me a hug and ran back towards the building.

I will never forget that afternoon.

Everything seemed surreal. Dazed and numb, feeling as if I was transported into someone else's life movie, I drove home as one crazy experience after another with this church flashed in my mind.

Maude? I helped her so much after her mother died, and helped her find a job, too! Yes, everyone knows she's a gossip, but there was nothing she could say about me that could be bad unless she made it up. Who are all these people?

As my garage door slowly opened, the sunlight shone directly on my three walls of professionally designed closets, cupboards, and shelving space filled with over ten thousand dollars' worth of exquisite silk flowers, trees, supplies, vases, and decorations in special storage containers created expressly for the purposes of blessing the church. As I beheld it all, the tears came.

It was painful to be so misunderstood, judged, slandered, and discarded without even the decency of a conversation. Heartbroken, I unloaded the salvaged flowers and went inside.

Jim and another friend came by later to console me. They were rattled at how I had been treated (again), and it was then they told me about the many others who had also been wrongly accused and terribly mistreated. After hearing all the sad scenarios, I finally understood the reasons behind "the mass exodus." Solid Christians, wonderful leaders, and other great pastors had, after such treatment, sought fellowship elsewhere.

A Hypocrite or Not a Hypocrite…That is the Question

"They were Pharisees!" Leah shouted. "Hypocrites, all of them!"

"Yes, the behaviors of these particular leaders were indeed contradictory to what they had been proclaiming, and I'd be lying if this last straw (especially since it was at church) wasn't the one that made me question God altogether. At that moment, I battled the knee-jerk reaction to blame God for not protecting me better and for letting madmen ruin yet another *home*, this time in *God's House*. On the heels of leaving the nuthouse with Barry, I thought I was at least safe in *His House*.

"The battle raged in my heart all night. It would *appear* God wasn't there for me—*again*. Everything tempted me to believe that God didn't love me, and maybe He wasn't even real.

"I couldn't help thinking, *If He loves me, why do these horrible things keep happening to me? I'm nice. I'm kind. I'm obedient and dutiful. I serve with love, and I serve selflessly, asking for nothing in return. What am I missing? Why does God let these things happen to me, and why isn't He 'smiting' these evil men and making them pay?*

"I was furious with the men at church, with Maude, with the pastors especially—and with God."

"Finally, you got good and mad!" Leah cheered. "Finally, some anger at the people hurting you!" After slapping her hand on knees, she took a breath and asked, "Now, I'm curious…what did God say when you asked Him why He didn't retaliate on your behalf and make those people pay?"

"You're not going to like this."

"Try me."

"He said He loved them. He was going to extend them grace and mercy. His goodness would one day bring them to a 'turnaround,' and He will use this to create 'mighty men (and women) of valor' in them. Their story wasn't over yet—and neither was mine."

"Well, that's convenient for them! But where does that leave you?" she said, unsatisfied. "You're left to clean up yet another mess! I don't get why God allows trouble, hardship, and persecution to visit you again and again!"

"We could talk forever about this, but for now, let me answer you with a few simple thoughts. Sometimes, God doesn't have to smite anyone. The consequences of their own actions are often painful enough. Plus, God didn't just extend grace and mercy to the pastors alone. He reminded me of the many times He had extended grace and mercy to me when I had failed and hurt others.

"And on the other side of the coin, when trials came, God gave me the grace and the strength to endure, persevere, *and* to overcome them. Every test and affliction was used to develop and strengthen my character, bolster my faith, deepen my maturity, and make me wiser. It was (and remains) part of the necessary training—"

"Training for w*hat*?" Leah interrupted. "Being a walking doormat?"

"No, Leah. By persevering and overcoming deep and diverse trials, my true colors are revealed, and anything unlovely will be made known for healing, cleansing, and renewal. Difficult situations occur to *reveal me to myself*. And as God uses these misfortunes to purify my heart and to transform my mind, I will then be able to help and comfort others, for I will know exactly what they are going through."

Leah's eyes opened wide as she began to understand. "Oh," she said softly, "like you're doing for me right now, I suppose."

I smiled.

"What else?" Leah asked slowly. "What else did God say?"

"Well, He has everything under control, and if we trust Him, He will bless us beyond measure for being faithful, even in the face of painful persecution. The joy of the Lord is our strength to undergo any adversity, and with Him, anything—and everything—is possible."

Leah sank back against her pillow, her eyes open, keen and alert. She wanted to believe.

"As the battle waged in my heart, I remembered the story of Jonah in the Old Testament. Like him, my anger and my desire for vengeance against 'the wicked' almost consumed me. I wanted to lash out against the injustices done to me, but vengeance was not mine to execute. I'm only to cling to what is good, and even if others can't, I'm to be patient in tribulation, stay steadfast in prayer, and speak blessings on those who persecute me. By being anything else, I would be *less like God, and more like them*—lost, confused, and yes, even wicked."

"That's easier said than done!" Leah observed.

"I know. In fact, it's impossible to do on our own. We need God's strength, His love, His wisdom, and His Spirit. Otherwise, I would have foolishly acted out of impulse and heated emotion and regretted my rash behavior. I already had enough regrets in my life, so I stayed silent and only poured my heart out to God.

"You're too good to be true," Leah said, shaking her head. "I wouldn't have been so obedient or generous."

"I wasn't always this way, and there are times I still struggle. But we all have opportunities for healing and growth, and one day this training will bring much fruit. We'll be lacking in nothing, and challenges like this will be stones we step over instead of mountains we don't think we can climb.

"It's so easy to forget that from God's perspective, this life is really all about that training, that each of us has our own race to run, and that this is what we need to focus on. One of my favorite verses is in Jeremiah. He's complaining to God about hypocrites—people for whom God is 'near in their mouth but far in their mind'—and saying, 'God, You don't let me get away with anything! Why aren't you dealing out consequences to these people?'—pretty much the same thing I was asking God about these pastors! And God answers, 'If racing against mere men makes you tired, how will you race against horses?' In other words, stop worrying about God holding other people to a standard and focus on the standard He's holding *you* to. He wants you to be like Him.

"When I stop looking other people, and even at myself, and look at God, I am quickly reminded that His thoughts are not our thoughts. His ways are not our ways. His nature is love, joy, peace, long-suffering, kindness, goodness, faithfulness, gentleness, and self-control. He isn't easily angered, is rich in love, is merciful, and filled with unfailing love. He doesn't seek destruction as justice. He seeks healing and restoration through His immense and immeasurable love. He extends mercy, not giving us what we deserve. And He extends grace, giving us *much more* than we deserve.

"And as I kept pressing into God, little by little, my anger subsided. By remembering the powerful lessons I learned from the Bible, my heart softened, and my spirit began to transform. From that place of equanimity, peace, and trust, I could see things more clearly. God had not changed. He was the same God who helped me before. He was the same God that delivered me from my painful past, and He was going to do something good with this too. I had no idea what that would look like, nor did I see how things could be brighter, but somehow, I found the courage to *choose* to believe in what I could not see. And to this day, I still *choose* to believe that God had a bigger and better plan that would bless me and prosper me in countless ways.

"Besides, blaming and accusing God (or anyone else) wouldn't have accomplished anything. I had seen God's fingerprints and felt His arms around me too many times. The louder the shadowy voices were telling me God didn't love me and that He failed me, the more powerful His sweet voice grew, and the more I remembered what God did do for me.

"Moreover, God's best for me isn't always about me getting *my* way. It's not about being comfortable or being acknowledged. Sometimes being disregarded and discarded 'just happens,' whether I deserve it or not. It is in these times that my character—*our* characters—are tested. Are we happy and nice just because we get what we want? Do we only love the gifts? Do we only adore the recognition or the flattery we get? Or do we love the Giver of the gifts, *even when we don't get what we want, or what we feel we are entitled to?*"

"I hadn't thought about it this way," Leah said thoughtfully.

"In life, no matter what title, role, or position people may have, they are still just people. Whether you're a pastor, chef, attorney, physician, rocket scientist, teacher, homemaker, or artist, we are all wounded. Just because someone has a title, doesn't mean they're perfect at their job, or that they've escaped being a human. Humans make mistakes, sometimes terrible mistakes, but that doesn't mean we're failures or hypocrites. We're simply people who make mistakes.

"And until this time, I had a faulty perception of what 'being a Christian' meant. Being a Christian does not mean one is perfect, living a flawless life, untainted by pain and suffering—far from it! We're simply everyday people who recognize we need help, hope, and a haven. It wasn't God's fault the pastors did what they did. The gift of free choice is a sharp and powerful tool. Even after two thousand plus years of practice, as a species we are far from mastering it. How much harder is it for one person who only has one short lifetime, maybe eighty to a hundred years, to master this? Individually, we're all only just learning how to use this tool.

"So when the cuts run deep, it is God who comes to heal us. He rescues us from the circus of lies, bad choices, painful consequences, and inexplicable tragedies. Without knowing there's a greater plan for all the randomness of life, there would be little to no meaning (or purpose) for our existence. To just die and enter an eternity of darkness (or worse) after that would be too much for us to bear.

"For me, being a Christian means we know that we're broken, we're lost, and we need someone greater than ourselves to *save us* from ourselves. We need *a Savior*."

"But, Manna, you may 'get it,' but the others didn't—they're hypocrites! They were pastors and are supposed to know better!" Leah protested.

"Yes, they're pastors, but as an entrepreneur, there are many things I'm supposed to know better, but I miss the mark also. Like I said, no matter what title we carry, we are all human first. These men were pastors as a vocation, but human first.

"Moreover, it seems like society believes pastors should be perfect because they studied God and His Word. But how many times have we studied great things, and even devoted our lives to great pursuits, but have still fallen short? If we can't remember where our keys are sometimes, how are we going to remember to do life just like the books tell us to? A top dermatologist can have the worst skin of anyone we know, no matter how much she studied and has achieved. A top chef will still overcook pasta and regularly eat greasy bad food and drink sodas. The best attorney will still miss key issues and lose cases. And a Buddhist monk will still get agitated, be tempted and make wrong choices, and fall away from the protocol.

"Getting a DD, Ph.D., Ed.D, MD, ND, DVM, MBA, JD, or any other designation doesn't mean you will be *perfect* at your craft. Life is not confined to a controlled educational environment or to books, theories, dissertations, labs, clinics, practicums, or internships. At some point, we have to just get out there and live life in a world we have no control over, with people we have no control over. We can only practice what we have learned whenever the opportunity arises, and we will *always* have ample opportunity *to practice*. Furthermore, not one situation will ever be the same as another. Perfection is impossible.

"I'm not trying to excuse these pastors, pastors in general, or anyone else. I'm just saying that Christians *and* non-Christians will always be imperfect. There is no way to live up to any standard of perfection, whether they are misguided and fickle manmade standards, or whether they are principles based on the truest measure of perfection itself—*God*. No *mere* man has ever been perfect, and no one ever will be. But that doesn't mean we can't sincerely seek to be the best at what we do and to be the best human we can be. God wants us to aspire to "run with the horses" and strive to reach our true potential for greatness in Him, refusing to settle for anything less.

"The test, then, is in what we do *after* we make a mistake. Do we apologize? Make amends? Work towards restoration? Do we learn from the situation and do better next time? If we do, then making mistakes and failing to reach perfection, by any standard, isn't the same as being a hypocrite. We've simply missed the mark, and we will try again. We fail forward—towards growth."

"You're too nice! But your old pastors didn't just miss the mark, they missed the boat!" Leah said unapologetically.

"Yes, they made a mistake, and while Pastor Earl didn't do the right thing afterwards, Pastor Scott did."

"I still say you're too nice."

"Leah, I'm not. I've experienced how pride (ego) can so easily slip into my own life, as I made my unforgettable trip down the stairs. If pride and rebellion could creep in and do such damage in a place where God's Word and His presence is focused on regularly, *how much more do I have to be aware, cautious, conscientious, and vigilant in my own life and in how I navigate in the world?*"

Leah sighed and nodded in agreement.

"Like I said, we could talk forever about this topic."

"No, I get it," Leah said slowly. "I understand what you're saying. Truth be told, I guess my issue is that I'd rather *not* understand and take the easy road. I would rather have things done *for me*, not take responsibility, keep blaming, and… complaining." She paused a moment before continuing. "I've had lots of chances to practice, but I guess I didn't do very well!"

I squeezed her hand.

Leah looked away before continuing. "I've missed so much. I wish I had chosen to trust God earlier in my life."

"Trust is faith in action, and you're doing it now."

She smiled.

I smiled, too as I remembered something. "There's a funny adage: even if we find a perfect church, it'll stop being perfect the second we go there!"

"That is funny!" Leah laughed. "But how do you know if your church is at least a good one?"

"Well, there are many factors to consider, and you'd have to consider many things, including your own personality and style. However, if I had to offer any advice, I'd look for some foundational components. First, it needs to be a Bible-teaching church, so you're getting the Truth and not manmade ideals. Second, the leadership should have vision, be qualified, pure-hearted, accountable, humble-hearted, virtuous, teachable, and of good character."

"That's quite a list!"

I laughed, then continued. "There should be a culture of servanthood, humility, unity, and a focus to reach the hurt, lost, lonely and poor. And lastly, they should be progressive in allowing the fullness of Christ to flow and work. You should see life, joy, fruit, and breakthrough in the people there.

"But no matter what, always, always, always listen and respond to the Holy Spirit. Whatever He tells you, listen, and follow. You can never go wrong that way."

"I wish I could have found a church like you're describing in my past. But I'd be too scared to step foot into another church again if I were in *your* shoes," Leah said warily.

"I was too. Thankfully, not all churches are like the one I told you about. And just as importantly, I didn't let the faults of misguided men steal my relationship with God. They had taken enough. They weren't going to have everything."

"What did you do?"

"I searched a long time, going to many, many churches, looking for the right one where I felt I belonged."

"But how do you know if you belong?"

"I'm not sure if there's a catchall answer for that either. All I can say is you will *know*. For me, I ended up going to literally dozens and dozens of churches. Most of them were very nice—*very, very nice,* and I even tried to talk myself into staying at a few of them.

"Then one Sunday, I walked into a church, and as soon as I heard the pastors speak, I knew. God was in that house. And my heart felt like I *belonged*."

Alien

"In the midst of all this drama, Michael was now in his teenage years," I said, changing the subject.

Leah rolled her eyes and sat up, "Oh, boy, here we go…how many heart attacks did you have during this time?" she asked somewhat sarcastically, but in her watchful eyes, I saw something only another parent who's been through those fires could know.

"A few dozen, and a wobbly banana-peel step away from a nervous breakdown or two! And I'm not trying to be facetious."

"Oh, I know, honey, I know!" she said, nodding her head firmly. "I'm tracking with you…been there, done that."

I looked directly at Leah. "Of all the difficult things I've been through and done, being a single mom has absolutely been the most difficult."

At first, Michael was just disrespectful, and that alone was hard enough because our relationship had never been like that. Instead of being kind and thoughtful, he was now rude, unappreciative, demanding, and selfish, flying into wild fits of rage whenever he didn't get his way.

Who is this alien? Where is my son?

When he was seven, he had come up with a special code so he wouldn't have to endure the embarrassment of having his mother say, "I love you" in front of his friends. When I suggested using the code "one-four-three" for the number of letters in each of those three magic words, he was thrilled.

Then, a few days later, he came running to me and said, "Mommy! Mommy! One four three *nine!*"

I smiled and asked, "What does nine stand for?"

"Massively!" he said, beaming ear to ear as he wrapped me in a breathtaking hug.

Oh, how I longed for those days back!

But now, there were no hugs and no sing-songy words of love. Instead, my son rebelled against me at every turn, and I was tossed back and forth daily in a hurricane of emotions.

When he was fourteen years old, while I was still at the former church volunteering for an event, he took my Mercedes convertible and gunned it down our street, leaving skid marks where he went. Thank God he didn't get far because the cameras in our gated community caught him, and the guards called me as they took him back to the house. I was shocked to the core to think my son would be so defiant as to risk doing such a dangerous and illegal thing, and that he would be so recalcitrant against me and all I had taught him.

Because of this incident (and many others), his increasing rebellion, and his escalating temper, I forbade him to drive until he was seventeen years old. I could not trust he would be rational behind the wheel, nor did I trust he would obey authorities. He was furious and screamed at me regularly, but I didn't care how loud he screamed, how much he threatened me, or what names he called me. He was not getting his license until he showed respect for me and for authority in general and demonstrated enough maturity to understand the great responsibilities of driving a car.

Many people might say this kind of behavior is typical for a teenager, but this was not how I had raised my son, and no matter what people said was normal, this was not a standard of behavior I was willing to accept. Sure, I was well aware of the relative changes that occur in puberty as these fledglings try to find their own wings, but what I saw in my son's eyes were not the conventional characteristics of a typical teenager. I was battling something much bigger than adolescence. It required me to be a weightier disciplinarian than I had thought (or hoped) would be necessary.

In an attempt to teach Michael the danger of what he had done and the peril we had escaped, I sat him down and explained, "Michael, we have a great responsibility with our free will, our freedom to choose. That's God's greatest gift to us, second to our gift of life and a life with Him. With every choice, there will be consequences. That is inescapable. You can't hide from them or pretend they don't exist. And the consequences can be good or bad, depending on what you choose to do.

"Further, these consequences always run deeper, farther, wider, and are always bigger than you can possibly imagine, good and bad. So, you must learn to choose wisely. Taking my car when you don't know how to drive, are still years away from learning how to drive, and don't have the understanding of what that responsibility means, could have had disastrous consequences. You could have died or been severely hurt, or you could have killed someone or maimed them for life. You must never, ever, ever, do that again."

In the moment, Michael got it, but whatever change I affected didn't last long.

Though I worked full time, I still made myself available for all of Michael's school requirements and extracurricular activities, provided and maintained a safe and loving home, and kept up with fun little routines and family traditions I hoped would one day be great memories for him when he was grown, all the while still training him, educating him, disciplining him and inspiring him in his daily life.

But my world with my beloved son had changed, and the air was now filled with his tirades, door slamming, screaming, and threats. Michael argued with me about everything, especially about school. He was intelligent and bright, but he didn't want to apply himself, choosing less demanding and more eye-catching activities like computer games overdoing his homework. I refused to let him sit in front of a hand-held machine or a computer screen (which seems to suck its users into a dark world hidden under clever marketing), but that only aggravated him more. So I found creative ways to help him learn, hiring countless personal tutors, and enrolling him in special tutoring programs to help him get through high school and prepare for university.

Michael was on a slippery slope with his teachers and had actually been impertinent enough to make enemies with an influential teacher who threatened to kick him out of school altogether. Were it not for his French teacher, who interceded on his behalf, Michael would not have made it through that year or graduated from that school.

I even sought counseling for us, and in one of the sessions I pleaded, "Michael, I'm not your enemy. I'm your mom! I love you! I'm your best friend and would do anything for you. We have to stick together. A house divided cannot stand. We're family."

That's when he blew up at me and snarled, "We're *not* family! That's a joke! There's 'you,' and there's 'me,' but we're not a family!"

My heart shattered upon hearing those words, and I was unable to speak for the rest of the session. I realized then that Michael had been blaming me for the divorce from his birth father and for marrying Barry, along with a host of other faults he deemed me to have.

We had much healing to do.

In his explosions, he blamed me for every one of his disappointments and for all of his perceived losses in life. During this difficult time, he never saw how much I had done for him. He only saw what he didn't have, and as evidence of my being a good parent, demanded I do more for him.

One Christmas, in an experiment to test his heart and to teach him a lesson about his entitlement issues, the only present I gave him was a book, a very good book. That night, he revealed his heart to me as he screamed at me for giving him a "piece of $#!^" gift.

No matter what I tried, no matter what counsel I sought, Michael's unruly behavior continued. I did my best to keep our "family" together, and to push through all I needed to do to support us, but I was still recovering myself, and often felt like a shell of a person.

On the way to school one day, Michael started in on me early, but I didn't have the strength to hold back anymore. He had crossed the line with his foul language and disrespect.

I'd had enough.

"*That's it!*" I shouted, slamming on the brakes so hard only our seatbelts kept us from hitting the windshield. Thankfully, the stretch of road we were on at the time was a remote one, and there were no other cars around. I skillfully handled the car to catch his attention, whipping it over to the curb. Michael stared at me in bewilderment, but when he saw me put the car into park, he again started with his pugnaciousness.

Not willing to endure another moment of it, I reached over and grabbed the front of his shirt and pulled him within inches of my face. I stared at him and slowly and firmly said, "Listen! I don't know who you think you are. And I don't know whom you've been listening to. But this bad behavior is stopping, right now, *to-day!*" I exhaled. "I hear what you say about me to your friends, so let me just clarify a few things. I'm not just a stupid old woman who doesn't know anything, and you may be arrogant enough to think you actually know more than me, or any other authority figure, but let me assure you, I know e*verything* that's going on! I'm simply choosing which battles I want to take on, and when!"

Michael rolled his eyes. "Yeah, yeah, whatever!" he snarled as he tried to pull away.

But I just held on tighter. "I'm not finished! You need to understand something else very clearly. You can fight me all you want, but I will always win!"

He stared at me as I was talking, searching my eyes for a weak spot, almost daring me, but when I said, "*I will always win!*" his eyes met the intensity of mine, and he knew I was serious, and he knew I was right. He also knew that when I said, "*I will always win,*" it was because I loved him more than he loved himself, and I was willing to do whatever it took to conquer the negative thoughts filling his mind, and I would ensure he would walk out his calling and fulfill his destiny.

I was fighting *for* him, not against him.

Looking back, that was one of those life-defining moments I truly believe changed the trajectory of our relationship. I didn't want to ever speak to Michael in that way. Nor did I ever want to grab his shirt collar like I did, but I had to take control, establish boundaries, and remind him that I was his mother. And as his mother, his covering, his caregiver, his protector, and his provider, I also had the authority of love over him, and not even the gates of hell would prevail against it!

There is no greater love and no devotion fiercer than that of a mother fighting for her child. This may sound dramatic, but there were many, many other situations occurring at that time that led me to this point of exasperation. Suffice it to say, this wasn't just about the simple exploits of a hormonal teenager trying to find himself.

Leah let out a huge sigh. "The power of a mother's love…that same power can take on a man twice her size if her child is threatened, and that same power can indeed fight the gates of hell. I believe it." Leah paused and thought quietly before adding, "You didn't have it easy, being both a mom and a dad…"

"Funny you should say that. My counselor said the same thing. And while it wasn't easy for me, I believe Michael had even more ambivalence about that fact. On the one hand, he loved me and to some degree appreciated all I did for him, but on the other hand, I think he was resentful that I couldn't simply be his mom—I also had to be the 'father figure,' the authoritarian and disciplinarian in his life. It may not have seemed right in his eyes for me to play this role, but there was no other option; I did the best I could…" I said slowly, remembering the heartache of this time. "I wish he had had a great father figure to teach him how to fix a car, change a tire, throw a football, or how to camp in the wilderness—"

"Stop right there!" Leah interrupted. "Trust me, I know how important it is for a child to have their father in their lives—but *a good father*. But that doesn't mean you didn't bless Michael with a great home and a great life also! Please don't underestimate what you did for your son, a son you fought for and lived for. You gave him the best of everything you had." Leah paused, and then added, "I know Michael missed out on having a good father at home, but he also had a mom who was willing to make up for that loss by going the extra mile anytime and every time she could. So go easy on yourself, honey. Maybe you didn't teach him how to shave or run with the bulls, but you did everything else you could."

I smiled in appreciation of her encouragement.

"Now, knowing you, I should qualify something, *did you* take Michael to run with the bulls?" Leah asked seriously.

"No," I laughed out loud. "I didn't have us run with the bulls, and I didn't teach him how to shave, but Luke did one Christmas. It was a tender evening that benchmarked a new season for Michael."

"That's lovely! See? You always provided for him," Leah said with a smile. Then she raised her eyebrow and asked, "Now, what about the birds and the bees? Who got *that* lucky job?"

"Actually, *I* did. I wanted to because I felt it was important for him to hear it from a woman's perspective so he could appreciate the significance and meaning of it from *our* context. Like most kids, I'm sure Michael also learned about this in school, in misinformed and exaggerated discussions with friends—and unfortunately, through the Internet."

Ain't No Mountain High Enough

I was also blessed with bringing Michael through a rite of passage at age sixteen. Many cultures and traditions celebrate their children's development and transformation into adulthood, and I, too, wanted to do something to honor Michael in this way.

Michael needed a new beginning; we both did. Remembering back to my own rite of passage my father gave me on that long-ago visit to the Hong Kong slums, and to my sweet time with my GongGong when I was a little girl, I resolved to do something memorable to commemorate this special time in Michael's life.

But this wasn't an easy task to figure out. This event had to also be appropriate for me as his mother to do, instead of a father-son event. But since mine had been with my father (and not my mother), I reasoned I could create a fun adventure for Michael and me, also.

But what would that be? What could we do together?

I wondered about a mission trip, but we had already served together for numerous organizations for many years. No. This event had to be different and something very significant, meaningful, and life changing. And, ideally, I would love it to be close to our family, so we could share the experience with them afterward.

Then, one day, after thinking long and hard about this for almost a year, the idea came to me. I was to climb a mountain with him!

Vancouver is home to Grouse Mountain, well-known for its ski runs and a challenging hiking trail that requires good physical strength and endurance. The climb is not recommended for anyone who isn't in good physical shape, as its summit is thirty-seven hundred feet, and the elevation gain is over twenty-eight hundred feet in less than two miles. The average person is said to require an hour and a half to climb the mountain, and it's advised that novice hikers go even slower, allowing themselves over two hours to complete the climb, with lots of water and rests in between.

Having hiked the mountain several times before, I knew this would be the perfect milestone to achieve together; it was demanding, but not dangerous. Climbing a mountain symbolized the meeting and the overcoming of challenges. Doing this together would be my way of showing him I would always be there for him—whether it was his first mountain or his one-thousandth mountain, he was never alone.

Believing Michael was also in good physical condition from playing soccer in a casual club, and playing tennis at the varsity level at school, I thought I could keep up with him, and we could finish the climb around the same time together.

I shared this idea with him, hoping we could strategize about the hike together and choose the right clothing and footwear for the climb, but that was not to be the case. He shut down the idea, calling it *stupid*. He resisted me every time I brought it up and refused to go.

"This is ridiculous! All my other friends get to go in limos and party at a restaurant, or they get to go golfing or fishing out of town—or other fun things. For my sixteenth birthday, I want to do something fun too, not go with my mother to climb some dumb mountain! That's just stupid!"

Ahh, but he had forgotten: *I will always win!*

As planned, we were with family in Vancouver on his sixteenth birthday. Michael wouldn't ride alone in the car with me for days when we first arrived because he thought I was going to hijack him to the mountain (which is exactly what I ended up doing). But after a few days there, and I had made no mention of it, he dropped his guard. Then, when he least expected it one afternoon, I headed to Grouse Mountain.

Michael yelled and complained during the entire thirty-minute car ride, but knowing nothing was going to change, he reluctantly surrendered to the event. I told him fun stories about others who had done the strenuous hike, the records that had been broken there, how athletes world-wide come to *run* this mountain, and how Olympiads trained on this mountain. As we got closer, he became more curious and started to show some interest in our little adventure together.

We pulled up to the parking lot, and with a few more gratuitous groans and moans, he seized on something he thought was his one last way out. "I only have flip flops on!" he told me. "Too bad! I guess we can't go now!"

That's when I opened the trunk of the car and revealed the clothes and shoes I had hidden there. He fought a smile, knowing he'd been beaten, and pretended to be upset with me as he put on his shoes.

As I checked the car and locked up, he went ahead of me and jogged towards the entrance of the gate, turning once to mutter, "Well, now that we're here, let's get this thing over with."

"I think we should start slowly, honey. It's a long hike, and it's pretty vertical at places—you'll literally be using your hands and feet in many spots. The air will also be different, so consider pacing yourself."

"Yeah, yeah, whatever," he retorted.

I watched from about twenty feet behind as my impetuous little boy was about to find out that this old woman was not so dumb, and that maybe I was someone to whom he should listen.

As I have already mentioned, I intended to use this event as a metaphor for life. And so, we set off. Michael charged the trail, but we weren't three minutes into the hike before the steep slope and thinner air proved too much for him. He began to slow down, and after another twenty feet, he stopped to rest on a rock.

When I caught up to him, I asked, "Why did you stop?"

"I'm tired...need to catch my breath," he puffed.

"It's not as easy as it looks, is it?"

Michael shook his head.

"It's good to always assess a situation before running into it too fast—no matter how easy or how fun it seems."

He nodded.

"It's great to be excited at the beginning of something, but we need to pace ourselves so we won't be discouraged on our journey, and we will finish well and finish happy!" I continued.

He looked at me, nodded, and with a sweep of his right arm, invited me to go ahead of him.

"No, you go ahead of me. I will follow behind," I said.

"Why, Mom? You know the way."

"Yes, I've been here a few times and know the path well. It's safe. You will now learn the markings yourself and know which steps to take and when, too. Plus, I want you to go first so you can have the experience of seeing the beauty and miracle of the forest unfold before your eyes—one stride at a time."

"But I want you to have that too, Mom."

"I've had my time. It's your turn now."

We had hiked a little longer when Michael suddenly stopped and looked back at me. "I have a feeling there's another reason you're behind me...isn't there?" he asked, panting.

I smiled. "Yes, Michael. There is. Why do you think that is?"

He thought a moment and shook his head.

"I'm behind you because I can catch you if you fall," I smiled.

Michael smiled back. In that instant, his hard shell fell off, and he was lighter than he'd been in years.

Now, this is the Michael I know...

We continued, but no sooner did we round a sharp bend than we met a group of youthful Asian tourists making their way clumsily and uncertainly down the path toward us. The girls were dressed in light, airy summer clothing—skirts, dresses, shiny sandals, and costume jewelry. Their expressions showed their concern, and their clothes were dirty and scuffed up; clearly, they had never done anything like this before.

"That was weird," Michael teased. "What was that all about? Didn't they know they were *climbing Grouse*?"

"Hmmm...maybe..."

"Well, it's obvious we're on a flippin' mountain! And they obviously headed up even though they were clearly *not prepared* and now *had* to come back down. They missed the chance to do the climb and slowed everyone else down in the process," he observed.

"Yes, but at least they decided to retreat before going further. It would have been dangerous for them to continue on a path they weren't equipped or trained to go on."

"But *hello?* We're at the base of a mountain! Signs are everywhere, warning people about what's ahead. Why did they even start?"

"Sometimes, people rush into things that look exciting or thrilling regardless of wise counsel. People doubt the authority behind the warning, doubt the seriousness of the situation, are too confident (or prideful) in themselves. Sometimes, people are rebellious and challenging in nature, undisciplined, and in some cases, just plain foolish. In this case, although they may be embarrassed, it's better to be humble and retreat than to continue and hurt themselves—and other people along the way."

"Yeah, they could have all gotten in trouble, and if one of them fell, that would have been a disaster. And getting the rangers up there with the right equipment wouldn't have been easy."

"Yes, the whole mountain would have been closed down, and well, the ongoing ramifications would have been horrible. I'm just glad they chose to come back down," I agreed.

"I guess people have to really think about what they're doing and the effect it could have on others," Michael added.

"Yes, better for all of us to be a little inconvenienced now and lose a little time, than to have a worse situation occur farther up. The good news is that they can always come back and try again. They may have missed the opportunity today, but if they prepare better next time, they'll have a greater chance of succeeding."

Michael smiled. He was beginning to understand the purpose of our adventure.

We continued in silence for a little while. The trail was getting harder and steeper. It was no longer a casual hike, but an arduous one that required our hands and upper body strength to pull us up. We were now climbing over rocks, roots, or wooden steps cut into the mountain for footing.

Michael stopped. He was panting and noticeably working on this trail.

"Why aren't *you* panting, Mom? You must be more fit than I thought—no offense."

I smiled. "Are you okay?"

"Yeah—do you have any water?"

I pulled some from the knapsack. "I could only grab a few water bottles before we left. Here, take this, but don't drink too much all at once. Take a few sips and then see how you feel."

"I'm sorry I was such a jerk about this," he apologized.

"It's okay." I smiled. "Let's ration what we have and see how we do."

"I didn't know you were carrying this extra weight in your backpack all this time. I don't have any pockets in these shorts. Here, put the water back in the bag, and I'll carry the knapsack."

My heart melted. "What do you think we can learn from this situation?"

Michael thought for a moment. "An opportunity can come at any time. We never know what that will look like, but we can be as prepared as possible." He beamed.

I nodded. "Take a little rest and use this time to get your wind back." I motioned for him to sit on a rocky outcropping nearby. "Honey, look down the path and see how far you've come. I don't usually suggest people look backward, but in this case, it's good to look back."

"Wow! That's steep!" Michael said with surprise.

I smiled. "Now, look ahead and see where the markers are." I turned my head back toward the face of the mountain. "In some areas, you'll see a few paths shooting off the main one. Just be aware of them for now. As you get closer, you'll be able to see which is the better one to take. Study the rocks and the footing."

Michael nodded, put the water back and headed upward.

When we rounded a bend, a few people ahead of us had stopped in the middle of the trail and were trying to catch their breath.

"Mom, what should we do? The path is blocked, and they don't look like they're going to go anywhere for a while. Do you want to go in front of me and talk to them?" Michael asked, uncertain.

"No, it's okay. Take a look again and see what our options are. Be open and flexible. Things may change once we reach that ledge."

"What do you mean?"

"You'll know what to do once we get there, whether or not we should pass them, slow down, or maybe stop and chat with them a while. Maybe they'll need assistance for the next leg. Maybe they need some encouragement, maybe they want some company, or maybe they're just enjoying a peaceful moment."

"Wow. I never thought hiking Grouse was going to be so philosophical!" Michael said half-jokingly. He turned back to continue the climb but stopped suddenly and looked back at me. "Thanks, Mom." He smiled and leaned over to kiss me on the cheek. *"Alrighty then,"* he said enthusiastically, *"Let's take this mountain!"*

This was one of the happiest moments of my life. My smile couldn't have been bigger, and my heart couldn't have been more overjoyed. My son was back, and my eyes welled with tears of joy.

Step by step, we passed one marker after another. Michael was feeling great about his accomplishment, and so was I. On the next break, he stopped and looked at me, sweat running down his forehead and the sides of his face. "How come you're not tired?"

"Because I know a little about taking mountains…" I smiled. "And I do my best to stay in shape and to be ready. One never knows when we're called to an unexpected adventure."

"Oh…is that why you love running so much? If it's anything like this, I don't think I'll ever get to where you are."

"Michael, you'll run faster. You'll go farther. And you'll take more mountains than I ever will. There's no mountain too high for you."

I took out the water and sat beside him on the rock. Michael thought about this as he drank his water. Thinking we had another bottle left, he downed the last of it and went to reach for the knapsack for the remaining one. But that was the last bottle of water, and we still hadn't reached the halfway point.

"Mom, I'm so sorry. I took the last bit of water, and you haven't had any!" he said, nervous.

"I'm fine. It's all good." I smiled. "You ready to keep going? We still have quite a bit to climb, and it gets steeper."

"What are we going to do without water?" he asked.

"Don't worry. God will provide," I said matter-of-factly, and stood up to continue our trek.

"*God will provide? Seriously?* Mom! What are you talking about? Unless there's a fresh, clean creek or a food and beverage stand coming up, I think we're toast until we get to the top."

"Don't worry. All we're responsible for is to take one step at a time." I nodded for him to start hiking.

"Mom! I can't do it! I'm exhausted, and there's no water. We should get help."

I looked at him calmly and then looked ahead at the next ledge. "Can you get to that ledge?"

He looked and then nodded.

"Don't let what you *think* you cannot do diminish what you know you can do. Let's do what we can do."

He shook his head at me, still unsure. He was tired, the air was much thinner than when we started, the top half of the mountain was still left to climb, and we were out of water. To him, what may have sounded foolish was faith in full action. Faith defies circumstances, and in my heart, I truly knew we would be okay. We just had to be smart, go slowly, rest when we needed to, and even if it took another hour for us to reach the top, we would be fine. I would never have put him in harm's way.

The next stretch was a long one. We hiked in focused silence until we stopped to take in the absolutely glorious scenery and views around us. The palette of colors was almost too much to take in. We were breathless—not because of the climb—but because of the beauty we were honored to witness in the everyday life of a forest. The sun illuminated all the vegetation underneath the majestic hundred-year-old trees, revealing the brilliance of life around us. Carefree birds flew over us, the Indian summer breeze rustled the leaves around us, and our eyes beheld the full spectrum of colors surrounding us—from royal red flowers to the dancing golden rays of the sun, from hundreds of nature-kissed bright-lime and yellows in the flora to the richest violets and the commanding blues of the Pacific

Ocean just over a ridge next to us. It was good. It was very good indeed.

At that moment, a small cluster of hikers rushed in between us. They weren't friendly like the others we had met on the trail, and a few even harshly demanded we move out of their way as they shouldered past us.

After they disappeared from view, I said, "There will always be those who are in a hurry, pushing their way through without much sensitivity to others."

I also shared that while they were on their mission, we were very happy to be on our own mission also. No offense was taken—only a reminder for us to still be kind to others during the times we are strained in our own pursuits.

Immediately following the last group was a lone man, huffing and puffing up the path. He didn't carry anything but a large rock, and by its size, I would say it was at least twenty-five pounds. He was sure-footed, and it was obvious he had done this many times before.

"The Grouse Grind is hard enough as it is!" Michael whispered. "Why would anyone want to carry a boulder on top of it all?"

"Maybe he's training for a competition. Sometimes the gain for the pain is greater than the speed we achieve without the inconvenience."

"But why would anyone want to carry more than they need to?"

"Because we grow stronger when we prepare in harsher conditions and under tougher circumstances. In life, we can choose to carry a *burden* for a specific goal for a season (or longer) also. The burden may not be easy or convenient, but carrying it serves a greater purpose—greater than our desire for immediate comfort or relief," I shared.

"I get it if it's a competition or a race, but what do you mean when you say 'in life' too?" Michael asked.

"Imagine if that stone was not a stone, but a 'life'? Maybe it's a wounded animal needing to be rescued; a little child in need of love and patience; a lost teenager who feels misunderstood; a broken woman floundering in a sea of mixed messages about her worth and value; a man mesmerized by his fame and fortune, ignoring the most precious of treasures in the relationships around him; or a community of misguided individuals who, without true guidance, are about to race off a cliff like lemmings. Whether it's a physical burden, a financial burden, an emotional burden, or a spiritual burden, we all need to be aware and sensitive to that 'stone,' that precious opportunity to bring someone less fortunate up the mountain with us. There will always be someone we can help. We can be like the group of men who just pushed us aside, focusing only on ourselves and our goals, or we can be like that gentleman who quietly and without causing pain or disruption to anyone else, carried a burden he didn't need to carry all the way up to the top of the mountain."

Michael nodded and smiled.

Just then, another passing hiker stopped and said, "Hey, do you guys need some water?" He pulled out a canteen, and I watched as he poured some into our water bottle. We thanked the man who gave us a knowing smile and moved on.

"Wow! Where did *he* come from?" Michael asked in awe.

"That was so nice of him to share his canteen of water!" I said.

"Mom, that guy came out of *nowhere!* How did he know we needed water? And his canteen wasn't even full! He offered us water even when he didn't have a full canteen himself!" Michael marveled.

I smiled.

"Wow…" Michael said, shaking his head with wonder. "I guess God really did provide! He sent someone to help us when I thought we'd be alone all the way to the end. He was an angel to us!"

"I couldn't have said it better."

We both chuckled and continued on up the path.

As we neared the summit, all of the hikers at the peak began cheering each other on, extending their arms to help one another climb up the last outcropping. There was joy, laughter, and warm displays of encouragement everywhere. It was magnificent.

We turned to take in the breathtaking panoramic view around us, and a great sense of gratitude and peace fell over us.

Michael turned to me and hugged me. I couldn't help but cry tears of joy.

"You climbed your first mountain," I cheered, "and now that you know you can do the most challenging of things, there's nothing to stop you or hold you back from your dreams! Those at the top of the mountain don't just fall there. It takes work, focus, persistence, faith, preparation—and heart."

Michael nodded knowingly.

After a few moments, I asked, "What do you see as you look around you?"

"Other mountains," he laughed.

"That's right, but not all of them are yours to climb. Part of growing up is knowing which mountain is yours to climb, and which ones aren't. If you're in doubt, ask God for wisdom. With God, you will be able to do anything; you will be able to climb every mountain He gives you."

He hugged me again and thanked me. My heart was overjoyed, and I felt we had achieved what I had hoped for Michael.

After walking around a bit, taking a few photos, and grabbing a snack, we allowed ourselves the luxury of taking the gondola back down, beholding the mountain as it slipped away under our feet.

"It's interesting…the way down is easy and smooth once you've reached the top," Michael noted.

"Yes, and we appreciate the view more once we know what it takes to get it," I reflected.

We rode the rest of the way in silence, appreciating the magnificence before us. As we neared the bottom, Michael asked, "Hey, Mom. It took us almost two hours to do this climb. How long does it normally take you?"

"Forty-five minutes."
"*What?*"

13 EVERYTHING THAT CAN BE SHAKEN WILL BE SHAKEN

Never give in…never, never, never, in nothing great or small, large or petty, never give in, except to convictions of honor and good sense. Never yield to force, never yield to the apparently overwhelming might of the enemy.

—Winston Churchill

Room 316

The next time I came to see Leah, she was sitting upright in her bed, and she practically pounced on me as soon as I walked in the door. She was weak, and it was becoming quite clear that her body was pushing towards a deadline, but her energy at seeing me buoyed my spirits.

"Finally!" she said. "I thought you would never get here!"

I laughed and looked up at the clock. I was ten minutes early.

"You look great today," I said, pulling my usual chair over towards her bed and settling in.

"I can't wait to hear the rest of your story. I know things must have turned around for you, especially after recovering your connection with Michael!" Leah said with a twinkle in her eye.

"Yes, they did," I admitted.

"I knew it! Here comes 'the happily ever after'!" Leah reached out and took my left hand in hers. She held it with her own featherlight hand and examined my ring. "Nice and shiny, just the way it's supposed to be," she winked. "What's his name?"

"I did get a happily ever after," I told her. "But not right away. It wasn't quite that simple or easy."

"It never is," Leah said. "Well then, pour me some more tea, dear, and let's get started. Tell me all about it…"

The Red String of Fate

It was another very busy time. I was finishing my schooling and had just finished writing the rough drafts of two books. I poured any extra ounce of energy into my health and wellness practice. I enjoyed my field so much that after I completed my formal studies, I continued to take as many courses as I could and invested a great deal into independent research and studies on my own.

This second growth spurt of learning was a wonderful time for me. I had never enjoyed learning like this, and by the grace of God, every concept, process, procedure, and system soaked into my mind as if I had a photographic memory.

In time, I had some of the best health practitioners as mentors. One doctor, in particular, was a renowned scientist, researcher, clinician, and lecturer. I attended every class and course he taught and repeatedly read everything he provided as work materials. I purchased every training CD he produced, listening to them throughout the day. On weekend nights, I stayed up late researching articles and reading medical journals.

Learning under this doctor was a joy. His intelligence and wisdom were inspiring, and I was fascinated by the depths and breadth of all he knew. One day, I counted every letter after his name, and he had forty-three letters symbolizing his titles, certifications, and designations. He was definitely a "lettered man."

I was under the tutelage of the best in the world, and he also helped me with my own personal health conditions resulting from my broken marriage. At one point, we even discussed a possible business venture together, but he was unwilling to move forward as long as my assistant was working for me (a very unfortunate situation which I will explain later).

Yes, this was a busy and exhilarating time, and I was excited about my growing practice. Through the unique programs I had created (private mentoring and coaching approaches, nutritional and herbal protocols, traditional Chinese medicinal programs, kinesiology, and other modalities), my clients were achieving great successes, reaching their health and wellness goals faster than they ever dreamed.

It was around this same time that I was introduced to Joshua, who, almost a decade later, would be my husband.

"Oooh…now we're talkin'! Leah giggled. "But a decade?"

"Yes. It was all very, well…unusual."

"Of course, it was! Everything about your life is unusual!" She winked. "But seriously, why was it unusual?"

"Because the craziest set of circumstances kept me in an inexplicable loop that brought about the most bizarre ways of meeting him, and eventually getting to know him."

"Hmmm…sounds like a movie! A destined red flame of love tied by a magical cord that may stretch and tangle, but never breaks! Start from the beginning! I want to know everything!"

During the time of my divorce, my friend Ellen invited Michael and me to join her on an impromptu all-inclusive package vacation to Europe. She had found a great deal on the Internet and thought it would be fun for the three of us to get away from the ugliness of the divorce proceedings.

The idea of an inexpensive vacation sounded wonderful, so I agreed. A month after the arrangements were made, Ellen told me she had also invited a few other friends to go along. I was surprised because she had originally wanted it to be a quiet time for the three of us. Going on a big social trip was not what we discussed—and *not* what I wanted. But canceling it was not an option, as it was a non-refundable package.

I was stuck.

When I asked her who was going, she shared the names of her friends, and one of them was Lilith.

"Is this the same crazy Lilith you used to tell me about?"

She replied, "Yes, I'm trying to be nice because her marriage is on the rocks again. This time it's really bad, and she needs a break too. She thought we could all commiserate over bad husbands and bad marriages."

"Ellen, no offense, but the last thing either Michael or I need is to keep talking about my bad marriage or hear about another one. I'd rather not do that, especially with someone I don't know, and someone with whom you have issues."

Ellen tried to reassure me. "No problem. If the topic comes up, you can excuse yourself and just say you're going to do a 'family thing' together with Michael."

"It sounds like a lot of work and not what we originally planned. I thought this was going to just be us, a time to simply relax and have some fun."

"I know, I'm sorry, but it's done now. Plus, everyone's really excited to meet you. It'll be good for you to meet new people. You've been in hiding way too long! It'll be *different*, but we'll still have fun! I promise," Ellen said in her typical silly and childlike way.

A few months later, Michael and I found ourselves in a distant land with a group of people we didn't know, except for Ellen.

Initially, everyone was very pleasant, but it wasn't long for our different personalities to set markers. After everything I had been through, I was unwilling to spend money and travel such great distances only to engage in more discord or conflict. Nonetheless, I was pleasant and gracious, and no one was aware Michael and I weren't comfortable on the trip.

I navigated myself carefully and often excused myself as planned. While the trip was not what I had expected, Michael and I ended up venturing out on our own much of the time. And we had great fun doing so.

However, for the times we were together as a group, I found it odd that Lilith always felt the need to correct and one-up me and the others. It was impossible to participate in simple conversation without being contradicted or minimized—and over the most ridiculous of things. After a while, I simply stopped engaging. I refused to be consistently challenged. And it didn't take long before everyone diplomatically agreed to enjoy the trip separately.

Once we separated, I hardly saw Ellen at all, and it wasn't until the end of our trip, en route to the airport, when we finally got to talk a bit. Unfortunately, our lighthearted conversation ended when we arrived at our gate to discover our flight had been delayed by inclement weather. It was a full flight, and naturally, every traveler was disappointed. They did the best they could to find alternate flights home, but since we were part of a package deal, there was little we could do but wait.

Since every flight that afternoon was delayed, the waiting areas at each gate were also jam-packed with travelers and their luggage. There were no extra seats, so people just found places to sit on the floor. Our group did too, and we sat in a circle playing card games.

Except for Lilith.

She stood at the gate, arguing with the flight attendant at the counter, raising her voice so loudly that eyes were starting to look her way. It was impossible not to overhear what she was saying, and we all shook our heads, before looking back to our card game.

As the next hand was dealt, one of the friends said with resignation, "You get used to her after a while."

I reflected on the entire trip and thought, *There is no way I would choose to get used to this.*

Ellen whispered, "I'm sorry. I told you she's a loose cannon."

Frustrated by the unnecessary added drama (which was what I thought I was avoiding by going on this vacation), I asked, "So, why did you invite her?"

"Well, she can be fun…sometimes," Ellen replied apologetically.

Meanwhile, the supervisor was called down to address the situation with Lilith. Still fuming, she walked off in a huff toward the oversized windows overlooking the tarmac.

"Why is she going off at those people? They can't control the snowstorm and make the pilots jeopardize lives by flying in it!" a nearby traveler commented.

"She should just sit down," said another traveler. "We're all going to arrive when we arrive—no need to add more upset!"

Seeing that everyone was upset by the commotion, Ellen nervously joked, "I'm sorry…but look on the bright side, you won't have to see her again once we deplane."

───◆───

Months passed, and Ellen had invited me to a large charity event she was co-hosting. The plan was for me to pick her up and for us to go together. However, the divorce proceedings were getting uglier by the day, and I was not in the mindset of socializing with the "Who's Who" of the city.

I asked Ellen if I could skip the event, but she had been planning and working on it for months, and after her determined pleading, I reluctantly agreed to go.

As I was on my way to pick her up, she called my cell phone and told me her plans had suddenly changed, and she had gotten an earlier ride. She was now at Lilith's house.

"Can you pick me up there? Lilith is going to ride with us," she asked.

"What? I'm almost at your house! Plus, after the disastrous trip, you said you weren't going to have much to do with her anymore."

"I know," she said sheepishly. "But she's better now. Oh! I have to go. Another call's coming in! Here's the address. See you soon!"

And with that, she hung up. I called her back several times, thinking maybe she could go with Lilith instead, and I could bow out of the entire ordeal, but she did not answer.

Aggravated, I changed direction and eventually pulled up Lilith's driveway. When Ellen saw me, she came running out to greet me and gave me a big hug.

"Thank you so, *sooo* much for doing this! It'll only be a few hours, and hopefully, there won't be any fireworks this time!" She giggled. "You're a trooper!"

"Ellen, I don't understand. If you are always walking on eggshells around Lilith, why do you still spend so much time with her?"

"I know. She is a porcupine, but she's really fun when you get past the prickly parts. And then, well, you learn to live with the jabs in between." With that, she looped her arm around mine and led me inside.

"But—" I started to speak, but Ellen suddenly pulled me closer to her.

"Shhh! Here she comes!" she whispered under her breath before grinning a wide smile at Lilith.

Lilith greeted me warmly and seemed to have no recollection of all the tension from our trip. I was polite and gracious but was intentional about moving on and asked if we could simply be on our way to the event. I wanted to fulfill my obligation to Ellen but then leave after an appropriate amount of time to get on with my day.

Without waiting for a response, I turned towards my car, but Ellen suddenly grabbed my hand to pull me back. Lilith's husband, who was on his way to catch a flight for a business trip, had come out of his office. Being the social butterfly that she was, Ellen wanted to introduce me to him before we all left.

Joshua stood about six feet tall, had light brown hair, and was dressed very professionally, but not in a way that would bring unnecessary attention to himself. He put down his suitcase, and as he extended his hand to greet me, I couldn't help but notice how kind he seemed. Even though he was rushing to get to the airport, he made time to ask Ellen some very thoughtful questions about the non-profit event we were about to attend and shared some genuine pleasantries with me before excusing himself.

Everything about Joshua seemed kind—his eyes, his smile, his countenance, and his interest in Ellen's event was authentic and sincere. In a flash, I recalled all the things I had heard about him—that he refused to marry Lilith because of her uncontrollable mood swings and volatile outbursts (even though they had unplanned children together). They had separated many times, and Lilith was equally fed up with him for being such a disappointment to her.

After Joshua had left, and Lilith went to answer the phone, I looked at Ellen in shock and whispered, "That's Joshua?"

She smiled and nodded.

As I headed toward my car, I thought, *This can't be the same man they are saying all these horrible things about.*

Ellen grabbed her purse, following behind me. When she got into my car, I turned to her and asked again, "*That* was Joshua?"

"Yes," she giggled. "Why do you keep asking that?"

"Because he doesn't look anything like the horrible fellow you guys have been talking about," I said, completely surprised. "He seems, well, really *nice*. I find it hard to believe this is the same person you described!"

"Individually, they are both nice, I guess. It's just when they're together, it's a hot mess," Ellen admitted.

"Well, you keep going back to Lilith, so I'm sure she has to be nice. I don't know Joshua, but he doesn't look like he has a mean bone in his body." I shook my head and started the engine. "I hope they can figure things out."

Ellen shook her head. "I don't know if that's possible. I honestly think it would be best if they just went their own ways. Then at least there's a chance for some kind of friendship. As it stands now, they're like fire and gasoline!" she chuckled. "Things are always blowing up over there."

At the last minute, Lilith insisted on taking her own car and followed us to the event. Ellen apologized for yet another mix-up, and I pulled out of the driveway, frustrated. That whole exercise of having gone to Lilith's house seemed pointless.

Time passed. My divorce was finalized, and I spent much of my time focusing on growing my practice. It was great to be free, and I was very happy rebuilding my life again.

One morning, Ellen called. She told me that Lilith wanted to see me at my practice and help her with some of her wellness goals. It had been months since I saw them, and while I had hardly spent time with Lilith at the event, I didn't want to be thrown into another social situation with her. I couldn't believe Ellen was making such a request of me and tried to deny her suggestion, making up many excuses. Unfortunately, no matter what I said, Ellen said I was being "rude."

"Manna, I know you guys are totally different; I'm not asking you to be friends! Just see her a couple of times as a client." She paused. "Honey, you *have to*, or you'll come across as hoity-toity, and turning down business when you only just got started is *not* a good idea!"

I didn't reply.

"Look," she continued, "Your time with her will be short and focused. It'll be okay. Plus…" she hesitated.

"Plus what, Ellen?"

"Well, I already told her that it wouldn't be a problem, and I'd help set it up."

I was shocked. "*Ellen!*" I yelled into the phone, "You have to stop volunteering me and including me on things without my permission!"

"I'm sorry! But it's already done. Please? Please? I promise it will be easy, and there won't be any drama."

"I've heard that before…"

I only saw Lilith a few times, and I did my best in my earnest and genuine desire to help her. My heart was in the right place, but in hindsight, I should have stuck to my decision and not have agreed to see her.

Unfortunately, I couldn't find a legitimately polite reason to deny the appointment, and that's why I conceded.

I was still on emotionally shaky ground myself. I suffered from PTSD brought on by my disturbing marriage, the ugly divorce, and the terrible disappointments at church. I had a great counselor helping me heal from those issues while learning how to establish healthy boundaries for relationships in my life, but I was still unable to assert myself proactively as I was still learning how to trust (and act on) my discernment. Until that became solidified, all I knew was how to do damage control. I hadn't yet mastered any preemptive techniques to prevent unnecessary drama from entering my life in the first place.

Even though my few appointments with Lilith went smoothly, she really didn't need my services. There were others much more suitable for the goals she wanted to pursue. It was then I realized that Ellen was trying to get me new business and that Lilith only came in as a courtesy to her.

Looking back, all three of us had good intentions, but like the group trip, and the non-profit event, it felt like another unnecessary exercise. After her last visit, Lilith had no valid reason to come back, and I had the sense that the purpose of our introduction had been completed. We wouldn't have to see each other again.

"Oh, dear," Leah said ominously. "Did you know the road to hell is paved with good intentions?"

"Yes," I sighed.

"So then how did you come to see Joshua again?"

"Ellen and I had plans to go to an early Halloween party, but once again, I found out things had drastically changed after I had already committed. Instead of going straight to a mutual friend's small gathering, she asked me to take her to Lilith's party first."

I sighed and began to relay the story.

"It's gonna be *huge*!" Ellen slurred. "There's a band, great food, and lots of games…plus you'll get to meet a ton of new people! It'll be good networking for your new center! Plus, I have to pick up something I left behind that I'll need on Monday."

"But what about Anne's party?" I protested.

"We'll go after!" she exclaimed.

Ellen had been drinking (while on pain medication for a health condition), and there was no reasoning with her. She was not capable of driving, so, once again, I was on my way to take her to Lilith's.

When we arrived, I couldn't believe how big this party was. People were everywhere—inside, outside, and on the streets. You could hear music booming, boisterous conversations, and eruptions of laughter down the block. But something didn't sit right with me, and I was immediately uncomfortable with it all.

I told Ellen I'd be happy to escort her in, but I wasn't staying. Frankly, I had lost interest in going out altogether and regretted not having said no, to begin with (again).

A nice quiet evening at home would have been much better.

While the party was of no interest to me, the excitement of it all seemed to charge Ellen, and she insisted on staying. There was no point in debating her, so I looked for someone Ellen knew, and once I was assured she was comfortable and safe, I planned to slip away.

People dressed in elaborate costumes were scattered throughout the house. Halloween decorations lined the walls, and music blared in the background. Down the hallway were signs on stands that read, "Tarot Card Readings," "Séance in Progress," and "Psychic Readings" in front of rooms with closed doors, along with sign-up sheets.

Yup, I should have stayed home.

We headed right towards the noisier part of the house to find friends Ellen would know. We saw Joshua first, though we didn't recognize him in his costume. He was gracious and offered us a drink. I shook my head and with a nod of my head, indicated I didn't think it would be a good idea for Ellen to drink either.

"Do you know where Lilith is? I want to get Ellen to her before I leave," I yelled so he could hear me through the loud music.

"You're not staying? There's great food and lots of great people here for you to meet! It'll be good networking for you!" he offered.

"That's exactly what I said!" Ellen added enthusiastically.

"That's very kind of you," I said politely as I scanned the kitchen area, hoping to catch a glimpse of Lilith.

Just then, she rushed in with a group of friends. I grabbed Ellen, thanked

Joshua, and headed over to the patio door where they were. After sharing a few pleasantries, I delicately explained Ellen's condition, and the group of friends assured me they'd take care of her.

Feeling relieved, I once again threaded my way back through the clusters of people. Going through the kitchen was like going through a pinball machine; as waves of people moved, I bounced from one side to another. But I didn't mind, the exit was in sight.

Just then, someone grabbed my right arm, and I was suddenly propelled into a group as photographs were being snapped. I forced a smile on the command, "Cheese!" I thought about all the times in my life, I had felt forced to smile, even though it was the last thing I wanted to do.

To my surprise, Ellen came rushing in out of nowhere and threw herself into the group photo, laughing uncontrollably, pleading for one more picture.

"Cheese!"

Another strained smile.

Although Ellen and I saw each other from time to time after that night, it was many months later before she asked me for another favor. This time, she asked if I would see Joshua, who wanted to improve his health after a comprehensive exam with his doctor. I was surprised, as I did not expect to have anything to do with either Lilith or Joshua again.

"He travels a lot for work, but I suspect it's an excuse to stay away from home," Ellen said matter-of-factly. "Can you please see him because he really wants to start a proper health program?"

I was adamant this time and said no. I wanted to limit my exposure to their dynamics and intensifying disputes.

But Ellen was insistent.

Over the next week, she called me many times. "You won't need to spend much time with him! Just help him get started." She paused. "Umm…and besides…I know you're gonna kill me for this, but I told him it wouldn't be a problem, and that you'd squeeze him in!"

"*Ellen!*"

Once again, I was put in an awkward position, and once again, I argued with her.

"Manna! You *have* to see Joshua! I already told him you would, and he wants to refer his friends to you, too, *if you're as good as your brochures say you are!*" she taunted. "You can't *not* see him! It will seem completely unprofessional. Plus, what good reason can you give him? That he and Lilith are hotheads? It's not going to fly! Plus, no offense, you already seem kind of flaky to him!"

"*What?*" I asked incredulously. "How in the world would *I* be the one that seems flaky?"

"Well, all he knows is you bolted out of the house before the charity event, and you bolted out of the Halloween party, leaving me there by myself! Oh, and by the way, I wasn't drunk! I was just really happy! And now, if you won't agree to see him when I've already told him it won't be a problem, you're gonna look *really, really bad!*"

I rolled my eyes.

Ellen continued, "The point is, you have to prove you're not some kind of social misfit and can at least keep appointments!"

"Ellen," I tried to find the words. "First of all, I didn't abandon you at a party where you didn't know anyone. I left you with your friends who promised to watch over you. And secondly, I never wanted to see *either one of them*. You set this up without my knowledge or permission, and that's not right!"

"I know…but I'm just trying to help you! You're finally on your own two feet, and you need help building your business! And it's not good for your reputation so early on in your practice to turn down clients when they've been handed to you, especially since you're new to this field. You're not in real estate anymore!"

I weighed her words.

She continued, "Trust me, he knows a lot of people, and turning him down wouldn't be a smart business move." She paused a moment and then added, "Just see him a few times. He'll get a strong start, and then he'll be good on his own."

As she described each point, I felt weaker and weaker in my position. What Ellen had said was true. I was starting all over, building a new business after leaving so much behind in my marriage. With my divorce fees costing a great deal of my savings, preparing Michael for university, and so on, the financial burden was wearing on me. Anxiety suddenly overwhelmed me, and I feared that if I didn't listen to her, I would lose both credibility and business.

I eventually succumbed and agreed to Ellen's request. I rationalized my uneasiness and talking myself into believing that a few appointments were an easy request to accommodate.

Joshua came in two weeks later for his first of several appointments. I recommended some testing and created an effective program that would meet his goals and work around his schedule. He seemed pleased with what we had discussed and the route we were going to take.

A week later, when all his test results arrived, he came in to review them. We talked about the results, what protocols would work best for him, and what the anticipated results would look like. The more we talked, the more I could see what a genuinely good person he was. My initial sense of him was confirmed, and I was happy to help him.

Joshua came in again a month later to review his progress. After making a few modifications to his plan, he was fully on the right track. The program had become second nature to him, and he was going to continue the routine on his own. He wouldn't have to check back in for another month. He was very pleased with his results so far and thanked me. As he was about to head out the office door, his cell phone rang. When he looked at his phone, his previously pleasant smile collapsed into a scowl, and I could feel the tension in the air. Uncomfortable, he excused himself and went outside to take the call.

When he returned to pick up his updated program and products, it was impossible not to notice the change in his demeanor and in his coloring.

"Joshua, are you okay?" I asked, concerned. "Do you want some water? Or do you want to go back and sit down for a bit? I don't have another client for another hour, so you can take your time."

"No, that's okay. I'll be fine. Thank you," he said.

Remembering his initial doctor's report, I became more insistent. "Joshua, no offense, but your ears are all red, and your face looks really pale. Please, come back into my office and sit down for a moment."

He took a deep breath to compose himself and nodded his head in agreement. I followed him back into my office and gave him a glass of water. When he sat down, he explained, "That was Lilith, and *another* blistering earful about *nothing*—the third one this morning."

I paused, fumbling for what to say. "Have you two seen a marriage counselor?"

He shook his head and admitted, "We could see a thousand people, and nothing would change. We've talked to everybody, but there's no point in talking endlessly if we don't follow up on it with actions. I've even read some self-help books. They all say to try and find the love we had for each other when we first dated. But we didn't have *love*. We had impetuousness. We had lust. I'm sorry to be so blunt, but that's the truth. And then we got pregnant." He exhaled and continued, "I stayed. But that's not *love*. We're not together because of *love*. For nearly a decade, I stayed and did the right things, but even the right things can't manufacture love."

He leaned back in the chair, looking up at the ceiling. After a few moments, he continued. "We've fought from day one, and I've just grown calloused to it all. This has cost me more than I ever thought it would."

Unsure of what he was referring to, I asked, "I'm sorry, I don't understand."

"I thought Ellen told you. I had a child from a previous marriage. But Lilith wanted nothing to do with my firstborn. We had constant battles over that. It's a long story, but essentially, my first wife moved with my child to another part of the country, and it was hard for me to visit without Lilith causing World War Three at home. Over time, to spare my second child—my child with Lillith—from more craziness, I relented and stopped fighting to see my firstborn. It was the only way I could keep a little peace in the house. I have great regrets about it, but hindsight is twenty-twenty, as they say. I'd do things so differently now," Joshua explained sadly.

I didn't know what to say.

Joshua took a sip of water and then added, "I left many times, but the threats of losing a relationship with another child always brought me back. I agreed to stay on the condition that we never have another child together. But she kept pushing and pushing for another baby. And that just became another thing we fought about all the time. Then, years later, she blindsided me and told me she was pregnant again. I was furious! She and everyone around us knew I was absolutely adamant about not having another child with her. Let's just say I felt deceived and totally betrayed. But that's Lilith, always insisting on having things her way; my wishes were never considered. To this day, I'm still sensitive about not being included in decisions that affect me. I've given up over half my life as a result of decisions that were made without my knowledge or consent.

"Over time, I retaliated in my own way, doing things that were important only to me. It was the only way I could find an outlet for everything else that had been stuffed down my throat for decades." He took a breath. "I'm sorry! I can't believe I told you all of that. I never talk about my personal life. I guess that last call was the straw that broke the camel's back."

"I'm so sorry," I said looking down.

"No, I'm the one who's sorry," Joshua apologized.

"Maybe there's another counselor you could talk to. I know of a few," I offered.

"No, thank you. I'm done. Too much has happened, and any illusions of hope I'd had were vaporized during that call. It's one thing to live with someone who disrespects and marginalizes me regularly. It's another thing to stay with someone who attacks me daily for my humanity."

He regained his composure. "I love my children with all my heart and can't imagine life without them, but I did not envision my life as being like *this!* Now that the kids are older, it's time I do something different. I will *not* live like this for the rest of my life."

The weight of his words hung in the air as he leaned forward and looked down at the carpet lost in his thoughts.

Whatever that call was about was enough to push him past the tipping point, and I didn't know what else to say. This was not a conversation either one of us expected to have.

All the stories I had been told about Joshua and Lilith years earlier flooded my mind—the firstborn, the fights, the separations, each pregnancy, and the aggravation they both felt for each other. At that time, they were simply stories of some people Ellen knew. I don't know why or how this came to be, but now these very people were somehow in my life, and I was watching their breakdown unfold before my very eyes.

Suddenly Joshua jumped up and said, "I'm sorry! I'm truly, *very sorry*. I didn't mean to dump all that out on you. The call just came in, you're seeing the worst of me…bad timing. I rarely talk about my personal life like this."

"Please, no need for apologies. I wish something could be done."

"No, don't worry about this," he interrupted awkwardly. "You have enough of your own troubles. You don't need mine. I truly do apologize." He put away his phone, and with a forced smile, he said, "I'm looking forward to implementing this new program. I'm traveling a lot in the next few weeks. I'll set up something when I get back."

"Good luck with everything," I said feebly.

And with that, he left.

Famous Last Words

Time went by, and Joshua came in every other month to pick up supplements and have review consultations. On the last consult, he shared that he had decided to file for a divorce and was doing his best to move forward calmly and amicably. He had found a place of his own and was in the process of moving a few personal things, but he was taking each step cautiously. His goal was to keep things harmonious, hopefully minimizing any eruptions for the children's sake. Once the details were finalized, he would tell them.

More time passed, and one day Joshua called to see if I had some training information for a local running event. He felt it was time to do something "big" as a symbolic act of taking his life back.

Being an avid runner and running coach myself, I asked Joshua to come by one of my training classes to pick up some resources. I invited him to join us for an afternoon run if he so wished. He liked the idea of having accountability with running partners and eventually joined our group. He was a great addition to the class, and his interesting running style and great sense of humor kept us amused. It didn't take long before everyone became comrades, encouraging each other in their respective races.

Joshua's updated lab work came in not long afterwards, but based on his travel schedule, he wouldn't be available to come in for a few weeks. During this conversation, we discovered that, ironically, I was going to be away for a health conference at the same time. We would be in the same city—me for the conference, and him to meet a client his company had been wooing.

"That's a crazy coincidence!" he said, surprised. "Well, if you happen to have a break in between sessions, maybe we could meet for a coffee? My meetings don't start until the day you leave. If it isn't too much trouble, maybe we could quickly review my results at the same time?"

I didn't see anything wrong with the request since we had become friends, and so we made arrangements to meet.

We had an afternoon coffee together after my last conference session of the day. By the time we finished discussing everything, it was time for me to leave, as I had promised to meet a few of my classmates for happy hour. Not wanting to be rude, and since he didn't have plans until his meetings started the following morning, I asked him to join us.

We headed to the restaurant, and we all ended up having a great time together. As we laughed and shared stories, I realized I was starting to enjoy Joshua's company more than I had noticed before, and I could see myself one day even *liking* him. Somewhat surprised by this awareness, I pulled back.

A hundred thoughts raced through my mind as I watched Joshua and my friends all engaged in great conversation.

Is he always this nice, this kindhearted? How can all the awful stories about him be true? Where is he in their divorce process? When it's all over, I wonder if he'd be interested in me? But that would be awkward since I met his future ex-wife before. Yes, this is awkward. Hmmm, this must be the wine talking. I only had one glass, but still… yes, I'm sure it's the wine. Tomorrow will be a new day, and this crazy thought will go away.

The evening came to a close, and after paying the entire bill, Joshua asked, "Hey, Manna, would you mind staying behind a minute?"

"Umm, sure," I answered nervously.

My friends and I arranged to meet for breakfast before the final session of the conference the next morning, and then we all said goodbye. After they left, I sat back down at the table.

Joshua asked, "What's wrong? You completely changed halfway through the evening. Did I say or do something to upset you?"

"Oh no! It's not you at all. Thank you for sharing your evening with us, and for treating! We weren't expecting that! That was very generous of you…thank you again."

"You're welcome, but you guys put up a good fight for the bill—very impressive!" He smiled. "So, if I didn't say or do anything to offend you, then why the change? What's going on?"

My heart was at my throat, and I couldn't speak. *What exactly am I going to say?* I tried to tell myself again, it was the wine that made me entertain emotions for Joshua, and I bit my tongue. After a few clumsy moments, all I could do was purse my lips and shake my head. "No, really, there's nothing," I insisted.

"Manna, something is going on. You're normally so happy and involved. You love laughing, and I gave you some of my best jokes!" He smiled. "Everyone else thought I was funny, and normally I can make you laugh too, but I could barely get a smile out of you. You looked like you were millions of miles away."

I smiled. Joshua's sensitivity was endearing. "I'm sorry, Joshua. I didn't mean to be distant, and yes, you do have some very funny stories to tell. Maybe I'm just tired—a full day of 'biochem' and endocrinology can be tiring—especially for an old student like me."

"I don't buy it. You love that stuff, and you soak it up like a sponge," he continued. "Well, if it's not obvious to you by now, I really care about you. You are one of the kindest people I know, and your heart is bigger than a thousand people put together. I've never met anyone like you, and seeing you so noticeably uncomfortable makes me sad. I never want you to be uncomfortable around me."

Oh dear…

I was flustered, unable to find the right words to say. "Awww, that's really sweet. I care about you too. I know I'm not myself for some reason, but I'm fine. Really."

He exhaled and addressed the elephant in the room, "Does being here with me make you feel uncomfortable?"

I waited a few moments and then responded, "Well, now that you mention it, yes." I took a deep breath and exhaled. "I feel a little awkward about how we met. And I don't know where you are in your divorce process, and most of all, I don't want Lilith to think…"

"Oh, okay. I see," he said assertively. "Look, Lilith and I have been like bleach and ammonia since day one. I'm sure you've heard that a thousand times from her, and Ellen, and anyone else who knows us! It's no secret our relationship was founded on obligation—not love. There's love for our children, but otherwise, it's been a roller coaster ride, somewhere between hell and an active volcano. Sure, there were some easier times, but the reality of our relationship never eluded us. I tried to make the best of things. We both did, but we still brought the worst out of each other." He took a sip of water and continued, "So, let me be absolutely clear—neither you nor anyone else is the reason for our failed relationship. *We are.* Some people stay together when they have children out of wedlock, and they do great together, but we were not one of them." He paused again, thinking. "What's that saying? 'One day, the pain of remaining the same will be greater than the pain of change.' It's been a long time coming. I can't change the past. I can only change the present, and by doing so, have a future."

I looked down, absent-mindedly playing with the silverware. There were many unfortunate historical factors involved in their relationship. It was a sad story. I'm sure they both did everything they thought was right in their own eyes. And of course, evaluation with hindsight is easy, but it's never easy when you're right in the middle of it.

I didn't know what to say right away, but after a few moments, I asked, "How about the kids…how are they with it all?"

"They've always been on pins and needles around us, so I want to make sure Lilith and I sort a few things out before we talk to them. That way, they're not stuck in the middle of another battle. It'll be fine, it's not like any of this will be a surprise."

"That's too bad. The children always get caught in the middle," I said somberly, remembering Michael and my two former stepchildren.

"This is going to be better for everyone, especially the kids. And Lilith will be happy to be done with me."

I gave him a dubious look. "I'm not usually skeptical, but—"

"Trust me. Lilith is unpredictable, but I can't imagine she'd do anything to hurt the kids in this process."

And so the conversation continued.

We ended up staying for dinner and talked about many things for the rest of the evening. Hours went by as if they were only minutes, and we were the last to leave the restaurant. I didn't have another drink for the rest of the evening, nor did he.

I don't think it was the wine talking.

"It *is* like a movie!" Leah exclaimed. "So many unexpected and inexplicable twists and turns, but that cord never broke. Is that when you started seeing each other?"

"No. Like I said before, 'happily ever after' didn't come so easily, or that quickly." I sighed. "Even though I was not a part of their volatile past or their breakdown, it was nonetheless awkward, and very strange to suddenly witness the end of it."

"That's *life*, Manna!" Leah almost shouted. "Life *is* strange. It *is* awkward, and it *is* most definitely complicated, confusing, and messy. *You*, of all people, know that! There are just some things in life we don't understand; it's beyond our grey matter! So, stop trying to figure it all out! You're smart, but not *that* smart!"

I sighed. "But sometimes I wonder how things would have been if I had met Joshua later…after their divorced was finalized."

"Look, it's obvious the *real divorce* had already happened ages ago; the papers were just a formality," Leah said, looking at me quizzically. "There's more in what you're not saying. Were you blamed for their breakup?"

"Yes." I sighed again.

"Ahhh…now I'm beginning to understand," Leah said slowly. "Isn't *that* convenient?"

"But it's not just about me. The children suffered so much."

"So, you were the scapegoat, and the kids were used as weapons of warfare!" Leah surmised.

I nodded.

"Oh, boy…" Leah shook her head. "Tell me what happened."

Well, as soon as I got back from my trip, I had to have a difficult conversation with Joshua. I apologized for being so direct, but I asked him not to come into the office anymore. I also asked that we put our friendship on the back burner until everything was finalized between the two of them. I shared again my discomfort with the awkward reality of having met Lilith first, and how I did not want to be linked to the two of them at this difficult time.

He was surprised by my request and didn't believe my concern was warranted. "Lillith won't care! Trust me!" he said, assuredly.

"But what about the children?" I insisted. "You both need time to sort things out with them. I'm still really concerned."

"Concerned about what?" Joshua asked.

"You seem so confident, but I have a whole different feeling about things. Even in the most amicable of divorces, it's still very emotional, and it's always painful for children. Plus, based on what you and others have said, I'm not convinced things will work out as gracefully as you think they will. In fact, I'm afraid it will be quite ugly."

"Please, stop worrying!" Joshua insisted. "Lilith won't do anything to hurt the kids or anyone else. She's a powder keg, but she's not evil!"

"Uh oh…" Leah said slowly. "Famous last words…sounds ominous. So what did you and Joshua eventually decide to do?"

"While he disagreed with my concerns and kept trying to reassure me, Joshua did honor my request to stop coming by the office and put our friendship on hold. But it was already too late, and my suspicions had already become a reality."

"Lilith didn't rise to the occasion," Leah surmised.

I shook my head.

"I'm sorry," Leah said, squeezing my hand. "What did Ellen have to say? She was the one that orchestrated everything, after all!"

"Ellen shared every horrible thing Lilith had said about me, and since Lilith's was the stronger current, Ellen sided with her. But after a few heated rounds between us, she acknowledged it was easier to blame me than to ask Lilith to take responsibility for the failed marriage. She started recalling the many difficult situations between Lilith and Joshua, and concluded with, 'I'm relieved, actually. At least now, they can both be out of their misery.'"

I did not comment.

"I'm sorry you're caught in the middle." Ellen paused, and then said forebodingly, "There's something else you have to know…"

"Now what?" I asked in exasperation.

"You're being blamed for everything. You need to be careful."

"What? What do you mean '*be careful*?'" I demanded.

"She's out of control!" Ellen cautioned. "Just watch your back."

"Ellen! What exactly are you saying?" I asked in shock.

She didn't answer.

"Ellen! Answer me!"

"Honey, all I can say is *be careful*," she said slowly before adding, "I wish you'd never met Lilith."

"No, really?" I said sarcastically.

"I know, I know! I'm sorry. It's my fault! You two are so different and would never have met if it weren't for me," Ellen reflected out loud.

Leah thought for a moment and then said, "Sorry, I'm an old woman and maybe a little slow on the uptake now, but I still don't get how you were blamed for their divorce? Sounds like the handwriting was on the wall from the very beginning. Plus, Joshua put things between you two on hold."

"Well, in Lilith's defense, it *was* awkward that I had met her beforehand. If I could do it over again, I would have been firmer with Ellen, and not have acquiesced to all her requests at the start."

"But, you may never have met Joshua!" Leah countered. "What if this isn't about *fault* or *blame* at all? What if all these strange and unexpected sets of circumstances had to occur so that the multiple layers of freedom and blessings could occur for everyone?"

My eyes widened, surprised at Leah's wiser perspective on things.

"Don't look at me like that! I'm learning! I'm not as dumb and arrogant as I used to be." She winked.

"What do you mean by 'freedom'?" I asked.

"Isn't that obvious? They were finally free of the torturous hamster wheel they were on. The kids were free from walking onto minefields every day, and everyone had a chance to create a better life, for starters!" Leah said pragmatically. "Do I have to explain everything to you?"

I smiled. "Should I start calling you 'Solomon'?"

"Don't you start with me, young lady," she snickered. "I may be an old crone, but I still have a little bit of fight in me."

"Leah, you're not an old crone! You're an angel."

"Call me whatever you want—just don't call me late for dinner!" She laughed so hard, she coughed.

My Best Friend

Right or wrong, while Joshua and I had originally agreed to not be in contact until his divorce was over, the unforeseen chaos that quickly ensued actually forced us to be in more conversation than ever. There are too many details to explain. Suffice it to say, the more alarming things became, the closer we drew together. Adversity, while not always the favorite catalyst in new (or long-term) relationships can strengthen the love, commitment, and devotion in the hearts of those involved. Such was the case with Joshua and me.

It's been said that one can only know the true character of someone when everything is going wrong. The American novelist, James Lane Allen, once penned, "Adversity does not build character, it reveals it." And as I watched Joshua endure one strike after another, I saw the nobility of his character revealed.

In fact, over what would be the next nine years, I witnessed Joshua being tested repeatedly. And his were not little speedbumps; his were Goliath-sized tests—and he had dozens of them. But not one ever caused his principles, ethics, morality, self-control, or faith to waver. He overcame each trial with integrity and a smile, never complaining or wallowing in self-pity. And he never blamed anyone for his adversities. Instead, he chose to learn from them and used those lessons to create more opportunities for joy and depth in his relationships. His uprightness, generosity of heart, and honor took my breath away.

Was he perfect? No. But when he made mistakes, he immediately apologized and did what he needed to do to bring wholeness back into our relationship. As we discussed before, mistakes will happen, but what you do immediately after it reveals more about your character clearer than anything else.

Did we have a few things to iron out as our relationship grew? Naturally. Did we annoy each other with some of our unique traits? Absolutely. But even through our quirks, Joshua taught me more about lovingkindness and the preciousness of life through a committed relationship than I've ever known.

In Joshua's presence, both my strengths and my shadows were illuminated. He helped me stretch to experience the fullness of my giftings, *and* he created safety so I could also honestly assess and work on my wounds. He showed me that I was valued, cherished, and loved, and that it was safe to trust again.

Admittedly, it wasn't easy for me to receive this kind of unconditional love and regard from Joshua at first. It was challenging to believe that my most sacred of dreams—to have a truly loving and honoring relationship—was actually happening. I had suppressed my hopes so much I had even called myself "Paulette" after the great disciple in the Bible who had the gift of singleness. But for the first time in my life, instead of barricading my heart, I felt safe to reveal it. Little by little, he coached me out of the cave in which I had been hiding and into the world of the living again.

Needless to say, the more time I spent with him, the deeper I fell in love with him.

Building Windmills

Before we knew it, the lease on Joshua's place had already come to an end, and since the landlord was moving back in himself, an extension of the lease was not possible. However, the economic crash at the time hit his industry hard. Dealing with the "war of all wars," while trying to maintain steadiness and safety for his children, Joshua had little to no time to look for another suitable place to live.

I helped as best I could, but the rental market was limited then, and not many choices were available. Anything suitable was rented within the day, and without Joshua able to see the properties on short notice, we were unsuccessful in securing a new home for him.

With no other option other than paying exorbitant hotel fees (and storage fees for his furniture), I suggested Joshua move in with me until he could find another place of his own. His older child was already an adult and had moved out, but his youngest child could easily stay with us in my guest room during Joshua's visitation weekends. I made sure that the room was warm, inviting, and safe, so his youngest would feel included and "at home."

There's a Chinese proverb that says: "When the winds of change blow, build windmills, not walls." I don't even know *how* to explain everything that happened during this turbulent time, but like this saying goes, we made the best of everything. Instead of tearing things down or building walls of separation, we chose to build a life that would beget and nurture life.

Honor's Reward

One evening after dinner, as we were reflecting on our lives—the good, the bad, and the ugly—we discussed our regrets, our gratitude (even for our difficulties), and the priceless lessons we learned from the experiences of our lives. As we recounted one story after another, it was impossible not to see God's love, protection, and grace upon us—especially when we had insisted on doing things our way (i.e., marrying out of fear, having children out of wedlock, etc.).

We reasoned if God is so kind to us when we were stubborn and rebellious, insisting on our own ways, how much more would He bless us if we trusted Him and did what He asks? And even more importantly, how much could *we bless God in return* by choosing and trusting Him over our own selfish desires? We weren't talking about trying to be perfect or trying to *will* ourselves to holiness by doing good works. We were simply very honest as we looked upon our past and how we wanted our future together to look.

There's a verse that says,

> *And so, dear brothers and sisters, I plead with you to give your bodies to God because of all He has done for you. Let them be a living and holy sacrifice...Don't copy the behavior and customs of this world, but let God transform you into a new person by changing the way you think. Then you will learn to know God's will for you, which is good and pleasing and perfect.*[6]

In that conversation, the consequences of stepping out of godly order and relying on our own limited thinking stood glaringly clear before us. Joshua realized that if he had only waited until marriage, he would never have lost decades of his life in a miserable relationship. And I reflected on the wasted years living in fear and in unhealthy and dangerous relationships because I didn't know my worth, didn't know how to say no, and naively believed that a man's desire for me was *love*.

As we continued to talk, it became evident that these sacred parts of ourselves had been given away too easily outside of a covenanted marriage, and we were fragmented. It was as though pieces of our souls had been fractioned off, and as quantum physics proves, we were still energetically bound with people from our past.

These "soul ties" had to be severed so we could start fresh with each other, and fresh with God. We wanted the fullness of everything He wanted for us, and we wanted to bless Him in return with our obedience and trust. So, that night, we prayed to break off those soul ties, and we decided to do something else…we chose to date *biblically*.

"I want to do things right," Joshua proclaimed excitedly. "I've made a lot of mistakes and have paid—and am still paying—dearly for them. Now that I have a chance to start over, I don't want anything to taint our relationship. You're too precious to me. I want to honor you. I want to honor God, and I want to honor our relationship."

"So wait…" Leah tilted her head, trying to be tactful and failing, as evidenced by the fire in her eyes, "So…no more…*you know?*" And with that, she gave me an exaggerated wink.

"No, Leah. No more '*you know,*'" I replied, with a matching exaggerated wink. "Not until our wedding night." I smiled.

"Wait…how far away was that?!" she asked incredulously.

"About seven years from that discussion."

Her jaw dropped, and she stuck her neck out like a turkey. I laughed out loud at the sight.

"Well, well, well. Will wonders never cease?"

"Come on, Leah. I know it's a long time, but it's not like God asked us to stop breathing!" I jested.

"Well, for some people, He might as well have!" she snickered, and after a pause, added, "Manna, if nothing else, you certainly are interesting! You have lived a most unconventional life indeed."

"I could write chapters about this topic alone, but for now, let's just say it was 'purpose over matter.' Joshua wanted to honor me more than his desires. He not only showed me that he loved me daily (in the routines of our relationship), he showed me he loved me sacrificially and wholly. Plus, by not having our relationship confused with physiological habits, we learned more about intimacy, love, and affection than if we had given in to old behaviors. Looking back, I can honestly say that had we not chosen this path, we wouldn't be as close as we are now."

"Sounds amazing." Leah smiled. "I don't know anyone who would do what you two did—and for so long!"

"We didn't think it would be seven years," I acknowledged.

"Let me guess. It's a long story!"

I smiled.

"Well, let's get on with it then!"

I paused, not knowing how to share the next part of my life in a way that could be understood. "If I told you everything that happened at this time, you'd think I was making it all up¾the heartaches, the miracles, and the blessings. Even if I did share everything with you, I wouldn't know where to begin, much less know *how* to explain it all."

"Just start at the beginning," Leah urged.

"Well, it would take years to tell you everything, so how about I just highlight some of the biggies?"

"Just don't rob me of the good stuff!" Leah ordered.

I exhaled deeply. "As I attempt to describe this next season of my life, it may get a little confusing. Timelines may appear skewed, and events may seem out of place, but that's because everything converged concurrently. Simple situations became complicated as layer after layer unfolded. My life was no longer just about me—that was complex enough on its own. My life was intricately interwoven with Michael's (more than ever) as he chose dangerous paths of self-destruction—and with Joshua's, his children, his work, and his divorce. Everyone and everything seemed unimaginably connected."

This time it was Leah who exhaled deeply. "Okay. I've been fairly forewarned and am strapped in for the ride!"

"I'm not trying to be melodramatic," I assured her. "I just didn't want the details of the whens and wheres of things to override the gist of the story."

"Got it!" she nodded. "I promise not to get stuck on the details and simply 'get the story.' Let her rip!"

I thought I had seen it all. Abandonment. Neglect. Racism. Abuse of every kind. Molestation. Sexual Assault. Abortion. Suicide attempts. Anorexia. Agoraphobia. Depression. Spousal abuse. Failed marriages. Divorces. Being a mom, and then a single mom. Starting new businesses as a single mom and being the sole provider for our family. I was stalked, my life was threatened, I went back to school while working full time, and lost cherished loved ones. I moved from country to country *twice*, starting over both times. I endured betrayals of all kinds from family and friends out of jealousy and greed. I lost almost all my assets and businesses, was a stepmother (and would be *twice*), suffered gossip, slander, libel, church trauma, and was scapegoated, to name *a few* life experiences. I thought I had been tried enough and tested enough. And in my simple thinking, I somehow believed there was a quota for the amount of tribulation one can be called upon to endure in life.

I was wrong.

While it had seemed hell itself had marked me since birth, I did not know its fury until it unleashed itself with one attack after another during this time.

Remove the Hedge

Joshua had only been living with me for a few months when one early morning, on my way to a business meeting, I was T-boned by a driver who sped through a red light with an older Dodge car built like a tank. He was clocked at seventy-five miles per hour in a forty-five zone. When I heard his brakes screech, I looked to my left, and all I saw was a large dark-brown car coming straight at me. I blacked out at impact. When I came to, I managed to make two calls before blacking out again, one to Joshua to let him know what happened and to come get me, and one to my business associate to tell him I was not going to make it to the meeting.

My car was struck with such force my eyelashes literally burst from my eyelids. The police and the firemen were shocked and amazed that I was not critically injured—even dead from the impact. I was extremely bruised, but miraculously, I had not one laceration, no broken bones, or any internal injuries. It was truly a miracle. The witnesses were aghast, and there was no doubt in anyone's mind that my life had been spared.

Joshua, devastated he had come so close to losing me in the accident, had an involuntary reactionary response. Out of nowhere, the next morning, his back seized, and he wasn't able to move for several days. He'd had serious back surgery years before, and we were worried the trauma of my accident triggered a relapse for him. Similar to the story of Job, while the attacks didn't escape me, my life was spared. And also like Job, I received one bad report after another.

In the following few weeks, every vehicle of ours was involved in some kind of accident. Joshua's cars were either randomly hit by bad drivers, keyed, or rear-ended in a parking lot. Michael was involved in a car accident, and even our boat was hit. What was happening was too bizarre to brush off as mere *coincidence*.

And this wasn't just with our vehicles. *We* were "attacked" in every aspect of our lives. Just when I thought I had extinguished one fire, another one flared. Yes, we shared some sweet moments, but sadness, troubles, and even tragedy followed closely behind.

Dancing in the Rain

As the saying goes, "Life isn't about waiting for the storm to pass, but about learning to dance in the rain."

In between all the bad reports, Joshua surprised me with a different message. A week after my car accident, he came home with a very serious look on his face. He was not his normal, jovial self.

I was in the kitchen preparing dinner when he walked straight up to me, put down his briefcase by my feet, and looked squarely at me. "Manna, you know I love you more than anything in this world. Even as a teenager, I knew *you* in my heart. I just didn't know how, where, or when I'd find you. I just *knew you were somewhere in the world, and one day we would be together.*" His voice started to tremble. "When I pulled up to the scene of the accident and saw the wreckage of your car, I had no idea what condition you'd be in once I got to you. The thought of losing you was too much for my heart to take, and I knew instantly I couldn't wait any longer. I want us to be together forever."

He reached into his jacket and pulled out a small, beautiful black velvet box with a stunning engagement ring inside.

"Will you please do me the honor of being my wife and make me the most blessed man ever in history?"

We had talked about marriage, but since his divorce was not finalized, and we were dealing with so many other challenges, it never occurred to me that he would ask me to marry him now.

I was torn; my heart was overjoyed, but my mind was pulled in a thousand directions with objections.

Joshua stared at me, and his eyes widened since I did not respond right away. "What's wrong?" he asked.

"Gosh, Joshua, it's just the timing of it all…" I hesitated. "It's not you; it's just that there's so much going on, and I don't feel the peace or the excitement I think a girl should feel when she's been proposed to. Plus, you're not divorced—"

"Don't worry about the divorce," he interrupted. "I'm filing a motion to bifurcate so the divorce will be official. The economics will be dealt with separately. We're free to do whatever we want," he assured me.

"But it's so soon. What about the children? That will be hard on them. They've been through so much already."

"If you're not comfortable, let's wait awhile. At least say yes!"

I hesitated again.

After a long silence, Joshua spoke. "Manna," he said softly. "What else is going on?"

My mind raced. I searched my heart for the seat of my uncertainty. Suddenly, the answer appeared. This was going to be my *third* marriage.

I was afraid.

I take full responsibility for my first marriage and its failure. I was foolish and made the decision out of fear. But with my second marriage, I had gone into it with my whole heart, and not only had I almost died fighting for it, he had also abused my child. But now, standing before me was a man of character, dignity, kindness, and love. Standing before me was a man I knew loved me more than life itself, and he truly loved Michael as if he was his own. *What was I to do?* I wanted to trust Joshua, but I was afraid I would make another mistake. And I was terrified there would be another father figure that would hurt my son.

Joshua slowly took my hand. "It's okay," he said softly. "I'm sorry if I upset you. I don't mean to pressure you. We don't have to get married. I love you and will care for you until my last breath. Whether you wear this ring or not, whether we have a piece of paper or not, I will never leave you. You will always be my one and only."

That was exactly what I needed to hear. Joshua didn't try to coerce me into anything, get angry, react out of wounded pride, or try to guilt or shame me. He only wanted me to feel safe and to be happy. He truly did love me; he put me first, again, ahead of what he wanted.

Just then, I suddenly heard myself say, "*Yes*! Yes! I'll marry you!"

Surprised, tears welled in his eyes. Seeing him cry made me cry, and soon we were giggling like little kids. In the excitement of it all, Joshua swept me in his arms, twirled me around, kissed me on the forehead, and held me for a very long time.

After dinner that night, we told Michael the news, and he was thrilled. He and Joshua had a great relationship, and they enjoyed each other's company very much. Michael and Joshua's children also had a great relationship, having become friends effortlessly. And when we were all together "as a family," it was fun, easy, and natural.

We were thankful for these sweet moments.

My Prodigal

Although Joshua and I were preparing to be married, we weren't "official" yet. As a result, though Michael wanted to bond with Joshua more, he was uncertain how much of his heart he could safely give again. Similarly, Joshua loved Michael, but also held back, unsure of his position since he wasn't Michael's official stepfather yet. Plus, with the background of Barry's abusiveness and Tristan's negligence, Joshua was sensitive to how much disciplining and "fathering" he should engage in. He didn't know what Michael would need and what would repel him. And yet, deep down, I know Michael was screaming to have a loving father come alongside of him—including disciplining him.

Yes, it was a delicate time juggling relationships, emotions, and assumptions. I was doing the best I could, believing I was making the right choices for everyone concerned.

I stopped just then, saddened by those memories, especially the breaches that occurred between Michael and myself.

"I wish I could have done more for Michael..." I sighed.

"Don't beat yourself up, Manna," Leah said gently. "You did better than most people I know in similar situations."

"Maybe..." I sighed.

"What would you have done differently?" Leah asked.

"I don't know," I responded absentmindedly, still distracted by the memories. "I know what I *want* to say, but I also know Michael wouldn't be who he is today were it not for those difficult times. While pain and suffering served their purposes for *me*, as a mother, I wanted to spare Michael from these difficulties in life. I wanted things to be easier for him." My tears clogged my sight.

"We all want that for our children," Leah said compassionately. "But if they didn't have these trials, how will they learn to be strong? They'd be eaten alive out there! I'm sure Michael's grown into a wonderful young man."

I nodded. "Yes. He is a wonderful young man, and definitely stronger and humbled by all that's happened."

"See? The blessings in disguise." Leah smiled. "The same is true with Joshua. If one thing had been different, then you two may not have ended up together."

"Yes, and had we not been in all those difficult times together, I would never have known his heart the way I do now. I would never have seen his character and integrity shine in such hardships. And Michael would never have had those tender and wonderful times with him either." I smiled, now remembering other memories. "Joshua ensured that we laughed and enjoyed each and every day. He refused to live life any other way."

"So, maybe it is true!" Leah exclaimed.

"What's true?" I asked, curiously.

"That God does turn everything together for good! All those bad and ugly things, all that pain and disappointment, all those betrayals and losses…happily ever after can come true in spite of them!"

I smiled and kissed the back of Leah's frail hands. "Yes, Leah. Happily ever after does come true because God does indeed turn all things together for good."

Leah beamed proudly. "Good girl. Even *you* need to be reminded every now and then! So, stop beating yourself up and finish telling me about your prodigal."

I took a deep breath and was about to start, but hesitated.

Leah looked at me expectantly, and then a strange expression came over her face. "You know what?" she said. "Why don't you *not* tell me those stories?"

I looked at her in surprise.

"I know the trials you had with Michael are part of your story. I also know from being a mother myself, and because of all of the difficulties I had with Peter, in the process of becoming a man, Michael probably broke your heart many times. But it sounds like he learned humility."

I nodded. "My GongGong once shared an old saying, 'He who returns from a journey is not the same as he who left.' This is true for Michael. He still has more to learn, but he's not as he was before." I let out a deep breath. "Yes, God answered all the tearful prayers I prayed on those many sleepless nights."

Leah continued, "And it sounds like your relationship with him has been restored and, maybe, is even better than before?"

I nodded again.

"Then that's good enough for me," Leah decided. "We are both mothers of exceptional young men who have taken the adventurous route to manhood. We don't have to speak the details; we can just look at each other on this point, and *understand*."

I smiled. "Agreed."

"Michael needed to go through a series of gauntlets so he could learn how to get to the other side," she said encouragingly. "You may have had your own special way of initiating him into maturity at sixteen, but God allowed all these other things to initiate him into being a powerful warrior—a messenger for other young prodigals. You'll see."

"It's already happening now," I confirmed.

"Good. So, from here on out, I will just assume that whatever you tell me is taking place against a formidable background of fighting *for* your son," she said with a knowing smile. "Now tell me something else juicy and exciting. Something I can really sink my teeth into!"

Empty Nesters with a Growing Family

There came a point when Joshua and I wanted something of our own. We were empty nesters (Michael had gone away for school), and we discussed selling my home, finding something where we could begin fresh together. I would buy the home on my own first, and once Joshua's divorce was finalized and his funds were released, he would contribute to our new home together. Unfortunately, that didn't work out as planned. More on that later.

Very long story short, I ended up purchasing a beautiful brand-new home with a one-hundred-and-eighty-degree panoramic white water view of the Pacific Ocean in the heart of a coveted local beach town.

But just before moving, Joshua and I also agreed to get another dog. Yes, we already had three Golden retrievers, but given how I am with dogs, I could have easily had a hundred dogs. Thankfully, Joshua loved dogs, too, and since he had to leave his behind in the divorce, he was excited about having a dog of his own again. Even though we didn't have children at home, our family was now growing in a different way.

We both love Bernese Mountain Dogs ('Berners' for short), and while they didn't seem to have a long lifespan, everything else that was written about them drew us to them. A renowned breeder once said of Berners: "You will never love a dog more, nor will you ever be loved more…and you will never cry more once they die."

I have loved many dogs in my life and losing them is like having your heart ripped out each time, but to think I could hurt even more at the loss of a Berner really caused me to rethink this breed. So, we did more research…but in spite of these reports, we still decided on getting a Berner.

Within a few weeks, we had found a breeder who recently had a litter. They weren't ready to leave yet, but we could go and see them. When I saw all twelve of those puppies run towards me, my knees buckled, and I fell to the ground, embracing as many of them as I could fit in my arms. Pulling me away from them was almost impossible to do, and seeing me so happy, Joshua agreed we could bring home *two* puppies. I immediately wrote out the check before he changed his mind, and we left knowing that in a few weeks, we would be returning home with two four-legged babies of our own.

I was in heaven.

The day came to pick up the puppies, but Joshua was in meetings all day and couldn't come with me, so I asked Michael (who happened to be home on a short school break) to join me. When we arrived, I bent down to play with all the puppies again. But one frail, tiny little one (he was the runt) came up to me. He awkwardly climbed on my knees, clumsily curled up in a ball, and fell asleep on my lap. My mouth fell open, and I looked up at Michael, eyes wide with joy.

"Oh boy," was all Michael could manage to say. He knew what was about to happen.

"I'll take this one too," were the words that came rolling out of my mouth to the breeder.

"Mom! What do you think Joshua will say?" Michael asked apprehensively.

"I don't know," I said quietly. "I'll figure it out later."

"But you know that will mean we have *six* dogs!"

I nodded, trying to hold back my secret joy.

Michael drove home, and I sat in the back with three puppies in my lap on a towel. I was in absolute bliss! All I could do was coo and stare at them as they stretched and slept and cuddled together as three little black, white, and brown balls of love.

Michael was worried about Joshua's reaction, and with each mile marker that passed indicating we were getting closer to home, I, too, was beginning to dread his reaction.

I then remembered Joshua telling me how he hated decisions being made without him that would affect his life and how disrespected he felt whenever Lilith had done that. Now, I was doing the same thing. I had made a decision that would affect him for years and years to come, and my heart sank.

"What did he do?" Leah asked.

"When we pulled up, all he said was, 'Why are there *three* puppies instead of two?' All I could do was tell him what happened and apologize."

"Then what did he say?" Leah demanded.

"He didn't say a word. He simply turned around, got into his car, and drove away. When he came back hours later, he told me he needed to think things through. After a long walk on the beach, he realized he loved me so much. He was just going to have to accept that dogs—a lot of dogs—were going to be a part of his life."

"What a man!" Leah shouted, applauding with her hands.

"Well…wait a minute. He also said something else."

Leah cocked her head and opened her eyes wide.

"He also said, and I quote, 'I see it as if you had an illness. Your love for dogs can be debilitating, but it's a part of you. In fact, it *is you*! I wouldn't be angry or leave you if you were handicapped for the rest of your life, and I won't be angry or leave you because you brought home three more dogs."

"Like I said, 'what a man!'" Leah cheered. "He called it for what it was—you're somewhat 'challenged.' And he loves you in spite of it!"

I chuckled. "Dogs have been my steady, loyal, loving, and devoted friends all my life. God totally knew what He was doing when He created them; they *are* 'love' to me."

Is This Really Happening?

Unfortunately, tragedy came the morning after I brought my three puppies home. One of them died in a terrible accident with another dog. I can barely talk about it. I had named her Skye and raced her to the vet, but nothing could be done. She died in my arms, and I was devastated.

As unimaginable as this may sound, the day after losing Skye, we were evacuated from our home. One of the worst fires to hit our city was less than a mile away, and heroic firefighters were fighting it day and night. We had to quickly evacuate (with five dogs and whatever precious items and documents we could grab) for several days.

Later *that same week*, as I was moving into my newly purchased home, news of the housing market collapse spread. I was in the process of selling the old house but rented it instead (for less than half the going rate) to help a friend. Before the year was out, she gave her notice to leave, and with the markets dropping faster and faster each day, I struggled to find a new renter carrying two mortgages in the meantime. As time wore on, I could no longer shoulder both payments and ended up short-selling my old house.

I couldn't believe this was happening.

Then, as soon as we moved into my new home, the homeowner in front of me appeared to be building higher than what we were told, which would affect some of my white water views. It was recommended I seek legal help for the realtor's misrepresentation. I was assured my "true" view, once the building was completed, would not breach its height restrictions. And after being told the realtor was put on notice and reprimanded by the real estate board, I put the situation behind me. Nonetheless, it was a very distressing situation as I had agreed to the purchase price based on what the realtor had declared would be my view.

In addition to the continuing economic breakdown, and the failing housing market, serious events were occurring for Joshua. Complications arose in negotiations for the sale of his half of the company, his divorce plummeted to unspeakable depths, and his children fell into greater flux.

Et Tu, Brutus?

But that wasn't all. Another storm was brewing in the distance.

Under the leadership of my mentor, and the careful oversight of another wonderful physician specializing in internal medicine, my wellness practice grew. I was excited to see new clients referred weekly from top physicians in their fields, and we even had patients from other countries call in for appointments.

In time, it became obvious that to reach and help more people, I needed a wider reach and a larger audience. Before I knew it, I was working on television treatments, scripts, and set designs for a television show in Los Angeles. The initial feedback from the networks was encouraging. They thought I would be a wonderful host for a talk show. Suddenly, my long-despised ethnicity worked in my favor. My health and wellness messages were relevant and timely, and despite the other challenges in my life, at least my career appeared to be coming together.

Unfortunately, the week my showrunner was going to pitch my program, the infamous writer's strike of 2007 began. There was no way to guess how long it would last. Under the advisement of my professional media team, we stepped up our networking program. That way, when the strike was over, *we* could *strike* and make a difference for TV programming that could help multitudes. But in preparation for this outreach, it was clear I had to sell my practice.

Brutus was a practitioner in another health discipline whom I had met through a local business group a few years earlier. Throughout our association, I had gotten to know him and became a strong ally for him. I promoted, helped, and supported him in a variety of ways with his own practice. He told me he wanted to purchase my practice to expand his own reach, and since I trusted him, I agreed to sell it to him.

Unfortunately, in the months to follow, he revealed a side of himself hidden behind empty words and untrue intentions. He paid me a small deposit, so I would be invested in the contract, but even that came several weeks late. He had misrepresented his finances (later verified by a mutual banker we knew) and did not follow through on other payments.

He had also developed an unusual friendship with my assistant Fanny.

Jezebel

After going through a string of unreliable assistants, I had hired Fanny because she appeared to be competent. She was rough around the edges, but something in my spirit stirred when I met her. I wanted to help her.

As I got to meet people who had also known her, I discovered she not only had a reputation for alienating friends (and suitors), but her family relationships had been severed as well.

Anyone else would have run. Looking back, I should have also. Instead, my heart foolishly went out to Fanny, and even with these facts in mind, I took her under my wing. I had hoped she would overcome her wounds and see that her safety was not in whom she could control and hurt, but in the goodness in her heart.

I knew it was a great risk to take her on, but I had often wondered where I would be if someone had only believed in me and come alongside of me when I was confused and lost. So, I persisted and fought for her. She became like another little sister to me, and I took her into my heart and into my family as if she was one of my own.

Despite all the trouble she also ended up causing at my office, and despite all the complaints from labs, clients, and my own mentors, including the doctor I have already mentioned, I stayed true to her, doing my best to help her heal and grow. I also paid for half of her education and training in the health and wellness fiel and treated her to many special gifts, rewards, and surprises. I did all of it to show her the kindness she never had. I received her with love, in spite of her callousness, her biting tongue, and her abrasive personality. I was a true friend to her and more of a family than she had ever had. Even in my negotiations with Brutus, I intentionally secured her a position in our contract, so she would have a job after I left. And in my negotiations with the television networks, I was even working on adding her to that contract so she could have hope for a better future with my show once it got going.

Unfortunately, I could not see how deeply corrupt and debased her heart really was, though it was soon fully exposed to me.

While I was innocently and eagerly working to protect her future, she was nefariously plotting against me. She had been copying and stealing all of my personal and business documents the whole time—including copyrighted materials and intellectual property. It was all illegal. In the most heinous of ways, she betrayed me without cause. And, in the end, all I had invested in her and believed about her was shattered and broken.

"Oh dear…there's a special place where it's really, *really hot* for her and people like that!" Leah said, resolutely.

"Sadly, things only got worse. By all accounts, it looked like both Fanny and Brutus were trying to steal my business from me. Fanny became extremely abusive, and her vindictiveness escalated dangerously—to the point where I locked my office door between clients. Still, I was unable to fire her because her job had been secured through the pending contract with Brutus.

My beloved, sacred practice became a living nightmare as her toxicity contaminated every aspect of it. Her hostility and dysfunction grew, and her verbal assaults knew no bounds.

I tried talking to Brutus about her, but he refused to listen to me. Instead of trusting me, *the owner, who had founded and created the entire practice,* he chose to trust Fanny, my receptionist. He also went on to breach several agreements in our contract and stalled with one excuse after another regarding his failure to comply.

I had no choice but to hire an attorney, who advised me to keep working on things so *I* wouldn't be the one to breach the contract. I continued my negotiations until it was clear that nothing would be resolved. But in the meantime, my wonderful practice was falling apart before my very eyes, and everything I had worked for was disintegrating, slipping through my hands.

The two of them were so caught up in their own lies and machinations that while I was away one afternoon, they *physically destroyed my practice.*

They took furniture, machines, supplies, products, and other personal property and literally dumped it all into a huge pile in my private office. Thankfully, my friends were with me to be witnesses when I returned to see what had been done. The police were involved, photos and videos were taken, and I had to file charges, including theft charges. The police sided with me and were kind enough to check in on me for weeks afterward to ensure I was safe. They also agreed to testify on my behalf.

Eventually, after trying everything possible to either restore the contract or to take my practice back, I had no choice but to file a lawsuit against Brutus and submitted all the evidence to the court. I did not want to pursue them legally, but my practice and my reputation had to be defended through the right channels.

The goodwill was gone, and the practice was destroyed with their poisonous hearts. Fanny had convinced Brutus she was the reason why the practice was so successful, and he believed her. Together, they successfully took my practice, paying nothing for it but a small deposit. In addition to my business and personal property, he also had my client files, which they put to use in another heinous way.

"Oh, my heavens!" Leah cried out in shock.

When I did not think things could get worse, clients, associates, mentors, physicians, labs, vendors, and even friends in different countries began calling me. Fanny was calling them at all hours of the day at their places of work, and even in the evenings on their cell phones. She used the information in the client files to locate them, and if they were local, she went door to door to their places of business, slandering me and making libelous statements against me. This wasn't just gossip. It was a full-on *slander campaign.*

For no logical reason, Fanny was at war—all-out war—against me. And she was leaving no stone unturned as she tried to ruin me.

Leah threw her hands in the air. "Why…why, why, why do horrible things happen to good people? It's amazing how the heart is so deceitfully wicked, isn't it? Did all her senses leave her? Did she not remember all the wonderful things you did for her that *no one else would have done for her*? No wonder all her friends left her! And no small wonder her family doesn't want anything to do with her either!" Leah said, disgusted at all the facts. After a few moments, she added, "And why do good deeds get punished? I just don't get it! You didn't deserve that. You were only good to her—and to that spurious charlatan, Brutus!"

"Yes, the ruthlessness and the viciousness of Fanny's attack were reprehensible. Her only bizarre accusation was that I tried to steal from Brutus. I wanted *my business* to pay for a five-dollar UPS delivery to a client. Brutus had not paid for my practice, had not complied with the terms of our agreement, and was in breach of most of its points. It hadn't been turned over to him yet, and it was still *my practice*! So, she accused me of stealing from myself! It was insane."

Leah's eyes opened wide. "I remember a story in the Bible about Jezebel! Or should I say, *Fanny*? I also remember Jezebel's ending! Ain't gonna be pretty!" She shook her head. "Don't worry. Consequences, especially the ones coming from this kind of evil, cannot be escaped. Justice will come. You won't have to do a thing."

"I'm not worried about that," I assured her. "I did the right things and can stand before anyone, and God, on this matter. Whether or not *they* can is no longer my concern. I have total trust that this will all be accounted for one day."

"Exactly! What happened next?" Leah asked eagerly.

"My attorneys insisted Fanny cease and desist from her slander and libel campaign, but she refused. So after half a dozen cease-and-desist letters, in addition to the lawsuit for breach of contract, breach of fiduciary duty (and many other points), we had no choice but to sue Fanny for slander and libel as well. Since this would pose a serious issue for Brutus, as Fanny was now his hire, we hoped this would wake him up, and he would rein her in. Unfortunately, neither one of them saw the depravity of their actions, so the lawsuits continued."

"Did you continue to see your clients?" Leah asked.

"No. Unfortunately. My attorney told me not to work in the same field until this matter was completed. I was advised to continue wearing 'the white hat' even though Brutus never paid for my practice, and they were clearly acting with evil intentions. The attorneys wanted to make sure Brutus and Fanny wouldn't accuse me of trying to steal back my clients if I worked in the same field. Then I would have grounds to file a countersuit.

"Then I heard about another practitioner named Benjamin who had also been victimized by Brutus and Fanny's unscrupulous business dealings. He, too, was trying to recoup after they had shattered his practice and had also filed a lawsuit against Brutus.

"*Two lawsuits* had now been brought against Brutus, and we were told yet *another practitioner* was also contemplating suing him."

"The truth always comes out!" Leah said assuredly.

"Yes, but with legal fees mounting and my preclusion to work in the field in which I had been educated and had trained, I was at a loss. Moreover, many of my clients were now my friends. As excruciatingly painful as this whole fiasco was, nothing was more painful than being unable to explain myself to them when they asked me for answers.

"Under the advisement of my attorneys, 'wearing the white hat' also meant I was not permitted to say a word about my case. My only response to those requesting discussion was, 'I am seeking legal action for all that has happened.' To my closest friends and confidants, I could share my heart openly, but even then, I discovered some of those I thought to be my friends were not—even some I had known for a very long time. That discovery was both very sobering and very sad. It was a lesson I didn't want to learn again, but this time, I learned it well. One such person was my dear friend from university whom I had loved with all my heart. Do you remember me talking about Molly?"

Leah paused a moment, then nodded, motioning for me to continue.

"During one of my darkest times, during the divorce from Barry, when I didn't think I was going to survive, I had given her some of my PoPo's jewelry, including her jade bracelet. I asked her to hold and treasure them for me because she knew and loved my PoPo also, and she knew how much my grandmother meant to me. Unfortunately, after that, she stopped returning my calls and emails. It's possible she may also have been contacted by Fanny and chosen to believe her lies…I don't know. I'm still at a loss. My heartfelt wish is that one day, our friendship can be restored. If nothing else, I still hope she finds it in her heart to return PoPo's jewelry to me."

"Oh, Manna, she will. She will." Leah took my hand with both of hers. "There may be some value in the article of jewelry itself, but the greater value is the love and relationship behind it. If she knows anything about legacy and the preciousness of your relationship with your PoPo, she will return it to you."

"I hope you're right. I would do the same for Molly if the situation were reversed."

"You went through so much together. No one escapes the trials of life, and as she makes mistakes of her own, she will remember all that you've been through, too." Leah looked at me tenderly. "I'm sure she thinks about you and the love and devotion you and your PoPo had together. God will make a way, and your PoPo's special pieces will come back to you."

I looked down sadly.

Then, out of the blue, Leah said, "How in the *hell* did you not say anything about what was going on with Brutus and Fanny? That would have been a killer for me and my big mouth!"

"Like I said, it was one of the hardest things I've ever done. Looking into the eyes of my wonderful clients, I was often humbled to tears. They deserved answers. I wanted to tell them everything, but I could say nothing. All I could do was pray that God would touch their hearts. I prayed He would let them know I could never have foreseen such evil and destruction and that I truly cared for them."

"You are an angel. 'To the pure, all things are pure; but to those who are defiled and unbelieving, nothing is pure. Even their mind and conscience are defiled.' That's Titus 1:15, by the way." Leah shook her head. "I would have been happy to waste a lot of saliva on those two double-crossing, blood-sucking, swindling nincompoops!"

I chuckled and returned to the story. "While I was able to eventually come to a place of acceptance about this, at the time, there was a battle waging in my heart and mind about the whole situation. I wanted to 'wear the white hat,' to take the high road and to totally trust God to serve justice. But as the reality of the situation sank in, a part of me badly wanted to retaliate. I wanted immediate justice, and I wanted everyone to know what they had done. Fortunately, I knew that when we seek to bury someone, we have to dig two graves—one for our enemy, and one for ourselves.

"And so, I continued wearing the white hat and doing the right things, including not defending myself except through the proper channels. To hold your head high when people are gossiping about you is one thing, but to be silent and to hold your head high during a vicious slander and libel campaign was a completely different life lesson.

"I steeled myself, remembering what I heard Coach John Wooden once said. 'Your character is what you *really* are, while your reputation is merely what others *think* you are.' I knew I was a good person. I knew I did the right things. I knew my character, and my honor could not be bought. And I knew it could stand up under the weight of this trial. So, I dug deep and refused to react to the lies, no matter how venomous and wicked they were. I was better than that. Plus, if you're not ready to be criticized for doing good, then you're not ready to be used to do good. Standing against malevolence when you know you are standing in integrity is not easy."

Leah nodded. "No, it's not easy to be lied about, especially when you're only doing good. Winston Churchill said, 'Having enemies isn't so bad; it simply means you stood up for something.' You're a good soul…I wouldn't have taken the high road. How did you do it?"

"Every time I wanted to react to the insanity of what was unfolding before me, I strengthened myself in God. Instead of screaming at the perpetrators, I cried out to God. Ultimately, I chose to listen to God instead of gossip. One of the most expensive things one can do is to pay attention to the wrong people. Brutus and Fanny had already taken enough.

"Like I said, it wasn't easy. At first, crying out to God and waiting for Him to respond almost felt useless. But little by little, with every prayer I uttered, I became more peaceful—and stronger. It was as though a supernatural ability came over me. Anytime I was in a position to justify myself, it became easier and easier for me to remain silent. Plus, I refused to defile myself by being like them, nor did I dignify their absurdities with a reactionary response."

"Just like that?" Leah challenged. "You got peace after such a betrayal and after enduring such losses, just with a few prayers?"

"It wasn't 'just a few prayers.' As I said, peace and strength didn't happen instantly, although I did feel some pressure release. It took time. *I had to want God and all that He offered more than I wanted to cling to my own perception of right and wrong. I had to pursue God more than I pursued retaliation.* Whenever I received another call from my clients or my attorneys or had to prepare more documentation for court, I had to *choose* my response. I had to choose to rise above the greed and the lies and take the higher road. It's always a matter of choice, faith, or fear.

"Even though I couldn't see the purpose for all this chaos, even though it didn't make sense to me, deep down, I knew God was allowing this to happen for a very specific reason. I didn't need to know 'why.' I just needed to trust that God did. I had to trust God, period.

"I also trusted that God would restore anything that was stolen, taken, or broken—a hundred-fold. He would restore my name, my reputation, my finances, and my time. Somehow, I knew that behind this attack, a great blessing was around the corner. Change isn't always easy at first, but He must have allowed this to pave the way for something better. I just had to be brave, keep grounded in faith, and keep believing.

"It's also important to mention that I didn't overcome this time alone. Great friends came alongside me. There's always a team—a tribe—who runs with you to victory. No one ever wins alone. I couldn't have overcome this without them.

"Finally, after almost two years of the legal process, I was awarded compensation for the damages. However, Brutus promptly filed for bankruptcy immediately after the papers were signed. I received a small amount from his insurance agency, but nothing compared to what was due. Interestingly, he still managed to take a two-week European vacation afterwards."

"Argh!" Leah moaned.

I looked calmly at her.

"I know. I know! It's just a matter of time! Then BAAM! Karma!" Leah exclaimed. "Still, it feels like criminals get away with so much. I don't know how you didn't become bitter!"

I sighed. "Out of their ignorance and jealousy, they sought to disgrace me, disregarding the price I had to pay for my successes. Small minds can't comprehend big spirits." I took a breath. "In order to fulfill your calling, you must be willing to stand in the face of hatred, mockery, lies, and attacks. And no, it wasn't easy to hold my head up high, nor was it easy to hold my tongue or hold back my anger. And yes, there were times when I was bitter; I'm human.

"But if I *stayed* bitter, then I would have been just like them. So, when I didn't know what to do next, I pressed into God, and He showed me the way. Solutions presented themselves to me every time I took a step of faith, and eventually, I overcame. There is never a victory without a battle."

Servant in Training

My lawsuit and the constraints to work occurred during the same time as the 2008 financial collapse. Without being able to work in the industry I was so passionate about, in which I had studied so hard to build a career, I had no idea what I was going to do next. True, I had savings and a strong portfolio *at first*, which sustained me longer than others, but that wasn't going to last forever.

I was getting worried and prayed for another career path based on my education and training to open up for me. But no answers came. God wasn't interested in *what I was going to do*, but in *who I was going to be*. He was in the process of taking me through another kind of training, and no schooling, certification, or designation could ever teach me. He was going to show me my true identity instead of my titles.

"What do you mean?" Leah asked.

"Well, as you know, I had been hurt by a lot of people. It wasn't easy to trust anyone because—"

"Because you were surrounded by crazy people!" Leah interrupted.

I smiled and went on with my story.

There was no logic, reason, or normalcy in my childhood, or in my adulthood. The irrational, the illogical, and the deviant seemed to surround me. When I questioned or challenged these behaviors, I was the one made to feel crazy, peculiar, or deficient. I was forced to cope with senseless family patterns and dynamics, apply outdated cultural standards to inappropriate situations. I lived in fear as a minority, a woman, a divorcée, and a single mother, while practicing a misunderstood idea of what being a "good Christian" was.

These forces were so strong and prevalent that they overrode my intuition, wisdom, and basic common sense. Many times, I didn't know what—or *who*—to believe, and I was often very confused and lost. Consequently, the only way to keep my sanity was to attach myself to something that would endure any contradiction or negative experience, like *dogs*, and to something indisputable and undeniable, like *education*.

My father always told me, "People may take away your things, but they can never take away your education or your dignity." So, I put my heart into the unwavering devotion of dogs, and my mind into the celebrated pursuit of education.

These became my pillars of strength.

At home, I had the love and loyalty of my five dogs, and at the office (before its destruction), I had my education—my "wall of fame." Behind my desk was a wall completely filled with all of my credentials—over thirty-five of them. Framed degrees, certifications, awards, letters of recognition, coveted membership standings to elite organizations, conferred plaques of distinction and achievements, and more were displayed. If knowledge was power, then *certainly*, this platform was powerful enough to insulate me from pain and the attacks of unkind people. After all, with sixteen letters following my name and accumulated assets after decades of hard work, wise investments, and savings, I had earned the right to be safe "on top of the mountain."

I was wrong.

Knowledge (which changes), letters after my name (which only showed *past* achievements and do not guarantee *future* security), and assets (which diminish depending on economic systems, trends, and fads totally out of anyone's control) did not shelter me from the trials of life. The *true me* was lost somewhere between the glass-framed pieces of paper and the alphabet following my name.

I had no idea who I was without my financial security, my office, and my "wall of fame" (which I hoped would prove I was special, that I was a "somebody"). I felt doomed. Until this time, my entire identity and security were wrapped up in what I did. The equation was simple: *What I do = who I am*.

While my father's exhortation to me had been accurate, I had taken its context to a whole other level. Nonetheless, this entire process, the gaining *and the losing*, was all a necessary part of my personal healing and growth. Looking back, I wish things didn't happen the way they did, but I'm still thankful, even to Brutus and Fanny.

"*What?*" Leah shouted.

"I know. It sounds crazy, but this entire mess was a gift. As valuable as education is, sometimes the things worth knowing can never be taught in a classroom. They have to be experienced and lived. As painful as losing my practice was, had it not happened, I would never have been freed. The internalized falsehoods would have kept me in bondage for the rest of my life. But I'm now free to accomplish my next assignment, and I have never felt more authentic and purposeful in my life. A 'wall of fame' or an alphabet after my name is no longer needed to define or protect me. The only letters after my name now are these: 'Manna Ko, S.I.T.'"

Leah cocked her head, quizzically. "What does S.I.T. stand for?"

"Servant in Training."

We both smiled.

"Why not just say 'servant'?" Leah inquired.

"Because if Jesus Himself was the Servant of all servants, I couldn't possibly claim that title. I can only be one 'in training'—endeavoring to be more like Him every day. I don't need to be a *somebody* anymore, always worrying if I'm going to be good enough or worthy enough. It was exhausting living that way. I now know I am safe, and even powerful, as a *nobody* because I serve a *Somebody* Who loves *everybody*."

"That's good!" Leah nodded. "Did you make that up?"

"I heard a version of this before, but I changed it to fit me better." I shrugged.

"With God, all things are possible…and I know you didn't make that one up!" Leah chuckled. "Your resolve is inspiring—even to a dying old woman. It may not look like it, but I'm learning, and every day I feel a little more hopeful."

The stories during this particular visit brought out more of Leah's fire than before, but I could tell she was becoming fatigued. I was about to suggest we make it a day when she spoke reflectively.

"It hasn't been easy to hear some of your stories…nor has it been easy for you to tell them either, I'm sure. But hearing each progression has made me stronger on the inside. I don't know if it will kill the cancer, but something inside of me feels 'alive' somehow."

"I'm glad, Leah," I said, as I reached to pull a shifting blanket back over her shoulder. "Let's call it a day, shall we?"

"No way, José! You're not leaving till you tell me how this nasty situation plays out!" she insisted.

I paused a moment then continued, hoping to leave on a high point.

"At the time, I couldn't see the end of it, but each day I was given a new page to write on and a new lesson to learn. Not only was I *not* to define myself by my achievements or my career, I was *not* to define myself by my situations either. I was learning *Whom* to trust and whom *not* to trust. I had to believe in something I *couldn't see*, and I had to believe in *something different than what I did see!* For what I didn't know, faith provided."

The Gift of Enemies

There's a Chinese proverb that says, "Men trip not on mountains, they trip on molehills." Though Brutus and Fanny had evil intentions to harm me, God turned it all together for my greater good. Their vision was so small; they thought their success was in robbing me of my practice, furniture, or supplies. Little did they know their schemes were actually allowed to happen so they could propel and position me to receive even greater gifts. I was strengthened and blessed in ways I never thought were possible. God broke off so many strongholds over my life; helped me to see more clearly, hear more accurately, and discern more wisely; and freed me from the fears and the lies that had been spoken over me most of my life.

I was cleaned up, refreshed, renewed, and emboldened. Had it not been for such disappointments, detours, and the proverbial "three steps forward, two steps back," I wouldn't have come so far. Monumental breakthroughs in my career and finances didn't happen immediately. And yet, I still knew deep down I was being prepared for something big one day. Before there are any public victories, there have to be private ones first.

Part of my private victory was that I emerged from this trial without resentment or hatred for Brutus and Fanny. If anything, I felt sad for them. They didn't know their own goodness, and consequently, sold their character, integrity, humanity, and soul for lesser things.

There's no way I could have overcome this on my own strength and abilities; it was all through God's grace. The gossip, lies, slander, and libel—I had to learn not to be affected by any of it. It's a lesson we all need to learn more deeply; to not fear what any man says. "Let God be true, but every man a liar."⁷

No one likes to be rejected or maligned. But when we're strong enough to withstand those arrows and know the proper tools to deflect the attacks, we can focus on what we're called to do and not be taken off track.

"You're too nice. Anyone else would have done more than just sue them! I know my friends in Chicago would have!" Leah jested.

"But what would that have proved? Except that I was messed up, just like them. Plus, I've learned the only people you should get even with are those who have *helped* you." I smiled.

"Well, I can't argue with that," Leah nodded. "Thomas always used to tell me not to worry about what people were saying behind my back—they were behind me for a reason."

We're Going to Need a Bigger Boat

In the midst of all the struggles with my practice, I had given up my television project. The writer's strike lasted a long time and was followed by an actor's strike. As it is with all strikes, one never knows how long they will take, and this situation was no different. After carefully assessing everything, I decided to stop pursuing the television program and focused on a new direction for work.

Now, here's where a lot of "life" started to happen *again*, and all simultaneously. Just hang on.

"I hear the theme from Jaws in the background," Leah winked, chuckling to herself. "I'm ready. Go for it!"

Joshua was a great source of strength and comfort to me during this time, but he, too, was in a season of great change. As I mentioned earlier, he had sold his company, and part of the requirements was a five-year non-compete clause. So, just like me, he was not permitted to work in the same capacity as he had before.

We were both reinventing ourselves professionally.

With no other option, I went back to an industry I knew well—real estate. Joshua, with his expansive business experiences, joined me in establishing global real estate markets for strategically identified products. Unfortunately, the economic climate, driven by all the real estate variables (loans, financing, pricing of products, etc.), was still on its downhill slide. We were never able to stabilize our business after its initial launch.

While I continued seeking alternate sources of income, I also sought ways to minimize expenses and contacted a friend who specialized in loan modifications. She reviewed my loan and discovered I was the victim of predatory lending. Though I had grounds to, I chose not to seek legal remedies for this (especially after what I had just been through with my practice) and was satisfied to move forward with a strong "loan mod" in my favor.

It was a desperate time for many. With the stock market crash, the depressed housing markets, businesses closing, and high unemployment rates, many friends were losing their homes, cars, and jobs. The financial stressors took their toll, and families were falling apart. Many had no money for food because every extra penny went towards paying their exorbitant mortgage loans. As one friend after another went through foreclosure, they came to my home. I emptied my pantry, freezer, and refrigerator no less than a dozen times. Some even stayed with me for short stints until they could get on their feet again. I purchased gas and groceries for them and did my best to help with childcare and any support avenues I knew. Calls came in left and right from people suffering from depression, divorce, addictions, and suicide threats. I took on clients for free, and by the grace of God, I was able to intervene for over half a dozen people on suicide watch. Local community mission efforts also reached out, and I spent many days with the despondent, seriously ill, or homeless.

Around this same time, a friend was diagnosed with cancer and died within three months of the report. On top of all of this, Michael (who was home from school and living on his own) called to tell me his lease was up, and because his roommates were moving on, he had to give up his apartment. His part-time job was also ending, and with no money, he was going to have to come home to live with me.

The transition of having Michael back home would be challenging, as he was accustomed to being on his own, and I wasn't sure how he would handle house rules again. I welcomed him back with cautious excitement, and prayed the new home environment and a fresh lifestyle at the beach would uplift and inspire him to try harder at pursuing his future.

One morning, after leaving the gym, I noticed almost a dozen missed calls from both Simone (Tristan's sister), and one of her sons, my godson, Taylor. I knew instantly something was wrong, but I never expected to hear what I did when we finally talked.

I called Taylor first. "Taylor, honey. I'm sorry to have missed your calls. What's wrong? Is everything okay?"

"Auntie...are you sitting down?"

"No, but I will. What is it?" Fear coursed through my body.

"Uncle Tristan passed away yesterday. He had a massive heart attack and died instantly."

"*What?*"

He'd only been forty-eight years old.

Taylor and I continued talking, and then he put his mom on the phone. Simone told me they were having difficulty getting any information from Tristan's girlfriend. All she knew was he had been smoking over five packs of cigarettes, drinking a bottle of liquor, and doing whatever drugs he did in between, *daily*. This lifestyle had finally caught up with him. Simone also told me Tristan had been estranged from the family for almost a decade because of his abusive treatment of them. And it was during one of those ugly episodes that she realized how he must have treated me when we were married.

Tristan was so young, and he had squandered his life and all his potential, one compromise, and one bad choice at a time. It was so sad…

That's when Simone also disclosed a dark secret, one Tristan and Nanny had kept silent for over two decades. He'd had a child with another girlfriend before he met me, but denied it was his.

"NO!" Leah was aghast. "That's the 'dark secret' you referred to earlier! Now I understand," Leah said somberly. "How did you break the news to Michael?"

"I called Joshua right after my call with Simone, and we brainstormed on what to do. Michael and his father had not had a relationship for over twelve years, and we weren't sure how he would react. Simone also told me Tristan's girlfriend (also estranged from the family) was in control of all his finances and the memorial. She had, in fact, forbidden Tristan's family to attend the service. She was not even going to disclose the date or the location of the funeral, to ensure no one on his side would come.

Michael was in the middle of final exams at the time, and in light of all this information, and since there were no services to we could attend, we thought it would be best to wait. We would tell Michael when he didn't have anything at risk—after his exams were over.

When it did come time to break the news to Michael though, I labored over how to tell him.

"Michael…I have something to tell you. It's not an easy thing to say…and we've struggled with how to share this news." I looked up at Joshua, stumbling over my words. Joshua nodded, and I proceeded.

"There's no way to say it, but to just speak it plainly." I took a deep breath. "Michael. Your father died of a massive heart attack a few weeks ago." I paused, took another breath, and continued. "Auntie Simone called me after she found out. Unfortunately, your father's girlfriend is in control of everything and has forbidden the family to attend the memorial. She won't even share the details about it. We all believe the service has already happened, but not even Auntie Simone, Auntie Marjorie, or Nanny went."

I stopped and watched Michael carefully.

Michael initially acted as if the news didn't hurt him, but no matter how much he tried to hold back the tears, they began to flow.

I could sense his sadness over missed past opportunities, and his hope of one day reconnecting (or at least having a conversation) with his father. But that was now gone. Joshua tried to add some comforting words as we continued to talk, but there was very little else we could say. It was a shock for all of us, especially for Michael. And while I had not had any thoughts or desires to see Tristan again, Michael had.

Michael knew about his father's past. No one (neither I, Simone, Marjorie, nor his cousins) had hidden the truth from him, though we were always sensitive as to how we answered his questions whenever the topic came up. But like most children with an estranged parent (myself included), he had romanticized what a reunion might look like.

When Michael began to cry, I went over and held him. After a while, he pulled away.

"Really, I'm okay," he said with a forced smile. "It's just a shock, that's all. It's not like I know him or anything. I guess it's just weird that I won't get to see him again, and I'm sad he chose such a bad life."

But Michael wasn't okay. This news came amid already painful lessons we were trying to work through with him, and sadly, it only spurred him onto other, more dangerous paths.

As a mother, I felt helpless. I could not take the pain away from my son, nor was I able to help him see that his thoughts and choices were erroneous and harmful. I did my best to support him, but he walled himself up to me.

For the next few years, I continued intervening where I could, but the majority of my battles were done on my knees. Through countless sleepless nights, I prayed and prayed for my son, fighting *for* his life. I could not afford to doubt in the valleys what God had already shown me on the mountaintops. I had to believe my son would overcome.

I had to.

One by one, more horrible news came regarding Michael, and I was desperate and growing weary. I did my best to stay lighthearted and kept praying, but my grip was slipping. I felt paralyzed, unable to help my son, and lived in fear for his life every waking moment. This fear played throughout my body—the latent back and neck strain after my car accident returned with ferocity, and panic attacks tormented me day and night.

I was losing hope.

For all my positive outlook and persistence, I was slowly falling into "clinical depression." I don't remember ever experiencing that kind of darkness—even as a child or as a young adult. It was a terrifying kind of dark emptiness and hopelessness. And it consumed me. I didn't understand what was happening to me, especially since my prayer life was solid, and I was involved in many good projects. This depression just didn't make sense. One moment I would rally and feel strong, but just as suddenly, I found myself piled up in a heap, wanting to die.

My life bounced between the duality of faith and fear, but I refused to let anyone see my anxieties; they only saw my optimism and my smile. I wanted to be strong and courageous for others because by being strong for them, I found strength for myself. However, when I came home, try as I might, I could not sustain that strength. I would go immediately to my room and collapse into bed. All my dogs would eagerly join me, and while it was wonderful to have them cuddled beside me, I often just stared out across the ocean and cried. I didn't know what to do. *How could I learn so much and feel so strong one minute and then fall apart the next?*

I desperately clung to a gossamer thread of hope.

Did I love God for what He did for me? Or did I love Him because of Who He is? Either God was for me, or He was not. Either He was with me all the time, or He was absent and distant. Who is God to me?

My faith was being tested.

The enemy's attack is often layered. First, he comes after our loved ones, especially our children. Then he comes after our property (possessions, homes, accomplishments, inheritances, careers, etc.). And then he attacks our relationship with God, challenging us to doubt His love, care, protection, and provision for us.

It was then when I began remembering everything He had done for me. I remembered His promises (verses in the Bible), and I even remembered Sunday school songs. Little by little, I grew stronger. I became braver, wiser, and I found a new resolve and a new expectation for my future.

"Just listening to this makes my hair stand on end!" Leah said, flustered. "How long did it take till you got back on your feet again?"

"It took a little while. Sometimes God allows the trials to last longer than we'd like them to because He is doing something *through* us. During these times, He's teaching us how to exercise our authority over our obstacles and hindrances. Other times, God removes the trials quickly, because He is doing *for* us. During these times, He is teaching us to know our 'sonship,' our belonging—that we belong to Him, and the battle is His. In my situation at the time (while God is always doing something wonderful *in and with* us at the core of our relationship), He was doing something *through* me.

"He was teaching me how to reign over my enemies—negative thoughts and beliefs, fear, intimidation, and even people."

"That's amazing. I never thought of delays or resistance in this way," Leah said thoughtfully.

"As I became stronger, new ideas came, and one by one, opportunities presented themselves to me. I obediently walked through each door that opened, but strangely, every door promising a new beginning only turned out to be a dead end. I tried every kind of business and did not leave one stone unturned, but nothing came to pass. Nothing could get off the ground, no matter how fervently I worked.

"I was confused, very confused. 'God,' I asked, 'why did You give me the strength to stand up, only for me to get knocked down again?'"

"What did you do?" Leah asked with anticipation.
"I did what I could do. I got up again. And I kept getting up."
Leah smiled.
"I had come so far, and I wasn't about to give up. God had breathed new life into my dry bones, and He had once again answered my prayers. Now, they may not always have been the answers I would have liked, or arrived in the way I thought they would come, but He always provided for me, *every single time*. And there was a purpose for this time, too—for all the 'dead ends' I had to keep trusting Him.

"Life has knocked me down too many times to count, and I've seen things I never wanted to see. People have said a lot of things about me—some true, some not—but one thing they'll always know about me: I will always get back up!"
"That's my girl!" Leah nodded.

Needless Casualties of War

Joshua and I were both under heavy financial and emotional stress as we dealt with all our personal and professional matters. We were doing our best under the weight of all our circumstances, but it was no time to be thinking about marriage and certainly no time to be planning a wedding. Amid everything, I "disengaged" us until we could start again, clean, and it wasn't long before we ended our relationship altogether—several times.

"What does that mean, several times?" Leah asked.

"Life was messy, and there were too many obstacles in the way of a normal relationship, so we took time apart from each other—sabbaticals, as I called them. However, since we had a natural love for each other, we always stayed in touch and even found our way back together now and then. But the burden of ongoing issues also found its way back into our lives, which resulted in more sabbaticals. We talked about dating other people, but with every new person I met, Joshua's special qualities were only illuminated to me more. Although we didn't get back together officially for a while, I knew no one could come close to being like my Joshua. We just needed some time to sort things out."

"I'm glad you two found your way back to each other, but what could cause so many separations?" Leah asked, puzzled.

"We were able to overcome many things together, but Joshua's divorce process took a heartbreaking toll on us, and on his children."

We had a good relationship. His children were amazing. Against a backdrop of ugly reports about me (and their instinct to defend their mother), they still demonstrated kindness towards me, in spite of all they heard—a true testimony to their intrinsic goodness and to the largeness of their hearts. Still, it wasn't a time to be "building" a relationship with me, per se. It was a time of healing for themselves and time to be with their father. They needed stability and safety, and they needed to know their father still loved them.

I insisted that Joshua spend more time with them and go to counseling with them. I even offered to go with the children as well, so they could feel free to discuss any issues they had with me in the safe presence of a professional they trusted. Unfortunately, Joshua did not believe that the damage was as bad as I was describing. He was more focused on rebuilding his business again, believing that would be the solution.

'Trust me, Manna," he said. "This is all about money."

"But you gave her everything already. That's not the answer. We need to focus on the kids."

"I'm doing my best. Don't worry. The kids will be fine. Keep praying, and just trust me, please," Joshua insisted.

But I'm sorry to say, I didn't trust him. He wasn't right about Lilith before, and I didn't believe he was right about her again. Unfortunately, I was mute in this situation. I had no formal role in their lives and no power to intercede. So I held my tongue and did the best with what I could whenever the children were with us.

Sadly, the only way to protect them was to keep them at arm's length with things we were doing, and we kept our conversations light so they would be safe from interrogation when they returned home. That way, when asked about us, they could honestly answer, "I don't know." We hoped that with no new information, the interrogations would stop, and they would be spared the confrontations. However, by taking this approach, we lost irreplaceable opportunities to share in special times with them in their younger years. But at least, we knew they were safe.

True to Joshua's nature, he never spoke poorly about Lilith in front of the kids. He told them the truth whenever they asked questions, as did I, and we were always forthcoming and available for them. But deep down, they didn't care about details; they simply wanted everyone to "be nice." They wanted to be free of all the drama. They were the innocent and unnecessary casualties of war.

Then one day, Joshua came to me very distraught. "Manna, things aren't good with Lilith and the youngest one. They have always been like oil and water, but now it's really bad."

"What do you mean 'really bad'?"

"Things have spiraled to almost irreparable conditions, and they can no longer live with each other. The youngest needs to get away from that toxic environment. She asked to live with us instead."

I gulped.

It wasn't that I didn't want to take care of Joshua's child. My first concern was that this would only put his child in the middle of *more* interrogations, and us under even greater and more constant scrutiny. But that thought went away quickly as I considered his child not feeling wanted, and not feeling safe. Memories of my own childhood popped up, and before I knew it, we were preparing to be a *family*. I knew we could provide a loving and consistent home for Joshua's little one, and I cried tears of joy as we started to make the necessary arrangements for the move-in day, only ten days away.

Michael and I discussed this, too, and he was eager to have a sibling at home. We considered the challenges we'd face, but in spite of them, we thought it would be worth it all to be together and to be *a family*.

After we had started to prepare a bedroom for full-time use, I received a call from one of my most trusted mentors. Her wisdom and experience exceeded her years, and I told her about the new developments. She responded with a long silence.

"What's wrong?" I asked nervously. "You're never this quiet…what's wrong?"

"Manna, I know you love Joshua's children. I know you want to give them a loving and happy home…" she hesitated.

"But what? I hear a 'but.' What is it?" I demanded.

"I'm afraid that if you take in this child, though it may seem fine at first, eventually your relationship will disintegrate," she warned.

"*What?*" I shouted. "How can that be? I only want to give that child something that's been missing. I can do it, and I *want* to do it. It will be great because Michael is home, too, and he loves Joshua's kids. They get along great together, and it will be a wonderful opportunity for everyone, including Lilith. She'll have some time alone, to get the support she needs, and they'll both have some peace." I defended my decision.

After a long silence, my mentor continued. "Yes, that may be true for a while, but what you're not seeing will cause great suffering and pain in the long run, for all of you," she stated definitively.

I pursed my lips, holding back the tears starting to pool.

Speaking to me was someone I respected greatly. Her insights, accuracy, and wisdom have seldom been challenged because she guards her words carefully. When she speaks, when she offers counsel, it's only because it's *truth*.

I was torn.

"I don't understand," I said, now weeping. "Why is it wrong to take in and love this child? How could I be hurt by doing so?"

"The child is *not yours*. The child, though happy to have some relief for a while, will always be loyal to their mother. The child will naturally and instinctively find things about you to dislike—despite liking and even loving you *now*. In time, you will be the topic of discussion and the common bond between the child and the mother. *Unconsciously*, you will be the tool used to somehow bring their relationship back together again. All unity needs is a common enemy."

I was speechless by her explanation.

"Your heart is in the right place," she continued. "But this isn't about you. This is about the child. Use discernment. Use wisdom."

"What am I supposed to do? Everything is already set! Everyone is waiting for the moving day next week—even Lilith! What am I supposed to say? How can I say no now, even if I did agree with what you're saying?" I struggled.

"Manna, do you love Joshua's children?"

"Yes! Of course I do! I've loved them from day one! I just haven't been given a formal role in their lives. Plus, how was I going to speak into their lives, or be a part of their lives, when all they knew was that I was the evil one? There was nothing I could do then, but now I have a chance!"

"Yes. You do have a chance," she said, almost cryptically.

"I have a feeling we're not talking about the same thing," I said quietly.

"Let me ask you again." She paused. "Do you love Joshua's children?"

"*Yes!*" I said without hesitation. "Of course, I do!"

"Then tell Joshua that his child cannot move in."

"*What?*"

Oh…my…goodness…!

Words escaped me for what seemed like hours, but after a long silent break, my friend spoke again, firmly, "Manna, if you truly love his kids, then you will spare them from any more onslaughts. If the youngest one lives with you, it brings the older one into the equation also. Both of them will now be thrown into the middle again. In time, the dissonance growing inside the youngest will be too great. Not only will you be the target again, you will lose all hope of having a real relationship with that child *ever again*—or with both children for that matter. They will always stick up for each other, and based on how they first heard about you, they will always align themselves with their mother. So, you have a choice," she said undeniably. "Suffer now, or suffer worse later."

I had no rebuttal to her words.

We talked for the next hour or so; I lost track of time. All I knew was I was in another whirlwind that left me ungrounded and unable to hold on.

I cried and cried and cried.

Joshua tried to convince me things would be fine, but since I no longer trusted his assessment of Lilith, and I was not willing to risk anymore upset or division with the children, I knew I had to say no.

I couldn't sleep for the rest of the week; I was tormented.

I don't know how I made it through that next day or the days ahead. I cried nonstop, but I was willing to risk my relationship with his child now—in the hopes that a better and more beautiful one in the future might be possible.

I prayed that one day, this little one would forgive me for making that heart-wrenching decision and know I did so at great cost. I placed my heart on the altar, sacrificing what I wanted, to pave the way for something better, more real, and much more beautiful in the future. I fell asleep many nights afterwards with tear-stained cheeks, praying Joshua's children would know how much I loved them, and for a chance to start fresh again one day.

A Place of Your Own

With all these considerations before us, it was time for Joshua to have a place of his own, a place where he could really have one-on-one time with both his children. They needed to remember who their father was, and not what they had been told. They needed to see he was the same person he had always been, loving and adoring of them, and they needed time to share, grieve, learn, and heal together. They needed their father (not necessarily the father and his girlfriend).

Even though finances were tight, we took a leap of faith and rented a wonderful apartment where Joshua could reclaim both his children and their relationship. I furnished and decorated it with my own things and made it a beautiful home for them.

As Joshua spent time with his children, I spent less time with him. Joshua did not want to put me in any more distressing situations, so he stayed away, but made it clear he hoped we would one day be back together.

These were sad times, but I was blessed with the introduction of new mentors and friends who poured into me.

One day, one of those mentors said to me, "Manna, you're on the fast track! You're learning quickly, and things will soon shift. Your life hasn't been easy, but God allowed all those trials to happen so things could be broken off of you, and you could finally know who you really are. No one could have done it for you. You had to do it for yourself." She smiled and held my hands. "All of these hardships have been essential parts of your training. Your preparation could be nothing less than vigorous, so you could be equipped and properly prepared for what's coming next. It will all be worth it. God has never left you, nor will He ever. You are stronger than you know. Your time is coming. You'll see."

Suddenly, I remembered the angel in the elevator. Over forty years had passed—just as the angel had said. *I haven't messed up so badly that He gave up on me. I haven't been forgotten. I have been preparing.*

I remember.

This was the encouragement I needed, and I grew spiritually. I developed even greater discernment, deeper and more accurate insights, and a greater understanding of things around me. I could talk on and on about that time of refreshing, but what I want to share most of all is this: God revealed to me that Joshua was "the one" for me. It would be safe to love him with all my heart. For all the times I had said I couldn't live with him, I knew now that I couldn't live *without* him.

The time just wasn't right yet.

In the meantime, Joshua's grueling five-year divorce finally came to an end, but only after paying staggering amounts of money to attorneys, the courts, all the specialists, and his ex-wife.

His relationship with his children had stabilized, and they were all moving forward excitedly with their respective plans and future goals. Unfortunately, almost all of Joshua's assets were now depleted. With economic conditions still at rock bottom and no reprieve in sight, we conceded to this state of affairs. We decided to live together again, pooling our finances to "stop the bleeding."

We renewed our relationship, and still remembering the promise we had made to each other many years ago, wanting our wedding night to be special, he insisted on sleeping on the couch.

"Like I said, what a man!" Leah sighed.

The Big Event

Michael moved abroad for one year. He was doing missions work and studying videography and photography, and Joshua and I were empty nesters once again. Despite the great burdens we still carried, we made sure we found joy in the simple things of life. We continued with our walks on the beach, made simple dinners at home, and spent time with new friends in the different businesses we were building. Then one day, I heard God say, *I want you to do something "big."* And in the days ahead, I learned what that was to mean.

Long gone were the days when people were drawn together to help one another authentically. Intentions were muddled between "service to others" and "self-serving" motives. This may seem naïve, but I was determined to change that—to take a stand for what I believed "true community service" and "love" ought to look like.

Everywhere I turned, the media reported the havoc in people's lives resulting from the devastating economic downturn. As I shared earlier, my phone constantly rang from people needing support, counseling, and interventions. But I was only one person. How could I help more people?

I needed a bigger platform.

This was the genesis of "The Big Event," a huge conference to draw people together and help businesses grow through strong networking groups. The focus was social entrepreneurship (a newer concept then, but one that spoke to my heart). I funded the entire event with the rest of my savings and spent seven months preparing for it. Everyone seemed happy and excited about The Big Event, and several colleagues even volunteered to do email pushes to their extensive client lists. No less than four million invitations and marketing pushes were going to go out in this manner. Even if only a small percentage of these guests actually attended, the event promised to be exactly what the name suggested—*big!*

However, the people who had given their word to send out invitations failed to do so. In the end, only hundreds showed up at an event that was prepared to take thousands.

Looming in the back of my mind was the fact that all the hotel rooms had not been booked, and I was about to receive a one-hundred-and-fifty-thousand-dollar bill for reserving them—a bill I had no idea how I would pay. We had released the rooms two weeks before the event, but the manager was not very hopeful they could sell, as it was their slower season.

Nonetheless, I still had those in the ballroom who believed in the message and all those who were watching in the wings, including my dedicated team and all the wonderful consultants I had hired. I was determined to give them even more than they had asked for, and we did. The gift of the event happened, regardless of people's broken promises, and regardless of the smaller crowd. Those who needed to hear the messages were blessed, and I was happy to have been a catalyst for them.

Billy Graham once said, "Courage is contagious. When a brave man takes a stand, the spines of others are often stiffened."

And so it was with "The Big Event."

I did what I could with what I had and where I was. Over the coming weeks, I received email after email, and call after call from people who had attended the event, sharing their wins, breakthroughs, and new beginnings with me. The event was a great success indeed, and I was genuinely grateful.

The following week, the hotel called. Joshua and I braced ourselves. After the final count, they could not believe what they had witnessed. Almost all the rooms had sold, and I was left having to pay for only a small fraction of what had been originally estimated. The manager herself emailed me and personally called me to share her astonishment at what she called, "This act of God."

"Never in my thirty-plus year career in the hotel business have I seen anything like this! You most certainly know 'The Big Guy' up there!" the hotel manager chuckled. "Manna, you are one of the nicest people I have met, and if anyone deserves this miracle, it's you!"

I wept with relief and gratitude.

My father, who attended the event, also wept tears of joy for me. "I've always known you were very capable, but I had never seen you in full action like this—creating, planning, organizing, hosting, speaking, and producing the entire event! Everything you did, from the beginning to the end, was wonderful. All the special surprises, the honor you showed to everyone there, and how you treated your team…I'm so proud of you! I now know why God asked me to name you 'Manna.' You were a gift to every hungry soul there."

Even though the event wasn't what we thought it would *look like*, God moved, creating *His Big Event*. All I had to do was to listen and obey. This act of faith stretched any logical reasoning and is still an event people talk about today. Great exploits and wild dreams often sound strange to other people. They may call you naïve, foolish, or even out of touch. But heroic visions cannot always be seen by others, and grand plans cannot be understood with small thinking. They require faith. They require obedience.

They require God.

How do you know if you have been given a powerful dream? When the dream is all you can think about, when it won't leave you alone, when your soul, heart, mind, and body stirs when you think upon it, and when you feel like a part of you would die if you didn't bring it to life.

How do you fulfill your dream? Pray. Ask God for wisdom, discernment, and favor. He will show you secret things which you do not yet know, and He will part seas for you. Just believe.

Rock of Ages

Although I was getting stronger spiritually and emotionally, my financial situation did not strengthen. In fact, it was now precarious. I had liquidated everything I had in my portfolio, and with no steady income (in spite of all the job applications and different businesses I pursued), I was at a loss as to how I was going to make the next month's mortgage payment and pay all the other bills.

I needed a miracle.

The next day, I received an investment statement in the mail. It had a very large balance in it and was *liquid*! I had forgotten about this account because it had been categorized in another way, and I had wrongly assumed everything was lost in the stock market crash. I called my financial planner right away, and she immediately took the necessary steps to release the funds to me.

My miracle arrived within twenty-four hours.

Joshua and I continued working on different ventures. Although we were able to get a little bit of work, it wasn't enough to meet all our expenses. My old theory—that the alphabet after my name would guarantee safety and security was definitely proven false. This time, instead of not having *enough* qualifications, I was told I was *over-qualified*. I was turned down for positions and salaries many times less than what I was earning before.

I had no choice but to continue pursuing my entrepreneurial path.

My mentoring clients were somewhat steady, but with many businesses folding, my corporate consulting practice dwindled. Eventually, to pay the bills, I was forced to sell my car and all my expensive jewelry. Over one hundred and fifty thousand dollars' worth of jewelry was sold for thirteen thousand dollars. But I wasn't the least bit upset. I was simply grateful I had these assets to sell and was able to take care of my family.

I also had the opportunity to get back into the world of media and was cast in a very progressive (and timely) reality television show. We did some early filming, but the company ran out of funding, so that project ended up being tabled.

With no other option available, I prepared to rebrand my company and then re-launch my business, hoping to stir up new interest and new clients. As it turned out, the timing was perfect to launch on my birthday.

One large component of my relaunch involved a heavy video feature, and a very dear friend offered to help me with the video and production aspects. In return, I agreed to pay him and also promote him to my friends in the media industry after they saw his work. The marketing push was massive, and the campaign was extensive. But with each passing day, I still had no deliverables. Not one product had been developed, and no one else on his team was returning my calls.

The evening before the launch, my friend confessed he had actually done nothing for me—no videos, no products, nothing. He told me his friends had been busy and unable to help, but no one had mentioned this to me. I didn't have time to find a replacement videographer or even search for relevant stock videos. It was 10 p.m., and the launch was supposed to be announced first thing the next morning.

I was devastated. Now only hours before midnight, I had nowhere else to go, and no one else to ask. I went to my room, rifling through my laptop to see what I could do. How could I mitigate the embarrassment of not being ready, having no videos or products for the *media work* I was promoting?. But this wasn't the first time that friend had said he would do something important for me and had not delivered as promised. I shouldn't have trusted him, but I wanted to show him that I believed in him and give him a platform to show off his talent to those I knew who would help promote him.

What am I to do about this one?

I was re-launching my career after being unable to work for almost five years in the field in which I had been trained, and I had nothing to present. It was humiliating. Tears rolled down my face as I frantically searched the Internet for anything that could help me.

The next morning, my friend came to see me. Instead of apologizing, he made up many reasons to justify his actions. When I did not—and *could* not—respond, he said something that pierced my heart like nothing else he had ever said. "Nothing you've done these past eight years have worked! You don't know what you're doing, and I doubt you even hear from God!"

I closed my eyes and told myself to forget this moment—to pretend it never happened. If I knew *anything*, it was that I did hear God. I had obeyed Him the best I could and diligently followed everything He had asked me to do, especially during those eight years. In fact, I had done the craziest of ideas out of blind faith. When things made no sense at all, I still obeyed. Did I get the results I hoped for? Not always, but that didn't mean I didn't hear Him, nor did it mean that results didn't happen. I may never know the final results of any situation. All that mattered was that I listened, and God knew He could trust me with what He asked of me.

There are times when you do everything right, but you don't see the fruits of your labor right away, or ever. But that doesn't mean you didn't hear God, or that He didn't answer your prayers. Patience is necessary because roots take time to grow deep. Everything is beautiful in its own time. Fruit picked too early is bitter and hard, even poisonous. But fruit picked at the right time is sweet. In the meantime, people may make fun of you and judge you, even those closest to you, but you must continue to believe. Stay the course. Do not waver. Keep believing.

There's a profound story of a young girl who, after playing in her backyard one day, decided to dedicate her life to God. Immediately after doing so, she heard Him say, "Pick up the rock." She did. Then she heard God say, "Put down the rock." She heard and obeyed those same two commands many times. Sometimes she held the rock for a few seconds. Sometimes she held the rock for hours, never putting it down until she heard Him say, "Put down the rock." Finally, she asked God, "Why are we doing this ridiculous exercise? It makes no sense at all! It's a dumb rock. I want to do big and important things for You!"

Only then did she hear the most life-changing words of all. She heard God say, "When you listen to me in the smallest and seemingly dumbest of things, then I can trust you with the biggest of things—the most important of things."

That *rocked* me, no pun intended! When I heard this story, I rededicated myself again, resolving myself to always trust God instead of what was happening, or what was being said.

As my friend walked away, I heard God say, "Forgive them for they know not what they do. I will turn all things together for good."

It's All Yours

Just when I didn't think I could bear anymore, my beloved dog Duke died. He was one of the Bernese Mountain dogs I had— and was only four-and-a-half years old. He was by far, my most favorite dog I had ever owned, and by this time, I'd had many. He was the kind of dog Disney would make movies of. If we had been separated, he would have traveled across the country to find me. While my other dogs loved me, "Dukie" was devoted to me.

Even other people noticed the incredible bond we had with each other. And when he died, I felt like a huge part of me had also died. It isn't enough to say I was devastated. Even to this day, now seven years later, I'm still emotional when I think of my Dukie.

Three months later, I lost my eleven-year-old Sadie, and seven months later, I lost Dakota. They were my two sweet Golden Retrievers. Inside the span of a single year, I had lost three dogs. I felt paralyzed with grief and was barely able to find the strength, some days, to get up.

Around this same time, my father and his wife had separated, going through a horrific divorce of their own. I won't go into all the details, but suffice it to say, my stepmother of thirty years acted as if she had never been a part of our family.

By the sound of things, I knew I had better come back home and spend some time with my father and my family. His health was very poor from all the upset of the divorce, and something told me I had to move—to leave my home and to be closer to my father.

I felt like I was in a tornado, and like Job in his trials, nothing, except my actual physical life itself, was spared. Everything else, though, was up for grabs—my son, my father, my brother, my pets, work, career, Joshua, finances, my home, my assets, my health, my accomplishments, my reputation, my friendships, and anything else you can think of.

And so, I put my beautiful home on the market.

It was a rare gem, and I received an immediate offer, but one so low I didn't even dignify it with a response. I received several other offers, but they were also very low. I knew my house was worth much more, even though we were still in the midst of a housing market crash. While I was ready to concede that I would never get all my money back, I was not willing to lose everything. Against all counsel, I held to my price, not because I was stubborn, but because I knew better.

One afternoon, after receiving more rounds of bad news warning that I "would lose it all if I didn't take that offer," I quietly went onto my deck and stared out onto the magnificent Pacific Ocean.

I had tried to be strong and very courageous. I had tried to trust God. I had tried to remember all the great experiences God had given me, and how He had proven Himself to me, but my home was all I had left.

I could take no more. It had all been too much.

I cried out to Him, "This…This…This whole thing—this whole thing You've allowed, or maybe even orchestrated these past eight years …it's just *reeeee-dic-uuuu-lousss*! I have no idea what You're trying to do, but it's a flippin' mess! And besides that, *this whole thing—whatever it is You're doing*—it's a *horrible* testimony for *You*! Everyone knows how much I love You! And no one, I repeat no one, understands *why Your faithful servant* (that would be me!), is being pummeled like this! The people who believe in You either think I'm crazy or that I have a secretly corrupt life for which I'm being punished. And the ones who don't believe in You are wondering if You even exist! After all, why would You allow so many bad things to happen to a good person? I've done everything You've asked, but every horrible thing keeps happening to me. Everything I've worked so hard for keeps getting stripped away! Don't you see me getting slaughtered out here?"

When I was completely spent, I stopped my blubbering and opened my eyes. All I could see was the stunning view of nature all around me—the Pacific Ocean rushing to the beach, the surfers out waiting for their break, dolphins playing through the waves, and pelicans flying south.

I took a deep breath and thought to myself. *God…I can't threaten You like I did as a child. I've experienced too much of You. Despite my rantings, I do know Your love, Your grace, Your mercy, Your provision, and Your kindness. I know You have protected* me against even worse crimes, and I know You have also saved me—many times. I know too much to deny You! But I'm in a horrible mess, and I have nothing left. I need a refuge from all the attacks. I have nothing with which to offer or negotiate with You. I can't even threaten to leave You because I never want to be without You. I'd die without You. I can't accuse You of not knowing what You're doing because as I look upon this view, I know You created it all, and You created, well, everything! I have nowhere to go, and I have nothing else left…

In a final surrender, I said, *"You've allowed everything I worked for, and everyone and everything I valued to be taken away. All I have left is this house. If You want this house too, You can have it! If You want me on the streets, then so be it. I don't want to fight You anymore. It's all Yours! Everything! All that I am—my whole life and everything in it—is Yours."*

I waited, but I didn't feel anything shift. I sighed with resignation and fell back into my patio chair, staring at the ocean.

About ten minutes later, I received an unexpected call from my dear friend, Dan, who encouraged me with words of wisdom. As soon as I finished that conversation, my realtor called, but this time she told me the buyer had come up in price and was willing to meet my requirements.

Within six weeks, I had sold my house, and almost everything inside it; anything else of value was packed away in storage.

With a U-Haul in tow and only two dogs now, (Noah and Harley), Joshua and I headed north. We were going to be with my family during my father's horrific divorce and left our lives in America behind.

Sorrowfully, my relationship with Michael had spiraled down to its lowest depths after he returned from his trip. He lived with me, but things had gotten so bad, I had no other option than to ask him to leave. This was one of the most difficult decisions I have ever made, and I cried day and night for weeks afterwards.

My heart was heavy and broken all at the same time. How my beloved son and I could have drifted so far apart, I did not know. Nonetheless, it was time he learned to stand on his own, and stop blaming me for his consequences.

It was also time I took care of my father now after all he had done for me.

Leah cleared her throat to find her voice. "Wow…well, I can honestly say you were *not* being melodramatic when you warned me about this part of your story." She let out a deep breath. "I'm beginning to understand; everything you have told me validates the lessons you've been trying to teach me. Were it not for the magnitude of your battles, you would never understand the magnitude of your blessings."

14 HAPPILY EVER AFTER

The greatest good you can do for another is not just to share your riches, but to reveal to him his own.

—Benjamin Disraeli

Peaceful Easy Feeling

Joshua and I love road trips. We travel well together, and someday we'd like to buy a large RV and vacation around the country. Although the trip to see my father wasn't such a holiday, and we didn't have an RV, we still made it fun.

In many ways, I was relieved to be leaving the city. I didn't know how long I'd be away, but I needed to have the flexibility and the freedom to stay, if necessary. We would be arriving just before my father's divorce trial, and my only goal was to help stabilize my father's health conditions and get him settled back into his fun routine with his friends.

My family had a vacation home in a lovely golf and marina resort community near the U.S./Canada border in Washington State. With my NEXUS pass, I was able to quickly cross the border when I needed to be with my family in Vancouver and just as quickly cross the border again back to the U.S., where I stayed in our family residence. This was much easier and less costly than establishing myself back in Canada for the time I was there. When I wasn't in Vancouver, I was able to have a lot of quiet time at home alone.

This arrangement couldn't have been more perfect.

In my eyes, this *sojourn* would only be for a very short time. Consequently, I didn't feel the need to announce I was "moving" (which felt permanent), nor did I make a big deal out of it. To that end, I didn't say goodbye to Michael either. Since we weren't on speaking terms anyway, I thought it best to have some distance between us and let him work things out on his own. I had talked to my friends before I left, and they agreed to keep an eye on him and support him in my absence.

Joshua only came with me to ensure my safety and make sure I was established and safe when we arrived. But he wouldn't be able to stay long because of his work commitments.

The impending trial was postponed (again) at the last minute—this time with another round of absurd allegations and threats, all made intending to inflict further pain and suffering on my family. No matter how illegitimate each additional allegation was, we were forced to spend more money on legal fees, court fees, and forensics to respond to them. This pattern was repeated several times, but my family stood strong and grew closer in spite of it all.

Christmas that year came quickly. It was the first time Michael and I were not together for the holidays, and there was an emptiness in my heart I could not describe. Joshua's youngest child was grown and finally able to get away, moving to another state, and that's where Joshua went for the holidays. Even though I was missing Michael terribly that Christmas, I was extremely thankful for the simplicity of that holiday.

Floor-to-ceiling windows and sliding glass doors lined the back of our home, with an unrestricted view of the tenth fairway adjoining our backyard. It had just begun to snow that particular morning, and a family of deer had come to graze on the berry bushes lining the side of our house. I was bundled in a blanket, sipping on a hot cup of tea, and my doggies were snuggled beside me. The sound of the crackling fire popped in the background, and as I took in the beauty all around me, I fell back into the sofa with a huge sigh.

Thank You, God.

I decided then to begin anew and make choices that would honor my life. I would not just blindly follow traditions or old habits. The degree to which I would live a purposeful, contributory life would be the degree to which I would choose those with whom I wanted to be in relationship. As Sylvia Boorstein once said, "Ultimately… it's not the stories that determine our choices, but the stories we continue to choose."

Dedicated

Shortly after Christmas, a wonderful opportunity arose for me to go to Israel on a very unique mission trip—something I had wanted to do for decades. We ministered to orphans, school children, and holocaust survivors, and we cleaned and refurbished bomb shelters.

To be in the Holy Land, walking where Jesus, the prophets, and the apostles had walked was overwhelming to me. I came to know myself better than I had in many years and felt closer to God than ever before.

On the plane ride home, I looked out over the Mediterranean Sea and gazed at the vivid expanse of blue. Sunlight played on the water's surface, and I felt God was there in everything I could see.

As I reflected on my life, I thought of my relationship with Joshua. We had now been together for nearly seven years—except for our "sabbaticals." Everything was behind us now, and we had no other distractions; we were finally at a place where we could really have clear-minded conversations about our future.

For me to even consider marriage again was an act of faith of exponential proportions. I had become pessimistic over the years, after all my experiences with men. Friendships were fine, but a relationship, let alone a marriage, was not a step to which I had been sincerely open. However, if I were to trust my life with another man again, there was no one else but Joshua.

With an open heart, I asked for God to show me what He wanted me to know. I promised that whatever He would tell me, I would do.

Just then, I felt the familiar warmth of the Holy Spirit infuse me, and I heard a soft voice say, *Joshua has never been baptized*. I repeated these words to myself, and I felt a sudden welling up of love and compassion for the man who had stayed by me through so many difficult years. The peace of God's love settled in my heart, and I knew in my core that not only was Joshua the one for me, it was soon time to get married.

Joshua greeted me when I landed, and when I saw him, I noticed something different about him. He was still the same, but something was new. During our months apart, he had taken the opportunity to dive deeper into his relationship with God also, and when I saw Joshua at the airport, I could see light all around him. He seemed to glow with strength, peace, love, and joy.

He took my breath away.

Serendipitously, the church I was attending when I moved to Washington was having a special baptism service the Sunday after I returned from my mission trip. Joshua was baptized that same Sunday—only three days after I returned home. He had accepted Jesus into his life before, but this time, he wholly dedicated his life to Him. It wouldn't be an exaggeration to say this was one of the most powerful and beautiful experiences we have ever shared together.

Thankfully, because of the conveniences of the Internet, Joshua was able to spend long periods with me in the Pacific Northwest, working from our family home. On weekends, he'd join my family and me at gatherings, and we all enjoyed many wonderful times together.

Then, through an uncanny set of circumstances, a miracle happened that set the stage for a settlement in my father's divorce proceedings, and after several hours of negotiations (and at a great financial cost to my family), the divorce was finalized.

It was, at long last, a season of rest, healing, and celebration. Luke and Elizabeth celebrated their twenty-fifth wedding anniversary, and my godparents celebrated their fiftieth wedding anniversary. My relationship with Joshua's children grew stronger and deepened. Yes, there were many celebrations that year. We had peace, and we had each other.

Mom! I'm Home!

And then there was my greatest joy of all—my prodigal left his old ways and came back to me.

Michael, who had been forced to find his own way in my absence, did just that. He was now surrounded by healthy new friendships and solid mentors. He had returned to his purpose and was growing stronger and deeper in his faith.

Admittedly, it was challenging to trust the "new" Michael at first, but he consistently proved himself to me. I had been away almost a year when a situation came up that I needed to address with him. I went into the discussion prepared for a battle, but Michael did not behave as I had expected. He responded kindly, responsibly, and maturely. He apologized for the mix-up and offered to rectify things on his own, and at his cost. I was shocked!

A few other instances came up after that as well, and each time Michael responded courteously and thoughtfully.

Just as Joshua had to develop his relationship with God, Michael, too, had to establish his own personal relationship with Him. And because of his honest seeking, Michael had now changed, also. Where he had once oozed brazenness, audacity, and haughtiness, he now exuded groundedness, maturity, and most noticeably of all, humbleness of heart. His countenance was not the same as it had been, and it was impossible not to see and feel his transformation.

Our relationship fell back into step, and now he even seeks my input and counsel on a variety of things. He stood as one of Joshua's groomsmen at our wedding. Michael married a wonderful young lady named Nava, the love of his life. They come over regularly, and together with Joshua's children and their families, we are at long last, *a family*.

Yes, my son has finally come *home*.

Oh, Happy Day!

"*Now that's what I've been waiting to hear!*" Leah cheered as she slapped her hand over her thigh. "Manna, I'm so happy for you! There's nothing, absolutely nothing like a mother's love for her child, especially her only child. You must have been beside yourself! You got your son back!" Leah smiled ear to ear, leaning into her pillow. "Did you stay in Washington much longer?"

"No, unfortunately. Once my father's health and family's life was back to normal, it was time to return to re-establish myself. It was a difficult and sad conversation to have with my family, telling them it was time to move back home. They were happy about our upcoming wedding but sad that I had to leave again. We had always been very close, but during this time, the depth of our relationship grew deeper still. I loved spending time with my family and our family friends, going to my nieces' sporting games, having dinners together, and just hanging out.

"I was also grateful to be home when my beloved Auntie Georgiana, my father's sister, passed away. Spending time with her that past year had been a gift. We reminisced over Luke's and my childhood and how she and Uncle William took care of us when we moved back to be with our father. In our last dinner together, only a week before she passed, she looped her arms into mine as I escorted her back to their car and said, 'Manna, you're all grown up now. I once held your arms to help you walk, and now you're looking after me!' She was a treasure to our family, and while we miss her terribly, we know heaven gained another angel with her passing.

"My time in the Pacific Northwest was wonderful. It was a time of rest, rejuvenation, restoration, renewal, and definitely peace, love, and joy. Now once again, with U-Hauls in tow, we headed back to begin again."

"So, I'm still waiting for the juicy details! How did Joshua propose, and when did you get married?" Leah persisted.

I chuckled. "I'm sorry. Yes—the details. On Christmas morning (my second Christmas there), Joshua surprised me with breakfast in bed. The dogs jumped up too, and on Harley's collar was the sign 'Mommy, will you please marry Daddy?' And on Noah's collar was the sign, 'Say *yes*!' together with the ring attached to a ribbon."

"Yup! I sure like your Joshua!" Leah shouted.

"There was no hesitation on my part this time, and after we finished breakfast, we spent the morning on a long walk along the water's edge by the marina. It was as sweet as any girl could dream it would be.

"As we discussed our wedding plans, I admitted I was too embarrassed to ask my father to walk me down the aisle *again*, and since this wasn't the first (or second) wedding for either one of us, I asked if we could keep things simple—a small ceremony with family, and possibly a larger (yet still simple) reception with friends later."

"What did Joshua think about that?" Leah asked.

"He didn't like that much."

"Why? What did he say?" Leah asked.

"He surprised me and said, 'I thought you said there was no condemnation in Christ? You shouldn't feel ashamed of anything. As far as I'm concerned, this is our first and *only* wedding because this is the first time I've ever been in love. You are my bride. You are pure, beautiful, and perfect. I want you to wear white, and I want to honor you with a true ceremony before God, our family, and our friends. You're not hiding behind a small ceremony. Someone like you should never be hidden. You were never meant to hide or to be kept under a basket. You're meant to shine.'"

Leah nodded. "What a man!" She liked saying that about Joshua.

"And so, with the loving care, support, and dedication of many wonderful friends helping me, we were married a few months later. I wore white. I was walked down the aisle by my father. My family was with us, and both Joshua's children and Michael were a part of the wedding party. We shared our vows under a glorious oak tree and then danced and sang with a Gospel choir who completed our ceremony with one of my favorite songs, 'Oh, Happy Day!' followed by many other wonderful favorites. We enjoyed an elegant afternoon reception afterwards and concluded our private celebration with an intimate family dinner that we will remember for the rest of our lives."

"A happy day *and a happily ever after!*" Leah cheered while clapping her hands.

"Yes, Leah. A happy day, *and at long last,* a Happily Ever After."

The Best Time of My Life

Leah became very quiet as she reflected upon my life story. She turned to look out that familiar window at the edge of her bed, deep in thought. After a little while, she cleared her throat to find her voice. "I don't know what to say, Manna."

I smiled and took her hand in both of mine.

She let out a long breath. "Through you, I feel like I've lived the lives of ten warriors in this past month or so!"

"I'm sorry, Leah. I've always been concerned it would all be too much for you," I said apologetically.

"Are you kidding me? It's been the best time of my life!" she assured me. "And because of you, I haven't wasted what time I had left with the misery of my own thoughts, frustrations, lost dreams, and regrets. Instead, I feel like I finally have a peace about everything." She took a moment. "And I'm amazed that I'm not feeling resentful or bitter at the offenses in my life anymore. The more we talked, the more I *knew*. The more I knew, the more I understood. The more I understood, the more I forgave. And the more I forgave, the more peace and joy I had."

I kissed the back of her hand.

"So, you see, it's not all about you, kid!" She winked. "Just wish I had met you earlier. I think we would have been great friends. I would have stood by you—like you have stood by me, sacrificing so much of your time to a stranger. You could have been doing a thousand more interesting things, I'm sure! But you chose to come faithfully to see me. You served and ministered to me more than I deserved…I don't know how to thank you." She started to cry.

"Leah, you are a treasure to me! You've got this reversed. *I'm* the one that should be thanking *you!* Thank you for caring about me and my loved ones. Thank you for being my cheerleader. I've enjoyed every second I've had with you. Because of you, my life is so much richer and beautiful," I responded, with tears now rolling down my face.

"You're one in a million, dear." Then, not wanting to be too vulnerable, Leah tried to change the topic. "Ummm, now that I've heard *everything* about your life, I can honestly say *I've heard it all!*" She laughed till she coughed a little. "Get it? *Heard it all?*"

"Yes, Leah," I obliged. "Yes, I get it."

"But in all seriousness, your life is *most unusual*, so extraordinary that it's kind of…weird! No offense! Hearing your story was like going to see ten back-to-back 3D action movies!"

We both chuckled.

"My life has been full, but I don't know if it was *that* exciting."

"You can't be serious!" Leah challenged. "Through you, I feel like I lived the life of a Chinese princess, a POW, the rich and famous, *Survivor*, *The Land of the Lost*, and even met *Dumb and Dumber*!" She paused to sip her tea, hiding the slightest cough. "I also had a sneak peek into the house of horrors—which I didn't mind only having a 'sneak peek' of, by the way. But the most amazing part is that I also really got to see *Heaven Is For Real*!"

"Did you see that movie?" I asked, surprised.

"Silly girl, I meant it literally!" She tapped the back of my hand. "Through your life, I know *heaven is for real!* And ironically, I did also just see the movie. Melody brought me her iPad last night, and I watched it on that. Quite a compelling story, but not as riveting as yours, in my humble opinion! Maybe your life story will be in a movie one day, too!"

"Now, that would be weird!"

At that moment, Melody came in to bring Leah her dinner tray.

"Speak of the devil," Leah said slyly.

Melody cocked her head, confused.

"Leah was just saying that you were kind enough to loan her your iPad so she could watch some good movies," I said while squeezing Leah's hand, reminding her to be nice.

Leah winked at me and then looked at Melody. "What kind of poisonous fare is for dinner tonight, little one?"

I shook my head, and so did Melody as she left the room.

"Okay, Leah, I'm going to go now, but I'll be back the day after tomorrow. Be good!" I leaned over and gave her a kiss on the forehead. She was cool to the touch, and an unsettling feeling came over me.

"Or maybe tomorrow, if you're lucky!" she bantered under her breath.

As I started to pull away, I felt her frail hand tug on mine. "Wait!" Leah looked serious. "I want you to know something…"

I sat back down.

"Every story, every moment—it was all worth it. Do you know what I'm trying to say?" Leah asked with intention.

I shook my head, unsure of the point she was trying to make.

"Everything that happened *to* you happened *for* you. And without all those lessons, nothing could happen *through* you for our lost world, desperately needing to hear your story. Remember this."

I smiled. "Thank you, Leah. I'll remember."

We held each other's hands for a long time. I wondered, *Now that I have finished telling my story, what will be next?*

I also felt Leah's concern about this, but neither one of us said anything out loud. Instead, we smiled awkwardly, and even giggled a few times, afraid to let go. Then we spent the next few minutes just looking at one another, saying more with unspoken words. It felt too much like my last few moments with my PoPo before she was given the morphine. An uneasiness fell upon me again, but I shook it off.

When the moment had passed, true to Leah's nature, she piped up, "Now, you'd better get going! My dinner's gettin' cold."

I smiled. "See you day after tomorrow, then."

She held my hand tightly and looked me squarely in the eyes. "Please come tomorrow."

The clarity in her eyes was inescapable, and I couldn't help but hold my breath. Finally, I nodded after swallowing hard. "Okay, after my morning appointments." Then, trying to lift her spirits up, I did my best Eastern European impression. *"I'll be back."*

"Good. What will we talk about, now that we're all caught up?" she asked, as I pushed back my chair and gathered my things.

"Oh, don't you worry there, Miss Leah. I have another surprise or two for you. Plus, you owe me a few stories, like the *times* you got arrested!" This time, it was I who raised my eyebrows.

I smiled and gave her feet a tender squeeze before leaving.

Just then, Leah's family began to filter back into the room, and I was relieved she wouldn't be alone.

As I greeted them with nods and an understanding smile, I caught Peter's eye. His face was contorted in pain and confusion, and as I passed by him on my way out of the door, I could feel the palpable energy of his anger and despair.

Room 316

My cell phone rang at 11:00 a.m. the next morning. I was in the middle of a meeting, but when I saw it was the hospital, I excused myself and took the call. It was Melody.

"Manna," she said, "I think you should come now."

My heart was in my throat, and I fought back the immediate tears. "I'll be there in twenty minutes," I told her.

Thankfully, my client was very understanding, and within moments I was out the door and driving much too quickly on the highway. I bolted through the familiar hospital entry, forcing the doors open with my hands as they opened unusually slowly that day. I pressed the elevator button a few times, but both elevators seemed to stop at every floor on their way down to me. I turned to take the stairs, and as I leapt up every other step, the echoing of my shoes and the sound of my heart drummed in my ears.

No... not yet, Leah... not yet...

I don't normally become so attached to my hospice clients. I loved them in terms of loving their souls, but I didn't generally *love them* like family as I had come to love Leah.

Dear God... if it is time, fill her with Your peace. Let her know You're with her.

I opened the large metal door and found my way into the correct corridor and past the doors to our familiar courtyard. Before entering her room, I stopped to catch my breath and to brace myself for whatever was about to happen.

The room was lit only by the sun's rays streaming through the window. A new set of IV bags had been brought to the side of her bed, and tubes ran to her frail, thin arms. She hadn't had an IV for weeks, so I knew this wasn't a good sign.

Melody stood beside her, adjusting the IV tube. She turned, and as soon as she saw me, she shook her head. "She had a bad night last night; difficulty breathing and...well, she was in pain. She's been refusing morphine all this time, but we had to start it. She insisted we didn't give her much until you arrived. Her next dosage time is coming soon." She looked down at Leah and then back at me. "I'm glad you're here. I called Thomas, and he said he'd call the rest of the family. Hopefully, they'll be here soon, too."

I put down my purse and stood next to her, holding one of her hands. She opened her eyes and blinked a few times as if to force herself awake. "Aahh, I knew it was you. I know your hands. I know your touch." She smiled.

The thin and faraway sound of her voice brought tears to my eyes. I pulled up my chair to the side of the bed and sat down. "You're a monkey, Leah," I said, trying to bring some levity to the situation. "I told you to be good. But now I come back to see all *this*!" I motioned my head toward the machine and the tubes.

She stretched her other arm out from under the covers and placed her bony hand on top of mine. The skin stretched across her thin frame looked different. Yes, the end was near.

"What's happening, Leah? Can you tell me what you've seen?" I asked, *knowing something* had transpired since I had last seen her.

"You *are* a bright cookie, aren't you?" she said weakly. "Well, I had a visitor last night."

"You did?" I asked lightheartedly. "Was it Thomas? Or one of your children?"

She snickered. "Nope! Try again."

"A neighbor?" I asked softly. "Who came to see you last night?"

She slowly turned her head toward me and opened her eyes. "You won't believe it..." she giggled. "It was *your* angel!" she said joyfully in a high-pitched, sing-songy tone.

What? What is she talking about?

I wondered how much the morphine was affecting her. "Leah, what do you mean, *my* angel?"

She smiled and exhaled, closing her eyes again. "Silly girl. You know…the one in the elevator with you."

Oh, my goodness…

"Oh…*that* angel!" I caught my breath. "Umm, Leah…tell me more. What did the angel say?"

"He told me everything you said, but he also told me something else," she said mysteriously.

I held my breath. *Is this really happening? How do I know she's telling the truth and not hallucinating?*

"What's that, Leah? Tell me what the angel said," I asked, almost whispering so as not to excite her.

"He said you were very sweet and a very good little girl," she answered slowly as if she was dreaming.

Then she stopped talking and seemed to drift back to some sort of reverie. The suspense was killing me, but I dared not rush her. I wanted to give her time to remember so she could tell me everything that the angel had said to her. I waited patiently in silence.

Finally, she started again.

"He said your dress was very pretty on you." She said each word slowly as if she wanted to repeat everything word for word back to me.

She has no way of knowing what I wore! I have the photo from that day, our last photo before "going to the park," so depending on what she says, I will know if she's telling me the truth, or if it's the morphine talking.

"Did he tell you what I was wearing?" I asked, sitting at the edge of my seat.

She smiled, nodded, and slowly said, "Yes. He said it was a pretty pink dress with a rounded collar, and you had a very cute two-sided little red purse with you, too."

I gasped. *That was exactly what I was wearing!*

Thank You, God! Thank You for making Yourself known to Leah. Thank You for sending the same angel You used to usher me into my journey, to usher Leah into hers. Oh, my goodness…I can't believe this is really happening!

"Yes, little one," Leah continued. "It's all real…and it is really happening. But you have to know, it's even more beautiful than you told me—much more beautiful."

She couldn't have known what I was thinking, and yet she had addressed my unspoken thoughts.

The palpable warmth of Holy Spirit was present. It was time.

"*No…*" I whispered, unable to believe the time had come to say goodbye to a woman who had become so dear to me.

Leah lay on the bed, unmoving. Her eyes closed, and her breathing was sporadic, sometimes missing a breath or two.

Just then, Leah opened her eyes and slowly turned towards me. "Thank you," she said, her voice struggling. "I would have died months ago if it hadn't been for you—" She started to cough.

"It's okay, Leah. You don't need to talk. I'm here, and your family is on their way," I said tearfully.

"Don't get sappy on me now. This isn't goodbye."

I nodded tearfully.

Then she suddenly gripped my hand with unexpected strength. "Now, before I go to 'la-la land,' I need you to promise me something."

I leaned forward. "Of course, Leah. Anything."

"Please talk to Peter. He's so angry and confused. He needs to know your story, and he needs to see all of this!" She feebly waved one of her arms around in a circle. "He'll get such a kick out of this!"

"Well, Leah...I don't know if he'll be interested, and besides—"

"You said you promise," she said firmly while giving me a wobbly, but still effective, all-knowing stare.

"Darn it, Leah! How is it you always get your way?" I shook my head. "Well, I'll try, but I can't guarantee he's going to be interested. Plus, he's young and very busy."

"Then you'd better get started right away. Besides, the more often you tell your story, the easier it'll be to write your memoir," she said. Then she added very clearly and matter-of-factly, "Don't forget to put me in there."

I smiled. "Leah, you will be the star."

She smiled. "I know I'll see you again," she said with her voice trailing. "In the meantime, I'll give my best regards to everyone up there for you."

I was speechless...words would not come.

At that moment, Thomas walked in the door, followed shortly by his children, their faces all solemn and tear-stained.

Leah heard the shuffling, turned to see her beloved family, and smiled. I stood up and went to Thomas, filling him in on Leah's condition. He asked me to sit back down as he pulled up another chair beside his beloved.

Leah turned to look me in the eyes, and I could see the intention in them. "I don't know what I'd do if it weren't for you." Her voice was small. "You showed me it was possible...that Love was real. I believe, now. I believe."

She turned to her husband and held his hand. I stepped back so her family could be close to her. Leah and Thomas shared their beautiful love for each other through their eyes as their children looked on. Not a word was spoken. It would have only diminished the sacredness of that moment.

My lips trembled as I fought to stay strong for the family. Leah turned back to look at me one more time, reaching for my hand. I walked back towards the bed and wove my fingers into hers.

Melody came in to check on things and took Leah's vitals. She nodded slightly, admitting to herself and to us what was happening. "It won't be long now," she whispered.

Within a few minutes, Leah's grip slowly loosened, and a smile began to spread across her face. She gasped a little, and something passed her lips that sounded like a giggle.

And with that hint of laughter in her voice, she was gone. Her children gathered around her and began to cry. With tears running down my own cheeks now, I glanced up at Peter. Profound grief was etched into his face. Despite the gracefulness and the ease of his mother's passing, he was still as surly as he had been the night before.

Thomas grabbed Leah's thin bony hands and kissed them over and over again as he repeated, "I love you, I love you, I love you. I thank you, I thank you, I thank you…"

His adoration took my breath away. *Such love…*

Then, as I looked upon Leah again, her last request of me replayed in my mind. *How in the world am I going to this?*

Peter stepped away from his mother's bed and left the room.

As if I was being guided by something larger than myself, I grabbed my things and headed out after him. He was down the hall, sitting in one of the waiting room chairs, his head in his hands. I approached him cautiously, suddenly unsure if I had done the right thing by following him. I was about to change my mind and leave when he looked up, and his red, swollen eyes met mine.

"Thank you very much for everything you did for my mother—for all of us," he said. "She told me you gave her peace. That, after a lifetime of having struggled, it was *you* that showed her how to be free." He sniffled and wiped his eyes, sitting up. "How?" he asked. "How did you do it? I…I would like…I think I need…"

I smiled.

"Peter," I began, "There's a beautiful courtyard just down the hall…do you have time for a little visit over coffee?"

She was fierce, she was strong. She wasn't simple. She was crazy and sometimes barely slept. She always had something to say, she had flaws and that was okay. And when she was down, she got right back up. She was a beast in her own way, but one idea describes her best; she was unstoppable and she took anything she wanted with a smile.

—R. M. Drake

The dress I wore on that fateful "day in the park."

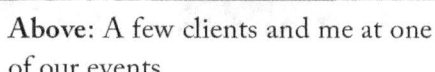

Above: A few clients and me at one of our events.

Above: My first business headshot after my divorce from Barry was finalized.

Right: Michael and me in Hawaii.

Above: Michael and me when I finally walked at the commencement ceremonies for my master's degree.

Right: PoPo after our last lunch together.

"The Big Event"

My father flew down to attend my Big Event. Below is us the week before, and on the left is us on the Red Carpet at the event.

Above: Me on the Red Carpet at my Big Event.

Right: Me with some of the attendees.

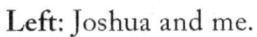

Left: Joshua and me.

Below: Sadie, Noah, Harley, Duke and Dakota.

Above: The view of the Pacific Ocean from my home.

Right: Michael and Joshua on a fishing trip to celebrate Michael's birthday.

Left: Michael and me when I picked him up from his mission's trip in South Africa.

Below: My father and me in Washington state after I moved there to be with him.

Above: My Godfather's 50th wedding anniversary celebration dinner with my father and Uncle Francis.

Happily Ever After

15 THE RACE SET BEFORE US

> Don't you realize that in a race, everyone runs, but only one person gets the prize? So run to win! All athletes are disciplined in their training. They do it to win a prize that will fade away, but we do it for an eternal prize. So, I run with purpose in every step. I am not just shadowboxing. I discipline my body like an athlete, training it to do what it should. Otherwise, I fear that after preaching to others I myself might be disqualified.
>
> 1 Corinthians 9:24-27 NLT

American writer Joseph Campbell famously codified "the hero's journey," which humans have captured in myths, legends, and stories for millennia. The final stage of this journey is The Return, in which the hero comes back from his adventures bringing the "elixir" of transformation, change, wisdom, and success to share with others.

The first edition of this book was my way of offering the "elixir" of my own story to a broader audience. I have been so blessed to hear readers tell me how my story reassured them, how they knew they were not alone in facing their hardships and adversities, and how it gave them fresh hope, courage, and tenacity to carry on in their own journeys.

Yet while "happily ever after" was a wonderful way to end the book then, as I mentioned in "A Message from the Author" at the beginning of this book, it was only the beginning of another set of adventures. Unlike the fairy tales we grew up with, in real life, "happily ever after" does not mean we are forever free from life's problems. In the last eight years since my autobiography was released, I have come to understand that living happily is not so much an outcome as it is a *lifestyle*—one that we choose both in losses and victories, betrayals and reconciliations, pain and delight, and endings and new beginnings. The real evidence of being happy and free is that we are not only stronger as challenges continue, but that we thrive regardless of them. After all, we humans were designed to overcome challenges. We've just become soft and accustomed to convenience.

The Last Eight Years

With that, let me share what I have been up to in the last eight years.

First, my marriage with Joshua has been truly blessed and both our family and our "furmily" has grown in every sense of the word. I am now a grandmother of *seven* precious grandchildren! My beloved son Michael and his bride Nava now have two beautiful children. Joshua's three kids are also married to wonderful spouses, and I have five grandchildren between them. My "furmily" has grown as well with the addition of two new rescue dogs.

Second, I have continued to stay productive with multiple creative projects, businesses, and endeavors. I wrote a series of four children's books called *Sophie and Solo's Fun Adventures*™, and several other leadership books and journals. I was asked to speak for several TEDx events, but because of the 2020 pandemic, I was only able to speak at two of them. Most recently, I redesigned my career path to focus on unique and specialized group trainings, and I started a second business with a dear friend where we cultivate, coach, and prepare both adult leaders for the big stage (such as TEDx Talks and others) and youths into their leadership platforms. Plus, I created my own nonprofit, *HuMannaTea For All*™, with unique initiatives to help eradicate child sex trafficking.

The blessings continued with the gifts of new and treasured friendships, deeper relationships with existing friends, and other personal miracles and dreams come true.

I have weathered a few big losses as well. My beloved father passed away in 2020, but due to the pandemic, I could not be with him. That was very painful. I also lost some friends to illnesses and said goodbye to the last two of my big pack of cherished furmily members—my Golden Retriever and my Bernese Mountain Dog, Noah and Harley.

Then in 2018—because thriving as an overcomer means continuing to overcome—I decided to take on a Mount Everest-level challenge, one that would stretch and push me emotionally, mentally, physically, and spiritually in ways I never imagined. As I briefly explained in "A Message from the Author," I went back to graduate school for my Doctorate in Education in Leadership for Change. It was certainly an adjustment going back into academia after a gap of more than twenty years. Not only did I have to create a whole new mindset to go back to grad school, but the educational processes have also changed. Classes were predominantly online and long gone were the microfiches and the quiet and intimidating ancient libraries with row after row of books. I no longer borrowed those library books and lugged them home to sit for days writing by hand all the excerpts and citations I needed for my classes, papers, and dissertation. Thank goodness! All in all, it was a grand adventure indeed, and one that gave me an opportunity to discover a new level of understanding of what it means to have the strength of heart, tenacity of character, and a vision greater than circumstances to be a trusted leader, especially in the storms.

It Chose Me

The most difficult and agonizing aspect of my graduate work lay in my chosen field of study: child sex trafficking. This research challenged me in so many ways and pushed me to my limits. With each book, article, and academic study I read, I was traumatized. Once you see something, you cannot unsee it. Once you know, you cannot pretend you don't know.

There was a time when I was so shocked by a particular sex trafficking case with an infant that I literally thought I was going to lose my mind. I needed the help of a specialized trauma therapist to help me work through the shock, heartbreak, rage, grief, and even the existential crisis I faced.

Many times, I found myself lying on the floor beside my desk, crying out to God, demanding explanations. I combed through scripture verses one after another, desperately trying to find answers, but no direct answer came. Then one day, in an uncanny set of circumstances, the Lord led me to something a wise and celebrated pulpit orator, J.M.L. Monsabré, once said: "If God would concede me His omnipotence for 24 hours, you would see how many changes I would make in the world. But if He gave me His wisdom too, I would leave things as they are." That humbled me deeply, and I fell on my knees, convicted of my ego and bitterness. Then, as if to ensure we didn't have to have another circuitous round of no-win argumentation from me, the Holy Spirit reminded me of Job 38. Yes, the chapter when God demands answers from Job:

> Then the LORD answered Job out of the whirlwind and said:
> "Who is this that darkens counsel by words without knowledge?
> Dress for action like a man; I will question you, and you make it known to me.
> Where were you when I laid the foundation of the earth?
> Tell me, if you have understanding.
> Who determined its measurements—surely you know!
> Or who stretched the line upon it?
> On what were its bases sunk, or who laid its cornerstone, when the morning stars sang together, and all the sons of God shouted for joy?"
>
> Job 38:1-7 NLT

The rest of the chapter continues in the same manner, with God asking question after question to remind Job of the powerful, exquisitely perfect, and intimately familiar way He runs everything in the universe—even the parts that are full of mystery, suffering, and evil. If you've never studied the chapter, I highly encourage you to do so!

If that isn't eating humble pie, I don't know what is. Instead of demanding God to answer my short-sighted questions, I asked God for His forgiveness and to just keep strengthening me.

And so, I persevered.

As time went on, whenever I was asked, "Why would you choose something like this?" at the risk of sounding trite, I can honestly say I didn't choose child sex trafficking—it chose me. There were a number of other research studies I wanted to conduct, but this topic was the one I could not stop thinking about—or escape from.

Sometimes, your calling isn't simply about what interests you, what you enjoy, or what you are passionate about. Sometimes your calling is defined by what you are willing to suffer for, what you are willing to pay the price for…and for me, it's the children.

And so, I kept having brave conversations with God, my dissertation committee, and anyone around me who would listen. Day after long day, I dug deep, and through tears, pursued this fight. There were times when the reality of this egregious and sickening industry was so dark, I didn't know if anything could be done to stop this insanity. But just when I didn't think anything was changing, I learned of others of who were also making great strides in fighting this heinous crime. I was encouraged. Soon, years passed, and in the fall of 2022, I completed my comprehensive research and graduated with EdD in Leadership for Change *for* the children, and on *behalf* of the children.

By God's grace, though the process was long and painful, the more I learned about the global crisis of child sex trafficking, with the United States arguably the epicenter of it, the more I became convinced that I could do more than telling my story to encourage others that they too can overcome. I wanted to take the hard-won "elixir" of my own struggle and triumph and use it in this war over the lives of women and children. It was important for me to not only be a part of the force that helps rescue and free those who were enslaved, but to educate and strengthen society so that, together, this evil is defeated, and our children don't have to take the long road back to recover their identity, dignity, integrity, and hope.

This undertaking taught me once again that when we do the hard thing once, we can do it again. We can build that muscle of courage and eventually do even harder things. As A.A. Milne said through his beloved Christopher Robin to Winnie the Pooh: "You are stronger than you seem, braver than you believe, and smarter than you think you are."

Mended with Gold

During this time, as I tried to find some answers regarding the atrocity of sex trafficking, I found myself inexorably drawn to a few women in the Bible. These women, young and old, also suffered loss, indentured servitude, sexual exploitation, bad marriages, divorces, demonic torment, barrenness, chronic illness, and social stigma—women like Hagar, Sarah, Leah, Rahab, Hannah, Abigail, Bathsheba, Gomer, the Shunammite woman, Mary Magdalene, the woman with the issue of blood, and the woman at the well, for example. We aren't told the details of their childhoods, but we do know that their lives were marked by great disappointments, wounding, brokenness, and trauma. Yet in each case, they became legends of hope, for they all played vital roles in the story of God. That which might have disqualified them only served to put on display how God saw them, chose them, and deemed them worthy no matter what they—or anyone else— pronounced against them.

Perhaps the one who captivated me most of these women was the one known as "the prostitute"— Gomer, who eventually became the wife of Hosea.

According to one Hebrew dictionary, the name Gomer actually means "whole," "complete," or "perfect."[1] That discovery was fascinating to me. While the world only saw her as a prostitute deemed contemptible by society as a scandalous outcast, her true identity was as a whole, complete, and even "perfect" person. Yet by the time Hosea married her, Gomer's life had been fractured and taken piece by piece by countless men.

Likewise, the damage done to our hearts, minds, and souls from our experiences, especially those who have been sex trafficked, can affect us in the same way, causing us to return to the familiar, no matter how ugly. On the inside, we too feel fractured and incomplete, and from the outside, people may deem us shameful and hopeless.

But what no one asks is, "What was the backstory?"

We aren't told this information for Hosea, or the other women in the Bible. Similarly, people may not know the whole story for you or me, either, just like they don't know the backstory of the young women we label as "prostitutes" today, many of whom were exploited or trafficked as children or youths. But there is a backstory for every one of us.

Women who have previous history with abuse, and I speak as one, may have an easier understanding as to why Gomer returned to a life in slavery. In addition to trauma bonding and sexual trauma bonding, we are unable to believe we are worth anything other than what is familiar, no matter how dark, abusive, or evil it is. And when this trauma is sustained, we lose hope. We not only stop fighting, we give into it. Hope is for "other people." Hopes and dreams belong to those who are clean, pure, and "chosen." Surviving the next day (or moment) only belong to the defiled, used, forgotten, and the "hopeless."

Until…

Until one day, something changes, and *stays* changed.

In the case of Gomer, her husband, Hosea, not only married her knowing her

---

[1] https://www.abarim-publications.com/Meaning/Gomer.html

lifestyle and despite the criticism of his community, he went back for her time and time again when she wandered back into slavery. It was through Hosea's consistent acts of sacrificial, unconditional love that she finally began to know her true worth.

The way God encountered Gomer, and encounters each one of us and weaves our individual stories into His greater story, reminds me of the Japanese art of *kintsugi*, which means "to mend with gold."

Broken porcelain vessels are repaired with gold, so that the cracks become even more distinct, yet incredibly beautiful. The philosophy of *kintsugi* is that instead of throwing out the broken pieces or crushing and reforming them into brand new items with no visible cracks, true and authentic restoration will preserve the unique history of each piece and show how the story of its brokenness has come to set it apart. After it has been restored, each piece of *kintsugi* is vastly more precious and valuable than it was before it was broken. In fact, you don't even see the broken sections anymore. You see the entire piece as a magnificent and stunning masterpiece. In the same way, when God encounters us and begins the process of restoring our lives and our stories, He takes the very places where we were most broken and mends them with the gold of His love, power, hope, authority, holiness, Spirit, and truth, so that we become testimonies of who He is and who we are in His eyes.

This is the hope I carry for myself, for you, and for every man, woman, and child living in this broken world. We may all be broken, and while we can't fix ourselves, we can be mended by the very One who created us in the first place. And as He mends us, He shows off His incredible power to redeem by taking even the most desperate, darkest of stories and filling them with gold and light. If we will let Him, God can weave the most amazing and breathtaking masterpieces out of pain, suffering, and loss. We can all become those priceless works of *kintsugi*, and can all carry the "elixir" of truth, hope, courage, and the power to transform to offer to others.

My Scars Are My Authority

As I studied the travesty of sex trafficking, I became more and more focused on trying to grasp its spiritual roots. It seemed clear that both the cause and the cure of child sex trafficking lie not at the level of law enforcement and social policies, but in the hearts and minds of human beings.

It is understandable that anyone forced to face the vastness of this horror might struggle to believe in the goodness or even the existence of a God who does not seem to be stopping it. In my case, remembering Monsabré's wisdom and Job 38's exhortation, I kept my heart humble and teachable. Although my simple mind had no immediate answers, I maintained that God was, in fact, the only hope for evil such as this. I determined to focus on God more than the problems, and to be in partnership with Him to see how He was at work bringing light and justice in the midst of such darkness—just as He brought me out of my own darkness.

As is the case with many who dedicate themselves to justice work, what I suffered as a child is precisely what sparked my passion to help those who are also being victimized. Though I was never sold or trafficked, I know firsthand how people who abuse children use psychological and sexual trauma to groom them into believing they are fit for nothing more than a life in slavery.

But like all worthy causes, choosing to make a difference has a price.

The reality of child sex trafficking is much more pervasive and devastating than I had ever known. I was no stranger to suffering, darkness, and evil, but even so, I was not prepared for what I eventually learned in this endeavor. No longer could I see the world with naïveté and simple-mindedness. I became aware—even hyper-aware—of everyone and every situation around me, especially in any situation regarding children. Instead of succumbing to the fear and size of the problem, I dug deep to the power, authority, and love of God. He was my strength, and I became more tenacious. I was also tireless, sometimes reading and writing for two days without sleep. I became fierce, vocal, and unapologetic in bringing empowered awareness to individuals, groups, organizations, communities, regions, and even national platforms. Some people thought I was being melodramatic, some didn't want to talk about this issue, and some just "canceled" me, accusing me of being a conspiracy theorist. But none of this mattered. I was unstoppable because I knew that children's lives were at stake, and people's approval was unnecessary and unimportant to the call.

It was then when the gold of *kintsugi* in my life became apparent. Everything I have endured, experienced, and overcome has given me the armor, knowledge, compassion, strength, and authority to now be a voice for the voiceless. And I became *Unapologetically for the Children*™.

I know without doubt that even the most severe and heart-wrenching of circumstances in my past were indispensable. They have given me a unique voice and message to contribute to humanity regarding social issues, cultural issues, and domestic and global justice issues. In the days ahead, I will be developing my dissertation into a resource that will help educate and empower people with tools and awareness to protect our children, join with other powerful organizations to one day abolish the trafficking trade, and rescue and restore victims to wholeness.

My dear friends, more than ever, it's time to use our gifts, talents, resources, anointing, skills, education, power, authority, influence, favor, and *our voice* to have brave conversations—with each other, and on behalf of those who need us to use our voices. You may not be called to fight child sex trafficking, but whatever injustices or issues you are meant to confront, do so with all your heart and with all you have. You will not regret it.

That said, in addition to your individual calling, would you still consider using your voice together with mine to help the children? Together, our individual voices can unite to not only be a choir, but a force for good so fierce we can break the neck of this unspeakably evil industry of child sex trafficking.

Edmund Burke once said, "The only thing necessary for the triumph of evil is that good men should do nothing...cowardice will suffice for its triumph. However, courage will suffice for its overthrow."

Together, our collective courage can be a great force to overthrow this evil.

Our Great Race to Run

The presence of evils such as child sex trafficking can seem so overwhelming and unassailable when you study them. And it can easily lead us to the common laments—Why is there so much evil in the world? Why do the perpetrators seem to get away with it? Where is God and His justice in these terrible situations?

As I shared in "A Message from the Author," the title of this second edition, *To Run with Horses*, is inspired by God's answer to Jeremiah when he asked Him these very questions:

> *So, Jeremiah, if you're worn out in this footrace with men,*
> *what makes you think you can race against horses?*
> *And if you can't keep your wits during times of calm,*
> *what's going to happen when troubles break loose like the Jordan in flood?*
>   Jeremiah 12:5 MSG

Jeremiah complained that not only were bad people getting way with the most nefarious of atrocities, they seemed to be thriving from it and living an easy, luxurious, and unencumbered life. Meanwhile, Jeremiah, who had committed to staying on the narrow path of righteousness, found himself constantly challenged, rebuffed, tested, and required to do hard things.

God's response to Jeremiah was essentially, *yes—that's how things work in this backward, upside-down broken world. The evil, selfish, cowardly things are easy, and the good, sacrificial, courageous things are hard. But in the long run, the broad way leads to darkness and destruction, and the narrow way to hope, new beginnings, and life eternal.*

Which do you want? And maybe even more importantly, who do you want to become? Do you want to be a run-of-the-mill, mediocre person who never takes risks, never achieves their potential, never fulfills their ultimate purpose and calling? Or do you want to be what you were actually created to be—a champion?

It's easier to blame others for our lack, but it only makes us weaker. It's easier to be a victim, but that's not our identity. It's easier to settle, but it's not a life of meaning. And it's easier to be small, dreamless, overly cautious, or neurotic, but that's not how champions are made, nor is that the destiny of champions.

Champions are meant to triumph, and this can only be achieved by facing challenges, obstacles, and enemies, and overcoming them. This is why God calls us to the narrow, difficult way.

Though God is not the author of the evil, pain, and suffering in the world, in His infinite wisdom He has allowed these realities to exist and is using them as the training ground for His champions to arise. This is why, once we commit to running the race He has laid out for us, we find that He will never let us settle for only small gains or a few victories. This race we are running is no mere footrace—it is a *great race*, a race that only the mighty can run. God has called us to stand against complacency and to be the light against destructive cultural trends. He has called us to compete as true champions, which is why we are required to live at a higher standard and endure far more rigorous training.

Do we really only want comfort and a small unbothered life? Or do we want to do great and mighty exploits for God? Will we retreat at the slightest discomfort, a slight from a stranger, an inconvenience, or many inconveniences? Will we retreat when our humanity—or the humanity of others, are challenged? Or will we stand in the face of opposition and engage in the fullness of our authority and anointing? While there may be times for a strategic retreat to gain a victory, retreating as a *lifestyle* is not acceptable. It's not how we are designed, and it's not our destiny.

As confronting as it was, when I finally understood that God had called me to have the heart of a champion, I was able to see that the many long seasons of hardship in my life were, in fact, gifts. As I noted in "A Message from the Author," a life of comfort and ease would have only lulled me into a path of least resistance, into entropy. I would never have been provoked to live the life of great promise and purpose that God had always planned for me. My hardships were truly the training ground that prepared and transformed me to run the race set before me, just as they are for you.

So, to quote Eugene Peterson's paraphrase, God challenges Jeremiah—as He does us—to consider, "If you are fatigued by this run-of-the-mill crowd of apathetic mediocrities, what will you do when the real race starts, the race with the swift and determined horses of excellence? What is it you really want, Jeremiah? Do you want to shuffle along with this crowd, or run with the horses?"[2]

A Final Charge

Ultimately, I believe that when we answer the call to the great race before us, the pain, suffering, hardship, and struggle will fade as the dominant theme and only be the backdrop of this fantastic journey. Like our great pioneer of faith, our Lord, Jesus Christ, we will persevere and endure through these things "for the joy set before us." Yes, there is a joy, a prize, a great reward, that lies ahead for us when we run our race with faithful intention, and it is nothing less than tasting the pure

---

[2] Eugene H. Peterson, *Run with the Horses*, (Intervarsity Press, 2009), 22.

pleasure of being *and* doing who God created us to be and to do. As Eric Liddell, the 1924 Olympic Gold Medal champion once said, "I believe God made me for a purpose…but he also made me fast…and when I run, I feel His pleasure." The great horse Secretariat knew this joy as well, and when he won the Belmont Stakes, "Secretariat was running at his own pleasure."[3]

There is nothing I could want more for you than to know the absolute thrill, pleasure, and joy of running *your* great race. And with that, I want to leave you with a final charge.

Please, never stop believing and never stop fighting until you break through your fears.

I lost so much precious time and missed so many opportunities because I lived with fear as a reality instead of with faith as my truth. I settled over and over *and over* again because I didn't think I deserved more than crumbs, or that I was worthy of having dreams. I was afraid of everything—and everyone. I was afraid of being rejected, abandoned, and hurt. My identity was wrapped up in all the wrong things and in the approval of all the wrong people.

Don't let this happen to you.

Fear is a liar.

Your *identity* is not in who you are with, what you have or haven't done, what you have or have not accomplished, what your title or position is in the marketplace, how much or how little is in your bank account, what size dress you wear, whether or not you are married or single, how old or young you are, or how attractive or desirable men or women think you are. And your identity, value, or worth certainly isn't determined by what others say about you, good or bad. Your identity is in who *God* says you are. He has a great plan for you, and no one and nothing can thwart it. Sure, it would be nice if everyone liked us and approved of us, but that isn't going to happen.

If it's true that a third of the people will like you, a third of the people will hate you, and a third of the people couldn't care less, then, why do we spend so much of our lives trying to please people who will *never* care what we do or like us? This is a guaranteed formula for failure. Live to manifest your truest expression, what you were created to do, and don't settle for anything less than the best for your life. In the words of Jeremiah, you weren't made for a mere footrace—you were made to run with the horses!

So never settle!

And don't sell yourself short, either. Don't sell yourself period. Your body, your integrity, your soul, your identity, your dreams, your dignity, your calling—none of it is for sale. Period. If I had only known this earlier in life… My world changed when I began to say "no" *and meant it.* "No" *is* a complete sentence, and it's more than enough when you know your value and worth. Just because you've experienced things you had no control over, and you've made a few (or a lot of)

---

[3] Paul Keith Davis, *Books of Destiny*, https://www.elijahlist.com/words/display_word/9081.

mistakes in your life, it doesn't mean you're less precious than anyone else, or that you've failed. Failure is not the same as having setbacks or making mistakes.

Confucius said, "Be not ashamed of mistakes and make them crimes." And George Bernard Shaw said, "A life spent making mistakes is not only more honorable but more useful than a life spent doing nothing." Mistakes and disappointments can be extraordinary portals to discovery. Our entire human history is founded on discoveries made from one mistake after another.

Failure, however, is completely different. Failure isn't a function of how many mistakes we make or how many times we fall. Failure is determined by our refusal to get up. Don't let anyone or anything stop you from getting up and trying again. Even if we can't change things for the better, we can allow the changes to make *us* better.

No, it's not easy to take a stand for yourself. It takes courage to say you deserve more, but almost everything is difficult before it becomes easy. Courage isn't action in the *absence* of fear, but action *in spite* of it. Andre Gide once said, "It's better to be hated for what you are than loved for what you are not."

And now, as we part ways for a time, may I offer you a little prayer?

> I pray that you will have "PoPos and GongGongs" who will call out the gifts in you because they "see" you, provide a safe sanctuary for you and teach you what love, and honor really means.
>
> I pray that you will have "Goomahs and Goozhengs" who will love you selflessly and wholly.
>
> I pray that you will have "MahMahs" who will be examples of courage, humility, and grace for you.
>
> I pray that you will have a "father" (or father figure) who will love you generously and sacrificially. That he is someone who will teach you the heart of a man for his children, and that no matter what is happening around you, your dignity can never be taken, and your aspirations can reach the highest of heights—that you can soar.
>
> I pray that you will have a "brother" (or friend) like Luke, whom you can "do life with" in good and bad times. Someone with whom you can share the power of trust, constancy, allegiance, and love, someone who is a living example of what a real-life hero truly is.
>
> I pray that you will have children (or spiritual children), who will show you the depth, breadth, width, and height of what love can be. I pray you will always be in awe and in wonder of the preciousness of life because of them. May this amazing gift awaken your spirit daily. May you enjoy and savor every moment

with your children, and may you never seek or believe that anything else is more of a treasure, for there is nothing on earth greater than this. May you, through this gift, learn to trust and rely on the power and authority of prayer. And as you lay your petitions at God's altar of love—daily, hourly, and even moment by moment—may you find peace, comfort, hope, and assurance that your children are in God's care and that they will always come back to you.

I pray that you will have a "Joshua" in your life. For those of you who have lost trust but still believe in love, may he be whole and complete on his own. May he lack nothing and need nothing from you but your trust, respect, and love. May he honor you, care for you, and be your armor-bearer, cheering you on and protecting you as you walk side by side in life together.

I pray that you will have family and true friends to love you, keep you accountable, fight alongside you (and for you), and to make you laugh. May they never waiver when you need them, and may you return the gift by being an even better friend to them.

I pray that you will have wise mentors and spiritual leaders to guide you, challenge you, inspire you, and keep you humble. May you have a teachable heart, a willing heart, and a soft heart to receive the precious gems they release to your care. And may you grow to surpass them in loving service by being a discerning steward of those gifts, nurturing them, and prospering in them so that you may have strong shoulders for others to stand one day.

I pray that you will have dogs (yes, I said *dogs*—plural ☺) around you to mirror your innocence, purity, trust, and childlike view on life. May you find comfort in their loyalty, devotion, and uncompromising love, and may this overflow of warmth spread to others. Dogs also teach us about contentment and living an uncomplicated life; about how to enjoy the moments you have sitting beside someone you love; how to be obedient, have manners, and learn the rules of the house; how to appreciate a simple meal; how it's good to have a treat now and then; how to chase something fun, play games, and be silly; how to go for long walks; how to stretch (i.e., downward dog ☺); how to have afternoon naps; and how to love others with everything that you are.

I pray that you will also have enemies to keep you strong, on point, sharp, and on top of your game—not too many, but enough to keep you brilliant. David could never have beaten Goliath if he didn't first know how to fight a lion and a bear. You, too, can face and defeat your giants when you are prepared and well trained.

And finally, and most importantly, I pray that you will know the meaning, the magnificence, the depth, and the joy of God's love for you. He is always with you, and because of that, you will always be in a place of grace. I pray that you will not only be open to this but that you will have a growing and blossoming relationship with Him. Only believe.

So, my friend, go now and live your fabulous, awesome, inspiring life! Cast fear aside, strap on wisdom, and let God lead you. Go run your race! You may not always understand the purpose of your circumstances but keep believing—keep pressing in. Don't put a period where God only intends for there to be a semicolon. It's not over. You may not have all the answers yet, but trust that in time, things will be much clearer.

As a Chinese proverb says, "A bird does not sing because it has an answer; it sings because it has a song." No matter where you are, no matter what circumstances you find yourself in, whether you are free or a slave, liberated or bound, caged or released, I hope you will always sing.

God's best and His utmost to you.

Unapologetically for the children™,

Manna Ko

RESOURCES

I may have had a tough break, but I have an awful lot to live for.
—Lou Gehrig

The following is a list of a few resources you may find helpful. This information is *not* a substitute for professional diagnosis and treatment. This list is provided without any warranty, expressed, or implied.*

Churches

- The River Family Church: http://www.theriverfamilychurchnc.org
- Jesus Culture San Diego: https://jesusculture.com/sandiego
- Third Day Churches: www.thirddaychurches.com

Abuse

- Rape, Abuse, Incest National Network: 800-656-HOPE www.rainn.org
- National Domestic Violence Hotline: 800-799-SAFE www.thehotline.org
- Child Abuse Hotline: 800-344-6000 www.childhelp.org
- Mercy Ministries: 615-831-6987 www.mercymultiplied.com (In USA, Canada, UK, and New Zealand)
- Safe Place (512) 267-SAFE www.safeplace.org
- Women's Health (800) 994-9662 www.womenshealth.gov

Child Sex Trafficking

- Call your local police department: 911
- HuMannaTea For All™ www.humannateaforall.org
- Missing Kids (National Center for Missing & Exploited Children): 800-THE-LOST (800-843-5678) www.ncmec.org
- Shared Hope International: 866-437-5433 www.sharedhope.org
- Saved In America: 760-348-8808 www.savedinamerica.org
- Association for the Recovery of Children www.recoveryofchildren.org
- Deliver Fund: 844-919-3863 www.deliverfund.org
- Save the Children: 800-728-3843 www.savethechildren.org
- Exodus Cry: 816-398-7490 www.exoduscry.com

Addiction

- L.A. Dream Center: 213-273-7000 www.dreamcenter.org
- The Center: 951-775-4000 www.thecenter4lifechange.com
- Alcoholics Anonymous: www.aa.org

- AL-Anon and Ala-Teen: 800-690-2666 www.al-anon.org
- Narcotics Anonymous: 800-479-0062 www.na.org
- Teen Challenge: 619-265-0337 www.teenchallengeusa.com

Crisis

- L.A. Dream Center: 213-273-7000 www.dreamcenter.org
- National Hope Line Network: 800-SUICIDE or 800-784-2433 www.hopeline.com
- National Center for Missing and Exploited Children: 800-843-5678 www.missingkids.com
- American Foundation for Suicide Prevention: 888-333-AFSP www.afsp.org
- National Suicide Prevention Lifeline: 800-273-8255 www.suicidepreventionlifeline.org

Counseling

- Turning Point Pregnancy Resource Center: 800-395-HELP (National Hotline) www.mmpregnancy.com
- Battered Women's Services: 619-234-3164 www.wrcsd.org
- National Institute of Marriage: 866-875-2915 www.nationalmarriage.com
- American Association of Christian Counselors: 800-526-8673 www.aacc.net
- Association of Christian Therapists: 502-632-3036 www.actheals.org

The contents of this list are for informational purposes only. Nothing contained in this list and/or in this book should be considered or used as a substitute for professional medical or mental health advice, diagnosis, or treatment. Never disregard medical advice from your doctor or other qualified health care provider(s) or delay seeking it because of something you have read on this list and/or in this book. We urge you to seek the advice of your physician or other qualified health professional(s) with any questions you may have regarding a medical, physical, emotional or mental, financial, or overall health and wellness condition. In case of an emergency, please call your doctor or 911 immediately. The information provided in this list and/or in this book is provided on an "as is" basis, without any warranty, expressed or implied. I receive no financial benefit whatsoever for offering these suggestions. Any usage of this book and/or of this list is voluntary and at your own risk.

This information is presented for use by the general public without a warranty or guarantee. Neither the author nor any of her companies (herein called "the Author") are liable to any user or anyone else for any decision made or action taken based on reliance upon the information contained in this list and/or in this book. The author does not make any express or implied warranties, representations, or endorsements of any kind whatsoever (including without limitation, warranties of title or non-infringement of third parties' rights, or any warranties of merchantability or fitness for a particular purpose) with regard to the service, or with respect to any information, product, service, merchandise, or other material provided on or through the service. The author does not warrant or guarantee the accuracy, completeness, correctness, timeliness, or usefulness of any information, services, or other material provided on or through this list and/or in this book. In no event shall the Author be liable for any damages whatsoever (including, without limitation, incidental and consequential damages, personal injury/wrongful death, lost profits, or damages resulting from the use or inability to use the information on this list and/or in this book, whether based on warranty, contract, tort, or any other legal theory, and whether the Author is advised of the possibility of such damages.)

SOURCES

Keller, Helen Adams. *Helen Keller's Journal: 1936-1937*. New York: Doubleday, Doran & Company, Inc. 1938, p. 60.

Boom, Corrie Ten. *The Hiding Place*. New York: Random House 1982, p. 15.

"Exclusive Interview With Maya Angelou on Her New Book, Mom & Me & Mom." Marianne Schnall. *The Huffington Post*. 10 May 2013. Web. http://www.huffingtonpost.com/marianne-schnall/maya-angelou-mothers-day-book_b_3202362.html

Congreve, William. *The Mourning Bride. Act i. Sc. 1.* 1697

"What is the Photograph of Frozen Water Crystals?" Dr. Masaru Emoto. Web. http://www.masaru-emoto.net/english/water-crystal.html.

Dickens, Charles. *A Tale of Two Cities*. New York: Dover Publications, Inc. 1999. All Rights reserved under Pan American and International Copyright Conventions.

Boorstein, Sylvia. *That's Funny, You Don't Look Buddhist*. New York: HarperCollins Publishers 1996. Reprinted courtesy of HarperCollins Publishers.

"Was This Maya Angelou's Final Interview?" Interview by Asha Bandele And Nicole Saunders. Ebony.com May 30, 2014. News & Views, Social Justice and Activism. https://www.ebony.com/was-this-maya-angelous-final-interview-987/#axzz3foEvON72

ABOUT THE AUTHOR

Manna Ko is a prolific writer and author, multiple TEDx Speaker, TEDx Speaker Trainer, International Speaker, Transformational Leader, Behavioral and Social Hope Scientist, Abolitionist, Founder and CEO of several companies, and Strategic Partner to many others.

Manna is affectionately known as Your Purpose Professor™ because she is passionate about helping people step into their calling, live extraordinary lives, prosper through chaos, be a forerunner with unseen opportunities, lead under pressure, and deliver results. Manna is called to teach, stretch, and equip others to live-out their gifts in a world hungry for authentic, honorable, and meaningful leadership and relationships.

Now with over thirty years of entrepreneurial experience, she has spoken to over 40,000 people in venues around the globe, shared the stage with other recognized leaders, worked with hundreds of different businesses and organizations, guided even more individuals seeking personal excellence, and has taught at numerous events, including a private writer's group in Oxford, England. She has worked with clients in over 10 countries, has contributed to numerous educational, disciplinary, and advisory boards, and is an Ordained Leader with Third Day Churches.

In the early 2000s, Manna went back to school and earned an MA in Psychology, a PhD in Philosophy, graduate certificates in many other health and wellness disciplines, and in 2022, she completed her EdD in *Leadership for Change* with her pioneering research on child sex trafficking in the United States. Manna has also achieved executive certifications from Harvard University's Kennedy School of Government, Harvard Business School, and Harvard T.C. Chan School of Public Health in *Leadership, and Positive Pyschology*, as well as executive certifications from MIT's Sloan's School of Management in *Negotiation and Conflict Resolution*.

She is also a marathon runner, a health and exercise enthusiast, an avid reader, is conversant in four languages, plays tennis and the piano, has studied martial arts, loves animals (dogs especially), and is active in her community.

As a prolific writer of many articles, curricula, manuals, and programs, Manna has also published over two dozen books (including her top-selling autobiographical novel, *To Run with Horses*, and her lauded children's book series, *Sophie and Solo's Fun Adventures*®).

Manna lives a grateful life with her family and furmily.

THE NEXT CHAPTER

My story continues, as does yours!

To find out more about what we're doing for children and youths, and our other fun projects, please contact us at *HuMannaTea.com* (our speaking and training company) or *HuMannaTeaForAll.org* (our non-profit to champion the voiceless) and join the family!

Find us at www.humannatea.com, and www.humannateaforall.org

- Facebook.com/humannatea
- Facebook.com/humannateaforall
- Instagram @HuMannaTea
- Instagram @HuMannaTeaForAll
- LinkedIn @HuMannaTea
- LinkedIn @HuMannaTeaForAll